LIKE A FISH
NEEDS A BICYCLE

LIKE A
FISH NEEDS
A BICYCLE

Edited by Anne Stibbs

BLOOMSBURY

This edition published in 1992
by Bloomsbury Publishing Limited
2 Soho Square, London W1V 5DE

The moral right of the authors has been asserted.

Extracts from the Authorized King James Version of the Bible, which is Crown Copyright, are reproduced by permission of Eyre and Spottiswoode, Her Majesty's Printers

A copy of the CIP entry for this book is available from the British Library.

ISBN 0 7475 1173 X

Designed by Geoff Green
Typeset by Market House Books Ltd, Aylesbury
Printed in Great Britain by Clay Ltd, St. Ives, PLC.

Contents

Acknowledgments

Elizabeth Bonham

John Daintith

Marie FitzPatrick

Joan Gallagher

Patrick Gallagher

Alan Isaacs

Amanda Isaacs

Jonathan Law

Sandra McQueen

Elizabeth Martin

David Pickering

Ruth Salomon

Jessica Scholes

Gwen Shaw

Tracey Smith

Barbara Standen

Gwendoline Stibbs

Leonard Stibbs

Brenda Tomkins

Linda Wells

Edmund Wright

INTRODUCTION

A quotation is something said or written that has a memorable quality — memorable, perhaps, because it is an astute observation, a clever use of words, or simply because it makes one laugh. There are those who believe that the value of a quotation rests solely on the words themselves. If this were true, it would not matter whether the quotation originated with a woman or a man. This book, however, is compiled on the assumption that the context in which the words first appeared can have a significant bearing on their relevance:

> *I realize that patriotism is not enough, I must have no hatred*
> *or bitterness towards anyone*

is a fairly bald statement, deprived of its context. As the last words of a brave and perceptive woman before a World-War I German firing squad, they say a great deal, not only about Edith Cavell, who said them, but more poignantly about the predominantly male preoccupation with patriotism, militarism, and war.

Even though the words do not have their full impact unless one knows that they were spoken by a woman, Edith Cavell was in no sense being feminist — the issues involved are wider than those of feminism. Christabel Pankhurst, however, referring to the 'Cat and Mouse Act' and the lunacy of forced feeding, *was* being feminist when she declared:

> *We are not ashamed of what we have done because, when*
> *you have a great cause to fight for, the moment of greatest*
> *humiliation is the moment when the spirit is proudest.*

Although Christabel Pankhurst was addressing a narrower issue than Edith Cavell, the two women have one thing in common. They are both members of that 'half the human race', which since the beginning of recorded history has been oppressed by the other half.

And that is what this book is about. It is a wide-ranging collection of quotations which builds into a commentary of attitudes to women. The book is divided into two parts: a chronological section that shows the prevailing attitudes to women through the ages; and a thematic section that deals with specific topics.

The chronological section explores the changing role of women over the last three or four thousand years. Perhaps it is true to say that in this period the condition of women in the various cultures to which they belong has traditionally been determined by the religions that have moulded these cultures. In many cases the emancipation of women is related to the extent to which they have escaped the trammels of these religions. This is not to say that every emancipated woman is an atheist — clearly that is not the case. Yet to achieve equality with men, with a right to make their own decisions, women in some religions have needed to discard certain customs, such as marriages that are arranged or involve a promise to obey their husbands. In the Old Testament, for example, women play a largely secondary role:

> And the rib which the Lord God had taken from man, made
> he a woman, and brought her unto the man.

The ancient Hebrews of the Bible lived in a period that was predominantly concerned with and written by men. Women are often seen as little more than childbearers or temptresses. Eve is the first and most devastating example. The story of Samson and Delilah presents another male view of the dangers of female temptation. Indeed the Book of Proverbs specifically warns men to be careful of adulterous women:

> Such is the way of an adulterous woman; she eateth, and
> wipeth her mouth, and saith, I have done no wickedness.

In the cradle of civilization — the lands around the Mediterranean — women maintained their secondary status even in the enlightened centuries of classical Greece. In Greek mythology, many of the women exhibit the treacherous habits of their biblical predecessors — the unfaithful Clytemnestra, the vengeful Medea, and the incestuous Phaedra are only three examples of a whole litany of unpleasant women, presumably invented by male mythologists. Perhaps they inspired Aeschylus in the 5th century BC to take such a dismissive view of motherhood: 'The mother is not the parent . . . the parent is he who mounts', or Aristotle, a hundred years later: 'woman is merely the passive incubator of his seed'.

By the time of the events related in the New Testament, world-class women rulers began to emerge — and for a brief moment Cleopatra and Salome Alexandra gave a new status to women. It was in the New Testament that a different view of women was portrayed in Mary, who was unsullied by the stain of original sin. This was in contrast with the Old Testament temptress Eve, who was blamed for all the evils in the world as 'the first deserter of the divine law'.

Yet this idealized view of woman was not carried over into everyday life. For the next eight centuries or so 'real-life' women were regarded as 'less perfect than the male' and therefore unworthy of being granted the full rights of citizenship. Justinian, in the 6th century, decreed that everything should belong to the husband regardless of 'whether the wife assisted', and in the 7th century the Koran is explicit:

> Men are in charge of women, because Allah hath made the
> one of them to excel . . . So good women are the obedient.

Yet it is from the Christian influence that medieval chivalry arose; closely associated with it is the literary concept of courtly love. The heroine of chivalry has idealized virtues unrelated to childbearing and motherhood. Indeed, the courtly lover is often unrequited — the object of his abject adoration is typically already married. The dilemma of the courtly lover is to decide between gallantly complying with the code of chivalry and seducing her.

This romanticized view of woman spread thoughout 12th-century Europe, especially in the works of such writers as Chretien de Troyes and later Petrarch and Chaucer. The 13th-century Robert de Blois describes the attributes of the new European woman:

> She could carry and fly falcon, tercel and hawk,
> She knew well how to play chess and tables,
> how to read romances, tell tales and sing songs.
> All things a well-bred lady ought to know she knew and
> lacked none.

However, the generally negative attitude towards women did not begin to change until around the beginning of the 15th century, when Christine de Pisan, among others, began agitating for education for girls as well as boys, although still 'for the purpose of developing her intelligence' and not for 'widening her field of ambition, dethroning man and reigning in his stead.' The advantages of education for women gradually became apparent until, in 1683, Gervase Markham was able to list skill in 'Physick, Chirurgery' among the virtues that enabled a woman to be 'profitable and necessary for all men'.

The demand for equal opportunities in education grew and, by the late 18th century, was coupled with the demand for equality in society. In 1791, for example, Olympe de Gouges was stating, that a 'woman's rights are the same as those of a man'. In 1808 Charles Fourier supported her statement, claiming that this was 'the basic principle of all social progess'. As the movement gathered strength many women banded together in their fight for the vote. In America, Angelina Grimké was fighting against women being 'governed by laws which *they* had no voice in making', and Elizabeth Cady Stanton was pronouncing the prolonged suppression of women as 'the darkest page in human history', while the French feminist Jeanne Deroin was demanding 'absolute equality between the sexes'. In Germany, Hedwig Dohm was querying the 'absurd talk about a woman's sphere' despite their earning 'their bread by the sweat of their brows', while the British suffragette Emmeline Pankhurst was demanding that women have 'full power to work their will in society'. Although there were still a number of people who felt, as Almroth Wright did in 1913, that a woman was insufferable when she insisted 'upon thrusting her society upon men everywhere', there were many who, with Stanley Baldwin, were urging that women should have 'with us, the fullest rights'. The Suffragette Movement, in both Britain and America, was a turning point in the fight for true equality; it was the first time that numbers of women had been seen to join together, to form a sisterhood with a common cause.

The 20th century has seen a transformation of the status of many women in society. The Sex Disqualification Removal Act of 1919 opened most professions to British women. This, together with equality in education and in voting, provided them with a means of determining their own financial security. However, the 'barriers to equality' were evident, from the practical difficulties that a wage-earning woman has in running a home and family to worries some men had (and still have) about the effects of women's employment on the job market. Although the US Equal Rights Amendment (ERA) bill, banning discrimination against women, was introduced in 1923 it was blocked by the House Judiciary Committee for 47 years. The Senate approved the Constitutional Amendment banning discrimination against women in 1972, and sent it to the states for ratification. It was defeated in 1982 after a 10-year effort to have 38 states ratify it.

From the early 1950s on, the 'problem of women's role in society' became a broader issue, and certain expectations were voiced, such as the Morton Commission report on divorce law that 'marriage . . . shall be an equal partnership', or the National Charter of Egypt that stated in 1962 that 'Woman must be regarded as equal to man'. This sense of expectation led to people, such as Betty Friedan, asking of their lives 'Is this all?', and set in motion the Women's Liberation Movement. The movement spread rapidly through many European countries, as well as the USA, Australia, and New Zealand, voicing among its concerns the problems of under-representation in politics, economic discrimination, when or if to start a family, and the stereotyped image of women as passive and dependent.

However, despite the widespread changes to the legal status of women there is a growing media image of women being unhappy and lonely because, as Susan Faludi puts it, 'they have grabbed at the gold ring of independence, only to miss the one ring that matters'. There is also a strong feeling that legislation has not been entirely successful in altering the entrenched attitudes that have persisted for centuries. Although women have won equality it could be, as Constance Rover said in 1982, 'on condition that they don't upset men, or interfere too much with men's way of life'.

The second section of the book includes a variety of quotations that have been sorted in two different ways. Some have been collected into various themes such as **adultery, birth control, language, musicians,** and **politics,** and have been arranged chronologically within the themes. In particular we have tried to select subjects that are relevant to women. Under, for example, **education** one can see how the attitudes of society have changed, from Euripides in 428 BC, who hated 'a learned women', through Rousseau in 1762, who felt that the 'whole education of woman should be relative to man', to Ruby Manikan in 1947 with her widely accepted sentiment that 'if you educate a woman you educate a family'. This arrangement has also been followed under themes in which there are only a few quotations; it can bring out some interesting contrasts. For example, one can see at a glance under **friendship**, that in the 14th century Richard Rolle was saying 'friendship between men and women can be a tricky business', whereas Agnes Smedley, in 1943, 'detested the belief that sex is the chief bond between man and woman. Friendship is far more human'.

This section of the book also includes a selection of biographical entries in their correct alphabetical position. Here are presented quotations by some 200 women, together with a short biography. These have been chosen for their prominence, their influence in the women's movement, and, above all, for their quotability.

The book also contains two indexes. The first is a key-word/key-phrase index, which enables the reader to locate a half-remembered quotation from its key words. The second is a name index to the authors of the quotations. Both indexes refer the reader to the quotation number (not the page number). References to the Chronology are marked CHRON, with the number of the quotation in this section. References to the thematic section are to the particular heading, followed by the quotation number under this heading.

In producing this dictionary, we have tried to put together the most comprehensive selection of quotations possible, and to provide the most useful indexes. The compiler of a dictionary of quotations is in the unusual position of producing a book of other people's words. Inevitably, there is a personal bias in making the selection; readers may therefore be disappointed to find that favourite or significant quotations are missing. We would welcome comments from readers that will help us to improve the book for future editions.

Finally, I would like to thank the many people have helped with the compilation of the book — their names are listed on the Acknowledgments page. In particular I would like to mention two people, for their support: Kathy Rooney of Bloomsbury, who wanted to do this book, and Robert Kerr, who is my bicycle.

A.S.
Aylesbury, 1992

CHRONOLOGY

Made he a woman...

1 And the rib, which the Lord God had taken from man, made he a woman, and brought her unto the man.
And Adam said, This is now bone of my bones, and flesh of my flesh: she shall be called Woman, because she was taken out of Man.
Bible: Genesis
2:22–23

2 And when the woman saw that the tree was good for food, and that it was pleasant to the eyes, and a tree to be desired to make one wise, she took of the fruit thereof, and did eat, and gave also unto her husband with her; and he did eat.
Bible: Genesis
3:6

3 And the man said, The woman whom thou gavest to be with me, she gave me of the tree, and I did eat.
Bible: Genesis
3:12

4 Unto the woman he said, I will greatly multiply thy sorrow and thy conception; in sorrow thou shalt bring forth children; and thy desire shall be to thy husband, and he shall rule over thee.
Bible: Genesis
3:16

5 And Adam called his wife's name Eve; because she was the mother of all living.
Bible: Genesis
3:20

6 And if a woman have an issue, and her issue in her flesh be blood, she shall be put apart seven days: and whosoever toucheth her shall be unclean until the even. And every thing that she lieth upon in her separation shall be unclean: every thing also that she sitteth upon shall be unclean.
Bible: Leviticus
15:19–20

7 You shall not approach a woman to have intercourse with her during her period of menstruation.
Bible: Leviticus
18:19

8 When a man takes a wife and after having intercourse with her turns against her...saying, 'I took this woman and slept with her and did not find proof of virginity in her,' then the girl's father and mother shall take the proof of her vir-ginity to the elders of the town, at the town gate...If, on the other hand, the accusation is true and no proof of the girl's virginity is found, then they shall bring her out to the door of her father's house, and the men of her town shall stone her to death.
Bible: Deuteronomy
22:13–15, 20–21

9 When a man comes upon a virgin who is not pledged in marriage and forces her to lie with him, and they are discovered, then the man who lies with her shall give the girl's father fifty pieces of silver, and she shall be his wife because he has dishonoured her. He is not free to divorce her all his life long.
Bible: Deuteronomy
22:28–29

10 Even warriors seized as booty in war are treated humanely.
At least, treat me like them!
Eristi-Aya (c. 1790–45 BC) Middle Eastern letter writer.
A letter to her mother. *A Book of Women Poets* (eds Aliki and Willis Barnstone) [18th century BC]

11 I bow before your rights as wife. From this day on, I shall never oppose your claims with a single word. I recognise you before all others as my wife, though I do not have the right to say you must be mine, and only I am your husband and mate.
Extract from an Egyptian marriage contract. *Mothers and Amazons: The First Feminine History of Culture* (Helen Diner) [15th century BC]

12 He...gave her speech and called the woman 'Pandora'...Up to this time the races of men had lived on earth free from harm, from toilsome labour and from the painful diseases which bring death to humankind. But the woman's hands raised the lid of the great jar, scattered the evils within it, and laid up harsh troubles for men. Only hope stayed where it was.
Hesiod (fl. c. 700 BC) Greek poet.
Works and Days [c. 700 BC]

13 I have received true prosperity from the golden Muses, and when I die shall not be forgot.
Sappho (c. 612–c. 580 BC) Greek poet.
Distinguished Women Writers (Virginia Moore) [6th century BC]

14 I hear that Andromeda –
that hayseed in her hay-
seed finery – has put

a torch to your heart
and she without even
the art of lifting her
skirt over her ankles.
Sappho (c. 612–c. 580 BC) Greek poet.
The Penguin Book of Women Poets [6th century BC]

15 You must remember that the two of us are
born women and as such do not fight with men;
since we are in the power of those who are
stronger, we must obey these orders, and orders
even more painful than these.
Sophocles (c. 496–406 BC) Greek dramatist.
Antigone [5th century BC]

16 The mother is not the parent of that which
is called her child: but only nurse of the newly
planted seed that grows. *The parent is he who
mounts.*
Aeschylus (c. 525–456 BC) Greek tragic dramatist.
Eumenides [458 BC]

17 Women, even though they are of full age,
because of their levity of mind shall be under
guardianship.
Roman Law
The Twelve Tables [450 BC]

18 Ask a Lycian who he is and he gives his
own name and that of his mother and of his
mother's mother, but never his father's name.
Moreover, if a free woman marry a slave their
children are free citizens; but if a free man
marry a slave, even though he be the first citizen
of the state, his children forfeit all the rights of
citizenship.
Herodotus (c. 480–c. 425 BC) Greek historian.
The Histories [5th century BC]

19 Your great glory is not to be inferior to what
God has made you, and the greatest glory of a
woman is to be least talked about by men,
whether they are praising you or criticizing you.
Aspasia (fl. c. 420s BC) Greek teacher.
History of the Peloponnesian War (Thucydides) [c. 420
BC]

20 Man is active, full of movement, creative in
politics, business and culture. The male shapes
and moulds society and the world. Woman, on
the other hand, is passive. She stays at home, as
is her nature. She is matter waiting to be formed
by the active male principle. Of course the
active elements are always higher on any scale,
and more divine. Man consequently plays a
major part in reproduction; the woman is
merely the passive incubator of his seed.
Aristotle (384–322 BC) Greek philosopher.
Politics, Bk I [4th century BC]

21 By nature, then, the female is marked off
from the slave...Among barbarians, it is true,

females and slaves rank together. But this is sim-
ply because barbarians lack the ruling element.
Aristotle (384–322 BC) Greek philosopher.
Politics, Bk I [4th century BC]

22 The male is by nature superior and the
female inferior; one rules and the other is ruled.
Aristotle (384–322 BC) Greek philosopher.
Politics, Bk I [4th century BC]

23 Men's courage is shown in commanding
and women's in obeying.
Aristotle (384–322 BC) Greek philosopher.
Politics, Bk I [4th century BC]

24 The male is naturally more fitted to command than the female (except where there is a
miscarriage of nature).
Aristotle (384–322 BC) Greek philosopher.
Politics, Bk I [4th century BC]

25 The law expressly forbids children and
women from being able to make a contract about
anything worth more than a bushel of barley.
Isaeus (c. 420–c. 350 BC) Greek speech writer.
[4th century BC]

26 Leaving women to do that they like is not
just to lose *half* the battle (as it may seem): a
woman's natural potential for virtue is inferior
to a man's, so she's proportionately a greater
danger, perhaps even twice as great. So the happiness of the state will be better served if we
reconsider the point and put things right, by providing that all our arrangements apply to men
and women alike.
Plato (429–347 BC) Greek philosopher.
Laws [4th century BC]

27 The gods created woman for the indoors
functions, the man for all others. The gods put
woman inside because she has less tolerance for
cold, heat and war. For woman it is honest to
remain indoors and dishonest to gad about. For
the man, it is shameful to remain shut up at
home and not occupy himself with affairs outside.
Xenophon (430–354 BC) Greek historian.
[4th century BC]

28 Men marry, indeed, so as to get a manager
for the house, to solace weariness, to banish
solitude.
Theophrastus (c. 372–c. 287 BC) Greek Peripatetic
philosopher.
On Marriage [4th century BC]

29 We have hetaerae for pleasure, concubines
for the daily care of the body and wives for the
production of full-blooded children and reli-
able guardians for the house.
Demosthenes (384–322 BC) Athenian orator and
statesman.
A hetaera is an educated courtesan. *Philippics* [344 BC]

30   Who then does not know that this is recent law, passed twenty years ago? Since our matrons lived for so long by the highest standards of behaviour without any law, what risk is there that, once it is repealed, they will yield to luxury?
Lucien Valerius
Defending the repeal of the Oppian Law. The Oppian Law was an emergency measure that limited women's use of expensive goods. Speech, 195 BC

31   If each man of us, fellow citizens, had established that the right and authority of the husband should be held over the mother of his own family, we should have less difficulty with women in general; now, at home our freedom is conquered by female fury, here in the Forum it is bruised and trampled upon, and, because we have not contained the individuals, we fear the lot.
Cato the Elder (Marcus Porcius C.; 234–149 BC) Roman statesman.
Opposing the repeal of the Oppian Law. Speech, 195 BC

32   Our ancestors did not want women to conduct any – not even private – business without a guardian; they wanted them to be under the authority of parents, brothers, or husbands; we (the gods help us!) even now let them snatch at the government and meddle in the Forum and our assemblies.
Cato the Elder (Marcus Porcius C.; 234–149 BC) Roman statesman.
Opposing the repeal of the Oppian Law. Speech, 195 BC

33   Women want total freedom, or rather total licence. If you allow them to achieve complete equality with men, do you think they will be any easier to live with? Not at all. Once they have achieved equality, they will be your masters.
Cato the Elder (Marcus Porcius C.; 234–149 BC) Roman statesman.
Opposing the repeal of the Oppian Law. Speech, 195 BC

34   Apollonia shall remain with Philiscus, obeying him as a wife should obey her husband, owning their property jointly with him. Philiscus, whether he is at home or away from home, shall furnish Apollonia with everything necessary and clothing and whatsoever is proper for a wedded wife, in proportion to their means. It shall not be lawful for Philiscus to bring home another wife in addition to Apollonia or to have a concubine or boy-lover, nor to beget children by another woman while Apollonia is alive nor to maintain another house of which Apollonia is not mistress, nor to eject or insult or illtreat her nor to alienate any of their property with injustice to Apollonia.
Marriage contract, Alexandria, 92 BC *Tebtunis papyrus*

35   You know how much I was with your father, and you are aware that it was he who placed the crown of Egypt upon my head.
Cleopatra VII (69–30 BC) Queen of Egypt (51–48, 47–30).
To Octavian, referring to Julius Caesar. *The Life and Times of Cleopatra* (Arthur Weigall) [1st century BC]

36   Nothing could part us while we lived, but death seems to threaten to divide us. You, a Roman born, have found a grave in Egypt. I, an Egyptian, am to seek that favour, and none but that, in your country.
Cleopatra VII (69–30 BC) Queen of Egypt (51–48, 47–30).
Said over Marc Antony's tombstone. *The Life and Times of Cleopatra* (Arthur Weigall) [1st century BC]

37   Many things which we consider proper are thought shocking in Greece. What Roman, for instance, has any scruples about taking his wife to a dinner-party? What Roman matron does not appear in the reception rooms of her own house and take part in its social life? But it is quite different in Greece, for there a wife may not be present at dinner, unless it is a family party, and spends her time in a remote part of the house called 'the gynaeceum' which is never entered by a man unless he is a close relative.
Cornelius Nepos (c. 100–c. 25 BC) Roman historian.
Vitae [1st century BC]

38   Why should we pay taxes when we have no part in the honours, the commands, the statecraft, for which you contend against each other with such harmful results?
Hortensia (fl. 50 BC) Roman noblewoman and orator.
Civil Wars (Appian) [1st century BC]

39   You assume the glorious title of reformers of the state, a title which will turn to your eternal infamy, if, without the least regard to the laws of equity, you persist in your wicked resolution of plundering those women of their lives and fortunes, who have given you no just cause of offence.
Hortensia (fl. 50 BC) Roman noblewoman and orator.
Civil Wars (Appian) [1st century BC]

40   Caesar's wife must be above suspicion.
Julius Caesar (100–44 BC) Roman general and statesman.
Said in justification of his divorce from Pompeia, after she was unwittingly involved in a scandal. *Lives*, 'Julius Caesar' (Plutarch) [1st century BC]

41 A virtuous wife rules her husband by obeying him.
Publilius Syrus (fl. 1st Century BC) Latin mime writer.
Opinions [1st century BC]

42 Is Priam to have fallen by the sword? Troy to be burnt in flames? The Dardan shore to be so often soaked in blood? Not so! For though there is no glorious renown in a woman's punishment and such victory wins no honour, yet I shall have praise for blotting out the unholy thing and exacting a just recompense.
Virgil (Publius Vergilius Maro; 70–19 BC) Roman poet.
Aeneid, Bk II [19 BC]

43 Woman is always fickle and changing.
Virgil (Publius Vergilius Maro; 70–19 BC) Roman poet.
Aeneid, Bk IV [19 BC]

44 To the same cave come Dido and the Trojan chief. Primal Earth and nuptial Juno give the sign; fires flashed in Heaven, the witness to their bridal, and on the mountain-top screamed the Nymphs. That day was the first day of death, that first the cause of woe. For no more is Dido swayed by fair show or fair fame, no more does she dream of a secret love: she calls it marriage and with that name veils her sins!
Virgil (Publius Vergilius Maro; 70–19 BC) Roman poet.
Aeneid, Bk IV [19 BC]

45 Whether a pretty woman grants or withholds her favours, she always likes to be asked for them.
Ovid (Publius Ovidius Naso; 43 BC–17 AD) Roman poet.
Ars Amatoria [c. 8 AD]

46 All men allow women to have been the founders of religion.
Strabo (64 BC–21 AD) Greek geographer.
Geography [c. 10 AD]

47 Choose someone rather who doesn't understand *all* she reads.
I hate these authority-citers, the sort who are always thumbing
Some standard grammatical treatise...
who with antiquarian zeal
Quote poets I've never heard of. Such matters are men's concern.
Juvenal (Decimus Junius Juvenalis; 60–130 AD) Roman satirist.
Satires, VI [1st century AD]

48 No one delights more in vengeance than a woman.
Juvenal (Decimus Junius Juvenalis; 60–130 AD) Roman satirist.
Satires, XIII [1st century AD]

49 Yet a musical wife's not so bad as some presumptuous
Flat-chested busybody who rushes around the town
Gate-crashing all-male meetings, talking back straight-faced
To a uniformed general – *and* in her husband's presence.
Juvenal (Decimus Junius Juvenalis; 60–130 AD) Roman satirist.
Satires [1st century AD]

50 It is very right too that married people should have the same kind of partnership in property. They should put everything they have into a common fund; neither of the two should think of one part as belonging to him and the other as not belonging; instead each should think of it all as his own, and none of it as not belonging to him.
Plutarch (?46–?120 AD) Greek biographer and philosopher.
Moralia [2nd century AD]

51 A wife ought not to make friends of her own, but to enjoy her husband's friends together with him.
Plutarch (?46–?120 AD) Greek biographer and philosopher.
Moralia [2nd century AD]

52 When the moon is a long way from the sun, she looks large and bright to us; but when she comes near she fades away and hides. With a good wife it is just the opposite; she ought to be most conspicuous when she is with her husband, and to stay at home and hide herself when he is not there.
Plutarch (?46–?120 AD) Greek biographer and philosopher.
Moralia [2nd century AD]

53 No part of their manners is more praiseworthy than their marriage code. The wife does not bring a dowry to the husband, but the husband to the wife. His marriage gifts are not such as a bride would deck herself with, but oxen, a caparisoned steed, a shield, a lance, and a sword. Lest the woman should think herself to stand apart from aspirations after noble deeds she is reminded by the ceremony that she is her husband's partner in danger, destined to share with him and dare with him both in peace and in war.
Tacitus (c. 55–c. 120 AD)
Referring to Celtic customs. *Germania* [2nd century AD]

You are an Eve...

54 For the parts were formed within her when she was still a foetus, but could not because of the defect in the heat emerge and project on the outside, and this, though making the animal itself that was being formed less perfect than one that is complete in all respects, provided no small advantage for the race; for there needs must be a female. Indeed, you ought not to think that our creator would purposely make half the whole race imperfect and, as it were, mutilated, unless there was to be some great advantage in such a mutilation.
Galen (?130–?200 AD) Greek physician.
On the Usefulness of the Parts of the Body [2nd century AD]

55 The female is less perfect than the male for one principal reason – because she is colder, for if among animals the warm one is the more active, a colder animal would be less perfect than a warmer.
Galen (?130–?200 AD) Greek physician.
On the Usefulness of the Parts of the Body [2nd century AD]

56 Wives have no right to bring criminal accusations for adultery against their husbands, even though they may desire to complain of the violation of the marriage vow, for while the law grants this privilege to men it does not concede it to women.
Lex Julia de Adulteriis [198 AD]

57 My soul doth magnify the Lord.
And my spirit hath rejoiced in God my Saviour.
For he hath regarded the low estate of his handmaiden: for, behold, from henceforth all generations shall call me blessed.
For he that is mighty hath done to me great things; and holy is his name.
Bible: Luke
I:46–49 Mary's song of rejoicing, known as the Magnificat.

58 A woman when she is in travail hath sorrow, because her hour is come: but as soon as she is delivered of the child, she remembereth no more the anguish, for joy that a man is born into the world.
Bible: John
16:21

59 …women should not address the meeting. They have no licence to speak, but should keep their place as law directs. If there is something that they want to know, they can ask their own husbands at home. It is a shocking thing that a woman should address the congregation.
Bible: I Corinthians
14:34

60 Woman must be a learner, listening quietly and with due submission. I do not permit a woman to be a teacher nor must woman domineer over man, but she should be quiet.
Bible: I Timothy
2:11–12

61 Likewise, ye husbands, dwell with them according to knowledge, giving honour unto the wife, as unto the weaker vessel, and as being heirs together of the grace of life; that your prayers be not hindered.
Bible: I Peter
3:7

62 And do you not know that you are an Eve? The sentence of God on this sex of yours lives in this age: the guilt must of necessity live too. *You* are the devil's gateway: *you* are the unsealer of that tree: *you* are the first deserter of the divine law: *you* are she who persuaded him whom the devil was not valiant enough to attack. *You* destroyed so easily God's image, man. On account of *your* desert – that is, death – even the Son of God had to die.
Tertullian (c. 160–225 AD) Carthaginian father of the church.
De cultu feminarum (*On Female Dress*) [3rd century AD]

63 It is our pleasure that no woman, on account of her own depraved desires, shall be permitted to send a notice of divorce to her husband on trumped-up grounds; as, for instance, that he is a drunkard or a gambler or a philanderer, nor indeed shall a husband be allowed to divorce his wife on every sort of pretext. But when a woman sends a notice of divorce, the following criminal charges only shall be investigated, that is, if she should prove that her husband is a homicide, a sorcerer, or a destroyer of tombs, so that the wife may thus earn commendation and at length recover her entire dowry.
Theodosian Code (438 AD)
Collection of laws, issued from 312 AD, which was sponsored by Theodosius II (401–50 AD) an eastern Roman emperor.

64 The woman taught once, and ruined all. On this account…let her not teach. But what is it to other women that she suffered this? It certainly

concerns them; for the sex is weak and fickle...The whole female race transgressed...Let her not, however, grieve. God hath given her no small consolation, that of childbearing.
St John Chrysostom (c. 347–407) Archbishop of Constantinople.
Works of Chrysostom (ed. P. Schaff) [5th century]

65 Where a husband makes clothing for his wife out of his own wool, although this is done for his wife and through solicitude for her, the clothing, nevertheless, will belong to the husband; nor does it make any difference whether the wife assisted in preparing the wool, and attended to the matter for her husband.
Justinian (483–565) Byzantine emperor.
Institutes [533]

66 On the death of the father or mother the inheritance goes to the son, not the daughter. When a man has a son and a daughter and the son marries, has a son, and then dies, the inheritance belongs to the son's son, that is, to the grandson, not to the daughter.
Leges Saxonum (ed. C. F. von Schwerin) [c. 6th century]

67 Men are in charge of women, because Allah hath made the one of them to excel the other, and because they spend of their property for the support of women. So good women are the obedient.
Koran
Ch. IV [7th century]

68 Suffer the women whom ye divorce to dwell in some part of the houses wherein ye dwell; according to the room and conveniences of the habitations which ye possess; and make them not uneasy, that ye may reduce them to straits.
Koran
Ch. LXV [7th century]

69 A sudden change was that for the men there when the Mother of Grendel found her way in among them – though the fury of her onslaught was less frightful than his; as the force of a woman, her onset in a fight, is less feared by men.
Beowulf (trans. Michael Alexander) [c. 9th century]

70 She may indeed say, whoever she be that brought into the world this young man here – if yet she lives – that the God of Old was gracious to her in her child-bearing.
Beowulf (trans. Michael Alexander) [c. 9th century]

71 A marriage that has been made legally cannot be unmade, except by spiritual separation decided on in common or for physical fornication attested by public confession or open conviction...These cases aside, a man must keep his wife *volens nolens*, even if she is a shrew, shameless, lewd, or greedy for the pleasures of this world.
Hincmar (c. 806–882) Archbishop of Reims.
On Divorce [860]

72 Between husband and wife there is established an affective relationship, which is primordial and excellent, except that in this conjunction the direction belongs to the man, and the submission to the woman.
Hincmar (c. 806–882) Archbishop of Reims.
On Divorce [860]

73 We order that marriages shall be confirmed by a nuptial blessing, so that if the future spouses fail to legitimize their union in this way from the beginning their marriage shall not be valid and shall not produce the effects of matrimony. For there is no intermediary situation between marriage and celibacy which is not open to reproach.
Leo the Wise (866–912) Byzantine emperor.
The Novels of Leo [9th century]

74 The beauty of a woman is only skin-deep. If men could only see what is beneath the flesh and penetrate below the surface with eyes like the Boeotian lynx, they would be nauseated just to look at women, for all this feminine charm is nothing but phlegm, blood, humours, gall.
Odo of Cluny (879–942) French monk, Abbot of Cluny (910–17).
[10th century]

75 To think that you who have been nurtured in the most profound philosophical studies and have attained knowledge in perfection, should have deigned to approve the humble work of an obscure woman!...admitting that I possess some little knowledge of those arts the subtleties of which exceed the grasp of my woman's mind.
Hroswitha of Gandersheim (c. 935–1000) German nun, poet, and playwright.

The Plays of Roswitha, 'Epistle of the Same to Certain Learned Patrons of this Book' (Christopher St John) [960]

Handicap of her sex...

76 So the Empire passed into the hands of the two sisters, and for the first time in our lives we saw the transformation of a gynaeconitis into an emperor's council chamber. What is more, both the civilian population and the military caste were working in harmony under empresses, and more obedient to them than to any proud overlord issuing arrogant commands.
Michael Psellus (1018–96) Byzantine philosopher and historian.
Referring to the joint reigns of Zoe (1042) and Theodora (1042). The gynaeconitis was the women's quarters. *Fourteen Byzantine Rulers* (*The Chronographia of Michael Psellus*) [11th century]

77 Everyone was agreed that for the Roman Empire to be governed by a woman, instead of a man, was improper...But if one removes this single objection, one must say that in everything else the Empire prospered and its glory increased.
Michael Psellus (1018–96) Byzantine philosopher and historian.
Referring to the reign of Theodora (1055–56). *Fourteen Byzantine Rulers* (*The Chronographia of Michael Psellus*) [11th century]

78 Women on account of modesty and the fragility and delicacy of the state of these parts dare not reveal the difficulties of their sicknesses to a male doctor.
Trotula of Salerno Italian gynaecologist and obstetrician.
Passionibus Muliernum Curandorum (The Diseases of Woman) [11th century]

79 Their fashion in dress is that they have no fashion and, whoever wants fashion, or does not refuse it if offered, loses the proof of her chastity. Any such person would be thought to be preparing herself not for religion but for fornication, and be judged not a nun but a whore.
Peter Abelard (1079–1142) French philosopher and theologian.
The Letters of Abelard and Heloise [12th century]

80 I need not say any more about the basic impossibility of combining matrimony and scholarship but think of the details of a good burgher's marriage...The spinning wheel charmingly combined with books and copybooks, style and pen with the spindle. You are immersed in your theological or philosophical ideas, and at that moment the infants begin to squall; the wet nurses try to quieten them with

their monotonous singsong...can then your attention remain uninterrupted?
Heloise (c. 1098–1164) French abbess and letter writer.
Historia Calamitatum (Abelard) [12th century]

81 Lady Carenza, I'd like to have a husband, but making babies I think is a huge penitence: your breasts hang way down and it's too anguishing to be a wife
Alais (12th century) French nun.
The Women Troubadours (Meg Bodin) [12th century]

82 She was a very wise woman, fully experienced in almost all spheres of state business, who had completely triumphed over the handicap of her sex so that she could take charge of important affairs.
William of Tyre (c. 1130–85) Syrian churchman and historian.
Referring to Melisende (c. 1140), Queen of Jerusalem. *Recueil des Historiens des Croisades, Historiens Occidentaux* (ed. Académie des Inscriptions et Belles-Lettres) [c. 1140]

83 The image of God is in man and it is one. Women were drawn from man, who has God's jurisdiction as if he were God's vicar, because he has the image of the one God. Therefore woman is not made in God's image.
Gratian (d. c. 1158) Italian monk.
Decretum [c. 1140]

84 By intermarriage and by every means in his power he bound the two peoples into a firm union.
Walter Map (c. 1140–c. 1209) Welsh cleric and writer.
Referring to Henry I of England, and specifically to his marriage (1100) to Matilda, a descendant of the Anglo-Saxon royal family. *De Nugis Curialium*, Pt V, Ch. 5 [1181–93]

85 For when a woman grows in virtue despite her inherited instincts and gladly keeps her honour, reputation, and person intact, she is only a woman in name, but in spirit she is a man!
Gottfried von Strassburg (fl. 1210) German poet.
Tristan [c. 1210]

86 Consider your sex and spare me! You are a woman, well born and of tender years. If you earn the name of murderess, enchanting Isolde will be dead to honour for ever.
Gottfried von Strassburg (fl. 1210) German poet.
Tristan [c. 1210]

87 After her husband's death, a widow shall have her marriage portion and her inheritance

at once and without any hindrance; nor shall she pay anything for her dower, her marriage portion, or her inheritance which she and her husband held on the day of her husband's death; and she may stay in her husband's house for forty days after his death, within which period her dower shall be assigned to her.
Magna Carta, 1215

88 No widow shall be compelled to marry so long as she wishes to live without a husband, provided that she gives security that she will not marry without our consent if she holds of us, or without the consent of the lord of whom she holds, if she holds of another.
Magna Carta, 1215

89 *Tear* the headdress from her even though her own hair should come away with it. Do this *not thrice or four times only*, and presently she will forbear.
Berthold of Regensburg German friar.
Advising husbands on how to stop their wives dressing their hair. *Sermons* [1250]

90 A necessary object, woman, who is needed to preserve the species or to provide food and drink.
St Thomas Aquinas (1225–74) Italian theologian.
[13th century]

91 She could carry and fly falcon, tercel and hawk,
She knew well how to play chess and tables,
how to read romances, tell tales and
sing songs. All the things a well-bred
lady ought to know she knew and lacked none.
Robert de Blois
Robert de Blois: Samtliche Werke (ed. J. Ulrich) [13th century]

92
But the intent of the King and his Council is that Women, that is to say Brewers, Bakers, Carders, Spinners and Workers as well of Wool as of Linen Cloth and of Silk, Brawdesters and Breakers of Wool and all other that do use and work all handy works may freely use and work as they have done before this time without any impeachment.
Statutes of the Realm, Vol. II [1363]

93 Here is an example to every good woman that she suffer and endure patiently, nor strive with her husband nor answer him before strangers, as did once a woman who did answer her husband before strangers with short words; and he smote her with his fist down to the earth; and then with his foot he struck her in her visage and brake her nose, and all her life after she had her nose crooked, the which so shent and disfigured her visage after, that she might not for shame show her face, it was so foul blemished. And this she had for her language that she was wont to say to her husband. And therefore the wife ought to suffer, and let the husband have the words, and to be master, for that is her duty.
Geoffrey de la Tour de Landry
Book of the Knight of the Tower [1371]

94 It is neither fitting nor safe that all the keys should hang from the belt of one woman.
Thomas Brinton (c. 1320–89) Bishop of Rochester.
Criticizing the influence of Alice Perrers over the ageing Edward III. Sermon, Westminster Abbey, 18 May 1376

95 But to say the truth in this instance the trade of regratery belongeth by right the rather to women. But if a woman be at it she in her stinginess useth much more machination and deceit than a man; for never alloweth she the profit on a single crumb to escape her, nor faileth to hold her neighbour to paying his price.
John Gower (1325–1408) English poet.
Referring to trickery in the selling trade; a regrater is a retailer. *Mirour de l'Omme* [14th century]

Woman should acquire learning...

96 This woman in love with scholarship intends, to be sure, that woman should acquire learning; but it must be for the purpose of developing her intelligence, or raising her heart to higher things, not of widening her field of ambitions, dethroning man and reigning in his stead.
Christine de Pisan (c. 1363–c. 1430) French author and poet.
La Cité des Dames, Prologue [1404]

97 If it were customary to send little girls to school and to teach them the same subjects as are taught to boys, they would learn just as fully and would understand the subtleties of all arts and sciences. Indeed, maybe they would understand them better...for just as women's bodies are softer than men's, so their understanding is sharper.
Christine de Pisan (c. 1363–c. 1430) French author and poet.
La Cité des Dames, Prologue [1404]

98 Since God chose his spouse from among women, most excellent Lady, because of your honour, not only should men refrain from reproaching women, but should also hold them in great reverence.
Christine de Pisan (c. 1363–c. 1430) French author and poet.
La Cité des Dames [1404]

99 Every man or woman of whatever state or condition that he be, shall be free to set son or daughter to take learning on any school that pleases them within the realm.
Statutes of the Realm [1405–1406]

100 Because that knights, esquires and gentlemen go upon journeys and follow the wars, it beseemeth wives to be wise and of great governance and to see clear, in all that they do, for that most often they dwell at home without their husbands who are at court or in divers lands.
Christine de Pisan (c. 1363–c. 1430) French author and poet.
Le Livre des Trois Vertus [1406]

101 A clarkes custume is whan he enditeth
Of wommen, be it prose, rhyme or verse
Seyn they be wicked, all honoure be the reverse.
Christine de Pisan (c. 1363–c. 1430) French author and poet.
Lepistre au Dieu Damour [c. 1420]

102 You men have more patience with the hen that befouleth thy table but layeth a fresh egg daily, than with thy wife when she bringeth forth a little girl. Consider the fruit of the woman, and have patience; not for *every* cause is it right to beat her.
Bernardino of Siena
Sermons [1427]

103 Surrender to the Maid sent hither, by God the King of Heaven, the keys of all the good towns you have taken and laid waste in France...And to you, King of England, if you do not thus, I am a chieftain of war and whenever I meet your followers in France, I will drive them out; if they will not obey, I will put them all to death.
St Joan of Arc (1412–31) French patriot.
Letter to the English, 1429

104 Not only did she wear short tunics, but she dressed herself in tabards and garments open at the sides, besides the matter is notorious since when she was captured she was wearing a surcoat cloak of gold, open on all sides, a cap on her head, and her hair cropped round in man's style. And in general, having cast aside all womanly decency, not only to the scorn of feminine modesty, but also of well instructed men, she had worn the apparel and garments of most dissolute men, and, in addition, had some weapons of defence.
One of the charges made against Joan of Arc at her trial.
The Trial of Jeanne d'Arc (W. P. Barrett) [1431]

105 And now let us examine the carnal desires of the body itself, whence has arisen unconscionable harm to human life. Justly may we say with Cato of Utica: If the world could be rid of women, we should not be without God in our intercourse. For truly without the wickedness of women, to say nothing of witchcraft, the world would remain proof against innumerable dangers.
Heinrich Kramer and Jakob Sprenger German Dominican monks.
Malleus Maleficarum: The Classic Study of Witchcraft [1486]

106 A womane is a worthy wyght
She serveth a man both daye and nyght,
Therto she puttyth alle her myght,
And yet she hathe but care and woo.
Anonymous
Medieval English Lyrics (ed. R. T. Davies) [15th century]

107 First, we see how women have been the cause of many troubles, have done great harm to

those who govern cities, and have caused in them many divisions...Among the primary causes of the downfall of tyrants, Aristotle puts the injuries they do on account of women, whether by rape, violation or the breaking up of marriages.
Machiavelli (1469–1527) Italian statesman.
Discourses on the First Decade of Livy, Bk III, Ch. 26, 'How Women have Brought the Downfall of States' [1513–19]

108 *A lesson for the wyfe...*alway be doyng of some good workes that the deuil may fynde the alway occupied, for as in a standyng water are engendred wormes, right so in an idel body are engendered ydel thoughtes.
Sir Anthony Fitzherbert (1470–1538) English barrister.
Boke of Husbandrye [1538]

109 And also to bye al maner of necessary thinges belonging to a houshold, and to make a true rekening & accompt to her husband what she hath receyued and what she hathe payed. And yf the husband go to the market to bye or sell as they ofte do, he then to shew his wife in lyke maner. For if one of them should use to disceiue the other, he disceyveth him selfe, and he is not lyke to thryve, & therefore they must be true ether to other.
Sir Anthony Fitzherbert (1470–1538) English barrister.
Boke of Husbandrye [1538]

110 The wife is entirely under the power and subjection of her husband.
James Balfour (d. 1583) Scottish judge.
The Practiks of Sir James Balfour of Pittendreich (ed. P. G. B. McNeill) [1550]

111 For the Holy Spirit says that there is neither male nor female in Christ...For the Lord has certainly not made married woman subservient to have her be polluted and tormented by the extortions and injuries of her husband but rather so that she may receive discipline from him, as if from her master and saviour, like the church from Christ.
Martin Bucer (1491–1551) German Protestant.
Arguing in favour of a woman being able to divorce her adulterous husband. *De Regno Christi* [1550]

112 Since a time has come, Mademoiselle, when the severe laws of men no longer prevent women from applying themselves to the sciences and other disciplines, it seems to me that those of us who can should use this long-craved freedom to study and to let men see how greatly they wronged us when depriving us of its honour and advantages.
Louise Labé (c. 1520–66) French poet.
Les poétes Lyonnais précurseurs de la Pléiade (ed. J. Aynard) [c. 1555]

113 I would have preferred to omit this chapter, that women might not become all the more arrogant by knowing that they also, like men, have testicles, and that they not only suffer the pain of having to nourish the child within their bodies...but also that they too put something of their own into it.
I. de Valverde Spanish anatomist.
Historia de la composicion del cuerpo humano [1556]

114 Under no other reign in English history during peacetime was so much Christian blood, so many Englishmen's lives been spilled, as under the said Queen Mary.
John Foxe (1516–87) English religious writer.
Referring to Mary I (1516–58) Queen of England. *Book of Martyrs* [1558]

115 After all the stormy, tempestuous, and blustering windy weather of Queen Mary was overblown, the darksome clouds of discomfort dispersed, the palpable fogs and mist of the most intolerable misery consumed, and the dashing showers of persecution overpast: it pleased God to send England calm and quiet season, a clear and lovely sunshine, a quitsest from former broils of a turbulent estate, and a world of blessings by good Queen Elizabeth.
Raphael Holinshed (d. 1580) English chronicler.
Chronicles [1558]

116 The First Blast of the Trumpet Against the Monstrous Regiment of Women.
John Knox (c. 1514–72) Scottish religious reformer.
The pamphlet states that the rule of women is contrary to both natural law and religion. It was aimed at three Catholic rulers: Mary Tudor, Mary Queen of Scots, and Catherine de Medici. Unfortunately, publication coincided with the accession of Protestant Elizabeth I. She immediately barred Knox from her realm. Title of pamphlet, 1558

117 To promote a Woman to bear rule, superiority, dominion or empire, above any Realm, Nation, or City, is repugnant to Nature; contumely to God, a thing most contrarious to his revealed will and approved ordinance, and finally it is the subversion of good Order, of all equity and justice.
John Knox (c. 1514–72) Scottish religious reformer.
Opening words. *First Blast of the Trumpet against the Monstrous Regiment of Women* [1558]

118 Woman in her greatest perfection was made to serve and obey man, not to rule and command him.
John Knox (c. 1514–72) Scottish religions reformer.
First Blast of the Trumpet against the Monstrous Regiment of Women [1558]

119   Most excellent Royall Majesty, of our *Elizabeth* (sitting at the *Helm* of this Imperial Monarchy: or rather, at the Helm of the Imperiall Ship).
John Dee (1527–1608) English mathematician and astrologer.
General and Rare Memorials pertaining to the Perfect Arte of Navigation [1566]

120   Since witches are usually old women of melancholic nature and small brains (women who get easily depressed and have little trust in God), there is no doubt that the devil easily affects and deceives their minds by illusions and apparitions that so bewilder them that they confess to actions that they are very far from having committed.
Johann Wier (1516–88) Belgian physician.
De Praestigiis Daemonum [1566]

121   If things were even worse than they are after all this war they might have laid the blame upon the rule of a woman; but if such persons are honest they should blame only the rule of men who desire to play the part of kings. In future, if I am not any more hampered, I hope to show that women have a more sincere determination to preserve the country than those who have plunged it into the miserable condition to which it has been brought.
Catherine de Medici (1519–89) Italian-born queen of France.
Letter to Ambassador of Spain, 1570

122   When thou wert in the world, Lord, thou didst not despise women...it is not right to repel minds which are virtuous and brave, even though they be the minds of women.
St Teresa of Avila (1515–82) Spanish mystic.
The Gospel According to Woman (Karen Armstrong) [1570]

123   The poets expressed this metaphorically when they said that Pallas Athena, goddess of wisdom, was born from the brain of Jupiter and had no mother: they meant to show that wisdom never comes from women, whose nature is nearer to that of brute beasts. We may as well add that Satan first addressed himself to woman, who then seduced man.
Jean Bodin (1530–96) French jurist.
De la Démonomanie des sorciers [1580]

124   I am your anointed Queen. I will never be by violence constrained to do anything. I thank God that I am endued with such qualities that if I were turned out of the Realm in my petticoat I were able to live in any place in Christome.
Elizabeth I (1533–1603) Queen of England.
Sayings of Queen Elizabeth (Chamberlin) [c. 1580]

125   I know I have the body of a weak and feeble woman, but I have the heart and stomach of a King, and of a King of England too.
Elizabeth I (1533–1603) Queen of England.
Speech at Tilbury on the approach of the Spanish Armada, 1588

126   Because great things by reason of my sexe, I may not doe, and that which I may, I ought to doe, I have according to my duety, brought my poore basket of stones to the strengthening of the walls of that Jerusalem, wherof (by Grace) we are all both Citizens and members.
Anne Locke (fl. 1590s) Scottish translator.
The Markes of the Children of God, Preface (J. Taffin) [1590]

127   England is the paradise of women, the purgatory of men, and the hell of horses.
John Florio (c. 1553–1625) English lexicographer.
Second Fruits [1591]

128   The common man believes that in order to be chaste a woman must not be clever: in truth it is doing chastity too little honor to believe it can be found beautiful only by the blind.
Marie de Jars (1565–1645) French writer.
Proumenoir [1594]

129   There is much to be said on the matter, which I refrain from setting down, fearing my arguments may be feeble beside those of the great...But however great the authority of the husband may be, what *sense* is there for him to be allowed to kill his wife?
Pierre de Bourdeille, Seigneur de Brantôme (c. 1540–1614) French writer.
The Lives of Gallant Ladies [16th century]

130   Though God hath raised me high, yet this I count the glory of my crown: that I have reigned with your loves.
Elizabeth I (1533–1603) Queen of England.
Speech to a deputation from the House of Commons (the Golden Speech), 30 Nov 1601

131   Common Artificers, as Smiths, Weavers, and Women, boldly and accustomably took upon them great Cures, and Things of great Difficulty, in the which they partly used Sorceries and Witchcraft, and partly applied such Medicines unto the Diseased, as were very noyous, and nothing meet therefore.
John Stow (?1525–1605) English chronicler and antiquary.
Survey of the cities of London and Westminster [1603]

132   These are rare attainments for a damsel, but pray tell me, can she spin?
James I (1566–1625) King of England.
On being introduced to a young girl proficient in Latin, Greek, and Hebrew. Attrib.

Let us have our Liberty...

133   Then let us have our Liberty again,
And challenge to your selves no Sovereignty;
You came not in the world without our pain,
Make that a bar against your cruelty;
Your fault being greater, why should you disdain
Our being your equals, free from tyranny?
Emilia Lanier (?1569–?1642) English poet.
Salve Deus Rex Judeorum, 'Eve's Apology' [1611]

134   A woman fit to be a man's wife is too good to be his servant.
Dorothy Leigh (d. 1616) English author.
The Mother's Blessing, Ch. 13 [1616]

135   Man was created of the dust of the earth, but woman was made of a part of man, after that he was a living soule: yet was shee not produced from Adam's foote, to be his too low inferiour; nor from his head to be his superiour, but from his side, neare his heart, to be his equall.
Rachel Speght (b. 1597) English author and poet.
A Mouzell for Melastomus, the Cynicall Bayter of, and foule mouthed Barker against Evahs Sex. Or an apologeticall Answere to that Irreligious and Illiterate Pamphlet made by Jo[seph] Sw[etnam] and by him intituled, The Arraignement of Women [1617]

136   Husbands should not account their wives as their vassals, but as those that are heires together of the grace of life.
Rachel Speght (b. 1597) English author and poet.
A Mouzell for Melastomus [1617]

137   Also wee most humbly desire your worship that you would have in remembrance that same develishe invention which was invented by strangers...which hath beene the utter overthrowe of many poore people...Wee meane those looms...which make tape, ribbon, stript garteringe and the like, which heretofore was made by poore aged woemen and children, but none nowe to be seene.
State Papers. Domestic Series [1621]

138   I desire her bringing up to bee learning the Bible, good huswifery, and good workes; other learning a woman needs not. I desired not much my owne, having seen that a woman hath no greater use for learning than a mainsaile to a flyeboat, which runs under water.
Elizabeth Joceline (1566–1622) English author.
The Mothers Legacie to her Unborne Childe, Ch. 10 [1624]

139   ...it being natural and comely to women to nourish their hair, which even God and nature

have given them for a covering, a token of subjection, and a natural badge to distinguish them from men.
William Prynne (1600–69) English Puritan.
Histriomastix [1632]

140   How...comes it to passe, that when a Father hath a numerous issue of Sonnes and Daughters, the sonnes forsooth are...trained up in the Liberall Arts and Sciences, and there (if they prove not Block-heads) they may in time be book-learned while...we...are set onely to the Needle, to pricke our fingers: or else to the Wheele to spinne a faire thread for our owne undoings.
Mary Tattlewell (fl. 1640) English author.
Mary Tattlewell and Joane Hit-him-home are both pseudonyms. *The Women's Sharpe Revenge* (with Joane Hit-him-home) [c. 1640]

141   Fervour is not placed in feelings but in will to do well, which women may have as well as men. There is no such difference between men and women that women may not do great things as we have seen by example of many saints who have done great things.
Mary Ward (1585–1645) English nun.
The Life of Mary Ward (Mary Catherine Elizabeth Chambers) [1645]

142   None ought to be lords or landlords over another, but the earth is free for every son and daughter of mankind to live free upon.
Gerrard Winstanley (c. 1609–c. 1660) Leader of the Diggers.
Letter to Lord Fairfax, 1649

143   Have we not an equal interest with the men of this Nation, in those liberties and securities contained in the Petition of Right, and the other good laws of the land? Are any of our lives, limbs, liberties, or goods to be taken from us more than from men, but by due process of law and conviction of twelve sworn men of the neighbourhood?
Following the arrest of the leaders of the Levellers, on whose behalf a group of anonymous women petitioned parliament. Their original petition (Apr 1649) was rejected on the grounds that the answer had been given to their husbands. Petition of 5 May 1649, *The Thomason Tracts*

144   Now say, have women worth? or have they none?
Or had they some, but with our queen is't gone?
Nay Masculines, you have thus taxt us long,
But she, though dead, will vindicate our wrong.
Let such as say our Sex is void of Reason,

Know 'tis a Slander now, but once was Treason.
Anne Bradstreet (?1612–72) English poet and
essayist.
*Several Poems Compiled with Great Variety of Wit and
Learning*, 'In Honour of that High and Mighty Princess,
Queen Elizabeth' [c. 1650]

145 ...Scotch-man, who pretended knowledge
to find out witches by pricking them with pins,
to come to Newcastle where he should try such
who should be brought to him, and to have
twenty shillings a piece for all he should condemn as witches...Thirty women were brought
into the townhall and stript, and then openly
had pins thrust into their bodies, and most of
them was found guilty, near twenty-seven of
them, by him and set aside.
Ralph Gardiner
England's Grievance Discovered [c. 1650]

146 If you please to make experience of my
Rules, they are very plain, and easie
enough...you need not call for the help of a Man-
Midwife, which is a disparagement, not only to
yourselves, but also to your Profession.
Nicholas Culpeper (1616–54) English astrologer
and physician.
Directory for Midwives [1651]

147 If my *Writing* please the *Readers*, though
not the *Learned*, it wil satisfie me...But I imagine I shall be censurid by my owne *Sex*, and
Men will cast a *smile* of *scorn* upon my *Book*,
because they think thereby, *Women* incroach
too much upon their Prerogatives.
Margaret Cavendish (1623–73) English poet,
playwright, and author.
Poems, and Fancies, 'To All Noble and Writing Ladies'
[1653]

148 Since all heroic actions, public employments, powerful governments, and eloquent
pleadings are denied our sex in this age, or at
least would be condemned for want of custom...I write.
Margaret Cavendish (1623–73) English poet,
playwright, and author.
Nature's Pictures, Drawn by Fancies Pencil to the Life,
'An Epistle to My Readers' [1656]

149 One tongue is sufficient for a woman.
John Milton (1608–74) English poet.
On being asked whether he would allow his daughters
to learn foreign languages. Attrib.

150 For though it be the part of every good
wife to desire children to keep alive the memory
of their husband's name and family by posterity, yet a woman has no such reason to desire
children for her own sake. For first her name is
lost as to her particular in marrying, for she
quits her own and is named as her husband;
also, her family, for neither name nor estate

goest to her family according to the laws and
customs of this country.
Margaret Cavendish (1623–73) English poet,
playwright, and author.
Sociable Letters, XCIII [1664]

151 Neither can women assure themselves of
comfort or happiness by them when they are
grown to be men, for their name only lives in
sons, who continue the line of succession,
whereas daughters are but branches which by
marriage are broken off from the root from
whence they sprange and engrafted into the
stock of another family.
Margaret Cavendish (1623–73) English poet,
playwright, and author.
Sociable Letters, XCIII [1664]

152 The Women, as they make here the Language and Fashions and meddle with Politicks
and Philosophy, so they sway also in Architecture.
Sir Christopher Wren (1632–1723) English
architect.
Comment to a friend on the idea of building the Palace
of Versailles. Letter, 1665

153 Ah, why did God,
Creator wise that peopled highest Heaven
With spirits masculine, create at last
This novelty on earth, this fair defect
Of nature, Woman?
John Milton (1608–74) English poet.
Paradise Lost [1667]

154 Adultery, according to canon law, is as
reprehensible in a husband as in a wife. But it is
different in the secular courts, for a woman's
infidelity has graver results. She gives her husband heirs who are not his children. It is theft to
foist heirs born of debauchery on an entire family: it is a usurpation of the property, nobility
and name of the family.
François Serpillon
*Code Criminel; on commentaire sur l'Ordonnance de
1670*

155 Some perhaps may think, that then it is
not proper for women to be of this profession,
because they cannot attain so rarely to the
knowledge of things as men may, who are bred
up in Universities...But that objection is easily
answered...for, though we women cannot deny
that men in some things may come to a greater
perfection of knowledge than women ordinarily
can, by reason of the former helps that women
want; yet the Holy Scriptures hath recorded
Midwives to the perpetual honour of the female
Sex.
Jane Sharp English writer.
*The Midwives Book, or the whole Art of Midwifery dis-
covered* [1671]

156 For waiving the examination why women having equal education with men, were not as capable of knowledge, of whatsoever sort as well as they: I'll only say as I have touched before, that plays have no great room for that which is men's great advantage over women, that is learning.
Aphra Behn (c. 1640–89) English writer.
The Dutch Lover [1672]

157 A learned woman is thought to be a comet, that bodes mischief whenever it appears.
Bathsua Makin (1612–1674) English scholar and author.
An Essay to Revive the Ancient Education of Gentlewomen [1673]

158 To offer the world the liberal education of women is to deface the image of God in man; it will make women so high and men so low. These things and worse than these are commonly talked of and verily believed by many who think themselves wise men.
Bathsua Makin (1612–74) English scholar and author.
An Essay to Revive the Ancient Education of Gentlewomen [1673]

159 Had God intended women only as a finer sort of cattle, He would not have made them reasonable. Brutes, a few degrees higher than…monkeys…might have better fitted some men's lust, pride, and pleasure; especially those that desire to keep them ignorant to be tyrannized over.
Bathsua Makin (1612–74) English scholar and author.
An Essay to Revive the Ancient Education of Gentlewomen [1673]

160 True it is, our sex make great complaints that men from their first creation usurped a supremacy to themselves, although we were made equal by nature, which tyrannical government they have kept ever since, so that we could never come to be free…which slavery has so dejected our spirits, as we are become so stupid that beasts are but a degree below us, and men use us but a degree above beasts.
Margaret Cavendish (1623–73) English poet, playwright, and author.
The World's Olio [1674]

161 Since *God* has determined subjection to be women's lot, there needs no other argument of its fitness, or for their acquiescence.
Anonymous
The Ladies' Calling [c. 1675]

162 Vain man is apt to think we were meerly intended for the Worlds propogation, and to keep its humane inhabitants sweet and clean; but by their leaves, had we the same Literature,

he would find our brains as fruitful as our bodies. Hence I am induced to believe, we are debar'd from the knowledge of humane learning lest our pregnant Wits should rival the towring conceits of our insulting Lords and Masters.
Mrs Hannah Woolley (1623–75) English governess.
The Gentlewoman's Companion [1675]

163 The right Education of the Female Sex, as it is in a manner everywhere neglected, so it ought to be generally lamented. Most in this depraved later Age think a Woman learned and wise enough if she can distinguish her Husbands Bed from anothers.
Mrs Hannah Woolley (1623–75) English governess.
The Gentlewoman's Companion [1675]

164 On the other hand, I flattered myself that I am not the first lady to have had something published; that minds have no sex and that if the minds of women were cultivated like those of men, and if as much time and energy were used to instruct the minds of the former, they would equal those of the latter.
Marie Meurdrac
La Chymie charitable et facile en faveur des dames [1680]

165 The inward and outward Vertues which ought to be in a Compleat Woman.
As her skill *in Physick, Chirurgery, Cookery, Extraction of Oyls, Banqueting stuff, Ordering of great Feasts, Preserving of all sort of Wines, conceited Secrets, Distillations, Perfumes,* Ordering of *Wool, Hemp, Flax:* Making *Cloath and Dying;* The knowledge of *Dayries:* Office of *Malting;* of *Oats,* their excellent uses in Families: Of *Brewing, Baking,* and all other things belonging to an Houshold.
A Work generally approved, and now *the Ninth time much Augmented, Purged, and made most profitable and necessary for all men, and the general good of this* NATION.
Gervase Markham (1568–1637) English writer.
The English Housewife, Title page [1683]

166 All I ask, is the privilege for my masculine part, the poet in me…if I must not, because of my sex, have this freedom, I lay down my quill and you shall hear no more of me.
Aphra Behn (1640–89) English writer.
The Lucky Chance, Preface [1686]

167 None of the said tenants or cottars that have daughters shall send them to any sewing school within the barony till they have been two full years reading at the said public school.
Baron Court of Stitchill, Lanarkshire
Attempting to encourage female literacy. *History of the Burgh and Parish Schools of Scotland* [1688]

168 The other sex, by means of a more expensive education to the knowledge of Greek and

Roman languages, have a vaster field for their imaginations to rove in, and their capacities thereby enlarged.
Aphra Behn (1640–89) English writer.
'Essay in Defence of the Female Sex' [1689]

169 The Education of their Children as well Daughters as Sons; all which, be they of never so great quality or estate, they always take care to bring up to write perfect good Hands, and to have the full knowledge and use of Arithmetick and Merchant Accounts
Sir Josiah Child (1630–99) English merchant.
Contrasting Dutch and English attitudes to the education of sons and daughters ('they' in the quotation refers to the Dutch). *A New Discourse of Trade* [1693]

170 For shame let's abandon that *Old*, and therefore one wou'd think, unfashionable employment of pursuing Butter-flies and Tri-fles! No longer drudge on in the dull beaten road of Vanity and Folly which so many have gone before us, but dare to break the enchanted Circle that custom has plac'd us in.
Mary Astell (1668–1731) English writer.
A Serious Proposal to the Ladies for the Advancement of Their True and Greatest Interest [1694]

171 Women are from their very Infancy debarr'd those advantages with the want of which they are afterwards reproached, and nursed up in those vices with which will hereaf-ter be upbraided them. So partial are Men as to expect Bricks when they afford no straw.
Mary Astell (1668–1731) English writer.
A Serious Proposal to the Ladies for the Advancement of their True and Greatest Interest [1694]

172 ...have omitted a Description of the parts in a woman destined to Generation, not being absolutely necessary to this purpose, and lest it might seem execrable to the more chaste and shamefaced through Baudiness and Impurity of words; and have also endeavoured to keep all Modesty, and a due Reverence to Nature.
James McMath English doctor.
The Expert Mid-wife [1694]

173 To write, or read, or think, or to inquire, Would cloud our beauty, and exhaust our time, And interrupt the conquests of our prime, Whilst the dull manage of a servile house Is held by some our utmost art and use.
Lady Winchilsea (1661–1720) English poet.
The Spleen [c. 1700]

174 How are we fallen! fallen by mistaken rules,
And Education's more than Nature's fools;
Debarred from all improvements of the mind,
And to be dull, expected and designed.
Lady Winchilsea (1661–1720) English poet.
The Spleen [c. 1700]

175 Boys have much time and care and cost bestowed on their education; girls have little or none. The former are early initiated in the sci-ences, study books and men, have all imagin-able encouragement: not only fame, but also authority, power and riches.
Mary Astell (b. 1666)
Reflections on Marriage [1706]

176 ...that nice unforgiving sex: who arbitrar-ily decide, that woman was only created (with all her beauty, softness, passions and complete tenderness) to adorn the husband's reign, per-fect his happiness, and propagate the kind.
Mary de la Rivière Manley (1663–1724) English author, playwright, and editor.
Secret Memoirs and Manners of Several Persons of Quality of Both Sexes [1709]

177 My sex is usually forbid studies of this nature, and folly reckoned so much our proper sphere, we are sooner pardoned any excesses of that, than the least pretensions to reading or good sense. We are permitted no books but such as tend to the weakening and effeminating of the mind.
Mary Wortley Montagu (1689–1762) British scientist and feminist.
Letter to the Bishop of Salisbury, 1709

178 Wife and servant are the same
But only differ in the name,
For when that fatal knot is tied,
Which nothing, nothing can divide,
When she the word *obey* has said,
And man by law supreme has made,
Then all that's kind is laid aside,
And nothing left but state and pride.
Mary Lee (1656–1710) English poet and author.
The Ladies' Defence [c. 1710]

179 The five worst maladies that afflict the female mind are: indocility, discontent, slan-der, jealousy and silliness. Without any doubt, these five maladies infest seven or eight out of every ten women, and it is from these that arises the inferiority of women to men...Such is the stupidity of her character that it is incumbent on her, in every particular, to distrust herself and to obey her husband.
Ekken Kaibaru
The Whole Duty of Women [c. 1716]

180 And, that the rest of the Fair Sex may be encourag'd to attempt Mathematics and Philo-sophical Knowledge, they here see that their Sex have as clear Judgements, a sprightly quick

Wit, a penetrating Genius, and as discerning and sagacious Faculties as ours.
Anonymous
The Ladies' Diary: or, The Woman's Almanack, Containing many Delightful and Entertaining Particulars, peculiarly adapted for the Use and Diversion of the Fair-Sex [1718]

181   Sundays being privileged from the needle, I have found time of late to read three short pamphlets.
Catherine Cockburn (1679–1749) British poet, playwright, and essayist.
Letter to her niece, 6 Oct 1732

182   Words are men's daughters, but God's sons are things.
Samuel Madden (1686–1765) Irish writer.
Boulter's Monument [1745]

183   Being married in 1708, I bid adieu to the muses, and so wholly gave myself up to the cares of a family, and the education of my children, that I scarce knew, whether there was any such thing as books, plays, or poems stirring in Great Britain.
Catherine Cockburn (1679–1749) British poet, playwright, and essayist.
The Works of Mrs Catherine Cockburn, Theological, Moral, Dramatic, and Poetical (ed. Thomas Birch) [1749]

184   You can come into no company of Ladies and or Gentlemen, where you shall not hear an open and Vehement exclamation against Learned Women.
Elizabeth Elstob (1683–1756) British Anglo-Saxon scholar and governess.
Letter to George Ballard, 1753

185   To say truth, there is no part of the world where our sex is treated with so much contempt as in England...I think it the highest injustice our knowledge must rest concealed, and be as useless to the world as gold in the mine.
Mary Wortley Montagu (1689–1762) British scientist and feminist.
Letter, 1753

186   Conceal whatever learning she attains, with as much solicitude as she whould hide crookedness or lameness; the parade of it can only serve to draw on her the envy, and consequently the most inveterate hatred, of all he and she fools.
Mary Wortley Montagu (1689–1762) British scientist and feminist.
Letter to her daughter, Jan 1753

187   Girls must be subject all their lives to the most constant and severe restraint...that they may the more readily learn to submit to the will of others...But is it not just that this sex should

partake of the sufferings which arise from those evils it hath caused *us*?
Jean Jacques Rousseau (1712–78) French philosopher.
Émile [1762]

188   A woman's thoughts, beyond the range of her immediate duties, should be directed to the study of men, or the acquirement of that agreeable learning whose sole end is the formation of taste; for the works of genius are beyond her reach, and she has neither the accuracy nor the attention for success in the exact sciences.
Jean Jacques Rousseau (1712–78) French philosopher.
Émile [1762]

189   A woman's preaching is like a dog's walking on his hinder legs. It is not done well; but you are surprised to find it done at all.
Samuel Johnson (1709–84) British lexicographer.
Life of Johnson, Vol. I (J. Boswell) [1763]

190   No vote can be given by lunatics, idiots, minors, aliens, females, persons convicted of perjury, subornation of perjury, bribery treating or undue influence, or by those tainted of felony or outlawed in a criminal suit.
William Blackstone (1723–80) British jurist.
Commentaries on the Laws of England [1765]

191   By marriage, the husband and wife are one person in law: that is, the very being or legal existence of the woman is suspended during the marriage, or at least is incorporated or consolidated into that of her husband, under whose wing, protection, and *cover*, she performs everything.
William Blackstone (1723–80) British jurist.
Commentaries on the Laws of England [1765]

192   But if you happen to have any learning, keep it a profound secret, especially from the men, who generally look with a jealous and malignant eye on a woman of great parts and a cultivated understanding. A man of real genius and candour is far superior to this meanness. But such a one will seldom fall in your way.
John Gregory Scottish doctor.
Advice to his daughters. *Scots Magazine*, 1774

193   If perticuliar care and attention is not paid to the Laidies we are determined to foment a Rebelion, and will not hold ourselves bound by any Laws in which we have no voice, or Representation.
Abigail Adams (1744–1818) US letter writer.
Letter to her husband, John Adams, 31 Mar 1776

194   Men of Sense in all Ages abhor those customs which treat us only as the vassals of your Sex.
Abigail Adams (1744–1818) US letter writer.
Letter to her husband, John Adams, 31 Mar 1776

195   I can not say that I think you very generous to the Ladies, for whilst you are proclaiming peace and good will to Men, Emancipating all Nations, you insist upon retaining an absolute power over Wives.
Abigail Adams (1744–1818) US letter writer.
Letter to her husband, John Adams, 7 May 1776

196   A man says what he knows, a woman what is agreeable: knowledge is necessary to the former, taste is sufficient to the latter.
Lord Kames (1696–1782) British lawyer and philosopher.
Loose Hints upon Education [1782]

197   A man is in general better pleased when he has a good dinner upon his table, than when his wife talks Greek.
Samuel Johnson (1709–84) British lexicographer.
Johnsonian Miscellanies Vol. II (ed. G. B. Hill) [1784]

198   Men know that women are an overmatch for them, and therefore they choose the weakest or the most ignorant. If they did not think so, they never could be afraid of women knowing as much as themselves.
James Boswell (1740–95) Scottish lawyer and writer.
Journal of a Tour to the Hebrides [1785]

199   Girls are sacrificed to family convenience, or else marry to settle themselves in a superior rank...if some widows did not now and then *fall* in love, Love and Hymen would seldom meet, unless at a village church.
Mary Wollstonecraft (1759–97) British writer.
A Vindication of the Rights of Men [1790]

Woman is born free...

200 Woman is born free and her rights are the same as those of a man...All citizens, be they men or women, being equal in its eyes, must be equally eligible for all public offices, positions and jobs, according to their capacity and without any other criteria than those of their virtues and talents.
Olympe de Gouges (1748–93) French writer and revolutionary.
Referring to the *Declaration of the Rights of Men and of the Citizen* (1789) in which Article 1 states: 'Men are born free and equal in rights.' *Déclaration des droits de la femme et la citoyenne* [1791]

201 In the government of the physical world it is observable that the female in point of strength is, in general, inferior to the male...But not content with this natural preeminence, men endeavor to sink us still lower, merely to render us alluring objects for a moment.
Mary Wollstonecraft (1759–97) British writer.
A Vindication of the Rights of Woman, Introduction [1792]

202 The *divine right* of husbands, like the divine right of kings, may, it is hoped, in this enlightened age, be contested without danger.
Mary Wollstonecraft (1759–97) British writer.
A Vindication of the Rights of Woman, Ch. 3 [1792]

203 The grand source of female folly and vice has ever appeared to me to arise from narrowness of mind; and the very constitution of civil governments has put almost insuperable obstacles in the way to prevent the cultivation of the female understanding.
Mary Wollstonecraft (1759–97) British writer.
A Vindication of the Rights of Woman, Ch. 3 [1792]

204 I do not wish them to have power over men; but over themselves.
Mary Wollstonecraft (1759–97) British writer.
Referring to women. *A Vindication of the Rights of Woman*, Ch. 4 [1792]

205 I really think that women ought to have representatives, instead of being arbitrarily governed without having any direct share allowed them in the deliberations of government.
Mary Wollstonecraft (1759–97) British writer.
A Vindication of the Rights of Woman, Ch. 7 [1792]

206 I cannot help thinking that the vows most women are made to take are very foolhardy. I doubt whether they would willingly go to the altar to swear that they will allow themselves to be broken on the wheel every nine months.
Suzanne Curchod Necker (1737–94) French author.
Mistress to an Age: A Life of Madame de Staël (J. Christopher Herold) [c. 1794]

207 Till of late, women were kept in Turkish ignorance; every means of acquiring knowledge was discountenanced by fashion, and impracticable even to those who despised fashion...Many things, which were thought to be above their comprehension, or unsuited to their sex, have now been found to be perfectly within the compass of their abilities, and peculiarly suited to their situation.
Maria Edgeworth (1767–1849) Irish novelist and essayist.
Letters for Literary Ladies [1795]

208 The state by recognizing marriage...abandons all claims to consider woman as a legal person. The husband supplies her place; her marriage utterly annuls her, so far as the state is concerned, by virtue of her own necessary will, which the state has guaranteed.
Johann Fichte (1762–1814) German philosopher.
The Science of Rights [1798]

209 Now if a woman holding public office were to marry, two possibilities would follow. First, she might not subject herself to her husband in matters regarding her official duties, which would be utterly against female dignity...secondly, she might subject herself utterly to her husband, as nature and morality require. But in that case she would cease to be the official and he would become it. The office would become his by marriage, like the rest of his wife's property and rights.
Johann Fichte (1762–1814) German philosopher.
The Science of Rights [1798]

210 I may be accused of enthusiasm, but such is my confidence in the sex, that I expect to see our young women forming a new era in female history.
Judith Sargent Murray (1751–1820) US author.
The Gleaner, Vol. III [1798]

211 Botany has lately become a fashionable amusement with the ladies. But how the study of the sexual systems of plants can accord with female modesty, I am not able to comprehend.
Richard Polwhele (1760–1838) British writer.
The Unsex'd Females: A Poem [1798]

212 Oppressed, degraded, enslaved, – must our unfortunate sex for ever submit to sacrifice their right, their pleasures, their *will*, at the altar of public opinion.
Maria Edgeworth (1767–1849) Irish novelist and essayist.
Angelina, Ch. 1 [1799]

213 Can anything be more absurd than keeping women in a state of ignorance, and yet so vehemently to insist on their resisting temptation?
Vicesimus Knox (1752–1821) British essayist.
Liberal Education, Vol. I, 'On the Literary Education of Women' [1800]

214 The entire social order...is arrayed against a woman who wants to rise to a man's reputation.
Germaine de Staël (1766–1817) French novelist, literary critic, and feminist.
The Influence of Literature upon Society [1800]

215 Nay, start not, gentle sirs; indeed, 'tis true,
Poor woman has her rights as well as you;
And if she's wise, she will assert them too.
Susanna Haswell Rowson (1762–1824) British author.
Miscellaneous Poems, 'Rights of Women' [1804]

216 What a misfortune it is to be born a woman!...Why seek for knowledge, which can prove only that our wretchedness is irremediable? If a ray of light break in upon us, it is but to make darkness more visible; to show us the new limits, the Gothic structure, the impenetrable barriers of our prison.
Maria Edgeworth (1767–1849) Irish novelist and essayist.
Leonora, Letter I [1805]

217 Is there a shadow of justice in the fate that has befallen women? Is not the young girl a piece of merchandise displayed for sale to any man willing to bargain for her possession and sole proprietary rights?
Charles Fourier (1772–1837) French social reformer.
Theory of the Four Movements [1808]

218 The extension of women's rights is the basic principle of all social progress.
Charles Fourier (1772–1837) French social reformer.
Theory of the Four Movements [1808]

219 She can have no illusions about her degradation, even in countries with an excessive fondness for philosophising, like England, where a man enjoys the right to lead his wife to market with a rope about her neck and deliver her like a beast of burden to anyone willing to pay the price.
Charles Fourier (1772–1837) French social reformer.
Theory of the Four Movements [1808]

220 I have lately been much occupied in forming a school in Newgate for the children of the poor prisoners as well as the young criminals, which has brought much peace and satisfaction with it.
Elizabeth Fry (1780–1845) British prison reformer.
Journal entry, 24 Feb 1817

221 The weakness of their reasoning faculty also explains why women show more sympathy for the unfortunate than men...and why, on the contrary, they are inferior to men as regards justice, and less honourable and conscientious.
Arthur Schopenhauer (1788–1860) German philosopher.
The World as Will and Representation [1819]

222 The numerous family and large domestic establishment of Mrs Fry are properly conducted with the utmost propriety...nor does her zeal in the holy cause of humanity ever lead her to infringe on those domestic duties which every female is called upon conscientiously to fulfil.
Defending Elizabeth Fry against charges that it was not fitting for her to neglect her home and family in her efforts to reform prison conditions. *The Gentleman's Magazine*, 'Cryptos', Aug 1820

223 When women stand at the head of government, the state is immediately plunged into danger because they conduct affairs not by the standard of universality but in accordance with random opinions and inclinations.
Hegel (1770–1831) German philosopher.
Foundations of the Philosophy of Right [1821]

224 The prejudices still to be found in Europe...which would confine...female conversation to the last new publication, new bonnet, and *pas seul* are entirely unknown here. The women are assuming their place as thinking beings.
Frances Wright (1795–1852) US feminist, social reformer, and author.
Views of Society & Manners in America [1821]

225 She is taught to believe that solid information is unbecoming her sex, almost her whole time is expended on light accomplishments... and when the natural consequences of his mode of treatment arise, all mankind agree that the

abilities of women are far inferior to those of men.
Harriet Martineau (1802–76) British writer and feminist.
Devotional Exercises [1823]

226　To man belong professions, dignities, authorities, and pleasures; for woman, there remain only duties, domestic virtue, and perhaps as the result of these, the happiness of tranquil submission.
Sarah Wentworth Morton (1759–1846) US poet.
My Mind and Its Thoughts, 'The Sexes' [1823]

227　One thing is pretty clear, that all those individuals whose interests are indisputably included in those of other individuals, may be struck off without inconvenience. In this light...women may be regarded, the interest of almost all of whom is involved either in that of their fathers or in that of their husbands.
James Mill (1773–1836) Scottish writer, historian, and philosophical radical.
Discussing who should have the right to vote. *Essay on Government* [1824]

228　Yes, injured Woman! rise, assert thy right!
Woman! too long degraded, scorned, opprest;
O born to rule impartial Laws despite,
Resume thy native empire o'er the breast!
Anna Letitia Barbauld (1743–1825) British poet, essayist, and editor.
The Works of Anna Letitia Barbauld, Vol. I, 'The Right of Woman' [c. 1825]

229　The modest and chaste woman may be assured that nothing is here meant to offend her. Instruction, upon a matter, of which both men and women are by far too ignorant, for their welfare and happiness, is the sole object of this publication. It may shock prejudices, but it will be approved by reason and due deliberation.
Richard Carlile (1790–1843) British journalist.
Every Woman's Book; Or What is Love? [1825]

230　It is a barbarous custom that forbids the maid to make advances in love, or that confines these advances to the eye, the fingers, the gesture, the motion, the manner...Equality and the right to make advances, in all the affairs of genuine love, are claimed for the female. The hypocrisy, the cruelty that would stifle or disguise a passion, whether in the male or in the female is wicked, and should be exposed, reprobated, and detested. Young Women! Assume an equality, plead your passion when you feel it, plead it to those to whom it applies.
Richard Carlile (1790–1843) English journalist.
Every Woman's Book; Or What is Love? [1825]

231　It is the nature of a woman...to cling to the man for support and direction, to comply with

his humours and feel pleasure in doing so, simply because they are his.
Thomas Carlyle (1795–1881) Scottish historian.
Correspondence of Thomas and Jane Welsh Carlyle (ed. C. R. Saunders and K. J. Fielding) [1826]

232　I wish to make a few remarks...respecting my own sex, and the place which I believe it to be their duty and privilege to fill in the scale of society...Far be it for me to attempt to forsake their right province. My only desire is that they should fill that province well; and although their calling in many respects, materially differs from that of the other sex and is not so exalted a one yet...if adequately fulfilled, it has nearly, if not quite, an equal influence on society.
Elizabeth Fry (1780–1845) British prison reformer.
Observations on the Visiting, Superintendance and Government of Female Prisoners [1827]

233　During the last ten years much attention has been successfully bestowed by women on the female inmates of our prisons...But a similar care is evidently needed for our hospitals, our lunatic asylums and our workhouses...Were ladies to make a practice of regularly visiting them, a most important check would be obtained on a variety of abuses, which are far too apt to creep into the management of these establishments.
Elizabeth Fry (1780–1845) British prison reformer.
Observations on the Visiting, Superintendance and Government of Female Prisoners [1827]

234　In this age of innovation perhaps no experiment will have an influence more important on the character and happiness of our society than the granting to females the advantages of a systematic and thorough education. The honour of this triumph, in favour of intellect over long established prejudice, belongs to the men of America.
Sarah Josepha Hale (1788–1879) US editor, writer, and poet.
First issue of the first woman's magazine in America *The Ladies' Magazine*, Jan 1828

235　Accomplished girls, portionless and homeless, were made into governesses, and for the less instructed there was nothing dreamed of but the dressmaking.
Elizabeth Grant (1745–1814) Scottish writer.
Memoirs of a Highland Lady 1797–1829

236　I consider every attempt to induce women to think they have a just right to participate in the public duties of government as injurious to

their best interests and derogatory to their character.
Sarah Josepha Hale (1788–1879) US editor, writer, and poet.
The Ladies' Magazine, Feb 1832

237 On the unjust rights which in virtue of this ceremony an iniquitous law tacitly gives me over the person and property of another, I cannot legally, but I can morally, divest myself. And I hereby distinctly and emphatically declare that I consider myself, and earnestly desire to be considered by others, as utterly divested, now and during the rest of my life, of any such rights, the barbarous relics of a feudal, despotic system.
Robert Owen (1771–1858) British social reformer.
Declaration made at his wedding. *The Oxford Book of Marriage* (ed. Helge Rubinstein) [1832]

238 I know that I am a slave, and you are my lord. The law of this country has made you my master. You can bind my body, tie my hands, govern my actions: you are the strongest, and society adds to your power; but with my will, sir, you can do nothing.
George Sand (Amandine Aurore Lucie Dupin; 1804–76) French writer.
Indiana, Preface [1832]

239 Equality may perhaps be a right, but no power on earth can ever turn it into a fact.
Honoré de Balzac (1799–1850) French novelist.
La Duchesse de Langeais [1834]

240 Oh, how immensely important is this work of preparing the daughters of the land to be good mothers!
Mary Lyon (1797–1849) US missionary and educator.
Letter to her mother, 12 May 1834

241 When we name the infliction of a wrong, we imply the existence of a right. Therefore, if we undertake to discuss the wrongs of women, we may be expected to set out by plainly defining what are the rights of women.
Charlotte Elizabeth Tonna (1790–1846) English poet, educator, and author.
The Wrongs of Women [1834]

242 It was of no importance to the farmer whether he employed the single or married labourer, inasmuch as the labourer's wife and family could provide for themselves. They are now dependent on the man's labour, or nearly so...the families hang as a dead weight upon the rates for want of employment.
The Gentleman's Magazine, 1834

243 While the tests of astronomical merit should in no case be applied to the works of a woman less severely than to those of a man, the sex of the former should no longer be an obstacle to her receiving any acknowledgement which might be held due to the latter.
Royal Astronomical Society
Recommending the granting of honorary membership of the society to Caroline Herschel (1750–1848), British astronomer and Mary Somerville (1780–1872), British astronomer and physical geologist. Report of the Council, 1835

244 Factory females have in general much lower wages than males, and they have been pitied on this account with perhaps an injudicious sympathy, since the low price of their labour here tends to make household duties their most profitable as well as agreeable occupation and prevents them from being tempted by the mill to abandon the care of their offspring at home.
Andrew Ure (1778–1857) British chemist and scientific writer.
The Philosophy of Manufactures [1835]

245 The forming of the minds of children in that early stage of their existence which, in nine cases out of every ten, determines their quality, character, and usefulness, through the whole period of life, is the most sacred duty which devolves upon the sex, and if they neglect this, or perform it in an improper manner, the character of the whole of society is lowered to the same extent.
The Magazine of Domestic Economy, 1835–36, 'Women in Domestic Life'

246 Our fathers waged a bloody conflict with England, because *they* were taxed without being represented...*They* were not willing to be governed by laws which *they* had no voice in making; but this is the way in which women are governed in this Republic.
Angelina Grimké (1805–79) US writer, abolitionist, feminist, and reformer.
Letters to Catherine Beecher [1836]

247 I know you do not make the laws but I also know that you are the wives and mothers, the sisters and daughters of those who do...
Angelina Grimké (1805–79) US writer, abolitionist, feminist, and reformer.
The Anti-Slavery Examiner, 'Appeal to the Christian Women of the South', Sept 1836

248 In everything that women attempt, they should show their consciousness of dependence. There is something so unpleasant in female self-sufficiency, that it not infrequently prejudices instead of persuading...Women, in this respect, are something like children: the more they show their need of support, the more engaging they are.
Anonymous
Magazine article, 'Woman in her Social and Domestic Character' [1837]

249 We must go walk the streets, my sisters, love is our shameful trade,
Never complain though the hours be long and our work so poorly paid,
Fate has decreed that we serve men's need and forfeit our worthless life,
All to defend the family home and protect the virtuous wife.
Auguste Barbier (1805–82) French poet and dramatist.
Lazare [1837]

250 The barbarous custom of wresting from women whatever she possesses, whether by inheritance, donation or her own industry, and conferring it all upon the man she marries, to be used at his discretion and will, perhaps waste it on his wicked indulgences, without allowing her any control or redress, is such a monstrous perversion of *justice* by *law*, that we might well marvel how it could obtain in a Christian community.
Sarah Josepha Hale (1788–1879) US editor, writer, and poet.
Godey's Lady's Book, 'The Rights of Married Women', May 1837

251 It is in vain to talk of the 'rights of women,' as long as they are obliged to confess the supremacy of the other sex in so many different ways. What spinster is there who has a few thousands, that is not obliged to call upon some kind brother, nephew, or friend, to transact her affairs? It matters not what the capacity of her mind may be for business; her education, or rather her want of business education, makes her a child in these affairs.
Hannah Farnham Lee (1780–1865) US author.
Elinor Fulton, Ch. 12 [1837]

252 She knew that it is only in the eyes of the vulgar-minded and the foolish, that a woman is degraded by exerting her ingenuity or her talents as a means of support.
Eliza Leslie (1787–1858) US author, editor, humorist, and cookery expert.
Pencil Sketches; or, Outlines of Character and Manners [1837]

253 It is pleaded that half the human race does acquiesce in the decision of the other half, as to their rights and duties...Such acquiescence proves nothing but degradation of the injured party. It inspires the same emotions of pity as the supplication of the freed slave who kneels to his master to restore him to slavery, that he might have his animal wants supplied, without being troubled with human rights and duties.
Harriet Martineau (1802–76) British writer and feminist.
Society in America [1837]

254 It is clear that the sole business which legislation has with marriage is with the arrangements of property; to guard the reciprocal rights of the children of the marriage and the community. There is no further pretence for the interference of the law, in any way.
Harriet Martineau (1802–76) British writer and feminist.
Society in America [1837]

255 In no country, I believe, are the marriage laws so iniquitous as in England, and the conjugal relation, in consequence, so impaired.
Harriet Martineau (1802–76) British writer and feminist.
Society in America [1837]

256 Is it to be understood that the principles of the Declaration of Independence bear no relation to half of the human race?
Harriet Martineau (1802–76) British writer and feminist.
Society in America [1837]

257 Keep them at home to look after their families; decrease the pressure on the labour market and there is then some chance of a higher rate of wages being enforced.
Anonymous
Referring to Lord Shaftesbury's bill banning women's underground work in the mines. The Coal Mines Act was passed in 1842. *The Northern Star* [1838]

258 'If the law supposes that,' said Mr Bumble...'the law is a ass – a idiot.'
Charles Dickens (1812–70) British novelist.
In reply to Mr Brounlow's statement that 'the law supposes that your wife acts under your direction'. *Oliver Twist*, Ch. 51 [1838]

259 They were both made in the image of God; dominion was given to both over every other creature, but not over each other. Created in perfect equality, they were expected to exercise the vice regence intrusted to them by their Maker, in harmony and love.
Sarah Moore Grimké (1792–1873) US abolitionist and women's rights pioneer.
Letters on the Equality of the Sexes, and the Condition of Woman [1838]

260 There is another way in which the general opinion, that women are inferior to men, is manifested...I allude to the disproportionate value set on the time and labor of men and women.
Sarah Moore Grimké (1792–1873) US abolitionist and women's rights pioneer.
Letters on the Equality of the Sexes, and the Condition of Woman [1838]

261 Woman, instead of being elevated by her union with man, which might be expected from an alliance with a superior being, is in reality lowered. She generally loses her individuality,

her independent character, her moral being. She becomes absorbed into him, and henceforth is looked at, and acts through the medium of her husband.
Sarah Moore Grimké (1792–1873) US abolitionist and women's rights pioneer.
Letters on the Equality of the Sexes, and the Condition of Woman [1838]

262 Let us then, gentlemen, whenever we feel our hearts hardening towards each other, or towards our political opponents, let us fly for counsel to those whose province and whose dearest task it is to soften, to bless, and to purify our imperfect nature.
Speech by the Mayor of Birmingham. *Birmingham Journal*, 23 Feb 1839

263 We have been told that the province of woman is her home, and that the field of politics should be left to men; this we deny; the nature of things renders it impossible, and the conduct of those who give the advice is at variance with the principles they assert. Is it not true that the interests of our fathers, husbands, and brothers, ought to be ours? If they are oppressed and impoverished, do we not share those evils with them? If so, ought we not to resent the infliction of those wrongs upon them?
Female Political Union Newcastle-on-Tyne branch. [1839]

264 We assume that it is never contemplated that the right of voting should be claimed for married women during their husbands' lives; or for unmarried women living under the protection of their parents. The divisions which would thereby be created in the heart of families, and the extensive injury consequent therefrom to domestic peace, are objections too obvious to require discussion.
Edinburgh Review, 1841

265 But I cannot doubt that a greater amount of happiness is produced in the married state from the mutual concession and forbearance which a sense that the union is indissoluble tends to produce, than could be enjoyed if the tie was less firm.
Judgment refusing a divorce petition by Cecilia Cochrane, 1841. *Reports of Cases argued and determined in the Queen's Bench Practice Courts* (A. Dowling) [1841]

266 A large proportion of the 500,000 English women who are lying-in every year and have any attendance at all, are attended by midwives, who, from one cause or other, probably delicacy of the national manners in point of this kind, receive no regular preliminary instruction in anatomy and other matters, some knowledge of which a glance at the causes of death in child-birth will show is indispensable in many emergencies.
Fifth Annual Report of the Registrar General, 1842

267 England is the seat of the most abominable despotism, where laws and prejudices submit women to the most revolting inequality! A woman may inherit only if she has no brothers; she has no civil or political rights, and the law subjects her to her husband in every respect.
Flora Tristan (1803–44) French writer, feminist, and revolutionary socialist.
The London Journal of Flora Tristan [1842]

268 O! men with sisters dear,
O! men with mothers and wives!
It is not linen you're wearing out,
But human creatures' lives!
Thomas Hood (1799–1845) British poet.
The Song of the Shirt [1843]

269 1. To constitute the working class by setting up a compact, solid, and indissoluble union...
9. To proclaim the fact that juridical equality between men and women is the only means of achieving the unity of humanity.
Flora Tristan (1803–44) French writer.
L'Union ouvrière [1843]

270 Mr. E., a manufacturer...informed me that he employed females exclusively at his power-looms...gives a decided preference to married females, especially those who have families at home dependent on them for support; they are attentive, docile, more so than unmarried females, and are compelled to use their utmost exertions to procure the necessities of life.
Lord Shaftesbury (1801–85) British politician and social reformer.
On the Ten Hours Bill; the Act was passed in 1847 achieving the ten-hour day for factory workers. Speech, House of Commons, 15 Mar 1844

271 It should be remarked that, as the principle of liberty is better understood, and more nobly interpreted, a broader protest is made on behalf of women. As men become aware that few have had a fair chance, they are inclined to say that no women have had a fair chance.
Margaret Fuller (1810–50) US journalist.
Woman in the 19th Century [1845]

272 Women are supposed to be very calm generally: but women feel just as men feel; they need exercise for their faculties and a field for their efforts as much as their brothers do; they suffer from too rigid a restraint, too absolute a stagnation, precisely as men would suffer; and it is narrow-minded in their more privileged fellow-creatures to say that they ought to confine themselves to making puddings and knitting stockings, to playing on the piano and

embroidering bags. It is thoughtless to condemn them, or laugh at them, if they seek to do more or learn more than custom has pronounced necessary for their sex.
Charlotte Brontë (1816–55) British novelist.
Jane Eyre [1847]

273 Always bear in mind that boys are naturally wiser than you. Regard them as intellectual beings, who have access to certain sources of knowledge of which you are deprived, and seek to derive all the benefit you can from their peculiar attainments and experience.
Mrs John Farrar
The Young Lady's Friend [1847]

274 In the married state there should be the strictest equality. The husband must come down from the position of master, not that his place may be taken by the woman – but that she may be the sharer of his pleasure, hopes and joys as she has been the partaker of his pains, fears, and sorrow.
The Family Economist, 1848

275 First: Jeanne Deroin, a schoolteacher. Founder of the newspaper *L'Opinion des Femmes*, Mme Desroches, as a sort of protest against marriage, has dropped her married name and uses her maiden name...For her, existing laws do not count...as a woman, she cannot submit to laws made without women's participation.
Reporting on the court proceedings charging Jeanne Deroin with conspiring to form an illegal political society. *Gazette des Tribuneaux*, 12 Nov 1850

276 Gentlemen of the jury, I want to protest against the words of the Advocate General, who reproached me for not using my husband's name. If I do not use it, it is, first, because I do not want to involve my husband in my actions and, second, because I protest against marriage, which is a condition of slavery for women. For my part, I demand absolute equality between the sexes.
Jeanne Deroin (1805–94) French journalist, schoolteacher, and feminist.
Replying to the above charge. *Gazette des Tribuneaux*, 14 Nov 1850

277 Let woman then go on – not asking as favour, but claiming as right, the removal of all the hindrances to her elevation in the scale of being – let her receive encouragement for the proper cultivation of all her powers, so that she may enter profitably into the active business of life; employing her own hands in ministering to her necessities, strengthening her physical being by proper exercise and observance of the laws of health.
Lucretia Mott (1793–1880) US abolitionist and Quaker.
Discourse on Women [1850]

278 The fundamental fault of the female character is that it has no sense of justice.
Arthur Schopenhauer (1788–1860) German philosopher.
Gedanken über vielerlei Gegenstände, XXVII [1850]

279 God made the woman for the man,
And for the good and increase of the world.
Alfred, Lord Tennyson (1809–92) British poet.
'Edwin Morris' [1850]

280 Because the revolutionary tempest, in overturning at the same time the throne and the scaffold, in breaking the chain of the black slave, forgot to break the chain of the most oppressed of all – of Woman, the pariah of humanity.
Jeanne Deroin (1805–94) French journalist, schoolteacher, and feminist.
Letter from the prison of St Lazare, Paris, 15 June 1851

281 Man was created independent because destined to govern the family, society, and nature; while woman was made dependent, tied to hearth and home by a long chain of never-ending infirmities, as if to point out the destined sphere where her activity could find more happiness, although a paler glory.
John Edward Tilt (1815–93) British doctor and president of the Obstetrical Society.
On the Preservation of the Health of Women [1851]

282 If the first woman God ever made was strong enough to turn the world upside down all alone, these women together ought to be able to turn it back, and get it right side up again!
Sojourner Truth (c. 1797–1883) US slave, abolitionist, and lecturer.
Speech, Ohio, 1851

Women want work...

283 The same reasons which make it no longer necessary that the poor should depend on the rich, make it equally unnecessary that women should depend on men, and the least which justice requires is that law and custom should not enforce dependence (when the correlative protection has become superfluous) by ordaining that a woman, who does not happen to have a provision by inheritance, shall have scarcely any means open to her of gaining a livelihood, except as a wife and mother. Let women who prefer that occupation, adopt it; but that there should be no option, no other career possible for the great majority of women, except in the humbler departments of life, is a flagrant social injustice.
John Stuart Mill (1806–73) British philosopher.
The Principles of Political Economy [1852]

284 I have…seen young unmarried women, of the middle class of society, reduced by the constant use of the speculum, to the mental and moral condition of prostitutes, seeking to give themselves the same indulgence by the practice of solitary vice, and asking every medical practitioner…to institute an examination of the sexual organs.
Dr Robert Brudenell Carter (1828–1918) British ophthalmic surgeon.
On the Pathology and Treatment of Hysteria [1853]

285 I do not ask for my rights. I have no rights; I have only wrongs.
Caroline Norton (1808–77) British poet and campaigner for women's rights.
Said when a court upheld her husband's refusal to maintain her. Remark, Aug 1853

286 Every young woman in our land should be qualified by some accomplishment which she may teach, or some art or profession she can follow, to support herself creditably, should the necessity occur.
Sarah Josepha Hale (1788–1879) US editor, writer, and poet.
Godey's Lady's Book, Mar 1854

287 It is time that legal protection be thrown over the produce of their (women's) labour and that in entering the state of marriage, they no longer pass from freedom into the condition of a slave, all of whose earnings belong to his master and not to himself.
Barbara Bodichon (1827–91) British suffragette and co-founder of Girton College.
Law Amendment Society's Journal, Vol. 1, 1855–56

288 My dearest – My days at Balaklava have been so busy as you may suppose. I have made a tour of inspection of Regimental Hosp'ls in camp – besides re-organizing the two Hospitals under our care, which were terribly 'seedy' – Nurses all in confusion.
Florence Nightingale (1820–1910) British nurse.
Letter to her sister, Parthenope Nightingale, 10 May 1855

289 The right to vote will yet be swallowed up in the real question, viz: has woman a right to herself? It is very little to me to have the right to vote, to own property, etc., if I may not keep my body, and its uses, in my absolute right.
Lucy Stone (1818–93) US suffragette and editor.
Letter to Antoinette Brown, 1855

290 We want rights. The flour-merchant, the house-builder, and the postman charge us no less on account of our sex; but when we endeavor to earn money to pay all these, then, indeed, we find the difference.
Lucy Stone (1818–93) US suffragette and editor.
Speech, 'Disappointment Is the Lot of Women', 17–18 Oct 1855

291 I almost regret that I did not make you aware at the risk of troubling you with trifles, of my experience of the goods & evils of the position of a woman, qua woman, in official life. It is difficult to overrate the disadvantages attached to her means of efficiency, as a public officer among men – public Officers. All their defects, qua men of business, are laden upon her – because 'a woman cannot be a man of business'.
Florence Nightingale (1820–1910) British nurse.
Letter to Sir John McNeill, 24 Oct 1856

292 It descended to the crowd and took the consistency and heat of a political passion, in such wise that general and abstract theories on the nature of society became the subject of daily conversation among those who had nothing to do, and inflamed the imagination even of women and peasants?
Alexis de Tocqueville (1805–59) French writer.
L'Ancien Régime [1856]

293 It must be clear that these are errors in the physical education of infants – errors in the habits of mothers, which are as wide-spread and deeply rooted as families themselves.
Dr R. Hall Bakewell
The British Mothers' Journal, 'Infant Mortality, and Its Causes', June 1857

294 Women want work both for the health of their minds and their bodies. They want it often because they must eat and because they have children and others dependent on them – for all the reasons that men want work.
Barbara Bodichon (1827–91) British suffragette and co-founder of Girton College.
Women and Work [1857]

295 So long as nearly every remunerative employment is engrossed by men only, so long must the wretchedness and slavery of women remain what it is.
Barbara Bodichon (1827–91) British suffragette and co-founder of Girton College.
Women and Work [1857]

296 What society wants from women is not labour, but refinement, elevation of mind, knowledge, making its power felt through moral influence and sound opinions. It wants civilizers of men, and educators of young. And society will suffer in proportion as women are either driven by necessity or tempted by seeming advantages to leave this their natural vocation, and to join the noisy throng in the busy markets of the world.
Eliza Shirreff (1814–97) British educationalist.
Intellectual Education and Its Influence on the Character and Happiness of Women [1858]

297 The whole process of home-making, housekeeping and cooking, which ever has been woman's special province, should be looked on as an art and a profession.
Sarah Josepha Hale (1788–1879) US editor, writer, and poet.
Godey's Lady's Book, c. 1859

298 So far from our country-women being all maintained as a matter of course by us, the breadwinners, 3 million out of 6 million adult Englishwomen work for subsistence; and two out of three for independence.
Harriet Martineau (1802–76) British writer and feminist.
Edinburgh Review, 'Female Industry', 1859

299 In a community where a larger proportion of women remain unmarried than at any known period; where a greater number of women depend on their own industry for subsistence...and where improved machinery demands more and more skilled labour which women can supply, how can there be doubt that women will work more and more.
Harriet Martineau (1802–76) British writer and feminist.
Edinburgh Review, 'Female Industry', 1859

300 No *man*, not even a doctor ever gives any other definition of what a nurse should be than this – 'devoted and obedient.' This definition would do just as well for a porter. It might even do for a horse. It would not do for a policeman.
Florence Nightingale (1820–1910) British nurse.
Notes on Nursing [1859]

301 Married life is a woman's profession and to this life her training, that of dependence, is modelled. Of course by not getting a husband, or by losing him, she may find she is without resources. All that can be said of her is, she has failed in her business, and no social reform can prevent such failures.
Saturday Review, Nov 1859

302 I should like to know what is the proper function of women, if it is not to make reasons for husbands to stay at home, and still stronger reasons for bachelors to go out.
George Eliot (Mary Ann Evans; 1819–80) British novelist.
The Mill on the Floss, Ch. 6 [1860]

303 Instead of wishing to see more Doctors made by women joining what there are, I wish to see as few Doctors, either male or female, as possible. For, mark you, the women have made no improvement – they have only tried to be 'Men', & they have only succeeded in being third-rate men.
Florence Nightingale (1820–1910) British nurse.
Letter to John Stuart Mill, 12 Sept 1860

304 We consider first that the promiscuous assemblage of the sexes in the same class is a dangerous innovation...That the presence of young females as passive spectators in the operating theatre is an outrage to our natural instincts and feelings and calculated to destroy those sentiments of respect and admiration with which the opposite sex is regarded by all right minded men, such feelings being a mark of civilization and refinement.
Medical school committee Middlesex Hospital
Minutes of meeting, 1861

305 Having taken pains to obtain and compare abundant evidence on the subject I should say that the majority of women (happily for them) are not very much troubled with sexual feelings of any kind...As a general rule, a modest woman seldom desires any sexual gratification for herself. She submits to her husband, but only to please him; and but for the desire of maternity would far rather be relieved from his attentions.
William Acton
See below for reply. *The Functions of the Reproductive Organs* [1862]

306 Sexual intercourse in marriage is a subject of vital importance, and one the bearing of which every medical man should be fully acquainted with. There is one statement of Mr Acton's which we think is open to question,

viz., that venereal pleasure is almost entirely on the side of the male. Now, this is unphysiological in the first place, and moreover, experience proves the contrary.
Replying to William Acton, above. The London Medical Review, 1862

307 If women want any rights more'n they got, why don't they just *take 'em*, and not be talkin' about it.
Sojourner Truth (c. 1797–1883) US slave, abolitionist, and lecturer.
Attrib. [c. 1863]

308 The woman's power is not for rule, nor for battle – and her intellect is not for invention or creation, but for sweet orderings, management and decision. She sees the qualities of things, their class, their places.
John Ruskin (1819–1900) British art critic and writer.
Sesame and Lilies [1865]

309 This, then, is the patriotism of woman; not to thunder in senates, or to usurp dominion, or to seek the clarion-blast of fame, but faithfully to teach by precept and example that wisdom, integrity, and peace which are the glory of a nation.
Lydia Howard Sigourney (1791–1865) US poet, author, teacher, and magazine editor.
Letters to Mothers [c. 1865]

310 It is important that young females should possess some employment by which they might obtain a livelihood in case they should be reduced to the necessity of supporting themselves.
Lydia Howard Sigourney (1791–1865) US poet, author, teacher, and magazine editor.
Letters to Mothers [c. 1865]

311 Among all the reasons for giving women the vote, the one which appears to me the strongest is that of the influence it might be expected to have in increasing public spirit...As it is, women of the middle class occupy themselves but little with anything beyond the immediate family circle.
Barbara Bodichon (1827–91) British suffragette and co-founder of Girton College.
Objections to the Enfranchisement of Women Considered [1866]

312 Women – one half the human race at least – care fifty times more for a marriage than a ministry.
Walter Bagehot (1826–77) British economist and journalist.
The English Constitution, 'The Monarchy' [1867]

313 We are told that we ought to ask for £30,000 at least...It is not a large sum, considering that there is to be but one college of this

sort...and considering how easy it is to raise immense sums for boys' schools. But considering how few people really wish women to be educated, it is a good deal.
Emily Davies (1830–1921) British suffragette and co-founder of Girton College, Cambridge.
Letter to Mme Bodichon, Jan 1867

314 But – what I want to see is – not, as Miss Garrett seems to wish – women obtaining exactly *the same* education as men, & exactly the same Diploma – & practising indiscriminately between the sexes as men do.
Very far otherwise.
Not that I conceive it is much more indelicate for a woman to doctor men than for a women to nurse men.
But the last is necessary.
The first is totally unnecessary.
Florence Nightingale (1820–1910) British nurse.
Letter to Sir Harry Verney, 16 Apr 1867

315 That women should have the suffrage, think no one can be more deeply convinced than I. It is so important for a woman, especially a married woman, especially a clever married woman, to be a 'person'. But it will probably be years before you obtain the suffrage for women. And, in the mean time, are there not evils which press much more hardly on women than not having a vote?
Florence Nightingale (1820–1910) British nurse.
Letter to John Stuart Mill, 11 Aug 1867

316 To employ women and children unduly is simply to run into debt with Nature.
The Times, 4 Mar 1867

317 Housekeeping ain't no joke.
Louisa May Alcott (1832–88) US novelist.
Little Women, Pt I [1868]

318 What is meant by the glib assertion, that woman is the equal of man? Is she equal in size? No. In physical strength? No. In intellect? Yes, replies the advocate; and if she received the same training as man, she would demonstrate her intellectual equality and her moral superiority to her masculine tyrant. I deny this assertion; and proceed to show why woman is incapable of receiving a training similar to that of man. My position is, that *there must be radical, natural, permanent distinctions in the mental and moral conformation, corresponding with those in the physical organisation of the sexes.*
J. M. Allan
Journal of the Anthropological Society, 'On the Differences in the Minds of Men and Women' [1869]

319 The most important thing women have to do is to stir up the zeal of women themselves.
John Stuart Mill (1806–73) British philosopher.
Letter to Alexander Bain, 14 July 1869

320 The power is a power given not to good men, or to decently respectable men, but to all men...How many men are there who...indulge the most violent aggressions of bodily torment towards the unhappy wife who alone of all persons cannot escape from their brutality...The law compels her to bear everything from him.
John Stuart Mill (1806–73) British philosopher.
On the Subjection of Women [1869]

321 It is a man's place to rule, and a woman's to yield. He must be held up as the head of the house, and it is her duty to bend so unmurmuringly to his wishes, that the rest of the household will follow her example, and treat him with the due respect his sex demands.
Sarah Ann Sewell (fl. 1870s) English writer.
Woman and the Times We Live In [1869]

322 Bread and Milk Flour is the name of the new compound designed for babies food – prepared in a few minutes with water only. When we consider that in addition to the natural grief of mothers who are denied the privilege of nursing their infants, they are in many cases compelled to submit to the worry, annoyance, and expense of maintaining a wet-nurse, we heartily welcome a substitution for the great desideratum the mother's milk.
The Englishwoman's Domestic Magazine, 'A New Food For Infants', Apr 1869

323 There is no comparison to be made between prostitutes and the men who consort with them. With the one sex the offence is committed as a matter of gain; with the other it is an irregular indulgence of a natural impulse.
Royal Commission into the Contagious Diseases Acts [1864, 1866, and 1869]

324 I am much pleased at Miss Garrett's success. She ought to have a vote for Westminster, but not to sit in Parliament. It would make too much confusion.
Lord John Russell (1792–1878) British statesman.
Letter to Lord Amberley, 1870

325 The days have long gone by when to be the fruitful mother of children was the happiest ambition to which, in public estimation, a woman could aspire...If it is still considered rather undignified to have no children at all, it is looked upon as supremely ridiculous to have a great many.
Anonymous
Beauty is Power [1871]

326 The chief distinction in the intellectual powers of the two sexes is shown by man attaining to a higher eminence, in whatever he takes up, than woman can attain – whether requiring deep thought, reason, or imagination, or merely the use of the senses and hands.
Charles Darwin (1809–82) British life scientist.
The Descent of Man [1871]

327 It is my opinion that by the higher and more thoroughly Christian education of women, what are called their 'wrongs' will be redressed, their wages will be adjusted, their weight of influence in reforming the evils of society will be greatly increased; as teachers, as writers, as mothers, as members of society, their power for good will be incalculably enlarged.
Sophia Smith (1796–1870) US philanthropist.
Last Will and Testament of Miss Sophia Smith, Late of Hatfield, Massachusetts [1871]

328 Age has not abated my zeal for the emancipation of my sex from the unreasonable prejudice too prevalent in Great Britain against a literary and scientific education for women.
Mary Somerville (1780–1872) British scientist and feminist.
Personal Recollections, From Early Life to Old Age (Martha Somerville) [1872]

329 Of all the little foxes that help destroy the domestic vines...the worst is that which makes it necessary for the wife to *ask* her husband for money to supply the daily recurring family necessities and her own.
Lucy Stone (1818–93) US suffragette.
Woman's Journal, 7 Sept 1872

330 For women there are, undoubtedly, great difficulties in the path, but so much the more to overcome. First, no woman should say, 'I am but a woman!' But a woman! what more can you ask to be?
Maria Mitchell (1818–89) US astronomer.
Address to students, 1874

331 The whole system is demoralizing and foolish. Girls study for prizes and not for learning, when 'honors' are at the end. The unscholarly motive is wearying. If they studied for sound learning, the cheer which would come with every day's gain would be health-preserving.
Maria Mitchell (1818–89) US astronomer.
Diary, 13 Mar 1874

332 The sexes in each species of beings...are always true equivalents – equals but not identicals.
Antoinette Brown Blackwell (1825–1921) US writer.
The Sexes Throughout Nature [1875]

333 Woman's share of duties must involve direct nutrition, man's indirect nutrition. She should be able to bear and nourish their young children, at a cost of energy equal to the amount expended by him as household provider. Beyond this, if human justice is to supplement

Nature's provisions, all family duties must be shared equitably, in person or by proxy.
Antoinette Brown Blackwell (1825–1921) US writer.
The Sexes Throughout Nature [1875]

334 Women must know something of the fundamental laws which explain the cosmic system of our planet and the simpler facts of meteorology and physics...They will be able to stop believing and making their children believe – thereby stunting the development of their intellects – that rain is sent to us by Jesus, that thunder is the sign of divine anger and menace, and that successful crops and a good or bad harvest are to be attributed rather to the will of Providence than to the merits of work and the course of natural events.
A. Angiulli
La Pedagogia, lo Stato e la Famiglia [1876]

335 How is it possible that this absurd talk about a woman's sphere is still heard in the face of those millions of women who earn their bread by the sweat of their brows in fields and factories, in streets and mines, behind the counter and in the office?
Hedwig Dohm (1833–1919) German writer.
Der Frauen Natur und Recht [1876]

336 We are slowly realizing that any knowledge calculated to improve the human mind should be communicated to women no less than men.
James Grant (1822–87) British novelist and miscellaneous writer.
History of the Burgh and Parish Schools of Scotland [1876]

337 The time has come which certainly will come, when women who are practically concerned in political life will have a voice in making the laws which they have to obey; but every woman who can think and speak wisely, and bring up her children soundly, in regards to rights and duties of society is advancing the time when the interests of women will be represented as well as those of men.
Harriet Martineau (1802–76) British writer and feminist.
Harriet Martineau's Autobiography with Memorials by Maria Weston Chapman [1876]

338 Can we force women to take up *Midwifery & Nursing* by legislation to prevent them from being *Doctors*?...Have we any right to shut women out?...
Let them try: Once we have 'free trade', supply & demand will, will they not?, adjust themselves: it will be seen, by the simple test of utility, of profit & loss, whether *women Doctors* can *get practice*, & *deserve practice*.

Florence Nightingale (1820–1910) British nurse.
Letter to Henry Acland, 19 Apr 1876

339 New avenues for higher culture and for good works are opening before them, which fifty years ago were unknown. That they may improve these opportunities, and be faithful to their high vocation, is my heartfelt prayer.
Sarah Josepha Hale (1788–1879) US editor, writer, and poet.
Godey's Lady's Book, Dec 1877

340 She was a gentlewoman, a scholar, and a saint, and after being married three times she took a vow of celibacy; what more could be expected of any woman?
Elizabeth Wordsworth (1840–1932) First principal of Lady Margaret Hall, Oxford.
Suggesting that the college should be named after Lady Margaret Beaufort (1443–1509) Countess of Richmond. Founding committee meeting, 1879

341 When I think over the sufferings of women in India in all ages, I am impatient to see the Western light dawn as the harbinger of emancipation.
Anandabai Joshee (1865–87) Indian physician; first Hindu woman to receive medical degree.
Letter to Mrs Carpenter, 1880

342 Walk wide o' the Widow at Windsor,
For 'alf o' Creation she owns:
We have bought 'er the same with sword an' the flame,
An' we've salted it down with our bones.
Rudyard Kipling (1865–1936) Indian-born British writer.
Referring to Queen Victoria. *The Widow at Windsor* [1880]

343 Gentlemen...Do you not see that so long as society says a woman is incompetent to be a lawyer, minister or doctor, but has ample ability to be a teacher, that every man of you who chooses this profession tacitly acknowledges that he has no more brains than a woman?
Susan B. Anthony (1820–1906) US editor.
Speech, State Convention of Schoolteachers, 1881

344 The whole moveable or personal estate of the wife, whether acquired before or during the marriage shall, by operation of law, be vested in the wife as her separate estate and shall not be subject to the *jus mariti*.
Married Women's Property (Scotland) Act [1881]

345 The prolonged slavery of women is the darkest page in human history.
Elizabeth Cady Stanton (1815–1902) US suffragette and abolitionist.
History of Woman Suffrage, Vol. I [1881]

346 We still wonder at the stolid incapacity of all men to understand that woman feels the

invidious distinctions of sex exactly as the black man does those of color, or the white man the more transient distinctions of wealth, family, position, place, and power; that she feels as keenly as man the injustice of disfranchisement.
Elizabeth Cady Stanton (1815–1902) US suffragette and abolitionist.
History of Woman Suffrage, Vol. I [1881]

347   The centennial will be but the celebration of the independence of one-half the nation. The men alone of this country live in a republic, the women enter the second hundred years of national life as political slaves.
Matilda Gage (1826–98) US social reformer.
Woman, Church and State (Sally Wagner) [1883]

348   It is strange to see into what unreasonable disrepute active housekeeping – women's first social duty – has fallen in England. The snobbish half of the middle-class hold housewifely work as degrading. A woman may sit in a dirty drawing room which the slip-shod maid has not had the time to clean, but she can not have a duster in her hands. There is no disgrace in the dust only in the duster.
Elizabeth Lynn Linton (1822–98) British writer.
The Girl of the Period and Other Social Essays [1883]

349   Oh pedants of these later days, who go on undiscerning,
To overload a woman's brain and cram our girls with learning,
You'll make a woman half a man, the souls of parents vexing,
To find that all the gentle sex this process is unsexing.
Leave one or two nice girls before the sex your system smothers,
Or what on earth will poor men do for sweethearts, wives and mothers?
Anonymous
Punch, 10 May 1884

350   A female professor of mathematics is a pernicious and unpleasant phenomenon – even, one might say, a monstrosity; and her invitation to a country where there are so many male mathematicians far superior in learning to her can be explained only by the gallantry of the Swedes toward the female sex.
August Strindberg (1849–1912) Swedish dramatist.
Referring to the appointment of Sonya Kovalévsky as professor of mathematics at Stockholm University (1884).

351   The moment a woman marries she is more or less the subject of every existing authority. Conventional society dictates her how, where, and in what manner it is proper for her to live. In the eyes of the law her personal liberty and her status are *nil*, her husband may lock her up and refuse her friends access to her; the guardianship of her children is not hers.
The Westminster Review, Jan 1884

352   It makes me mad to hear people talk about unemployed women. If they are unemployed it is because they won't work. The highest salaries given to women at all we can secure to women trained by us. But we can't find the women. They won't come.
Florence Nightingale (1820–1910) British nurse.
Referring to the difficulty of recruiting women for the nursing profession. *Florence Nightingale, 1820–1910* (Cecil Woodham-Smith) [1885]

353   Women are the creatures of an organised tyranny of men, as the workers are the creatures of an organised tyranny of idlers.
The Westminster Review, 1885

354   The right of private contract is a right very dear to a liberty-loving people; yet in the most important matter of their lives, they have consented to forego it.
Mona Caird (d. c. 1935)
Referring to marriage. *Daily Telegraph*, 1887

355   Probably the most successful mode of rearing girls, so as to bring them to the full perfection of womanhood, is to retard the period of puberty as much as possible…It is the duty, therefore, of the mother to enjoin on her daughter the frequent use of cold baths, free exercise in the open air, or in cool, well-ventilated rooms, to provide plain and digestible diet for her, and to insist on abstinence from *hot* tea and coffee.
E. H. Ruddock
The Common Diseases of Women [1888]

356   But you must know the class of sweet women – who are always so happy to declare 'they have all the rights they want'; 'they are perfectly willing to let their husbands vote for them' – are and always have been numerous, though it is an occasion for thankfulness that they are becoming less so.
Eliza 'Mother' Stewart (1816–1908) US temperance leader.
Memories of the Crusade, Ch. 7 [1888]

357   Women must remain in industry despite all narrow-minded caterwauling; in fact the circle of their industrial activity must become broader and more secure daily.
Clara Zetkin (1857–1933) German political activist and co-founder of the Communist Party of Germany.
The Question of Women Workers and Women at the Present Time [1889]

358   The organization and enlightenment of working women, the struggle to attain their eco-

nomic and political equal rights is not only desirable for the socialist movement. It is and will become more and more a life-and-death question for it.
Clara Zetkin (1857–1933) German political activist and co-founder of the Communist Party of Germany.
The Question of Women Workers and Women at the Present Time [1889]

359   Taken as a whole, the legal status of the Mohammedan woman is not more unfavourable than that of a European woman, whilst in many respects she occupies a decidedly better position.
Amir 'Ali (1849–1928) Indian writer.
The Nineteenth Century, 'The Real Status of Women in Islam' [1891]

360   This clamour for political rights is woman's confession of sexual enmity. Gloss over it as we may, it comes to this in the end. No woman who loves her husband would wish to usurp his province. It is only those whose instincts are inverted, or whose anti-sexual vanity is insatiable, who would take the political reins from the strong hands which have always held them to give them to others – weaker, less capable, and wholly unaccustomed.
Elizabeth Lynn Linton (1822–98) British writer.
The Wild Women as Politicians [1891]

361   The modern woman stands with the prospect of shrinking fields of labour on every hand. She is brought face-to-face with two possibilities. Either, on the one hand, she may remain quiescent and, as her old fields of labour fall from her, seek no new...On the other hand, woman may determine not to remain quiescent...she may determine to find labour in the new and to obtain that training which...shall fit her to take as large a share in the labours of her race in the future as in the past.
Olive Schreiner (1855–1920) South African writer.
Thoughts on South Africa, Ch. 4 [1892]

362   ...the fatal perils awaiting female aspirants to intellectual fame...there is a decided difference between the sexes in their physical and intellectual capacity and power of endurance. This is the result of the direction which the evolution of each sex has taken.
John Clarence Webster (1863–1930) British gynaecologist.
Puberty and the Change of Life. A Book for Women [1892]

363   Poor Mrs John Smith, her life is one long slavery. Cooking, cleaning, managing, mending, washing clothes, waiting on husband and children, her work is never done. What are her *hours of labour*, my trade union friend? What pleasure has she, what rest, what prospect?
Robert Blatchford (1851–1943) British journalist.
Merrie England [1893]

364   He does not yet discern her equal right with himself to impress her own opinions on the world. He still interprets governments and religions as requiring from her an unquestioning obedience to laws she had no share in making.
Matilda Gage (1826–98) US social reformer.
Woman, Church and State: the Original Exposé of Male Collaboration Against the Female Sex [1893]

365   The most stupendous system of organized robbery known has been that of the church towards woman, a robbery that has not only taken her self-respect but all rights of person; the fruits of her own industry; her opportunities of education; the exercise of her judgment, her own conscience, her own will.
Matilda Gage (1826–98) US social reformer.
Woman, Church and State: the Original Exposé of Male Collaboration Against the Female Sex [1893]

366   Were we not employed others would have to be, and if of the opposite sex, I venture to say, sir, would have to be paid on a very different scale. Why, because we are weak women, without pluck and grit enough to stand up for our rights, should we be ground down to this miserable wage?
Ada Nield Chew (1870–1945) British suffragette.
Crewe Chronicle, 19 May 1894

367   The general tone of this influence is against the idea that women should assert their rights as human beings, or that they should be loyal to a cause, and to their comrades, known and unknown in that cause, sooner than to their own immediate interests.
Isabella Ford (c. 1860–1924) British feminist.
Referring to the education of girls. *Industrial Women and How to Help Them* [c. 1895]

368   I would earnestly advise everybody thinking of going to any out of the way part of our Colonies to learn to a certain extent how to do everything for himself or herself. Cooking, baking and washing, besides making and mending are duties which a woman may very likely have to undertake herself, or to teach an untrained servant to perform. I should be inclined to add to the list of desirable accomplishments, riding, driving and the art of shearing and saddling a horse in case of emergency, for the distances from place to place are great and the men are often all out on the run or in the bush.
Lady Brassey
Report following a visit to Australia, 1896

369 While in most states the divorce laws are the same for men and women, they never can bear equally upon both while all the property earned during marriage belongs wholly to the husband.
Susan B. Anthony (1820–1906) US editor.
The Arena, 'The Status of Women, Past, Present and Future', May 1897

370 Public opinion has largely altered for the better; education for women has progressed, and is steadily progressing; women have obtained entrance into many eminently suitable callings, chiefly by their own brave efforts; they have gained a strong footing in Local Self-Government; they now, as married women, control and administer their own property or results of their earnings; and are even recognized as legal guardians of their children!...But much remains to be done.
Enid Stacey British suffragette.
Forecasts of the Coming Century, 'A Century of Women's Rights' (E. Carpenter) [1897]

371 Working women want to make themselves felt in public life for definite purposes – to improve the social laws and administration, and particularly to watch over the lives of women and children. To reject from the electorate public-spirited workers like these is a folly which nothing but voluntary ignorance can account for.
Women's Co-operative Guild
Report of a Guild meeting. *Co-operative News*, 27 Mar 1897

372 Rock-a-bye, baby, for father is near,
Mother is 'biking' she never is here!
Out in the park she's scorching all day
Or at some meeting is talking away!
She's the king-pin at the women's rights show,

Teaching poor husbands the way they should go!
Close then, your eyes; there's dishes to do.
Rock-a-bye, baby; 'tis pa sings to you.
Anonymous
Monthly Herald, Apr 1898

373 The labor of women in the house, certainly, enables men to produce more wealth than they otherwise could; and in this way women are economic factors in society. But so are horses.
Charlotte Perkins Gilman (1860–1935) US writer and lecturer.
Women and Economics, Ch. 1 [1898]

374 The mother as a social servant instead of a home servant will not lack in true mother duty...From her work, loved and honored though it is, she will return to the home life, the child life, with an eager, ceaseless pleasure, cleansed of all the fret and fraction and weariness that so mar it now.
Charlotte Perkins Gilman (1860–1935) US writer and lecturer.
Women and Economics, Ch. 13 [1898]

375 Possessed by a restless discontent of their appointed work, and fired with a mad desire to dabble in all things unseemly, which they call ambition; blasphemous to the sweetest virtues of their sex, which until now have been accounted with their own pride and the safeguard of society...these women of the doubtful gender have managed to drop all their own special graces while unable to gather up any of the more valuable virtues of men.
Elizabeth Lynn Linton (1822–98) British writer.
The Epicene Sex [c. 1890s]

Votes for Women!

376 We want the electoral franchise not because we are angels oppressed by the wickedness of 'the base wretch man' but because we want women to have the ennobling influence of national responsibility brought into their lives.
Millicent Garrett Fawcett (1847–1929) British suffragette.
Speech, Women's Debating Society, The Owen's College, Manchester, 13 Feb 1899

377 Many a young life is battered and forever crippled in the breakers of puberty; if it cross these unharmed and is not dashed to pieces on the rock of childbirth, it may still ground on the ever-recurring shallows of menstruation, and lastly, upon the final bar of the menopause e'er protection is found in the unruffled waters of the harbor beyond reach of sexual storms.
George J. Engelmann (1809–84) US physician and botanist.
President's Address, American Gynecology Society, 1900

378 Many Lancashire women are keeping on homes, and even worthless husbands, and yet the latter when it becomes a matter of voting have the only voice in the affairs of the nation. The children are led by this to think little of their mothers and much of their fathers.
Sarah Dickenson (1868–1954) British suffragette.
Englishwoman's Review, 15 Apr 1901

379 To the Right Honourable the Commons of Great Britain and Ireland, in Parliament assembled. The HUMBLE PETITION of the undersigned women workers in the cotton factories of Lancashire.
Sheweth:
That in the opinion of your petitioners the continued denial of the franchise to women is unjust and inexpedient.
In the home, their position is lowered by such an exclusion from the responsibilities of national life.
In the factory, their unrepresented condition places the regulation of their work in the hands of men who are often their rivals as well as their fellow workers.
North of England Society for Women's Suffrage
Englishwoman's Review, 15 Apr 1901

380 What a Woman may be, and yet not have the Vote
Mayor   Nurse   Mother   Doctor or Teacher Factory Hand

What a Man may have been, & yet not lose the Vote
Convict   Lunatic   Proprietor of White Slaves Unfit for Service   Drunkard
Poster used during the suffragette campaign [c. 1901]

381 Women, methinks, have waited long enough, without standing aside until the men get more than they appear to have been contented with for so many years. Women are the most downtrodden and sweated workers in all the industrial world. Taxation without representation has been their lot for so long that they are sick of it.
Julia Dawson (d. 1945) British writer.
The Clarion, 15 Aug 1902

382 Naive conclusions to draw from man's brutality! Because man is a brute, woman has to be locked up so that she will remain unharmed.
Hedwig Dohm (1833–1919) German writer.
Die Antifeministen [The Antifeminists; 1902]

383 More pride, you women! How is it possible that you do not rebel against the *contempt* with which you are met?
Hedwig Dohm (1833–1919) German writer.
Die Antifeministen [The Antifeminists; 1902]

384 Mr Bell was speaking about the way in which women are used to bring down wages. How far are men responsible for that fact? Treat the woman as an inferior and she will play the part, if only in self-defence.
Keir Hardie (1856–1915) British politician.
Speech, Chelsea Town Hall, 18 Feb 1902

385 There are no herbs against death but there are many herbs against the early death of woman. The most effective is unconditional emancipation for women and with it the salvation from that brutal myth that her right of existence is based on her sexuality only.
Hedwig Dohm (1833–1919) German writer.
Die Mütter [The Mother; 1903]

386 To women the enjoyment of University life brought home a knowledge of the infinite power and force that lie in the idea of…fellowship with those associated with us in study, but differing from us in experience, in the object of their work, and in the destinies that await them.
Ethel Hurlbatt (d. 1934) British educator, principal of Bedford College, London.
Speech, Sixteenth Annual General Meeting of the Women's University Settlement, 1903

387   A man thinks himself badly off if he cannot earn more than 17s a week…there are…skilled women who can never hope to earn more than 12s to the end of their lives…These workers are living very near the subsistence level. Without any industrial or political defence, they are fully exposed to the crushing and numbing force of the bare struggle for life.
Manchester and Salford Women's Trade Union Council
Annual Report, 1903

388   Give women the vote, and in five years there will be a crushing tax on bachelors.
George Bernard Shaw (1856–1950) Irish dramatist and critic.
Man and Superman, Preface [1903]

389   These two movements have had in the past, as now, the same object, and have therefore been largely interdependent, in that both have fallen and risen together, and the same events have affected each, more or less in the same manner. Also that the same powers have been and are still, hostile to both.
Isabella Ford British feminist.
Referring to feminism and socialism. *Women and Socialism* [1904]

390   He had fancied that a woman can shed her past like a man.
Edith Wharton (1862–1937) US writer.
The Descent of Man, Ch. 4 [1904]

391   And yet, in the schoolroom more than any other place, does the difference of sex, if there is any, need to be forgotten.
Susan B. Anthony (1820–1906) US editor.
Elizabeth Cady Stanton, Vol. II (eds Theodore Stanton and Harriot Stanton Blatch) [1906]

392   Just so long as there is a degraded class of labor in the market, it always will be used by the capitalists to checkmate and undermine the superior classes.
Susan B. Anthony (1820–1906) US editor.
Speech, 1906, 'Woman Wants Bread, Not the Ballot!'

393   Why do women take so little interest in the affairs of the world? It is not because they are denied votes. It is because they do not understand. I would give them votes if I could. But I would a thousand times rather they should learn and understand.
Robert Blatchford (1851–1943) British journalist.
The Clarion, 24 Aug 1906

394   Every woman in England is longing for her political freedom in order to make the lot of the worker pleasanter and to bring about reforms which are wanted. We do not want it as a mere plaything!
Selina Cooper (1864–1946) British suffragette.
Addressing an open-air meeting in Wigan. *Wigan Observer*, 6 Jan 1906

395   If all women were enfranchised they would at once swamp the votes of men.
Samuel Evans MP for Glamorgan, Wales.
House of Commons, 1906

396   Sir – It will be of interest to many of your readers to learn that we have in Manchester founded a Women's Social and Political Union, its objects being to secure for women complete equality with men, both social and political. As in the other political parties, so in the Labour party, the help of women is welcomed in the work of elections, but when our leaders and men members of the party are asked for efforts to be made to secure the enfranchisement of women, they express, at best, vague sympathy.
Rachel Scott British suffragette.
Labour Leader, 31 Oct 1906

397   Oh, to be alone!
To escape from the work, the play,
The talking every day;
To escape from all I have done,
And all that remains to do!
To escape – yes, even from you,
My only love, and be
Alone and free.
…
I am only you!
I am yours, part of you, your wife!
And I have no other life.
I cannot think, cannot do;
I cannot breathe, cannot see;
There is 'us', but there is not me: –
And worst at your kiss I grow
Contented so.
Anonymous
The Woman Socialist (Ethel Snowden) [1907]

398   I think they are too hysterical, they are too much disposed to be guided by feeling and not by cold reason, and…to refuse any kind of compromise. I do not think women are safe guides in government, they are very unsafe guides.
Earl of Halstead

399   I view with considerable apprehension the steady rise in the number of female factory employees, and the consequent deterioration of that best of all institutions – home life, the interference with the training of housewives, and, in spite of the most perfect of factory legislation, the manufacture of bodily diseases in the younger employees, unfitting them to fulfill their highest obligation to the State, viz., Motherhood.
Inspector-General for the Insane, Victoria, Australia
Report, 1907

400   Extraordinarily important parts of the brain necessary for spiritual life, the frontal convolutions and the temporal lobes, are less well

developed in women and this difference is inborn.
Paul Moebius (b. 1853) German neurologist.
The physiological intellectual feebleness of women [1907]

401 For, consider what man-rule, man-made religion, man's moral code has implied to woman. She has seen her female child, Nature's highest development in organic evolution, ruthlessly murdered as superfluous. She has seen her son, the 'defective variation' biologically, the outcome of malnutrition and adverse conditions, and thereby imperfect, placed over her as master, Lord and tyrant.
Francis Swiney
The Bar of Isis [1907]

402 We went to men's lectures, unless the professor objected. I had very few lectures in college – we had tutors up there. But practically all my lectures – I was doing history – and some of the other subjects also, were the same with the men. We rode up and down to lectures on bicycles. And if you met men at lectures, you didn't know them.
Description by a British bishop's daughter of her time at Cambridge. *Nothing to Spare* (Jan Carter) [1907]

403 Votes for Women.
Slogan [c. 1907]

404 I think there can be no doubt that the suffragists did influence voters. Their activity, the interest shown in their meetings, the success of their persuasive methods in enlisting popular sympathy, the large numbers of working women who acted with them as volunteers – these are features of the election which although strangely ignored by most of the newspapers, must have struck visitors to the constituency.
Report of the Newton Abbot by-election. *Manchester Guardian*, Jan 1908

405 I used to think women could hardly do anything, that it all depended on men. Now it seems to me that there is nothing brave women cannot do if they are only given the chance. Only look at the women who are taking the chair at our Hyde Park demonstrations.
Anonymous
Labour Leader, 5 June 1908

406 Here's to the lot of them, murderer, thief, Forger and lunatic too, Sir –
Infants, and those who get parish relief,
And women, it's perfectly true, Sir –
Please to take note, they are in the same boat:
They have not a chance of recording the vote.
H. Crawford
Referring to the women's suffrage movement. *In the Same Boat* [c. 1908]

407 I see some rats have got in; let them squeal, it doesn't matter.
David Lloyd George (1863–1945) British Liberal statesman.
Said when suffragettes interrupted a meeting. *The Faber Book of English History in Verse* (Kenneth Baker) [c. 1908]

408 The women we do pity, the women we think unwomanly, the women for whom we have almost contempt, if our hearts could let us have that feeling, are the women who can stand aside, who take no part in this battle – and perhaps even more, the women who know what the right path is and will not tread it, who are selling the liberty of other women in order to win the smiles and favour of the dominant sex.
Christabel Pankhurst (1880–1958) British suffragette.
Speech, Albert Hall, London, 19 Mar 1908

409 We are not ashamed of what we have done, because, when you have a great cause to fight for, the moment of greatest humiliation is the moment when the spirit is proudest.
Christabel Pankhurst (1880–1958) British suffragette.
Speech, Albert Hall, London, 19 Mar 1908

410 We have taken this action, because as women…we realize that the condition of our sex is so deplorable that it is our duty even to break the law in order to call attention to the reasons why we do so.
Emmeline Pankhurst (1858–1928) British suffragette.
Speech in court, 21 Oct 1908. *Shoulder to Shoulder* (ed. Midge Mackenzie)

411 If civilisation is to advance at all in the future, it must be through the help of women, women freed of their political shackles, women with full power to work their will in society. It was rapidly becoming clear to my mind that men regarded women as a servant class in the community, and that women were going to remain in the servant class until they lifted themselves out of it.
Emmeline Pankhurst (1858–1928) British suffragette.
My Own Story [c. 1908]

412 Women had always fought for men, and for their children. Now they were ready to fight for their own human rights. Our militant movement was established.
Emmeline Pankhurst (1858–1928) British suffragette.
My Own Story [c. 1908]

413 Women are one-half of the world but until a century ago…it was a man's world. The laws were man's laws, the government a man's gov-

ernment, the country a man's country...The man's world must become a man's and a woman's world. Why are we afraid? It is the next step forward on the path to the sunrise, and the sun is rising over a new heaven and a new earth.
Martha Thomas (1857–1935) US writer.
Address, North American Woman Suffrage Association, Oct 1908

414 Nothing would induce me to vote for giving women the franchise. I am not going to be henpecked into a question of such importance.
Winston Churchill (1874–1965) British statesman.
The Amazing Mr Churchill (Robert Lewis Taylor) [c. 1910]

415 Women have suffered too much from the Conspiracy of Silence to allow that conspiracy to last one minute longer. It has been an established and admitted rule in the medical profession to keep a wife in ignorance of the fact that she has become the victim of venereal disease.
Christabel Pankhurst (1880–1958) British suffragette.
The Great Scourge [c. 1910]

416 Until changing economic conditions made the thing actually happen, struggling early society would hardly have guessed that woman's road to gentility would lie through doing nothing at all.
Emily James Putnam (1865–1944) US writer; first dean of Barnard College, New York.
The Lady, Introduction [1910]

417 Said the Socialist to the Suffragist:
'My cause is greater than yours!
You only work for a Special Class,
We for the gain of the General Mass,
Which every good ensures!'
Said the Suffragist to the Socialist:
'You underrate my Cause!
While women remain a Subject Class,
You never can move the General Mass,
With your Economic Laws!'
'A lifted world lifts women up,'
The Socialist explained.
'You cannot lift the world at all
While half of it is kept so small,'
The Suffragist maintained.
The world awoke, and tartly spoke:
'Your work is all the same:
Work together or work apart,
Work, each of you, with all your heart –
Just get into the game!'
Charlotte Perkins Gilman (1860–1935) US writer and lecturer.
Suffrage Songs and Verses [1911]

418 True, the movement for women's rights has broken many old fetters, but it has also forged new ones.
Emma Goldman (1869–1940) US editor.
Anarchism and Other Essays, 'The Tragedy of Women's Emancipation' [1911]

419 Merely external emancipation has made of the modern woman an artificial being...Now, woman is confronted with the necessity of emancipating herself from emancipation, if she really desires to be free.
Emma Goldman (1869–1940) US editor.
Anarchism and Other Essays, 'The Tragedy of Women's Emancipation' [1911]

420 As to the great mass of working girls and women, how much independence is gained if the narrowness and lack of freedom of the home is exchanged for the narrowness and lack of freedom of the factory, sweatshop, department store, or office?
Emma Goldman (1869–1940) US editor.
Anarchism and other Essays, 'The Tragedy of Women's Emancipation' [1911]

421 The important and only God of practical American life: Can the man make a living? Can he support a wife? That is the only thing that justifies marriage.
Emma Goldman (1869–1940) US editor.
Anarchism and Other Essays, 'Marriage and Love' [1911]

422 I heard only the other day that whereas the man who (whether married or single) makes constant and promiscuous advances when circumstances favour him is a fairly well recognised phenomenon of modern society, the woman who does so – if she happens to be a married woman – is liable to be regarded as insane, and, by the connivance of her husband and the medical profession, to be shut up for life in a mad-house.
Laurence Housman (1865–1959) British artist and author.
The Immoral Effects of Ignorance in Sex Relations [1911]

423 It is time that the women took their place in Imperial politics.
Emmeline Pankhurst (1858–1928) British suffragette.
The Standard, 5 Oct 1911

424 Our spinning wheels are all broken, and we dare no longer say proudly as of old, that we and we alone clothe our peoples...today steam often shapes our bread and the loaves are set down by our very door.
Olive Schreiner (1855–1920) South African writer.
Woman and Labour [1911]

425 The story of women's work in gainful employments is a story of constant changes or shiftings of work and workshop, accompanied by long hours, low wages, insanitary conditions, overwork, and the want on the part of the woman of training, skill, and vital interest in her work.
Helen L. Sumner (1876–1933) US government official and children's rights activist.
Senate Report [1911]

426 The history of women's work in this country shows that legislation has been the only force which has improved the working conditions of any large number of women wage-earners.
Helen L. Sumner (1876–1933) US government official and children's rights activist.
Senate Report [1911]

427 Are you who are in authority at the Home Office unaware that the modern woman writes as well as sews? Perhaps you may be anxious to press upon us some permanent prejudice of your own in the form of the needle rather than the pen as a suitable implement for women. If this be so may I beg you to choose some other time and place for exalting the needle at the expense of the pen?
Marion Wallace-Dunlop
Written during her imprisonment for suffragist activities. Letter to the home secretary, 5 Dec 1911

428 These intrepid 'typewriter pounders', instead of being allowed to gloat over love novels or do fancy crocheting during the time they are not 'pounding' should fill in their space time washing out the offices and dusting same, which you will no doubt agree is more suited to their sex and maybe would give them a little practice and insight into the work they will be called upon to do should they so far demean themselves as to marry one of the poor male clerks whose living they are doing their utmost to take out of his hands at the present time.
Letter from a male clerk, *Liverpool Echo*, 1911

429 I hold that militant Suffragettes stand in an analogous position to soldiers. You do not regard the latter as murderers because they fight in a good cause and neither am I as a militant Suffragist a criminal. Because I fight in a cause as good as any for which men have fought, I say, my lord, that I am morally guiltless.
Helen Craggs
Defending herself in court following her arrest for arson. *The Suffragette*, 25 Oct 1912

430 The Militant Suffragettes, whose passionate idealism and daring imagination are in striking contrast to the sluggish respectability of the 'plain man' who insists upon regarding them as criminals and lunatics.
Elaine Kidd
Materialism and the Militants [c. 1912]

431 There are parts of the world, including a country no less distinguished as a pioneer of education than Scotland, where serious mental strain is now being imposed upon girls…official regulations demand that at just such ages as thirteen, fourteen, and fifteen large numbers of girls – and picked girls – shall devote themselves to the strain of preparing for various examinations, upon which much depends.
Caleb Williams Saleeby (1878–1940) British physician.
Woman and Womanhood [1912]

432 The whole course of evolution in industry, and in the achievements of higher education and exceptional talent, has shown man's invariable tendency to shut women out when their activities have reached a highly specialized period of growth.
Anna Garlin Spencer (1851–1931) US minister and social reformer.
Woman's Share in Social Culture [1912]

433 When womanhood declares that she is no longer helpless, dislikes being penniless, and refuses to be subservient, the men become indignant and inarticulate, and find themselves caught in a contradictory position.
Rebecca West (Cicely Isabel Fairfield; 1892–1983) British novelist and journalist.
Manchester Daily Despatch, 26 Nov 1912

434 The patriarchal system is the ideal for which he longs. He likes to dream of himself sitting on the verandah after dinner, with his wife beside him and the children in the garden, while his unmarried sisters play duets in the drawing room and his maiden aunts hand around the coffee. This maintenance of helpless, penniless, subservient womanhood is the nearest he can get in England to the spiritual delights of the harem.
Rebecca West (Cicely Isabel Fairfield; 1892–1983) British novelist and journalist.
Manchester Daily Despatch, 26 Nov 1912

435 Pure selfishness is the motive of men's desire to oppress women… Antifeminists from Chesterton down to Dr Lionel Tayler want women to specialise in virtue. While men are rolling round the world having murderous and otherwise sinful adventures of an enjoyable nature, in commerce, exploration or art, women

are to stay at home earning the promotion of the human race to a better world.
Rebecca West (Cicely Isabel Fairfield; 1892–1983) British novelist and journalist.
The Clarion, 20 Dec 1912

436 You cannot expect the Suffragettes to give you a quiet life unless you in return will give them the Vote…We have been very patient with you hitherto. Even now we feel no bitterness. When all is over we will give you a free pardon for your neglect of our interests and liberties. But there can be no peace without honour – no end to fighting till the Vote is won. – Yours for peace or for war,
The Suffragette, 20 Dec 1912

437 On behalf of all women who will win freedom by the bondage which you have endured for their sake, and dignity by the humiliation which you have gladly suffered for the uplifting of our sex.
We the Members of the Women's Social and Political Union, herewith express our deep sense of admiration for your courage in enduring a long period of privation and solitary confinement in prison for the Votes for Women Cause, also our thanks to you for the great service that you have thereby rendered to the Woman's Movement.
Inspired by your passion for freedom and right may we and the women who come after us be ever ready to follow your example of self-forgetfulness and self-conquest, ever ready to obey the call of duty and to answer to the appeal of the oppressed.
Women's Social and Political Union
Certificate of thanks to Victoria Lidiard, signed by Emmeline Pankhurst [1912]

438 Marriage is the aim and end of all sensible girls, because it is the meaning of life.
Elinor Glyn (1864–1943) English writer.
Harper's Bazaar, Sept 1913

439 So greatly did she care for freedom that she died for it. So dearly did she love women that she offered her life as their ransom. That is the verdict given at the great Inquest of the Nation on the death of Emily Wilding Davison.
Christabel Pankhurst (1880–1958) British suffragette.
Emily Davison threw herself under the King's horse at the Epsom Derby in protest at the imprisoning of suffragettes. *The Suffragette*, 13 June 1913

440 The vote is the symbol of freedom and equality. Any class which is denied the vote is branded as an inferior class…The inferiority of women is a hideous lie which has been enforced by law and woven into the British Constitution, and it is quite hopeless to expect

reform between the relationship of the sexes until women are politically enfranchised.
Christabel Pankhurst (1880–1958) British suffragette.
The Great Scourge and How to End It [1913]

441 People are led to reason thus: a woman who is a wife is one who has made a permanent sex bargain for her maintenance; the woman who is not married must therefore make a temporary bargain of the same kind.
Christabel Pankhurst (1880–1958) British suffragette.
The Great Scourge and How to End It [1913]

442 From the moment I leave this court I shall deliberately refuse to eat food – I shall join the women who are already in Holloway on the hunger strike. I shall come out of prison, dead or alive, at the earliest possible moment…I do not want to commit suicide. I want to see the women of this country enfranchised, and I want to live until that is done.
Emmeline Pankhurst (1858–1928) British suffragette.
Speech to the Court, 2 Apr 1913

443 Over one thousand women have gone to prison in the course of this agitation, have suffered their imprisonment, have come out of prison injured in health, weakened in body, but not in spirit.
Emmeline Pankhurst (1858–1928) British suffragette.
My Own Story [1913]

444 I blushed with shame that the cup of tea should have such power over me. I kept going to it and looking at it – the steam fascinated me…Would one little sip matter? Quite possibly no one was hunger striking.
S. I. Stevenson
Describing her first experience of prison and hunger striking. *No Other Way* [1913]

445 One would wish for every girl who is growing up to womanhood that it might be brought home to her by some refined and ethically-minded member of her own sex how insufferable a person woman becomes when, like a spoilt child, she exploits the indulgence of man; when she proclaims that it is his duty to serve her and to share with her his power and possessions; when she makes an outcry when he refuses to part with what is his own; and when she insists upon thrusting her society upon men everywhere.
Almroth Wright (1861–1947) British doctor.
The Unexpurgated Case Against Woman Suffrage [1913]

446 For mothers who must earn, there is indeed no leisure time problem. The long hours

of earning are increased by the hours of domestic labor, until no slightest margin for relaxation or change of thought remains.
Katharine Anthony (1877–1965) US writer.
Mothers Who Must Earn, Ch. 6 [1914]

447 More than all should women discourage the fostering of the ideal of the domestic tabby-cat-woman as that to which womanhood should aspire…Marriage and motherhood should not be for sale. They should be dissociated from what is for sale – domestic drudgery.
Ada Nield Chew (1870–1945) British suffragette.
Common Cause, 27 Feb 1914

448 The socially pernicious, racially wasteful, and soul-withering consequences of the working of mothers outside the home must cease. And this can only come to pass, either through the programme of institutional upbringing, *or* through the intimated renaissance of the home.
Ellen Key (1849–1926) Swedish writer.
The Renaissance of Motherhood, Pt III, Ch. 2 [1914]

449 The Government use brute force to keep women in subjection. The anti-militant women bow down before brute force. The women in prison refuse to let brute force rule the world. They defy and by defying they are conquering it.
Christabel Pankhurst (1880–1958) British suffragette.
The Suffragette, 19 June 1914

450 I will not be examined by you because your intention is not to help me as a patient, but merely to ascertain how much longer it will be possible to keep me alive in prison. I am not prepared to assist you or the government in any such way. I am not prepared to relieve you of any responsibility in this matter.
Emmeline Pankhurst (1858–1928) British suffragette.
Speaking to a prison doctor during a hunger strike. *My Own Story* [1914]

451 If there is to be any romance in marriage woman must be given every chance to earn a decent living at other occupations. Otherwise no man can be sure that he is loved for himself alone, and that his wife did not come to the Registry Office because she had no luck at the Labour Exchange.
Rebecca West (Cicely Isabel Fairfield; 1892–1983) British novelist and journalist.
The Clarion, 14 Feb 1914

452 'Votes for Women!' there is a cracked and treble sound about that. The call for 'votes' can never be a call to freedom. For what is it to vote? To vote is to register assent to being ruled by one legislator or another…Rebel women struggle to be free from bondage and they struggle not against the men who share their interests in life, but side by side with these men.
Lily Gair Wilkinson
Women's Freedom [1914]

453 Why is it that men's blood-shedding militancy is applauded and women's symbolic militancy punished with a prison-cell and the forcible feeding horror?…Men make the moral code and they expect women to accept it.
Emmeline Pankhurst (1858–1928) British suffragette.
My Own Story [1914]

454 What is the use of fighting for a vote if we have not got a country to vote in? With that patriotism which has nerved women to endure torture in prison for the national good, we ardently desire that our country shall be victorious.
Emmeline Pankhurst (1858–1928) British suffragette.
Announcing a cessation of militant suffragette activities during the war. Statement, 10 Aug 1914

455 The cult of 'arms and the man' must reckon with a newer cult, that of 'schools and the woman'. Schools, which exalt brains above brawn, and women, who exalt life-giving above life-taking, are the natural allies of the present era.
Katharine Anthony (1877–1965) US writer.
Feminism in Germany and Scandinavia, Ch. 2 [1915]

456 I was in domestic service and 'hated every minute of it' when war broke out, earning £2 a month working from 6.00 a.m. to 9.00 p.m. So when the need came for women 'war workers' my chance came to 'out'.
Mrs H. A. Felstead
Women at War, 1914–1918 (Arthur Marwick) [1915]

457 In time of war the rules of peace must be set aside and we must put ourselves without delay upon a war basis, let the women stand shoulder to shoulder with the men to win the common victory which we all desire.
Emmeline Pankhurst (1858–1928) British suffragette.
Speech, London Pavilion, 5 Oct 1915

458 War is a thing of fearful and curious anomalies…It has shown that government by men only is not an appeal to reason, but an appeal to arms; that on women, without a voice to protest, must fall the burden. It is easier to die than to send a son to death.
Mary Roberts Rinehart (1876–1958) US writer.
Kings, Queens, and Pawns, Ch. 37 [1915]

459 The natural vocation for every woman is that of wife and mother, and in the training of every girl provision should be made for the

acquisition of definite and accurate knowledge of the essentials of domestic economy and mothercraft.
Mary Scharlieb (1845–1930) British gynaecological surgeon.
The Seven Ages of Woman. A Consideration of the Successive Phases of Woman's Life [1915]

460 Dainty skirts and delicate blouses,
Aren't much use for pigs and cowses.
Anonymous
Explaining why women landworkers wore breeches.
Rhyme from World War I [c. 1916]

461 The grant of the Parliamentary franchise to women in this country would be a political mistake of a very disastrous kind.
H. H. Asquith (1852–1928) British statesman.
Speech, 1916

462 No, it is not because woman is lacking in responsibility, but because she has too much of the latter that she demands to know how to prevent conception.
Emma Goldman (1869–1940) US editor.
Mother Earth, 'The Social Aspects of Birth Control', Apr 1916

463 I wasn't told anythink about marriage and the husbands didn't know anything either...I know right up till my first boy was born, I knew nothing. When he was born, I got the shock of my life...This morning, I got up and got the old man's breakfast and then I went with him when he went to work over to me mother's place...And after I'd been there a while, I started to get these pains in me stomach as I thought. I was in the bedroom doin' somethin' and I felt this terrible bearin' down. So there was an old chamber pot under the bed, so I got that out and I was lettin' this water run away into this chamber. And the next thing, a baby was there, almost into the chamber.
Report of a butcher's daughter, born in Australia, 1899.
Nothing to Spare (Jan Carter) [c. 1916]

464 There has grown up a masculine mythology suppressing and distorting all the facts of women's sexual and maternal emotions.
Stella Browne (1882–1955) British socialist and founder member of the Abortion Law Reform Association.
Women and Birth Control [1917]

465 ...the entire individual responsibility of women in regard to the acceptance or refusal of motherhood, the fundamental human right of the mother to bear life gladly or not at all and of the unborn to be wanted and welcomed.
Stella Browne (1882–1955) British socialist and founder member of the Abortion Law Reform Association.
Women and Birth Control [1917]

466 I do not believe in sex distinction in literature, law, politics, or trade – or that modesty and virtue are more becoming to women than to men, but wish we had more of it everywhere.
Belva Lockwood (1830–1917) US lawyer.
Lady for the Defense, Pt II, Ch. 8 [1917]

467 I know we can't abolish prejudice through laws, but we can set up guidelines for our actions by legislation. If women are given equal pay for Civil Service jobs, maybe other employers will do the same.
Belva Lockwood (1830–1917) US lawyer.
Lady for the Defense, Pt III, Ch. 11 [1917]

468 I have been told that there is no precedent for admitting a woman to practice in the Supreme Court of the United States. The glory of each generation is to make its own precedents. As there was none for Eve in the Garden of Eden, so there need be none for her daughters on entering the colleges, the church, or the courts.
Belva Lockwood (1830–1917) US lawyer.
Lady for the Defense, Pt III, Ch. 13 [1917]

469 Russia still writhed and stumbled. The wave of revolts and uprisings, the constant agitations, the incessant inflammatory orations of men possessed of little political competence, had by this time cowed the emperor and the ruling class into bewildered and sullen inertia.
Maria, Grand Duchess of Russia (1890–1958)
Referring to the Russian Revolution of 1917. *Education of a Princess*, Ch. 8

470 We men and women of today have now to pay the price of man's economic dominance over women which has existed for centuries. Content to treat women as subjects instead of equals, men are now faced with problems not to their liking.
J. T. Murphy
The Workers Committee. An Outline of its Principles and Structure [1917]

471 We want the vote so that we may serve our country better. We want the vote so that we shall be more faithful and more true to our allies. We want the vote so that we may help to maintain the cause of Christian civilisation for which we entered this war. We want the vote so that in future such wars if possible may be averted.
Emmeline Pankhurst (1858–1928) British suffragette.
Speech, Queen's Hall, 23 Apr 1917

472 Women of the working class, especially wage workers, should not have more than two children at most. The average working man can support no more and the average working

woman can take care of no more in decent fashion.
Margaret Sanger (1883–1966) US nurse and writer.
Family Limitations [1917]

473 A mutual and satisfied sexual act is of great benefit to the average woman, the magnetism of it is health giving. When it is not desired on the part of the woman and she has no response, *it should not take place*. This is an act of prostitution and is degrading to the woman's finer sensibility, all the marriage certificates on earth to the contrary notwithstanding.
Margaret Sanger (1883–1966) US nurse and writer.
Family Limitations [1917]

474 The idea that because the State called for women to help the nation, the State must continue to employ them is too absurd for serious women to entertain. As a matter of grace, notice should be at least a fortnight and if possible a month. As for young women formerly in domestic service, they at least should have no difficulty in finding vacancies.
Anonymous
Newspaper article. *Women on the Warpath* (David Mitchell) [1918]

475 A sense of inferiority is one of the prime requisites for a continued state of subjection, and nothing contributes to this sense so much, as a marked inferiority of education and training in a society accustomed to rate everything according to its money value. The difference in earning capacity which the want of education produces, is in itself sufficient to stamp a class as inferior.
Alice Clark (1874–1934) British writer, and a director of Clark's shoe firm.
Working Life of Women in the Seventeenth Century [1918]

476 We may even ask ourselves whether the instability, superficiality and spiritual poverty of modern life, do not spring from the organisation of a State which regards the purposes of life solely from the male standpoint.
Alice Clark (1874–1934) British writer, and a director of Clark's shoe firm.
Working Life of Women in the Seventeenth Century [1918]

477 Party managers think that for the most part women over 30 voting for the first time have followed the allegiance of husbands or other close relatives.
The Daily Telegraph, 28 Dec 1918

478 Shamed, dishonored, wading in blood and dripping with filth, thus capitalist society stands.
Rosa Luxemburg (1870–1919) Polish-born German revolutionary.
The Crisis in the German Social Democracy [1919]

479 It is a foolish delusion to believe that we need only live through the war, as a rabbit hides under the bush to await the end of a thunderstorm, to trot merrily off in his old accustomed gait when all is over.
Rosa Luxemburg (1870–1919) Polish-born German revolutionary.
The Crisis in the German Social Democracy [1919]

480 Without general elections, without freedom of the press, freedom of speech, freedom of assembly, without the free battle of opinions, life in every public institution withers away, becomes a caricature of itself, and bureaucracy rises as the only deciding factor.
Rosa Luxemburg (1870–1919) Polish-born German revolutionary.
The Crisis in the German Social Democracy [1919]

481 Thousands of American women know far more about the subconscious than they do about sewing.
H. L. Mencken (1880–1956) US journalist.
Prejudices [1919]

482 The right of citizens of the United States to vote shall not be denied or abridged by the United States or by any State on account of sex.
Constitution of the United States, Amendment XIX [1920]

Barriers to equality...

483 Foremost among the barriers to equality is the system which ignores the mother's service to Society in making a home and rearing children. The mother is still the unchartered servant of the future, who receives from her husband, at *his* discretion, a share in *his* wages.
Katharine Anthony (1877–1965) US writer.
The Endowment of Motherhood, Introduction [1920]

484 Life is nothing but a series of crosses for us mothers.
Colette (1873–1954) French novelist.
Cheri [1920]

485 Life as a child and then as a girl had taught her patience, hope, silence; and given her a prisoner's proficiency in handling these virtues as weapons.
Colette (1873–1954) French novelist.
Cheri [1920]

486 The great question...which I have not been able to answer, despite my thirty years of research into the feminine soul, is 'What does a woman want?'
Sigmund Freud (1856–1939) Austrian psychoanalyst.
Psychiatry in American Life (Charles Rolo) [1920]

487 The 'homo' is the legitimate child of the 'suffragette'.
Wyndham Lewis (1882–1957) British novelist.
The Art of Being Ruled, Pt VIII, Ch. 4 [1920]

488 I think the reason my generation bobbed and shingled their hair, flattened their bosoms and lowered their waists, was not that we wanted to be masculine, but that we didn't want to be emotional. War widows, many of them still wearing crepe and widows' weeds in the Victorian tradition, had full bosoms, full skirts and fluffed-out hair. To shingle was to cut loose from the maternal pattern; it was an anti-sentiment symbol, not an anti-feminine one.
Barbara Cartland (1902–) British romantic novelist.
We Danced all Night [1920s]

489 I have gone to war too...I am going to fight capitalism even if it kills me. It is wrong that people like you should be comfortable and well fed while all around you people are starving.
Sylvia Pankhurst (1882–1960) British suffragette.
The Fighting Pankhursts (David Mitchell) [1921]

490 Those love children always suffer because their mothers have crushed them under their stays trying to hide them, more's the pity. Yet after all, a lovely unrepentant creature, big with child is not such an outrageous sight.
Colette (1873–1954) French novelist.
My Mother's House, 'My Mother and Illness' [1922]

491 I do think if women were a little more willing to take their share in the fight against present working class conditions and a little less ready to talk about the evils of child-bearing and the domination of men, we should be nearer to that true equality of the sexes only to be attained when we have established true economic freedom.
S. Francis
The Communist, 19 Aug 1922

492 To the old saying that man built the house but woman made of it a 'home' might be added the modern supplement that woman accepted cooking as a chore but man has made of it a recreation.
Emily Post (1873–1960) US writer.
Etiquette, Ch. 34 [1922]

493 I think it is wicked and scandalous to call Dr Marie Stopes Birth Control method an experiment or even to suggest that we women are her victims...Can any of these people imagine what it is, or means to a woman like myself my last 2 children I had in 18 months. My husband being out of work I had to leave my children to be looked after by their father while I had to go into a poor law institute to have my baby because I did not have the means of providing for it at home.
Anonymous
Referring to Halliday Sutherland, a Roman Catholic doctor, who accused Marie Stopes of experimenting on the poor. Letter to Marie Stopes, Jan 1923

494 Mercifully, we have no political past; we have all the mistakes of one-sex legislation, with its appalling failures, to guide us. We should know what to avoid. It is no use blaming the men – we made them what they are – and now it is up to us to try and make ourselves – the makers of men – a little more responsible.
Nancy Astor (1879–1964) US-born British politician; first woman MP to sit in the House of Commons.
My Two Countries, Ch. 1, 'America' [1923]

495 (Love, by whom I was beguiled,
Grant I may not bear a child.)
Edna St Vincent Millay (1892–1952) US writer.
'Humoresque' [1923]

496 With respect to the admission to New Zealand of the book entitled 'Wise Parenthood' by Dr Marie Stopes, I have to inform you that the matter has again been under consideration and it has been decided that this book is in future to be regarded as an indecent document within the meaning of the Indecent Publications Act, 1910. The importation of this publication will therefore in future not be permitted.
Letter from the New Zealand Customs Department, 24 Mar 1924

497 In days of old, as we've been told
The women ruled the men
The men, like fools, did make new rules
And ruled them back again.
But womenkind were not content
They wanted the franchise,
The world is topsy turvy now
And that is no surprise.
Some females in the labour cause
Have got great intellect
They have a system of their own
And that is most perfect.
But take all women, good and bad,
There is this much about them
To keep this world as it is
We cannot do without them.
'Percy the Poet'
'Why Women Rule the Men' [c. 1925]

498 Now the legal barriers are down, there is still some debris left which we must clear away...We can demand what we want for women, not because it is what men have got but because it is what women need to fulfil the potentialities of their own natures and to adjust themselves to the circumstances of their own lives.
Eleanor Rathbone (1872–1946) British suffragette and president (1919–28) of the National Union of Societies for Equal Citizenship (NUSEC).
Speech, NUSEC, 1925

499 In 1918 they bestowed the vote, just as they dropped about a few Dames and MBES as a reward for our services in helping the destruction of our offspring...They gave the vote to the older women who were deemed less rebellious.
Dora Russell (1894–   ) British writer.
Hypatia [1925]

500 To me the important task of modern feminism is to accept and proclaim sex; to bury for ever the lie that the body is a hindrance to the mind, and sex is a necessary evil to be endured for the perpetuation of our race.
Dora Russell (1894–   ) British writer.
Hypatia [1925]

501 I sorely need advice concerning birth control I have only been married Four years and have just given birth for the Fifth time and it has made us desperately poor financially as my husband's wages are but small. It is through my weakness of body that I become pregnant every single time we submit to Marital Rights.
Anonymous
Mother England [Marie Stopes]

502 Out in the East...the average woman may not eat at the same table with the husband, speak lovingly of her mate in the hearing of her older in-laws, or let the lady doctor examine her with female instruments.
Anonymous
Letter to Marie Stopes, from India, 26 Aug 1926

503 They should also be shown that on efficient care and management of the home depend the health, happiness and prosperity of the nation. Distaste for the work of the home has arisen, in great measure, from the fact that housecraft has not been generally regarded as a skilled occupation for which definite training is essential, and it has too often been practised by those who, through lack of training or through undeveloped intelligence, have been incapable of performing it efficiently and of commanding the respect of their fellows.
Board of Education (1926)
The Education of the Adolescent

504 Many times last year I went to meetings organised by Trade Union officials to ask women to join various unions; these women came in small numbers to the meeting place; sat down on a seat in weariness so profound that no propaganda could get into their heads; and all the time children played about the door calling, 'Mum, aren't you coming home? I want my tea.'
Leonora Eyles (1889–1960) British author.
Women's Problems of Today [1926]

505 You're a modern woman...You can't live with strong men, because you're damned if you're going to be ruled; and you can't live with weak men because you're damned if you're going to be bothered to manage them.
W. L. George (1882–1926) British writer.
Gifts of Sheba [1926]

506 It is a commonplace in this century that women form the leisure class; and this leisure class of women, like leisured classes everywhere, has its leisure at the expense of other people, who in this case are the husbands.
Suzanne LaFollette (1893–   ) US politician and writer.
Concerning Women, 'The Beginnings of Emancipation' [1926]

507 Nothing could be more grotesquely unjust than a code of morals, reinforced by laws, which relieves men from responsibility for irreg-

ular sexual acts, and for the same acts drives women to abortion, infanticide, prostitution and self-destruction.
Suzanne LaFollette (1893–   ) US politician and writer.
Concerning Women, 'Women and Marriage' [1926]

508   The claim for alimony…implies the assumption that a woman is economically helpless.
Suzanne LaFollette (1893–   ) US politician and writer.
Concerning Women, 'Women and Marriage' [1926]

509   Now comrade, do let us have some information and discussion in the 'Woman Worker' soon about birth control…between illness and worry and babies, it's no wonder that lots of women get too tired and dull to bother with politics.
Letter, *The Woman Worker*, June 1926

510   I believe, as a wage-earning woman, that if I make the great sacrifice of strength and health and even risk my life, to have a child, I should certainly not do so if, on some future occasion, the man can say that the child belongs to him by law and he will take it from me and I shall see it only three times a year!
Isadora Duncan (1878–1927) US dancer.
My Life [1927]

511   Trade unions in the past have thought to remedy this evil by ignoring it, or by attempting to drive women out of industry altogether. Agreements between unions and employers have been made to ensure that women shall be employed on certain operations only – these operations being invariably the worst paid. There are still trade union leaders, some of whom are regarded as left wingers, who oppose strenuously the principle of equal pay for equal work.
Beth Turner
The Communist, Nov 1927

512   I would rather trust a woman's instinct than a man's reason.
Stanley Baldwin (1867–1947) British statesman.
Referring to the Equal Franchise Bill, 1928. Speech, Queen's Hall, 1928

513   The subjection of women, if there be such a thing, will not now depend on any creation of the law, nor can it be remedied by any action of the law…Women will have, with us, the fullest rights.
Stanley Baldwin (1867–1947) British statesman.
During the debate on the Equal Franchise Bill. Speech, House of Commons, 29 Mar 1928

514   The principle of women working with equal status is accepted. The principle of married women so working is equally accepted.
British Broadcasting Corporation
Most women were barred from continuing with their jobs after marriage. Internal memo, Nov 1928

515   When children cease to be altogether desirable, women cease to be altogether necessary.
John Langdon Davies (1897–1971) British author.
A Short History of Women [1928]

516   Of Mlle Germaine Tailleferre one can only repeat Dr Johnson's dictum concerning a woman preacher, transposed into terms of music. 'Sir, a woman's composing is like a dog's walking on his hind legs. It is not done well, but you are surprised to find it done at all.'
Cecil Gray (1895–1951) British music critic and writer.
A Survey of Contemporary Music [1928]

517   The emancipation of today displays itself mainly in cigarettes and shorts. There is even a reaction from the ideal of an intellectual and emancipated womanhood, for which the pioneers toiled and suffered, to be seen in painted lips and nails, and the return of trailing skirts and other absurdities of dress which betoken the slave-woman's intelligent companionship.
Sylvia Pankhurst (1882–1960) British suffragette.
News of the World, Apr 1928

518   Idiots are always in favour of inequality of income (their only chance of eminence), and the really great in favor of equality.
George Bernard Shaw (1856–1950) Irish dramatist and critic.
The Intelligent Woman's Guide to Socialism and Capitalism [1928]

519   Instead of this absurd division into sexes they ought to class people as static and dynamic.
Evelyn Waugh (1903–66) British novelist.
Decline and Fall, Pt III, Ch. 7 [1928]

520   If American politics are too dirty for women to take part in, there's something wrong with American politics.
Edna Ferber (1887–1968) US writer.
Cimarron, Ch. 23 [1929]

521   She ascribed all the wrong in the world to male domination and narrowness, and would not see my experiences in the war as anything comparable with the sufferings that millions of working-class women went through without complaint.
Robert Graves (1895–1985) British poet and novelist.
Goodbye to All That [1929]

522 Marriage is for women the commonest mode of livelihood, and the total amount of undesired sex endured by women is probably greater in marriage than in prostitution.
Bertrand Russell (1872–1970) British philosopher.
Marriage and Morals [1929]

523 These cases also disclosed that prices may range between $70 or $80 for a baby child and $500 for children of more mature age. Generally speaking, a boy commands the better price, as he is much fancied by those who are childless. And then his lot is a happier one than that of a girl, over whom many evils associated with the nefarious traffic hang heavily.
Referring to the discovery of an organized system of brokerage in children in Hong Kong. *South China Morning Post*, 10 Aug 1929

524 All this pitting of sex against sex, of quality against quality; all this claiming of superiority and imputing of inferiority, belong to the private-school stage of human existence where there are 'sides', and it is necessary for one side to beat another side.
Virginia Woolf (1882–1941) British novelist.
A Room of One's Own [1929]

525 It would be a thousand pities if women wrote like men, or lived like men, or looked like men, for if two sexes are quite inadequate, considering the vastness and variety of the world, how should we manage with one only? Ought not education to bring out and fortify the differences rather than the similarities?
Virginia Woolf (1882–1941) British novelist.
A Room of One's Own [1929]

526 I was actually at the door which leads into the library itself. I must have opened it, for instantly there issued, like a guardian angel barring the way with a flutter of black gown instead of white wings, a deprecating, silvery, kindly gentleman, who regretted in a low voice as he waved me back that ladies are only admitted to the library if accompanied by a Fellow of the College or furnished with a letter of introduction.
Virginia Woolf (1882–1941) British novelist.
A Room of One's Own [1929]

527 Women have served all these centuries as looking-glasses possessing the magic and delicious power of reflecting the figure of man at twice its natural size.
Virginia Woolf (1882–1941) British novelist.
A Room of One's Own [1929]

528 If you do not consent to be awakened your husband will be deeply disappointed...He will not call it purity, he will call it prudery; and he will be right...He will know that you have not fully *given* yourself in marriage: and married joys are for those who *give* with royal generosity.
Reverend Gray
Introduction, *The Sex Factor* (Dr Helena Wright) [1930]

529 In their quest for rights they have naturally placed emphasis on their wrongs, rather than their achievements and possessions, and have retold history as a story of their long Martyrdom.
Mary Ritter Beard (1876–1958) US historian.
Referring to women. *Understanding Women*, Ch. 1 [1931]

530 Political equality is Dead Sea fruit unless it leads to economic equality.
Vera Brittain (1893–1970) British writer and feminist.
Nation, 3 Jan 1931

531 Childbirth has always been women's travail and always will be...The broad fact remains, first that childbirth is a heavy strain on the physique of any woman and the bodies of many must, therefore, be impaired. Secondly, that there is in modern civilised nations an insufficient number of organised facilities for effective treatment.
George Newman (1870–1948) British doctor, Chief Medical Officer, Ministry of Health (1919–35).
Replying to the demand for better maternity and child welfare services [1931]

532 Married women are kept women, and they are beginning to find it out.
Logan Pearsall Smith (1865–1946) US writer.
Afterthoughts, 'Other people' [1931]

533 By underlining constantly the fact that the emancipation of woman can be brought about only by paid work, we have excluded from our ranks women who were ready and willing to come to us.
Fourth International Women's Conference, 1931. *Labour and Socialist International, Reports and Proceedings*

534 I don't think a woman's place is in industry. If we were to take women out of industry I believe we could absorb all the unemployment. I think the men ought to be doing the work instead of the women.
Herbert Austin (1866–1941) British industrialist and engineer.
The Times, 25 Sept 1933

535 A caress is better than a career.
Elisabeth Marbury (1856–1933) US playwright.
Careers for Women [1933]

536 Persons of both sexes would continue to share the burdens of house-keeping and child production, maintenance and education.
Aleo Craig
Sex and the Revolution [1934]

537 Mothers who can share their children's interests, mothers who have some knowledge of the wider world outside the family circle, are far better equipped than purely domestic house-wives, to help their sons and daughters as they pass from school to the shops and offices and factories and universities in which they complete their education.
Winifred Holtby (1898–1935) British writer.
Women, and a Changing Civilisation [1934]

538 In view of the persistently high maternal death rate and the evils arising from the illegal practice of abortion, this Congress calls upon the Government to revise the abortion laws of 1861 by bringing them into harmony with modern conditions and ideas, thereby making of abortion a legal operation that can be carried out under the same conditions as any other surgical operation.
It further asks that women now suffering imprisonment for breaking these antiquated laws be amnestied.
Women's Co-operative Guild
Resolution, 1934

539 Modern young women know amazingly little of what life was like before the war, and show a strong hostility to the word 'feminism' and all which they imagine it to connote.
Ray Strachey (1887–1940) US feminist, writer, and editor.
Our Freedom and its Results [1936]

540 The art of woman must be born in the wombcells of the mind. She must be the link between synthetic products of man's mind and the elements.
Anaïs Nin (1903–77) US writer and lecturer.
Diary entry, Aug 1937

541 Fascism recognizes women as a part of the life force of the country, laying down a division of duties between the two sexes, without putting obstacles in the way of those women who by their intellectual gifts reach the highest positions.
Maria Castellani (fl. 1930s) Italian writer.
Italian Women, Past and Present [1937]

542 They sit down and drink tea, and the procuress leads in a shou ma saying, 'Pay your respects to the guests' and the girl does so. Then she commands 'Walk forward' – 'Turn around' – so the girl turns around to face the light, and thus to show her face. Then the woman asks 'Let us see your hands' so the girl pushes up her sleeves to reveal her hands, arms, and her skin. At the command 'Look at the guest' she glances sidelong at him, thus showing her eyes. Then she is asked 'How old are you' and she gives her reply, so the customer can hear her voice. The procuress says 'Walk around again', and pulls back the girl's skirt to reveal her feet.
Chen Dong-yuan Chinese writer.
Describing the ritual of selecting a young girl for shou ma (concubinage). *Zhongguo funü shenghuo shi* [1937]

543 The selling of young girls as concubines for mere profit is one of the evils that arises from the transference of infants and girl children for valuable consideration, and from this it is right and reasonable to protect them.
Suggesting reform in the Chinese practice of adoption of young girls. *Mui Tsai Commission*, 1937

544 Anyway I had a very bad stomach ache one day so I went upstairs to lie down. The pain got worse and worse then all of a sudden out popped a baby. And I thought 'Where has that come from? I haven't got to go through the rest of my life with that attached to me.' Then the mistress came in and she was furious. She said: 'Betty, you wicked girl.' She dismissed me there and then and said I'd have to pay for the sheets I'd soiled. After that they took me off to a home.
Betty Jones (1920–) British domestic servant.
Relating her experience in 1938. *Independent*, 6 Apr 1991

545 AN APPEAL TO WOMEN
Will *You* drive to the Rescue?
London Volunteer Ambulance Service
World War II poster [c. 1939]

546 Children by Choice not Chance.
Slogan of the Family Planning Association [1939]

547 As an old soldier, if I were offered the choice of commanding a mixed battery or an all male battery, I say without hesitation I would take the mixed battery. The girls cannot be beaten in action, and in my opinion they are definitely better than the men on the instruments they are manning.
Comment by the officer commanding the first mixed battery to bring down a German bomber. *Roof Over Britain, The Official Story of the AA Defences* [c. 1940]

548 The menace is the woman who thinks she ought to be flying a high speed bomber when she really has not the intelligence to scrub the floor of a hospital properly...There are men like that too so there is no need to charge us with anti-feminism...This combination is perhaps more common amongst women than men.
Charles G. Grey (1875–1953) Editor of *Aeroplane*.
Forgotten Pilots (Lettice Curtis) [c. 1940]

549 I felt that we were doing a job of morale boosting, and after a year or so even the govern-

ment ministers realized that women's magazines had an influence. In a practical way the Ministry of Food would see that we had plenty of material about the coming shortages well in advance, so that we could arrange cookery recipes that were suitable. They gave us press conferences earlier than the daily newspapers because we had full colour for certain pages, and we went to press three weeks ahead.
Constance Holt British magazine editor.
Don't You Know There's a War On? (Jonathan Croall) [c. 1940]

550 The good operator needs a well developed conscience, a sense of duty, patience and freedom from any tendency to panic. Qualities in which women predominate.
Robert Watson-Watt (1892–1973) Scientific advisor, author, and lecturer.
Referring to radio operators. *Their Finest Hour* (Edward Bishop) [c. 1940]

551 The women were awfully keen to do war work. People who really weren't fit and couldn't give up the time, they all joined things. There was a sewing bee, they used to make nightshirts and bandages, and they all got themselves up in white nursing caps and aprons and white overalls. There was a great deal of activity. There was a Women's Volunteer Service, the WVS, who had a rather nice uniform, which was supposed to be designed by one of the top dress-makers. They looked quite nice in it.
Joyce Dennys British writer.
Don't You Know There's a War On? (Jonathan Croall) [c. 1941]

552 A War Comforts meeting was a solemn affair, everyone in awe of the Chairman. Lulu appealed to us to sew badges on to the Durhams' tunics, they are going to Egypt soon. So I went to the Red X depot to do this. A b— awful job – takes ages.
Anne Lee-Mitchell (1908–) British housewife.
Diary entry, 2 Apr 1941. *People at War* (ed. Michael Moynihan) [1941]

553 But the real difficulty about this proposal is accommodation on board. In all designing today the utmost and absolute economy of space has to be effected, and, quite obviously, if men and women are serving alongside, you cannot have the same economy of space as if there are men only.
Richard Anthony Pilkington (1908–76) Civil Lord of the Admiralty.
Replying to the proposal that women should be allowed to go to sea. House of Commons, 10 Mar 1941

554 The average women takes to welding as readily as she takes to knitting once she has overcome any initial nervousness due to sparks. Indeed the two occupations have much in com-

mon, since they both require a small, fairly complex manipulative movement which is repeated many times combined with a kind of subconscious concentration at which women excel.
Ministry of Labour leaflet [c. 1941]

555 Taken as a whole, the plan for Social Security puts a premium on marriage in place of penalizing it...In the next thirty years housewives as mothers have vital work to do in ensuring the adequate continuance of the British race and of British ideals in the world.
Lord Beveridge (1879–1963) British economist.
Suggesting the introduction of a family allowance.
Report on Social Insurance and Allied Services [1942]

556 The wave of feminism which swept Britain after 1918 caused widespread unemployment, a general trade depression, and an alarming decline in our birthrate...As soon as Hitlerism has been defeated the combined forces of various men's organisations will launch their campaign against a menace just as threatening to Britain as Hitlerism – Feminism.
National Men's Defence League British servicemen's association.
Leaflet, distributed during World War II, c. 1942

557 British women have proved themselves in this war. They have stuck to their posts near burning ammunition dumps, delivered messages afoot after their motor-cycles have been blasted from under them. They have pulled aviators from burning planes. They have died at their gun-posts, and as they fell another girl has stepped directly into the position and 'carried on'. There isn't a single record of any British woman in uniformed service quitting her post, or failing in her duty under fire. When you see a girl in a uniform with a bit of ribbon on her tunic, remember she didn't get it for knitting more socks than anyone else in Ipswich.
United States War Department
From a booklet issued to all US soldiers entering Britain during World War II.

558 It has transpired since the appeals that the girls were directed to wash bottles in breweries or to wash dishes in luxury restaurants, and that at the most appalling wages. Surely, if luxury restaurants are allowed to employ girls they should be expected to pay for the luxury, and not continue with the sweated labour they were used to before the war. In any case, the girls resent being sent to such jobs when they could undertake engineering jobs, and their general feeling is that they should be directed to wash dishes in hospitals rather than in luxury restaurants, if that is the only kind of work available for them.
Kay Ekevall British shop steward in World War II.
Letter to F. W. Pethick-Lawrence, c. 1943

559 The Board of Trade issues a moral little booklet 'Make and Mend', exhorting us to cut the feet from old stockings, pick up the stitches and knit new feet, with creased turn-downs to hide the joins. Am doing this, but for other tips such as 'Sew up all pleats and button-holes before putting clothes away' and 'Reinforce all elbows, knees and pockets on new clothes before putting them on' I've little use and less time.
Anne Lee-Mitchell (1908–) British housewife.
Diary entry, 28 Sept 1943 *People at War* (ed. Michael Moynihan) [1943]

560 Only a few women went to prison, I think it's not generally known that there were women conscientious objectors as well as men during the war, though not many of them. Many of them had been called up into the services. One woman I remember was called out of our office to go into the war office. She refused, and was called to a tribunal, which gave her a six-month sentence for continuing to say no.
Doris Nicholls British pacifist.
Don't You Know There's a War On? (Jonathan Croall) [c. 1943]

561 I am much impressed by the achievement of the Organization under your command in making more than 200,000 aircraft ferryings on behalf of the Royal Navy and the Royal Air Force during the past four years; this is indeed a wonderful record.
That this formidable task should have been performed with so low an accident record redounds greatly to the credit of both your pilots and ground staff...The time may come when many of your pilots will be delivering aircraft to the R.A.F. bases that are to be established on the Continent, and I am confident that this important task, which is being entrusted to the Organization under your command, will be carried out with the same efficiency and devotion to duty as has been shown by the personnel of the Air Transport Auxiliary since its inception.
Winston Churchill (1874–1965) British statesman.
Personal minute to Commodore d'Erlanger, Air Transport Auxiliary, 28 May 1944

562 He wondered why sexual shyness, which excites the desire of dissolute women, arouses the contempt of decent ones.
Colette (1873–1954) French novelist.
'Armande' [1944]

563 There was some opposition to women pilots to start with. People wrote in to the *Aeroplane* saying how wicked and contemptible it all was to employ them. The editor of the magazine wrote about women being a menace thinking they could cope with piloting a high-speed bomber, when some of them weren't intelligent enough to scrub a hospital floor decently. But I personally didn't come across any prejudice against women. We were soon treated equally and there was very little bias against us; eventually we got equal pay with men. After all, when there's a war on, you get on with your job.
Lettice Curtis British pilot in World War II.
Don't You Know There's a War On? (Jonathan Croall) [c. 1944]

564 It's absolutely disgusting. We men are furious, the women are there sitting in the ambulances in the centre, the bombs dropping, and if anything happens to them we know very well that their compensation will only be four-fifths of ours and yet they're as much in the danger zone as we are.
General Secretary of the Fireman's Union
Deputation to Clement Attlee (then deputy prime minister), negotiating equal compensation with men for war injuries. *Out of the Doll's House* (Angela Holdsworth) [1944]

565 These Women's Auxiliary Services, whose trim khaki, light and dark blue uniforms are now seen everywhere, are being sensibly managed; the girls look healthy and happy, and clearly most of them will make better wives and mothers and citizens, if only because they have had some physical and mental training, and been given a glimpse of wider horizons after their years of national service.
Her Majesty's Stationery Office.
The Story of Britain's Mobilisation for War [1944]

566 The feminine character, and the ideal of femininity on which it is modelled, are products of masculine society...Where it claims to be humane, masculine society imperiously breeds in woman its own corrective, and shows itself through this limitation implacably the master. The feminine character is a negative imprint of domination.
Theodor Adorno (1903–69) German philosopher.
Minima Moralia [1945]

567 Until my experience in London I had been opposed to the use of women in uniform. But in Great Britain I had seen them perform so magnificently in various positions, including service with anti-aircraft batteries, that I had been converted.
Dwight D. Eisenhower (1890–1969) US general and statesman.
Crusade in Europe [c. 1945]

568 Women took part in most of the jobs, such as crane-driving, burning, buffing, painting, welding and such-like. I became a welder when there were both men and women trainees, but the men were paid more than the women. We had several battles over equal pay after we were used on the same jobs as the men, many of whom were as new to the skills as we were. By the end of my time we had managed to get close to the men's wage, but we only got equality in the case of the crane-drivers.

Kay Ekevall British shop steward in World War II.
Don't You Know There's a War On? (Jonathan Croall) [c. 1945]

569 The dogma of woman's complete historical subjection to men must be rated as one of the most fantastic myths ever created by the human mind.

Mary Ritter Beard (1876–1958) US historian.
Woman as a Force in History [1946]

570 Women's intellectuality is to a large extent paid for by the loss of valuable feminine qualities: it feeds on the sap of the affective life and results in impoverishment of this life...All observations point to the fact that the intellectual woman is masculinized; in her, warm intuitive knowledge has yielded to cold unproductive thinking.

Helene Deutsch (1884–1982) US psychoanalyst.
Psychology of Women, I [1946]

571 I am sorry that Governments in all parts of the world have not seen fit to send more women as delegates, alternates or advisors to the Assembly. I think it is in these positions that the women of every nation should work to see that equality exists.

Eleanor Roosevelt (1884–1962) US writer and wife of Franklin D. Roosevelt (1882–1945) US president.
Ladies' Home Journal, 28 Jan 1946

572 Most woman...unlike most men, do not expect either now or in the future, to support a married partner or a family of children out of the proceeds of their labour; on the contrary most of them look forward to being themselves supported in the relatively near future.
Royal Commission on Equal Pay [1946]

573 We turn in our sleep and groan because we are parasites – we women – because we produce nothing, say nothing, find our whole world in the love of a man. – For shame! We are become the veriest Philistines – in this matter of woman's sphere. I suppose it is too soon to expect us to achieve perspective on the problem of women's rights.

Ruth Benedict (1887–1948) US anthropologist and writer.
An Anthropologist at Work (Margaret Mead) [1948]

574 At medical school we were taught that a mixture of oestrogen and progestogens is excellent to prevent heavy bleeding or pain with menstruation but, as it is a contraceptive, you never give it to a married woman. That is treatment only for single women and widows. No one realised the demand. There was a feeling that every woman who was married would automatically want to conceive.

Katharina Dalton British doctor.
Out of the Doll's House (Angela Holdsworth) [c. 1948]

575 It is of very doubtful value to enlist the gifts of women if bringing women into fields that have been defined as male frightens the men, unsexes the women, muffles and distorts the contribution women could make.

Margaret Mead (1901–78) US anthropologist and writer.
Male and Female [1948]

Not born a woman...

576 One is not born a woman, one becomes one.
Simone de Beauvoir (1908–86) French writer.
Le Deuxième Sexe (*The Second Sex*) [1949]

577 For him she is sex – absolute sex, no less. She is defined and differentiated with reference to man and not he with reference to her; she is the incidental, the inessential as opposed to the essential. He is the Subject, he is the Absolute – she is the Other.
Simone de Beauvoir (1908–86) French writer.
Le Deuxième Sexe (*The Second Sex*) [1949]

578 Between women love is contemplative... There is no struggle, no victory, no defeat; in exact reciprocity each is at once subject and object, sovereign and slave; duality becomes mutuality.
Simone de Beauvoir (1908–86) French writer.
Le Deuxième Sexe (The Second Sex) [1949]

579 The Professor of Gynaecology began his course of lectures as follows: Gentlemen, woman is an animal that micturates once a day, defecates once a week, menstruates once a month, parturates once a year and copulates whenever she has the opportunity.
W. Somerset Maugham (1874–1965) British novelist.
A Writer's Notebook [1949]

580 For a woman to get a rewarding sense of total creation by way of the multiple monotonous chores that are her daily lot would be as irrational as for an assembly line worker to rejoice that he had created an automobile because he tightened a bolt.
Edith Mendel Stern (1901–75) US writer.
American Mercury, 'Women Are Household Slaves', Jan 1949

581 Women have always been the guardians of wisdom and humanity which makes them natural, but usually secret, rulers. The time has come for them to rule openly, but together with and not against men.
Charlotte Wolff (1904–) German-born British writer.
Bisexuality: A Study, Ch. 2 [c. 1950]

582 It certainly must have been a relief for the women of the country to realize that one could be a woman and a lady and yet be thoroughly political.
Agnes Meyer (1887–c. 1970) US writer.
Letter to Eleanor Roosevelt, 25 July 1952

583 What are we educating women for? To raise this question is to face the whole problem of women's role in society. We are uncertain about the end of women's education precisely because the status of women in our society is fraught with contradictions and confusion.
Mirra Komarovsky (1906–) Russian-born US writer.
Women in the Modern World [1953]

584 Gradually the women of Egypt pulled down the silken curtain that separated them from the free world – the world of men. The voluntary removal of the veil by Egyptian women marked the beginning of a process of gradual emancipation.
Aziza Husain Egyptian social reformer.
Middle East Journal, 'The Role of Women in Social Reform in Egypt', 1954

585 Women are no longer content to endure the treatment which in past times their inferior position obliged them to suffer. They expect of marriage that it shall be an equal partnership; and rightly so. But the working out of this ideal exposes marriages to new strains.
Morton Commission report on divorce law [1955]

586 Women are equal because they are not different any more.
Erich Fromm (1910–80) US writer.
The Art of Loving [1956]

587 The Gordian knot of a seemingly insoluble feminine dilemma has been cut. The technical and social developments of the last few decades have given women the opportunity to integrate their two interests in Home and Work...The best of both worlds has come within their grasp, if only they reach out for it.
A. Myrdal and V. Klein
Woman's Two Roles [1956]

588 Why not put up that pane of glass called passion between us? It may distort things at times, but it's wonderfully convenient. But no, we were two of a kind, allies and accomplices. In terms of grammar, I could not become the object, or he the subject. He had neither the capacity nor the desire to define our roles in any such way.
Françoise Sagan (1935–) French writer.
A Certain Smile, Pt II, Ch. 2 [1956]

589 When we stopped short of treating women as people after providing them with all the paraphernalia of education and rights, we set up a

condition whereby men also became less than full human beings and more narrowly domestic.
Margaret Mead (1901–78) US anthropologist and writer.
The New York Times Magazine, 'American Man in a Woman's World', 10 Feb 1957

590 The keeping of an idle woman is a badge of superior social status.
Dorothy L. Sayers (1893–1957) English writer.
Essay [1957]

591 You may think that one of the ways in which you can test this book, and test it from the most liberal outlook, is to ask yourselves the question when you have read it through:
'Would you approve of your young sons and daughters – because girls can read as well as boys – reading this book?' Is it a book you would have lying around in your own house? Is it a book you would even wish your wife or your servants to read?
Mervyn Griffith-Jones (1909–78) British lawyer.
As counsel for the prosecution in the *Lady Chatterley's Lover* trial, 1960

592 People call me a feminist whenever I express sentiments that differentiate me from a doormat or a prostitute.
Rebecca West (Cicely Isabel Fairfield; 1892–1983) British novelist and journalist.
Attrib. [c. 1960]

593 The incentive for girls to equip themselves for marriage and home-making is genetic.
Kathleen Ollerenshaw (1912–) British educationalist.
Education for Girls [1961]

594 It has simply been taken for granted that men and women are equal and even though some centuries separated the period when woman functioned as a free citizen in her own right and her re-emergence after India's independence, the theoretical acceptance of equality has always remained.
Vijaya Lakshmi Pandit (1900–) Indian government official.
Punch, 16 May 1962

595 Woman must be regarded as equal to man and must shed the remaining shackles that impede her from taking a constructive part in life.
National Charter of Egypt, 1962

596 You may marry or you may not. In today's world that is no longer the big question for women. Those who glom on to men so that they can collapse with relief, spend the rest of their days shining up their status symbol and figure they never have to reach, stretch, learn, grow, face dragons or make a living again are the ones

to be pitied. They, in my opinion, are the unfulfilled ones.
Helen Gurley Brown (1922–) US writer.
Sex and the Single Girl [1963]

597 It was a strange stirring, a sense of dissatisfaction, a yearning that women suffered in the middle of the twentieth century in the United States. Each suburban wife struggled with it alone. As she made the beds, shopped for groceries, matched slip cover material, ate peanut butter sandwiches, chauffeured Cub Scouts and Brownies, lay beside her husband at night, she was afraid to ask even of herself the silent question, 'Is this all?'
Betty Friedan (1921–) US writer.
The Feminine Mystique [1963]

598 The glorification of the 'woman's role', then, seems to be in proportion to society's reluctance to treat women as complete human beings; for the less real function that role has, the more it is decorated with meaningless details to conceal its emptiness.
Betty Friedan (1921–) US writer.
The Feminine Mystique [1963]

599 That we have not made any respectable attempt to meet the special educational needs of women in the past is the clearest possible evidence of the fact that our educational objectives have been geared exclusively to the vocational patterns of men.
Betty Friedan (1921–) US writer.
The Feminine Mystique [1963]

600 In the dust and strife of life in Parliament, I often longed for the peace and leisure of the days in *purdah*. But there could be no turning back, no return to the secluded and sheltered existence of the past…I had to continue on this new road on which the women of my country had set out.
Shaista Ikramullah Pakistani politician.
From Purdah to Parliament [1963]

601 Girls should be educated in terms of their own social function – which is to make for themselves, their children and their husbands a secure and suitable home, and to be mothers.
Sir John Newsom (1910–) Chairman of British Government advisory panel on women's education.
Report, 1963

602 At no previous period has mankind been faced by a half-century which so paradoxically united violence and progress. Its greater and lesser wars and long series of major assassinations have been strangely combined with the liberation of more societies and individuals than ever before in history, and by the transformation of millions of second-class citizens –

women, workers, and the members of subject races – to a stage at which first-rate achievement is no longer inhibited even if opportunities are not yet complete.
Vera Brittain (1893–1970) British writer and feminist.
The Rebel Passion, Ch. 12 [1964]

603 What I call the destructive anxieties are not the growth of women's minds and powers, but quite the contrary: the pressures of society and the mass media to make woman conform to the classic and traditional images in men's eyes.
Marya Mannes (1904–   ) US writer.
Journal of Neuropsychiatry, 'The Roots of Anxiety in Modern Women', May 1964

604 Such is the fear of women that it has been, by tradition, essential to a man's education that he should from an early age be removed from feminine influence – sons were taken from their mothers to begin a process of hardening for knighthood, or to go to the monastery for learning: at a later date we find the young hustled off to prep school.
Dora Russell (1894–   ) British writer.
In a Man's World: The Eclipse of Women [1965]

605 As the world has changed so radically, so has the status of woman changed from that of a follower or marginal person to one who has the status of a full and equal person and citizen.
Aminah al-Sa'id (1914–   ) Egyptian feminist.
Lecture, 'The Arab Woman and the Challenge of Society', 12 Dec 1966

Rumblings of women's liberation...

606   SCUM Society for Cutting Up Men Manifesto
Valerie Solanas (1940–   ) US writer.
Book title [1967]

607   The nicest women in our 'society' are raving sex maniacs. But, being just awfully, awfully nice they don't, of course, descend to fucking – that's uncouth – rather they make love, commune by means of their bodies and establish sensual rapport.
Valerie Solanas (1940–   ) US writer.
SCUM Manifesto [1967]

608   A true community consists of individuals – not mere species members, not couples – respecting each other's individuality and privacy.
Valerie Solanas (1940–   ) US writer.
SCUM Manifesto [1967]

609   The male is a biological accident: the y (male) gene is an incomplete x (female) gene, that is, has an incomplete set of chromosomes. In other words, the male is an incomplete female, a walking abortion, aborted at the gene stage.
Valerie Solanas (1940–   ) US writer.
SCUM Manifesto [1967]

610   The practice of abortion is as old as pregnancy itself...historically the opposition to abortion and birth control...stemmed from the urgency of the need to decrease the mortality and morbidity rates and to increase the population...Today, literate people of the space age, in well-populated countries, are not prepared to accept taboos without question; and in the matter of abortion the human rights of the mother with her family must take precedence over the survival of a few weeks' old foetus without sense or sensibility.
Edith Summerskill (1901–80) English politician and writer.
A Woman's World, Ch. 19 [1967]

611   The contraceptive pill may reduce the importance of sex not only as a basis for the division of labor, but as a guideline in developing talents and interests.
Caroline Bird (1915–   ) US writer.
Born Female, Foreword [1968]

612   A career woman who has survived the hurdle of marriage and maternity encounters a new obstacle: the hostility of men.
Caroline Bird (1915–   ) US writer.
Born Female, Ch. 3 [1968]

613   I had explained that a woman's asking for equality in the church would be comparable to a black person's demanding equality in the Ku Klux Klan.
Mary Daly (1928–   ) US writer and theologian.
The Church and the Second Sex [1968]

614   You say being a housewife is the noblest call in the world...You remind me of those company executives who...praise the 'little guys' of their organization in their speeches.
Françoise Parturier (1919–   ) French writer.
Open Letter to Men [1968]

615   There was never lipstick to contrast with her straight black hair, while at the age of thirty-one her dresses showed all the imagination of English blue-stocking adolescents. So it was quite easy to imagine her the product of an unsatisfied mother who unduly stressed the desirability of professional careers that could save bright girls from marriages to dull men.
James Dewey Watson (1928–   ) US geneticist.
Referring to Rosalind Franklin, whose X-ray crystallography work contributed to the discovery of the structure of DNA. *The Double Helix* [1968]

616   The fact that the adult American Negro female emerges a formidable character is often met with amazement, distaste and even belligerance. It is seldom accepted as an inevitable outcome of the struggle won by survivors, and deserves respect if not enthusiastic acceptance.
Maya Angelou (1928–   ) US writer.
I Know Why the Caged Bird Sings [1969]

617   In sheer quantity, household labor, including child care, constitutes a huge amount of socially necessary production. Nevertheless, in a society based on commodity production, it is not usually considered as 'real work' since it is outside of trade and the marketplace.
Margaret Lowe Benston (1937–   ) US physical chemist and educator.
Monthly Review, 'The Political Economy of Women's Lib', Sept 1969

618   Personally, Freud's 'anatomy is destiny' has always horrified me. *Kirche, Kusse, Kuche, Kinde* made me sick...The-pill'll-make-you-gals-run-wild a lot of male chauvinist anxiety. Dump-the-pill a truncated statement...the fam-

ily unit being the last word in socializing institutions to prepare us all for the ultimate rip-off and perpetuate the status quo, and abortion fatalities being what they are – of course the pill.
Toni Cade (c. 1937–   ) US writer.
Onyx, 'The Pill', Aug 1969

619   The care of children, even from the period when their cognitive powers first emerge, is infinitely better left to the best-trained practitioners of both sexes who have chosen it as a vocation, rather than to harried and all too frequently unhappy persons with little time or taste for the work of educating minds however young or beloved.
Kate Millett (1934–   ) US sculptor and writer.
Sexual Politics [1969]

620   I sometimes think the sex war for equality may have gone a bit too far. I think absolute equality is impossible. Aggressive women make me shudder. Militant feminists who take a determined stand on women's rights seem to forget that women still have an advantage simply because they *are* women.
Janet Morgan (1945–   ) First woman secretary of the Oxford Union Society.
Daily Mail, 1969

621   Because woman's work is never done and is underpaid or unpaid or boring or repetitious and we're the first to get the sack and what we look like is more important than what we do and if we get raped it's our fault...for lots and lots of other reasons we are part of the women's liberation movement.
Taken from a leaflet/poster produced by the NUS Women's Campaign [1970s]

622   Raising a family and doing housework are the common tasks of a society, to be done equally by men and women; along with this equality of shared necessity will come the equal pursuit of work, love, amusement, thought, emotional independence, and any other damn thing that increases life and gives peace and pleasure.
Vivian Gornick
SCUM Manifesto, Introduction (Valerie Solanas) [1970]

623   Women, who are beginning to understand that it has benefited a patriarchal society to make adults of men by giving them all the real responsibility, and to make children of women by depriving them of all the real responsibility.
Vivian Gornick
SCUM Manifesto, Introduction (Valerie Solanas) [1970]

624   Mother is the dead heart of the family, spending father's earnings on consumer goods to enhance the environment in which he eats, sleeps and watches the television.
Germaine Greer (1939–   ) Australian-born British writer and feminist.
The Female Eunuch [1970]

625   Women fail to understand how much men hate them.
Germaine Greer (1939–   ) Australian-born British writer and feminist.
The Female Eunuch [1970]

626   The only logical choice for us is to reject motherhood as long as procreation and childcare are considered as one and the same thing. What makes motherhood unbearable are the conditions imposed on mothers in our society, obviously not motherhood in and of itself.
Les Chimères A specially formed collective who were members of the Féministes Révolutionnaires.
Maternité esclave [1970]

627   Legislation and case law still exist in some parts of the United States permitting the 'passion shooting' by a husband of a wife; the reverse, of course, is known as homicide.
Diane B. Schulder (1937–   ) US lawyer and educator.
Sisterhood Is Powerful [1970]

628   What makes Soviet Russia the new land of the machine are the new social relationships of the men and women around the machine. The new man...and with him, on an equal footing, the new woman – operating drill presses, studying medicine and engineering – are integral parts of a people working collectively toward a common goal.
Margaret Bourke-White (1906–71) US photographer and writer.
The Woman's Eye [1971]

629   In order to function as slave, the black woman had to be annulled as woman, that is, as woman in her historical stance of wardship under the entire male hierarchy. The sheer force of things rendered her equal to her man.
Angela Davis (1944–   ) US political activist and writer.
The Black Scholar, Dec 1971

630   There are no such things as women's issues! All issues are women's issues...the difference that we bring is that we are going to bring the full, loud, clear determined voice of women into deciding how those issues are going to be addressed.
Aileen Clarke Hernandez (1926–   ) US business executive.
Address, National Conference of the National Organization for Women, Los Angeles, Sept 3–6, 1971

631 For sheer, ingrained, insufferable masculine prejudice, with a dollop of self-righteousness thrown in, it would be hard to beat this statement from British European Airways. 'We may be old-fashioned perhaps but we prefer to have women in the home and not as airline pilots.'
Commenting on British European Airways refusal to grant an interview to a qualified female pilot. *Daily Mirror*, 2 Feb 1971

632 A million women abort every year in France. They do it under dangerous conditions because they are condemned to clandestinity, although, when done under medical supervision, this operation is extremely simple.
No-one ever mentions these millions of women. I declare that I am one of them. I declare that I have had an abortion.
Just as we demand free access to contraception, we demand freedom of abortion.
A statement, signed by 343 French women, and headed by Simone de Beauvoir, marking the beginning of the campaign for free legal abortion on demand in France. *Le Nouvel Observateur*, 5 Apr 1971

633 There they were, all the lovely sisters, giggling and shivering and bawdy and prim and I turned and turned again, gloating at the numbers before and behind my motley, frost-defying sex. Because sex is all we really had in common.
Jill Tweedie (1936–) British writer and journalist.
Reporting the first large Women's Liberation demonstration, 6 Mar 1971. *Telegraph Weekend Magazine*, Mar 1991

634 Lesbianism is far more than a sexual preference: it is a political stance.
Sidney Abbott (1937–) US writer.
Sappho Was a Right-On Woman [1972]

635 For human reality, existing means existing in time: in the present we look towards the future by means of plans that go beyond our past, in which our activities fall lifeless, frozen and loaded with passive demands. Age changes our relationship with time: as the years go by our future shortens, while our past grows heavier.
Simone de Beauvoir (1908–86) French writer.
The Coming of Age, Pt II, Ch. 6 [1972]

636 When modern woman discovered the orgasm it was (combined with modern birth control) perhaps the biggest single nail in the coffin of male dominance.
Eva Figes (1932–) English writer.
The Descent of Woman (Elaine Morgan) [1972]

637 We had taken the first step along the tortuous road that led to the sex war, sadomasochism, and ultimately to the whole contemporary snarl-up, to prostitution, prudery,

Casanova, John Knox, Marie Stopes, white slavery, women's liberation, *Playboy* magazine, *crimes passionels*, censorship, strip clubs, alimony, pornography, and a dozen different brands of mania. This was the Fall. It had nothing to do with apples.
Elaine Morgan (1920–) Welsh writer.
The Descent of Woman, Ch. 4 [1972]

638 Housewives and mothers seldom find it practicable to come out on strike. They have no union, anyway. But the rumblings of women's liberation are only one pointer to the fact that you already have a discontented work force.
Elaine Morgan (1920–) Welsh writer.
The Descent of Woman, Ch. 11 [1972]

639 According to civil law, women are equal to men. But I have to go to a religious court as far as personal affairs are concerned. Only men are allowed to be judges there – men who pray every morning to thank God He did not make them women. You meet prejudice before you open your mouth. And because they believe women belong in the home, you are doubly discriminated against if you work.
Shulamit Aloni (1905–) Israeli lawyer, politician, and writer.
'Women in Israel', Nov 1973

640 Women get more unhappy the more they try to liberate themselves and act like men. A woman is a tender and sweet person and she'll lose that if she tries to be like a man.
Brigitte Bardot (1934–) French film actress.
Television interview, 1973

641 The embattled gates to equal rights indeed opened up for modern women, but I sometimes think to myself: 'That is not what I meant by freedom – it is only "social progress."'
Helene Deutsch (1884–1982) US psychoanalyst.
Confrontations with Myself, Ch. 1 [1973]

642 The uniqueness of today's Women's Liberation Movement is that it dares to challenge what is, including the male chauvinism not only under capitalism but within the revolutionary movement itself.
Raya Dunayevskaya (?1911–) US author and philosopher.
Philosophy and Revolution, Ch. 9 [1973]

643 The wait seemed interminable, but finally Justice Blackmun read: 'This right of privacy... is broad enough to encompass a woman's decision whether or not to terminate her pregnancy.' This privacy right to abortion...was grounded in either the 'Fourteenth Amendment's concept of personal liberty or...in the Ninth Amendment's reservation of rights to the

people'...The Court had ruled that a woman's right to abortion was constitutionally protected.
Marian Faux US writer.
Referring to a Supreme Court decision in the Roe v. Wade case concerning the right to abortion [1973]

644 I wish women in the gay liberation movement God-speed, although I take issue with their premise that all men, without exception, are intruding vandals bent only on the oppression of womankind. I submit that some of them can be welcome guests.
Jane Howard (1935–) US writer.
A Different Woman, Ch. 9 [1973]

645 I'm furious about the Women's Liberationists. They keep getting up on soapboxes and proclaiming that women are brighter than men. That's true, but it should be kept very quiet or it ruins the whole racket.
Anita Loos (1891–1981) US novelist.
Observer, 'Sayings of the Year', 30 Dec 1973

646 Alimony is one way of compensating women for those financial disabilities aggravated, or caused, by marriage: unequal educational opportunities; unequal employment opportunities; and an unequal division of family responsibilities, with no compensation for the spouse who works in the home.
Susan C. Ross (1942–) US lawyer and writer.
The Rights of Women, Ch. 7 [1973]

647 Equal pay for equal work continues to be seen as applying to equal pay for men and women in the same occupation, while the larger point of continuing relevance in our day is that some occupations have depressed wages because women are the chief employees. The former is a pattern of sex discrimination, the latter of institutionalized sexism.
Alice Rossi (1922–) US editor.
The Feminist Papers, 'A Feminist Friendship' [1973]

648 Without the means to prevent, and to control the timing of conception, economic and political rights have limited meaning for women. If women cannot plan their pregnancies, they can plan little else in their lives.
Alice Rossi (1922–) US editor.
The Feminist Papers, 'The Right to One's Body' [1973]

649 What the emergence of woman as a political force means is that we are quite ready now to take on responsibilities as equals, not protected partners.
Jill Ruckelshaus (?1937–) US government official and lecturer.
Saturday Evening Post, 3 Mar 1973

650 The Equal Rights Amendment is designed to establish in our Constitution the clear moral value judgment that all Americans, women and men, stand equal under the law...It will give woman's role in the home new status, recognizing that the homemaker's role in a marriage has economic value.
Jill Ruckelshaus (?1937–) US government official and lecturer.
The ERA, which was introduced in Congress in 1923 and approved in 1972, states that 'Equality of rights under the law shall not be denied or abridged by the United States or any State on account of sex'. It has not been ratified. *Saturday Evening Post*, 3 Mar 1973

651 It is misleading and unfair to imply that an intelligent woman must 'rise above' her maternal instincts and return to work when many intelligent, sensitive women have found that the reverse is better for them.
Sally E. Shaywitz (1942–) US paediatrician and writer.
The New York Times Magazine, 'Catch 22 for Mothers', 4 Mar 1973

652 Whether we regard the Women's Liberation movement as a serious threat, a passing convulsion, or a fashionable idiocy, it is a movement that mounts an attack on practically everything that women value today and introduces the language and sentiments of political confrontation into the area of personal relationships.
Arianna Stassinopoulos (1950–) Greek writer.
The Female Woman, 'The Emancipated Woman' [1973]

653 Emancipation means the removal of all barriers to female opportunities. Liberation would compel women into male roles by devaluing female ones.
Arianna Stassinopoulos (1950–) Greek writer.
The Female Woman [1973]

654 She will be challenging a system that is still wedded to militarism and that saves billions of dollars a year by underpaying women and using them as a reserve cheap labor supply.
Bella Abzug (1920–) US lawyer and congresswoman.
Referring to a woman politician. *Ms*, 'Bella's-Eye View of Her Party's Future', Apr 1974

655 ...the torment that so many young women know, bound hand and foot by love and motherhood without having forgotten their former dreams.
Simone de Beauvoir (1908–86) French writer.
All Said and Done [1974]

656 Women are not a special interest group in the usual sense of the term. We are half the population. When the image of women presented in the media is offensive, it is offensive to women

of all social classes, races, religions and ethnic origins.
Toni Carabillo (1926–   ) US writer.
Address, National Association of Broadcasters, 'Womanpower and the Media', 1974

657 If divorce has increased one thousand percent, don't blame the woman's movement. Blame our obsolete sex roles on which our marriages were based.
Betty Friedan (1921–   ) US writer.
Speech, 20 Jan 1974

658 In commercial law, the person duped was too often a woman. In a section on land tenure, one 1968 textbook explains that 'land, like women, was meant to be possessed.'
Ruth Bader Ginsberg (1933–   ) US educator and lawyer.
Ms, 'Portia Faces Life – The Trials of Law School', Apr 1974

659 The emphasis must be not on the right to abortion but on the right to privacy and reproductive control.
Ruth Bader Ginsberg (1933–   ) US educator and lawyer.
Ms, 'Portia Faces Life – The Trials of Law School', Apr 1974

660 Those black males who try to hold women down are expressing in sexist terms the same kinds of expressions in racist terms which they would deny.
Jacquelyne Jackson (1932–   ) US writer.
Speech, First National Conference on Black Women, Mar 1974

661 There are very few jobs that actually require a penis or vagina. All other jobs should be open to everybody.
Florynce R. Kennedy (1916–   ) US lawyer and civil rights activist.
Writer's Digest, 'Freelancer with No Time to Write', Feb 1974

662 The American Republic is now almost 200 years old, and in the eyes of the law women are still not equal with men. The special legislation which will remedy that situation is the Equal Rights Amendment. Its language is short and simple: *Equality of rights under the law shall not be abridged in the United States or by any state on account of sex.*
Clare Boothe Luce (1903–   ) US politician and writer.
Bulletin of the Baldwin School, Pennsylvania, Sept 1974

663 Once in a Cabinet we had to deal with the fact that there had been an outbreak of assaults on women at night. One minister suggested a curfew: women should stay home after dark. I said, 'But it's the men who are attacking the

women. If there's to be a curfew, let the men stay home, not the women.'
Golda Meir (1898–1978) Israeli politician and prime minister.
Against Rape (Andra Medea and Kathleen Thompson) [1974]

664 The freer that women become, the freer will men be. Because when you enslave someone – you *are* enslaved.
Louise Nevelson (1900–   ) US sculptor and feminist.
AFTRA, Summer 1974

665 The astonishing fact of human history is that religion, philosophy, political, social and economic thought have been reserved as the prerogative of men. Our cultural world is the product of male consciousness.
Dora Russell (1894–   ) British writer.
The New Humanist [1974]

666 I earn and pay my own way as a great many women do today. Why should unmarried women be discriminated against – unmarried men are not.
Dinah Shore (1920–   ) US singer and actress.
Referring to taxation. *Los Angeles Times*, 16 Apr 1974

667 It will be years – and not in my time – before a woman will lead the party or become Prime Minister.
Margaret Thatcher (1925–   ) British politician and prime minister (1979–91).
Said when she was minister for health; she became leader of the Conservative party the following year, and prime minister in 1979. Speech, 1974

668 If you have a psychotic fixation and you go to the doctor and you want these two fingers amputated, he will not cut them off. But he *will* remove your genitals. I have more trouble getting a prescription for Valium than I do having my uterus lowered and made into a penis.
Lily Tomlin (1936–   ) US actress.
Rolling Stone, 24 Oct 1974

669 The Rubicons which women must cross, the sex barriers which they must breach, are ultimately those that exist in their own minds.
Freda Adler (1934–   ) US educator.
Sisters in Crime, Epilogue [1975]

670 When two people marry they become in the eyes of the law one person, and that one person is the husband!
Shana Alexander (1925–   ) US writer.
State-by-State Guide to Women's Legal Rights, Introduction [1975]

671 I wonder anew whether and how the human female will ever transcend the lower, more dependent, less rights-ful station to which

her reproductive nature has until the last-minute invention of The Pill confined her.
Shana Alexander (1925–) US writer.
State-by-State Guide to Women's Legal Rights, Introduction [1975]

672 Compared to riot-ridden suffragette movements in the Western countries, the feminist movement in Pakistan has been comparatively uneventful.
Dr Parveen Shaukat Ali Pakistani historian.
Status of Women in the Muslim World [1975]

673 The feeling is that until men are comfortable working in some of these fields that are traditionally considered to be female...women end up doing two jobs, and the men are still doing just one.
Rosemary Brown (1920–) Canadian politician.
Branching Out, Aug 1975

674 In our party, being a woman is no problem. After all, it is a revolutionary party.
Isabel do Carmo (1940–) Portuguese revolutionary.
Time, 30 Oct 1975

675 Our motto: Life is too short to stuff a mushroom.
Shirley Conran (1932–) British designer and journalist.
Superwoman, Epigraph [1975]

676 We were born in an era in which it was a disgrace for women to be sexually responsible. We matured in an era in which it was an obligation.
Janet Harris (1915–) US writer.
The Prime of Ms. America [1975]

677 The IRS has stolen from me over the past 20 years because I am single. It is unconstitutional to impose a penalty tax of 40 percent on me because I have no husband.
Vivien Kellems (1896–1975) US industrialist, feminist, and lecturer.
Reader's Digest, Oct 1975

678 Women's battle for financial equality has barely been joined, much less won. Society still traditionally assigns to woman the role of money-handler rather than money-maker, and our assigned specialty is far more likely to be home economics than financial economics.
Paula Nelson (1945–) US economist, business executive.
The Joy of Money, Ch. 1 [1975]

679 Critics say ERA will open the draft to women. At the moment, the United States has an oversubscribed volunteer army, many of whom are women. ERA means that women who serve will get equal benefits.
Jill Ruckelshaus (c. 1937–) US government official and lecturer.
Ladies' Home Journal, Aug 1975

680 It's ridiculous to think that half the brains in the country are locked up in female heads and are not being used.
Baroness Seears (1913–) British politician.
Speaking in support of the Sex Discrimination Act (1975). Speech, House of Lords, 1975

681 An act to render unlawful certain kinds of sex discrimination and discrimination on the ground of marriage and establish a Commission with the function of working towards the elimination of such discrimination and promoting equality of opportunity between men and women generally.
Sex Discrimination Act [1975]

682 It is interesting to hear some of the arguments in opposition to the Equal Rights Amendment. Some of them are the same ones that were made at the time when women, after a tremendous thrust of energy and effort, were enfranchised...There is no question that under ERA there will be debates at times, indecision at times, litigation at times. Has anyone proposed that we rescind the First Amendment on free speech because there is too much litigation over it?
Sissy Farenthold (1926–) US politician.
Speech for International Women's Year, 26 Feb 1977

683 I try to talk to one person. I've got this picture of a woman, a housewife, young or young at heart. She's probably on her own virtually all day. She's bored with the routine of housework and her own company and just for her I'm the chatty, slightly cheeky romantic visitor.
David Hamilton British disc-jockey.
Is This Your Life? Images of Women in the Media (eds Josephine King and Mary Stott) [1977]

684 In almost all Arab countries the veil has been abolished, but not by force or by occidental criticism. It has been abolished by the women who decided one day that they did not want it any more.
Nouha Alhegelan Wife of Sheik Alhegelan.
Irish Arab World, 'Women in the Arab World', 1978

685 Women's Liberation is just a lot of foolishness. It's the men who are discriminated against. They can't bear children. And no one's likely to do anything about that.
Golda Meir (1898–1978) Israeli politician and prime minister.
Attrib.

686 Legislation is not going to change discrimination. That is like trying to legislate morality.

The quality of representation is neither hindered nor helped by gender; the quality is with the individual.
Beverly Butcher Byron (1932–) US politician.
Speech, Congress, Jan 1979

687   Anybody against women, against the ERA, should never be voted into office again.
Liz Carpenter (1920–) US writer and feminist.
Speech, New York City, 22 Mar 1979

688   The women's movement was very significant to my career. Without it people would have continued to assume that women could not be in high positions. It changed tradition, if it hasn't yet changed all the minds. I would not have been promoted so many times without that as a backdrop.
Joan Manley (1932–) US publisher.
Working Woman, Feb 1979

689   This amendment, if passed, would be like a beacon which should awaken nine sleeping Rip Van Winkles to the fact that the twentieth century is passing into history…I seek justice, not in some distant tomorrow, not in some study commission, but now while I live.
Martha Wright Griffiths (1912–) US politician.
Referring to the Equal Rights Amendment. *American Political Women* (Esther Stineman) [c. 1980]

690   The best thing a woman can do is to marry, have children and bring them up herself.
Elizabeth Lane (1905–) British judge.
Speech, Malvern Girl's College, 1980

691   I liked the *name* of the amendment. I couldn't help feeling uneasy that the church was opposing something with a name as beautiful as the *Equal Rights* Amendment.
Sonia Johnson (c. 1936–) US writer.
From Housewife to Heretic [1981]

I'm not a feminist...

692 But I think women dwell quite a bit on the duress under which they work, on how hard it is just to do it at all. We are traditionally rather proud of ourselves for having slipped creative work in there between the domestic chores and obligations. I'm not sure we deserve such big A-pluses for all that.
Toni Morrison (1931–) US author.
Newsweek, 30 Mar 1981

693 My first child was born in 1967 when I was twenty-two and had accomplished a university degree. I thought it was my vocation to be a mother…but the time that followed was an unhappy haze of nappy washing and pill taking, as I found I could not make my dream of domestic contentment come true. I felt depressed and oppressed. I felt constantly tired. I felt isolated. I felt resentful of my husband's freedom. I felt my life was at an end.
Ann Oakley (1944–) British sociologist.
From Here to Maternity [1981]

694 Women's intellect, who wants it?
Not her nearest, nor her dearest.
They all want three meals a day.
It's hard to say them nay.
…
In these days of liberation,
Conditional emancipation,
At least there's toleration.
A little learning adds distinction
Gives rise to some congratulation
Always provided (need one say?)
There are still three meals a day.
Constance Rover (1910–) British lecturer and feminist.
Three Meals a Day [1981]

695 If the men in the room would only think how they would feel graduating with a 'spinster of arts' degree they would see how important this is.
Gloria Steinem (1934–) US writer and feminist.
Referring to language reform. Speech, Yale University, Sept 1981

696 We will be ourselves and free, or die in the attempt. Harriet Tubman was not our great-grandmother for nothing.
Alice Walker (1944–) US writer.
Harriet Tubman (c. 1820–1913) was a US slave who escaped and became a leading Abolitionist. *You Can't Keep a Good Woman Down* [1981]

697 Women have been emancipated on condition that they don't upset men, or interfere too much with men's way of life.
Constance Rover (1910–) British lecturer and feminist.
There's Always been a Women's Movement this Century (Dale Spender) [1982]

698 A lot of women seem to have a similar attitude, – 'I'm not a feminist' – and it gets wearying. What's wrong with being a feminist? I'm proud to be a feminist. It's been one of the most positive things in my life. It's one of the best traditions there is. It's admirable to be a feminist and to stand up for one's sex, to fight against inequality and injustice and to work for a better society.
Mary Stott (1907–) British journalist.
There's Always been a Women's Movement this Century (Dale Spender) [1982]

699 In politics, if you want anything said, ask a man; if you want anything done, ask a woman.
Margaret Thatcher (1925–) British politician and prime minister (1979–91).
The Changing Anatomy of Britain (Anthony Sampson) [1982]

700 The battle for women's rights has been largely won.
Margaret Thatcher (1925–) British politician and prime minister (1979–91).
Guardian, 1982

701 If we had left it to the men *toilets* would have been the greatest obstacle to human progress. *Toilets* was always the reason women couldn't become engineers, or pilots, or even members of parliament. They didn't have women's toilets.
Rebecca West (Cicely Isabel Fairfield; 1892–1983) British novelist and journalist.
There's Always been a Women's Movement this Century (Dale Spender) [1982]

702 I feel that equality is equality and that feminist goals will not have been realised until all human beings are equal, and this means an end to existing social arrangements which structure inequality – be they based on nationality, ethnicity, class, political position, education, sexual preference, disability or age.
Dale Spender (1943–) Australian writer and feminist.
Feminist Theorists, 'Modern Feminist Theorists: Reinventing Rebellion' [1983]

703 Women are here today to express their objection to the sexism, racism and war-mongering in the press, including the gross misrepresentation of the women's peace camp.

We accuse the press of creating a climate of distrust and prejudice against women working for peace. Our voices are silenced and facts are distorted in ways which incite more violence and bigotry against us. We demand fair and honest reporting for all women, including peace workers and victims of male violence.

Issued by the women protesting at Greenham Common, following a number of slanderous articles in the popular press. Press statement, Sept 1983

704 To get to the top women, like men, will simply have to put their careers and companies first for some part of their working lives...men in power have always been willing to pay this price.

Katharine Graham (1917–63) US editor and chairman of the *Washington Post*.

Speech, New York Women in Communication Matrix Awards, 1984

705 An executive who opts to bear a child, an opportunity not open to men, becomes a mother. Physiology has specified the nature of the maternal role and the relationship to the child which, if the child were asked and given priority, should continue to be direct and close for 5–7 years. In short, the mother should stay at home at least for that period...perhaps the spread of feminist denial of the natural law explains why women do not often reach the upper limbs of the executive tree; they are being encouraged to revolt against their nature.

J. M. Reid

The Financial Times, Letter to the editor, June 1984

706 I have yet to hear a man ask for advice on how to combine marriage and a career.

Gloria Steinem (1934–) US writer and feminist.

LBC radio interview, 2 Apr 1984

707 Wedding day, well, is compulsory. Political women are tortured and raped before execution. Especially young women. They rape nine-year-old women in the prison because it is against God if they execute a virgin woman. Women are attacked in various horrific ways, such as acid being thrown in their faces, their hair being burnt if it is not covered. It means that just to be a woman in Iran is a political crime.

Selma James (1930–) US-born British feminist.

Strangers and Sisters: Women, Race and Immigration [1985]

708 It's not an accident that when God became 'man' He chose to be a male. There's no doubt that He could have chosen to be a woman if He'd wanted to.

Graham Leonard (1921–) British churchman; Bishop of London (1981–91).

Arguing against women priests in the Church of England. *The Sunday Times*, 22 Dec 1985

709 Everything is all right until you start having children. Society gives no help at all, and every couple has to work it out for themselves. Women have in the past shouldered the double burden unquestioningly, but the next generation is starting to think in these terms – will he get up at 3 a.m. and feed the baby if she has got a meeting the next morning?

Mary Moore (1930–) Principal of St Hilda's College, Oxford.

[1985]

710 All males should deposit their sperm in a sperm bank and then present themselves for compulsory vasectomy. In future all children would be conceived by artificial insemination, thus ensuring a responsible attitude to planned parenthood and eliminating unwanted pregnancies. Try to get this on to the Statute Book and I confidently expect to be deafened by the sound of men demanding their right to choose.

Standard, Letter to the editor, 6 Feb 1985

711 The idea of equal pay now has majority support among both men and women, which it didn't ten years ago. There is some understanding of shared work at home and shared parenthood. It would be hard to find anyone who didn't have a changed idea of what women expect.

Gloria Steinem (1934–) US writer and feminist.

Women and Power (Rosalind Miles) [1985]

712 A man may be hesitant about encouraging a woman as a protégé. He may be delighted to have her as an assistant, but not see her as a colleague. He may believe that she is less likely to be a good gamble, that she is financially less dependent on a job.

Martha White Social psychologist

Women and Power (Rosalind Miles) [1985]

713 In 1978–9, educated women donned the *chador* as a protest against the Shah, while Ayatollah Khomeini denounced the Shah's attitude to women...

Today, women who expose too much hair can be sent to camps for 'corrective moral re-education'. The veil is seen as the symbol of independence from the Western values that the Shah used merely to consolidate his family's power. Failure to observe correct wearing of 'hejab' (correct religious dress) is counter-revolutionary.

Tim Hodlin
The Listener, 'Veil of Tears', 12 June 1986

714 Words such as 'beast', 'brute', 'monster' and 'sex fiend' are commonly used to describe the rapist. Yet we rarely see the simple word 'man', which the rapist invariably is.
Cambridge Rape Crisis Centre
Out of Focus [1987]

715 I don't believe in equal opportunity. I think it's terribly tiresome. The whole thing is absolutely terrible now because we've got vast unemployment. It's still a stigma for a man to be unemployed, and to be kept by a woman. It's not a stigma for the woman to be kept by a man.
Barbara Cartland (1902–) British romantic novelist.
Women (Naim Attalah) [1987]

716 Women are exploited at the lower end of the workforce by part-time work and once a job becomes a woman's job people tend to pay slightly worse rates for it. An interesting example is word processing and the new technology: once women master it, the rate for the job goes down slightly. When it is still a masculine preserve, as in computer science, it is well paid and highly regarded.
Margaret Drabble (1939–) British novelist.
Women (Naim Attallah) [1987]

717 Now a woman can get married or not as she likes, she doesn't mind. Nobody throws things at her, or sneers. It has allowed women to be themselves, to choose their own future, or their own present; to choose things for themselves and not to be tied up by tradition. They're free agents to act as they want and as they feel they really need to act, without people sneering or people talking. It's a marvellous feeling to feel free to do just what you want to do after being down so long.
Elizabeth Dean (1885–) British suffragette.
Commenting on whether she thought the vote had brought equality to women. *Out of the Doll's House* (Angela Holdsworth) [1988]

718 However the right to abortion and improved contraception transformed many women's lives. Although the pill, with its threatening side effects, has not turned out to be the perfect contraceptive everyone hoped for, it has brought women – particularly those under thirty – security from unplanned pregnancy, affording extra years between childhood and motherhood.
Angela Holdsworth British television journalist.
Out of the Doll's House [1988]

719 I shrug my shoulders in despair at women who moan at the lack of opportunities and then take two weeks off as a result of falling out with their boyfriends.
Sophie Mirman British business woman.
On receiving the Business Woman of the Year Award. Speech, 1988

720 Saudi Arabia's religious sages…faced a dilemma yesterday after about 50 Saudi women drove a convoy of cars through the centre of Riyadh in protest at the country's ban on women drivers…Eventually the Ulema issued a fatwa, or ruling, that smacked of compromise. While technically the women had not broken the law of the Koran, which was written some years before the invention of the motor car, they were adjudged to have offended the spirit of pious Islamic practice.
Anonymous
Daily Telegraph, 8 Nov 1990

721 I do not think British industry has made any recognition whatsoever of the social revolution of the 1980s and 1990s. Two out of every three families are dual-career families, but industry has not designed itself in any way to help women – or, indeed, men who have working wives – to cope with the new family circumstance.
Cary Cooper (1940–) British psychologist.
Move Over Darling (Kathy Barnby and Loretta Loach) [1990]

722 What we still need to do is to infiltrate the mainstream with feminine values. Allow women to think and behave like women. There is no point in having women Cabinet ministers or managing directors or editors if they think and behave exactly like men. Their whole value lies in their difference.
Lesley Garner British journalist.
Daily Telegraph, 5 Dec 1990

723 You can see exactly what your next step should be, but you realise there are all sorts of obstacles…a brick wall: a solid united front of male clubbability.
Valerie Hammond British management consultant.
The Times, 12 Dec 1990

724 Over the years of working towards equality between men and women, company after company has realised that without financial and moral commitment from the very top, progress will be, if not non-existent, then at least as slow as to be imperceptible.
Hansard Society Commission on Women at the Top
Report, Jan 1990

725 In this era of opening opportunity, women are beginning to move into positions of authority. At first we assumed they could simply talk the way they always had, but this often doesn't work. Another logical step is that they should

change their styles and talk like men. Apart from the repugnance of women's having to do all the changing, this doesn't work either, because women who talk like men are judged differently – and harshly.
Deborah Tannen US writer and professor of linguistics.
You Just Don't Understand [1990]

726 The most dramatic thing is that, even when you look at women who are working full time outside the home – as full time as their men – when it comes to ironing and cleaning, 60 or 70 per cent of that work is still done by the women. That simply means that many women are doing two jobs in society: they've still got the traditional role of housewife and mother, they're still running the home, but in the daytime, they're helping to run the economy, too.
Malcolm Wicks Director, Family Policy Studies Institute.
Move Over Darling (Kathy Barnby and Loretta Loach) [1990]

727 My mother taught me to stir in the sugar before giving my husband the cup. But in the last six months we have learnt many things. Before we thought it was impolite to let the man pour the tea. But that is changing.
Hissa al-Shaheen Kuwaiti feminist.
Independent, 18 Feb 1991

728 I think it is still rather early to work in space. But I think the time will come when women can work in more comfortable conditions. For a short expedition it is acceptable. I just think it is hard work, not a woman's work.
Commander Artsebarsky (1955–) Russian astronaut, commander of the Soviet-British space mission.
Commenting on Helen Sharman, the first British astronaut. *The Times*, 18 May 1991

729 The idea that only a male can represent Christ at the altar is a most serious heresy.
Dr George Carey (1935–) British churchman and Archbishop of Canterbury (1991–).
Reader's Digest, Apr 1991

730 In a man's world, a woman in a position of power is still likely to be either a token woman or an imitation man. There are significant and hopeful exceptions. But as a general rule, role is more powerful than gender; and roles are still largely defined in traditional male ways. A woman Prime Minister is likely to be the best man in the cabinet.
Philip Crowe (1936–) British theologian.
The Times, 18 Feb 1991

731 At last, women have received their full citizenship papers.
And yet...

Behind this celebration of the American woman's victory, behind the news, cheerfully and endlessly repeated, that the struggle for women's rights is won, another message flashes. You may be free and equal now, it says to women, but you have never been more miserable.
Susan Faludi US writer.
Backlash 1991

732 Women are unhappy precisely *because* they are free. Women are enslaved by their own liberation. They have grabbed at the gold ring of independence, only to miss the one ring that really matters...The women's movement, as we are told time and again, has proved women's own worst enemy.
Susan Faludi US writer.
Backlash 1991

733 Under the umbrella of NAWO we have all kinds of women coming together because they recognise that there is a woman's common ground. There are young women who may be interested in their own advancement, but that doesn't mean they don't have any solidarity with other women.
Jane Grant British feminist, director of the National Alliance of Women's Organisations.
Daily Telegraph, 20 Feb 1991

734 We take the view that the time has now arrived when the law should declare that a rapist remains a rapist and is subject to the criminal law, irrespective of his relationship with his victim.
Geoffrey Dawson Lane (1918–) British judge and Lord Chief Justice.
Dismissing the appeal of a man who argued on the 1736 principle of Chief Justice Hale, that he could not be guilty of raping his wife. *The Times*, 15 Mar 1991

735 Marriage in modern times is regarded as a partnership of equals and no longer one in which the wife must be the subservient chattel of the husband.
Lord Keith of Kinkel (1922–) British judge.
Giving judgment in the House of Lords that rape can occur within marriage. *Independent*, 24 Oct 1991

736 I strongly feel that a rapist is a rapist, whether he is married to his victim or not.
John Patten (1945–) British politician.
Commenting on the Law Lords ruling that a husband can be guilty of raping his wife. *Independent*, 24 Oct 1991

737 Do we have to begin from scratch again and prove that women are people, too, just like we did at the dawn of Soviet power?
Tatyana Khudyakova Russian essayist.
Independent, 15 Nov 1991

738 The demise of the housewife is entirely to be welcomed, because it was a grossly oppressive thing for women to be confined to little boxes like brood mares or hens in a chicken house.
Rosalind Miles British writer.
The Times, 10 July 1991

739 One should not be sanguine when, at one end of the spectrum, one in four women is still being battered by partners and there is but a handful of women in Parliament at the other, but equally we should guard against sweeping statements on having sold out.
Angela Neustatter British writer.
Daily Telegraph, 20 Feb 1991

740 I think it was the stridency of the feminists I disliked so much. And I think it's had an appalling effect on men. There are no manners any more. I watched a woman in her seventies struggling to push her shopping trolley over an awkward pavement. There was a young man walking past and I wondered if he would help her. He just walked on. I thought, if that were my son I'd be angry and ashamed.
Kate Wharton British journalist.
Telegraph Weekend Magazine, Mar 1991

741 Female size, especially brain size, has always been held to explain their unfitness for this or that; whole nineteenth-century theories were based on the smaller size of the brain of women and 'inferior races' – until it was found that elephants' brains were even larger than men's.
Katharine Whitehorn (1926–) British journalist.
Observer, 18 Aug 1991

742 For the thing has been blown up out of all proportion. PC language is *not* enjoined on one and all – there are a lot more places where you can say 'spic' and 'bitch' with impunity than places where you can smoke a cigarette.
Katharine Whitehorn (1926–) British journalist.
PC stands for Politically Correct. *Observer*, 25 Aug 1991

743 Why is it so universally upsetting for men to have women around them on anything like a footing of equality? Why is the resentment as

deep-seated as ever, even if it is now underground?…Individual men may have no desire whatever to put women in their place, but everywhere women are made subordinate by traditions to which these men subscribe.
Katharine Whitehorn (1926–) British journalist.
Observer, 25 Aug 1991

744 There is no doubt that the type of techniques available are going to enable women who are past the menopause to have babies and society is going to have to grasp and deal with this.
Robert Winston (1940–) British doctor, head of the infertility unit at Hammersmith Hospital.
Referring to the possibility of delaying the menopause until the age of 60 or 70. *Independent*, 16 Dec 1991

745 The more legal and material hindrances women have broken through, the more strictly and heavily and cruelly images of female beauty have come to weigh upon us…After years of much struggle and little recognition, many older women feel burned out; after years of taking its light for granted, many younger women show little interest in touching new fire to the torch.
Naomi Wolf US writer.
The Beauty Myth (1991)

746 There is no legitimate historical or biological justification for the beauty myth; what it is doing to women today is a result of nothing more exalted than the need of today's power structure, economy, and culture to mount a counteroffensive against women.
Naomi Wolf US writer.
The Beauty Myth (1991)

747 The time is right for action. We are at a stage, worldwide, when women's rights could leap into the future – or be thrust back into a Dark Age. There is a window of opportunity. The question is, can women hold that window open and help each other through to the next stage, or will it be slammed shut in their faces with the force of the backlash?
Vanessa Baird Journalist and coeditor of 'New Internationalist Cooperative'.
New Internationalist, Jan 1992

THEMATIC SECTION

ABBOTT, Berenice (1898–)

US photographer, best known for her photographic record of New York in the late 1930s, some of which were published in the book *Changing New York* (1939). She is also well-known for her work in classifying and promoting the work of photographer Eugène Atget, after his death in 1927.

1 Photography can never grow up if it imitates some other medium. It has to walk alone; it has to be itself.

Infinity, 'It Has to Walk Alone', 1951

2 If a medium is represented by nature of the realistic image formed by a lens, I see no reason why we should stand on our heads to distort that function. On the contrary, we should take hold of that very quality, make use of it, and explore it to the fullest.

Infinity, 'It Has to Walk Alone', 1951

3 Some people are still unaware that reality contains unparalleled beauties. The fantastic and unexpected, the ever-changing and renewing is nowhere so exemplified as in real life itself.

Photographers on Photography (ed. Nathan Lyons)

ABORTION

1 She should use diuretic decoctions which also have the power to bring on menstruation... If this is without effect, one must also treat locally by having her sit in a bath of a decoction of linseed, fenugreek, mallow, marsh mallow, and wormwood.

Soranus of Ephesus (2nd century AD) Greek physician.

Gynaecology [2nd century AD]

2 Some women behave like harlots; when they feel the life of a child in their wombs, they induce herbs or other means to cause miscarriage, only to perpetuate their amusement and unchastity. Therefore I shall deprive them from everlasting life and send them to everlasting death.

Bridget of Sweden (1303–73) Swedish nun and visionary.

Revelations, Vol. VII

3 It serves me right for putting all my eggs in one bastard.

Dorothy Parker (1893–1967) US writer and wit.

On going into hospital for an abortion. *You Might As Well Live* (J. Keats)

4 Abortions will not let you forget.
You remember the children you got that you did not get...

Gwendolyn Brooks (1917–) US poet and writer.

A Street in Bronzeville, 'The Mother' [1945]

5 The 'immorality' of women, favourite theme of misogynists, is not to be wondered at; how could they fail to feel an inner mistrust of the presumptuous principles that men publicly proclaim and secretly disregard? They learn to believe no longer in what men say when they exalt woman or exalt man: the one thing they are sure of is this rifled and bleeding womb, the shreds of crimson life, this child that is not there. It is at her first abortion that woman begins to 'know'.

Simone de Beauvoir (1908–86) French writer.

Le Deuxième Sexe (*The Second Sex*) [1949]

6 Historically the opposition to abortion and birth control...stemmed from the urgency of the need to decrease the morality and morbidity rates and to increase the population...in the matter of abortion the human rights of the mother with her family must take precedence over the survival of a few weeks' old foetus without sense or sensibility.

Edith Summerskill (1901–80) British politician, gynaecologist, and writer.

A Woman's World, Ch. 19 [1967]

7 A million women abort every year in France. They do it under dangerous conditions because they are condemned to clandestinity, although, when done under medical supervision, this operation is extremely simple.
No-one ever mentions these millions of women. I declare that I am one of them. I declare that I have had an abortion.
Just as we demand free access to contraception, we demand freedom of abortion.

A statement, signed by 343 French women, and headed by Simone de Beauvoir, marking the beginning of the campaign for free legal abortion on demand in France. *Le Nouvel Observateur*, 5 Apr 1971

8 Abortion leads to an appalling trivialization of the act of procreation.

Donald Coggan, Archbishop of York (1909–) British churchman.

Speech to the Shaftesbury Society, 2 Oct 1973

9 The wait seemed interminable, but finally Justice Blackmun read: 'This right of privacy... is broad enough to encompass a woman's decision whether or not to terminate her pregnancy.' This privacy right to abortion...was grounded in either the 'Fourteenth Amendment's concept of personal liberty or...in the Ninth Amendment's reservation of rights to the people'...The Court had ruled that a woman's right to abortion was constitutionally protected.

Marian Faux US writer.

Referring to a Supreme Court decision in the Roe v. Wade case concerning the right to abortion [1973]

10 If men could get pregnant, abortion would be a sacrament.
Florynce R. Kennedy (1916–   ) US lawyer, civil rights activist, and feminist.
Ms, 'The Verbal Karate of Florynce R. Kennedy, Esq.' Gloria Steinem, Mar 1973

11 Contrary to the folklore of abortion as life-long trauma, it is not necessarily a profoundly scarring one either.
Helen Dudar US writer.
Saturday Review of the Society, 'Abortion for the Asking', Apr 1973

12 I'm opposed to abortion because I happen to believe that life deserves the protection of society.
Ella Grasso (1919–81) US politician.
Ms, Oct 1974

13 The greatest destroyer of peace is abortion because if a mother can kill her own child what is left for me to kill you and you to kill me? There is nothing between.
Mother Teresa (1910–   ) Yugoslavian missionary in Calcutta.
Nobel Peace Prize Lecture [1979]

14 Until that day when women, and only women, shall determine which American males must, by law, have vasectomies, then – and only then – will you or any man have the right to determine which American women can have abortions.
Betty Beale
Ms, Mar 1982

15 Most women decide to have abortions reluctantly, and with trepidation, as the lesser of two evils. No woman has an abortion for *fun*. They do not see why they should take on the responsibility of an unwanted child after their method of contraception has let them down… their circumstances – bad housing, lack of money, ill health – are such that they cannot cope with a new baby.
Joan Smith (1953–   ) British writer and journalist.
Misogynies [1989]

ACHIEVEMENT

1 Now my heart turns to and fro,
In thinking what will the people say,
They who shall see my monument in after years,
And shall speak of what I have done.
Hatshepsut (fl. 1503–1482 BC) Egyptian queen.
Inscription on her obelisk. *Ancient Egyptian Literature*, Vol. II, 'The New Kingdom' (ed. Miriam Lichtheim) [2nd century BC]

2 We must be silent no longer about those women whom neither the condition of their nature nor the cloak of modesty could keep silent in the Forum or the courts. Amasia Sentia, a defendant, pled her case before a great crowd…and was acquitted, almost unanimously, in a single hearing. Because she bore a man's spirit under the appearance of a woman, they called her *Androgyne*.
Valerius Maximus (fl. c. 20 AD) Roman historian.
Memorable Deeds and Sayings, VIII [c. 31 AD]

3 I have been led to imagine that the few extraordinary women who have rushed in eccentrical directions out of the orbit prescribed to their sex were *male* spirits, confined by mistake in female frames.
Mary Wollstonecraft (1759–97) British writer.
A Vindication of the Rights of Woman, Ch. 1 [1792]

4 When men bring forward as a second proof of their superiority the assertion that women have not achieved as much as men, they use poor arguments which leave history out of consideration. If they kept themselves more fully informed historically, they would know that great women have lived and achieved great things in the past, and that there are many living and achieving great things today.
'Abdu'l-Bahá (1844–1921) Persian leader of the Baha'i faith.
Speech, Women's Freedom League, London, Jan 1913

5 I cannot understand any woman's wanting to be the first woman to do anything…It is a devastating burden and I could not take it, could not be a pioneer, a Symbol of Something Greater.
Nora Ephron (1941–   ) US writer.
Crazy Salad, 'Bernice Gera, First Lady Umpire', Jan 1973

6 You have to admit that most women who have done something with their lives have been disliked by almost everyone.
Françoise Gilot Artist and mistress of Picasso.
Remark, Oct 1987

ACTING

1 Ladies, just a little more virginity, if you don't mind.
Herbert Beerbohm Tree (1853–1917) British actor and theatre manager.
Directing a group of sophisticated actresses. *Smart Aleck* (H. Teichmann) [1917]

2 The idea that acting is quintessentially 'feminine' carries with it a barely perceptible sneer, a suggestion that it is not the noblest or most dignified of professions. Acting is role-playing, role-playing is lying, and lying is a woman's game.
Molly Haskell (1940–   ) US film critic and writer.
From Reverence to Tape [1973]

3 An actor is something less than a man, while an actress is something more than a woman.
Richard Burton (Richard Jenkins; 1925–84) British actor.
Halliwell's Filmgoer's and Video Viewer's Companion [1984]

ADAMS, Abigail (1744–1818)

US letter-writer and feminist. Wife of the US president John Adams, she wrote many letters to her husband during their frequent separations, caused by his public commitments. She addressed her husband as 'Friend' and often signed herself as 'Portia', after the lawyer in *The Merchant of Venice*. Although she felt conscious of her lack of education her letters were fascinating and often reflected her views on the rights of women.

Quotations about Adams

1 The central and conspicuous fact about Abigail Adams' letters is that she hardly knew how to write a full paragraph.
L. H. Butterfield (1919–82) US historian and author. *The Book of Abigail and John*

2 Mrs President not of the United States but of a faction.
Albert Gallatin (1761–1849) US statesman. *Dictionary of American Biography*, I

Quotations by Adams

3 I am more and more convinced that man is a dangerous creature and that power, whether vested in many or a few, is ever grasping, and like the grave, cries 'Give, give.'
Letter to John Adams, 27 Nov 1775

4 Men of Sense in all Ages abhor those customs which treat us only as the vassals of your Sex.
Letter to John Adams, 31 Mar 1776

5 A habit the pleasure of which increases with practise, but becomes more irksome with neglect.
Referring to letter-writing. Letter to her daughter, 8 May 1808

ADDAMS, Jane (1860–1935)

US social reformer. Awarded the Nobel peace prize in 1931, she was a supporter of racial equality, feminism, and pacifism. She opened the Social Settlement of Hull House, Chicago, in 1889 and was president of the Women's International League for Peace and Freedom.

Quotations about Addams

1 She simply inhabits reality and everything she says necessarily expresses its nature. *She can't help writing truth.*
William James (1842–1910) US psychologist and philosopher. *American Journal of Sociology*

2 She had compassion without condescension. She had pity without retreat into vulgarity. She had infinite sympathy for common things without forgetfulness of those that are uncommon. That, I think, is why those who have known her say she was not only good, but great.
Walter Lippman (1889–1974) US editor and writer. *American Heroine, The Life and Legend of Jane Addams* (Allen F. Davis)

3 Jane Addams is to Chicago what Joan of Arc was to her people, she is sacrificing all for the masses.
Springfield Caxton, Aug 1910

Quotations by Addams

4 Doubtless the clashes and jars which we feel most keenly are those which occur when two standards of morals, both honestly held and believed in, are brought sharply together.
Democracy and Social Ethics, 'Filial Relations'

5 Old-fashioned ways which no longer apply to changed conditions are a snare in which the feet of women have always become readily entangled.
Newer Ideals of Peace, 'Utilization of Women in City Government'

6 Civilization is a method of living, an attitude of equal respect for all men.
Speech, Honolulu 1933

ADULTERY

See also UNFAITHFULNESS

1 Why should marriage bring only tears?
All I wanted was a man
With a single heart,
And we would stay together
As our hair turned white,
Not somebody always after wriggling fish
With his big bamboo rod.
Chuo Wên-chün (c. 179–117 BC) Chinese poet.
'A Song of White Hair' [2nd century BC]

2 If you should take your wife in adultery, you may with impunity put her to death without a trial; but if you should commit adultery or indecency, she must not presume to lay a finger on you, not does the law allow it.
Cato the Elder (Marcus Porcius C; 234–149 BC) Roman statesman.
On the Dowry [2nd century BC]

3 The *lex Julia* declares that wives have no rights to bring criminal accusations for adultery against their husbands, even though they may desire to complain of the violation of the marriage vow, for while the law grants this privilege to men it does not concede it to women.
Justinian I (482–565 AD) Byzantine emperor.
Codex, IX [6th century AD]

4 If any of your women be guilty of whoredom, then bring your witnesses against them from among themselves; and if they bear witness to the fact, shut them up within their houses till death release them, or God make some way for them.
Koran
Ch. IV [7th century]

5 A father will have compassion on his son. A mother will never forget her child. A brother will cover the sin of his sister. But what husband ever forgave the faithlessness of his wife?
Margaret of Navarre (1492–1549) French poet, writer, and patron of literature.
Mirror of the Sinful Soul [1531]

6 Force your husband to take you away. Do not fear that you are taking measures too harsh and too difficult: however terrible they may appear at first, they will be more pleasant in the end than the evils of an illicit love-affair.
Marie Madeleine de La Fayette (1634–c. 1692) French novelist and salonist.
The Princess of Clèves, First Part [1678]

7 If the husband is the criminal, he escapes with little or no injury either to fame or fortune. If the wife be the criminal, the persecutions of the world and her incapacity to make honorable provision for herself, compel her to join the ranks of prostitutes.
T. Bell British doctor.
Kalogynomia [1821]

8 An interviewer asked me what book I thought best represented the modern American woman. All I could think of to answer was: *Madame Bovary*.
Mary McCarthy (1912–89) US novelist.
On the Contrary [1962]

9 Lady, lady, should you meet,
One whose ways are all discreet,
One who murmurs that his wife
Is the lodestar of his life,
One who keeps assuring you
That he never was untrue,
Never loved another one...
Lady, lady, better run!
Dorothy Parker (1893–1967) US writer.
'Social Note' [1960s]

10 ALEX. I can't see why having an affair with someone on and off is any worse than being married for a course or two at mealtimes.
Penelope Gilliatt (1932–) British writer, film critic, and scenarist.
Sunday Bloody Sunday, 'Monday' [1971]

11 I say I don't sleep with married men, but what I mean is that I don't sleep with happily married men.
Britt Ekland (1942–) Swedish film actress.
Attrib. [c. 1980s]

AGE

1 A woman, till five-and-thirty, is only looked upon as a raw girl, and can possibly make no noise in the world till about forty. I don't know what your ladyship may think of this matter; but 'tis a considerable comfort to me, to know there is upon earth such a paradise for old women.
Mary Wortley Montagu (1689–1762) English poet, letter writer, and essayist.
Letter to Lady Rich, 20 Sept 1716

2 This day I am thirty years old. Let me now bid a cheerful adieu to my youth. My young days are now surely over, and why should I regret them? Were I never to grow old I might be always here, and might never bid farewell to sin and sorrow.
Janet Colquhoun (1781–1846) Scottish writer, diarist, and philanthropist.
Diary entry, 18 Apr 1811

3 A lady of a 'certain age', which means Certainly aged.
Lord Byron (1788–1824) British poet.
Don Juan, VI [1819–24]

4 She may very well pass for forty-three
In the dusk, with a light behind her!
W. S. Gilbert (1836–1911) British dramatist.
Trial by Jury [1875]

5 A man is as old as he's feeling,
A woman as old as she looks.
Mortimer Collins (1827–76) British writer.
The Unknown Quantity [1876]

6 One should never trust a woman who tells one her real age. A woman who would tell one that, would tell one anything.
Oscar Wilde (1854–1900) Irish-born British dramatist.
A Woman of No Importance, I [1893]

7 No woman should ever be quite accurate about her age. It looks so calculating.
Oscar Wilde (1854–1900) Irish-born British dramatist.
The Importance of Being Earnest, III [1895]

8 A man is only as old as the woman he feels.
Groucho Marx (Julius Marx; 1895–1977) US comedian.
Attrib. [c. 1950]

9 I refuse to admit that I am more than fifty-two, even if that does make my sons illegitimate.
Nancy Astor (1879–1964) US-born British politician.
Attrib. [1964]

10 I have always felt that a woman has the right to treat the subject of her age with ambiguity until, perhaps, she passes into the realm of over ninety. Then it is better she be candid with herself and with the world.
Helena Rubinstein (1882–1965) Polish-born US cosmetics manufacturer.
My Life for Beauty, Pt I, Ch. 1 [1965]

11 One searches the magazines in vain for women past their first youth. The middle-aged face apparently sells neither perfume nor floor wax. The role of the mature woman in the media is almost entirely negative.
Janet Harris (1915–) US writer and educator.
The Prime of Ms America [1975]

AIDS

1 My message to the businessmen of this country when they go abroad on business is that there is one thing above all they can take with them to stop them catching Aids, and that is the wife.
Edwina Currie (1946–) British politician.
Observer, 'Sayings of the Week', 15 Feb 1987

2 Every time you sleep with a boy you sleep with all his old girlfriends.
Government-sponsored AIDS advertisement, 1987

3 It could be said that the Aids pandemic is a classic own-goal scored by the human race against itself.
Princess Anne (1950–) The Princess Royal, only daughter of Elizabeth II.
Remark, Jan 1988

AIKIN, Lucy (1781–1864)

British poet and historian. Her works include *Epistles on Women* (1810), *Memoirs of the Court of Queen Elizabeth* (1818), and *The Life of Addison* (1843).

Quotations about Aikin
1 Nor are the immunities of sex the only immunities which Miss Aikin may rightfully plead. Several of her works…have fully entitled her to the privileges enjoyed by good writers.
T. B. Macaulay (1800–59) British historian. *Essays*

2 Miss Lucy Aikin…pert as a pear-monger.
Robert Southey (1774–1843) British poet. Letter to Caroline Bowles, 8 Feb 1835

Quotations by Aikin
3 Their kindness cheer'd his drooping soul;
And slowly down his wrinkled cheek

The big round tears were seen to roll,
And told the thanks he could not speak.
The children, too, began to sigh,
And all their merry chat was o'er;
And yet they felt, they knew not why,
More glad than they had done before.
'The Beggar Man'

4 And often o'er the level waste
The stifling hot winds fly;
Down falls the swain with trembling haste,
The gasping cattle die.
Shepherd people on the plain
Pitch their tents and wander free;
Wealthy cities they disdain,
Poor, – yet blest with liberty.
'Arabia'

5 That life may not be prolonged beyond the power of usefulness is one of the most natural, and apparently of the most reasonable wishes man can form for the future.
Memoirs (Sarah Josepha Hale)

AMBITION

1 Fervour is not placed in feelings but in will to do well, which women may have as well as men. There is no such difference between men and women that women may not do great things as we have seen by example of many saints who have done great things.
Mary Ward (1585–1645) English nun.
The Life of Mary Ward (Mary Catherine Elizabeth Chambers) [c. 1640]

2 I dare not examine the former times, for fear I should meet with such of my sex that have outdone all the glory I can aim at, or hope to attain; for I confess my ambition is restless, and not ordinary; because it would have an extraordinary fame.
Margaret Cavendish (c. 1623–c. 1673) English poet, playwright, and writer.
Nature's Pictures, Drawn by Fancies Pencil to the Life, 'An Epistle to My Readers' [1656]

3 When people inquire I always just state, 'I have four nice children, and hope to have eight.'
Aline Murray Kilmer (1888–1941) US poet.
'Ambition' [c. 1941]

4 We are all right in our place, we are told – as controllers of the household budget, educators of the minds of children, folders of election addresses, but beware the efforts of those who aspire to higher things.
Norah Willis (1924–91) British feminist and president of the Cooperative Congress.
Speech, Cooperative Congress, 1983

ANGER

1 Women are like wasps in their anger.
Proverb

2 Those two conflicting qualities, those warring contradictions, womanhood and anger, which accord so ill together, fought a hard battle in her breast. When anger in Isolde's breast was about to slay her enemy, sweet womanhood intervened. 'No, don't!' it softly whispered.
Gottfried von Strassburg (fl. 1210) German poet.
Tristan [c. 1210]

3 She left me as an enemy!
Joseph Stalin (1879–1953) Soviet statesman.
Remark, November 1932, on viewing the open coffin of his wife, Nadezhda, who had committed suicide after a quarrel with him; he did not attend her funeral, nor openly visit her grave. *Let History Judge* (Roy Medvedec) [1932]

4 There is no fury like an ex-wife searching for a new lover.
Cyril Connolly (1903–74) British journalist.
The Unquiet Grave [1944]

5 Oh, the utter unpredictability of a quarrel! How inflammable words were to ignite each other until the blaze of them scorched and seared.
Agnes Sligh Turnbull (b. 1888) US writer.
The Golden Journey, Ch. 10 [1955]

6 Anger repressed can poison a relationship as surely as the cruelest words.
Joyce Brothers (c. 1925–   ) US psychologist and journalist.
Good Housekeeping, 'When Your Husband's Affection Cools', May 1972

ANNE (1665–1714)

Queen of England and Scotland (Great Britain from 1707) and Ireland (1702–14). Daughter of James II, Anne was the last Stuart monarch and, although her father was converted to Roman Catholicism, she was brought up a Protestant. She became heir to the throne in 1689 following the overthrow of her father. Her marriage to Prince George of Denmark in 1683 was followed by eighteen pregnancies; however, as none of her children lived beyond childhood she agreed to the Act of Settlement which paved the way for the Hanovarian succession after her death. Anne was persuaded away from her Tory loyalties by her friends Sarah and John Churchill (Duke of Marlborough). In 1710, faced with a dissatisfied country and having quarrelled with the Marlboroughs, Anne again appointed a Tory ministry.

Quotations about Anne

1 I believe sleep was never more welcome to a weary traveller than death was to her.
John Arbuthnot (1667–1735) Scottish writer and physician. Letter to Jonathan Swift, 12 Aug 1713

2 Her friendships were flames of extravagant passion ending in aversion.
Sarah Churchill (1914–82) British actress and author. *Character of Queen Anne*

3 She has been called stupid: she was not stupid in the policies she adopted, but there is a certain stupidity in her personal relations with anyone against whom she had taken umbrage.
George Macauley Trevelyan (1876–1962) British historian. *England in the Reign of Queen Anne*

Quotations by Anne

4 As I know my heart to be entirely English, I can very sincerely assure you that there is not one thing you can expect or desire of me, which I shall not be ready to do for the happiness or prosperity of England.
1st speech to Parliament, 11 Mar 1702

5 I have changed my Ministers, but I have not changed my measures; I am still for moderation and will govern by it.
Speech, to the new Tory government, Jan 1711

ANNE (Elizabeth Alice Louise) (1950–   )

Princess of the United Kingdom and only daughter of Elizabeth II. In 1973 she married Lieutenant Mark Phillips (1948–   ) from whom she is now separated. A keen horsewoman, she won silver medals at the European Championship in 1975 and was an Olympic competitor in 1976. In recognition for her committed support as president of the Save the Children Fund, and for her involvement in many other charitable organizations, she was granted the title Princess Royal in 1987.

Quotations about Anne

1 Don't irritate Princess Anne by asking opinions about women's hats. Although she will be receptive to chat about tanks and submachine guns.
Life

2 She'll wear the pants in that marriage.
Harvey Smith (1938–   ) British showjumper.

Quotations by Anne

3 When I appear in public people expect me to neigh, grind my teeth, paw the ground and swish my tail – none of which is easy.
Observer, 'Sayings of the Week', 22 May 1977

4 It's a very boring time. I am not particularly maternal – it's an occupational hazard of being a wife.
TV interview, talking about pregnancy. *Daily Express*, 14 Apr 1981

5 Why don't you naff off!
To reporters. *Daily Mirror*, 17 Apr 1982

6 It could be said that the Aids pandemic is a classic own-goal scored by the human race against itself.
Remark, Jan 1988

ANTHONY, Susan B(rownell) (1820–1906)

US editor and campaigner for women's suffrage. From 1850 she collaborated with Elizabeth Stanton in compiling *The Revolution*, a women's rights newspaper, and with Mathilda Gage on *The History of Woman Suffrage*. In 1872 she was arrested after leading a group of women to the voting polls in Rochester to test the right of women to vote. Although she was convicted of violating the voting laws, she was successful in her refusal to pay the fine. She organized the International Council of Women (1888) and was president (1892–1900) of the National American Woman Suffrage Association.

Quotations about Anthony

1 Who does not feel sympathy for Susan Anthony? She has striven long and earnestly to become a man. She has met with some rebuffs, but has never succumbed. She has never done any good in the world, but then she doesn't think so.
Ida Husted Harper *Life and Work of Susan B. Anthony*, Vol. I

2 We touch our caps, and place to night
The visitor's wreath upon her,
The woman who outranks us all
In courage and honor.
Ida Husted Harper *Life and Work of Susan B. Anthony*, Vol. I

Quotations by Anthony

3 There never will be complete equality until women themselves help to make laws and elect lawmakers.
The Arena, 'The Status of Women, Past, Present and Future', May 1897

4 And yet, in the schoolroom more than any other place, does the difference of sex, if there is any, need to be forgotten.
Elizabeth Cady Stanton, Vol. II (ed. Theodore Stanton and Harriot Stanton Blatch)

5 Men their rights and nothing more; women their rights and nothing less.
The Revolution, Motto

6 …and I shall earnestly and persistently continue to urge all women to the practical recognition of the old Revolutionary maxim, 'Resistance to tyranny is obedience to God.'
Speech in court, 18 June 1873. *Jailed for Freedom* (Doris Stevens)

ANTRIM, Minna (b. 1861)

US writer.

1 A fool bolts pleasure, then complains of moral indigestion.
Naked Truth and Veiled Allusions

2 Experience is a good teacher, but she sends in terrific bills.
Naked Truth and Veiled Allusions

3 Man forgives woman anything save the wit to outwit him.
Naked Truth and Veiled Allusions

4 To control a man a woman must first control herself.
Naked Truth and Veiled Allusions

APPEARANCE

See also BEAUTY; CLOTHES; COSMETICS; STYLE

1 But if a woman have long hair, it is a glory to her: for her hair is given her for a covering.
Bible: I Corinthians
11:15

2 Because of the death you merited, the Son of God had to die. And yet you think of nothing but covering your tunics with ornaments?
Tertullian (c. 160–225 AD) Carthaginian father of the church.
De Cultu Feminarum [3rd century AD]

3 What else do they want in life but to be as attractive as possible to men? Do not all their trimmings and cosmetics have this end in view, and all their baths, fittings, creams, scents, as well – and all those arts of making up, painting, and fashioning the face, eyes and skin? Just so. And by what other sponsor are they better recommended to men than by folly?
Erasmus (1467–1536) Dutch humanist, scholar, and writer.
In Praise of Folly [1509]

4 There is a garden in her face,
Where roses and white lilies grow;
A heav'nly paradise is that place,
Wherein all pleasant fruits do flow.
There cherries grow, which none may buy
Till 'Cherry ripe' themselves do cry.
Thomas Campion (1567–1620) English poet.
Fourth Book of Airs [1617]

5 Had Cleopatra's nose been shorter, the whole face of the world would have changed.
Blaise Pascal (1623–62) French philosopher and mathematician.
Pensées, II [1669]

6 A woman with cut hair is a filthy spectacle, and much like a monster; and all repute it a very great absurdity for a woman to walk abroad with shorn hair; for this is all one as if she should take upon her the form or person of a man, to whom short cut hair is proper.
William Prynne (1600–69) English Puritan pamphleteer.
Histrio-Mastix [1669]

7 There was a young lady from Skye,
With a shape like like a capital I;
She said, 'It's too bad!
But then I can pad,'
Which shows you that figures can lie.
Ethel Watts Mumford (1878–1940) US writer, playwright, and humorist.
The Limerick Up to Date Book 'Appearances Deceitful' [1903]

8 That although artificial teeth are a great blessing, and although a suitable wig may be a charitable covering for a bald head, yet she is committing a sin against her personal appearance as well as against her self-respect if she dyes her hair.
Mary Scharlieb (1845–1930) British gynaecological surgeon.
The Seven Ages of Woman [1915]

9 It was a blonde. A blonde to make a bishop kick a hole in a stained-glass window.
Raymond Chandler (1888–1959) US novelist.
Farewell, My Lovely, Ch. 13 [1940]

10 One girl can be pretty – but a dozen are only a chorus.
F. Scott Fitzgerald (1896–1940) US novelist.
The Last Tycoon [1941]

11 In high school and college my sister Mary was very popular with the boys, but I had braces on my teeth and got high marks.
Betty MacDonald (1908–58) US writer.
The Egg and I, Ch. 2 [1945]

12 A woman can look both moral and exciting – if she also looks as if it was quite a struggle.
Edna Ferber (1887–1968) US writer and scenarist.
Reader's Digest, Dec 1954

13 Manners are especially the need of the plain. The pretty can get away with anything.
Evelyn Waugh (1903–66) British novelist.
Observer, 'Sayings of the Year', 1962

14 The two women gazed out of the slumped and sagging bodies that had accumulated around them.
Nadine Gordimer (1923–) South African writer and lecturer.
Not for Publication and Other Stories, 'Vital Statistics', 1965

15 Men seldom make passes
At girls who wear glasses.
Dorothy Parker (1893–1967) US writer.
Attrib. [1967]

16 Her body is arranged the way it is, to display it to the man looking at the picture. The picture is made to appeal to *his* sexuality. It has nothing to do with her sexuality…Women are there to feed an appetite, not to have any of their own.
John Berger (1926–) British writer and art critic.
Describing the construction of advertising images. *Ways of Seeing* [1972]

17 If people think I'm a dumb blonde because of the way I look, then they're dumber than they think I am. If people think I'm not very deep because of my wigs and outfits, then they're not very deep.
Dolly Parton (1946–) US singer and songwriter.
Ms, June 1979

18 All the little hoops were set up for me to jump through, and when you jump, you get a reward – an image. But it's the image *they* supply…you become the Perfect Couple, or the Faded English Rose, or the Wronged Woman, or the Rock And Roll Slut, or whatever. It has very little to do with real, manageable emotions.
Marianne Faithfull (1947–) British singer and actress.
Referring to her relationship with Mick Jagger. *City Limits*, Dec 1981

19 The affluent, educated, liberated women of the First World…do not feel as free as they want to…This lack of freedom has something to do with – with apparently frivolous issues, things that really should not matter. Many are ashamed to admit that such trivial concerns – to do with physical appearance, bodies, faces, hair, clothes – matter so much.
Naomi Wolf US writer.
The Beauty Myth [1991]

ARDEN, Elizabeth (1878–1966)

Canadian beautician and businesswoman. She was born in Ontario, the youngest child of a Scottish grocer. With little education behind her, she set off for New York, where she became an assistant in a shop selling cosmetics. Her sharp wits and business acumen led to promotion, enabling her soon to become a partner in a beauty salon; in 1909 she opened her own business on Fifth Avenue. In 1918 she married Thomas Lewis, who acted as her business manager until their divorce in 1935, when he went to work for her rival, Helena Rubinstein. Undeterred, Elizabeth Arden went on to build a familiar and prestigious image (invariably dressed in shades of pink). She finally owned more than 100 salons in America and Europe and her firm manufactured over 300 cosmetic products.

Quotations about Arden

1 Elizabeth Arden was a pioneer in an industry which was backward and insanitary when she entered it, and prosperous, modern and a real contribution to human happiness when she died.
Anne Scott-James (1913–) British journalist. *1000 Makers of the 20th Century*

2 She took a high-handed attitude with her staff and did not like her managers to marry without her permission.
Anne Scott-James (1913–) British journalist. *1000 Makers of the 20th Century*

Quotations by Arden

3 Nothing that costs only a dollar is worth having.
Fortune, 'In Cosmetics the Old Mystique Is No Longer Enough' (Eleanore Carruth), Oct 1973

4 I'm not interested in age. People who tell you their age are silly. You're as old as you feel.
Attrib.

ARENDT, Hannah (1906–75)

German-born US political philosopher, well known for her work on totalitarianism and for her writing on Jewish affairs. She was educated at Marburg and Freiburg, before obtaining her doctorate (1928) at Heidelburg. Forced by the rise of the Nazis to flee to Paris in 1933, she became a social worker until again becoming a fugitive from the Nazis in 1940. She then moved to the USA where she established her reputation with the publication of *The Origins of Totalitarianism* (1951). She provoked controversy with her work *Eichmann in Jerusalem* (1963) in which she argued that the cooperation of Jewish community leaders had facilitated Nazi extermination of the Jews in World War II.

Quotation about Arendt

1 She interpreted rather than created systems. She forces us to think about the nature of the world, not simply about problems in disciplines.
Bernard Crick *Makers of Modern Culture*

Quotations by Arendt

2 Under conditions of tyranny it is easier to act than to think.
A Certain World (W. H. Auden)

3 The defiance of established authority, religious and secular, social and political, as a world-wide phenomenon may well one day be accounted the outstanding event of the last decade.
Crises of the Republic, 'Civil Disobedience'

4 No punishment has ever possessed enough power of deterrence to prevent the commission of crimes. On the contrary, whatever the punishment, once a specific crime has appeared for the first time, its reappearance is more likely than its initial emergence could have been.
Eichmann in Jerusalem: A Report on the Banality of Evil

5 Wars and revolutions…have outlived all their ideological justifications…No cause is left but the most ancient of all, the one, in fact, that from the beginning of our history has determined the very existence of politics, the cause of freedom versus tyranny.
On Revolution, Introduction

ARTISTS

1 I have the greatest sympathy for your lordship, because the name of a woman makes one doubtful until one has seen the work.
Artemisia Gentileschi (1593–c. 1652) Italian painter.
Letter to Don Antonio Ruffo, a patron, 30 Jan 1649

2 She took up once more her old painting position with the dim eyes and the absent-minded manner, subduing all her impressions as a woman, to something more general; becoming once more under the power of that vision which she had seen clearly once and must now grope for among hedges and houses and children – her picture.
Virginia Woolf (1882–1941) British writer and literary critic.
To the Lighthouse [1937]

3 Remember I'm an artist. And you know what that means in a court of law. Next worst to an actress.
Joyce Cary (1888–1957) British novelist.
The Horse's Mouth, Ch. 14 [1944]

4 The proletariat was my idea of beauty. The appearance of typical members of the working class fascinated me, and it was a challenge to reproduce it. It was only later, when I really got to know about the want and misery of the working classes through my close and personal contact with them, that I felt I also had a duty to serve them through my art.

Käthe Kollwitz (1867–1945) German lithographer and sculptor.
Women Artists: Recognition and Reappraisal from the Early Middle Ages to the Twentieth Century (Karen Petersen and J. J. Wilson) [1945]

5 Why should I paint dead fish, onions and beer glasses? Girls are so much prettier.
Marie Laurencin (1885–1956) French painter.
Time, 18 June 1956

ASHLEY, Laura (1925–85)

British designer. Her designs, which encompassed clothing, fabrics, linens, and household appliances, were evocative of the English countryside and the Welsh retreat in which she established a studio and a school. Her business was to become international but went into decline after her death, caused by a fall at her home.

Quotation about Ashley

1 She knew what was right and wrong in fabrics just the same as she did in life, there were no grey areas.
Lynda Kee-Scott *Laura Ashley – A Life by Design* (Anne Sebba)

Quotation by Ashley

2 No wonder I am so keen on Florence Nightingale, she just worked all the time for her whole life. There is something to be said for that once you have discovered a cause (or an art!).
Laura Ashley – A Life by Design (Anne Sebba)

ASQUITH, Margot (1864–1945)

British hostess and socialite. Daughter of Sir Charles Tennant and second wife of the reformist Liberal prime minister Herbert Henry Asquith, 1st Earl of Oxford and Asquith, she was famous for her political dinner parties and for her indiscreet memoirs, *The Autobiography of Margot Asquith* (1922).

Quotations about Asquith

1 Beneath a bony, witchlike head, with a big hooked nose and sharp dark eyes moved and attitudinised a small skinny body dressed usually in the height of fashion.
Lord David Cecil (1869–1956) British politician.
Observer, 'Staying with Margot', 20 Dec 1981

2 The affair between Margot Asquith and Margot Asquith will live as one of the prettiest love stories in all literature.
Dorothy Parker (1893–1967) US writer. *Wit's End* (ed. Robert Drennan)

Quotations by Asquith

3 If Kitchener was not a great man, he was, at least, a great poster.
Kitchener: Portrait of an Imperialist, Ch. 14 (Sir Philip Magnus)

4 I do not say that I was ever what is called 'plain', but I have the sort of face that bores me when I see it on other people.
Lilliput, 1938

5 To marry a man out of pity is folly; and, if you think you are going to influence the kind of fellow who has 'never had a chance, poor devil,' you are profoundly mistaken. One can only influence the strong characters in life, not the weak; and it is the height of vanity to suppose that you can make an honest man of anyone.
The Autobiography of Margot Asquith, Ch. 6

6 Rich men's houses are seldom beautiful, rarely comfortable, and never original. It is a constant source of surprise to people of moderate means to observe how little a big fortune contributes to Beauty.
The Autobiography of Margot Asquith, Ch. 17

ASTOR, Nancy Witcher, Viscountess (1879–1964)

US-born British politician, who became the first woman to take a seat in the British House of Commons (1919) when she was elected to her husband's seat on his elevation to the peerage. She devoted herself to women's rights, the welfare of women and children, temperance, and education.

Quotations about Astor

1 She could exchange compliments or insults on equal terms with dukes or dockers.
Clement Attlee (1883–1967) British statesman and Labour prime minister. *Observer*, 3 May 1964

2 Viscount Waldorf Astor owned Britain's two most influential newspapers, *The Times* and the *Observer*, but his American wife, Nancy, had a wider circulation than both papers put together.
Emery Kelen (1896–1978) US journalist. *Peace in Their Time*

Quotations by Astor

3 I married beneath me – all women do.
Dictionary of National Biography

4 Nobody wants me as a Cabinet Minister and they are perfectly right. I am an agitator, not an administrator.
Address to a women's luncheon.

5 Take a close-up of a woman past sixty! You might as well use a picture of a relief map of Ireland!
When asked for a close-up photograph. Attrib.

ATTITUDES

1 It is a great glory in a woman to show no more weakness than is natural to her sex, and not be talked of, either for good or evil by men.
Thucydides (c. 460–c. 400 BC) Greek historian and general.
History of the Peloponnesian War, Bk II, Ch. 45 [5th century BC]

2 No one delights more in vengeance than a woman.
Juvenal (Decimus Junius Juvenalis; 60–130 AD) Roman satirist.
Satires, XIII [c. 100 AD]

3 There is no worse evil than a bad woman; and nothing has ever been produced better than a good one.
Euripides (c. 480–406 BC) Greek dramatist.
Melanippe [5th century BC]

4 I have no other but a woman's reason: I think him so, because I think him so.
William Shakespeare (1564–1616) English dramatist.
The Two Gentlemen of Verona, I:2 [1595]

5 Do you not know I am a woman? When I think, I must speak.
William Shakespeare (1564–1616) English dramatist.
As You Like It, III:2 [1600]

6 Frailty, thy name is woman!
William Shakespeare (1564–1616) English dramatist.
Hamlet, I:2 [1601]

7 Were't not for gold and women, there would be no damnation.
Cyril Tourneur (1575–1626) English dramatist.
The Revenger's Tragedy, II:1 [1607]

8 The souls of women are so small, That some believe they've none at all.
Samuel Butler (1612–80) English satirist.
Miscellaneous Thoughts [17th century]

9 A woman seldom asks advice until she has bought her wedding clothes.
Joseph Addison
Spectator, 475 [1712]

10 Men, some to business, some to pleasure take;
But every woman is at heart a rake.
Alexander Pope (1688–1744) British poet.
Moral Essays, II [1732]

11 Words are men's daughters, but God's sons are things.
Samuel Madden (1686–1765) Irish writer.
Boulter's Monument [1745]

12 What female heart can gold despise? What cat's averse to fish?

Thomas Gray (1716–71) British poet.
Ode on the Death of a Favourite Cat [1747]

13 Every woman is infallibly to be gained by every sort of flattery, and every man by one sort or other.
Earl of Chesterfield (1694–1773) English statesman.
Letter to his son, 16 Mar 1752

14 Were it not for imagination, Sir, a man would be as happy in the arms of a chambermaid as of a Duchess.
Samuel Johnson (1709–84) British lexicographer.
Life of Johnson, Vol. III (J. Boswell) [1778]

15 How lucky we are that women defend themselves so poorly! We should, otherwise, be no more to them than timid slaves.
Pierre Choderlos de Laclos (1741–1803) French novelist.
Les Liaisons dangereuses, Letter 4 [1782]

16 There is a tide in the affairs of women, Which, taken at the flood, leads – God knows where.
Lord Byron (1788–1824) British poet.
Don Juan, VI [1819]

17 His sayings are generally like women's letters; all the pith is in the postscript.
William Hazlitt (1778–1830) British essayist.
Referring to Charles Lamb. *Conversations of Northcote* [1826–27]

18 There are some meannesses which are too mean even for man – woman, lovely woman alone, can venture to commit them.
William Makepeace Thackeray (1811–63) British novelist.
A Shabby-Genteel Story, Ch. 3

19 When the Himalayan peasant meets the he-bear in his pride,
He shouts to scare the monster, who will often turn aside.
But the she-bear thus accosted rends the peasant tooth and nail
For the female of the species is more deadly than the male.
Rudyard Kipling (1865–1936) Indian-born British writer.
The Female of the Species

20 If men knew how women pass their time when they are alone, they'd never marry.
O. Henry (William Sidney Porter; 1862–1910) US short-story writer.
The Four Million Memoirs of a Yellow Dog [1906]

21 Because women can do nothing except love, they've given it a ridiculous importance.
W. Somerset Maugham (1874–1965) British novelist.
The Moon and Sixpence, Ch. 41 [1919]

22 The great question…which I have not been able to answer, despite my thirty years of research into the feminine soul, is 'What does a woman want'?
Sigmund Freud (1856–1939) Austrian psychoanalyst.
Psychiatry in American Life (Charles Rolo) [1939]

23 There is no spectacle on earth more appealing than that of a beautiful woman in the act of cooking dinner for someone she loves.
Thomas Woolfe (1900–38)
The Web and the Rock [1939]

24 Women do not find it difficult nowadays to behave like men; but they often find it extremely difficult to behave like gentlemen.
Compton Mackenzie (1883–1972) British writer.
On Moral Courage

25 Love is based on a view of women that is impossible to those who have had any experience with them.
H. L. Mencken (1880–1956) US journalist.
Attrib. [1956]

26 Why can't a woman be more like a man? Men are so honest, so thoroughly square; Eternally noble, historically fair.
Alan Jay Lerner (1918–86) US songwriter.
My Fair Lady, II:4 [1956]

27 There are two kinds of women – goddesses and doormats.
Pablo Picasso (1881–1973) Spanish painter.
Attrib. [1973]

AUSTEN, Jane (1775–1817)

British novelist. She was born at Steventon, Hampshire, the daughter of a clergyman. She settled in Chawton in Hampshire with her mother and sister, Cassandra, in 1809. Her six major novels are *Sense and Sensibility* (1811), *Pride and Prejudice* (1813), *Mansfield Park* (1814), *Emma* (1815–16), *Northanger Abbey* (1818), and *Persuasion* (1818). Her heroines are drawn from the small country society in which she lived, and the novels explore the moral and economic problems facing young women in that society. The quality and accessibility of her novels made them popular; the Prince Regent kept a complete set in each of his residences. In 1817 Jane Austen's health deteriorated and she and her sister moved to Winchester to be near her doctor. She died of Addison's disease in July 1817 and was buried in Winchester Cathedral.

Quotations about Austen

1 More can be learnt from Miss Austen about the nature of the novel than from almost any other writer.
Walter Allen (1911–) British author and literary journalist. *The English Novel*

2 That young lady has a talent for describing the involvements and feelings and characters of ordinary life which is to me the most wonderful thing I ever met with.
Walter Scott (1771–1832) Scottish novelist. *Journals*, 14 Mar 1826

3 Jane Austen's books, too, are absent from this library. Just that one omission alone would make a fairly good library out of a library that hadn't a book in it.
Mark Twain (Samuel Langhorne Clemens; 1835–1910) US writer. *Following the Equator*, Pt II

Quotations by Austen

4 Human nature is so well disposed towards those who are in interesting situations, that a young person, who either marries or dies, is sure to be kindly spoken of.
Emma, Ch. 22

5 Business, you know, may bring money, but friendship hardly ever does.
Emma, Ch. 34

6 Let other pens dwell on guilt and misery.
Mansfield Park, Ch. 48

7 One does not love a place the less for having suffered in it unless it has all been suffering, nothing but suffering.
Persuasion, Ch. 20

8 It is a truth universally acknowledged, that a single man in possession of a good fortune must be in want of a wife.
The opening words of *Pride and Prejudice*

9 Happiness in marriage is entirely a matter of chance.
Pride and Prejudice, Ch. 6

10 One cannot be always laughing at a man without now and then stumbling on something witty.
Pride and Prejudice, Ch. 40

11 What dreadful hot weather we have! It keeps me in a continual state of inelegance.
Letter, 18 Sept 1796

12 Mrs Hall of Sherbourne was brought to bed yesterday of a dead child, some weeks before she expected, owing to a fright. I suppose she happened unawares to look at her husband.
Letter, 27 Oct 1798

13 I do not want people to be very agreeable, as it saves me the trouble of liking them a great deal.
Letter, 24 Dec 1798

14 The little bit (two inches wide) of ivory on which I work with so fine a brush as produces little effect after much labour.
Letter, 16 Dec 1816

BABIES

See CHILDBIRTH; CHILDREN

BAEZ, Joan (1941–)

US folk and protest singer. Her performance at the Newport Festival (1959) led to her recording career. She also received a considerable amount of publicity as a result of her relationship with the young Bob Dylan, accompanying him on several of his early tours. By 1965 her political activity, particularly her opposition to the Vietnam War, had become more important than her music; this led to her foundation of the Institute for the Study of Non-Violence. She returned to music in 1975, releasing the album *Diamonds and Rust*. Her later recordings include *European Tour* (1981) and *Ballad Book* (1984).

1 If it's natural to kill why do men have to go into training to learn how?
Daybreak

2 By the middle of the twentieth century men had reached a peak of insanity. They grouped together in primitive nation-states, each nation-state condoning organized murder as the way to deal with international differences.
Daybreak

3 Instead of getting hard ourselves and trying to compete, women should try and give their best qualities to men – bring them softness, teach them how to cry.
Los Angeles Times, 'Sexism Seen But Not Heard' (Tracy Hotchner), 26 May 1974

BARDOT, Brigitte (1934–)

French actress. She enjoyed tremendous success as a sex symbol and actress in the 1950s and 1960s, making her debut in *Le Trou normand* (*Crazy for Love*; 1952). She achieved international fame in *Et Dieu créa la femme* (*And God Created Woman*; 1956) and later appeared in such films as *Vie privée* (*A Very Private Affair*; 1961), *Viva Maria* (1965), and *The Novices* (1970). After three unsuccessful marriages she now lives in seclusion in the south of France, devoting her time to animal welfare.

Quotations about Bardot

1 If Canada is underdeveloped, so is Brigitte Bardot.
H. R. MacMillan

2 B.B. on the screen is not simply a selfish delinquent. She has freshness, charm and a touch of mischievousness. She is irresponsible and immoral, but not deliberately cruel.
Observer, 'Profile', 27 Sept 1959

3 She has made 40 films, attempted suicide at least twice, married three men and has shared passion with many more. Her rampant sexuality made her a fantasy figure for men worldwide.
TV Times, 20 Oct 1983

Quotations by Bardot

4 I leave before being left. I decide.
Newsweek, 5 Mar 1973

5 I'm a woman who has undoubtedly made a success of her career but not of her life. The myth of Bardot is finished, but Brigitte is me.
Said on her 40th birthday. *TV Times*, 20 Oct 1983

6 Men are beasts and even beasts don't behave as they do.
Attrib.

BARTON, Clara (1821–1912)

US nurse, founder of the American National Red Cross. Originally a schoolteacher, she organized relief for wounded soldiers during the American Civil War.

1 It is wise statesmanship which suggests that in time of peace we must prepare for war, and it is no less a wise benevolence that makes preparation in the hour of peace for assuaging the ills that are sure to accompany war.
The Red Cross, Ch. I

2 An institution or reform movement that is not selfish, must originate in the recognition of some evil that is adding to the sum of human suffering, or diminishing the sum of happiness. I suppose it is a philanthropic movement to try to reverse the process.
The Red Cross, Ch. I

BEAUTY

1 A wife is sought for her virtue, a concubine for her beauty.
Chinese proverb

2 The day was good for Enheduanna, for she was dressed in jewels.
She was dressed in womanly beauty.
Like the moon's first rays over the horizon,
how luxuriously she was dressed!
Enheduanna (b. c. 2300 BC) Sumerian moon priestess.
'The Restoration of Enheduanna to Her Former Station' [3rd century BC]

3 My Love in her attire doth show her wit,
It doth so well become her:
For every season she hath dressings fit,
For winter, spring, and summer.
No beauty she doth miss,
When all her robes are on;
But beauty's self she is,
When all her robes are gone.

Anonymous
Madrigal [16th century]

4   A fair woman is a paradise to the eye, a purgatory to the purse, and a hell to the soul.
Elizabeth Grymeston (?1563–1603) English writer.
Miscelanea: Prayer, Meditations, Memoratives, Ch. 2 [1603]

5   Shall I compare thee to a summer's day?
Thou art more lovely and more temperate.
Rough winds do shake the darling buds of May,
And summer's lease hath all too short a date.
William Shakespeare (1564–1616) English dramatist.
Sonnet 18 [1609]

6   There is nothing so lovely as to be beautiful. Beauty is a gift of God and we should cherish it as such.
Marie de Sévigné (1626–96) French letter writer and salonist.
Letters of Madame de Sévigné to her daughters and friends [1696]

7   Beauty in distress is much the most affecting beauty.
Edmund Burke (1729–97) British politician.
On the Sublime and Beautiful, Pt III [1757]

8   LADY MARY. Beauty in London is so cheap, and consequently so common to the men of fashion, (who are prodigiously fond of novelty) that they absolutely begin to fall in love with the ugly women, by way of change.
Elizabeth Inchbald (1753–1821) British playwright, translator, and writer.
Appearance is against Them, I:1 [1785]

9   She walks in beauty, like the night
Of cloudless climes and starry skies;
And all that's best of dark and bright
Meet in her aspect and her eyes.
Lord Byron (1788–1824) British poet.
She Walks in Beauty

10   For she was beautiful – her beauty made
The bright world dim, and everything beside
Seemed like the fleeting image of a shade.
Percy Bysshe Shelley (1792–1822) British poet.
The Witch of Atlas, XII [1820]

11   SONYA. I'm not beautiful.
HELEN. You have lovely hair.
SONYA. No, when a woman isn't beautiful, people always say, 'You have lovely eyes, you have lovely hair.'
Anton Chekhov (1860–1904) Russian dramatist.
Uncle Vanya, III [1897]

12   I always say beauty is only sin deep.
Saki (Hector Hugh Munro; 1870–1916) British writer.
Reginald's Choir Treat [1904]

13   You're the most beautiful woman I've ever seen, which doesn't say much for you.
Groucho Marx (Julius Marx; 1895–1977) US comedian.
Animal Crackers [1930]

14   Unnecessary dieting is because everything from television and fashion ads have made it seem wicked to cast a shadow. This wild, emaciated look appeals to some women, though not to many men, who are seldom seen pinning up a *Vogue* illustration in a machine shop.
Peg Bracken (1918–) US writer and humorist.
The I Hate to Cook Book [1960]

15   In Britain, an attractive woman is somehow suspect. If there is talent as well it is overshadowed. Beauty and brains just can't be entertained; someone has been too extravagant.
Vivien Leigh (1913–67) British actress.
Light of a Star (Gwen Robyns) [1967]

16   The beauty myth of the present is more insidious than any mystique of femininity yet: A century ago, Nora slammed the door of the doll's house; a generation ago, women turned their backs on the consumer heaven of the isolated multiapplianced home; but where women are trapped today, there is no door to slam. The contemporary ravages of the beauty backlash are destroying women physically and depleting us psychologically. If we are to free ourselves from the dead weight that has once again been made out of femaleness, it is not ballots or lobbyists or placards that women will need first; it is a new way to see.
Naomi Wolf US writer.
The Beauty Myth [1991]

17   The more legal and material hindrances women have broken through, the more strictly and heavily and cruelly images of female beauty have come to weigh upon us.
Naomi Wolf US writer.
The Beauty Myth [1991]

BEAUVOIR, Simone de (1908–)

French writer and feminist. A powerful writer and philosopher, she will always be associated with Jean-Paul Sartre, with whom she had an intense relationship, which lasted from their meeting in 1929 until his death in 1980. They were the leading exponents of existentialism and founded the review *Les Temps Modernes* (1945). She has written a number of novels reflecting various aspects of existentialist thought, including *Le Sang des autres* (*The Blood of Others*; 1944) and *Tous les hommes sont mortels* (*All Men are Mortal*; 1946). However, her most influential work remains *Le Deuxième Sexe* (*The Second Sex*; 1949), in which she argues that marriage and mother-hood constitute submission to male domination.

1 What is an adult? A child blown up by age.
La Femme rompue

2 A man would never get the notion of writing a book on the peculiar situation of the human male.
Le Deuxième Sexe (The Second Sex)

3 One is not born a woman, one becomes one.
Le Deuxième Sexe (The Second Sex)

4 If you live long enough, you'll see that every victory turns into a defeat.
Tous les hommes sont mortels

5 If you haven't been happy very young, you can still be happy later on, but it's much harder. You need more luck.
Observer, 'Sayings of the Week', 19 May 1975

6 I cannot be angry at God, in whom I do not believe.
Observer, 7 Jan 1979

BEHN, Aphra (1640–89)

English novelist and dramatist. Although she is believed to have been born in Kent the details of her life are uncertain. It is known that she was an ardent supporter of the Stuarts and acted as a government spy during the Dutch wars, which followed the accession of Charles II. From 1670 onwards she earned her living as a writer. She had 17 plays performed in London, the most notable of which was *The Rover* (1678). She is, however, chiefly remembered for her exotic novel *Oronooko* (1688), containing the first attack on slavery in English literature.

Quotations about Behn

1 Mrs Behn is still to be found here and there in the dusty worm eaten libraries of old country houses, but as a rule we imagine she has been ejected from all *decent* society for more than a generation or two.
Anonymous *Saturday Review*, 'Literary Garbage', 27 Jan 1862

2 She was involved in an insurrection of slaves, thus going one better than Harriet Beecher Stowe, who merely preached abolition-ism.
Anthony Burgess (John Burgess Wilson; 1917–) British novelist. *Observer*, 30 Dec 1980

3 Mrs Behn was the first woman in history to earn her living as an author and her remains were appropriately entombed in the cloisters of Westminster Abbey.
Frank Muir (1920–) British writer and broadcaster. *The Frank Muir Book*

Quotations by Behn

4 Since Man with that inconstancy was born,
To love the absent, and the present scorn,
Why do we deck, why do we dress
For a short-liv'd happiness?
Poems on Several Occasions, 'To Alexis'

5 Who is't that to women's beauty would sub-mit,
And yet refuse the fetters of their wit?
The Forced Marriage, Prologue

6 Love ceases to be a pleasure, when it ceases to be a secret.
The Lover's Watch, 'Four o'clock'

7 Faith, Sir, we are here to-day, and gone tomorrow.
The Lucky Chance, IV

8 The Devil's in her tongue, and so 'tis in most women's of her age; for when it has quitted the tail, it repairs to the upper tier.
The Town Fop

BERNHARDT, Sarah (1844–1923)

French actress. Nicknamed the 'Divine Sarah', her beautiful, pure voice and emotional acting brought her fame in both tragedy and comedy. She travelled extensively during her 60-year career and achieved worldwide fame, appear-ing often in London and New York. Amongst the plays in which she gave notable perfor-mances were Racine's *Phèdre*, in which she played the title role, *La Dame aux Camelias*, and *L'Aiglon*. After the amputation of her right leg in 1915, roles were specially created for her. Her memoirs, *Ma Double Vie*, were published in 1907.

Quotation about Bernhardt

1 Sarah took it for granted that she was the greatest actress in the world, just as Queen Vic-toria took it for granted that she was Queen of England.
Maurice Baring (1874–1945) British author. *Sarah Bernhardt*

Quotations by Bernhardt

2 For the theatre one needs long arms; it is bet-ter to have them too long than too short. An *artiste* with short arms can never, never make a fine gesture.
Memories of My Life, Ch. 6

3 I do love cricket – it's so very English.
On seeing a game of football. *Nijinsky* (R. Buckle)

BESANT, Annie (1847–1933)

British theosophist and political campaigner. After an unhappy marriage to a clergyman, who she divorced in 1873, Annie Besant promoted the causes of atheism and birth control; in the

1880s, under the influence of George Bernard Shaw, she turned to Fabianism. In 1889 she became a pupil of Madame Blavatsky and converted to Theosophy. After 1893 she spent much of her life in India, where she founded the Indian Home Rule League (1916), taking up the causes of women's education and the abolition of the caste system.

Quotations about Besant

1 (Her fanaticism built up unnecessary hostility against her, as well as excessive adulation.) No doubt the main body of secularists hailed her as a lady of refinement and genius; she was so witty, sparkling, sarcastic and intelligent, their new 'star of freedom'. But there were enemies who called her shrewish, a vixen, an animal, bestial, foul.
Elizabeth Longford *Eminent Victorian Women*

Quotations by Besant

2 There is no birthright in the white skin that it shall say that wherever it goes, to any nation, amongst any people, there the people of the country shall give way before it, and those to whom the land belongs shall bow down and become its servants.
Wake Up, India: A Plea for Social Reform

3 For I believe that the colour bar and all it implies are largely due to thoughtlessness, to silly pride, to the pride of race, which has grown mad in a country where there is no public opinion to check it.
Wake Up, India: A Plea for Social Reform

4 ...no differences save by merit of character, by merit of ability, by merit of service to the country. Those are the true tests of the value of any man or woman, white or coloured; those who can serve best, those who help most, those who sacrifice most, those are the people who will be loved in life and honoured in death, when all questions of colour are swept away and when in a free country free citizens shall meet on equal grounds.
Wake Up, India: A Plea for Social Reform

BETRAYAL

See also ADULTERY; UNFAITHFULNESS

1 When lovely woman stoops to folly,
And finds too late that men betray,
What charm can soothe her melancholy,
What art can wash her guilt away?
Oliver Goldsmith (1728–74) Irish-born British writer.
The Vicar of Wakefield, Ch. 9 [1761–62]

2 There is, indeed, no perfidy so unjustifiable, as that which wins but to desert the affections of an innocent female. It is still, if possible, more cowardly than it is cruel.
Fanny Burney (1752–1840) British novelist.
Camilla, Bk III, Ch. 9 [1796]

3 The breach of promise...I can think of no action more basically insincere than one conducted with the maximum publicity, for damages for a broken heart by a young woman who must already loathe the man who has rejected her.
Edith Summerskill (1901–80) British politician, gynaecologist, and writer.
A Woman's World, Ch. 4 [1967]

BIBLE

See RELIGION

BIRTH

See CHILDBIRTH

BIRTH CONTROL

1 ...wherefore, since if the parts be smooth conception is prevented, some anoint that part of the womb on which the seed falls with oil of cedar, or with ointment of lead or with frankincense, comingled with olive oil.
Aristotle (384–322 BC) Greek philosopher.
History of Animals [347–335 BC]

2 It also aids in preventing conception to smear the orifice of the uterus all over before with old olive oil or honey or cedar resin or juice of the balsam tree, alone or together with white lead; or with a moist cerate containing myrtle oil and white lead; or before the act with moist alum, or with galbanum together with wine; or to put a lock of fine wool into the orifice of the uterus; or, before sexual relations to use vaginal suppositories which have the power to contract and to condense.
Soranus of Ephesus (fl. 2nd century AD) Greek physician.
On Midwifery and the Diseases of Women [2nd century AD]

3 The remedy, for preventing conception shocks the mind of a woman, at the first thought; but prejudice soon flies.
Richard Carlile
Every Woman's Book or What is Love? [1838]

4 It is therefore a real sin when a young married woman refuses to bear a family or neglects the nurture and the welfare of her children, in the pursuit of pleasure, or even in the performance of works which are indeed good, and which ought to be accomplished, but not by her.
Mary Scharlieb (1845–1930) British gynaecological surgeon.
The Seven Ages of Woman [1915]

5 Any protestant woman in her senses would object to marrying a Roman Catholic...They prohibit the use of proper hygienic Birth Control methods preferring that a woman's health should be entirely ruined and that she should bring forth feeble, dying or imbecile infants rather than that proper hygienic methods should be used.
Marie Stopes (1880–1958) British birth-control campaigner.
Letter to an Irish Catholic, 18 Oct 1920

6 I read about what you were going to do and about the Mothers Clinic that you have opened what I would like to know is how I can save having any more children as I think that I have done my duty to my Country having had 13 children 9 boys and 4 girls.
Anonymous
Letter to Marie Stopes, 22 Mar 1921

7 1. What did Christ put you on this Earth for? 2. What is a Womens Comfort? What did Christ make in his Commandments? Did he say, did he make birth Control?
Well Madam No Women can have a Child without Gods help? No law in England can make Birth Control. Nor you either. I Remain, a Married Man, and a Lover of Children
Anonymous
Letter to Marie Stopes, Mar 1923

8 If instead of birth control every one would preach drink control, you would have little poverty, less crime, and fewer illegitimate children...I speak feelingly; for as my brother Harold John Tennant and I were the last of twelve children, it is more than probable we should never have existed had the fashion of birth control been prevalent in the eighties.
Margot Asquith (1865–1945) The second wife of Herbert Asquith.
Places and Persons [1925]

9 We want far better reasons for having children than not knowing how to prevent them.
Dora Russell (1894–1986)
Hypatia, Ch. 4 [1925]

10 The command 'Be fruitful and multiply' was promulgated according to our authorities, when the population of the world consisted of two people.
Dean Inge (1860–1954) British churchman.
More Lay Thoughts of a Dean [1931]

11 'Yes, yes – I know, Doctor,' said the patient with trembling voice, 'but,' and she hesitated as if it took all of her courage to say it, '*what* can I do to prevent getting that way again?'
'Oh, ho!' laughed the doctor good naturedly. 'You want your cake while you eat it too, do you? Well, it can't be done...I'll tell you the

only sure thing to do. Tell Jake to sleep on the roof!'
Margaret Sanger (1883–1966) US nurse, editor, writer, and civil rights activist.
My Fight for Birth Control [1931]

12 It is now quite lawful for a Catholic woman to avoid pregnancy by a resort to mathematics, though she is still forbidden to resort to physics and chemistry.
H. L. Mencken (1880–1956) US journalist.
Notebooks, 'Minority Report'

13 Contraceptives should be used on every conceivable occasion.
Spike Milligan (1918–) British comic actor and author.
The Last Goon Show of All [c. 1960]

14 The contraceptive pill may reduce the importance of sex not only as a basis for the division of labor, but as a guideline in developing talents and interests.
Caroline Bird (1915–) US writer.
Born Female, Foreword [1968]

15 Protestant women may take the Pill. Roman Catholic women must keep taking the *Tablet*.
Irene Thomas (1920–) British writer.
The Tablet is a British Roman Catholic newspaper. Attrib. [1970s]

16 Biological *possibility* and desire are not the same as biological *need*. Women have child-bearing equipment. For them to choose not to use the equipment is no more blocking what is instinctive than it is for a man who, muscles or no, chooses not to be a weightlifter.
Betty Rollin US writer, editor, and actress.
Look, 16 May 1971

17 He no play-a-da game. He no make-a-da rules!
Earl Butz (1909–) US politician.
Referring to the Pope's strictures against contraception. Remark, 1974

18 I wonder anew whether and how the human female will ever transcend the lower, more dependent, less rights-ful station to which her reproductive nature has until the last-minute invention of The Pill confined her.
Shana Alexander (1925–) US writer.
State-by-State Guide to Women's Legal Rights, Introduction [1975]

19 I want to tell you a terrific story about oral contraception. I asked this girl to sleep with me and she said 'no'.
Woody Allen (Allen Stewart Konigsberg; 1935–) US film actor.
Woody Allen: Clown Prince of American Humor, Ch. 2 (Adler and Feinman) [c. 1977]

BLACK, Shirley Temple (1928–   )

US politician and former child film star. She was spectacularly successful in many films during the 1930s, including *Little Miss Marker* (1934), *Heidi* (1937), and *Little Princess* (1939). She won a special Academy Award in 1934. During the 1960s she became active in politics as a Republican and was appointed US representative to the United Nations (1969–70), US ambassador to Ghana (1974–76), chief of protocol at the White House (1976–77), and US ambassador to Czechoslovakia (1989–   ).

1   Nonsense, all of it. Sunnybrook Farm is now a parking lot; the petticoats are in the garbage can, where they belong in this modern world; and I *detest* censorship.
McCall's, Jan 1967

2   I stopped believing in Santa Claus at an early age. Mother took me to see him in a department store and he asked me for my autograph.
Halliwell's Filmgoers and Video Viewer's Companion

3   Our whole way of life today is dedicated to the *removal of risk*. Cradle to grave we are supported, insulated, and isolated from the risks of life – and if we fall, our government stands ready with Bandaids of every size.
Speech, Kiwanis International Convention, Texas, June 1967

BLACKWELL, Elizabeth (1821–1910)

US physician; the first woman in the US to gain an MD degree. In 1857 she cofounded, with her sister Emily Blackwell, the Women's Medical College of New York Infirmary and in 1869 she moved to England, where she was one of the founders of the London School of Medicine for Women.

1   The total deprivation of sex produces irritability.
The Human Element in Sex

2   I must have something to engross my thoughts, some object in life which will fill this vacuum and prevent this sad wearing away of the heart.
Pioneer Work for Women

3   I, who so love a hermit life for a good part of the day, find myself living in public, and almost losing my identity.
Pioneer Work for Women

4   Do you think I care about medicine? Nay, verily, it's just to kill the devil, whom I hate so heartily – that's the fact, mother.
Letter to her mother

BLACKWELL, Emily (1826–1910)

US physician. She was one of the founders, with her sister Elizabeth Blackwell, and later dean, of the Women's Medical College of New York Infirmary. She was later connected with the New York Infirmary for Women and Children.

1   Social intercourse – a very limited thing in a half civilized country, becomes in our centers of civilization a great power.
Medicine as a Profession for Women

2   Our school education ignores, in a thousand ways, the rules of healthy development.
Medicine as a Profession for Women

3   As teachers, then, to diffuse among women the physiological and sanitary knowledge which they need, we found the first work for women physicians.
Medicine as a Profession for Women

4   For what is done or learned by one class of women becomes, by virtue of their common womanhood, the property of all women.
Medicine as a Profession for Women

BLAVATSKY, Elena Petrovna (1831–91)

Russian religious leader. After 20 years of travelling in the East, during which she claimed to have spent 7 years studying in Tibet under the Hindu Mahatmas. Blavatsky toured the world as a spirit medium. Together with Col H. S. Olcott and others she formed the Theosophical Society in New York in 1875. Although she was denounced in 1885 as a fraud by the London Society for Psychical Research, her popularity did not diminish. Her works include *Isis Unveiled* (1887) and *The Secret Doctrine* (1888).

1   This idea of passing one's whole life in moral idleness, and having one's hardest work and duty done by another – whether God or man – is most revolting to us, as it is most degrading to human dignity.
The Key to Theosophy

2   It is the worst of crimes and dire in its results…Voluntary death would be an abandonment of our present post and of the duties incumbent on us, as well as an attempt to shirk karmic responsibilities, and thus involve the creation of new Karma.
The Key to Theosophy

3   We must prepare and study truth under every aspect, endeavoring to ignore nothing, if we do not wish to fall into the abyss of the unknown when the hour shall strike.
La Revue theosophique, 21 Mar 1889

4 The Christians were the first to make the existence of Satan a dogma of the church.
Attrib.

BLOOMER, Amelia (1818–94)

US reformer who campaigned for temperance and women's rights. She was interested in dress reform and was one of the originators of bloomers (full trousers, gathered at the ankle). Although this idea was ridiculed at the time, the eponym has survived for any type of baggy knickers.

Quotations about Bloomer

1 You must take Mrs Bloomer's suggestions with great caution, for she has not the spirit of the true reformer. At the first Woman's Rights Convention, but four years ago, she stood aloof and laughed at us.
Letter to Elizabeth Cady Stanton

2 Heigh ho,
Thro' sleet and snow,
Mrs Bloomer's all the go.
Twenty tailors take the stitches,
Plenty of women to wear the breeches,
Heigh ho,
Carrion crow!
Anonymous *Life and Work of Susan B. Anthony* (Ida Harper)

Quotations by Bloomer

3 In the minds of some people the short dress and woman's rights were inseparably connected. With us, the dress was but an incident, and we were not willing to sacrifice greater questions to it.
The Bloomer Girls (Charles N. Gattey)

4 Ah how steadily do they who are guilty shrink from reproof!
The Lily, Apr 1853

5 The costume of women should be suited to her wants and necessities. It should conduce at once to her health, comfort, and usefulness; and, while it should not fail also to conduce to her personal adornment, it should make that end of secondary importance.
Letter to Charlotte A. Joy, 3 June 1857

BOADICEA (Latin name: Boudicca; d. 60 AD)

Queen of the Iceni, who ruled in the east of England in what is now Norfolk. She led the Iceni in a revolt against the Romans after they had tried to seize the wealth of her dead husband Prasutagus and raped her and her daughters. Her troops sacked Colchester, London, and St Albans, and (according to Tacitus) killed many thousands of Roman soldiers. She committed suicide after her defeat by Suetonius Paulinus at or near Fenny Stratford.

Quotations about Boadicea

1 Great glory, equal to that of our old victories, was won on that day. Some indeed say that there fell little less than eighty thousand of the Britons, with a loss to our soldiers of about four hundred, and only as many wounded. Boadicea put an end to her life by poison.
Tacitus (c. 55–c. 120 AD) Roman historian. *Annals*

2 She was very tall and her aspect was terrifying, for her eyes flashed fiercely and her voice was harsh. A mass of red hair fell down to her hips, and around her neck was a twisted gold necklace.
Dio Cassius (c. 150–235) Roman administrator and historian. *Roman History*, Bk 42, Vol. VIII

Quotation by Boadicea

3 But now it is not as a woman descending from noble ancestry, but as one of the people that I am avenging lost freedom, my scourged body, the outraged chastity of my daughters. Roman lust has gone so far that not our very persons, not even age or virginity, are left unpolluted…This is a woman's resolve; as for men, they may live and be slaves.
Annals (Tacitus)

BOLEYN, Anne (c. 1507–36)

English queen. The second wife of Henry VIII and the mother of Elizabeth I; Henry's infatuation with her led to his divorce from Katharine of Aragon and the subsequent ecclesiastical breach with Rome. They were married in 1533, but three years later Henry had tired of her and her inability to give him a male heir. She was accused of treason for committing adultery and beheaded in the Tower of London on 19 May 1536.

Quotations about Boleyn

1 She is not one of the handsomest women in the world. She has a swarthy complexion, long neck, wide mouth, bosom not much raised, and in fact has nothing but the king's great appetite, and her eyes, which are black and beautiful and take great effect.
Report of the Venetian ambassador

2 For something like five years she succeeded in holding him at arms' length, a remarkable performance, all things considered, and probably indicative that there was considerably more of cold calculation than of passion in Anne's attitude.
Conyers Read (1881–1959) US author. *The Tudors*

Quotations by Boleyn

3 You have chosen me from a low estate to be your queen and companion, far beyond my desert or desire.
Her last letter to Henry VIII

4 The king has been very good to me. He promoted me from a simple maid to be a marchioness. Then he raised me to be a queen. Now he will raise me to be a martyr.
Notable Women in History (W. Abbot)

5 I heard say the executioner is very good and I have a little neck.
Letter from Sir W Kingston, Constable of the Tower, to Thomas Cromwell, 19 May 1536

BOMBECK, Erma (1927–)

US journalist. Born in Dayton, Ohio, she was educated at the University of Dayton. In 1949 she joined the *Dayton Journal Herald*, where she remained until 1965, when she began writing her column 'At Wit's End' for *Newsday*. From 1969 she was the author of a column 'Up the Wall', which appeared in *Good Housekeeping*. A collection of her columns was published in *At Wit's End* (1967).

1 I worry about scientists discovering that lettuce has been fattening all along.
If Life is a Bowl of Cherries – What am I Doing in the Pits?

2 The selling of the suburbs made the coronation of Queen Elizabeth look like an impulse.
The Grass is Always Greener Over the Septic Tank

3 Humorists can never start to take themselves seriously. It's literary suicide.
Detroit Free Press, 10 Aug 1978

4 You hear a lot of dialogue on the death of the American family. Families aren't dying. They're merging into big conglomerates.
San Francisco Examiner, 'Empty Fridge, Empty Nest', 1 Oct 1978

BORGIA, Lucrezia (1480–1519)

Italian noblewoman. Daughter of Rodrigo, who became Pope Alexander VI and sister of Cesare Borgia. Although she was notorious for her alleged immorality, her three marriages and betrothals were arranged to further the political ambitions of her father. Her first marriage was to Don Gasparo de Procida, but the marriage was annulled by her father and she was betrothed to Giovanni Sforza. This engagement was later cancelled by her father, for political reasons, and Lucrezia was married to Alfonso of Aragon, a relative of the King of Naples. Her brother Cesare arranged for Alfonso to be murdered, enabling Lucrezia to be finally married to Alfonso d'Este, heir to the Duke of Ferrara. She

was by this time 22. When her husband became Duke of Este, her life was more settled, their court becoming a haven for the arts and the pursuit of knowledge.

Quotations about Borgia

1 Far from being the poisoning Messalina of legend she was a gay, charming pleasure-loving girl whose high spirits made her the centre of the Vatican circle.
Sarah Bradford (1938–) British manuscript consultant. *Cesare Borgia, His Life and Times*

2 This beautiful woman, whose character has been the subject of so much controversy and who has been accused, probably unjustly, of the most unmentionable crimes, seems to have been a person of colourless disposition who was made the puppet of the schemes of her father and brother.
A. H. Johnson (1845–1927) British historian. *Europe in the Sixteenth Century*

Quotations by Borgia

3 So great is the favour which our merciful Creator has shown me, that I approach the end of my life with pleasure, knowing that in a few hours, after receiving for the last time all the holy sacraments of the Church, I shall be released.
Letter, 22 June 1519

4 My husbands have been very unlucky.
Remark to her father after the murder of her second husband. *Lucrezia Borgia* (Rachel Erlanger)

5 The more I try to do God's will the more he visits me with misfortune.
Remark on hearing of the death of her brother. *Lucrezia Borgia* (Rachel Erlanger)

BOUDICCA

See BOADICEA

BOW, Clara (1905–65)

US film actress. Known as the 'It' girl after her role in the film version of Elinor Glyn's *It* (1927), she was the epitome of Hollywood sex-appeal and the carefree spirit of the 1920s. She was an enormous success in the era of silent films, appearing in, amongst others, *Mantrap* (1926), *The Fleet Is In* (1928), and *The Wild Party* (1929). She was not successful in sound films, and a series of highly publicized scandals led to her declining popularity. She retired from films in the 1930s.

Quotations about Bow

1 In Miss Bow, the emergent flapper found her predestined model, pointing to such novelties as a boyish figure, short shirts, step-ins, chain smoking, a vanity case of precious metal with

flask to match, necking, petting parties and the single standard.
Lloyd Morris (1893–1954) US biographer and essayist. *Not So Long Ago*

2   Even if the whole thing, including what she did on the screen, was evolved from the sort of girl she was, her life and career still seem to have been dreamed up by one of her script-writers.
David Shipman (1932–   ) British publisher. *The Great Movie Stars*

3   The 20's would have been quite different without Clara Bow: she was totally representative of the era, but to what extent she created the flapper and how much derived from her could probably never be calculated.
David Shipman (1932–   ) British publisher. *The Great Movie Stars*

Quotation by Bow
4   Being a sex symbol is a heavy load to carry, especially when one is tired, hurt and bewildered.
A Pictorial History of Sex in the Movies (Clyde Jeavons and Jeremy Pascal)

BREASTFEEDING

1   To be sure, other things being equal, it is better to feed the child with maternal milk, for this is more suited to it, and the mothers become more sympathetic towards the offspring, and it is more natural to be fed from the mother after parturition just as before parturition.
Soranus of Ephesus (fl. 2nd century AD) Greek physician.
Gynaecology, I [2nd century AD]

2   It is the express ordinance of God that mothers should nurse their own children, and, being his ordinance, they are bound to it in conscience.
Elizabeth Clinton (1574–c. 1630) English writer.
The Countess of Lincoln's Nurserie [1622]

3   A mother, if physically capable, whether regal or otherwise, ought to supply nature's food to her own offspring.
Referring to Queen Victoria's refusal to breastfeed her children. Letter to *Lancet*, 1840

4   Every mother should consider it her absolute duty, unless her health is delicate, and her medical man's opinion is against her so doing, to suckle her infant for at least six months.
Lionel A. Weatherly
The Young Wife's Own Book [1882]

5   ...on second cry I woke
fully and gave to feed and fed on feeding.
Muriel Rukeyser (1913–80) US poet.
Selected Poems, 'Night Feeding' [1951]

6   Like marriage, nursing was turning out to be one of those painful addictions; damned if you do, damned if you don't.
Viva (1943–   ) US actress.
The Baby [1975]

BRITTAIN, Vera (1893–1970)

British writer. Her book, *Testament of Youth* (1933), describes her early education and service as a nurse during the World War I, expressing her attitude to the horrendous suffering which was responsible for the death of her fiancé and her brother. On her return to Oxford after the war she formed a deep friendship with the novelist Winifred Holtby, described in her book *Testament of Friendship* (1940). In 1937 she became a sponsor of the Peace Pledge Union, chaired the *Peace News* board from 1958 to 1964, and actively supported the Campaign for Nuclear Disarmament. The final volume of her biography is *Testament of Experience* (1957).

Quotation about Brittain
1   And in retrospect, my mother was not essentially a novelist, but a chronicler of her times…a promoter of causes rather than a woman of creative imagination.
John Catlin *Family Quartet*

Quotations by Brittain
2   It is probably true to say that the largest scope for change still lies in men's attitude to women, and in women's attitude to themselves.
Lady into Woman, Ch. 15

3   The idea that it is necessary to go to a university in order to become a successful writer, or even a man or woman of letters (which is by no means the same thing), is one of those phantasies that surround authorship.
On Being an Author, Ch. 2

4   Meek wifehood is no part of my profession;
I am your friend, but never your possession.
Poems of the War and After, 'Married Love'

5   Politics are usually the executive expression of human immaturity.
The Rebel Passion

THE BRONTËS

1   Literary criticism of the Brontës has been a long game of masculine prejudice wherein the player either proves they can't write and are hopeless primitives, whereupon the critic sets himself up like a schoolmaster to edit their stuff and point out where they went wrong, or converts them into case histories from the wilds, occasionally prefacing his moves with a few pseudo-sympathetic remarks about the windy

house on the moors, or old maidhood, following with an attack on every truth the novels contain, waged by anxious pedants who fear Charlotte might 'castrate' them or Emily 'unman' them with her passion.

Kate Millett (1934–) British author and feminist. *Sexual Politics*

BRONTË, Anne (1820–49)

British novelist. Youngest of the three Brontë sisters and daughter of Patrick Brontë, the rector of Haworth, Yorkshire. Her best known works, *Agnes Grey* (1847) and *The Tenant of Wildfell Hall* (1948), were published under the pseudonym Acton Bell. The first of these books was based on her unhappy experiences as a governess at Thorp Green Hall; the second contains a portrait of a wasted drunk, Arthur Huntingdon, which is believed to be modelled on her brother, Branwell. She developed tuberculosis soon after the death of her sister Emily, and died at Scarborough.

Quotations about Anne Brontë

1 A sort of literary Cinderella.

George Moore (1852–1933) Irish writer and art critic. *Conversations in Ebury Street*

2 Anne Brontë was a gentle, quiet, rather subdued person, by no means pretty, yet of a pleasing appearance. Her manner was curiously expressive of a wish for protection and encouragement, a kind of constant appeal which invited sympathy.

George Smith (1859–1919) British publisher. *Cornhill Magazine*

3 Her gentle and delicate presence, her sad short, short story, her hard life and early death entered deeply into the poetry and tragedy that have always been entwined with the memory of the Brontës, as women and as writers.

Mrs Humphrey Ward (1851–1920) British writer and philanthropist. Preface to the collected edition of the Brontës' works

Quotations by Anne Brontë

4 But he that dares not grasp the thorn
Should never crave the rose.

The Complete Poems of Anne Brontë (ed. Clement Shorter), 'The Narrow Way'

5 Well, but you affirm that virtue is only elicited by temptation; – and you think that a woman cannot be too little exposed to temptation, or too little acquainted with vice, or anything connected therewith. It must be either that you think she is essentially so vicious, or so feeble-minded, that she cannot withstand temptation.

The Tenant of Wildfell Hall, Ch. 3

6 What is it that constitutes virtue, Mrs. Graham? Is it the circumstance of being able and willing to resist temptation; or that of having no temptations to resist?

The Tenant of Wildfell Hall, Ch. 3

7 Keep a guard over your eyes and ears as the inlets of your heart, and over your lips as the outlet, lest they betray you in a moment of unwariness.

The Tenant of Wildfell Hall, Ch. 16

BRONTË, Charlotte (1816–55)

British novelist. Eldest daughter of Patrick Brontë, the rector of Haworth, Yorkshire. Her best known works, *Jane Eyre* (1847), *Shirley* (1849), and *Villette* (1853), were published under the pseudonym Currer Bell. Her writing draws heavily on her own experiences, as pupil, teacher, and governess, and shows concern for the position of women in society. Eventually she agreed to marry her father's curate, A. B. Nicholls, but died a few months later of an illness probably connected with pregnancy.

Quotations about Charlotte Brontë

1 If these remarkable works are the productions of a woman we shall only say she must be a woman pretty nearly unsexed; and Jane Eyre strikes us as a personage much more likely to have sprung ready-armed from the head of a man and that head a pretty hard one, than to have experienced, in any shape, the softening influence of a female creation.

James Lorimer (1818–90) British jurist and philosopher. *North British Review*, Aug 1849

2 Two gentlemen came in leading a tiny, delicate, serious little lady with fair straight hair and steady eyes. She may be a little over thirty; she is dressed in a little barège dress with a pattern of faint green moss. She enters in mittens, in silence, in seriousness; our hearts are beating with wild excitement. This then is the authoress, the unknown power whose books have set all London talking, reading, speculating.

Anne, Lady Ritchie (1837–1919) British writer. *Chapters From Some Memoirs*

3 I believe she would have given all her genius and all her fame to be beautiful. Perhaps few women ever existed more anxious to be pretty than she, and more angrily conscious of the circumstance that she was *not* pretty.

George Smith (1859–1919) British publisher. *The Critic*, Jan 1901

Quotations by Charlotte Brontë

4 Vain favour! coming, like most other favours long deferred and often wished for, too late!

Jane Eyre, Ch. 3

5 I grant an ugly *woman* is a blot on the fair face of creation; but as to the *gentlemen*, let them be solicitous to possess only strength and valour: let their motto be:– Hunt, shoot, and fight: the rest is not worth a fillip.
Jane Eyre, Ch. 17

6 The soul fortunately, has an interpreter – often an unconscious, but still a truthful interpreter – in the eye.
Jane Eyre, Ch. 28

7 Reader, I married him.
Jane Eyre, Ch. 38

8 An abundant shower of curates has fallen upon the north of England.
Shirley, Ch. 1

BRONTË, Emily (1818–48)
British novelist. Daughter of Patrick Brontë, the rector of Haworth, Yorkshire she was educated mostly at home. She spent much time on the wild moors surrounding Haworth, which are portrayed so vividly in her major work *Wuthering Heights* (1847), published under the pseudonym Ellis Bell. She died of tuberculosis three months after the death of her brother, Branwell.

Quotations about Emily Brontë
1 Indeed, I have never seen her parallel in anything, stronger than a man simpler than a child, her nature stood alone.
Charlotte Brontë (1816–55) British novelist. *Wuthering Heights*, Preface

2 Posterity has paid its debt to her too generously, and with too little understanding.
Ivy Compton-Burnett (1892–1969) British novelist. Letter to Anthony Powell

3 Emily Brontë remains the sphinx of literature.
W. Robertson Nicoll (1851–1923) British writer. *Chambers Encyclopedia of English Literature*

Quotations by Emily Brontë
4 No coward soul is mine,
No trembler in the world's storm-troubled sphere:
I see Heaven's glories shine,
And faith shines equal, arming me from fear.
Last Lines

5 Vain are the thousand creeds
That move men's hearts: unutterably vain;
Worthless as wither'd weeds.
Last Lines

6 O! dreadful is the check – intense the agony –
When the ear begins to hear, and the eye begins to see;
When the pulse begins to throb – the brain to think again –

The soul to feel the flesh, and the flesh to feel the chain.
The Prisoner

7 Once drinking deep of that divinest anguish,
How could I seek the empty world again?
Remembrance

8 A good heart will help you to a bonny face, my lad…and a bad one will turn the bonniest into something worse than ugly.
Wuthering Heights, Ch. 7

BROWN, Olympia (1835–1900)
US Universalist minister and feminist. A keen supporter of the suffrage campaign, she was president of the Federal Suffrage Association and a life member of the National American Suffrage Association. She was ordained in 1863 and from 1893 to 1900 was secretary and treasurer of the Times Publishing Company. She is the author of a book entitled *Old and New Among Reformers*.

1 As the oldest of the children many household duties fell upon me, but there are always compensations for every adverse experience.
The Annual Journal of the Universalist Historical Society, Vol. IV, Ch. 2, 'Olympia Brown, An Autobiography'

2 I used to say that Susan B. Anthony was my pole star until I learned to make no one my guide but to follow truth wherever it might lead and to do the duty of the hour at whatever cost.
The Annual Journal of the Universalist Historical Society, Vol. IV, Ch. 6, 'Olympia Brown, An Autobiography'

3 How natural that the errors of the ancients should be handed down and, mixing with the principles and system which Christ taught, give to us an adulterated Christianity.
Sermon, Mukwonago, Wisconsin, 13 Jan 1895

4 He who never sacrificed a present to a future good or a personal to a general one can speak of happiness only as the blind do of colors.
Sermon, Mukwonago, Wisconsin, 13 Jan 1895

BROWNING, Elizabeth Barrett (1806–61)
British poet. An invalid for many years, Elizabeth Browning made an amazing recovery after secretly marrying Robert Browning in 1846, against the wishes of her father. They settled in Florence and remained happily married until Robert Browning's death 15 years later. Although she is now chiefly remembered for her *Sonnets from the Portuguese* (1850) and *Aurora Leigh* (1857), during her lifetime her poetry and espousal of liberal causes made her more famous than her husband. Her other works include *The Seraphim and Other Poems*

(1838), *Poems Before Congress* (1860), and *Last Poems* (1862).

Quotations about Browning

1 Mrs Browning's death is rather a relief to me, I must say. No more *Aurora Leigh*, thank God. A woman of real genius, I know. But what is the upshot of it all? She and her sex had better mind the kitchen and the children and perhaps the poor.

Edward Fitzgerald (1809–83) British poet. Letter, 1861

2 Her physique was peculiar; curls like the pendant ears of a water spaniel and poor little hands – so thin that when she welcomed you she gave you something like the foot of a young bird.

Frederick Locker (1821–95) British writer. *My Confidences*

3 Fate has not been kind to Mrs Browning. Nobody reads her, nobody discusses her, nobody troubles to put her in her place.

Virginia Woolf (1882–1941) British novelist. *Second Common Reader*

Quotations by Browning

4 Since when was genius found respectable?

Aurora Leigh, Bk VI

5 Do you hear the children weeping, O my brothers,
Ere the sorrow comes with years?

The Cry of the Children

6 God's gifts put man's best gifts to shame.

Sonnets from the Portuguese, XXVI

7 I love thee with a love I seemed to lose
With my lost saints – I love thee with the breath,
Smiles, tears, of all my life! – and, if God choose,
I shall but love thee better after death.

Sonnets from the Portuguese, XLIII

BUCK, Pearl S(ydenstricker) (1892–1973)

US writer. Daughter of Presbyterian missionaries, much of her writing was influenced by the years she spent with them in China, and later as a university teacher in Nanking. Her book *The Good Earth* (1931) won the Pulitzer prize in 1932; this was followed by *Sons* (1932) and *A House Divided* (1935). In 1938 she received the Nobel prize for literature. After World War II she instituted the Pearl S. Buck Foundation to aid the illegitimate children of US servicemen in Asian countries. Her later works include *The Child Who Never Grew* (1950), about her retarded daughter, and *The Three Daughters of Madame Liang* (1969).

Quotations about Buck

1 A capable, bustling novelist of the journalist school.

V. S. Pritchett (1900–) British short-story writer. *Pearl S. Buck* (Paul A. Doyle)

2 East versus West, Victorian versus twentieth-century values: her life and work turn on their interplay.

Dody Weston Thompson *American Winners of the Nobel Literary Prize* (ed. Warren G. French and Walter E. Kidd)

Quotations by Buck

3 In this unbelievable universe in which we live there are no absolutes. Even parallel lines, reaching into infinity, meet somewhere yonder.

A Bridge for Passing

4 Euthanasia is a long, smooth-sounding word, and it conceals its danger as long, smooth words do, but the danger is there, nevertheless.

The Child Who Never Grew, Ch. 2

5 Ah well, perhaps one has to be very old before one learns how to be amused rather than shocked.

China, Past and Present, Ch. 6

6 It is better to be first with an ugly woman than the hundredth with a beauty.

The Good Earth, Ch. 1

7 I feel no need for any other faith than my faith in human beings.

I Believe

BUSINESS

See OCCUPATIONS; WORK

CALAMITY JANE (Martha Jane Burke; 1852–1903)

US frontierswoman. A prostitute in various frontier towns, she built up a reputation for her skills as a scout, rider, and sharpshooter. She appeared in Wild West shows in the 1890s and at the Buffalo Pan American Exposition (1901).

1 There are thousands of Sioux in this valley. I am not afraid of them. They think I am a crazy woman and never molest me...I guess I am the only human being they are afraid of.

Letter to her daughter, 28 Sept 1877

2 During the month of June I acted as a pony express rider carrying the U.S. mail between Deadwood and Custer, a distance of fifty miles...It was considered the most dangerous route in the Hills, but as my reputation as a rider and quick shot was well known, I was molested very little, for the toll gatherers looked on me as being a good fellow, and they knew that I never missed my mark.

Life and Adventures of Calamity Jane

3 I Jane Hickok Burke better known as Calamity Jane of my own free will and being of sound mind do this day June 3, 1903 make this confession. I have lied about my past life...People got snoopy so I told them lies to hear their tongues wag. The women are all snakes and none of them I can call friends.

Document to James O'Neill, 3 June 1903

CALDWELL, Sarah (1924–)

US opera conductor, producer, and impresario. She was educated at the University of Arkansas and the New England Conservatory of Music, Boston, later becoming chief assistant to Boris Goldovsky at the New England Opera Company. In 1957 she founded the Operatic Company of Boston, where she established a reputation for innovative productions of standard works. Included among the company's productions are Verdi's *Don Carlos* and Schoenberg's *Moses und Aron*.

1 If you approach an opera as though it were something that always went a certain way, that's what you get. I approach an opera as though I didn't know it.

Ms, 'Sarah Caldwell: The Flamboyant of the Opera' (Jane Scovell Appleton), May 1975

2 The conductor and director must create the atmosphere, but a situation must exist where the singers can think and use their own remarkable faculties. It's like bringing up a gifted child.

Ms, 'Sarah Caldwell: The Flamboyant of the Opera' (Jane Scovell Appleton), May 1975

3 It was a place where gods strode the earth.

She was referring to Tanglewood, a famous US music school, and the site of the annual (summer) Tanglewood Music Festival. *Time*, 'Music's Wonder Woman', 10 Nov 1975

CALLAS, Maria (1923–77)

US-born Greek opera singer. The combination of her coloratura voice and unusual dramatic ability contributed to her enormous success, particularly in Verdi and earlier Italian opera. From 1950 she was prima donna at La Scala in Milan and made her debut at Covent Garden, singing the title role in Bellini's *Norma*, in 1952. She retired from the stage in 1965, but continued to be actively associated with opera, giving masterclasses at the Juilliard School, New York (1971–72) and coproducing (with Giuseppe di Stefano) Verdi's *Sicilian Vespers* in 1973.

Quotations about Callas

1 The vocal tone of Callas, sporadically beautiful, but never easily or artlessly produced, takes second place to the sheer power of her interpretative abilities.

Felix Aprahamian (1914–) British music critic and writer. *1000 Makers of the 20th Century*

2 Her magnetic stage personality and her passionate and conscientious artistry have made her the outstanding diva of our time.

Felix Aprahamian (1914–) British music critic and writer. *1000 Makers of the 20th Century*

Quotation by Callas

3 The more 'up' we go, you see, the more is expected of us and the harder we must work...Right now I have only one hope – that I will not be a disappointment.

Referring to her debut in Chicago. *New York Herald Tribune*, 7 Nov 1954

CARSON, Rachel (1907–64)

US biologist and writer. She is remembered as a popularizer of science, and, in particular, for her warnings about the effects of pesticides and weed killers on the environment. Her works include *The Sea Around Us* (1951) and *Silent Spring* (1955).

Quotation about Carson

1 She is that rare phenomenon, a writer who combines scientific ability and observation with a command of the English language.

Kenneth Richardson *20th Century Writing*

Quotations by Carson

2 For all at last return to the sea – to Oceanus, the ocean river, like the ever-flowing stream of time, the beginning and the end.

The closing words of the book. *The Sea Around Us*

3 As cruel a weapon as the cave man's club, the chemical barrage has been hurled against the fabric of life.

The Silent Spring

4 Over increasingly large areas of the United States, spring now comes unheralded by the return of the birds, and the early mornings are strangely silent where once they were filled with the beauty of bird song.

The Silent Spring

5 The ocean is a place of paradoxes.

Atlantic Monthly, 'Under Sea', Sept 1937

CASSATT, Mary (1844–1926)

US painter. A friend and disciple of Degas, she worked mainly in Paris and exhibited with the Impressionists. Initially a figure painter, whose subjects were groups of women drinking tea or on outings with friends, her later paintings were often mother-and-child scenes, as in 'La Toilette' (c. 1892).

1 A woman artist must be…capable of making the primary sacrifices.
Arts Weekly, 1932, 'Mary Cassatt' (Forbes Watson)

2 I am independent. I can live alone and I love to work. Sometimes it made him furious that he could not find a chink in my armor, and there would be months when we just could not see each other, and then something I painted would bring us together again.
Referring to Degas. *Sixteen to Sixty, Memoirs of a Collector* (Louisine W. Havemeyer)

3 You know how hard it is to inaugurate anything like independent action among French artists, and we are carrying on a despairing fight and need all our forces, as every year there are new deserters.
Letter to J. Alden Weir, 10 Mar 1878

4 Why do people so love to wander? I think the civilized parts of the World will suffice for me in the future.
Letter to Louisine Havemeyer, 11 Feb 1911

CASTLE, Barbara (Baroness Castle of Blackburn) (1910–)

British Labour politician. She was born in Chesterfield, Derbyshire and educated at Bradford Girls Grammar School and St Hugh's College, Oxford. During World War II she became an administrative officer at the Ministry of Food (1941–44). In 1944 she married Edward Castle, the following year becoming MP for Blackburn; she remained a member of the House of Commons for the following 34 years. During this period she held a number of important cabinet posts, including those of minister of transport (1965–68) and Secretary of State for Employment and Productivity (1968–70). She is remembered for her controversial policy *In Place of Strife* and for carrying the Equal Pay Act through parliament, which became effective in 1975.

Quotations about Castle
1 When she left the Ministry for Overseas Development it was as though someone had switched off the current.
Peter Dunn (1926–) British writer and lecturer. *The Sunday Times*, 2 July 1967

2 Her total commitment, combined with her warmth, spontaneity and fearlessness, were the secrets of much of her success. And a very considerable success it was.
Roy Jenkins (1920–) British politician. *Observer*, 11 Nov 1984

3 She was the ablest Labour politician of her generation. On grounds of ability alone she ought to have become Britain's first woman Prime Minister. But there is no justice in politics.
Paul Johnson (1928–) British editor. *Sunday Telegraph*, 28 Nov 1980, 'In Face of Strife'

Quotations by Castle
4 It has always been an endless worry as to whether I would ever have a whole garment and an unladdered pair of stockings to wear. Poor old Ted pointed out to me that his jacket was torn. My riposte was to pull out my winter coat, whose lining is falling apart for want of a stitch, and tell him how embarrassed I was when people at functions insisted on helping me into it.
Diaries 1974–78

5 I have never consciously exploited the fact that I am a woman. I wouldn't dare try that, even if I knew how to. I have too much respect for my male colleagues to think they would be particularly impressed.
Observer, 5 Oct 1969

6 I've never regretted being in the government. I love responsibility and I don't mind unpopularity.
The Sunday Times, 2 July 1967

CATHER, Willa Sibert (1873–1947)

US writer. Although born in Virginia, she was brought up in Nebraska, which is reflected in her writings about the American pioneers. Her works include *Alexander's Bridge* (1912), *O Pioneers!* (1913), *The Song of the Lark* (1915), *A Lost Lady* (1923), and *Lucy Gayheart* (1935).

Quotations about Cather
1 For the whole range of Cather's values, standards, tastes, and prejudices, her tone is that of an inherent aristocrat in an equalitarian order, of an agrarian writer in an industrial order, of a defender of the spiritual graces in the midst of an increasingly materialistic culture.
Maxwell Geismar (1909–79) US author and critic. *The Last of the Provincials*

2 The disappearance of the old frontier left Miss Cather with a heritage of the virtues in which she had been bred but with the necessity of finding a new object for them. Looking for the new frontier she found it in the mind.
Lionel Trilling (1905–75) US author. *After the Genteel Tradition* (Malcolm Cowley)

Quotations by Cather
3 Old men are like that, you know. It makes them feel important to think they are in love with somebody.
My Antonia, Bk III, Ch. 4

4 The history of every country begins in the heart of a man or woman.
O Pioneers!, Pt II, Ch. 4

5 I have never faced the typewriter with the thought that one more chore had to be done.
The World of Willa Cather (Mildred R. Bennett)

CATHERINE THE GREAT (1729–96)

Empress of Russia (1762–96), who came to the throne after the murder of her husband, Emperor Peter III, and who was to significantly change the role of Russia in Europe. Her reign was marked by successful expansionist wars and the partition of Poland and she was much inspired by Voltaire and Diderot and other leading figures of The Enlightenment. However, because of her autocratic domestic policies she became known as an enlightened despot. She is renowned for her many lovers and voracious sexual appetite.

Quotations about Catherine the Great

1 At the age of fourteen she made the threefold resolution, to please her Consort, [Empress] Elizabeth, and the Nation.
Epitaph, written by herself, 1789

2 I'm glad you like my Catherine. I like her too. She ruled thirty million people and had three thousand lovers. I do the best I can in two hours.
Mae West (1892–1980) US actress. Speech from the stage after her performance in *Catherine the Great*

Quotations by Catherine the Great

3 If Fate had given me in youth a husband whom I could have loved, I should have remained always true to him. The trouble is that my heart would not willingly remain one hour without love.
Letter to Prince Potemkin, 1774

4 In my view he who goes ahead is always the one who wins.
Letter to Baron F. M. Grimm, 11 Aug 1778

5 Do you know, it is not praise that does me good, but when men speak ill of me, then, with a noble assurance I say to myself, as I smile at them, 'let us be revenged by proving them to be liars'.
Letter to Baron F. M. Grimm, 4 Dec 1793

6 I shall be an autocrat: that's my trade. And the good Lord will forgive me: that's his.
Attrib.

CATT, Carrie (1859–1947)

US suffragette. She grew up in Wisconsin, Iowa where she had great success in the educational system, being appointed one of the first women school superintendents in 1883. From 1887 she became active in the suffrage movement; in 1902 she founded the International Woman Suffrage Alliance, serving as its president until 1923. After women were granted the vote in America she reorganized the National American Woman Suffrage Association into the League of Women Voters to continue working for progressive legislation throughout America.

1 The sacrifice of suffering, of doubt, of obloquy, which has been endured by the pioneers in the woman movement will never be fully known or understood.
Speech, 8–14 Feb 1900, 'For the Sake of Liberty'

2 There are two kinds of restrictions upon human liberty – the restraint of law and that of custom. No written law has ever been more binding than unwritten custom supported by popular opinion.
Speech, 8–14 Feb 1900, 'For the Sake of Liberty'

3 The Government evidently nurses a forlorn hope that by delay it may tire out the workers and destroy the force of the campaign.
Speech, Stockholm 1911, 'Is Woman Suffrage Progressing?'

4 When a just cause reaches its flood-tide, as ours has done in that country, whatever stands in the way must fall before its overwhelming power.
Speech, Stockholm 1911, 'Is Woman Suffrage Progressing?'

CAULKINS, Frances Manwaring (1795–1869)

US author and historian.

1 The purest and noblest love of the olden time is that which draws from its annals, motives of gratitude and thanksgiving for the past – counsels and warnings for the future.
History of New London, Connecticut, Preface

2 The tendency of man among savages, without the watch of his equals and the check of society, is to degenerate; to decline from the standard of morals and gradually to relinquish all Christian observances.
History of New London, Connecticut, Ch. 6

3 Many excellent men in that day, were believers in impressions, impulses and ecstacies. Imagination was trusted more than judgment and transports of feeling were valued beyond the decisions of reason. Such a state of things naturally tends to destroy the equilibrium of the character.
History of New London, Connecticut, Ch. 26

CAVELL, Edith (1865–1915)

British nurse who became a heroine of World War I. She entered the nursing profession in 1895 and was appointed the first matron of the Berkendael Medical Institute, Belgium in 1907.

She continued in her post after the German occupation of Belgium, treating both German and Allied wounded; however, she also became involved in an underground group formed to help stranded Allied soldiers. Edith Cavell was arrested on 5 August 1915, sentenced to death and, despite interventions by the US minister in Brussels, executed by firing squad at 02.00 on 12 October 1915.

Quotations about Cavell

1 A fragile, middle-aged little woman, grey eyes that could be tender or critical, a mouth of masculine firmness, a woman to cling to her standards at all costs.
A. E. Clark-Kennedy Lecture to the London Hospital League of Nurses, 8 May 1965

2 She was introspective, deeply religious, possessed by a sense of duty and with neither inclination nor capacity to make friends; a solitary, withdrawn figure, who loved suffering humanity as a whole, rather than a particular member of it.
A. E. Clark-Kennedy Lecture to the London Hospital League of Nurses, 8 May 1965

Quotations by Cavell

3 If we are, we shall all be punished, whether we have done much or little. So let us go ahead and help these men as much as possible.
Discussing the risk of arrest. A. E. Clark-Kennedy Lecture to the London Hospital League of Nurses, 8 May 1965

4 I realize that patriotism is not enough. I must have no hatred or bitterness towards anyone.
Last words

CHANEL, Coco (Gabrielle C.; 1883–1971)
French fashion designer, remembered for her elegant but simple designs, combining comfort with style, that revolutionized women's clothing. Her first shop was opened in Deauville in 1913; within 5 years her original use of jersey material had attracted the attention of fashionable women, leading them to abandon their corsetted, uncomfortable clothes. Her perfume Chanel No. 5, introduced in 1922, was extremely successful and formed the financial basis of her empire.

Quotations about Chanel

1 Coco Chanel has been distinguished in a business overburdened with chi-chi by the simplicity of her approach to everything concerning fashion.
Meriel McCooey *1000 Makers of the 20th Century*

2 In her own life, Chanel epitomised the New Woman, free and independent in every sense.
Kaori O'Connor *Makers of Modern Culture* (ed. J. Wintle)

Quotations by Chanel

3 There goes a woman who knows all the things that can be taught and none of the things that cannot be taught.
Coco Chanel, Her Life, Her Secrets (Marcel Haedrich)

4 Youth is something very new: twenty years ago no one mentioned it.
Coco Chanel, Her Life, Her Secrets (Marcel Haedrich)

5 Wherever one wants to be kissed.
When asked where one should wear perfume. *Coco Chanel, Her Life, Her Secrets* (Marcel Haedrich)

6 Fashion is architecture: it is a matter of proportions.
Coco Chanel, Her Life, Her Secrets (Marcel Haedrich)

CHARACTER

1 The female is an empty thing and easily swayed: she runs great risks when she is away from her husband. Therefore, keep females in the house…and come home often to keep an eye on your affairs and to keep them in fear and trembling.
Paolo da Certaldo (fl. 1330–70) Italian businessman.
Handbook of Good Customs [c. 1360]

2 Most women have no characters at all.
Alexander Pope (1688–1744) British poet.
Moral Essays, II [1732]

3 Just the disposition for a woman, a wife; a spirit that can accommodate itself to the wishes and humours of those on whom it is dependent for happiness, and yet retain sufficient firmness to act with decision when circumstances shall require its exertion.
Sarah Josepha Hale (1788–1879) US editor, writer, and poet.
Sketches of American Character [1829]

4 The fundamental fault of the female character is that it has no sense of justice.
Arthur Schopenhauer (1788–1860) German philosopher.
Gedanken über vielerlei Gegenstände, XXVII

5 Character contributes to beauty. It fortifies a woman as her youth fades. A mode of conduct, a standard of courage, discipline, fortitude and integrity can do a great deal to make a woman beautiful.
Jacqueline Bisset (1946–   ) British actress.
Los Angeles Times, 16 May 1974

CHARM

1 Charm is a delusion and beauty fleeting; it is the God-fearing woman who is honoured. Extol her for the fruit of her toil,

and let her labours bring her honour in the city gate.
Bible: Proverbs
31:30–31

2 On Richmond Hill there lives a lass,
More sweet than May day morn,
Whose charms all other maids surpass,
A rose without a thorn.
Leonard MacNally (1752–1820) Irish dramatist and poet.
The Lass of Richmond Hill [c. 1790]

3 It's a sort of bloom on a woman. If you have it, you don't need to have anything else; and if you don't have it, it doesn't much matter what else you have.
J. M. Barrie (1860–1937) British novelist and dramatist.
What Every Woman Knows, I [1906]

CHASTITY

See also VIRTUE

1 In the old days poverty
Kept Latin women chaste: hard work, too little sleep,
These were the things that saved their humble homes from corruption.
Juvenal (Decimus Junius Juvenalis; 60–130 AD) Roman satirist.
Satires, VI [1st century AD]

2 Women have one great advantage…A man must be courteous, generous, brave and wise. But if a woman keeps her body intact, all her other defects are hidden and she can hold her head high.
Philippe de Navarre (d. c. 1261)
Les Quatre Ages de l'Homme [13th century]

3 Only one woman in thousands has been endowed with the God-given aptitude to live in chastity and virginity…God fashioned her body so that she should be with a man, to have and to rear children. No woman should be ashamed of that for which God made and intended her.
Martin Luther (1483–1546) German Protestant.
Kritische Gesamtausgabe [1524]

4 …made of iron, and consisting of a belt and a piece which came up under and was locked in position, so neatly made that once a woman was bridled it was out of the question for her to indulge in the gentle pleasure, as there were only a few little holes for her to piss through.
Pierre de Bourdeille, Seigneur de Brantôme (c. 1540–1614) French writer.
Describing a chastity belt. *The Lives of Gallant Ladies* [16th century]

5 Nothing makes women more esteemed by the opposite sex than chastity; whether it be that we always prize those most who are hardest to come at, or that nothing beside chastity, with its collateral attendants, truth, fidelity and constancy, gives the man a property in the person he loves, and consequently endears her to him above all things.
Anonymous
Spectator, 23 June 1711

6 The advantages are manifold. Not only will the purity of the virgin be maintained, but the fidelity of the wife exacted. The husband will leave the wife without fear that his honour will be outraged and his affections estranged.
A French merchandising house advertising a chastity belt. *The Girdle of Chastity* (Eric Dingwall) [1880]

7 There is no doubt that the practice is a means of suppressing and controlling the sexual behaviour of women. Female circumcision is a physiological chastity belt.
Sue Armstrong South African journalist.
New Scientist, 2 Feb 1991

8 Female circumcision, a traditional practice that affects an estimated 80 million women in the world today…entails different things in different cultures. The mildest form – known to Muslims as 'sunna' and the least common – involves the removal of the prepuce or hood of the clitoris. It is the only operation analogous to male circumcision. Excision involves the removal of the clitoris and the labia minora: while infibulation involves the removal of all the external genitalia and the stitching up of the two sides of the vulva to leave only a tiny opening for the passage of urine and menstrual blood.
Sue Armstrong South African journalist.
New Scientist, 2 Feb 1991

CHILD, Lydia (1802–80)

US abolitionist and writer. She established the first children's periodical in the US, the *Juvenile Miscellany* (1826), and wrote the novels *Hobomok* (1824) and *The Rebels* (1825). However, following her meeting with abolitionist William Lloyd Garrison in 1931, she wrote *An Appeal in Favor of that Class of Americans Called Africans* (1833), which relates the history of slavery and denounces inequality for blacks. This work led to her being socially ostracized and caused her magazine to fail in 1834. From 1841 to 1843 she edited the *National Anti-Slavery Standard* and allowed her home to become part of the Underground Railroad that helped escaping slaves.

1 But men never violate the laws of God without suffering the consequences, sooner or later.
The Freedmen's Book, 'Toussaint L'Ouverture'

2 Not in vain is Ireland pouring itself all over the earth…The Irish, with their glowing hearts and reverent credulity, are needed in this cold age of intellect and skepticism.
Letters from New York, Vol. I, No. 33, 8 Dec 1842

3 England may as well dam up the waters from the Nile with bulrushes as to fetter the step of Freedom, more proud and firm in this youthful land.
The Rebels, Ch. 4

CHILDBIRTH

1 There is nothing encourageth a woman sooner to be barren than hard travail in child bearing.
Pliny the Elder (Gaius Plinius Secundus; 23 AD–79 AD) Roman writer.
Natural History [1st century AD]

2 A woman when she is in travail hath sorrow, because her hour is come: but as soon as she is delivered of the child, she remembereth no more the anguish, for joy that a man is born into the world.
Bible: John
16:21

3 I am not giving permission for a woman to teach or tell a man what to do. A woman ought not to speak, because Adam was formed first and Eve afterwards, and it was not Adam who was led astray but the woman who was led astray and fell into sin. Nevertheless, she will be saved by childbearing.
Bible: I Timothy
2:12–15

4 Many pregnant women in confinement and small children of noble as well as of common rank are often miserably neglected, injured, harmed and crippled at the time of the birth or in the following six weeks, all through the clumsiness, arrogance, and rashness of the midwives and assisting women; few sensible midwives are to be found in this country.
Anna of Saxony (fl. c. 1587) German medical practitioner.
Women in the Middle Ages (Sibylle Harksen) [c. 1587]

5 My mother groan'd, my father wept,
Into the dangerous world I leapt;
Helpless, naked, piping loud,
Like a fiend hid in a cloud.
William Blake (1757–1827) British poet.
Songs of Experience, 'Infant Sorrow' [1789]

6 The husband persisted in being at the bedside…I confess it did not square with my old-fashioned notions of delicacy or propriety.
Letter from a country doctor, *Lancet*, 11 Dec 1841

7 I think a medical man steps very far beyond his province when he endeavours to prevent a husband being present at the accouchement of his wife. Man and wife are one, and it is a matter between themselves with which we have nothing whatever to do.
John Chatto
Lancet, 18 Dec 1841

8 You cannot really wish me to be the '*mamma d'une nombreuse famille*'…men never think, at least seldom think, what a hard task it is for us women to go through this very often.
Victoria (1819–1901) Queen of the United Kingdom.
Letter to Leopold I, 1841

9 I must confess that I have a great dislike to it; not because I have anything to apprehend from the observation of the husband, but *because I do not think it is delicate or decent.*
Referring to the presence of husbands at childbirth. Letter, *Lancet*, 1842

10 That women *will* die from their effect, no one will deny, and that they *have* done so is certainly true; but to esteem this as a proof of the usefulness of anaesthesia is showing an ignorance of the means always at the command of those who scientifically practise midwifery, which, if properly employed, will, in all cases, effectually prevent the occurrence of death from the prolonged pains of labour.
G. T. Gream
Lancet, 1 Jan 1848

11 *Childbirth* is that natural process by which the womb expels its contents, and returns to the condition in which it was previously…I am well aware that some degree of suffering is connected with child-birth; and this applies equally to the whole animal creation, whether human or brute, – though the former suffer more than the latter, because the habits of brutes are less unnatural.
Dr John T. Conquest
Letters to a Mother [1848]

12 Dr Snow gave that blessed Chloroform & the effect was soothing, quieting & delightful beyond measure.
Victoria (1819–1901) Queen of the United Kingdom.
Describing her labour. *Journal*, 1853

13 What you say of the pride of giving life to an immortal soul is very fine, dear, but I own I cannot enter into that; I think much more of our being like a cow or a dog at such moments;

when our poor nature becomes so very animal and unecstatic.
Victoria (1819–1901) Queen of the United Kingdom.
Letter to her daughter, 15 June 1858

14 *Should the husband be present during the labour?* Certainly not; but as soon as the labour is over, and all the soiled clothes have been put out of the way, let him instantly see his wife for a few minutes, to whisper in her ear words of affection, of gratitude, and consolation.
Pye Henry Chavasse
Advice to a Wife on the Management of Her Own Health [1889]

15 In this country if a farmer's mare has a foal she is turned out to rear it in idleness, if his cow or sheep has a baby, it is given every chance to be a good one, but if his wife has a child in ten days or even less (evidently that absolute minimum time allowed to weakness) she does her own housework, milks perhaps ten cows night and morning, feeds calves, pigs, hens etc and suckles her baby.
Anonymous
Letter to Marie Stopes, from New Zealand, Mar 1926

16 I'll simply say here that I was born Beatrice Gladys Lillie at an extremely tender age because my mother needed a fourth at meals.
Beatrice Lillie (Constance Sylvia Munston, Lady Peel; 1898–1989) Canadian-born British actress.
Every Other Inch a Lady, Ch. 1 [1927]

17 It is unheard of, uncivilized barbarism that any woman should still be forced to bear such monstrous torture. It should be remedied. It should be stopped. It is simply absurd that with our modern science painless childbirth does not exist as a matter of course.
Isadora Duncan (1878–1927) US dancer, educator, and writer.
My Life [1927]

18 When they first brought the baby in to her...she stared, inert, and thought, This is the author of my pain.
Bessie Breuer (b. 1893) US writer.
The Actress, Ch. 21 [1955]

19 At the moment of childbirth, every woman has the same aura of isolation, as though she were abandoned, alone.
Boris Pasternak (1890–1960) Russian writer.
Doctor Zhivago [1957]

20 It is a great pity that a man should stand back, helpless and inadequate, *de trop*, while his wife alone knows the profound experience

of the birth of the child they have created together.
Marjorie Karmel US writer.
Thank You, Dr Lamaze, Ch. 3 [1959]

21 Publication is the male equivalent of childbirth.
Richard Acland (1906–) British politician and writer.
Observer, 'Sayings of the Week', 19 May 1974

22 Birth may be a matter of a moment. But it is a unique one.
Frédérick Leboyer (1918–) French obstetrician.
Birth Without Violence [1975]

23 There are women who like to be allowed to be women, who like to have their babies *with* gravity instead of against it to please some obstetrician.
Margaret Mead (1901–78) US anthropologist, writer, editor, and museum curator.
New Realities, Vol. 2, No. 2, June 1978

24 It is not ultimately a matter of High Tech versus natural childbirth. The doctor does not necessarily always know best. A woman having a baby is doing what she was designed for and that equips her with a kind of knowing. Surely humility and respect on both sides is what is needed...The awareness of the paper-thin divide between life and death can be life-enhancing or can shake your confidence completely.
Mary Ellis
British Medical Journal, 25 Jan 1986

CHILDREN
See also MOTHERHOOD

1 There's only one pretty child in the world, and every mother has it.
Proverb

2 The joys of parents are secret, and so are their griefs and fears.
Francis Bacon (1561–1626) English philosopher.
Essays, 'Of Parents and Children' [1597]

3 There is nothing so strong as the force of love; there is no love so forcible as the love of an affectionate mother to her natural child.
Elizabeth Grymeston (c. 1563–1603) English writer.
Letter to her son Bernye Grymeston, 1603

4 We are transfused into our children, and...feel more keenly for them than for ourselves.
Marie de Sévigné (1626–96) French letter writer and salonist.
Letter to her daughter, 27 Feb 1685

5 Since marriage, which is a human institution invented for purely practical purposes, is so frail and so full of stumbling-blocks, how is it that so many marriages hold together? They do so because both partners have one interest in common, the thing for which nature has always intended marriage, namely children.
August Strindberg (1849–1912) Swedish dramatist.
Getting Married, Preface [1884]

6 Oh my son's my son till he gets him a wife,
But my daughter's my daughter all her life.
Dinah Mulock Craik (1826–87) British writer and poet.
'Young and Old' [c. 1887]

7 My father was frightened of his mother. I was frightened of my father, and I'm damned well going to make sure that my children are frightened of me.
George V (1865–1936) King of the United Kingdom.
Attrib. [1936]

8 There are only two things a child will share willingly – communicable diseases and his mother's age.
Dr Benjamin Spock (1903–) US pediatrician and psychiatrist.
Attrib. [c. 1945]

9 Literature is mostly about having sex and not much about having children; life is the other way round.
David Lodge (1935–) British author.
The British Museum is Falling Down, Ch. 4 [1965]

10 Parents are the bones on which children sharpen their teeth.
Peter Ustinov (1921–) British actor.
Dear Me [1977]

11 The State's attitude to motherhood is ambivalent...In France, for instance, childcare is subsidised by the government, with crèches for children up to the age of three, kindergartens for three- to four-year-olds and special arrangements at elementary schools for older children...In Britain, mothers are expected to make private arrangements and receive no tax concessions for the expenses they incur.
Angela Holdsworth British television journalist.
Out of the Doll's House [1988]

CHIVALRY

1 True chivalry respects all womanhood, and no one who reads the record, as it is written in the faces of the million mulattoes in the South, will for a minute conceive that the southern white man had a very chivalrous regard for the honor due the women of his race or respect for the womanhood which circumstances placed in his power.
Ida B. Wells (1862–1931) US abolitionist, educator, writer, and lecturer.
A Red Record [1895]

2 Remember, men, we're fighting for this woman's honour; which is probably more than she ever did.
Groucho Marx (Julius Marx; 1895–1977) US comedian.
Duck Soup [1933]

3 Even nowadays a man can't step up and kill a woman without feeling just a bit unchivalrous.
Robert Benchley (1889–1945) US humorist.
Chips off the Old Benchley, 'Down in Front' [1949]

4 A gentleman is any man who wouldn't hit a woman with his hat on.
Fred Allen (1894–1956) US comedian.
Attrib. [1956]

5 But there is another side to chivalry. If it dispenses leniency, it may with equal justification invoke control.
Freda Adler (1934–) US educator.
Sisters in Crime, Ch. 4 [1975]

6 Every man I meet wants to protect me. I can't figure out what from.
Mae West (1892–1980) US actress.
Attrib. [c. 1980]

CHRISTIE, Agatha (1891–1975)

British author and dramatist. Known as the 'Queen of Crime', she created the characters Hercule Poirot and Miss Marple, who have become household names. Her first book *The Mysterious Affair at Styles* (1920), in which she introduced Hercule Poirot, was the start of a phenomenally successful career. She was divorced from her first husband, Archibald Christie, in 1928, and two years later married Max Mallowan, an archaeologist. Their travels in the Middle East form the background for some of her later novels, such as *Appointment With Death* (1938). Other novels include *The Murder of Roger Ackroyd* (1926), in which the narrator is revealed to be the murderer, and *Murder on the Orient Express* (1934), in which the murder is committed by all the suspects. She is also famous for her play *The Mousetrap* (1952), which holds the record for the longest continuous run in the history of the London theatre.

Quotations about Christie

1 Outsold only by the Bible and Shakespeare and translated into over 100 foreign languages, writer of the longest-running play on the British stage, the most popular entertainer the world has ever known.

Robert Barnard (1936–) British writer. *A Talent to Deceive*

2 She is a comely, ample woman with no outward traces of brilliance.

Sir Henry Channon (1897–1958) British politician and writer. Diary, 14 Feb 1944

Quotations by Christie

3 One doesn't recognize in one's life the really important moments – not until it's too late.

Endless Night, Bk II, Ch. 14

4 Where large sums of money are concerned, it is advisable to trust nobody.

Endless Night, Bk II, Ch. 15

5 Hercule Poirot tapped his forehead. 'These little grey cells, It is 'up to them' – as you say over here.'

The Mysterious Affair at Styles

6 Curious things, habits. People themselves never knew they had them.

Witness for the Prosecution

7 An archaeologist is the best husband any woman can have: the older she gets, the more interested he is in her.

Attrib.

CHRISTINE DE PISAN (1364–1430)

French poet, author, and scholar, who took up writing to support herself and her three children after the death of her husband. Although she wrote on a number of different subjects, including a biography of Charles V of France and many courtly ballads, she was much concerned with the question of women and attitudes towards them. *L'Epistre du dieu d'amours* (1399) defended women against the satire of Jean de Meun in the *Roman de la Rose* (*Romance of the Rose*; c. 1275); *La Cité des Dames* (*The City of Ladies*; 1405) tells of women who were famous for their heroism and virtue; *Livre des trois vertus* (1406) is a treatise on women's education.

Quotations about Christine de Pisan

1 *The Book of the City of Ladies* represents a determined and clear-headed woman's attempt to take apart the structure of her contemporaries' prejudices.

Marina Warner (1946–) British writer and critic. *La Cité des Dames*, Introduction

2 Christine alters her source material in the most surprising ways, sometimes refreshing, sometimes bizarre.

Marina Warner (1946–) British writer and critic. *La Cité des Dames*, Introduction

Quotations by Christine de Pisan

3 You ask whether woman possesses any natural intelligence. Yes. It can be developed to become wisdom, and then it is most beautiful.

La Cité des Dames, Prologue

4 If it were customary to send little girls to school and to teach them the same subjects as are taught to boys, they would learn just as fully and would understand the subtleties of all arts and sciences. Indeed, maybe they would understand them better…for just as women's bodies are softer than men's, so their understanding is sharper.

La Cité des Dames, Prologue

5 Honour to Womankind. It needs must be That God loves Woman, since He fashioned Thee.

Of Six Medieval Women (Alice Kemp-Welch)

CHURCH

See RELIGION

CLEOPATRA VII (69–30 BC)

Egyptian Queen (51–48, 47–30). She was coruler of Egypt with her brother Ptolemy XIII, who ousted her in 48. Restored as queen by Julius Caesar the following year, she accompanied him to Rome where she bore him a son, Caesarion. After Caesar's murder she returned to Egypt and in 41 she met Mark Antony. They married in 37, destroying Antony's popularity in Rome. The Roman Senate declared war against them in 31, defeating them at Actium. They fled to Egypt where they both committed suicide.

Quotations about Cleopatra

1 The kingdom of the Romans endured much evil through Cleopatra, Queen of Egypt, that worst of women. And so with others. Therefore it is no wonder that the world now suffers through the malice of women.

Heinrich Kramer and Jakob Sprenger German Dominican monks. *Malleus Maleficarum: The Classic Study of Witchcraft* (1486)

2 If Cleopatra's nose had been shorter the whole face of the earth would have changed.

Blaise Pascal (1623–62) French philosopher and mathematician. *Pensées*

3 At last, as if in mockery of them, she came sailing up the river Cydnus, in a barge with gilded stern and outspread sails of purple, while oars of silver beat time to the music of flutes and fifes and harps. She herself lay all alone under a canopy of cloth of gold, dressed as Venus in a picture, and beautiful young boys, like painted Cupids, stood on each side to fan her. Her maids were dressed like sea nymphs and graces, some steering at the rudder, some working at the ropes. The perfumes diffused themselves from the vessel to the shore, which was covered with multitudes, part following the galley up the river on either bank, part running out of the city to see the sight.

Plutarch (c. 46–119 AD) Greek biographer and author. *Life of Mark Anthony*, XXV

4   Gaius Octavius had a desire to have reserved Cleopatra as a captive to adorn his Triumph, therefore he sent for the Psylli, a people whose faculty and employment is to suck out poison, and made them apply themselves to her wounds, to see if they could draw forth that venom which her asps had infused there, and which was thought to be the occasion of her death. He did Anthony and Cleopatra that favour as to let them be buried together, and ordered that monument to be finished which was begun by themselves.

Suetonius (c. 69–c. 122 AD) Roman biographer and antiquarian. *Lives of the Caesars*

Quotations by Cleopatra

5   As surely as one day I shall administer justice on the Capitol...

Her favourite oath, referring to the capital of the Roman Empire. *Cleopatra of Egypt* (Philip W. Sergeant), Ch. 9

6   Fool! Don't you see now that I could have poisoned you a hundred times had I been able to live without you!

Remark to Mark Antony. *Cleopatra's Daughter, The Queen of Mauretania* (Beatrice Chanler), Ch. 5

7   I *will not* be exhibited in his Triumph.

Remark concerning Octavian's victory. *The Life and Times of Cleopatra* (Arthur Weigall), Ch. 20

CLOTHES

See also APPEARANCE

1   Today I dressed to meet my father's eyes; yesterday it was for my husband's.

Julia (39 BC–14 AD) Daughter of Augustus.
On being complimented by her father, the emperor Augustus, on her choice of a more modest dress than the one she had worn the previous day. *Saturnalia* (Macrobius) [1st century AD]

2   It is an amazing thing to see in our city the wife of a shoemaker, or a butcher, or a porter dressed in silk with chains of gold at the throat, with pearls and a ring of good value...and then in contrast to see her husband cutting the meat, all smeared with cow's blood, poorly dressed... but whoever considers this carefully will find it reasonable, because it is necessary that the lady, even if low-born and humble, be draped with such clothes for her natural excellence and dig-

nity, and that the man be less adorned as if a slave, or a little ass, born to her service.

Lucrezia Marinella (fl. 1600) Italian writer.
The Nobility and Excellence of Women together with the Defects and Deficiencies of Men [1600]

3   There can be no doubt that the hand which first encloses the waist of a girl in these cruel contrivances, supplying her with a fictitious support, where the hand of God has placed bones and muscles that ought to be brought into vigorous action, that hand lays the foundation of bitter suffering.

Charlotte Elizabeth Tonna (1790–1846) English poet, educator and author.
She was referring to stays. *Personal Recollections*, Letter I [1841]

4   She had a womanly instinct that clothes possess an influence more powerful over many than the worth of character or the magic of manners.

Louisa May Alcott (1832–88) US writer and editor.
Little Women, Pt II [1868]

5   To a woman, the consciousness of being well-dressed gives a sense of tranquility which religion fails to bestow.

Helen Olcott Bell (1830–1918) US writer.
Letters and Social Aims: R. W. Emerson [1876]

6   Her frocks are built in Paris but she wears them with a strong English accent.

Saki (Hector Hugh Munro; 1870–1916) British writer.
Reginald on Women [1895]

7   As an article of dress for the girl the corset must be looked upon as distinctly prejudicial to health, and as entirely unnecessary.

Howard A. Kelly (b. 1858) US gynaecologist.
Medical Gynecology [1909]

8   There is no such thing as a moral dress...It's people who are moral or immoral.

Jennie Jerome Churchill (1854–1921) British hostess, editor, and playwright.
Daily Chronicle, 16 Feb 1921

9   Brevity is the soul of lingerie.

Dorothy Parker (1893–1967) US writer.
While Rome Burns (Alexander Woollcott) [1934]

10   So fashion is born by small facts, trends, or even politics, never by trying to make little pleats and furbelows, by trinkets, by clothes easy to copy, or by the shortening or lengthening of a skirt.

Elsa Schiaparelli (d. 1973) Italian fashion designer.
Shocking Life, Ch. 9 [1954]

11   What caused this...renaissance of the dandy in an era of technology? As women became more aggressive, invaded masculine professions and usurped male prerogatives,

men fell back on being peacocks. With clothes, men were reconstructing their diminished manhood.
Marilyn Bender (1925–) US journalist.
The Beautiful People, Ch. 10 [1967]

12 An after-dinner speech should be like a lady's dress – long enough to cover the subject and short enough to be interesting.
R. A. Butler (1902–82) British Conservative politician.
Remark made at an Anglo-Jewish dinner [1970s]

13 Elegance does not consist in putting on a new dress.
Coco Chanel (1883–1971) French fashion designer.
Coco Chanel, Her Life, Her Secrets (Marcel Haedrich) [1971]

COHABITING

See MARRIAGE; PARTNERSHIP

COLETTE (Sidonie-Gabrielle C.; 1873–1954)

French writer. Regarded as the outstanding French woman writer of the first half of the 20th century, she was honoured by being made a member of the Belgian Royal Academy (1935) and was the first woman president of the Académie Goncourt (1945). After the divorce in 1906 from her first husband, Henri Gauthier-Villars, in whose name the *Claudine* novels (1900–03) were published, she became a music-hall performer. These experiences led to *La Vagabonde* (1910) and *L'Envers du music-hall* (1913). Outstanding among her later works are *Chéri* (1920), *La Find e Chéri* (1926), and *Gigi* (1944).

Quotations about Colette
1 Colette wrote of vegetables as if they were love objects and of sex as if it were an especially delightful department of gardening.
Brigid Brophy (1929–) British author. *1000 Makers of the 20th Century*

2 Her concrete, always intelligent never intellectualised prose lifts sensuousness to the pitch of sanctity.
Brigid Brophy (1929–) British author. *1000 Makers of the 20th Century*

Quotations by Colette
3 Total absence of humour renders life impossible.
Chance Acquaintances

4 When she raises her eyelids it's as if she were taking off all her clothes.
Claudine and Annie

5 My virtue's still far too small, I don't trot it out and about yet.
Claudine at School

6 Don't ever wear artistic jewellery; it wrecks a woman's reputation.
Gigi

7 Don't eat too many almonds; they add weight to the breasts.
Gigi

COMMITMENT

1 'We don't want her to take music too seriously.' Real concern came into her voice. 'We don't want her to become intense over something, and warped and queer. Such women are unhappy in later life. They don't,' she rang the bell for more tea, 'they don't make good wives.'
Catherine Drinker Bowen (1897–1973) US writer and historian.
Friends and Fiddlers, Ch. 4 [1934]

2 Miss Brodie said: 'Pavlova contemplates her swans in order to perfect her swan dance, she studies them. This is true dedication. You must all grow up to be dedicated women as I have dedicated myself to you.'
Muriel Spark (1918–) British writer and poet.
The Prime of Miss Jean Brodie, Ch. 3 [1961]

3 It isn't until you begin to fight in your own cause that you (a) become really committed to winning, and (b) become a genuine ally of other people struggling for their freedom.
Robin Morgan (1941–) US writer.
Sisterhood Is Powerful, Introduction [1970]

4 Total commitment to family and total commitment to career is possible, but fatiguing.
Muriel Fox (1928–) US business executive and feminist.
New Woman, Oct 1971

COMMUNICATION

See LANGUAGE

COMPLIMENTS

1 She, and comparisons are odious.
John Donne (1573–1631) English poet.
Elegies, 8, 'The Comparison' [1590]

2 She isn't a bad bit of goods, the Queen! I wish all the fleas in my bed were as good.
Miguel de Cervantes (1547–1616) Spanish novelist.
Don Quixote, Pt I, Ch. 30 [1605]

3 Won't you come into the garden? I would like my roses to see you.
Richard Brinsley Sheridan (1751–1816) British dramatist.
Said to a young lady. Attrib. in *The Perfect Hostess* [1781]

4 The rose was awake all night for your sake,
Knowing your promise to me;
The lilies and roses were all awake,
They sighed for the dawn and thee.
Alfred, Lord Tennyson
Maud, I [1855]

5 Roses are flowering in Picardy,
But there's never a rose like you.
Frederic Edward Weatherly (1848–1929) British lawyer and songwriter.
Roses of Picardy [1919]

CONSERVATION

1 I am acquainted with several ladies who have worn birds in their hats for years, who wear them no longer, whatever the fashion may be, and who grieve when they remember how, sinning from want of thought, they once used such ornaments.
W. H. Hudson (1841–1922) British naturalist and writer.
Osprey, or, Egrets and Aigrettes [1891]

2 The movement began in a small way, and for the first few months of its existence was confined to efforts to enlist the sympathy of women in support of protests against the wanton slaughter of birds for the sake of their plumage.
Margaretta Louisa Smith (1860–1953) British founder-member of the Royal Society for the Protection of Birds.
For love of birds: the story of the RSPB [c. 1892]

3 Do our soldiers fight the better for their busbies made of egrets' crests? Would our lovely ladies not look ever fair if no plumes waved upon their heads?
Mrs Archibald Little
Our Pet Herons [1900]

4 As cruel a weapon as the cave man's club, the chemical barrage has been hurled against the fabric of life.
Rachel Carson (1907–64) US marine biologist and writer.
The Silent Spring [1962]

5 We are living beyond our means. As a people we have developed a life-style that is draining the earth of its priceless and irreplaceable resources without regard for the future of our children and people all around the world.
Margaret Mead (1910–78) US anthropologist, writer, editor, and museum curator.
Redbook, 'The Energy Crises – Why Our World Will Never Again Be the Same', Apr 1974

CONSTANCY

1 Through perils both of wind and limb,
Through thick and thin she follow'd him.
Samuel Butler (1612–80) English satirist.
Hudibras, Pt II [1663–78]

2 We only part to meet again.
Change, as ye list, ye winds; my heart shall be
The faithful compass that still points to thee.
John Gay (1685–1732) English poet and dramatist.
Sweet William's Farewell [1720]

3 But I'm always true to you, darlin', in my fashion,
Yes, I'm always true to you, darlin', in my way.
Cole Porter (1893–1964) US songwriter.
Kiss Me, Kate, 'Always True to You in My Fashion' [1953]

CONTEMPT
See also ATTITUDES; MISOGYNY

1 A woman's preaching is like a dog's walking on his hinder legs. It is not done well; but you are surprised to find it done at all.
Samuel Johnson (1709–84) British lexicographer.
Life of Johnson, Vol. I (J. Boswell) [1763]

2 And a woman is only a woman, but a good cigar is a smoke.
Rudyard Kipling (1865–1936) Indian-born British writer.
The Betrothed

3 I expect that Woman will be the last thing civilized by Man.
George Meredith (1828–1909) British novelist.
The Ordeal of Richard Feverel, Ch. 1 [1859]

4 'I will not stand for being called a woman in my own house,' she said.
Evelyn Waugh (1903–66) British novelist.
Scoop, Bk I, Ch. 5 [1938]

CONTRACEPTION
See BIRTH CONTROL

CONTRARINESS

1 Forbid a thing, and that women will do.
Proverb

2 Woman is always fickle and changing.
Virgil (Publius Vergilius Maro; 70–19 BC) Roman poet.
Aeneid, Bk IV [19 BC]

3 Women that are chaste when they are trusted, prove often wantons when they are causelesse suspected.
R. M. (fl. 1630) English author.
The Mothers Counsell or, Live within Compasse. Being the last Will and Testament to her dearest Daughter [1630]

4 Woman's at best a contradiction still.
Alexander Pope (1688–1744) British poet.
Moral Essays, II [1732]

5 Girls are so queer you never know what they mean. They say No when they mean Yes, and drive a man out of his wits for the fun of it.
Louisa May Alcott (1832–88) US novelist.
Little Women, Pt II [1868]

6 When Venus said 'Spell no for me,'
'N-O' Dan Cupid wrote with glee,
And smiled at his success:
'Ah, child,' said Venus, laughing low,
'We women do not spell it so,
We spell it Y-E-S.'
Carolyn Wells (1869–1942) US writer and humorist.
'The Spelling Lesson' [c. 1920]

7 Women would rather be right than reasonable.
Ogden Nash (1902–71) US poet.
Frailty, Thy Name Is a Misnomer

8 I was seized by the stern hand of Compulsion, that dark, unseasonable Urge that impels women to clean house in the middle of the night.
James Thurber (1894–1961) US humorist.
Alarms and Diversions, 'There's a Time for Flags' [1957]

COSMETICS
See also APPEARANCE

1 I am too pretty to bother with an eyebrow pencil.
Spring hills paint themselves
With their own personality.
Chao Luan-luan (8th century) Chinese poet and courtesan.
'Willow Eyebrows' [8th century]

2 Beauty with all the Helps of Art, is of no long Date; the more it is help'd, the sooner it decays.
Mary Astell (c. 1666–1731) English pamphleteer.
Reflections Upon Marriage [1700]

3 Most women are not as young as they're painted.
Max Beerbohm (1872–1956) British writer.
A Defence of Cosmetics [1922]

4 I did not use paint. I made myself up morally.
Eleanora Duse (1859–1924) Italian actress.
Le Gaulois, 27 July 1922

5 The intoxication of rouge is an insidious vintage known to more girls than mere man can ever believe.
Dorothy Speare (1898–1951) US writer and scenarist.
Dancers in the Dark [1922]

6 The feminine vanity-case is the grave of masculine illusions.
Helen Rowland (1876–1950) US writer, journalist, and humorist.
'Personally Speaking', *The Book of Diversion* [1925]

7 Twentieth-century woman appears to regard sunlight as a kind of cosmetic effulgence with a light aphrodisiac content – which makes it a funny thing that none of her female ancestors are recorded as seeing it the same way. Men, of course, just go on sweating in it from century to century.
John Wyndham (1903–69) British science-fiction writer.
The Kraken Wakes [1953]

8 It is a sad woman who buys her own perfume.
Lena Jaeger
Remark, 1955

9 There are no ugly women, only lazy ones.
Helena Rubinstein (1882–1965) Polish-born US cosmetics manufacturer.
My Life for Beauty, Pt II, Ch. 1 [1965]

10 In the factory we make cosmetics. In the store we sell hope.
Charles Revson (1906–75) US business tycoon.
Fire and Ice (A. Tobias) [1975]

11 All the cosmetics names seemed obscenely obvious to me in their promises of sexual bliss. They were all firming or uplifting or invigorating. They made you *tingle*. Or *glow*. Or feel *young*.
Erica Jong (1942–) US poet and writer.
How to Save your Own Life [1977]

COURAGE

1 Nature gave me the form of a woman; my actions have raised me to the level of the most valiant of men.
Semiramis (8th century BC) Assyrian queen.
Women of Beauty and Heroism (Frank B. Goodrich) [8th century BC]

2 I have a woman's fears, but they cannot make me into a hypocrite or a slave.
Germaine de Staël (1766–1817) French novelist, literary critic, and feminist.
Letter to Charles de Lacretelle, c. May 1802

3 The back is fitted to the burden, they say; and I always *did* pray that if I had work to do, I might be able to do it; and I always was, somehow.
Susan Warner (1819–85) US writer.
What She Could, Ch. 3 [1870]

4 I am not belittling the brave pioneer men, but the sunbonnet as well as the sombrero has helped to settle this glorious land of ours.
Edna Ferber (1887–1968) US writer and scenarist.
Cimarron, Ch. 23 [1929]

5 We dip our colours in honour of you, dear women comrades, who march into battle together with the men.
Dolores Ibarruri (1895–   ) Spanish-born Russian revolutionary and editor.
Speeches and Articles, 1936–1938 [1938]

6 Women, wronged in one way or another, are given the overwhelming beauty of endurance, the capacity for high or low suffering, for violent feeling absorbed, finally tranquilized, for the radiance of humility, for silence, secrecy, impressive acceptance. Heroines are, then, heroic.
Elizabeth Hardwick (1916–   ) US writer, educator, drama and literary critic.
Seduction and Betrayal: Women in Literature [1974]

CURIE, Marie Sklodowska (1867–1934)

Polish chemist, who emigrated to France in 1891 and pioneered research into radioactivity. In 1895 she married Pierre Curie (1859–1906), a French physicist. In 1903 she shared the Nobel prize for physics with Pierre Curie and Henri Becquerel, for their work on radioactivity. Marie was also awarded the 1911 Nobel prize for chemistry for her discovery of polonium and radium. At the time the dangers of radiation were not appreciated and no precautions were taken – her notebooks are still too dangerous to handle. She died of radiation sickness.

Quotations about Marie Curie

1 Women cannot be part of the Institute of France.
Emile Hilaire Amagat (1841–1915) French physicist. Comment following the rejection of Marie Curie by the Académie des Sciences, for which she had been nominated in 1910. She was rejected by one vote, and refused to allow her name to be submitted again or, for ten years, to allow her work to be published by the Académie.

2 Marie Curie is, of all celebrated beings, the only one whom fame has not corrupted.
Albert Einstein (1879–1955) German-born US physicist. *Madame Curie* (Eve Curie)

3 That one must do some work seriously and must be independent and not merely amuse oneself in life – this our mother has told us always, but never that science was the only career worth following.
Irène Joliot-Curie (1897–1956) French scientist. Recalling the advice of her mother, Marie Curie. *A Long Way from Missouri* (Mary Margaret McBride), Ch. 10

Quotations by Marie Curie

4 After all, science is essentially international, and it is only through lack of the historical sense that national qualities have been attributed to it.
Memorandum, 'Intellectual Co-operation'

5 All my life through, the new sights of Nature made me rejoice like a child.
Pierre Curie

6 I have no dress except the one I wear every day. If you are going to be kind enough to give me one, please let it be practical and dark so that I can put it on afterwards to go to the laboratory.
Referring to a wedding dress. Letter to a friend, 1849

7 One never notices what has been done; one can only see what remains to be done.
Letter to her brother, 18 Mar 1894

DEATH

1 I envy aire because it dare
Still breathe, and he not so;
Hate earthe, that doth entomb his youth,
And who can blame my woe?
Anne Dacre Howard (1557–1630) English poet.
'Elegy on the Death of Her Husband' [1595]

2 The thought of death came and stayed with her and lent her a sort of drowsy cheer. It would be nice, nice and restful, to be dead.
Dorothy Parker (1893–1967) US writer, poet, and humorist.
Laments for the Living [1929]

3 I learned early to keep death in my line of sight, keep it under surveillance, keep it on cleared ground and away from any brush where it might coil unnoticed.
Joan Didion (1935–   ) US journalist and writer.
The Book of Common Prayer [1977]

DECEPTION

1 When Dogs fall on snarling, Serpents on hissing, and Women on weeping, the first meanes to bite, the second to sting, and the last to deceive.
R. M. (fl. 1630) English writer.
The Mothers Counsell or, Live within Compasse. Being the last Will and Testament to her dearest Daughter [1630]

2 For a priest to turn a man when he lies a-dying, is just like one that has a long time solicited a woman, and cannot obtain his end; at length makes her drunk, and so lies with her.
John Selden (1584–1654) English historian.
Table Talk [1689]

3 Mother is far too clever to understand anything she does not like.
Arnold Bennett (1867–1931) British novelist.
The Title [1918]

DEDICATION

See COMMITMENT

DELANEY, Shelagh (1939–)

British playwright. One of the group of 1950s dramatists who rejected the drawing-room dramas of Coward and Rattigan for 'kitchen sink' realism. Her first successful play was *Taste of Honey* (1958). Her other works include *The Lion in Love* (1961) and *The House That Jack Built* (1977).

1 I'm not frightened of the darkness outside. It's the darkness inside houses I don't like.
A Taste of Honey, I:1

2 Women never have young minds. They are born three thousand years old.
A Taste of Honey, I:1

3 In this country there are only two seasons winter and winter.
Referring to England. *A Taste of Honey*, I:2

4 Why don't you learn from my mistakes? It takes half your life to learn from your own.
A Taste of Honey, I:2

DESIRE

See LUST; SEX

DETERMINATION

1 I cannot and will not cut my conscience to fit this year's fashions, even though I long ago came to the conclusion that I was not a political person and could have no comfortable place in any political group.
Lillian Hellman (1906–) US playwright and writer.
Letter to the House Committee on Un-American Activities. *The Nation*, 31 May 1952

2 I've got a woman's ability to stick to a job and get on with it when everyone else walks off and leaves it.
Margaret Thatcher (1925–) British politician and prime minister (1979–90).
Observer, 'Sayings of the Week', 16 Feb 1975

3 I knew what I wanted and determined at an early age that no man would ever tell me what to do. I would make my own rules and down with the double standard.
Mae West (1892–1980) US actress, playwright, and scenarist.
Working Woman, Feb 1979

DICKINSON, Emily (1830–86)

US poet who has been called 'the New England mystic'. Daughter of a successful lawyer, she began writing verse around 1850; it was not, however, until 1860 that her experiments in both language and form began. She wrote over 1700 poems on themes of love, death, nature, and religion of which only seven were published in her lifetime. Posthumous collections include *Poems by Emily Dickinson* (1890), *The Single Hound: Poems of a Lifetime* (1914), and *Bolts of Melody: New Poems of Emily Dickinson* (1945).

Quotations about Dickinson

1 I saw her but twice, face to face, and brought away the impression of something as unique and remote as Undine or Mignon or Thekla.
Bookman, Oct 1924

2 In a life so retired it was inevitable that the main events should be the death of friends, and Emily Dickinson became a prolific writer of notes of condolence.
Northrop Frye (1912–83) Canadian critic. *Major Writers of America* (ed. Perry Miller)

Quotations by Dickinson

3 Because I could not stop for Death,
He kindly stopped for me;
The carriage held but just ourselves
And Immortality.
The Chariot

4 Parting is all we know of heaven,
And all we need of hell.
My Life Closed Twice Before its Close

5 Pain – has an Element of Blank –
It cannot recollect
When it begun – or if there were
A time when it was not –.
Pain

6 Success is counted sweetest
By those who ne'er succeed.
Success is Counted Sweetest

DISAPPOINTMENT

1 In education, in marriage, in religion, in everything, disappointment is the lot of women. It shall be the business of my life to deepen this disappointment in every woman's heart until she bows down to it no longer.
Lucy Stone (1818–93) US suffragette, abolitionist, editor, and lecturer.
Speech, 'Disappointment Is the Lot of Women', 17–18 Oct 1855

2 Ah, 'All things come to those who wait,'
(I say these words to make me glad),
But something answers soft and sad,
'They come, but often come too late.'
Violet Fane (1843–1905) British poet.
'Tout Vient á Qui Sait Attendre'

3 Like most men, my father is interested in action. And this is also why he disappoints my mother when she tells him she doesn't feel well and he offers to take her to the doctor. He is focused on what he can do, whereas she wants sympathy.
Deborah Tannen US writer and professor of linguistics.
You Just Don't Understand [1990]

DISCRIMINATION

See also PREJUDICE

1 There are already so many women in the world! Why then…was I born a woman, to be scorned by men in words and deeds?
Isotta Nogarola (1418–1466) Italian scholar and author.
Letter to Guarino Veronese [15th century]

2 Had I had a beard I would have been the King of France. I have been defrauded by that confounded Salic law.
Renée de France (1510–75) French patron of the arts.
This law prevented women from succeeding to the throne. *Women of the Reformation* (ed. Roland H. Bainton) [16th century]

3 The entire social order…is arrayed against a woman who wants to rise to a man's reputation.
Germaine de Staël (1766–1817) French novelist, literary critic, and feminist.
De la littérature considérée dans ses rapports avec les institutions sociales (*The Influence of Literature upon Society*) [1800]

4 Persecution for opinion, punishment for all manifestations of intellectual and moral strength, are still as common as women who have opinions and who manifest strength.
Harriet Martineau (1802–76) British writer, social critic, and feminist.
Society in America, 'Women', Vol. III [1837]

5 Man is a creature who lives not upon bread alone, but principally by catchwords; and the little rift between the sexes is astonishingly widened by simply teaching one set of catchwords to the girls and another to the boys.
Robert Louis Stevenson (1850–94) Scottish writer.
Virginibus Puerisque [1881]

6 Many women do not recognize themselves as discriminated against; no better proof could be found of the totality of their conditioning.
Kate Millett (1934–) US sculptor, writer, and feminist.
Sexual Politics [1969]

7 NORA. When a man can't explain a woman's actions, the first thing he thinks about is the condition of her uterus.
Clare Boothe Luce (1903–) US politician and writer.
Slam the Door Softly [1970]

8 When a man gives his opinion he's a man. When a woman gives her opinion she's a bitch.
Bette Davis (Ruth Elizabeth D.; 1908–89) US film star.
Attrib. [1989]

9 In the UK aid programme only one in six training places goes to Third World women, and in the category which includes agriculture ('renewable natural resources') only one in nine. Of the ODA's own British staff working in poor countries, only one in 18 are women, and of those working on renewable natural resources the figure is one in 60.
A critique of the UK government's response to the World Commission on Environment and Development. The ODA is the Overseas Development Administration. *Brutland in the Balance* [1989]

10 Most countries now have anti-discrimination laws…So what is holding back women? If they are not getting ahead is it maybe because they don't want to?
Perhaps. Centuries of being viewed as inferior to men has left women, collectively, with a pretty low self-image. After all oppression does not exist to encourage or propel its victims forward.
Vanessa Baird Journalist and coeditor of the New Internationalist Cooperative.
New Internationalist, Jan 1992

DIVORCE

1 Caesar's wife must be above suspicion.
Julius Caesar (100–44 BC) Roman general and statesman.
Said in justification of his divorce from Pompeia, after she was unwittingly involved in a scandal. *Lives*, 'Julius Caesar' (Plutarch) [c. 62 BC]

2 If any woman leaves (puts aside) her husband to whom she is legally married, let her be smothered in mire....If by chance a man wishes to put away his wife, and is able to prove one of these three crimes against her, that is, adultery, witchcraft, or violation of graves, let him have full right to put her away.
The Burgundian Code [16th century]

3 Should a husband be or become of so cold a nature as to be unable to have carnal relations with his wife of the sort proper between husband and wife, then the prelate grants perpetual divorce to the couple and the woman may remarry according to her will and pleasure.
Jean Boutillier (fl. 14th century) French jurist.
Referring to the divorce laws in France. *Somme Rurale* [14th century]

4 Nobody, I believe, defends the arrangement by which...divorce is obtainable only by the very rich. The barbarism of granting that as a privilege!
Harriet Martineau (1802–76) British writer, social critic, and feminist.
Society in America, 'Women', Vol. III [1837]

5 The wife's child was actually taken from her and given into the custody of the woman with whom the husband cohabited: the husband being then imprisoned for debt...in spite of the gross circumstances of the case, the courts decided against her.
Pearce Stevenson, Esq (Caroline Norton; 1808–77) British writer.
A Plain Letter to the Lord Chancellor on the Infant Custody Bill [1839]

6 It shall be lawful for any wife to present a petition to the said Court, praying that her marriage may be dissolved, on the ground that since the celebration thereof her husband has been guilty of incestuous adultery, or of bigamy with adultery, or of rape, or of sodomy or bestiality, or of adultery coupled with such cruelty as without adultery would have entitled her to a divorce *à mensâ et thoro*, or of adultery coupled with desertion, without reasonable excuse, for two years or upwards.
Statutes of the United Kingdom of Great Britain and Ireland [1857]

7 The Commons passed the second reading of the Matrimonial Causes Bill...The Bill will put the sexes on an equal footing by allowing a wife to petition for a husband's adultery.
The Daily Telegraph, 2 Mar 1923

8 So many persons think divorce a panacea for every ill, who find out, when they try it, that the remedy is worse than the disease.
Dorothy Dix (1861–1951) US journalist and columnist.
Dorothy Dix, Her Book, Ch. 13 [1926]

9 Where divorce is allowed at all...society demands a specific grievance of one party against the other...The fact that marriage may be a failure spiritually is seldom taken into account.
Suzanne Lafollette (b. 1893) US politician, feminist, writer, and editor.
Concerning Women [1926]

10 LITTLE MARY. You know, that's the only good thing about divorce; you get to sleep with your mother.
Clare Boothe Luce (1903–) US politician and writer.
The Women, I [1936]

11 Judges, as a class, display, in the matter of arranging alimony, that reckless generosity that is found only in men who are giving away somebody else's cash.
P. G. Wodehouse (1881–1975) British humorous novelist.
Louder and Funnier [1963]

12 If divorce has increased one thousand percent, don't blame the woman's movement. Blame our obsolete sex roles on which our marriages were based.
Betty Friedan (1921–) US writer.
Speech, 20 Jan 1974

DIX, Dorothea (1802–87)

US social reformer who brought public awareness to mental health. In 1821 she opened a school for girls in Boston, where she taught until 1935. However, her work for the mentally ill did not begin until 1941 when, after accepting an invitation to teach a Sunday school class in a Massachusetts jail, she was shocked to find mentally ill patients imprisoned with criminals of both sexes. Following a tour of Massachusetts institutions she submitted a report to the state legislature (1943), which resulted in some improvement. She instigated special hospitals for the mentally ill in over 15 states as well as in Canada.

Quotation about Dix
1 She studied language as the soldier guards his sword, to make it cut.
The Century Illustrated Monthly Magazine, Jan 1893

Quotations by Dix
2 The present state of insane persons, confined within this commonwealth, in cages, clos-

ets, cellars, stalls, pens! Chained, naked, beaten with rods, and lashed into obedience.
Memorial to the Legislature of Massachusetts

3   I am naturally timid and diffident, like all my sex.
Dictionary of American Biography

4   In a world where there is so much to be done, I felt strongly impressed that there must be something for me to do.
Letters from New York, Vol. II (ed. Lydia Maria Child)

5   I think even lying on my bed I can still do something.
Last words Attrib.

DIX, Dorothy (Elizabeth Merriwether Gilmer; 1861–1951)

US newspaper columnist and writer. Born in Mongomery County, she began her writing career in the 1890s, when she joined the *New Orleans Picayune*. She was given her own column 'Sunday Salad', which she devoted to articles on the problems arising in human relationships (particularly within the family). In 1901 she joined the *New York Journal*, in which her daily column 'Dorothy Dix Talks' appeared, until her retirement in 1949. Her books include *Hearts a la Mode* (1915), *Mirandy Exhorts* (1925), and *How to Win and Hold a Husband* (1939).

1   It is only the women whose eyes have been washed clear with tears who get the broad vision that makes them little sisters to all the world.
Dorothy Dix, Her Book, Introduction

2   I have learned to live each day as it comes, and not to borrow trouble by dreading tomorrow. It is the dark menace of the future that makes cowards of us.
Dorothy Dix, Her Book, Introduction

3   Now one of the great reasons why so many husbands and wives make shipwreck of their lives together is because a man is always seeking for happiness, while a woman is on a perpetual still hunt for trouble.
Dorothy Dix, Her Book, Ch. 1

4   The reason that husbands and wives do not understand each other is because they belong to different sexes.
Newspaper article

DOMINATION

1   Athens holds sway over all Greece; I dominate Athens; my wife dominates me; our newborn son dominates her.
Themistocles (c. 528–462 BC) Athenian statesman.
Explaining an earlier remark to the effect that his young son ruled all Greece. Attrib. [5th century BC]

2   Your wives are your field: go in, therefore, to your field as you will.
Koran
Ch. II [7th century]

3   In losing a husband one loses a master who is often an obstacle to the enjoyment of many things.
Madeleine de Scudéry (1607–1701) French novelist and poet.
Clelia, An Excellent New Romance, Vol. IV [1656–61]

4   She who ne'er answers till a husband cools,
Or, if she rules him, never shows the rules;
Charms by accepting, by submitting sways,
Yet has her humour most, when she obeys.
Alexander Pope (1688–1744) British poet.
'Epistle to a Lady'

5   The lust of dominion was probably the first effect of the fall; and as there was no other intelligent being over whom to exercise it, woman was the first victim of this unhallowed passion.
Sarah Moore Grimké (1792–1873) US abolitionist and women's rights pioneer.
Letters on the Equality of the Sexes, and the Condition of Woman [1838]

6   I have no wish for a second husband. I had enough of the first. I like to have my own way – to lie down mistress, and get up master.
Susanna Moodie (1803–85) Canadian writer and poet.
Roughing It in the Bush, Ch. 12 [1852]

7   The creation of a new woman of necessity demands the creation of a new man. The domination of women is at once the most complex and the most fundamental of links in the chain. Accordingly in moments of acute social unrest the question of our position leaps to the surface.
Sheila Rowbotham
Once a Feminist (Michelene Wandor) [1969]

8   It is…possible that the women of the old gynocracies brought on their own downfall by selecting the phallic wild men over the more civilized men of their own pacific and gentle world.
Elizabeth Gould Davis (1925–74) US librarian and writer.
The First Sex, Pt I, Ch. 5 [1971]

DRABBLE, Margaret (1939–)

British writer. Popular and skilful writer whose female characters explore the growth towards maturity through the experiences of love, marriage, and motherhood. Her books include *The Millstone* (1965), *The Needle's Eye* (1972), *The Middle Ground* (1980), *The Radiant Way* (1987), and *The Gates of Ivory* (1991). She also edited the 1985 edition of the *Oxford Companion to Literature*.

Quotation about Drabble

1 She is becoming the chronicler of contemporary Britain, the novelist people will turn to a hundred years from now to find out how things were, the person who will have done for the late 20th century London what Dickens did for Victorian London, what Balzac did for Paris.
Phyllis Rose *The New York Times Book Review*, Sept 1980

Quotations by Drabble

2 Sex isn't the most important thing in life, she decided, wriggling her body slightly to see if her movement would affect Anthony. It did: he stiffened slightly, but slept on. But if sex isn't the most important, what is?
The Ice Age, Part II

3 When nothing is sure, everything is possible.
The Middle Ground

4 Civilized woman can't do the right thing without paying too high a price.
The Middle Ground

5 Poverty, therefore, was comparative. One measured it by a sliding scale. One was always poor, in terms of those who were richer.
The Radiant Way

6 And there isn't any way that one can get rid of the guilt of having a nice body by saying that one can serve society with it, because that would end up with oneself as what? There simply doesn't seem to be any moral place for flesh.
A Summer Bird-Cage, Ch. 10

DRINKING

1 A fuddled woman is a shameful sight, a prey to anyone, and serve her right.
Ovid (Publius Ovidius Naso; 43 BC–17 AD) Roman poet.
Ars Amatoria [1 BC]

2 And Nature herself has made provision for our being safely granted a mild indulgence in any kind of food, for our sex is protected by greater sobriety. It is well known that women can be sustained on less nourishment and at less cost than men, and medicine teaches that they are not so easily intoxicated.
Heloise (c. 1100–c. 1163) French abbess.
The Letters of Abelard and Heloise [12th century]

3 Another cannot make fit to eat without wine or brandy. A third must have brandy on her apple dumplings, and a fourth comes out boldly and says she likes to drink once in a while herself too well…That lady must be a wretched cook indeed who cannot make apple dumplings, mince pie or cake palatable without the addition of poisonous substances.
Amelia Jenks Bloomer (1818–94) US temperance leader, reformer, and writer.
Water Bucket [1842]

4 No power on earth or above the bottomless pit has such influence to terrorize and make cowards of men as the liquor power. Satan could not have fallen on a more potent instrument with which to thrall the world. Alcohol is king!
Eliza Stewart (1816–1908) US temperance leader.
Memories of the Crusade, Ch. 1 [1888]

5 Gin was mother's milk to her.
George Bernard Shaw (1856–1950) Irish dramatist and critic.
Pygmalion, III [1912]

6 All along the line, physically, mentally, morally, alcohol is a weakening and deadening force, and it is worth a great deal to save women and girls from its influence.
Beatrice Potter Webb (1858–1943) British sociologist, reformer, writer, and historian.
Health of Working Girls, Ch. 10 [1917]

7 If instead of birth control every one would preach drink control, you would have little poverty, less crime, and fewer illegitimate children…I speak feelingly; for as my brother Harold John Tennant and I were the last of twelve children, it is more than probable we should never have existed had the fashion of birth control been prevalent in the eighties.
Margot Asquith (1865–1945) The second wife of Herbert Asquith.
Places and Persons [1925]

8 She commenced drinking alone, short drinks all through the day…It blurred sharp things for her. She lived in a haze of it. Her life took on a dream-like quality. Nothing was astonishing.
Dorothy Parker (1893–1967) US writer, poet, and humorist.
Laments for the Living [1929]

9 Alcohol was a threat to women, for it released men from the moral control they had

learned from a diet of preaching and scolding from ministers and mothers alike.
Alice Rossi (1922–) US educator, scholar, and editor.
The Feminist Papers, Pt II, Introduction [1973]

10 Mr Williams told the court he did not consider it ladylike for women to drink pints in his lounge and said if they wanted to drink like men they should go to the public bar or skittle alley.
Report on the case of Harold Williams, publican of the Maltsters Arms, Whitchurch. *The Times*, 1980

DU MAURIER, Daphne (1907–89)

British writer. Granddaughter of George du Maurier, the *Punch* artist, and daughter of Gerald du Maurier, an actor manager, she was born in London and educated in Paris. Her first novel, *The Loving Spirit*, was published in 1931, but her reputation was established with *Rebecca* (1938). She lived much of her life in Cornwall where many of her romances are set. Later works include *The Flight of the Falcon* (1965), *The House on the Strand* (1969), and *Rule, Britannia* (1972). She was made a Dame of the British Empire in 1969.

1 'The trouble is,' said Laura, 'walking in Venice becomes compulsive once you start. Just over the next bridge, you say, and then the next one beckons.'
Don't Look Now

2 She could not separate success from peace of mind. The two must go together; her observation pointed to this truth. Failure meant poverty, poverty meant squalor, squalor led, in the final stages, to the smells and stagnation of Bowling Inn Alley.
Mary Anne, Pt I, Ch. 10

3 One second's hesitation. Tears, or laughter? Tears would be an admission of guilt, so laughter was best.
Mary Anne, Pt II, Ch. 7

4 Last night I went to Manderley again.
Rebecca, Ch. I

5 We can never go back again, that much is certain. The past is still too close to us. The things we have tried to forget and put behind us would stir again, and that sense of fear, of furtive unrest…might in some manner unforeseen become a living companion, as it had been before.
Rebecca, Ch. 2

DUNCAN, Isadora (1878–1927)

US dancer. A highly innovative dancer, she gained as much fame for her lifestyle as for her dancing. As a child she rejected the rigidity of classic ballet training and developed a new technique of natural rhythms and movements. As her first public appearances in America were unsuccessful, at the age of 21 she booked herself a passage on a cattle boat to England. Here, through the patronage of Mrs Patrick Campbell, she was invited to perform at private receptions and parties. In 1905 she visited Russia, where she caught the attention of the ballet impresario Sergei Diaghilev, who was deeply influenced by her revolutionary dancing.
Her private life was renowned for her defiance of traditional values; publicly rejecting marriage, she lived openly with both Gordon Craig, a stage designer, and Paris Singer, a prominent patron of the arts, having a child by each. Both children died in 1913 in an accident in which the car in which they were travelling rolled out of control into the Seine. She never fully recovered from this tragedy. After an unhappy marriage to the poet, Sergei Yesenin, who was 17 years her junior, and a disastrous tour of America in 1922, she abandoned America and settled in Nice, where she met her death by strangulation when her scarf became entangled in a wheel of the car in which she was travelling.

Quotations about Duncan

1 As a dancer she was probably one of the greatest who ever lived. Nor was she any less great as a woman – a wild, impetuous and extravagant creature of whims and what is called 'artistic temperament'.
John o' London's Weekly, 5 Oct 1929

2 Isadora Duncan probably represents the maximum possible development of emotion at the expense of intellect. She was a creature of impulse, and the impulses were usually bad ones. She drank champagne as a thirsty horse drinks water.
John o' London's Weekly, 15 Feb 1933

Quotations by Duncan

3 I have discovered the dance. I have discovered the art which has been lost for two thousand years.
My Life

4 I believe, as a wage-earning woman, that if I make the great sacrifice of strength and health and even risk my life, to have a child, I should certainly not do so if, on some future occasion, the man can say that the child belongs to him by law and he will take it from me and I shall see it only three times a year!
My Life

5 Any intelligent woman who reads the marriage contract, and then goes into it, deserves all the consequences.
My Life

6 So that ends my first experience with matrimony, which I always thought a highly overrated performance.
The New York Times, 1923

7 People do not live nowadays – they get about ten percent out of life.
This Quarter Autumn, 'Memoirs'

DU PRÉ, Jacqueline (1945–87)
British cellist, who began her career as a soloist with a recital at the Wigmore Hall at the age of 16. In 1965 she toured America with the BBC Symphony Orchestra, making an international reputation for herself, particularly with the Elgar cello concerto. In 1967 she converted to Judaism in order to marry the Israeli pianist and conductor Daniel Barenboim, with whom she gave many recitals. Her career was cut short by multiple sclerosis in 1973. However, although confined to a wheelchair, she continued to teach and gave a series of masterclasses.

Quotations about du Pré
1 Jacqueline was born to play the cello. She thoroughly understands its genius, and so instinctive is her reaction to the music that one feels the subtlest ideas of the composer to be embraced.
Reviewing Jacqueline du Pré's debut. Percy Cater *Daily Mail*, 1981

2 There was a very strong feeling of goodness about Jackie. Her whole inner nature shone through whatever she did…So people might have thought she was just a smiley laughing girl who played the cello. Later, the things she said about her illness showed there was far more to her than that.
Anthea Goehr *Jacqueline du Pré* (William Wordsworth)

Quotations by du Pré
3 But after all, I'm a woman. A woman can't play as a man plays. She hasn't the physique and energy. A woman's hand is a limitation in itself.
The New York Times, 26 Feb 1967

4 I love to walk. I love the rain and all the things Danny can't stand. It's boring to be too much in the sun.
Referring to her husband, Daniel Barenboim.
Nova, 1968

DUTY
See also WOMAN'S ROLE

1 It is the highest and eternal duty of women – namely, to sacrifice their lives and to seek the good of their husbands.
Adi Parva
Hindu text. *Mahabharata* [c. 400 BC–200 AD]

2 Sisters should be always willing to attend their brothers, and consider it a privilege to be their companions…Consider the loss of a ball or a party, for the sake of making the evening pass pleasantly for your brothers at home, as a small sacrifice.
Mrs John Farrar
The Young Lady's Friend [1847]

3 She's the sort of woman who lives for others – you can always tell the others by their hunted expression.
C. S. Lewis (1898–1963) British academic and writer.
The Screwtape Letters [1942]

4 The fact of the matter is that the prime responsibility of a woman probably is to be on earth long enough to find the best mate possible for herself, and conceive children who will improve the species.
Norman Mailer (1923–) US writer.
The Presidential Papers [1963]

5 Like their personal lives, women's history is fragmented, interrupted; a shadow history of human beings whose existence has been shaped by the efforts and demands of others.
Elizabeth Janeway (1913–) US writer.
Women: Their Changing Roles, 'Reflections on the History of Women' [1973]

EARHART, Amelia (1898–1937)
US aviator. Born in Kansas she worked for the Canadian Red Cross during World War I and, after the war, as a social worker in Boston. In June 1928 she became a celebrity as the first woman passenger to fly across the Atlantic. In 1932 she made a solo flight across the Atlantic and later that year was the first woman to fly solo nonstop across the USA, taking off from Los Angeles and landing in Newark, New Jersey, 19 hrs and 4 mins later. Her achievements enabled her to take an active part in opening up flying to women.
On 1 June 1937 Amelia Earhart left Miami, Florida, accompanied by navigator Fred Noonan, on the first stage of a round-the-world flight. After completing over two thirds of the distance her plane vanished without trace in the central Pacific.

1 Courage is the price that Life exacts for granting peace.
Courage

2 There are two kinds of stones, as everyone knows, one of which rolls.
20 Hours: 40 Minutes – Our Flight in the Friendship, Ch. 1

3 In soloing – as in other activities – it is far easier to start something than it is to finish it.
20 Hours: 40 Minutes – Our Flight in the Friendship, Ch. 2

4 Of course I realized there was a measure of danger. Obviously I faced the possibility of not returning when first I considered going. Once faced and settled there really wasn't any good reason to refer to it.
Referring to her flight in the 'Friendship'. *20 Hours: 40 Minutes – Our Flight in the Friendship*, Ch. 5

EDDY, Mary Baker (1821–1910)

US theologian. Born at Bow, New Hampshire, and brought up a Congregationalist she suffered for most of her life from a spinal problem, which led to her preoccupation with questions of health. After achieving some success with homeopathy and faith healing, she had a severe fall, from the effects of which she believed she would never recover. However she was treated later that year after reading the New Testament and marked this as the point of her discovery of Christian Science. She spent the following years developing her system and teaching it to others.
The First Church of Christ, Scientist, was founded in Boston in 1879, followed, in 1881, by the Massachusetts Metaphysical College. The doctrine is explained in *Science and Health with Key to the Scriptures* (1875); other works include *Retrospection and Introspection* (1892) and *Rudimental Divine Science* (1908).

Quotations about Eddy

1 I hail with joy your voice speaking an assured word for God and Immortality, and my joy is heightened that these words are of woman's devisings.
Amos Bronson Alcott *Address to Mary Baker Eddy*

2 You can no more separate Mrs. Eddy from Science and Health than you can Moses from the Commandments, or Jesus from the Sermon on the Mount.
Anonymous *We Knew Mary Baker Eddy*

Quotations by Eddy

3 Christian Science explains all cause and effect as mental, not physical.
Science and Health, with Key to the Scriptures

4 Sin brought death, and death will disappear with the disappearance of sin.
Science and Health, with Key to the Scriptures

5 Sickness, sin and death, being inharmonious, do not originate in God, nor belong to His government.
Science and Health, with Key to the Scriptures

EDUCATION

See also INTELLECT; INTELLECTUALS; INTELLIGENCE

1 I hate a learned woman.
Euripides (c. 480–406 BC) Greek dramatist.
Hippolytus [428 BC]

2 The girls must be trained in precisely the same way, and I'd like to make this proposal without any reservations whatever about horseriding or athletics being suitable activities for males but not for females.
Plato (429–347 BC)
Laws, VII [4th century BC]

3 A man who teaches women letters feeds more poison to a frightful asp.
Menander (c. 341–c. 290 BC) Greek dramatist.
Fragments [3rd century BC]

4 If you have a female child, set her to sewing and not to reading, for it is not suitable for a female to know how to read unless she is going to be a nun.
Paolo da Certaldo (c. 1300–70)
Libro di buoni costumi [14th century]

5 My daughters, your brother has brought you my summary of Logic in French...I am letting you have it on condition that you make use of it only for yourselves and not against your companions or superiors, as it is dangerous for women to use such things against their husbands...I do not blame your eagerness to learn with your brothers, but I would be loath either to discourage or encourage you.
Agrippa d'Aubigné (1552–1630) French writer and historian.
Letter to his daughters [16th century]

6 Learned ladies are not to my taste.
Molière (Jean Baptiste Poquelin; 1622–73) French dramatist.
Les Femmes savantes [1672]

7 Merely to teach gentlewomen to frisk and dance, to paint their faces, to curl their hair, to put on a whisk, to wear gay clothes, is not truly to adorn, but to adulterate their bodies; yea (what is worse) to defile their souls.
Bathsua Makin (c. 1612–c. 1674) English scholar and writer.
A whisk is a woman's scarf, worn around the neck. *An Essay to Revive the Ancient Education of Gentlewomen* [1673]

8 Objection: Women do not desire learning. Answer: Neither do many boys…yet I suppose you do not intend to lay fallow all children that will not bring forth fruit of themselves.
Bathsua Makin (c. 1612–c. 1674) English scholar and writer.
An Essay to Revive the Ancient Education of Gentlewomen [1673]

9 One tongue is sufficient for a woman.
John Milton (1608–74) English poet.
On being asked whether he would allow his daughters to learn foreign languages. Attrib. [1674]

10 Teach your daughters to read and write correctly. It is disgraceful but common to see women of wit and good manners unable to pronounce what they read.
François Fénelon (1651–1715) French writer and prelate.
Traité de léducation des filles [1683]

11 The other sex, by means of a more expensive education to the knowledge of Greek and Roman languages, have a vaster field for their imaginations to rove in, and their capacities thereby enlarged.
Aphra Behn (1640–89) English novelist, dramatist, poet, translator, and spy.
'Essay in Defense of the Female Sex' [1696]

12 As if a woman of education bought things because she wanted 'em.
John Vanbrugh (1664–1726) English architect and dramatist.
The Confederacy, II:1 [1705]

13 The whole education of women should be relative to man. To be pleasing in his sight, to win his respect and love, to be useful to him, to make themselves loved and honoured by him, to train him in childhood, to tend him in manhood, to counsel and console, to make his life pleasant and happy, these are the duties of woman for all time, and this is what she should be taught from her infancy. Woman was made to yield to man and put up with his injustice.
Jean Jacques Rousseau (1712–78) French philosopher.
Émile [1762]

14 Can anything be more absurd than keeping women in a state of ignorance, and yet so vehemently to insist on their resisting temptation?
Vicesimus Knox (1752–1821) British essayist.
Liberal Education, Vol. I, 'On the Literary Education of Women' [1778]

15 Will it be said that the judgment of a male two years old, is more sage than that of a female's of the same age? I believe the reverse is generally observed to be true. But from that period what partiality! how is the one exalted and the other depressed, by the contrary modes of education which are adopted! the one is taught to aspire, and the other is early confined and limited.
Judith Sargent Murray (1751–1820) US writer.
The Massachusetts Magazine, 'On the Equality of the Sexes', Mar and Apr 1790

16 And if it be granted that woman was not created merely to gratify the appetite of man, or to be the upper servant, who provides his meals and takes care of his linen, it must follow that the first care of those mothers or fathers who really attend to the education of females should be…not to destroy the constitution by mistaken notions of beauty and female excellence.
Mary Wollstonecraft (1759–97) British writer.
A Vindication of the Rights of Woman, Ch. 2 [1792]

17 Necessity never makes prostitution the business of men's lives; though numberless are the women who are thus rendered systematically vicious. This, however, arises, in a great degree from the state of idleness in which women are educated, who are always taught to look up to man for a maintenance, and to consider their persons as the proper return for his exertions to support them.
Mary Wollstonecraft (1759–97) British writer.
A Vindication of the Rights of Woman, Ch. 3 [1792]

18 The sum and substance of female education in America, as in England, is training women to consider marriage as the sole object in life, and to pretend that they do not think so.
Harriet Martineau (1802–76) British writer, social critic, and feminist.
'Women', *Society in America*, Vol. III [1837]

19 I wish you had not sent me Jane Eyre. It interested me so much that I have lost (or won if you like) a whole day in reading it at the busiest period, with the printers I know waiting for copy. Who the author can be I can't guess – if a woman she knows her language better than most ladies do, or has had a 'classical' education.
W. M. Thackeray (1811–63) British novelist.
Referring to Charlotte Brontë. Letter to W. S. Williams, 23 Oct 1847

20 A learned girl is one of the most intolerable monsters of creation.
Saturday Review, 1870

21 Women must withdraw themselves from the influence of the Church and, with a new culture, make themselves fit to work at forming free citizens. Elementary education for girls must therefore be obligatory, in the hands of the laity, and identical to that of boys.
A. Angiulli
La Pedagogia, lo Stato e la Famiglia [1876]

22 In regard to the possible effect on health and physical vigour of women students, it was feared that the opening of new facilities for study and intellectual improvement would result in the creation of a new race of puny, sedentary and unfeminine students, and would destroy the grace and charm of social life, and would disqualify women for their true vocation, the nurture of the coming race and the governance of well-ordered, healthy and happy homes.
Joshua Fitch (1824–1903) British educational writer.
'Women in the Universities', *Contemporary Review*, 1890

23 Now, what is the aim in the training of girls? To make them as perfect *women* as possible; not as perfect human beings as possible, but as perfect women. The idea of sex is never lost sight of, a method of education which would be positively dangerous in the case of boys, and which is only saved from the full consequences of its foolishness by the better moral nature and less strongly developed animal passions of girls.
Harriet E. Mahood
The Modesty of Englishwomen [1901]

24 The cost of activity, and especially of cerebral activity, which is very costly, has to be met…The reproductive capacity is diminished in various degrees – sometimes to the extent of inability to bear children, more frequently to the extent of inability to yield milk, and in numerous cases to a smaller extent which I must leave unspecified.
Herbert Spencer
The Principles of Ethics [1904]

25 It will be found that there are womanly concerns, of profound importance to a girl and therefore to an empire, which demand no less of the highest mental and moral qualities than any of the subjects in a man's curriculum, and the pursuit of which in reason does not compromise womanhood, but only ratifies and empowers it.
C. W. Saleeby
Woman and Womanhood [1912]

26 The natural vocation for every woman is that of wife and mother, and in the training of every girl provision should be made for the acquisition of definite and accurate knowledge of the essentials of domestic economy and mothercraft.
Mary Scharlieb (1845–1930) British gynaecological surgeon.
The Seven Ages of Woman [1915]

27 If you educate a man you educate a person, but if you educate a woman you educate a family.
Ruby Manikan (20th century) Indian Church leader.
Observer, 'Sayings of the Week', 30 Mar 1947

28 The dream of college apparently serves as a substitute for more direct preoccupation with marriage: girls who do not plan to go to college are more explicit in their desire to marry, and have a more developed sense of their own sex role.
Elizabeth Douvan (1926–) US psychologist.
The American College, 'Motivational Factors in College Entrance' (with Carol Kaye) [1960s]

29 To me education is a leading out of what is already there in the pupil's soul. To Miss Mackay it is a putting in of something that is not there, and that is not what I call education, I call it intrusion.
Muriel Spark (1918–) British novelist.
The Prime of Miss Jean Brodie, Ch. 2 [1961]

30 A society in which women are taught anything at all but the management of a family, the care of men and the creation of the future generation is a society which is on the way out.
L. Ron Hubbard (1911–86) US founder of the Church of Scientology.
Questions for Our Time [1980]

ELIOT, George (Mary Ann Evans; 1819–80)

British writer. Daughter of Robert Evans, an agent for the Arbury Hall estate in Warwickshire, she became one of the leading Victorian novelists. Her major works include *Adam Bede* (1859), *The Mill on the Floss* (1860), *Silas Marner* (1861), *Middlemarch* (1871–72), and *Daniel Deronda* (1876). Her early life was strongly influenced by the Evangelical movement but, following her friendship with Charles and Caroline Bray, both freethinkers, she broke with orthodox religion. From 1851 to 1854 she was assistant editor of *The Westminster*, during which time she met George Henry Lewes, a married man who, under 19th-century law, was unable to divorce his wife. George Eliot began living with Lewes in 1854 and, in spite of a period of social ostracism, their partnership continued happily until his death in 1878. In May 1880 she married John Walter Cross, a banker who had been her financial adviser. She died seven months later and was buried at Highgate cemetery.

Quotations about Eliot

1 I found out in the first two pages that it was a woman's writing – she supposed that in making a door, you last of all put in the *panels*!
Referring to *Adam Bede*. Thomas Carlyle (1795–1881) Scottish historian and essayist. *George Eliot* (G. H. Haight)

2 I never saw such a woman. There is nothing a bit masculine about her; she is thoroughly feminine and looks and acts as if she were made for nothing but to mother babies. But she has a power of *stating* an argument equal to any man; equal to any man do I say? I have never seen any man, except Herbert Spencer, who could state a case equal to her.
John Fiske (1842–1901) US historian. Letter to his wife, 1873

Quotations by Eliot

3 It's but little good you'll do a-watering the last year's crop.
Adam Bede

4 He was like a cock who thought the sun had risen to hear him crow.
Adam Bede

5 A different taste in jokes is a great strain on the affections.
Daniel Deronda

6 I should like to know what is the proper function of women, if it is not to make reasons for husbands to stay at home, and still stronger reasons for bachelors to go out.
The Mill on the Floss, Ch. 6

7 Women who are content with light and easily broken ties do *not* act as I have done. They obtain what they desire and are still invited to dinner.
Referring to her life with George Lewes. *The New Encyclopedia Britannica*

ELIZABETH I (1533–1603)
Queen of England and Ireland (1558–1603). Elizabeth was the daughter of Henry VIII and his second wife Anne Boleyn. Her early years were troubled – she was declared illegitimate in 1536 after the execution of her mother and was imprisoned in 1554 during the reign of her Catholic half-sister Mary I. After Mary's death she succeeded to the throne and established a Protestant establishment, despite continuous difficulties from Catholic factions. Her cousin, Mary Queen of Scots, complicated the situation by plotting with Catholic dissidents, for which she was imprisoned for 18 years. Elizabeth finally agreed to her execution in 1587. Elizabeth's excommunication in 1570 marked the beginning of greater Catholic resistance to her rule, leading to the attempted invasion by the Spanish

and the defeat of the Spanish Armada (1588), which established both her own position and that of Protestantism in England. She is generally regarded as one of the greatest English monarchs, whose reign brought an increase in stability at home and in influence overseas. She never married – hence her nickname 'the Virgin Queen' – although there was speculation about her relationship with some courtiers. Possibly her 'virginity' was a political decision to preserve her independence.

Quotations about Elizabeth I

1 The queen did fish for men's souls, and had so sweet a bait that no one could escape her network.
Christopher Hatton. Attrib.

2 ...her face oblong, fair but wrinkled; her eyes small, yet black and pleasant; her nose a little hooked, her lips narrow and her teeth black (a defect the English seem subject to from their too great use of sugar)...She wore false hair and that red.
Paul Hentzner (fl. 1590s) German tutor. *Journey into England*

3 As just and merciful as Nero and as good a Christian as Mahomet.
John Wesley (1703–91) British religious leader. *Journal*, 29 Apr 1768

Quotations by Elizabeth I

4 Though God hath raised me high, yet this I count the glory of my crown: that I have reigned with your loves.
The Golden Speech, 1601

5 God may pardon you, but I never can.
To the Countess of Nottingham. *History of England under the House of Tudor* (Hume), Vol. II, Ch. 7

6 Good-morning, gentlemen both.
When addressing a group of eighteen tailors. *Sayings of Queen Elizabeth* (Chamberlin)

7 I will make you shorter by a head.
Sayings of Queen Elizabeth (Chamberlin)

8 I am your anointed Queen. I will never be by violence constrained to do anything. I thank God that I am endued with such qualities that if I were turned out of the Realm in my petticoat I were able to live in any place in Christome.
Sayings of Queen Elizabeth (Chamberlin)

9 To me it shall be a full satisfaction both for the memorial of my name, and for the glory also, if when I shall let my last breath, it be engraven upon my marble tomb, 'Here lieth Elizabeth, who reigned a virgin and died a virgin'.
Reply to a petition from the House of Commons, 6 Feb 1559

10 As for me, I see no such great cause why I should either be fond to live or fear to die. I have had good experience of this world, and I know what it is to be a subject and what to be a sovereign. Good neighbours I have had, and I have met with bad: and in trust I have found treason.
Speech to Parliament, 1586

11 I know I have the body of a weak and feeble woman, but I have the heart and stomach of a King, and of a King of England too.
Speech at Tilbury on the approach of the Spanish Armada

12 Of myself I must say this, I never was any greedy, scraping grasper, nor a strait fast-holding prince, nor yet a waster; my heart was never set on wordly goods, but only for my subjects' good.
Speech to a deputation from the House of Commons (the Golden Speech), 30 Nov 1601

13 Must! Is *must* a word to be addressed to princes? Little man, little man! thy father, if he had been alive, durst not have used that word.
Said to Robert Cecil, on her death bed. *A Short History of the English People* (J. R. Green), Ch. 7

EMANCIPATION

See also EQUALITY; FREEDOM; SUFFRAGETTES; WOMEN'S LIBERATION MOVEMENT

1 I thought a woman was a free agent, as well as a man, and was born free, and could she manage herself suitably, might enjoy that liberty to as much purpose as the men do; that the laws of matrimony were indeed otherwise...and those such that a woman gave herself entirely away from herself, in marriage, and capitulated only to be, at best, but an upper servant.
Daniel Defoe (1660–1731) British journalist and writer.
Roxana [1724]

2 The most important thing women have to do is to stir up the zeal of women themselves.
John Stuart Mill (1806–73) British philosopher.
Letter to Alexander Bain, 14 July 1869

3 The Queen is most anxious to enlist every one who can speak or write to join in checking this mad, wicked folly of 'Woman's Rights', with all its attendant horrors, on which her poor feeble sex is bent, forgetting every sense of womanly feeling and propriety.
Victoria (1819–1901) Queen of the United Kingdom.
Letter to Sir Theodore Martin, 29 May 1870

4 The prolonged slavery of women is the darkest page in human history.
Elizabeth Stanton (1815–1902) US suffragette.
History of Woman Suffrage, Vol. I (with Susan B. Anthony and Mathilda Gage) [1880]

5 The Bible and Church have been the greatest stumbling block in the way of woman's emancipation.
Elizabeth Cady Stanton (1815–1902) US suffragette and abolitionist.
Free Thought Magazine, Sept 1896

6 The emancipation of women is practically the greatest egoistic movement of the nineteenth century, and the most intense affirmation of the right of the self that history has yet seen.
Ellen Key (Karolina Sofia Key; 1849–1926) Swedish writer.
The Century of the Child, Ch. 2 [1909]

7 Merely external emancipation has made of the modern woman an artificial being...Now, woman is confronted with the necessity of emancipating herself from emancipation, if she really desires to be free.
Emma Goldman (1869–1940) Russian-born US anarchist, political agitator and organizer, lecturer, and editor.
'The Tragedy of Women's Emancipation', *Anarchism and Other Essays* [1911]

8 It is the effeminate man – when it is not the prejudiced and jealous male – who dislikes woman and fears her emancipation. It is the abnormal woman whose conception of the movement after freedom is one of antagonism to the 'stronger sex'...A vast amount of energy is wasted in futile argument as to the relative superiority of men and women.
Elizabeth Chesser
Woman, Marriage and Motherhood [1913]

9 Time and trouble will tame an advanced young woman, but an advanced old woman is uncontrollable by any earthly force.
Dorothy L. Sayers (1893–1957) British writer.
Clouds of Witness, Ch. 16 [1956]

10 By the time I grew up, the fight for the emancipation of woman, their rights under the law, in the office, in bed, was stale stuff.
Lillian Hellman (1906–   ) US playwright and writer.
An Unfinished Woman [1969]

EMOTION

1 I was, and I still am convinced that women, being the victims of all social institutions, are destined to misery if they make the least concession to their feelings and if, in any way whatever, they lose control of themselves.
Germaine de Staël (1766–1817) French novelist, literary critic, and feminist.
Delphine, Preface [1802]

2 The old chestnut about women being more emotional than men has been forever destroyed by the evidence of the two world wars. Women under blockade, bombardment, concentration-camp conditions survive them vastly more successfully than men. The psychiatric casualties of populations under such conditions are *mostly* masculine.
Ashley Montagu
'The Natural Superiority of Women' [1957]

3 Hysteria is a natural phenomenon, the common denominator of the female nature. It's the big female weapon, and the test of a man is his ability to cope with it.
Tennessee Williams (1911–83) US dramatist.
The Night of the Iguana [1961]

4 Women are emotional and an emotional approach is the best approach...Reiterate that the prime function in life is to reproduce; that is what God placed her on earth for.
Training booklet used by the Royal Canadian Mounted Police (The Mounties), 1975

EMPLOYMENT
See OCCUPATIONS; WORK

EPITAPHS

1 Here lies my wife; here let her lie!
Now she's at rest, and so am I.
John Dryden (1631–1700) British poet and dramatist.
Epitaph Intended for Dryden's Wife [c. 1680]

2 Here lies my wife,
Here lies she;
Hallelujah!
Hallelujee!
Epitaph, Leeds churchyard [c. 1800]

3 And when I lie in the green kirkyard,
With mould upon my breast,
Say not that she did well – or ill,
Only 'she did her best'.
Dinah Mulock Craik (1826–87) British writer and poet.
Obituary [1887]

4 She sleeps alone at last.
Robert Benchley (1889–1945) US humorist.
Suggested epitaph for an actress. Attrib. [1945]

5 When I die, my epitaph should read: *She Paid the Bills.* That's the story of my private life.
Gloria Swanson (1899–1983) US actress.
Saturday Evening Post, 22 July 1950

6 Excuse my dust.
Dorothy Parker (1893–1967) US writer, poet, and humorist.
'Epitaph'

7 Goodbye Norma Jean
Though I never knew you at all
You had the grace to hold yourself
While those around you crawled.
They crawled out of the woodwork
And they whispered into your brain
Set you on the treadmill
And made you change your name.
Bernie Taupin (1950–) British songwriter.
Lyrics for a song by Elton John; referring to Marilyn Monroe. *Candle in the Wind* [1973]

EQUALITY

1 By the enactment of a single...law...Romulus brought the women to great prudence and orderly conduct...The law was as follows: A woman united with her husband by a sacred marriage shall share in all his possession and in his sacred rites.
A sacred marriage (confarreatio) was exclusively for patricians. Laws attributed to Romulus [753–716 BC]

2 Are you asking why I don't want to take a rich wife? I don't want a husband for a wife. Let the matron, Priscus, stay beneath the husband: otherwise woman and man can't be equals.
Martial (Marcus Valerius Martialis; c. 38–103 AD) Roman poet.
Epigram, VIII [1st century AD]

3 Woman does not have a soul of a different sex from that which animates man. Both received a soul which is absolutely the same and of an equal condition. Women and men were equally endowed with the gifts of spirit, reason, and the use of words; they were created for the same end, and the sexual difference between them will not confer a different destiny.
Cornelius Heinrich Agrippa (c. 1486–1535) German physician and philosopher.
On the Nobility and Excellence of Women [1529]

4 The let us have our Liberty again,
And challenge to your selves no Sovereignty;
You came not in the world without our pain,
Make that a bar against your cruelty;
Your fault being greater, why should you disdain
Our being your equals, free from tyranny?
Emilia Lanier (c. 1569–c. 1640) English poet.
Salve Deus Rex Judeorum, 'Eve's Apology' [1611]

5 Think me all man: my soul is masculine,
And capable of as great things as thine.
Joan Philips (fl. 1679–82) English poet.
Female Poems on Several Occasions, 'To Phylocles, Inviting Him to Friendship' [1679]

6 The wise Author of nature has endowed the female mind with equal powers and faculties,

and given them the same right of judging and acting for themselves, as he gave to the male sex.
Hannah Mather Crocker (1752–1829) US writer.
Observations on the Real Rights of Women [1818]

7 Is it to be understood that the principles of the Declaration of Independence bear no relation to half of the human race?
Harriet Martineau (1802–76) British writer.
Society in America, Vol. III, 'Marriage' [1837]

8 The more women become rational companions, partners in business and in thoughts, as well as in affection and amusement, the more highly will men appreciate *home* – that blessed work, which opens to the human heart the most perfect glimpse of Heaven, and helps to carry it thither, as on an angel's wings.
Lydia M. Child (1802–80) US abolitionist, writer, and editor.
Letters from New York, Vol. I, Jan 1843

9 Men their rights and nothing more; women their rights and nothing less.
Susan B. Anthony (1820–1906) US editor.
The Revolution, Motto [1868]

10 The higher the animal or plant in the scale of being, the more slowly does it reach its utmost capacity of development. Girls are physically and mentally more precocious than boys. The human female arrives sooner than the male at maturity, and furnishes one of the strongest arguments against the alleged equality of the sexes.
J. M. Allan
Journal of the Anthropological Society, 'On the Differences in the Minds of Men and Women' [1869]

11 *Declaration of Sentiments*:…We hold these truths to be self-evident: that all men and women are created equal.
Elizabeth Stanton (1815–1902) US suffragette.
History of Woman Suffrage, Vol. I (with Susan B. Anthony and Mathilda Gage) [1880]

12 Above the titles of wife and mother, which, although dear, are transitory and accidental, there is the title human being, which precedes and out-ranks every other.
Mary Livermore (c. 1820–1905) US social reformer, lecturer, and writer.
What Shall We Do with Our Daughters?, Ch. 7 [1883]

13 There never will be complete equality until women themselves help to make laws and elect lawmakers.
Susan B. Anthony (1820–1906) US editor.
The Arena, 'The Status of Women, Past, Present and Future', May 1897

14 Humanity is like a bird with its two wings – the one is male, the other female. Unless both wings are strong and impelled by some common force, the bird cannot fly heavenwards. According to the spirit of this age, women must advance and fulfill their mission in all departments of life, becoming equal to men. They must be on the same level as men and enjoy equal rights.
'Abdu'l-Bahá (1844–1921) Persian leader of the Baha'i faith.
Speech, Women's Freedom League, London, Jan 1913

15 Just as the difference in height between males is no longer a realistic issue, now that lawsuits have been substituted for hand-to-hand encounters, so the difference in strength between men and women is no longer worth elaboration in cultural institutions.
Margaret Mead (1901–78) US anthropologist, writer, editor, and museum curator.
Sex and Temperament in Three Primitive Societies [1935]

16 Women have always been the guardians of wisdom and humanity which makes them natural, but usually secret, rulers. The time has come for them to rule openly, but together with and not against men.
Charlotte Wolff (1904–86) German-born British writer.
Bisexuality: a Study, Ch. 2 [1960]

17 But we are all creatures in a way, aren't we? And both men and women are wretched.
Alice Neel (1908–) US painter.
Ms, Oct 1973

18 Our time has come. We will no longer content ourselves with leavings and bits and pieces of the rights enjoyed by men…we want our equal rights, nothing more but nothing less. We want an equal share of political and economic power.
Bella Abzug (1920–) US lawyer and congresswoman.
Gullible's Travels (Jill Johnston) [1974]

19 Equality, Child, like freedom, exists only where you are now. Only as an egg in the womb are we all equal.
Oriana Fallaci (1930–) Italian writer.
Letter to a Child Never Born [1975]

20 I do, and I also wash and iron them.
Denis Thatcher (1915–) British businessman married to Margaret Thatcher.
Replying to the question 'Who wears the pants in this house?' *The Los Angeles Times*, 21 Apr 1981

21 The battle for women's rights has been largely won.
Margaret Thatcher (1925–) British politician and prime minister (1979–90).
Guardian, 1982

22 I'm not a believer in equality and my attitude is that women are supposed to be pretty and nice. A woman should be a woman.
Jim Davidson (1954–) British comedian.
Remark, 1986

23 A man is designed to walk three miles in the rain to phone for help when the car breaks down – and a woman is designed to say, 'You took your time' when he comes back dripping wet.
Victoria Wood (1953–) British writer and comedian.
Attrib. [1991]

EQUAL OPPORTUNITIES

1 As men become aware that few have had a fair chance, they are inclined to say that no women have had a fair chance.
Margaret Fuller (1810–50) US journalist, social critic, educator, translator, editor, and feminist.
Woman in the 19th century [1845]

2 The only jobs for which no man is qualified are human incubators and wet nurse. Likewise, the only job for which no woman is or can be qualified is sperm donor.
Wilma Scott Heide (1926–) US nurse and feminist.
NOW Official Biography [1971]

3 Equal pay for equal work continues to be seen as applying to equal pay for men and women in the same occupation, while the larger point of continuing relevance in our day is that some occupations have depressed wages because women are the chief employees. The former is a pattern of sex discrimination, the latter of institutionalized sexism.
Alice Rossi (1922–) US educator, scholar, and editor.
The Feminist Papers, 'A Feminist Friendship' [1973]

4 I've always wanted to equalize things for us…Women can be great athletes. And I think we'll find it the next decade that women athletes will finally get the attention they deserve.
Billie Jean King (c. 1943–) US professional tennis player.
Interview, Sept 1973

5 I don't believe in equal opportunity. I think it's terribly tiresome. The whole thing is absolutely terrible now because we've got vast unemployment. It's still a stigma for a man to be unemployed, and to be kept by a woman. It's not a stigma for the woman to be kept by a man.
Barbara Cartland (1902–) British romantic novelist.
Women (Naim Attallah) [1987]

6 It is not just a matter of some women getting into the mainstream, but of shifting its very

course; with the realisation that if it leaves out half the human race it cannot be as main as all that.
Katherine Whitehorn (1926–) British journalist.
Observer, 18 Aug 1991

EVANS, Dame Edith Mary Booth (1888–1976)

British actress who was made a DBE in 1946. She made her debut as Cressida in *Troilus and Cressida* (1912), directed by William Poel. Her range was considerable, from Shakespearean roles to modern plays. In 1925 she joined the Old Vic and during World War II she was a member of ENSA, entertaining the troops overseas. She is mainly remembered for her great performances in such roles as the Nurse in *Romeo and Juliet*, Judith Bliss in Coward's *Hay Fever*, and Lady Bracknell in Wilde's *The Importance of Being Earnest*.

Quotations about Evans

1 She had a faculty for endowing a stage character and its more striking passages of dialogue with such life that no other actress who subsequently attempted the part could escape unfavourable comparison.
W. A. Darlington (1890–) British author and journalist. *Daily Telegraph*, 15 Oct 1976

2 She grew to hate her success as Lady Bracknell though it was perhaps the most popular and famous of all her impersonations…she disliked the imitations of her trumpet tone in the famous line '*A handbag*' which many people seemed to think was the alpha and omega of her performance as Lady Bracknell. For me there was so much else to admire.
John Gielgud (1904–) British actor. *An Actor and His Time*

3 She always refused the part of Lady Macbeth because she found the character incredible.
The Times, Obituary, 15 Oct 1976

Quotations by Evans

4 What does he think they pay me for?
On being told by Peter Brook how to time her entrance while rehearsing *The Dark is Light Enough*. Attrib.

5 When a woman behaves like a man, why doesn't she behave like a nice man?
Observer, 'Sayings of the Week', 30 Sept 1956

EXPLOITATION

1 MEDEA. We women are the most unfortunate creatures.
Firstly, with an excess of wealth it is required
For us to buy a husband and take for our bodies
A master; for not to take one is even worse.
Euripides (c. 480–406 BC) Greek dramatist.
Medea [431 BC]

2 They used to call us to the various ministries when they had something they wanted to put over – if they wanted women to do or not to do certain things such as join up, or go into factories or to evacuate children or whatever it was they wanted. Of course, *Vogue* was a very minor thing, our circulation, but the mass circulation people had got enormous power and the ministries used to say, 'they will listen to what you tell them when they won't read our pamphlets' which was absolutely true.
Audrey Withers British magazine editor.
Out of the Doll's House (Angela Holdsworth) [c. 1941]

3 There are two kinds of women – goddesses and doormats.
Pablo Picasso (1881–1973) Spanish painter.
Attrib. [1973]

FAILINGS

1 It is the usual frailty of our sex to be fond of flattery. I blame this in other women, and should wish not to be chargeable with it myself.
Marguerite of Valois (1553–1615) French queen and diarist.
Memoirs [1594–1600]

2 Does it always end so with a woman? When they build their palaces they are never finished. Women can do nothing that has permanence.
Selma Lagerlöf (1858–1940) Swedish writer. First woman elected to Swedish Academy. Nobel prize (1909).
The Miracles of Anti-Christ, Bk II, Ch. 2 [1899]

FAMILY

1 I have a wife, I have sons: all of them hostages given to fate.
Lucan (Marcus Annaeus Lucanus; 39–65 AD) Roman poet.
Works, VII [45 AD]

2 He that loves not his wife and children, feeds a lioness at home and broods a nest of sorrows.
Jeremy Taylor (1613–67) English Anglican theologian.
Sermons, 'Married Love' [17th century]

3 Sisters should be always willing to attend their brothers, and consider it a privilege to be their companions…Consider the loss of a ball or a party, for the sake of making the evening pass pleasantly for your brothers at home, as a small sacrifice.
Mrs John Farrar
The Young Lady's Friend [1847]

4 Two mothers-in-law.
Lord John Russell (1792–1878) British statesman.
His answer when asked what he would consider a proper punishment for bigamy. *Anekdotenschatz* (H. Hoffmeister) [c. 1850]

5 All happy families resemble one another, each unhappy family is unhappy in its own way.
Leo Tolstoy (1828–1910) Russian writer.
Anna Karenina, Pt I, Ch. 1 [1875–77]

6 Home is the girl's prison and the woman's workhouse.
Florence Farr (Mrs Edward Emery; 1860–1917) British actress and director.
Attrib. [1917]

7 No man is responsible for his father. That is entirely his mother's affair.
Margaret Turnbull (fl. 1920s–1942) US writer.
Alabaster Lamps [1925]

8 What a marvellous place to drop one's mother-in-law!
Marshal Foch (1851–1929) French soldier.
Remark on being shown the Grand Canyon Attrib. [1929]

9 And Her Mother Came Too.
Ivor Novello (David Ivor Davies; 1893–1951) British actor, composer, and dramatist.
Title of song

10 The sink is the great symbol of the bloodiness of family life. All life is bad, but family life is worse.
Julian Mitchell (1935–   ) British writer.
As Far as You Can Go, Pt I, Ch. 1 [1963]

11 Far from being the basis of the good society, the family, with its narrow privacy and tawdry secrets, is the source of all our discontents.
Edmund Leach (1910–   ) British social anthropologist.
In the BBC Reith Lectures for 1967. Lecture reprinted in *The Listener* [1967]

12 They fuck you up, your mum and dad.
They may not mean to, but they do.
They fill you with the faults they had
And add some extra, just for you.
Philip Larkin (1922–85) British poet.
This be the Verse

13 Mother is the dead heart of the family, spending father's earnings on consumer goods to enhance the environment in which he eats, sleeps and watches the television.
Germaine Greer (1939–   ) Australian-born British writer and feminist.
The Female Eunuch [1971]

14 It is always the woman who must keep the thread straight, to save the marriage. Women

choose for the family – though sometimes they must sacrifice themselves.
Sophia Loren (1934–) Italian film actress.
Sunday Telegraph, 2 Sept 1984

FASHION
See CLOTHES

FEAR

1 It takes a brave man to face a brave woman, and man's fear of women's creative energy has never found expression more clear than in the old German clamor, renewed by the Nazis, of 'Kinder, Kuchen und Kirche' for women.
Pearl Buck (1892–1973) US novelist.
To My Daughters with Love [1967]

2 My literary reputation – or rather the lack of it – is the work of male reviewers who fear female sexuality and don't like successful women.
Erica Jong
Observer, 12 Oct 1980

FEMININITY
See also WOMAN'S NATURE

1 The virtues of women are not brilliant talent, nor distinction and elegance. The virtues of women are reserve, quiet, chastity, orderliness, governing herself to maintain a sense of shame, and conducting herself according to the rules of Confucian etiquette.
Pan Chao (c. 45–c. 115) Chinese historian and poet.
Nü Chieh (Precepts for Women) [2nd century AD]

2 The ten properties of a woman:
Ye.i. is to be merry of chere, ye.ii. to be wel placed, ye.iii. to haue a broad forhed, ye.iiii. to haue brod buttocks, ye.v. to be hard of ward, ye.vi. to be easy to leap upon, ye.vii. to be good at long iourney, ye.viii. to be wel sturring under a man, ye.ix. to be always busy wt ye mouth, ye.x. euer to be chewing on ye bridle.
Fitzherbert's Boke of Husbandry [1568]

3 Who is Silvia? What is she,
That all our swains commend her?
Holy, fair, and wise is she.
William Shakespeare (1564–1616) English dramatist.
The Two Gentlemen of Verona, IV:2 [1595]

4 These are rare attainments for a damsel, but pray tell me, can she spin?
James I (1566–1625) King of England.
On being introduced to a young girl proficient in Latin, Greek, and Hebrew. Attrib. [1625]

5 She is Venus when she smiles;
But she's Juno when she walks,
And Minerva when she talks.
Ben Jonson (1573–1637) English dramatist.
The Underwood, 'Celebration of Charis, V. His Discourse with Cupid' [1640]

6 I am a source of satisfaction to him, a nurse, a piece of furniture, a *woman* – nothing more.
Sophie Tolstoy (1844–1919) Russian writer.
A Diary of Tolstoy's Wife, 1860–1891 [1863]

7 She must be enduringly, incorruptibly good; instinctively, infallibly wise – wise not for self-development, but for self-renunciation: wise, not that she may set herself above her husband, but that she may never fail from his side: wise, not with the narrowness of insolent and loveless pride, but with the passionate gentleness of an infinitely variable, because infinitely applicable, modesty of service – the true changefulness of woman.
John Ruskin (1819–1900) British art critic and writer.
Sesame and Lilies [1865]

8 In all countries, then, the ideal woman changes, chameleon-like, to suit the taste of man; and the great doctrine that her happiness does somewhat depend on his liking is part of the very foundation of her existence.
Anonymous
Saturday Review, 1867

9 For Shelley's nature is utterly womanish. Not merely his weak points, but his strong ones, are those of a woman. Tender and pitiful as a woman; and yet, when angry, shrieking, railing, hysterical as a woman...The nature of a woman looks out of that wild, beautiful, girlish face – the nature: but not the spirit.
Charles Kingsley (1819–75) British writer.
Thoughts on Shelley and Byron

10 God is a gentleman. He prefers blondes.
Joe Orton (1933–67) British dramatist.
Loot, II [1965]

11 As though femininity is something you can lose the way you lose your pocketbook: hmm, where in the world did I put my femininity?
Françoise Giroud (1916–) Swiss-born French politician, journalist, editor, and French Minister of Women.
I Give You My Word [1974]

12 I don't mind...the fun and games of being treated like a fragile flower. But as a physiologist working with the unromantic scientific facts of life, I find it hard to delude myself about feminine frailty.
Estelle R. Ramey (1917–) US endocrinologist, physiologist, biophysicist, and educator.
The Prime of Ms. America (Janet Harris) [1975]

FEMINISM

See also EMANCIPATION; SUFFRAGETTES; WOMEN'S LIBERATION MOVEMENT

1 The extension of women's rights is the basic principle of all social progress.
Charles Fourier (1772–1837) French social reformer.
Théorie des quatre mouvements [1808]

2 Let woman then go on – not asking as favour, but claiming as right, the removal of all the hindrances to her elevation in the scale of being – let her receive encouragement for the proper cultivation of all her powers, so that she may enter profitably into the active business of life.
Lucretia Mott (1793–1880) US abolitionist, Quaker, and suffragist.
Discourse on Women [1850]

3 The rights of women who demand,
Those women are but few:
The greater part had rather staid
Exactly as they do.
Beauty has claims for which she fights
At ease with winning arms;
The women who want women's rights
Want mostly, women's charms.
Punch, 1870

4 The struggle for self-consciousness is the essence of the feminist movement. Slowly but inevitably, the soul of a sex is emerging from the dim chamber of instinct and feeling into the strong sunshine of reason and will.
Katharine Anthony (1877–1965) US writer and educator.
Feminism in Germany and Scandinavia, Ch. 9 [1915]

5 We must rid England of all traces of feminism and purge her of these antimale influences…Feminism, by striking nearer the roots of life, is perhaps even more dangerous to civilization and to the Race, than Democracy itself.
Anthony Ludovici
Women, a Vindication [1923]

6 So – against odds, the women inch forward, but I'm rather old to be carrying on this fight!
Eleanor Roosevelt (1884–1962) US First Lady, government official, writer, humanitarian, and lecturer.
Letter to Joseph P. Lash, 13 Feb 1946

7 We turn in our sleep and groan because we are parasites – we women – because we produce nothing, say nothing, find our whole world in the love of a man. – For shame! We are become the veriest Philistines – in this matter of woman's sphere. I suppose it is too soon to expect us to achieve perspective on the problem of women's rights.
Ruth Benedict (1887–1948) US anthropologist, biographer, and poet.
An Anthropologist at Work (Margaret Mead) [1948]

8 It is probably true to say that the largest scope for change still lies in men's attitude to women, and in women's attitude to themselves.
Vera Brittain (1893–1970) British writer and poet.
Lady into Woman, Ch. 15 [1953]

9 First the sweetheart of the nation, then the aunt, woman governs America because America is a land of boys who refuse to grow up.
Salvador de Madariaga y Rogo (1886–1978) Spanish diplomat and writer.
The Perpetual Pessimist (Sagitarius and George) [1958]

10 The thought could not be avoided that the best home for a feminist was in another person's lab.
James Dewey Watson (1928–) US geneticist.
The Double Helix, Ch. 2 [1968]

11 To be a liberated woman is to renounce the desire of being a sex object or a baby girl. It is to acknowledge that the Cinderella-Prince Charming story is a child's fairy tale.
Clare Boothe Luce (1903–) US politician and writer.
Bulletin of the Baldwin School, Pennsylvania, Sept 1974

12 We have been looking at it warily. Black women need economic equality but it doesn't apply for me to call a black man a male chauvinist pig. Our anger is not at our men. I don't think they have been the enemy.
Marcia Gillespie (1944–) US editor.
Los Angeles Times, 12 May 1974

13 The whole idea of the feminist struggle being a peripheral kind of thing that you do in your spare time is something that has to be changed.
Rosemary Brown (c. 1920–) Jamaican-born Canadian politician.
Branching Out, 'The Radical Tradition of Rosemary Brown', JulyAug 1975

14 I am a feminist because I feel endangered, psychically and physically, by this society and because I believe that the women's movement is saying that we have come to an edge of history when men – insofar as they are embodiments of the patriarchal idea – have become dangerous to children and other living things, themselves included.
Adrienne Rich (1929–) US poet and educator.
On Lies, Secrets and Silence [1979]

15 There is a danger today in feminist rhetoric, rigidified in reaction against the past, harping

on the same old problems in the same old way, leaving unsaid what's really bothering women and men.
Betty Friedan (1921–) US writer.
The Second Stage [1981]

16 Feminism is an entire world view or gestalt, not just a laundry list of 'women's issues'.
Charlotte Bunch (1944–) US editor, feminist, educator, and writer.
New Directions for Women, SeptOct 1981

17 People call me a feminist whenever I express sentiments that differentiate me from a doormat or a prostitute.
Rebecca West (Cicely Isabel Fairfield; 1892–1983) British novelist and journalist.
Attrib. [1983]

18 Men *would* support us (the feminists) we are told, if only we learned how to ask for their support in the right way. It's a subtle and effective way of blaming the victim.
Gloria Steinem (1934–) US writer.
Outrageous Acts and Everyday Rebellions [1984]

19 If you want to know I'm really tired of feminists, sick of them. They've really dug themselves into their own grave. Any man would be a fool who didn't agree with equal rights and pay, but some women, now, juggling with career, lover, children, wifehood, have spread themselves too thin and are very unhappy.
Michael Douglas (1945–) US actor and producer.
You, 6 Mar 1988

20 I was born into the first generation of women who could actually choose – without risking death in an illegal abortion – when and whether we would have children. It seems hard to believe that we flower children of the 1960s and 1970s never doubted for a second that we would eventually find fulfilling jobs. All the radical soul-searching was born of basic economic security.
Debbie Taylor British writer.
New Internationalist, Oct 1989

21 If establishing masculinity depends most of all on succeeding as the prime breadwinner, then it is hard to imagine a force more directly threatening to fragile American manhood than the feminist drive for economic equality.
Susan Faludi US writer.
Backlash: The Undeclared War Against American Women [1991]

22 I disagree with the current phase of feminism. Women's sexual power is an enormous force. Feminists think only in terms of social power.
Camille Paglia
Independent, 'Quote Unquote', 30 Nov 1991

23 We are in the midst of a violent backlash against feminism that uses images of female beauty as a political weapon against women's advancement: the beauty myth.
Naomi Wolf US writer.
The Beauty Myth [1991]

24 But there is another more subtle form of backlash…'Feminism has failed women badly. Instead of liberating them it has actually created a new set of problems. Professional women in the West are particularly ill and unhappy,' write the experts in scientific journals, popular books and magazines on both sides of the Atlantic.
Vanessa Baird Journalist and coeditor for the New Internationalist Cooperative.
New Internationalist, Jan 1992

FERTILITY

1 Why should human females become sterile in the forties, while female crocodiles continue to lay eggs into their third century?
Aldous Huxley (1894–1964) British writer.
After Many a Summer [1939]

2 The management of fertility is one of the most important functions of adulthood.
Germaine Greer (1939–) Australian-born British writer and feminist.
Sex and Destiny [1984]

3 Scientists on IVF programmes often describe the women they treat as 'non-achievers' and 'failures' with 'defective' bodies which can only be fixed with technology. Many are punitive, and blame women's infertility on supposed infections contracted from sexual promiscuity, or on earlier abortions, or they chastise patients for pursuing careers and postponing childbearing until it is too late.
Celia Kitzinger British psychologist.
New Internationalist, Mar 1991

4 As babies become products, mothers become producers, pregnant women the unskilled workers on a reproductive assembly line…Mothers, rather like South African diamond miners, are the cheap, expendable, not-too-trustworthy labour necessary to produce the precious product.
Barbara Katz Rothman
Describing the possible effects of the IVF programme.
Recreating Motherhood: Ideology and Technology in a Patriarchal Society [1991]

FLYNN, Elizabeth Gurley (1890–1964)

US political civil-rights activist and Communist. She began her political career at the age of 16, and in 1907 became a speaker for the Socialist Party, the Socialist Labor Party, and the Industrial Workers of the World. In 1918 she helped establish a Workers' Liberty Defense Union, and from 1926 to 1930 was chairman of the International Labor Defense. In 1936 she joined the Communist party, becoming a columnist for the *Daily Worker*, and in 1961 was chairman of the Communist Party USA. She died on a visit to the Soviet Union in 1964 and was given a state funeral in Red Square.

1 One of my correspondents asked me: 'What do you think are the main differences between a women's prison and a men's prison?' I replied: 'You would never see diapers hung on a line at a men's prison or hear babies crying in the hospital on a quiet Sunday afternoon.' The physiological differences – menstruation, menopause, and pregnancy – create intense emotional problems among many women in prison.
The Alderson Story, Ch. 13

2 A popular saying in Alderson went as follows: 'They work us like a horse, feed us like a bird, treat us like a child, dress us like a man – and then expect us to act like a lady.'
The Alderson Story, Ch. 25

3 We hated the rich, the trusts they owned, the violence they caused, the oppression they represented.
The Rebel Girl, Pt I

4 I said then and am still convinced that the full opportunity for women to become free and equal citizens with access to all spheres of human endeavor cannot come under capitalism, although many demands have been won by organized struggle.
The Rebel Girl, Pt I

FONDA, Jane (1937–)

US actress, political activist, and aerobics expert. Daughter of Henry Fonda, she began her career as a model by appearing on the cover of *Vogue*. She became recognized as an actress in *They Shoot Horses Don't They?* (1969) for which she received a New York Critics Best Actress Award and an Oscar nomination. Her other films include *Klute* (1971), for which she was awarded an Oscar, *On Golden Pond* (1981), and *Old Gringo* (1989). Although admired for her acting ability she attracted much opprobrium in the United States for her anti-Vietnam war activities. She has also become internationally famous for her fitness programme, *Jane Fonda's Workout*.

Quotation about Fonda

1 Jane Fonda – exasperating at times, inspiring at times – is a modern-day version of the mythical bird, the phoenix, rising constantly from the ashes.
Bill Davidson *Jane Fonda – An Intimate Biography*

Quotations by Fonda

2 Back then…women were not survivors. If you didn't want to be like your mother – if you wanted to be stronger and survive – you had to align yourself with a man or be a tomboy or whatever.
Referring to the 1950s. *Mother Jones*, 'The Essential Tom & Jane' (Jeffrey Klein), FebMar 1980

3 But the whole point of liberation is that you get out. Restructure your life. Act by yourself.
Los Angeles Weekly, 'At Home with Tom and Jane' (Danae Brook), 28 Nov 1980

4 Well, what is a relationship? It's about two people having tremendous weaknesses and vulnerabilities, like we all do, and one person being able to strengthen the other in their areas of vulnerability. And vice versa. You need each other. You bolster each other. You complete each other, passion and romance aside.
Los Angeles Weekly, 'At Home with Tom and Jane' (Danae Brook), 28 Nov 1980

5 I am not a do-gooder. I am a revolutionary. A revolutionary woman.
Los Angeles Weekly, 'At Home with Tom and Jane' (Danae Brook), 28 Nov 1980

FORGIVENESS

1 Forgive you? – Oh, of course, dear,
A dozen times a week!
We women were created
Forgiveness but to speak.
Ella Higginson (1862–1940) US poet, writer, and historian.
'Wearing Out Love'

2 She intended to forgive. Not to do so would be un-Christian; but she did not intend to do so soon, nor forget how much she had to forgive.
Jessamyn West (c. 1902–) US writer.
The Friendly Persuasion, 'The Buried Leaf' [1945]

3 Once a woman has forgiven her man, she must not reheat his sins for breakfast.
Marlene Dietrich (Maria Magdalene von Losch; 1904–) German-born film star.
Marlene Dietrich's ABC [1962]

FRANCHISE

See EMANCIPATION; SUFFRAGETTES

FRANK, Anne (1929–45)

A German-Jewish girl who has achieved lasting fame for the diary she kept while hiding for two years from the Nazis in occupied Amsterdam during World War II. She died of typhus in Bergen-Belsen after being betrayed by Dutch informers in 1944. Her diary, published in 1947, has become a symbol of Jewish reistance and courage.

Quotations about Frank

1 Her diary endures, full-blooded, unselfpitying, a perpetual reminder that the enormity of the Nazi crime amounted not to the abstraction of 'genocide' but the murder of six million individuals.
Simon Schama (1945–) British historian. *1000 Makers of the 20th Century*

2 Through her diary she remains the most vivid and poignant symbol of Jewish suffering in the 20th century.
Simon Schama (1945–) British historian. *1000 Makers of the 20th Century*

Quotations by Frank

3 I soothe my conscience now with the thought that it is better for hard words to be on paper than that Mummy should carry them in her heart.
The Diary of a Young Girl, 2 Jan 1944

4 Mummy herself has told us that she looked upon us more as her friends than her daughters. Now that is all very fine, but still, a friend can't take a mother's place. I need my mother as an example which I can follow, I want to be able to respect her.
The Diary of a Young Girl, 15 Jan 1944

5 We all live with the objective of being happy; our lives are all different and yet the same.
The Diary of a Young Girl, 6 July 1944

6 Laziness may *appear* attractive, but work *gives* satisfaction.
The Diary of a Young Girl, 6 July 1944

7 Parents can only give good advice or put them on the right paths, but the final forming of a person's character lies in their own hands.
The Diary of a Young Girl, 15 July 1944

FREEDOM

1 Women do many things, just because they are forbidden…Women of this kind are children of mother Eve, who flouted the first prohibition…But indeed it is my firm belief today that Eve would never have done so, had it never been forbidden her.
Gottfried von Strassburg (fl. 1210) German poet.
Tristan [c. 1210]

2 I have no wish for a second husband. I had enough of the first. I like to have my own way – to lie down mistress, and get up master.
Susanna Moodie (1803–85) Canadian writer and poet.
Roughing It in the Bush, Ch. 12 [1852]

3 Women, like men, ought to have their youth so glutted with freedom they hate the very idea of freedom.
Vita Sackville-West (1892–1962) British writer.
Letter to Harold Nicolson, 1 June 1919

4 We have not owned our freedom long enough to know exactly how it should be used.
Phyllis McGinley (1905–78) US poet and humorist.
The Province of the Heart, 'The Honor of Being a Woman' [1959]

5 The freer that women become, the freer will men be. Because when you enslave someone – you *are* enslaved.
Louise Nevelson (1900–) Russian-born US sculptor and feminist.
AFTRA, Summer 1974

FRIEDAN, Betty (1921–)

US writer and feminist. Cofounder (1966), and president of the National Organisation for Women she became active in the women's movement after the publication of her book *Feminine Mystique* (1966). This work was prompted by her frustration with the role of housewife and mother, and by the discovery that other women felt the same dissatisfaction. In 1973 she helped to found the First Women's Bank. Other works include *It Changed My Life* (1976) and *The Second Stage* (1981). Her work has earned her the reputation of 'mother of the New Feminist Movement'.

Quotations about Friedan

1 She is deeply and honestly sceptical about what it is that feminism has achieved for women…a down-to-earth scrutiny of the self-deceptions, hypocrisies and blind alleys of feminism.
Review of *The Second Stage. New Statesman*, 1981

2 The most influencial feminist of the last 20 years.
The Sunday Times, 1982

Quotations by Friedan

3 It can be less painful for a woman not to hear the strange, dissatisfied voice stirring within her.
The Feminine Mystique, Ch. 1

4 Over and over women heard in voices of tradition and Freudian sophistication that they could desire no greater destiny than to glory in their own femininity…to pity the neurotic,

unfeminine, unhappy women who want to be poets or physicians or presidents.
The Feminine Mystique, Ch. 1

5 How did Chinese women, after having their feet bound for many generations, finally discover they could run?
The Feminine Mystique, Ch. 4

6 It is easier to live through someone else than to become complete yourself.
The Feminine Mystique, Ch. 14

FRIENDSHIP

1 But friendship between men and women can be a tricky business because a pretty face all too easily attracts a weak soul, and visual temptation kindles carnal lust, often to produce a defiled mind and body. Familiarity between men and women is apt to turn to virtue's disadvantage.
Richard Rolle (c. 1300–49) English writer.
The Fire of Love [14th century]

2 And much more am I sorrier for my good knights' loss than for the loss of my fair queen; for queens I might have enough, but such a fellowship of good knights shall never be together in no company.
Thomas Malory (1400–71) English writer.
Morte d'Arthur, Bk XX, Ch. 9 [c. 1469]

3 I have always detested the belief that sex is the chief bond between man and woman. Friendship is far more human.
Agnes Smedley (c. 1894–1950) US author and lecturer.
Battle Hymn of China [1943]

4 Learn to reject friendship, or rather the dream of friendship. To want friendship is a great fault. Friendship ought to be a gratuitous joy, like the joys afforded by art, or life (like aesthetic joys). I must refuse it in order to be worthy to receive it.
Simone Weil (1910–43) French writer, philosopher, and revolutionary.
First and Last Notebooks, 'The Pre-War Notebook' (ed. Richard Rees) [1970]

FRY, Elizabeth (1780–1845)

British social reformer. A Quaker, she paid her first visit in 1813 to Newgate prison, where she was appalled by the situation of women convicts. Much of her subsequent work was concerned with improving the conditions for female inmates of British prisons and, later, hospitals and mental institutions. Although she was often accused of neglecting her husband and family, she justified herself on the grounds of her religious vocation.

Quotations about Fry
1 Known as the 'Angel of the prison', E. Fry became a symbol of saintliness soon after she began to visit Newgate Prison in Dec. 1816.
June Rose *Makers of 19th Century Culture 1800–1914* (ed. Justin Wintle)

2 I am glad you like what I said of Mrs Elizabeth Fry. She is very unpopular with the clergy; examples of living, active virtue disturb our repose and give one to distressing comparisons; we long to burn her alive.
Sydney Smith (1771–1845) British clergyman and essayist. Letter

Quotations by Fry
3 Does capital punishment tend to the security of the people? By no means. It hardens the hearts of men, and makes the loss of life appear light to them; and it renders life insecure, inasmuch as the law holds out that property is of greater value than life.
Biography of Distinguished Women (Sarah Josepha Hale)

4 Punishment is not for revenge, but to lessen crime and reform the criminal.
Biography of Distinguished Women (Sarah Josepha Hale)

GAGE, Mathilda Joslyn (1826–98)

US suffragette and writer. She joined the National Woman Suffrage Association in 1869, and in 1875 was elected president. From 1878 to 1881 she published *National Citizen and Ballot Box*, the National Woman Suffrage Association's newspaper. In 1890 she founded the Woman's National Liberal Union, which was a group dedicated to the separation of church and state. Her writings include *History of Woman Suffrage* (with Susan B. Anthony and Elizabeth Cady Stanton; 1881–87) and *Woman, Church and the State* (1893).

1 But when at last woman stands on an even platform with man, his acknowledged equal everywhere, with the same freedom to express herself in the religion and government of the country, then, and not until then...will he be able to legislate as wisely and generously for her as for himself.
History of Woman Suffrage, Vol. I

2 Wherever the skilled hands and cultural brain of women have made the battle of life easier for man, he has readily pardoned her sound judgment and proper self-assertion.
History of Woman Suffrage, Vol. I

3 The queens in history compare favorably with the kings.
History of Woman Suffrage, Vol. I

4 The woman is uniformly sacrificed to the wife and mother.
History of Woman Suffrage, Vol. I

GANDHI, Indira (1917–84)

Indian politician; prime minister (1966–77; 1980–84). Daughter of the first Indian prime minister, Jawaharlal Nehru, she attended Visva-Bharati University, West Bengal, and Somerville College, Oxford. She joined the All-India Congress Party in 1938, at the age of 21, and in 1942 married fellow member Feroze Gandhi (unrelated to Mahatma Gandhi). In 1959 she was elected president of the Congress Party and, following Lal Bahadur Shastri's death in 1966 became leader of the Congress Party and prime minister. A skilful and controversial stateswoman, she was praised for her handling of the Pakistani civil war (1971) leading to the independence of East Pakistan as Bangladesh (1972). Political unrest and a worsening of India's economy caused Mrs Gandhi to introduce a state of emergency in June 1975. During this period she introduced a number of unpopular reforms, including large-scale sterilization as a form of birth control. In the elections of 1977 she was defeated by the Janata Party. However, the new government proved unpopular and she was returned to power in 1980. Her second term of office was troubled by religious disturbances. In June 1984 she ordered the army to attack the Sikhs' holiest shrine, the Golden Temple at Amritsar, which led to the deaths of more than 450 Sikhs. Five months later she was assassinated by her own Sikh bodyguard in revenge for the attack on the Golden Temple.

Quotations about Gandhi

1 Her weapon is the snub, a regal, chilling silence. Her silences, as could be testified by ex-President Nixon, whom she disliked, can be disconcerting.
Trevor Fishlock (1941–) British journalist. *The Times*, 'Empress Indira', 22 Mar 1982

2 After the portrayal of her as a ruthless natural autocrat it was stunning to meet her; to see with what composure and courtesy she managed her entourage and her Cabinet colleagues.
Michael Foot (1913–) British Labour politician and journalist. *Observer*, 4 Nov 1984

3 Mrs Gandhi never gives a performance less than the occasion demands.
Observer, 'Profile', 21 Mar 1982

Quotations by Gandhi

4 There exists no politician in India daring enough to attempt to explain to the masses that cows can be eaten.
New York Review of Books, 'Indira's Coup' (Oriana Fallaci)

5 You cannot shake hands with a clenched fist.
Remark at a press conference, New Delhi, 19 Oct 1971

6 There are moments in history when brooding tragedy and its dark shadows can be lightened by recalling great moments of the past.
Letter to Richard Nixon, 16 Dec 1971

7 I don't mind if my life goes in the service of the nation. If I die today every drop of my blood will invigorate the nation.
Said the night before she was assassinated by Sikh militants, 30 Oct 1984. *The Sunday Times*, 3 Dec 1989

GARBO, Greta (Greta Gustafson; 1905–90)

Swedish actress; a film star of legendary beauty and mystery who retired in 1941. She was born in Stockholm and started work at 14, first as a lather girl in a barber shop, then as a clerk in a department store, and later as a model. She appeared in her first film, *Luffar-Petter* in 1922. From 1922 to 1924 she studied at the Royal Dramatic Theatre, Stockholm, where she met Mauritz Stiller, the director who gave her her stage name and her first starring role in *Gösta Berlings Saga* (1924). Her later films, made in Hollywood, include *Queen Christina* (1934), *Anna Karenina* (1935), and *Ninotchka* (1939).

Quotations about Garbo

1 She is every man's fantasy mistress. She gave you the impression that, if your imagination had to sin, it could at least congratulate itself on its impeccable taste.
Alistair Cooke (1908–) British journalist.

2 What, when drunk one sees in other women, one sees in Garbo sober.
Kenneth Tynan (1927–80) British theatre critic. *The Sunday Times*, 25 Aug 1963

Quotations by Garbo

3 Why can't we avoid being followed and examined? It is cruel to bother people who want to be left in peace. This kills beauty for me.
Newspaper interview, Naples 1938

4 I want to be alone.
Words spoken by Garbo in the film *Grand Hotel*, and associated with her for the rest of her career.

5 I never said, 'I want to be alone.' I only said, 'I want to be *left* alone.' There is all the difference.
Garbo (John Bainbridge)

6 I am not a versatile actress.
Attrib.

GASKELL, Elizabeth (1810–65)

British novelist. Born in Chelsea, the daughter of William Stevenson, Keeper of the Treasury Records, she was, after the death of her mother, brought up by a maternal aunt in an atmosphere of rural gentility. She married a Unitarian minister in 1832 and settled in Manchester, the setting of her first novel *Mary Barton* (1848). Other works include *Cranford* (1853), based on her childhood in Knutsford, *Ruth* (1853), advocating more lenient treatment of unmarried mothers, and *North and South* (1855). She also wrote the first biography of her friend Charlotte Brontë (1857).

Quotations about Gaskell

1   A natural unassuming woman whom they have been doing their best to spoil by making a lioness of her.
Jane Welsh Carlyle (1801–66) Wife of Thomas Carlyle. Letter, 17 May 1849

2   She is neither young nor beautiful; very retiring but quite capable of talking when she likes – a good deal of the clergyman's wife about her.
Arthur Hugh Clough (1819–61) British poet. Letter to his wife, 9 Feb 1849

Quotations by Gaskell

3   A man...is *so* in the way in the house!
Cranford, Ch. 1

4   'It is very pleasant dining with a bachelor,' said Miss Matty, softly, as we settled ourselves in the counting-house. 'I only hope it is not improper; so many pleasant things are!'
Cranford, Ch. 4

5   That kind of patriotism which consists in hating all other nations.
Sylvia's Lovers, Ch. 1

GILMAN, Caroline (1794–1888)
US author and poet.

1   One clear idea is too precious a treasure to lose.
Recollections of a Southern Matron, Ch. 3

2   Intellectual women are the most modest inquirers after truth, and accomplished women often the most scrupulous observers of social duty.
Recollections of a Southern Matron, Ch. 7

3   Men are not often unreasonable, their difficulties lie in not understanding the moral and physical structure of our sex. They often wound through ignorance, and are surprised at having offended. How clear is it, then, that woman loses by petulance and recrimination! Her first study must be self-control, almost to hypocrisy.
Recollections of a Southern Matron, Ch. 35

4   You must know I've resolved and agreed
My books from room not to lend,
But you may sit by my fire and read.
Verses of a Life-Time, 'One Good Turn Deserves Another'

GILMAN, Charlotte Perkins (1860–1935)
US writer. She began her literary career in the 1890s with the publication of poetry and short stories. Her major work is *Women and Economics* (1898) in which she proposed that only economic independence could bring freedom to women. In 1909 she founded the socialist magazine *Forerunner* and, in 1915, she cofounded the Women's Peace Party.

1   However, one cannot put a quart in a pint cup.
The Living of Charlotte Perkins Gilman

2   New York...that unnatural city where every one is an exile, none more so than the American.
The Living of Charlotte Perkins Gilman

3   Where young boys plan for what they will achieve and attain, young girls plan for whom they will achieve and attain.
Women and Economics, Ch. 5

GOOD AND EVIL

1   What is beautiful is good, and who is good will soon also be beautiful.
Sappho (fl. c. 610–635 BC) Greek poet.
Fragments, No. 101 [7th century BC]

2   A bad woman always has something she regards as a curse – a real bit of goodness hidden away somewhere.
Lady Troubridge (Laura Gurney; fl. early 1900s–46) British writer.
The Millionaire [1907]

GOSSIP

1   The gossip of two women will destroy two houses.
Arabic proverb

2   Men have always detested women's gossip because they suspect the truth: their measurements are being taken and compared.
Erica Jong (1942–) US poet and writer.
Fear of Flying, Ch. 6 [1973]

GREER, Germaine (1939–)
Australian writer and feminist. She was born in Melbourne and studied at the universities of Melbourne and Sydney before taking a doctorate in literature at Cambridge. Her book *The Female Eunuch* (1970) thrust her into the limelight, with its exposé of women's frustration in a male-dominated society. Later writings include *Sex and Destiny* (1984), *Daddy, We Hardly Knew You* (1989), and *The Change* (1991).

Quotation about Greer

1   The combination of her dazzling appearance, erudition and fondness for sharp repartee

made her an obvious choice for mass media, as a TV personality, broadcaster and popular journalist.
Monica Petzal *Makers of Modern Culture*

Quotations by Greer

2 Probably the only place where a man can feel really secure is in a maximum security prison, except for the imminent threat of release.
The Female Eunuch

3 Mother is the dead heart of the family, spending father's earnings on consumer goods to enhance the environment in which he eats, sleeps and watches the television.
The Female Eunuch

4 Love, love, love – all the wretched cant of it, masking egotism, lust, masochism, fantasy under a mythology of sentimental postures, a welter of self-induced miseries and joys, blinding and masking the essential personalities in the frozen gestures of courtship, in the kissing and the dating and the desire, the compliments and the quarrels which vivify its barrenness.
The Female Eunuch

5 When the life of the party wants to express the idea of a pretty woman in mime, he undulates his two hands in the air and leers expressively. The notion of a curve is so closely connected to sexual semantics that some people cannot resist sniggering at road signs. The most popular image of the female despite the exigencies of the clothing trade is all boobs and buttocks, a hallucinating sequence of parabolas and bulges.
The Female Eunuch

6 Buttock fetishism is comparatively rare in our culture…Girls are often self-conscious about their behinds, draping themselves in long capes and tunics, but it is more often because they are too abundant in that region than otherwise.
The Female Eunuch

GRIMKÉ, Angelina (1805–79)

US abolitionist, writer, and feminist. She and her sister Sarah were daughters of one of the most aristocratic families in the south. Having witnessed at first hand the excesses of slavery, she developed deep moral objections to it. She joined the Anti-slavery Association and, in 1836, produced the pamphlet *An Appeal to the Christian Women of the South* in which she exhorted Southern women to use moral persuasion to help overcome oppression. In 1838 she married the abolitionist Theodore Dwight Weld. Ill health forced her to retire shortly afterwards.

1 I know you do not make the laws but I also know that you are the wives and mothers, the sisters and daughters of those who do.
The Anti-Slavery Examiner, 'Appeal to the Christian Women of the South', Sept 1836

2 So that precious a talent as intellect never was given to be wrapt in a napkin and buried in the earth.
The Anti-Slavery Examiner, 'Appeal to the Christian Women of the South', Sept 1836

3 Duty is ours and events are God's.
The Anti-Slavery Examiner, 'Appeal to the Christian Women of the South', Sept 1836

4 I recognize no rights but *human* rights – I know nothing of men's rights and women's rights; for in Christ Jesus there is neither male nor female. It is my solemn conviction that, until this principal of equality is recognized and embodied in practice, the church can do nothing effectual for the permanent reformation of the world.
Letters to Catherine Beecher, Letter No. 12

GRIMKÉ, Sarah Moore (1792–1873)

US abolitionist and feminist. Like her sister, Angelina, she developed deep moral objections to slavery and, in 1836, wrote a pamphlet *An Epistle to the Clergy of the Southern States*. With Angelina she spoke out in public in favour of abolition, which prompted a letter from the General Association of Congregational Ministers of Massachusetts decrying women preachers and reformers. Because of this opposition both sisters became pioneers in the women's rights movement.

1 All I ask our brethren is that they will take their feet from off our necks and permit us to stand upright.
Prudery and Passion (Milton Rugoff)

2 Adam's ready acquiescence with his wife's proposal, does not savor much of that superiority *in strength of mind*, which is arrogated by man.
Letter to Mary S. Parker, 17 July 1837

3 In most families, it is considered a matter of far more consequence to call a girl off from making a pie, or a pudding, than to interrupt her whilst engaged in her studies.
Letter, 1837

4 They are early taught that to appear to yield, is the only way to govern.
Letter, 1837

GUILT

1 Dread remorse when you are tempted to err, Miss Eyre: remorse is the poison of life.
Charlotte Brontë (1816–55) British novelist and poet.
Jane Eyre, Ch. 14 [1847]

2 HICKEY. Christ, can you imagine what a guilty skunk she made me feel! If she'd only admitted once she didn't believe any more in her pipe dream that some day I'd behave!
Eugene O'Neill (1888–1953) US dramatist.
The Iceman Cometh [1946]

3 It is quite gratifying to feel guilty if you haven't done anything wrong: how noble! Whereas it is rather hard and certainly depressing to admit guilt and to repent.
Hannah Arendt (1906–75) German-born US philosopher and historian.
Eichmann in Jerusalem, Ch. 15 [1963]

GWYNN, Nell (1650–87)

English actress. Originally she was a seller of fruit and fish in Covent Garden, later becoming an orange seller at the Theatre Royal, Drury Lane. Here she graduated to comedy acting and subsequently became the mistress of Charles II. Her sons by Charles were Charles (who later became Duke of St Albans) and James, Lord Beauclerc. She helped to establish the Royal Hospital at Chelsea.

Quotations about Gwynn
1 Let not poor Nelly starve.
Charles II (1630–85) King of England. Said on his deathbed, to his brother James, 5 Feb 1685

2 Pretty, witty Nell.
Samuel Pepys (1633–1703) English diarist. *Diary*, 3 Apr 1665

Quotations by Gwynn
3 Pray, good people, be civil. I am the Protestant whore.
On being surrounded in her coach by an angry mob in Oxford at the time of the Popish Plot. The mob, thinking that the coach contained the King's Catholic mistress, Louise de Kéroualle, shouted 'It is the Catholic whore!' *Nell Gwyn* (Bevan), Ch. 13

4 Here is a sad slaughter at Windsor, the young mens taking your Leaves and going to France, and, although they are none of my Lovers, yet I am loathe to part with the men.
Letter to Madam Jennings, 14 Apr 1684

5 Shall the dog lie where the deer once couched?
Refusing a lover after the death of Charles II.

HAPPINESS

1 Here and in the other world happiness comes to a person, not a gender.
Honnamma (fl. 1665–99) Indian poet.
A Book of Women Poets (eds. Aliki and Willis Barnstone) [c. 1699]

2 Be good, sweet maid, and let who can be clever;
Do lovely things, not dream them, all day long;
And so make Life, and Death, and that For Ever,
One grand sweet song.
Charles Kingsley (1819–75) British writer.
A Farewell. To C. E. G.

3 There is only one happiness in life, to love and be loved.
George Sand (Amandine Aurore Dupin; 1804–76) French writer.
Letter to Lina Calamatta, 31 Mar 1862

4 When a small child...I thought that success spelled happiness. I was wrong. Happiness is like a butterfly which appears and delights us for one brief moment, but soon flits away.
Anna Pavlova (1881–1931) Russian ballerina.
Pavlova: A Biography (ed. A. H. Franks) [1931]

HATE

1 No one delights more in vengeance than a woman.
Juvenal (Decimus Junius Juvenalis; 60–130 AD) Roman satirist.
Satires, XIII [c. 100 AD]

2 Heaven has no rage like love to hatred turned,
Nor hell a fury like a woman scorned.
William Congreve (1670–1729) British Restoration dramatist.
The Mourning Bride, III [1697]

HAYES, Helen (1900–)

US actress. Born in Washington, she made her first stage appearance at the age of six, playing such roles as Peaseblossom in *Midsummer Night's Dream*. Her adult stage appearances included parts in Shaw's *Caesar and Cleopatra* (1925), Laurence Housman's *Victoria Regina* (1935), Tennessee Williams's *The Glass Menagerie* (1956), and Eugene O'Neill's *Long Day's Journey into Night* (1971). She also acted in radio drama and received the Best Radio Actress Award in 1940. She appeared in many films including *The Sin of Madelon Claudet* (1932), for which she received an Oscar, *Anastasia* (1956), *Airport* (1970) for which she received an Academy Award, and *Candleshoe* (1978).

1 One has to grow up with good talk in order to form the habit of it.
A Gift of Joy (with Lewis Funke), Introduction

2 Actors cannot choose the manner in which they are born. Consequently, it is the one gesture in their lives completely devoid of self-consciousness.
On Reflection (with Sandford Dody), Ch. 1

3 When I was very young, I half believed one could find within the pages of these memoirs the key to greatness. It's rather like trying to find the soul in the map of the human body. But it is enlightening – and it does solve some of the mysteries.
On Reflection (with Sandford Dody), Ch. 6

4 An actress's life is so transitory – suddenly you're a building.
Referring to a New York theatre named after her. News item, Nov 1955

HEALTH AND HEALTHY LIVING

1 Young ladies should take care of themselves. Young ladies are delicate plants. They should take care of their health and their complexion. My dear, did you change your stockings?
Jane Austen (1775–1817) British novelist.
Emma, Ch. 34 [1815]

2 There can be no doubt that the hand which first encloses the waist of a girl in these cruel contrivances, supplying her with a fictitious support, where the hand of God has placed bones and muscles that ought to be brought into vigorous action, that hand lays the foundation of bitter suffering.
Charlotte Elizabeth Tonna (1790–1846) English poet, educator and author.
She was referring to stays. *Personal Recollections*, Letter I [1841]

3 Other books have been written by men physicians…One would suppose in reading them that women possess but one class of physical organs, and that these are always diseased. Such teaching is pestiferous, and tends to cause and perpetuate the very evils it professes to remedy.
Mary Ashton Livermore (c. 1820–1905) US writer.
What Shall We Do with Our Daughters?, Ch. 2 [1860]

4 Conventionality has indeed curtailed feminine force by hindering healthful and varied activity.
Antoinette Brown Blackwell (1825–1921) US feminist, writer, and minister.
The Sexes Throughout Nature [1875]

5 As an article of dress for the girl the corset must be looked upon as distinctly prejudicial to health, and as entirely unnecessary.
Howard A. Kelly (b. 1858) US gynaecologist.
Medical Gynecology [1909]

6 Unnecessary dieting is because everything from television and fashion ads have made it seem wicked to cast a shadow. This wild, emaciated look appeals to some women, though not to many men, who are seldom seen pinning up a *Vogue* illustration in a machine shop.
Peg Bracken (1918–) US writer and humorist.
The I Hate to Cook Book [1960]

7 Our body is a magnificently devised, living, breathing mechanism, yet we do almost nothing to insure its optimal development and use…The human organism needs an ample supply of good building material to repair the effects of daily wear and tear.
Indra Devi (1899–) Russian-born US yogini and writer.
Renewing Your Life Through Yoga, Ch. 2 [1963]

8 Nutritional research, like a modern star of Bethlehem, brings hope that sickness need not be a part of life.
Adelle Davis (1904–74) US nutritionist and writer.
The New York Times Magazine, 'The Great Adelle Davis Controversy', 20 May 1973

9 They have to run the house, bring up a family and many of them now work as well. So much for the weaker sex! They have to be a lot tougher than men to cope with three jobs in one. I don't think women are under any more stress than our grandmothers were, if you can imagine the days when our grandmothers were short of money, living in very poor conditions. I think the stress is different. It's a much more refined stress than it used to be. It used to be gross and grotesque stress in the living conditions.
John Fry British doctor.
Explaining why women are more likely to visit a doctor with problems of depression, anxiety, or panic. *Out of the Doll's House* (Angela Holdsworth) [1988]

HEPWORTH, Dame Barbara (1903–75)

British sculptor. An outstanding abstract sculptor who, with Ben Nicholson and Henry Moore, led the abstract movement in Britain in the 1930s. She was born in Wakefield, Yorkshire, and studied at the Leeds School of Art and at the Royal College of Art (1921–24). In 1931 she met Ben Nicholson, who became her second husband. Her work, at this time, was becoming increasingly abstract, as in 'Reclining Figure' (1932). In 1933 she became a member of the Abstraction-Création association and of the British Unit One group. In the 1930s and 1940s her work became larger and more complex; one of the prime examples of this period is 'Wave' (1943–44). In the late 1950s she began to work in bronze, producing large works for landscape and architectural settings, such as 'Four-Square (Walk Through)' (1966). She was awarded the Grand Prix at São Paulo Biennale in 1959, and was made a DBE in 1965.

Quotations about Hepworth

1   However abstract, Hepworth's sculptures nearly always suggest a human presence or a relationship of one person to another.
Richard Calvocoressi *Makers of Modern Culture*

2   What she does she does admirably. It is rather like the work of a maker of musical instruments. If anyone would know how to make a beautiful belly to a mandolin or a lute it is she. If she were a potter, she would be a potter of distinction and resource. But she comes at a time – as does Mr. Moore – when artists are working in a vacuum.
Wyndham Lewis (1882–1957) British novelist. *The Listener*, Oct 1946

Quotations by Hepworth

3   It's so natural to work large – it fits one's body. This doesn't mean that I don't like working small because I do. It's refreshing, like painting or drawing, but I've always wanted to go to my arm's length and walk around things, or climb up them. I kept on thinking of large works in a landscape: this has always been a dream in my mind.
The Complete Sculpture of Barbara Hepworth (A. Bowness)

4   I rarely draw what I see. I draw what I feel in my body.
World of Art (A. M. Hammersmith)

HINKLE, Beatrice (1874–1953)

US psychiatrist. Born in San Francisco she was educated privately and received her MD from Cooper Medical College (now the medical department of Stanford University) in 1899. She was appointed city physician for San Francisco (1899–1905), becoming the first woman physician to hold a public health position. In 1905 she moved to New York and began to specialize in psychoanalysis, opening the first psychotherapeutic clinic in America, at Cornell Medical College, in 1908. Her writings include *Recreating the Individual* (1923).

1   Woman is a being dominated by the creative urge and…no understanding of her as an individual can be gained unless the significance and effects of that great fact can be grasped.
Recreating the Individual, 'The Psychology of the Artist'

2   The artist has always been and still is a being somewhat apart from the rest of humanity.
Recreating the Individual, 'The Psychology of the Artist'

3   The mystics are the only ones who have gained a glimpse into what is possible.
Recreating the Individual, 'The Psychology of the Artist'

4   The creator does not create only for the pleasure of creating…but he also desires to subdue other minds.
Recreating the Individual, 'The Psychology of the Artist'

HOMOSEXUALITY

See also LESBIANISM

1   Postumus, are you *really*
Taking a wife?…
isn't it better to sleep with a pretty boy?
Boys don't quarrel all night, or nag you for little presents
While they're on the job, or complain that you don't come
Up to their expectations, or demand more gasping passion.
Juvenal (Decimus Junius Juvenalis; 60–130 AD) Roman satirist.
Satires, VI [1st century AD]

2   People who have a low self-esteem…have a tendency to cling to their own sex because it is less frightening.
Clara Thompson (1893–1958) US physician, psychiatrist, writer, lecturer, and educator.
A Study of Interpersonal Relations, New Contributions to Psychiatry, 'Changing Concepts of Homosexuality in Psychoanalysis' (ed. Patrick Mullahy) [1949]

HOUSEKEEPING

1   It is certainly true that housekeeping cares bring with them a thousand endearing compensations. They are a woman's peculiar joy, and women are apt to be light-hearted.
Marceline Desbordes-Valmore (1786–1859) French actress and poet.
Letter to Hippolyte and Undine, her son and daughter, 1 Nov 1840

2   The whole process of home-making, housekeeping and cooking, which ever has been woman's special province, should be looked on as an art and a profession.
Sarah Josepha Hale (1788–1879) US editor, writer, and poet.
Editorial, *Godey's Lady's Book* [c. 1859]

3   Housekeeping ain't no joke.
Louisa May Alcott (1832–88) US novelist.
Little Women, Pt I [1868]

4 It is not motherhood that keeps the housewife on her feet from dawn till dark; it is house service, not child service.
Charlotte Perkins Gilman (1860–1935) US writer and lecturer.
Women and Economics, Ch. 1 [1898]

5 To housekeep, one had to plan ahead and carry items of motley nature around in the mind and at the same time preside, as mother had, at table, just as if everything, from the liver and bacon, to the succotash, to the French toast and strawberry jam, had not been matters of forethought and speculation.
Fannie Hurst (1889–1968) US writer.
Cosmopolitan [1917]

6 Cleaning your house while your kids are still growing
Is like shoveling the walk before it stops snowing.
Phyllis Diller (1917–) US writer and comedienne.
Phyllis Diller's Housekeeping Hints [1966]

7 Housework isn't bad in itself – the trouble with it is that it's inhumanely lonely.
Pat Loud (1926–) US writer and television personality.
Pat Loud: a Woman's Story (with Nora Johnson) [1974]

8 I make no secret of the fact that I would rather lie on a sofa than sweep beneath it. But you have to be efficient if you're going to be lazy.
Shirley Conran (1932–) British designer and journalist.
Superwoman, 'The Reason Why' [1975]

9 There is now no sort of work in the home strictly reserved for 'the wives', even clothes-washing and bed-making, still ordinarily thought of as women's jobs, were frequently mentioned by husbands as things they did as well.
M. Young and P. Willmott
The Symmetrical Family [1975]

10 Any woman who understands the problems of running a home will be nearer to understanding the problems of running a country.
Margaret Thatcher (1925–) British politician and prime minister (1979–90).
Observer, 8 May 1979

HOWE, Julia Ward (1819–1910)

US writer and lecturer. She wrote the Battle Hymn of the Republic, first published in *The Atlantic Monthly* (Feb 1862), after visiting the army at the Potomac in 1861. Her aim was to provide more dignified words to the tune of 'John Brown's body lies a'mouldering in the grave'. In 1943 she married Samuel Gridley Howe, a reformer and teacher of the blind, with whom she conducted an anti-slavery campaign before the Civil War. After the slavery question was settled she became active in woman suffrage, prison reform, and campaigning for peace. Her writings include *Sex and Education* (n.d.), *Reminiscences* (1899), and *Sketches of Representative Women of New England* (1905).

Quotations about Howe

1 ...a personality serenely throned as queen among her American sisters; yet apparently unconscious of her sovereignty.
Ellen M. Mitchell *Julia Ward Howe*

2 She could aways discover sunlight behind the shadows and the clouds; evil to her was but the promise of good, and good the promise of something better.
Ellen M. Mitchell *Julia Ward Howe*

Quotations by Howe

3 Mine eyes have seen the glory of the coming of the Lord:
He is trampling out the vintage where the grapes of wrath are stored.
Battle Hymn of the American Republic

4 O Land, the measure of our prayers,
Hope of the world in grief and wrong!
'Our Country'

5 'Twas red with the blood of freemen and white with the fear of the foe;
And the stars that fit in their courses 'gainst tyrants its symbols know.
'The Flag'

6 The very intensity of our feeling for home, husband and children gives us a power of loving and working outside our homes, to redeem the world as love and work only can.
Women and Politics (Vicky Randall)

HUMILITY

1 To think that you who have been nurtured in the most profound philosophical studies and have attained knowledge in perfection, should have deigned to approve the humble work of an obscure woman!
Hroswitha of Gandersheim (c. 935–1000) German nun, poet, essayist, and translator.
The Plays of Roswitha, 'Epistle of the Same to Certain Learned Patrons of this Book' [c. 960]

2 Let them lower their gaze before the men at whom it is not lawful for them to look, and let them guard their private parts by veiling them, or by bewaring of (or guarding against) fornication. The lowering of glances is presented because the glance is the messenger of fornication.
al Baydawi (Islamic text) [c. 10th century]

3 It is annoying and impossible to suffer proud women, because in general Nature has given men proud and high spirits, while it has made women humble in character and submissive, more apt for delicate things than for ruling.
Giovanni Boccaccio (1313–75) Italian writer and poet.
Concerning Famous Women, 'Niobe' [14th century]

4 Many of you no doubt will see it as audacious, that I, a maiden…have come forth to speak in this radiance of learned men.
Cassandra Fedele (1465–1558) Italian scholar.
Beyond Their Sex (ed. Patricia Labalme) [16th century]

5 Virtuous women wisely understand
That they were born to base humility.
Edmund Spenser (c. 1552–99) English poet.
The Fairie Queene [1590]

6 Humility becomes our fallen nature.
Mary Martha Sherwood (1775–1851) British writer.
The Lady of the Manor; being a Series of Conversations on the Subject of Confirmation intended for the use of the Middle and Higher Ranks of Young Female, Vol. I, Ch. 2 [c. 1851]

7 So I am beginning to wonder if maybe girls wouldn't be happier if we stopped demanding so much respeckt for ourselves and developped a little more respeckt for husbands.
Anita Loos (1888–1981) US writer, playwright, humorist, and screenwriter.
A Mouse Is Born, Ch. 19 [1951]

HUMOUR

1 Wit in women is apt to have bad consequences; like a sword without a scabbard, it wounds the wearer and provokes assailants. I am sorry to say the generality of women who have excelled in wit have failed in chastity.
Elizabeth Montagu (1720–1800) British essayist and letter writer.
Reconstructing Aphra (Angeline Goreau) [1750]

2 Why have they been telling us women lately that we have no sense of humor – when we are always laughing?…And when we're not laughing, we're smiling.
Naomi Weisstein (1939–) US experimental psychologist, educator, feminist, writer, pianist, and comedienne.
All She Needs, Introduction (Ellen Levine) [1973]

3 Few women care to be laughed at and men not at all, except for large sums of money.
Alan Ayckbourn (1939–) British dramatist.
The Norman Conquests, Preface [1974]

HYPATIA (c. 370–415)

Egyptian Neoplatonist philosopher and mathematician. The daughter of Theon (fl. 4th century AD), also a mathematician and philosopher, she became head of the Neoplatonist school of philosophy at Alexandria. Her eloquence, wisdom, and beauty endeared her to both pagans and Christians, making her a focal point in the tensions between these two factions. Following the accession of Cyril to the patriarchate of Alexandria, she was brutally murdered by a fanatical mob of Christian followers, supposedly because of her intimacy with Orestes, the city's pagan prefect.

Quotations about Hypatia

1 Donning the philosopher's cloak, and making her way through the midst of the city, she explained publicly the writings of Plato, or Aristotle, or any other philosopher, to all who wished to hear.
Hesychius *Critic*, 1903 (Joseph McCabe)

2 She was a person who divided society into two parts those who regarded her as an oracle of light, and those who looked upon her as an emissary of darkness.
Elbert Hubbard *Little Journeys to the Homes of the Great*

3 All men did both reverence and had her in admiration for the singular modesty of her mind. Wherefore she had great spite and envy owed unto her, and because she conferred oft, and had great familiarity with Orestes, the people charged her that she was the cause why the bishop and Orestes were not become friends. To be short, certain heady and rash cockbrains whose guide and captain was Peter, a reader of that Church, watched this woman coming home from some place or other, they pull her out of her chariot: they hail her into the Church called Caesarium: they stripped her stark naked they raze the skin and rend the flesh of her body with sharp shells, until the breath departed out of her body: they quarter her body: they bring her quarters unto a place called Cinaron and burn them to ashes.
Socrates Scholasticus *A Treasury of Early Christianity* (ed. Anne Freemantle)

Quotations by Hypatia

4 Men will fight for a superstition quite as quickly as for a living truth – often more so, since a superstition is so intangible you cannot get at it to refute it, but truth is a point of view, and so is changeable.
Little Journeys to the Homes of Great Teachers (Elbert Hubbard), 'Hypatia'

5 He who influences the thought of his times, influences all the times that follow. He has made his impress on eternity.
Little Journeys to the Homes of Great Teachers (Elbert Hubbard), 'Hypatia'

6 To rule by fettering the mind through fear of punishment in another world, is just as base as to use force.
Little Journeys to the Homes of Great Teachers (Elbert Hubbard), 'Hypatia'

HYPOCRISY

1 In France or Italy...women, in losing one virtue, are not necessarily exposed to the loss of all. There, our sex are saved from the necessity of hypocrisy; and are not compelled to pull down the reputations of their contemporaries, in order to erect on the ruins a pedestal for the elevation of their own.
Marguerite Blessington (1789–1849) Irish novelist, poet, and salonist.
The Victims of Society, 'Miss Montressor to La Marquise Le Villeroi' [1837]

2 To insist that a young girl should be pure, chaste and innocent, and then to prescribe for her reading a book containing the stories of Lot, David, Absalom, Ruth and the Song of Songs; to allow her to read St Paul's sermons on fornicators and regale her mind with scenes of rape, orgy, adultery and prostitution expressed in the picturesque language of the Bible; and then to tell her that the words breeches, shift, drawers, thigh, bitch etc., must never pass her lips!
Flora Tristan (1803–44) French writer, feminist, and revolutionary socialist.
The London Journal of Flora Tristan [1842]

3 Virtue consisted in avoiding scandal and venereal disease.
Robert Cecil (1913–) British writer.
Life in Edwardian England [1969]

IBARRURI, Dolores (1895–1989)

Spanish revolutionary. Known as La Pasionaria she earned a legendary reputation as an orator during the Spanish Civil War, coining the phrase 'No pasarán!' ('They shall not pass!'). Forced into exile after the Spanish Civil War in 1939, she was only able to return to retirement in Spain in 1977 after the death of Franco and the subsequent legalization of the Communist party.

Quotations about Ibarruri
1 One of the most despicable and self-seeking careerists of the communist movement.
Franz Borkenau *European Communism*

2 Her early poverty, her severe black dress and her gifts as a popular orator gave her a moral and romantic appeal to left wing intellectuals and direct contact with the masses.
Raymond Carr (1919–) British historian. *1000 Makers of the 20th Century*

Quotations by Ibarruri
3 They shall not pass!
The Spanish Civil War (H. Thomas), Ch. 16

4 It is better to die on your feet than to live on your knees.
Speech, Paris, 1936

5 It is better to be the widow of a hero than the wife of a coward.
Speech, Valencia, 1936

6 We shall very soon achieve victory and return to our children.
Speeches and Articles, 1936–38

ILLEGITIMACY

1 There are no illegitimate children – only illegitimate parents.
Léon R. Yankwich US lawyer.
Quoting columnist O. O. McIntyre. Decision, State District Court, Southern District of California, June 1928

2 The child is different, not because he is illegitimate, but because he is fatherless and he is going to miss a father in the same way that any child who loses his father early, through death or separation, misses him.
Lena Jeger British politician, Member of Parliament, civil rights activist, and writer.
Illegitimate Children and Their Parents, Foreword [1951]

3 The American woman, when she is an unmarried mother, simply disappears for a while from her community and then comes back, childless, her secret hidden for life.
Pearl S. Buck (1892–1973) US writer.
Children for Adoption, Ch. 1 [1964]

INDEPENDENCE

1 Whilst they are absolutely dependent on their husbands they will be cunning, mean, and selfish, and the men who can be gratified by the fawning fondness of spaniel-like affection have not much delicacy, for love is not to be bought, in any sense of the words, its silken wings are instantly shriveled up when anything beside a return in kind is sought.
Mary Wollstonecraft (1759–97) British writer.
A Vindication of the Rights of Woman, Ch. 7 [1792]

2 But, to render her really virtuous and useful, she must not, if she discharge her civil duties, want, individually, the protection of civil laws; she must not be dependent on her husband's bounty for her subsistence during his life, or support after his death.
Mary Wollstonecraft (1759–97) British writer.
A Vindication of the Rights of Woman, Ch. 7 [1792]

3 Women are brought up to depend on men to sort out financial things...But we are getting more clued up. It's interesting how there is always one woman who asks how she can put money away without her husband knowing. That's when they all sit up and start scribbling furiously.

Susan Fieldman British solicitor.

Discussing 'Money Matters' – a seminar run for women. *The Sunday Times*, 21 Oct 1984

INJUSTICE

See also DISCRIMINATION; LAW

1 I would, without a doubt, rather be a simple soldier than be a woman, because to be truthful, a soldier can become king, but a woman can never become free.

Madeleine de Scudéry (1607–1701) French novelist and poet.

Clelia, An Excellent New Romance, Vol. I [1656–61]

2 What has poor woman done, that she must be debar'd from sense, and sacred poetry?

Aphra Behn (1640–89) English novelist, dramatist, poet, translator, and spy.

The Rover [1677]

3 MARIA. Men rail at weakness themselves create,
And boldly stigmatize the female mind,
As though kind nature's just impartial hand
Had form'd its features in a baser mould

Mercy Otis Warren (1728–1814) US poet, historian, and playwright.

The Ladies of Castile, I:5 [c. 1770]

4 From the day of my mother's death, he has withheld entirely and with perfect impunity my income as a wife. I do not receive, and have not received for the last three years, a single farthing from him.

Caroline Norton (1808–77) British writer.

Referring to her husband. *A Letter to the Queen on Lord Chancellor Cranworth's Marriage and Divorce Bill* [1855]

5 If I had been born a man, I would have conquered Europe. As I was born a woman, I exhausted my energy in tirades against fate, and in eccentricities.

Marie Konstantinovna Bashkirtseff (1860–84) Russian artist and diarist.

The Journal of a Young Artist, 25 June 1884

6 They invent a legend to put the blame for the existence of humanity on women and, if she wants to stop it, they talk about the wonders of civilizations and the sacred responsibilities of motherhood. They can't have it both ways.

Dorothy Miller Richardson (1873–1957) British writer.

Pilgrimage, Vol. II, Ch. 24 [1938]

INTELLECT

1 And from the soul three faculties arise,
The mind, the will, the power; then wherefore shall
A woman have her intellect in vain,
Or not endeavor Knowledge to attain.

Rachel Speght (b. 1597) English writer and poet.

Mortalitie's Memorandum, with a Dreame Prefixed, imaginarie in manner, reall in matter [1621]

2 Whereas in nature we have as clear an understanding as men, if we were bred in schools to mature our brains and to manure our understandings, that we might bring forth the fruits of knowledge.

Margaret Cavendish (c. 1623–c. 1673) English poet, playwright, and writer.

The World's Olio [c. 1670]

3 When women stand at the head of government, the state is immediately plunged into danger because they conduct affairs not by the standard of universality but in accordance with random opinions and inclinations.

Hegel (1770–1831) German philosopher.

The Philosophy of Right [1821]

4 The weakness of their reasoning faculty also explains why women show more sympathy for the unfortunate than men…and why on the contrary they are inferior to men as regards justice, and less honourable and conscientious.

Arthur Schopenhauer (1788–1860) German philosopher.

On Women [1851]

5 Women are intellectually more desultory and volatile than men; they are more occupied with particular instances than with general principles; they judge rather by intuitive perceptions than by deliberate reasoning.

W. E. H. Lecky (1838–1903) British historian.

History of European Morals, II [1869]

6 It is generally admitted that with woman the powers of intuition, of rapid perception, and perhaps of imitation, are more strongly marked than in man; but some, at least, of these faculties are characteristic of the lower races, and therefore of a past and lower state of civilisation.

Charles Darwin (1809–82) British life scientist.

The Descent of Man [1871]

7 The chief distinction in the intellectual powers of the two sexes is shewn by man attaining to a higher eminence, in whatever he takes up, than woman can attain – whether requiring deep thought, reason, or imagination, or merely the use of the senses and hands.

Charles Darwin (1809–82) British life scientist.

The Descent of Man [1871]

8 A woman cannot grasp that one must act from principle; as she has no continuity she does not experience the necessity for logical support of her mental processes…she may be regarded as 'logically insane'.
Otto Weininger (1880–1903) Philosopher who influenced the Nazi movement.
Sex and Character [1906]

9 In general, it can be said that feminine mentality manifests an undeveloped, childlike, or primitive character; instead of the thirst for knowledge, curiosity; instead of judgment, prejudice; instead of thinking, imagination or dreaming; instead of will, wishing.
Emma Jung (1882–1955) Swiss scholar and lecturer.
'On the Nature of Animus' [1931]

10 Now he disliked talking business with her as much as he had enjoyed it before they were married. Now he saw that she understood entirely too well and he felt the usual masculine indignation at the duplicity of women. Added to it was the usual masculine disillusionment in discovering that a woman has a brain.
Margaret Mitchell (1900–49) US writer.
Gone with the Wind, Pt IV, Ch. 36 [1936]

11 I had no reason to doubt that brains were suitable for a woman. And as I had my father's kind of mind – which was also his mother's – I learned that the mind is not sex-typed.
Margaret Mead (1901–78) US anthropologist, writer, editor, and museum curator.
Blackberry Winter [1972]

INTELLECTUALS

1 A learned woman is thought to be a comet, that bodes mischief whenever it appears.
Bathsua Makin (c. 1612–c. 1674) English scholar and writer.
An Essay to Revive the Ancient Education of Gentlewomen [1673]

2 He says a learned woman is the greatest of all calamities.
Marie Ebner von Eschenbach (1830–1916) Austrian writer.
The Two Countesses [1893]

3 The higher mental development of woman, the less possible it is for her to meet a congenial mate who will see in her, not only sex, but also the human being, the friend, the comrade and strong individuality, who cannot and ought not lose a single trait of her character.
Emma Goldman (1869–1940) Russian-born US lecturer and editor.
'The Tragedy of Women's Emancipation', *Anarchism and Other Essays* [1911]

4 What is a highbrow? It is a man who has found something more interesting than women.
Edgar Wallace (1875–1932) British thriller writer.
Interview [1931]

5 I've been called many things, but never an intellectual.
Tallulah Bankhead (1903–68) US actress.
Tallulah, Ch. 15 [1952]

6 She cooks, she cleans, she wins the Nobel prize.
Referring to Rosalyn Yarrow (1921–), who was awarded the Nobel prize for Physiology and Medicine in 1977, for her work which led to a breakthrough in the treatment of diabetes. Newspaper headline [1977]

INTELLIGENCE

See also EDUCATION; INTELLECT

1 A woman cuts her wisdom teeth when she is dead.
Proverb

2 A woman has the form of an angel, the heart of a serpent, and the mind of an ass.
German proverb

3 Women have long hair and short brains.
Proverb

4 The most beautiful woman in the world would not be half so beautiful if she was as great at mathematics as Sir Isaac Newton or as great a metaphysician as the noblest and profoundest school man.
The Gentleman's Magazine, 1738

5 A woman with a beard is not so disgusting as a woman who acts the freethinker.
Johann Kaspar Lavater (1741–1801) Swiss writer and Protestant.
Essays on Physionomy [1775–78]

6 A man is in general better pleased when he has a good dinner upon his table, than when his wife talks Greek.
Samuel Johnson (1709–84) British lexicographer.
Johnsonian Miscellanies, Vol. II (ed. G. B. Hill) [1784]

7 A woman, especially if she have the misfortune of knowing anything, should conceal it as well as she can.
Jane Austen
Northanger Abbey, Ch. 14 [1818]

8 Women are certainly capable of learning, but they are not made for the higher forms of science, such as philosophy and certain types of artistic creativity; these require a universal ingredient. Women may hit on good ideas and they may, of course, have taste and elegance, but they lack the talent for the ideal.
Hegel (1770–1831) German philosopher.
The Philosophy of Right [1821]

9 Even if woman possessed a brain equal to man's – if her intellectual powers were equal to his – the eternal distinction in the physical organisation of the sexes would make the average man in the long run, the mental superior of the average woman. In intellectual labour, man has surpassed, does now, and always will surpass woman.
J. M. Allan
Journal of the Anthropological Society of London, 'On the Differences in the Minds of Men and Women' [1869]

10 When a woman becomes a scholar there is usually something wrong with her sexual organs.
Friedrich Wilhelm Nietzsche (1844–1900) German philospher.
Bartlett's Unfamiliar Quotations (Leonard Louis Levinson) [1900]

11 Extraordinarily important parts of the brain necessary for spiritual life, the frontal convolutions and the temporal lobes, are less well developed in women and this difference is inborn.
Paul Moebius (1853–) German neurologist.
'The Physiological Intellectual Feebleness of Women' [1907]

12 Mother is far too clever to understand anything she does not like.
Arnold Bennett (1867–1931) British novelist.
The Title [1918]

13 Women decide the larger questions of life correctly and quickly, not because of intuition, but simply and solely because they have sense…It is a rare, rare, man who is as steadily intelligent, as constantly sound in judgment, as little put off by appearance, as the average woman.
H. L. Mencken (1880–1956) US journalist.
In Defense of Women [1922]

14 So this gentleman said a girl with brains ought to do something else with them besides think.
Anita Loos (1891–1981) US novelist.
Gentlemen Prefer Blondes, Ch. 1 [1928]

15 In those rare individual cases where women approach genius they also approach masculinity.
Waverley Root
'Women are Intellectually Inferior' [1949]

16 A short neck denotes a good mind…You see, the messages go quicker to the brain because they've shorter to go.
Muriel Spark (1918–) British novelist.
The Ballad of Peckham Rye, Ch. 7 [1960]

17 Do you think it pleases a man when he looks into a woman's eyes and sees a reflection of the British Museum Reading Room?
Muriel Spark (1918–) British novelist.
The Wit of Women (L. and M. Cowan) [c. 1960s]

18 In general all curvaceousness strikes men as incompatible with the life of the mind.
Françoise Parturier (1919–) French writer, feminist, and columnist.
Open Letter to Men [1968]

19 NORA. But if God had wanted us to think with our wombs, why did He give us a brain?
Clare Boothe Luce (1903–) US politician and writer.
Slam the Door Softly [1970]

20 Women have smaller brains than men.
Hojatolislam Rafsanjani Iranian politician.
Remark, July 1986

JARS, Marie de (1566–1645)

French writer. Adopted daughter of the French essayist Montaigne (1533–92), she issued an edition of his *Essais*, after his death, defending him from the grammatical censures of the school of Malherbe. She was an early bluestocking and a staunch defender of women's rights.

1 Society is a cage of idiots.
Essais (Montaigne), 'A Lenten'

2 Concern for individual well-being is for private citizens…but Princes, who enjoy public possessions, should be concerned with the public good.
Proumenoir

3 The common man believes that in order to be chaste a woman must not be clever: in truth it is doing chastity too little honor to believe it can be found beautiful only by the blind.
Proumenoir

4 Even if a woman has only the name of being educated she will be evilly spoken of.
Proumenoir

JEALOUSY

1 If someone with whom one is having an affair keeps on mentioning some woman whom he knew in the past, however long ago it is since they separated, one is always irritated.
Sei Shonagon (c. 966–c. 1013) Japanese poet and diarist.
The Pillow-Book of Sei Shonagon [10th century]

2 Though jealousy be produced by love, as ashes are by fire, yet jealousy extinguishes love as ashes smother the flame.
Margaret of Navarre (1492–1549) French poet, writer, and patron of literature.
'Novel XLVIII, the Fifth Day' [1558]

3 People may go on talking for ever of the jealousies of pretty women; but for real genuine, hard-working envy, there is nothing like an ugly woman with a taste for admiration.
Emily Eden (1797–1869) British-born Indian novelist.
The Semi-Attached Couple, Pt I, Ch. 1 [1830]

4 The 'Green-Eyed Monster' causes much woe, but the absence of this ugly serpent argues the presence of a corpse whose name is Eros.
Minna Antrim (b. 1861) US writer.
Naked Truth and Veiled Allusions [1902]

JHABVALA, Ruth Prawer (1927–   )
German-born novelist who, after marrying an Indian architect, lived for 24 years in India. Also known for her work as a screenwriter with the director James Ivory, she achieved considerable success with her novels set in her adopted country, India. She won the Booker prize for *Heat and Dust* (1975). Other novels include *Esmond in India* (1958), *A New Dominion* (1973), and *In Search of Love and Beauty* (1983).

1 These diseases that people get in India, they're not physical, they're purely psychic. We only get them because we try to resist India – because we shut ourselves up in our little Western egos and don't want to give ourselves. But once we learn to yield, then they must fall away.
Travelers

2 Take me, make what you will of me, I have joy in my submission.
Travelers

3 India…is not a place that one can pick up and down again as if nothing had happened. In a way it's not so much a country as an experience, and whether it turns out to be a good or a bad one depends, I suppose, on oneself.
Travelers

JOAN OF ARC, St (Jeanne d'Arc; c. 1412–31)
French martyr. Also known as the Maid of Orléans, she was the illiterate daughter of a Meuse Valley farmer. From the age of 13 she heard voices telling her that she must save France from the English. Having persuaded Charles VII to allow her to lead an army to relieve the besieged city of Orléans in 1429, she won a great victory that enabled the coronation of Charles to take place at Rheims in July of that

year. The following year she was captured and imprisoned, condemned as a heretic, and in 1431 she was convicted and burned at the stake. She was canonized in 1920.

Quotations about Joan of Arc
1 …a disciple and limb of the fiend, called the Pucelle, that used false enchantments and sorcery.
John of Lancaster, Duke of Bedford (1389–1435) Brother of Henry V. *Proceeding and Ordinances of the Privy Council* (ed. N. H. Nicolas), Vol. IV

2 I saw her mount her horse, armed all in white except her head, a little battle-axe in her hand, on a great black courser which at the door of her lodging pranced boldly and would not at first suffer her to mount; and then she said 'Lead him to the Cross.' This cross was close to the church at the edge of the road. And then she mounted while he stood as quiet as though he had been bound.
Gui de Laval. Letter to his mother.

3 Pity was the inspiration of Jeanne, not the pity of a woman who weeps and groans, but the magnanimous pity of a heroine who feels called to a mission and takes the sword to succour others.
C. A. Sainte-Beuve (1804–69) French writer. *Les Causeries du lundi*

Quotations by Joan of Arc
4 Deliver the keys of all the good towns you have taken and violated in France to the Maid who has been sent by God the King of Heaven! Go away, for God's sake, back to your own country; otherwise, await news of the Maid, who will soon visit you to your great detriment.
Letter to the English, 1429, *Saint Joan of Arc* (Vita Sackville-West)

5 I was in my thirteenth year when God sent a voice to guide me. At first, I was very much frightened. The voice came towards the hour of noon, in summer, in my father's garden.
Said at her trial

6 If I said that God did not send me, I should condemn myself; truly God did send me.
Said at her trial

JOHNSON, Amy (1903–41)
British aviator. One of the great pioneers of aviation, she first came to public notice when she flew solo from England to Australia in 1930. After graduating in economics, from Sheffield University, in 1925 she moved to London, where she joined the London Aeroplane Club. She was the first woman to obtain a ground engineer's licence followed by her pilot's certificate in December 1929. On 5 May the following year she set off on her solo flight to Darwin in an

attempt to beat the record. Although she missed the record by three days she became a national heroine, being called 'Queen of the Air' by the British press. She joined the Air Transport Auxiliary in World War II and, whilst on a flying mission disappeared over the Thames Estuary.

Quotations about Johnson

1 She hung around aerodromes and learned to fly.

Terry Coleman (1931–) British reporter and author. *1000 Makers of the 20th Century*

2 Wonderful Amy the Aeroplane Girl.

Song title

Quotation by Johnson

3 Had I been a man I might have explored the Poles or climbed Mount Everest, but as it was my spirit found outlet in the air.

Myself When Young (ed. Margot Asquith)

JOHNSON, Lady Bird (Claudia Alta J.; 1912–)

Born in Texas, she studied at the University of Texas until her marriage to Lyndon Baines Johnson in 1934. In 1941 she became manager of Lyndon Johnson's congressional office and in 1942 took over as station-owner and manager of KTBC-Radio, Austin, Texas (from 1963 the Texas Broadcasting Company). She participated actively in her husband's political campaigns, acting as hostess to government and diplomatic leaders. *A White House Diary* (1970) gives an account of her five years as First Lady of the United States, beginning on the day (22 Nov 1963) of John F. Kennedy's assassination.

1 It all began so beautifully. After a drizzle in the morning, the sun came out bright and clear. We were driving into Dallas. In the lead car were President and Mrs. Kennedy...

A White House Diary, 22 Nov 1963

2 Lyndon [Johnson] acts like there was never going to be a tomorrow.

The New York Times Magazine, 29 Nov 1964

3 It's odd that you can get so anesthetized by your own pain or your own problem that you don't quite fully share the hell of someone close to you.

A White House Diary, 8 Feb 1965

4 This was one of those terrific, pummeling White House days that can stretch and grind and use you – even I, who only live on the periphery. So what must it be like for Lyndon!

A White House Diary, 14 Mar 1968

JONG, Erica (1942–)

US novelist. Her semi-autobiographical novel *Fear of Flying* (1974) achieved fame with its comic and erotic writing. She has written several novels since then, including *Fanny* (1980) and *How to Save Your Life* (1977).

Quotation about Jong

1 I get the impression that she loves life, and people too...She doesn't write like a man but like a 100% woman, a female, sometimes, a 'bitch'. In many ways she is more forthright, more honest, more daring than most male authors.

Henry Miller *The New York Times* (on *Fear of Flying*), 7 Sept 1974

Quotations by Jong

2 He never regarded himself as crazy. The world was.

Fear of Flying

3 Growing up female in America. What a liability! You grew up with your ears full of cosmetic ads, love songs, advice columns, whoreoscopes, Hollywood gossip, and moral dilemmas on the level of TV soap operas. What litanies the advertisers of the good life chanted at you! What curious catechisms!

Fear of Flying

4 Gossip is the opiate of the oppressed.

Fear of Flying

5 Everyone has talent. What is rare is the courage to follow the talent to the dark place where it leads.

The First Ms. Reader (ed. Francine Klagsbrun), 'The Artist as Housewife: The Housewife as Artist'

JULIAN OF NORWICH (c. 1342–c. 1417)

English mystic and writer. Also known as Juliana, she wrote *Revelations of Divine Love* while living as a recluse in a cell attached to the Church of Julian in Norwich. This work describes visions of Christ's suffering and of the Virgin Mary, which she had received 20 years earlier during a serious illness.

1 He is to us all-thing that is good and comfortable for our help. He is our clothing, for love; He enwraps us and envelops us, embraces and encloses us; He hovers over us for tender love, that He may never leave us.

Revelations of Divine Love, Ch. 4

2 Sin is behovely, but all shall be well and all shall be well and all manner of thing shall be well.

Revelations of Divine Love, Ch. 27

3 I saw not sin; for I believe that it had no manner of substance, nor no part of being, nor it might not be known but by the pain that it caused thereof. And this pain...maketh us to know our self, and ask mercy.

Revelations of Divine Love, Ch. 27

4 And then our good Lord opened my ghostly eye, and shewed me my soul in the midst of my heart. I saw the soul so large as it were an endless world, and also as it were a blessed kingdom. And by the conditions that I saw therein, I understood that it is a worshipful city.
Revelations of Divine Love, Ch. 68

5 He said not, 'thou shalt not be troubled, thou shalt not be travailed, thou shalt not be diseased;' but He said, 'Thou shalt not be overcome.'
Revelations of Divine Love, Ch. 68

JUSTICE

1 Surveillance…the maddening fetter that galls reputation and robs many a woman of her honour who would otherwise gladly have kept it, had she received just treatment. But when in fact she is treated unjustly, her desire for honour begins to flag; so far as this is concerned, close-keeping spoils her character.
Gottfried von Strassburg (fl. 1210) German poet.
Tristan [c. 1210]

2 We know that the solid foundation of a Communist Party are the workers and that our Party must be rooted in their struggle…Negro and white workers, young workers, women workers – will come to understand the need of being a member of the Communist Party.
Elizabeth Gurley Flynn (1890–1964) US political and civil rights activist.
Labor's Own: William Z. Foster [1949]

3 I am a warrior in the time of women warriors; the longing for justice is the sword I carry, the love of womankind my shield.
Sonia Johnson (c. 1936–) US feminist and writer.
From Housewife to Heretic [1981]

KELLER, Helen (1880–1968)

US writer and lecturer. The daughter of a newspaper editor she lost her sight and hearing at the age of 19 months after contracting scarlet fever. When she was nearly seven her parents employed Annie Sullivan, herself partially sighted, to teach Helen Keller the manual alphabet and to lip-read by placing her thumb and forefingers on the speaker's face. She learned to read and write in Braille and, with the help of Annie Sullivan, who 'spelled' the lectures into her hand, graduated *cum laude* from Radcliffe College. She used these experiences to work and help the handicapped by lecturing and writing. Her books include *The Story of My Life* (1902), *The Song of the Stone Wall* (1910), and *Teacher* (1956).

Quotation about Keller
1 She likes stories that make her cry – I think we all do, it's so nice to feel sad when you've nothing particular to be sad about.
Annie Sullivan (1866–1936) US teacher of the handicapped. Letter, 12 Dec 1887

Quotations by Keller
2 Militarism…is one of the chief bulwarks of capitalism, and the day that militarism is undermined, capitalism will fail.
The Story of My Life

3 We could never learn to be brave and patient, if there were only joy in the world.
Atlantic Monthly, May 1890

4 How reconcile this world of fact with the bright world of my imagining? My darkness has been filled with the light of intelligence, and behold, the outer day-light world was stumbling and groping in social blindness.
The Cry for Justice (ed. Upton Sinclair)

KENNY, Elizabeth (1886–1952)

Daughter of an Australian veterinary surgeon in the 'outback', she studied anatomy while staying in a doctor's house after she had broken her wrist. In 1907 she began her training as a nurse. While helping to treat a child suffering from poliomyelitis in 1910, in desperation she applied hot cloths to the convulsed limbs. The treatment was so effective that she developed it for others, later opening her own hospital in South Queensland. Although regarded as a charlatan by orthodox medical practitioners, her excellent results in combating an epidemic of poliomyelitis in 1942 vindicated her treatment.

1 Panic plays no part in the training of a nurse.
And They Shall Walk (with Martha Ostenso)

2 O sleep, O gentle sleep, I thought gratefully, Nature's gentle nurse.
And They Shall Walk (with Martha Ostenso)

3 Some minds remain open long enough for the truth not only to enter but to pass on through by way of a ready exit without pausing anywhere along the route.
And They Shall Walk (with Martha Ostenso)

4 My mother used to say, 'He who angers you, conquers you!' But my mother was a saint.
And They Shall Walk (with Martha Ostenso)

KEY, Ellen (1849–1926)

Swedish feminist writer. She took up teaching in Stockholm in the late 1870s and lectured at the workers' institute for the next 20 years. In 1900 she published *Barnets århundrade* (*The Century of the Child*; 1909) which made her world famous, dealing with the issues of marriage, motherhood, and family life. Her controversial ideas on sex, love, and marriage led to her being called the 'Pallas of Sweden'.

1 The emancipation of women is practically the greatest egoistic movement of the nineteenth century, and the most intense affirmation of the right of the self that history has yet seen.
The Century of the Child, Ch. 2

2 At every step the child should be allowed to meet the real experiences of life; the thorns should never be plucked from his roses.
The Century of the Child, Ch. 3

3 Love is moral even without legal marriage, but marriage is immoral without love.
The Morality of Woman and Other Essays, 'The Morality of Woman'

4 Everything, everything in war is barbaric...But the worst barbarity of war is that it forces men collectively to commit acts against which individually they would revolt with their whole being.
War, Peace, and the Future, Ch. 6

LA FAYETTE, Marie de (1634–93)

French novelist. Her novel *La Princesse de Clèves* (1678), with its description of the conflict between duty and passion, earned her a lasting place in French literature. Her friends included such literary figures as La Rochefoucauld. Other novels are *La Princesse de Montpensier* (1662) and *Zaÿde* (1670).

1 Most mothers think that to keep young people away from love-making it is enough never to speak of it in their presence.
The Princess of Clèves, Part 1

2 I know too much of life to be ignorant of the fact that appreciation of the husband does not prevent a man from falling in love with the wife.
The Princess of Clèves, Part 3

3 I was wrong in believing there was a man capable of hiding what pleases his vanity.
The Princess of Clèves, Part 3

4 You had forgotten, then, that I loved you to distraction, and that I was your husband? One or the other can drive a man to extremities – how much more so the two together!
The Princess of Clèves, Part 4

LANGTRY, Lily (1853–1929)

British actress. Known as 'the Jersey Lily', her success on the stage owed as much to her beauty as to her acting ability. Daughter of the dean of Jersey, she married Edward Langtry in 1874; after his death (1897), she married Hugo de Bathe in 1899. She was the first publicly

acknowledged mistress of the Prince of Wales (later Edward VII) who, when her colt won the Cesarewitch, gave the order that she should become the first woman member of the Jockey Club. The first woman of high society to make a career on the stage, her first appearance was as Kate Hardcastle in *She Stoops to Conquer*; her most successful part was as Rosalind in *As You Like It*.

1 Anyone who limits his vision to his memories of yesterday is already dead.
Because I Loved Him (Noel B. Gerson)

2 The sentimentalist ages far more quickly than the person who loves his work and enjoys new challenges.
New York Sun, 1906

LANGUAGE

1 Give us that grand word 'woman' once again,
And let's have done with 'lady'; one's a term
Full of fine force, strong, beautiful, and firm,
Fit for the noblest use of tongue or pen;
And one's a word for lackeys.
Ella Wheeler Wilcox (1855–1919) US poet and journalist.
'Woman' [1883]

2 *Miss*, *n*. A title with which we brand unmarried women to indicate that they are in the market. Miss, Missis (Mrs) and Mister (Mr) are the three most distinctly disagreeable words in the language, in sound and sense. Two are corruptions of Mistress, the other of Master...If we must have them, let us be consistent and give one to the unmarried man. I venture to suggest Mush, abbreviated to Mh.
Ambrose Bierce (1842–?1914) US writer and journalist.
The Devil's Dictionary [1906]

3 If the English language had been properly organized...then there would be a word which meant both 'he' and 'she', and I could write, 'If John or Mary comes heesh will want to play tennis,' which would save a lot of trouble.
A. A. Milne (1882–1956) British writer.
The Christopher Robin Birthday Book [1931]

4 Call me madame.
Frances Perkins (1882–1965) US social worker and politician.
Deciding the term of address she would prefer when made the first woman to hold a cabinet office in the USA. *Familiar Quotations* (J. Bartlett) [1933]

5 As hunting takes place in the open air and is ever so English and ever so traditional, the word bitch can be frequently employed without offence, and indeed is a rare pleasure for a lady to be able to look fearlessly into the eyes of

another lady, even though she be on four legs, and say loudly and clearly, 'Bitch!'
Virginia Graham (1912–) US writer and broadcaster.
Say Please, Ch. 14 [1949]

6 Although the witch, incarnate or in surrogate mother disguise, remains a universal bogey, pejorative aspects of the wizard, her masculine counterpart, have vanished over the patriarchal centuries. The term *wizard* has acquired reverential status – wizard of finance, wizard of diplomacy, wizard of science.
Dena Justin (1912–) US writer and educator.
Natural History, 'From Mother Goddess to Dishwasher', Feb 1973

7 Animals which are traditionally referred to as female include the cow, sow, bitch and cat – all derogatory words in our language when they are applied to human beings. English does not use gender extensively, but its linguistic sexism is intact because sexism is intact.
Arlene Raven (1944–) US art historian and feminist.
Womanspace, FebMar 1973

8 The liberation of language is rooted in the liberation of ourselves.
Mary Daly (1928–) US educator, writer, and theologian.
The Church and the Second Sex [1975]

9 For most women, the language of conversation is primarily a language of rapport: a way of establishing connections and negotiating relationships...For most men, talk is primarily a means to preserve independence and negotiate and maintain status in a hierarchical social order.
Deborah Tannen US writer and professor of linguistics.
You Just Don't Understand [1990]

10 For many people, feminism has almost been equated with a tiresome insistence on 'chair' and 'dustperson', and plenty of strong-minded women who've never had the slightest difficulty with language think the whole thing is absurd – it's certainly given an easy target to its enemies. But they underestimate the cumulative effect of always hearing Stone-Age man, postman, chairman; of the different reactions you have to 'landlord' and 'landlady' of 'a bit of a bitch' and 'a bit of a dog'.
Katherine Whitehorn (1926–) British journalist.
Observer, 18 Aug 1991

LAW

1 Guardians are appointed for males as well as for females, but only for males under puberty, on account of their infirmity of age; for females,

however, both under and over puberty, on account of the weakness of their sex as well as their ignorance of business matters.
Ulpian (Domitius Ulpianus; d. 228 AD) Roman jurist.
Rules, V [3rd century AD]

2 Down to the fifth generation the males in the paternal line shall succeed. After the fifth, however, the daughter shall succeed to everything coming both from her father's and mother's side; not until then does the inheritance pass from the spear to the spindle.
Lex Thuringorum [6th century]

3 These three are not to be accepted as a witness: a woman, a young serving boy, and a man slave.
Dînâ-Maînôg-î Khirad (Zoroastrian text) [c. 10th century]

4 We uphold the custom which, rectifying the errors of the law, denies women the right to give evidence. We hereby give this custom legal force and forbid women's evidence to be taken in matters connected with contracts. But in purely feminine affairs, where men are not permitted to be present – I refer to childbirth and other things which only the female eye may see – women may testify.
Leo the Wise (886–912) Byzantine emperor.
The Novels of Leo (P. Noailles and A. Dain) [10th century]

5 Every Feme Covert is a sort of infant...It is seldom, almost never, that a married woman can have any action to use her wit only in her own name: her husband is her stern, her prime mover, without whom she cannot do much at home, and less abroad.
Anonymous
A 'Feme Covert' is a married woman. *The Lawes Resolutions of Women's Rights* [16th century]

6 By marriage the very being or legal existence of woman is suspended, or at least it is incorporated and consolidated into that of a husband.
Sir William Blackstone (1723–80) British jurist.
Commentaries on the Laws of England [1780]

7 No vote can be given by lunatics, idiots, minors, aliens, females, persons convicted of perjury, subornation of perjury, bribery treating or undue influence, or by those tainted of felony or outlawed in a criminal suit.
Sir William Blackstone (1723–80) British jurist.
Commentaries on the Laws of England [1780]

8 But, to render her really virtuous and useful, she must not, if she discharge her civil duties, want, individually, the protection of civil laws; she must not be dependent on her husband's

bounty for her subsistence during his life, or support after his death.
Mary Wollstonecraft (1759–97) British writer.
A Vindication of the Rights of Woman, Ch. 7 [1792]

9 The barbarous custom of wresting from women whatever she possesses, whether by inheritance, donation or her own industry, and conferring it all upon the man she marries, to be used at his discretion and will, perhaps waste it on his wicked indulgences, without allowing her any control or redress, is such a monstrous perversion of *justice* by *law*, that we might well marvel how it could obtain in a Christian community.
Sarah Josepha Hale (1788–1879) US editor, writer, and poet.
Godey's Lady's Book, 'The Rights of Married Women', May 1837

10 A married woman in English law has no legal existence: her being is absorbed in that of her husband. Years of separation or desertion cannot alter this position. Unless divorced by special enactment of the House of Lords, the legal fiction holds her to be 'one' with her husband, even though she may never hear of him.
Caroline Norton (1808–77) British writer.
A Letter to the Queen on Lord Chancellor Cranworth's Marriage and Divorce Bill [1855]

11 There remain no legal slaves – except for the woman in every man's home.
John Stuart Mill (1806–73) British philosopher.
Referring to Britain. *On the Subjection of Women* [1860]

12 The whole theory of the law where it concerns women, is a slavish one. The merging of the wife's name with that of her husband is emblematic of all her legal rights. The Torch of Hymen serves but to light the Pyre on which these rights are offered up.
Luillius Alonzo Emery US judge.
Common Legal Principles (F. W. Marshall) [c. 1890]

13 It is about my daughter…She is unfortunate in having a bad husband…he is very ready in useing his hands to her…she applied for a seperation order in the sheriff court she was told by the sherriff that he did not count it illtreatment for a husband to put his wife out unless he marked her…the sheriff told her she would have to go back to her husband or loose her baby as the husband got full control of her.
Letter to Marie Stopes. *Mother England* (Marie Stopes) [1926]

14 There are only about 20 murders a year in London and many not at all serious – some are just husbands killing their wives.
Commander G. H. Hatherill
Scotland Yard, 1954

15 Legislation and case law still exist in some parts of the United States permitting the 'passion shooting' by husband of a wife; the reverse, of course, is known as homicide.
Diane B. Schulder (1937–) US lawyer and educator.
Sisterhood is Powerful (ed. Robin Morgan) [1970]

16 A trial at Bradford Crown Court yesterday was ajourned *sine die* after a barrister had objected because 11 members of the jury were women.
The Times, 1980

17 He would stand the chance of violent sexual abuse and becoming a homosexual if sent to a state prison.
Judge Robert C. Abel US judge.
Explaining why he had given a sentence of only 120 days for the raping and beating of a woman. [1982]

18 I am not saying that a girl hitching home late at night should not be protected by the law, but she was guilty of a great deal of contributory negligence.
Bertrand Richards (1913–) British judge.
Ipswich, 1982

LEARNING
See EDUCATION

LESBIANISM

1 *The Well of Loneliness*, a novel by Radclyffe Hall, which treats of intimate relationships between women, was withdrawn on the advice of the Home Secretary, to whom the publishers submitted it for an opinion. But this was not before it had been condemned by the editor of the Sunday Express, who declared he 'would sooner give a healthy boy or girl a dose of prussic acid than a copy of it.'
The Daily Telegraph, 20 Dec 1928

2 You're neither unnatural, nor abominable, nor mad; you're as much a part of what people call nature as anyone else; only you're unexplained as yet – you've not got your niche in creation.
Radclyffe Hall (1886–1943) British writer and poet.
The Well of Loneliness [1928]

3 Refusal to make herself the object is not always what turns women to homosexuality; most lesbians, on the contrary, seek to cultivate the treasures of their femininity.
Simone de Beauvoir (1908–86) French writer and feminist.
Le Deuxième Sexe (*The Second Sex*) [1949]

4 Lesbian is a label invented by the man to throw at any woman who dares to be his equal,

who dares to challenge his prerogatives…who dares to assert the primacy of her own needs.
Radicalesbians
The Woman-Identified Woman [1970s]

5 I have no doubt that lesbianism makes a woman virile and open to *any* sexual stimulation, and that she is more often than not a more adequate and lively partner in bed than a 'normal' woman.
Charlotte Wolff (1904–) German-born British psychiatrist and writer.
Love Between Women [1971]

6 It is only when she can denounce the idiocy of religious scriptures and legal strictures that bind her and can affirm her Lesbian nature as but a single facet of her whole personality that she can become fully human.
Del Martin (1921–) US civil rights activist, feminist, and writer.
LesbianWoman (with Phyllis Lyon) [1972]

7 I never said I was a dyke even to a dyke because there wasn't a dyke in the land who thought she should be a dyke or even thought she was a dyke so how could we talk about it.
Jill Johnston (1929–) British-born US writer and feminist.
Lesbian Nation: The Feminist Solution [1973]

8 Lesbianism is not a matter of sexual preference, but rather one of political choice which every woman must make if she is to become woman-identified and thereby end male supremacy.
Lesbianism and the Women's Movement (ed. N. Myron and C. Burch) [1975]

LIFE

1 LORD ILLINGWORTH. The Book of Life begins with a man and a woman in a garden.
MRS ALLONBY. It ends with Revelations.
Oscar Wilde (1854–1900) Irish-born British dramatist.
A Woman of No Importance, I [1893]

2 Life has got to be lived – that's all there is to it. At 70, I would say the advantage is that you take life more calmly. You know that 'this, too, shall pass!'
Eleanor Roosevelt (1884–1962) US First Lady, government official, writer, humanitarian, and lecturer.
The New York Times, 8 Oct 1954

3 You don't get to choose how you're going to die. Or when. You can only decide how you're going to live. Now.
Joan Baez (1941–) US folksinger and civil rights activist.
Daybreak [1966]

4 I've looked at life from both sides now
From up and down, and still somehow
It's life's illusions I recall
I really don't know life at all.
Joni Mitchell (1943–) US songwriter and singer.
'Both Sides, Now' [1969]

LONELINESS

1 I grow lean
in loneliness,
like a water lily
gnawed by a beetle.
Kaccipettu Nannakaiyar (3rd century) Indian poet.
Interior Landscape: Love Poems from a Classical Tamil Anthology (ed. A. K. Tamanaujan) [3rd century]

2 So lonely am I
My body is a floating weed
Severed at the roots
Were there water to entice me,
I would follow it, I think.
Ono no Komachi (834–880) Japanese poet.
Kokinshu, Anthology of Japanese Literature (ed. Donald Keene) [9th century]

3 But who can count the beatings of the lonely heart?
Susan Edmonstone Ferrier (1782–1854) Scottish novelist.
The Inheritance, Ch. 1 [1824]

LONGWORTH, Alice Roosevelt (1884–1980)
Daughter of President Theodore Roosevelt and wife of Congressman Nicholas Longworth, she was noted for her social gatherings, sharp wit, and political acumen.

1 I have a simple philosophy. Fill what's empty. Empty what's full. And scratch where it itches.
The Best (Peter and Leonard Ross)

2 He looks as if he had been weaned on a pickle.
Longworth was referring to Calvin Coolidge (1872–1933), US president (1923–9). *Crowded Hours*

3 Were it not for Czolgosz we'd all be back in our brownstone-front houses. That's where we'd be. And I would have married for money and been divorced for good cause.
Czolgosz assassinated President McKinley in 1901.
Saturday Evening Post, 4 Dec 1965

LOOS, Anita (1893–1981)
US novelist and screenwriter. She began as a child actress, both on stage and screen, but by the age of 20 she was working as a professional screenwriter, on such films as *The Perfect Woman* (1920) and *Learning to Love* (1925). Later screenwriting credits include the films

Saratoga (1937), *Blossoms in the Dust* (1941), and *I Married an Angel* (1942). She is chiefly remembered for her novel *Gentlemen Prefer Blondes* (1925), which looked at the Jazz Age with a cool satirical eye and introduced the character of Lorelei Lee, the archetypal flapper. She also wrote *But Gentlemen Marry Brunettes* (1928).

1 Gentlemen always seem to remember blondes.
Gentlemen Prefer Blondes, Ch. 1

2 So this gentleman said a girl with brains ought to do something else with them besides think.
Gentlemen Prefer Blondes, Ch. 1

3 Kissing your hand may make you feel very very good but a diamond and safire bracelet lasts forever.
Gentlemen Prefer Blondes, Ch. 4

4 Any girl who was a lady would not even think of having such a good time that she did not remember to hang on to her jewelry.
Gentlemen Prefer Blondes, Ch. 4

5 I'm furious about the Women's Liberationists. They keep getting up on soapboxes and proclaiming that women are brighter than men. That's true, but it should be kept very quiet or it ruins the whole racket.
Observer, 'Sayings of the Year', 30 Dec 1973

LOVE

1 All is fair in love and war.
Proverb

2 All the world loves a lover.
Proverb

3 Love laughs at locksmiths.
Proverb

4 Love makes the world go round.
Proverb

5 Love will find a way.
Proverb

6 Lucky at cards, unlucky in love.
Proverb

7 No love like the first love.
Proverb

8 Salt water and absence wash away love.
Proverb

9 True love never grows old.
Proverb

10 When poverty comes in at the door, love flies out of the window.
Proverb

11 Although love dwells in gorgeous palaces, and sumptuous apartments, more willingly than in miserable and desolate cottages, it cannot be denied but that he sometimes causes his power to be felt in the gloomy recesses of forests, among the most bleak and rugged mountains, and in the dreary caves of a desert...
Giovanni Boccaccio (1313–75) Italian poet.
Decameron, 'Third Day' [c. 1350]

12 Love built on beauty, soon as beauty, dies.
John Donne (1573–1631) English poet.
Elegies, 2, 'The Anagram' [1590]

13 Come live with me, and be my love;
And we will all the pleasures prove
That hills and valleys, dales and fields,
Woods or steepy mountain yields.
Christopher Marlowe (1564–93) English dramatist.
The Passionate Shepherd to his Love [16th century]

14 If all the world and love were young,
And truth in every shepherd's tongue,
These pretty pleasures might me move
To live with thee, and be thy love.
Walter Raleigh (1554–1618) English explorer.
Answer to Marlowe [16th century]

15 For aught that I could ever read,
Could ever hear by tale or history,
The course of true love never did run smooth.
William Shakespeare (1564–1616) English dramatist.
A Midsummer Night's Dream, I:1 [1596]

16 But love is blind, and lovers cannot see
The pretty follies that themselves commit.
William Shakespeare (1564–1616) English dramatist.
The Merchant of Venice, II:6 [1597]

17 If thou rememb'rest not the slightest folly
That ever love did make thee run into,
Thou hast not lov'd.
William Shakespeare (1564–1616) English dramatist.
As You Like It, II:4 [1600]

18 Let me not to the marriage of true minds
Admit impediments. Love is not love
Which alters when it alteration finds,
Or bends with the remover to remove.
O, no! it is an ever-fixed mark,
That looks on tempests and is never shaken.
William Shakespeare (1564–1616) English dramatist.
Sonnet 116 [1609]

19 Come live with me, and be my love,
And we will some new pleasures prove
Of golden sands, and crystal brooks,
With silken lines, and silver hooks.
John Donne (1573–1631) English poet.
The Bait [c. 1610]

20   I am two fools, I know,
For loving, and for saying so
In whining Poetry.
John Donne (1573–1631) English poet.
The Triple Fool [c. 1610]

21   Those have most power to hurt us that we love.
Francis Beaumont (1584–1616) English dramatist.
The Maid's Tragedy, V:6 [1611]

22   There are very few people who are not ashamed of having been in love when they no longer love each other.
Duc de la Rochefoucauld (1613–80) French writer.
Maximes, 71 [1665]

23   Love ceases to be a pleasure, when it ceases to be a secret.
Aphra Behn (1640–89) English novelist and dramatist.
The Lover's Watch, 'Four o'clock' [17th century]

24   Once a woman has given you her heart you can never get rid of the rest of her.
John Vanbrugh
The Relapse, II:1 [1696]

25   Say what you will, 'tis better to be left than never to have been loved.
William Congreve (1670–1729) British Restoration dramatist.
The Way of the World, II:1 [1700]

26   She who has never loved has never lived.
John Gay (1685–1732) English poet and dramatist.
Captives [18th century]

27   To men, love is an incident; to women a vocation. They live by and for their emotions.
Denis Diderot (1713–84) French writer.
Celibate's Apology

28   Love is the wisdom of the fool and the folly of the wise.
Samuel Johnson (1709–84) British lexicographer.
Johnsonian Miscellanies, Vol. II (ed. G. B. Hill) [1784]

29   *Plaisir d'amour ne dure qu'un moment,
Chagrin d'amour dure toute la vie.*
Love's pleasure lasts but a moment; love's sorrow lasts all through life.
Jean-Pierre Claris de Florian (1755–94) French writer of fables.
Celestine

30   Next to being married, a girl likes to be crossed in love a little now and then.
Jane Austen (1775–1817) British novelist.
Pride and Prejudice, Ch. 24 [1813]

31   Love is above the laws, above the opinion of men; it is the truth, the flame, the pure element, the primary idea of the moral world.
Germaine de Staël (1766–1817) French novelist, literary critic, and feminist.
Zulma, and Other Tales [1813]

32   It is said there is no happiness, and no love to be compared to that which is felt for the first time. Most persons erroneously think so; but love like other arts requires experience, and terror and ignorance, on its first approach, prevent our feeling it as strongly as at a later period.
Caroline Lamb (1785–1828) British novelist.
Glenarvon, Vol. I, Ch. 11 [1816]

33   Man's love is of man's life a thing apart,
'Tis woman's whole existence.
Lord Byron (1788–1824) British poet.
Don Juan, I [1819–24]

34   Love in a hut, with water and a crust,
Is – Love, forgive us! – cinders, ashes, dust;
Love in a palace is perhaps at last
More grievous torment than a hermit's fast.
John Keats (1795–1821) British poet.
Lamia, II [1820]

35   All mankind love a lover.
Ralph Waldo Emerson (1803–82) US poet and essayist.
Essays, 'Love' [c. 1840]

36   My love for Linton is like the foliage in the woods: time will change it, I'm well aware, as winter changes the trees. My love for Heathcliff resembles the eternal rocks beneath: a source of little visible delight, but necessary. Nelly, I *am* Heathcliff!
Emily Brontë (1818–48) British novelist and poet.
Wuthering Heights, Ch. 9 [1847]

37   How do I love thee? Let me count the ways.
I love thee to the depth and breadth and height
My soul can reach.
Elizabeth Barrett Browning (1806–61) British poet.
Sonnets from the Portuguese, XLIII [1850]

38   I love thee with a love I seemed to lose
With my lost saints – I love thee with the breath,
Smiles, tears, of all my life! – and, if God choose,
I shall but love thee better after death.
Elizabeth Barrett Browning (1806–61) British poet.
Sonnets from the Portuguese, XLIII [1850]

39   I hold it true, whate'er befall;
I feel it, when I sorrow most;
'Tis better to have loved and lost
Than never to have loved at all.
Alfred, Lord Tennyson (1809–92) British poet.
In Memoriam A.H.H., XXVII [1850]

40 'Tis strange what a man may do, and a woman yet think him an angel.
William Makepeace Thackeray (1811–63) British novelist.
Henry Esmond, Ch. 7 [1852]

41 Here with a Loaf of Bread beneath the Bough,
A Flask of Wine, a Book of Verse – and Thou
Beside me singing in the Wilderness –
And Wilderness is Paradise enow.
Edward Fitzgerald (1809–83) British poet.
The Rubáiyát of Omar Khayyám [1859]

42 Love's like the measles – all the worse when it comes late in life.
Douglas William Jerrold (1803–57) British dramatist.
Wit and Opinions of Douglas Jerrold, 'A Philanthropist' [1859]

43 Such ever was love's way; to rise, it stoops.
Robert Browning (1812–89) British poet.
A Death in the Desert [1864]

44 I doubt whether any girl would be satisfied with her lover's mind if she knew the whole of it.
Anthony Trollope (1815–82) British novelist.
The Small House at Allington, Ch. 4 [1864]

45 What the gods taught me I have given you –
a rich hoard of holy runes;
but of the strength of my maidenly inheritance
I was bereft by the hero to whom I now bow.
Drained of knowledge but full of desire;
rich in love but deprived of strength;
do not despise the poor creature
who can grudge you nothing but give no more!
Richard Wagner (1813–83) German composer.
Said by Brünnhilde to Siegfried. *Götterdämmerung*, Prologue [1876]

46 A woman despises a man for loving her, unless she returns his love.
Elizabeth Drew Stoddard (1823–1902) US novelist and poet.
Two Men, Ch. 32 [1888]

47 Love is like the measles; we all have to go through with it.
Jerome K. Jerome (1859–1927) British humorist.
Idle Thoughts of an Idle Fellow [1889]

48 And I was desolate and sick of an old passion.
Ernest Dowson (1867–1900) British lyric poet.
Non Sum Qualis Eram Bonae Sub Regno Cynarae (1896)

49 Look not in my eyes, for fear
They mirror true the sight I see,
And there you find your face too clear
And love it and be lost like me.
A. E. Housman (1859–1936) British scholar and poet.
A Shropshire Lad, 'March' [1896]

50 'Tis better to have loved and lost than never to have lost at all.
Samuel Butler (1835–1902) British writer.
The Way of All Flesh, Ch. 77 [1903]

51 Women who love the same man have a kind of bitter freemasonry.
Max Beerbohm (1872–1956) British writer.
Zuleika Dobson, Ch. 4 [1911]

52 God is Love – I dare say. But what a mischievous devil Love is!
Samuel Butler (1835–1902) British writer.
Notebooks [1912]

53 Because women can do nothing except love, they've given it a ridiculous importance.
W. Somerset Maugham (1874–1965) British novelist.
The Moon and Sixpence, Ch. 41 [1919]

54 Love one another, but make not a bond of love:
Let it rather be a moving sea between the shores of your souls.
Fill each other's cup but drink not from one cup.
Give one another of your bread but eat not from the same loaf…
And stand together yet not too near together:
For the pillars of the temple stand apart,
And the oak tree and the cypress grow not in eath other's shadow.
Kahlil Gibran (1833–1931) Lebanese mystic and poet.
The Prophet [1923]

55 This is what I know:
Lover's oaths are thin as rain;
Love's a harbinger of pain –
Would it were not so!
Dorothy Parker (1893–1967) US writer, poet, and humorist.
Enough Rope, 'Somebody's Song' [1927]

56 Everyone has experienced that truth: that love, like a running brook, is disregarded, taken for granted; but when the brook freezes over, then people begin to remember how it was when it ran, and they want it to run again.
Kahil Gibran (1833–1931) Lebanese mystic and poet.
Beloved Prophet (ed. Virginia Hilu) [c. 1930]

57 It is better to be first with an ugly woman than the hundredth with a beauty.
Pearl Buck (1892–1973) US novelist.
The Good Earth, Ch. 1 [1931]

58   Oh, love is real enough, you will find it some day, but it has one arch-enemy – and that is life.
Jean Anouilh (1910–87) French dramatist.
Ardèle [1948]

59   Love is, above all, the gift of oneself.
Jean Anouilh (1910–87) French dramatist.
Ardèle [1948]

60   Many a man has fallen in love with a girl in a light so dim he would not have chosen a suit by it.
Maurice Chevalier (1888–1972) French singer and actor.
Attrib. [1955]

61   Every little girl knows about love. It is only her capacity to suffer because of it that increases.
Françoise Sagan (1935–   ) French writer.
Daily Express, 1957

62   Time was away and somewhere else,
There were two glasses and two chairs
And two people with one pulse.
Louis MacNeice (1907–63) Irish-born British poet.
Meeting Point

63   Love means never having to say you're sorry.
Erich Segal (1937–   ) US writer.
Love Story [1970]

64   To the men and women who own men and women
those of us meant to be lovers
we will not pardon you
for wasting our bodies and time.
Leonard Cohen (1934–   ) Canadian poet.
The Energy of Slaves [1972]

65   Perhaps at fourteen every boy should be in love with some ideal woman to put on a pedestal and worship. As he grows up, of course, he will put her on a pedestal the better to view her legs.
Barry Norman (1933–   ) British cinema critic and broadcaster.
The Listener, 1978

LOVE AND FRIENDSHIP

1   Most friendship is feigning, most loving mere folly.
William Shakespeare (1564–1616) English dramatist.
As You Like It, II:7 [1600]

2   Friendship is a disinterested commerce between equals; love, an abject intercourse between tyrants and slaves.
Oliver Goldsmith (1728–74) Irish-born British writer.
The Good-Natured Man, I [1768]

3   If we *let* our friend become cold and selfish and exacting without a remonstrance, we are no true lover, no true friend.
Harriet Beecher Stowe (1811–96) US writer and social critic.
Little Foxes, Ch. 3 [1865]

4   A woman can become a man's friend only in the following stages – first an acquaintance, next a mistress, and only then a friend.
Anton Chekhov (1860–1904) Russian dramatist.
Uncle Vanya, II [1897]

5   I'm not sure if a mental relation with a woman doesn't make it impossible to love her. To know the *mind* of a woman is to end in hating her. Love means the pre-cognitive flow…it is the honest state before the apple.
D. H. Lawrence (1885–1930) British novelist and poet.
Letter to Dr Trigant Burrow, 3 Aug 1927

6   No human relation gives one possession in another – every two souls are absolutely different. In friendship or in love, the two side by side raise hands together to find what one cannot reach alone.
Kahil Gibran (1833–1931) Lebanese mystic and poet.
Beloved Prophet (Virginia Hilu) [c. 1930]

LOVE AND MARRIAGE

1   …she is offering herself for sale. Certainly any woman who comes to marry through desires of this kind deserves wages, not gratitude, for clearly her mind is on the man's property, not himself, and she would be ready to prostitute herself to a richer man, if she could.
Heloise (c. 1100–c. 1163) French abbess.
The Letters of Abelard and Heloise [12th century]

2   Nuptial love maketh mankind; friendly love perfecteth it; but wanton love corrupteth and embaseth it.
Francis Bacon (1561–1626) English philosopher.
Essays, 'Of Love' [1597]

3   Any one must see at a glance that if men and women marry those whom they do not love, they must love those whom they do not marry.
Harriet Martineau (1802–76) British writer.
Society in America, Vol. III, 'Marriage' [1837]

4   Love in the heart of a wife should partake largely of the nature of *Gratitude*. She should fill her soul with gratitude to God and to the

Man who has chosen *her* to be his helpmate for time and for Eternity.
Mrs John Farrar
The Young Lady's Friend [1847]

5 The amount of women in London who flirt with their own husbands is perfectly scandalous. It looks so bad. It is simply washing one's clean linen in public.
Oscar Wilde (1854–1900) Irish-born British dramatist.
The Importance of Being Earnest, I [1895]

6 After all, the rosy love-making and marrying and Epithalamy are no more than the dawn of things…Try as we may to stay those delightful moments they fade and pass remorselessly…We go on – we grow. At least we age.
H. G. Wells (1866–1946) British writer.
Love and Mr Lewisham [1900]

LUST

1 All witchcraft comes from carnal lust which in women is insatiable.
Jacob Sprenger and Hendrich Kramer German Dominican monks.
The indispensable handbook for the Inquisition. *Malleus Maleficarum* [1489]

2 How a man must hug, and dandle, and kittle, and play a hundred little tricks with his bedfellow when he is disposed to make that use of her that nature designed for her.
Erasmus (1466–1536) Dutch humanist, scholar, and writer.
The Praise of Folly [1511]

3 Have you not as yet observed that pleasure, which is undeniably the sole motive force behind the union of the sexes, is nevertheless not enough to form a bond between them? And that, if it is preceded by desire which impels, it is succeeded by disgust which repels? That is a law of nature which love alone can alter.
Pierre Choderlos de Laclos (1741–1803) French novelist.
Les Liaisons dangereuses, Letter 131 [1782]

4 Those who restrain Desire, do so because theirs is weak enough to be restrained.
William Blake (1757–1827) British poet.
The Marriage of Heaven and Hell, 'Those who restrain Desire…' [1793]

5 Man in his lust has regulated long enough this whole question of sexual intercourse. Now let the mother of mankind, whose prerogative it is to set bounds to his indulgence, rouse up and give this whole matter a thorough, fearless examination.
Elizabeth Cady Stanton (1815–1902) US suffragette and abolitionist.
Letter to Susan B. Anthony, 1853

6 A mutual and satisfied sexual act is of great benefit to the average woman, the magnetism of it is health giving. When it is not desired on the part of the woman and she has no response, *it should not take place*. This is an act of prostitution and is degrading to the woman's finer sensibility, all the marriage certificates on earth to the contrary notwithstanding.
Margaret Sanger (1883–1966) US nurse, editor, writer, and civil rights activist.
Family Limitations [1917]

7 She gave me a smile I could feel in my hip pocket.
Raymond Chandler (1888–1959) US novelist.
Farewell, My Lovely, Ch. 18 [1940]

MANN, Erika (1905–69)
German writer and actress. Daughter of Thomas Mann (1875–1955), she was born in Munich, moving to Berlin to study with Max Reinhardt in preparation for an acting career. In 1925 she played the lead in the first play, *Anja and Esther*, by her brother (Klaus Mann; 1906–49). She married Gustaf Gründgens, an actor who became a Nazi, and who she divorced after the Nazi conquest of Germany. She left Germany in 1933, moving to Britain, when she met and married (1935) the poet W. H. Auden, with whom she moved to the United States at the beginning of World War II. Her works include *School for Barbarians* (1938), *Escape to Life* (with Klaus Mann; 1939), *The Other Germany* (with Klaus Mann; 1940), and *The Lights Go Down* (1940).

1 The nightmare dreamer is delivered up to the horror he himself has created, and derives not the slightest relief from the neutral world, such as would be granted by feeling that it is hot or windy, that other people are present, or that the day or the night is coming to an end. The dreamer knows and perceives nothing but the horror of his dream.
The Last Year of Thomas Mann, a Revealing Memoir by His Daughter

2 There's absolutely no discipline in the democracies. The other day our propaganda minister said that the democracies strike him as being a collection of comical old fogies. But I've got to say it myself; they're rotten and corrupt to the marrow.
The Lights Go Down, 'The City'

3 I want the child to become a human being, a good and decent man who knows the difference

between lies and truth, aware of liberty and dignity and true reason, not the opportunistic reason dictated by policy which turns black white if it's useful at the moment. I want the boy to become a decent human being – a man and not a Nazi!
School for Barbarians, Prologue

4 But the Hitler Youth organization, that third circle around the child, is the most expansive, most important and by far the most comprehensive of his influences.
School for Barbarians, 'The State Youth'

MARIE ANTOINETTE (1755–93)

The wife of Louis XVI of France. Daughter of Emperor Francis I and Maria Theresa of Austria, she married Louis while he was still dauphin. Her extravagant lifestyle, uncompromising attitude to reform, and sympathy for Austria were contributing factors to his overthrow in the French Revolution. She was guillotined nine months after her husband.

Quotations about Marie Antoinette

1 It is now sixteen or seventeen years since I saw the Queen of France at Versailles, and surely never lighted on this orb a more delightful vision, glittering like the morning star full of life and splendour and joy.
Edmund Burke (1729–97) British politician. *Reflections on the Revolution in France*

2 Little did I dream that I should have lived to see disasters fallen upon her in a nation of gallant men, in a nation of men of honour and of cavaliers. I thought ten thousand swords must have leapt from their scabbards to avenge even a look that threatened her with insult. But the age of chivalry is gone.
Edmund Burke (1729–97) British politician. *Reflections on the Revolution in France*

Quotations by Marie Antoinette

3 I cannot consent to be separated from my son. I can feel no enjoyment without my children; with them I can regret nothing.
Remark, 21 Jan 1793, day of Louis XVI's execution. *Women of Beauty and Heroism* (Frank B. Goodrich)

4 Courage! I have shown it for years; think you I shall lose it at the moment when my sufferings are to end?
Remark on the way to the guillotine, 16 Oct 1793. *Women of Beauty and Heroism* (Frank B. Goodrich)

5 Let them eat cake.
On being told that the people had no bread to eat; in fact she was repeating a much older saying. Attrib.

MARKOVA, Dame Alicia (Lilian Alicia Marks; 1910–)

British ballerina. She made her debut with the Diaghilev Ballet at the age of 14 and, in 1931, joined the Vic-Wells Ballet where she was prima ballerina from 1933 to 1935. She became the first English dancer to take the lead in *Giselle* and the full-length *Swan Lake*. She also distinguished herself in the fields of jazz and contemporary dance, in such ballets as Massine's *Rouge et Noir* (1939) and Antony Tudor's *Romeo and Juliet* (1943). She retired from the stage in 1963, when she was made a DBE, and was appointed director of New York's Metropolitan Ballet, holding this post until 1969. In 1986 she became president of the London Festival Ballet.

1 Glorious bouquets and storms of applause…These are the trimmings which every artist naturally enjoys. But to *move* an audience in such a role, to hear in the applause that unmistakable note which breaks through good theatre manners and comes from the heart, is to feel that you have won through to life itself. Such pleasure does not vanish with the fall of the curtain, but becomes part of one's own life.
Giselle and I, Ch. 18

MARRIAGE

1 Men marry, indeed, so as to get a manager for the house, to solace wariness, to banish solitude; but a faithful slave is a far better manager, more submissive to the master, more observant of his ways, than a wife who thinks she proves herself mistress if she acts in opposition to her husband, that is, if she does what pleases her not what she is commanded.
Theophrastus (c. 372–287 BC) Greek philosopher. *On Marriage* [3rd century BC]

2 Though destitute of virtue or seeking pleasure elsewhere, or devoid of good qualities, a husband must be constantly worshipped as a god.
Hindu text. *Laws of Manu* [c. 200 BC–200 AD]

3 Husbands, love your wives, and be not bitter against them.
Bible: Colossians
3:19

4 Let the husband render unto the wife due benevolence: and likewise also the wife unto the husband.
Bible: I Corinthians
7:3

5 But if they cannot contain, let them marry: for it is better to marry than to burn.
Bible: I Corinthians
7:9

6 But he that is married careth for the things that are of the world, how he may please his wife.
Bible: I Corinthians
7:33

7 Wherefore they are no more twain, but one flesh. What therefore God hath joined together, let not man put asunder.
Bible: Matthew
19:6

8 Likewise, ye husbands, dwell with them according to knowledge, giving honour unto the wife, as unto the weaker vessel, and as being heirs together of the grace of life; that your prayers be not hindered.
Bible: I Peter
3:7

9 If a man avoids
Marriage and all the troubles women bring
And never takes a wife, at last he comes
To a miserable old age, and does not have
Anyone to care for the old man.
Hesiod (8th century BC) Greek epic poet.
Theogony, 602–7 [8th century BC]

10 He that hath wife and children hath given hostages to fortune; for they are impediments to great enterprises, either of virtue or mischief.
Francis Bacon (1561–1626) English philosopher.
Essays, 'Of Marriage and Single Life' [1597]

11 Wives are young men's mistresses, companions for middle age, and old men's nurses.
Francis Bacon (1561–1626) English philosopher.
Essays, 'Of Marriage and Single Life' [1597]

12 He was reputed one of the wise men, that made answer to the question, when a man should marry? A young man not yet, an elder man not at all.
Francis Bacon (1561–1626) English philosopher.
Essays, 'Of Marriage and Single Life' [1597]

13 For a light wife doth make a heavy husband.
William Shakespeare (1564–1616) English dramatist.
The Merchant of Venice, V:1 [1597]

14 But what if a man of lewd and beastly conditions, as a drunkard, a glutton, a profane swaggerer, an impious swearer and blasphemer, be married to a wise, sober, religious matron, must she account him her superior and worthy of an husband's honour? Surely she must. For the evil quality and disposition of his heart and life doth not deprive a man of that civil honour which God hath given unto him.
William Gouge
Of Domesticall Duties [1634]

15 To have and to hold from this day forward, for better for worse, for richer for poorer, in sickness and in health, to love and to cherish, till death us do part.
The Book of Common Prayer
Solemnization of Matrimony [1662]

16 I am to be married within these three days; married past redemption.
John Dryden (1631–1700) British poet and dramatist.
Marriage à la Mode, I [1673]

17 Courtship is to marriage, as a very witty prologue to a very dull Play.
William Congreve (1670–1729) British Restoration dramatist.
The Old Bachelor, V:10 [1693]

18 The triumph of hope over experience.
Samuel Johnson (1709–84) British lexicographer.
Referring to the hasty remarriage of an acquaintance following the death of his first wife, with whom he had been most unhappy. *Life of Johnson* (J. Boswell), Vol. II [1770]

19 What is your fortune, my pretty maid?
My face is my fortune, sir, she said.
Then I can't marry you, my pretty maid.
Nobody asked you, sir, she said.
Archaeologia Cornu-Britannica (William Pryce) [1790]

20 The *divine right* of husbands, like the divine right of kings, may, it is hoped, in this enlightened age, be contested without danger.
Mary Wollstonecraft (1759–97) British writer.
A Vindication of the Rights of Woman, Ch. 3 [1792]

21 It is a truth universally acknowledged, that a single man in possession of a good fortune must be in want of a wife.
Jane Austen (1775–1817) British novelist.
The opening words of the book. *Pride and Prejudice*, Ch. 1 [1813]

22 Without thinking highly either of men or of matrimony, marriage had always been her object, it was the only honourable provision for well-educated young women of small fortune, and however uncertain of giving happiness, must be their pleasantest preservative from want.
Jane Austen (1775–1817) British novelist.
Pride and Prejudice, Ch. 22 [1813]

23 Marrying merely to be married, to manage her own affairs, and have her own way – so childish! – or marrying merely to get an establishment – so base! How women, and such

young creatures, *can* bring themselves to make these venal matches.
Maria Edgeworth (1767–1849) Irish novelist and essayist.
Ormond, Ch. 11 [1817]

24 The most happy marriage I can picture or imagine to myself would be the union of a deaf man to a blind woman.
Samuel Taylor Coleridge (1772–1834) British poet.
Recollections (Allsop) [1834]

25 The early marriages of silly children…where…every woman is married before she well knows how serious a matter human life is.
Harriet Martineau (1802–76) British writer.
Society in America, Vol. III, 'Marriage' [1837]

26 Of course the fate of the married woman is very much sadder than that of the spinster; at least the unmarried woman enjoys a certain freedom, she can enter society and travel with her family or with friends, whereas once a woman is married, she cannot stir from the house *without the permission of her husband*.
Flora Tristan (1803–44) French writer, feminist, and revolutionary socialist.
The London Journal of Flora Tristan [1842]

27 This I set down as a positive truth. A woman with fair opportunities and without a positive hump, may marry whom she likes.
William Makepeace Thackeray (1811–63) British novelist.
Vanity Fair, Ch. 4 [1847]

28 Remember, it is as easy to marry a rich woman as a poor woman.
William Makepeace Thackeray (1811–63) British novelist.
Pendennis, Ch. 28 [1848]

29 No man should marry until he has studied anatomy and dissected at least one woman.
Honoré de Balzac (1799–1850) French novelist.
La Physiologie du mariage

30 The general aim of English wives is practically to convince their husbands how much happier they are married than when living in bachelor solitude, or when vainly roaming after happiness; for except domestic happiness, what does man gain by marriage? A great increase of expenses, of duties, and of cares.
John Edward Tilt (1815–93) British doctor and president of the Obstetrical Society.
Elements of Health and Principles of Female Hygiene [1852]

31 'Old girl,' said Mr Bagnet, 'give him my opinion. You know it.'
Charles Dickens (1812–70) British novelist.
Bleak House, Ch. 27 [1853]

32 Women – one half the human race at least – care fifty times more for a marriage than a ministry.
Walter Bagehot (1826–77) British economist and journalist.
The English Constitution, 'The Monarchy' [1867]

33 Every woman should marry – and no man.
Benjamin Disraeli (1804–81) British statesman.
Lothair, Ch. 30 [1870]

34 Lastly (and this is, perhaps, the golden rule), no woman should marry a teetotaller, or a man who does not smoke.
Robert Louis Stevenson (1850–94) Scottish writer.
Virginibus Puerisque [1881]

35 If a man stays away from his wife for seven years, the law presumes the separation to have killed him; yet according to our daily experience, it might well prolong his life.
Lord Darling (1849–1936) British judge.
Scintillae Juris [1889]

36 The husband was a teetotaller, there was no other woman, and the conduct complained of was that he had drifted into the habit of winding up every meal by taking out his false teeth and hurling them at his wife.
Arthur Conan Doyle (1856–1930) British writer.
A Case of Identity [1892]

37 Twenty years of romance make a woman look like a ruin; but twenty years of marriage make her something like a public building.
Oscar Wilde (1854–1900) Irish-born British dramatist.
A Woman of No Importance, I [1893]

38 I married beneath me – all women do.
Nancy Astor (1879–1964) US-born British politician.
Dictionary of National Biography [1900]

39 When a woman gets married it is like jumping into a hole in the ice in the middle of winter; you do it once and you remember it the rest of your days.
Maxim Gorky (Aleksei Maksimovich Peshkov; 1868–1936) Russian writer.
The Lower Depths [1903]

40 When you see what some girls marry, you realize how they must hate to work for a living.
Helen Rowland (1876–1950) US writer.
Reflections of a Bachelor Girl [1903]

41 It is a woman's business to get married as soon as possible, and a man's to keep unmarried as long as he can.
George Bernard Shaw (1856–1950) Irish dramatist and critic.
Man and Superman, II [1903]

42 Bricklayers kick their wives to death, and dukes betray theirs; but it is among the small clerks and shopkeepers nowadays that it comes most often to the cutting of throats.
H. G. Wells (1866–1946) British writer.
Short Stories, 'The Purple Pileus' [1904]

43 *Marriage*, n. The state or condition of a community consisting of a master, a mistress and two slaves, making in all two.
Ambrose Bierce (1842–?1914) US writer and journalist.
The Devil's Dictionary [1906]

44 Marriage is distinctly and repeatedly excluded from heaven. Is this because it is thought likely to mar the general felicity?
Samuel Butler (1835–1902) British writer.
Notebooks [1912]

45 Being a husband is a whole-time job. That is why so many husbands fail. They cannot give their entire attention to it.
Arnold Bennett (1867–1931) British novelist.
The Title, I [1918]

46 No man is genuinely happy, married, who has to drink worse gin than he used to drink when he was single.
H. L. Mencken (1880–1956) US journalist.
Prejudices, 'Reflections on Monogamy' [1919–27]

47 So that ends my first experience with matrimony, which I always thought a highly overrated performance.
Isadora Duncan (1878–1927) US dancer, educator, and writer.
Interview, *The New York Times* [1923]

48 Now one of the great reasons why so many husbands and wives make shipwreck of their lives together is because a man is always seeking for happiness, while a woman is on a perpetual still hunt for trouble.
Dorothy Dix (Elizabeth Meriwether Gilmer; 1861–1951) US journalist and writer.
Dorothy Dix, Her Book, Ch. 1 [1926]

49 Never feel remorse for what you have thought about your wife; she has thought much worse things about you.
Jean Rostand (1894–1977) French biologist and writer.
Le Mariage [1927]

50 Married women are kept women, and they are beginning to find it out.
Logan Pearsall Smith (1865–1946) US writer.
Afterthoughts, 'Other people' [1931]

51 Marriage I think
For women
Is the best of opiates.
It kills the thoughts
That think about the thoughts,
It is the best of opiates.
Stevie Smith (Florence Margaret Smith; 1902–71) British poet.
'Marriage I Think' [1937]

52 The man who marries always makes the woman a present because she needs marriage and he does not…woman is made for man, man is made for life.
Henri de Montherlant (1896–1972) French novelist.
Girls [1936–39]

53 A loving wife will do anything for her husband except stop criticising and trying to improve him.
J. B. Priestley (1894–1984) British novelist.
Rain on Godshill [1939]

54 You can measure the social caste of a person by the distance between the husband's and wife's apartments.
Alfonso XIII (1886–1941) Spanish monarch.
Attrib. [1941]

55 There must be several young women who would render the Christian life intensely difficult to him if only you could persuade him to marry one of them.
C. S. Lewis (1898–1963) British academic and writer.
The Screwtape Letters [1942]

56 It has been discovered experimentally that you can draw laughter from an audience anywhere in the world, of any class or race, simply by walking on to a stage and uttering the words 'I am a married man'.
Ted Kavanagh (1892–1958) British radio scriptwriter.
News Review, 10 July 1947

57 The others were only my wives. But you, my dear, will be my widow.
Sacha Guitry (1885–1957) French actor and dramatist.
Allaying his fifth wife's jealousy of his previous wives.
Speaker's and Toastmaster's Handbook (J. Brawle) [c. 1950]

58 A man should not insult his wife publicly, at parties. He should insult her in the privacy of the home.
James Thurber (1894–1961) US humorist.
Thurber Country [1953]

59 The trouble with my wife is that she is a whore in the kitchen and a cook in bed.
Geoffrey Gorer (1905–85) British writer and anthropologist.
Exploring the English Character [1955]

60 Marrying a man is like buying something you've been admiring for a long time in a shop window. You may love it when you get it home,

but it doesn't always go with everything else in the house.
Jean Kerr
The Snake Has All the Lines [1960]

61 When you're bored with yourself, marry and be bored with someone else.
David Pryce-Jones (1936–   ) British author and critic.
Owls and Satyrs [1960]

62 Those who marry God…can become domesticated too – it's just as humdrum a marriage as all the others.
Graham Greene (1904–91) British novelist.
A Burnt-Out Case, Ch. 1 [1961]

63 To Crystal, hair was the most important thing on earth. She would never get married because you couldn't wear curlers in bed.
Edna O'Brien (1936–   ) Irish novelist.
Winter's Tales, 8, 'Come into the Drawing Room, Doris' [1968]

64 And let her learn through what kind of dust
He has earned his thirst and the right to quench it
And what sweat he has exchanged for his money
And the blood-weight of money. He'll humble her.
Ted Hughes (1930–   ) British poet.
Selected Poems 1957–1981, 'Her Husband' [c. 1970]

65 I think women are basically quite lazy. Marriage is still a woman's best investment, because she can con some man into supporting her for the rest of his life.
Alan Whicker (1925–   ) British television broadcaster and writer.
Observer, 'Sayings of the Week', 10 Sept 1972

66 Of course, I do have a slight advantage over the rest of you. It helps in a pinch to be able to remind your bride that you gave up a throne for her.
Duke of Windsor (1894–1972) King of the United Kingdom; abdicated 1936.
Discussing the maintenance of happy marital relations. Attrib. [1972]

67 It has been said that a bride's attitude towards her betrothed can be summed up in three words: Aisle. Altar. Hymn.
Frank Muir (1920–   ) British writer and broadcaster.
Upon My Word!, 'A Jug of Wine' (Frank Muir and Dennis Norden) [1974]

68 Writing is like getting married. One should never commit oneself until one is amazed at one's luck.
Iris Murdoch (1919–   ) Irish-born British novelist.
The Black Prince, 'Bradley Pearson's Foreword' [1974]

69 'We stay together, but we distrust one another.'
'Ah, yes…but isn't that a definition of marriage?'
Malcolm Bradbury (1932–   ) British academic and novelist.
The History Man, Ch. 3 [1975]

70 Like so many substantial Americans, he had married young and kept on marrying, springing from blonde to blonde like the chamois of the Alps leaping from crag to crag.
P. G. Wodehouse (1881–1975) British humorous novelist.
Wodehouse at Work to the End, Ch. 2 (Richard Usborne) [1975]

71 Margot is a good wife; she allows her husband to sap her energy and youth, and tax her good nature, and feels no resentment.
Fay Weldon (1933–   ) British novelist and dramatist.
Remember Me [1976]

72 Personally I know nothing about sex because I've always been married.
Zsa Zsa Gabor (1919–   ) Hungarian-born US film star.
Observer, 'Sayings of the Week', 16 Aug 1987

73 When a man opens the car door for his wife, it's either a new car or a new wife.
Prince Philip (1921–   ) The consort of Queen Elizabeth II.
Remark, Mar 1988

74 I don't think a prostitute is more moral than a wife, but they are doing the same thing.
Prince Philip (1921–   ) The consort of Queen Elizabeth II.
Remark, Dec 1988

75 Marriage is a wonderful invention; but then again so is a bicycle repair kit.
Billy Connolly (1942–   ) British comedian.
The Authorized Version

MARTYRDOM

See also DUTY; WOMAN'S ROLE

1 Fate has always been upheld by sacrifice; and who so fit to make it as woman?
Sydney Owenson Morgan (c. 1776–1859) British novelist, poet, historian, and actress.
The O'Briens and the O'Flahertys, Vol. II, Ch. 4 [1827]

2 To bear and rear the majestic race to which they can never fully belong! To live vicariously forever, through their sons, the daughters being

only another vicarious link! What a supreme and magnificent martyrdom!
Charlotte Perkins Gilman (1860–1935) US writer and lecturer.
Women and Economics, Ch. 9 [1898]

3 Women in drudgery knew
They must be one of four:
Whores, artists, saints, and wives.
Muriel Rukeyser (1913–80) US poet.
Beast in View, 'Wreath of Women' [1944]

MATURITY

1 From a timid, shy girl I had become a woman of resolute character, who could not longer be frightened by the struggle with troubles.
Anna Dostoevsky (1846–1918) Russian diarist and writer.
Dostoevsky Portrayed by His Wife [c. 1871]

2 From birth to age eighteen, a girl needs good parents. From eighteen to thirty-five, she needs good looks. From thirty-five to fifty-five, she needs a good personality. From fifty-five on, she needs good cash.
Sophie Tucker (Sophia Abuza; 1884–1966) Russian-born US singer.
Attrib. [1953]

3 She takes just like a woman, yes, she does
She makes love just like a woman, yes, she does
And she aches just like a woman
But she breaks just like a little girl.
Bob Dylan (Robert Allen Zimmerman; 1941–) US popular singer.
Just Like a Woman [1966]

4 I gave my beauty and my youth to men. I am going to give my wisdom and experience to animals.
Brigitte Bardot (1934–) French film actress.
Referring to her animal-rights campaign. *Guardian*, 1987

MEIR, Golda (1898–1978)
Israeli politician and prime minister (1969–74). Born in Kiev, Russia she emigrated with her parents to Milwaukee in 1907. She moved to Palestine in 1921 and began her political activities as secretary of the Histradut Women's Labour Council (1928–32) and later on the Histradut executive committee (1934–39). She was appointed ambassador to the Soviet Union, following Israel's independence in 1948. She subsequently became minister for labour (1949–56) and minister for foreign affairs (1956–66). In 1969 she was elected prime minister, a position which she held until 1974, when she resigned in the wake of the Yom Kippur War. She died in 1978 after a twelve-year struggle against leukaemia.

Quotation about Meir
1 Ask her what it is like to be a woman Foreign Minister and she will reply with a puckish smile that she does not know what it is like to be a man Foreign Minister.
The Times, 6 Feb 1981

Quotations by Meir
2 A leader who doesn't hesitate before he sends his nation into battle is not fit to be a leader.
As Good as Golda (ed. Israel and Mary Shenker)

3 I can honestly say that I was never affected by the question of the success of an undertaking. If I felt it was the right thing to do, I was for it regardless of the possible outcome.
Golda Meir: Woman with a Cause (Marie Syrkin)

4 There's no difference between one's killing and making decisions that will send others to kill. It's exactly the same thing, or even worse.
L'Europeo (Oriana Fallaci)

5 We intend to remain alive. Our neighbors want to see us dead. This is not a question that leaves much room for compromise.
Reader's Digest, 'The Indestructible Golda Meir', July 1971

6 Being seventy is not a sin.
Reader's Digest, 'The Indestructible Golda Meir', July 1971

7 Pessimism is a luxury that a Jew never can allow himself.
Observer, 'Sayings of the Year', 29 Dec 1974

8 There are not enough prisons and concentration camps in Palestine to hold all the Jews who are ready to defend their lives and property.
Speech, 2 May 1940

MELBA, Dame Nellie (Helen Armstrong; 1861–1931)
Australian operatic soprano, whose immense popularity caused Escoffier to name his ice-cream dish *pêche melba* after her. (Melba toast was also named after her.) Although she was a skilled pianist and organist she did not study singing until after her marriage to Charles Nesbitt Armstrong in 1882. She made her operatic debut at the Théâtre de la Monnaie, Brussels, as Gilda in Verdi's *Rigoletto*, singing under her stage name Melba, taken from her native city Melbourne. She made regular appearances in all the major European and American opera houses, in such roles as Violetta in Verdi's *La traviata* and Mimi in Puccini's *La Bohème*. She gave her last Covent Garden performance in 1926 and retired to Australia to become president of the Melbourne Conservatory. She was created a DBE in 1918.

Quotations about Melba

1 It is a nice question whether the pleasure Melba gave with her own singing was not outweighed by the pleasure she deprived London of by blocking the careers of so many other singers.
Ronald Hastings *Daily Telegraph*, 21 Sept 1967

2 She retained a keen sense of her own fiscal value. When she was invited to dinner by a rich hostess who suggested that after the meal she might 'sing a little song' Melba declined. It was no trouble, she agreed, to sing a little song. But it was even less arduous to sign a little cheque.
Joseph Wechsberg (1907–) US writer. *Red Plush and Black Velvet*, 1962

Quotations by Melba

3 So you're going to Australia! Well, I made twenty thousand pounds on my tour there, but of course *that* will never be done again. Still, it's a wonderful country, and you'll have a good time. What are you going to sing? All I can say is – sing 'em muck! It's all they can understand!
Speaking to Clara Butt. *Clara Butt: Her Life Story* (W. H. Ponder)

4 Music is not written in red, white and blue. It is written in the heart's blood of the composer.
Melodies and Memories

5 One of the drawbacks of Fame is that one can never escape from it.
Melodies and Memories

6 The first rule in opera is the first rule in life: see to everything yourself.
Melodies and Memories

MEN

1 Wealth makes them lavish, wit knavish, beauty effeminate, poverty deceitful, and deformity ugly. Therefore, of me take this counsel:
Esteem of men as of a broken reed,
Mistrust them still, and then you well shall speed.
Jane Anger (fl. 1589) English feminist and pamphleteer.
Protection for Women [1589]

2 It is an ancient contention of my wife that I, in common with all other men, in any dispute between a female relative and a tradesman, side with the tradesman, partly from fear, partly from masculine clannishness, and most of all from a desire to stand well with the tradesman.
E. Œ. Somerville (1858–1949) Irish writer.
Experiences of an Irish R.M., 'The Pug-nosed Fox' [1899]

3 Why are women...so much more interesting to men than men are to women?
Virginia Woolf (1882–1941) British novelist.
A Room of One's Own [1929]

4 The average man is more interested in a woman who is interested in him than he is in a woman – any woman – with beautiful legs.
Marlene Dietrich (Maria Magdalene von Losch; 1904–) German-born film star.
News item, 13 Dec 1954

5 Most women set out to try to change a man, and when they have changed him they do not like him.
Marlene Dietrich (Maria Magdalene von Losch; 1904–) German-born film star.
Attrib. [c. 1960s]

6 The male ego with few exceptions is elephantine to start with.
Bette Davis (Ruth Elizabeth D.; 1908–89) US actress.
The Lonely Life, Ch. 9 [1962]

7 Happy is the man with a wife to tell him what to do and a secretary to do it.
Lord Mancroft (1917–87) British businessman and writer.
Observer, 'Sayings of the Week', 18 Dec 1966

8 All men are rapists and that's all they are. They rape us with their eyes, their laws and their codes.
Marilyn French (1929–) US novelist.
The Women's Room

9 Men are frustrated when their sincere attempts to help a woman solve her problems are met not with gratitude but with disapproval. One man reported being ready to tear his hair out over a girlfriend who continually told him about problems she was having at work but refused to take any of the advice he offered.
Deborah Tannen US writer and professor of linguistics.
You Just Don't Understand [1990]

MEN AND WOMEN

1 Yang – positive cosmic force, the heavens, man.
Yin – negative cosmic force, earth, woman.
Confucian text. *Tung Chung Shu* [2nd century BC]

2 So too the woman is less perfect than the man in respect to the generative parts. For the parts were formed within her when she was still a foetus, but could not because of the defect in the heat emerge and project on the outside, and this, though making the animal itself that was being formed less perfect than one that is complete in all respects, provided no small advantage for the face; for there needs must be a

female. Indeed, you ought not to think that our creator would purposely make half the whole race imperfect and, as it were, mutilated, unless there was to be some great advantage in such a mutilation.
Galen (129–c. 199 AD) Greek physician.
On the Usefulness of the Parts of the Body, XIV [2nd century AD]

3 We are the grief of man, in that we take all the grief from man: we languish when they laugh, we lie sighing when they sit singing, and sit sobbing when they lie slugging and sleeping.
Jane Anger (fl. 1589) English feminist and pamphleteer.
Protection for Women [1589]

4 Women run to extremes; they are either better or worse than men.
Jean de La Bruyère (1645–96) French satirist.
Les Caractères [1688]

5 Women are much more like each other than men: they have, in truth, but two passions, vanity and love; these are their universal characteristics.
Earl of Chesterfield (1694–1773) English statesman.
Letter to his son, 19 Dec 1749

6 Man's love is of man's life a thing apart,
'Tis woman's whole existence.
Lord Byron (1788–1824) British poet.
Don Juan, I [1819–24]

7 The woman whose life is of the head will strive to inspire her husband with indifference; the woman whose life is of the heart, with hatred; the passionate woman, with disgust.
Honoré de Balzac (1799–1850) French novelist.
The Physiology of Marriage [1829]

8 What are little boys made of?
Frogs and snails
And puppy-dogs' tails,
That's what little boys are made of.
What are little girls made of?
Sugar and spice
And all that's nice,
That's what little girls are made of.
Nursery Rhymes (J. O. Halliwell) [1844]

9 Man for the field and woman for the hearth:
Man for the sword and for the needle she:
Man with the head and woman with the heart:
Man to command and woman to obey;
All else confusion.
Alfred, Lord Tennyson (1809–92) British poet.
The Princess, V [1847]

10 Man has his will, – but woman has her way.
Oliver Wendell Holmes (1809–94) US writer.
The Autocrat of the Breakfast Table, Prologue [1857]

11 Where young boys plan for what they will achieve and attain, young girls plan for whom they will achieve and attain.
Charlotte Perkins Gilman (1860–1935) US writer and lecturer.
Women and Economics, Ch. 5 [1890]

12 Women represent the triumph of matter over mind, just as men represent the triumph of mind over morals.
Oscar Wilde (1854–1900) Irish-born British dramatist.
The Picture of Dorian Gray, Ch. 4 [1891]

13 'Boys will be boys – '
'And even that…wouldn't matter if we could only prevent girls from being girls.'
Anthony Hope (Anthony Hope Hawkins; 1863–1933) British novelist.
The Dolly Dialogues [1894]

14 It is only rarely that one can see in a little boy the promise of a man, but one can almost always see in a little girl the threat of a woman.
Alexandre Dumas, fils (1824–95) French writer.
Attrib. [1895]

15 All women become like their mothers. That is their tragedy. No man does. That's his.
Oscar Wilde (1854–1900) Irish-born British dramatist.
The Importance of Being Earnest, I [1895]

16 No matter how hard a man may labor, some woman is always in the background of his mind. She is the one reward of virtue.
Gertrude Atherton (1857–1948) US writer.
The Conqueror, Bk IV, Ch. 3 [1902]

17 It takes a woman twenty years to make a man of her son, and another woman twenty minutes to make a fool of him.
Helen Rowland (1876–1950) US writer.
Reflections of a Bachelor Girl [1903]

18 When a man confronts catastrophe on the road, he looks in his purse – but a woman looks in her mirror.
Margaret Turnbull (fl. 1920s–1942) US writer.
The Left Lady [1926]

19 Instead of this absurd division into sexes they ought to class people as static and dynamic.
Evelyn Waugh (1903–66) British novelist.
Decline and Fall, Pt III, Ch. 7 [1928]

20 I often want to cry. That is the only advantage women have over men – at least they can cry.
Jean Rhys (1894–1979) Dominican-born British novelist.
Good Morning, Midnight, Pt II [1939]

21 The reason that husbands and wives do not understand each other is because they belong to different sexes.
Dorothy Dix (Elizabeth Meriwether Gilmer; 1861–1951) US journalist and writer.
News item [1940s]

22 In the sex-war thoughtlessness is the weapon of the male, vindictiveness of the female.
Cyril Connolly (1903–74) British journalist.
The Unquiet Grave [1944]

23 Sylvia said, 'Men are stronger than women. They don't need such complete rest.' Kimi said, 'Nonsense, it is because the Medical Director is also a man. He thinks, "The woman's mind is little. She can lie twenty-four hours a day for thirty days, a total of seven hundred and twenty hours, doing nothing. The man's mind is big. He must give it something to think about. I will let him read the paper immediately."'
Betty MacDonald (1908–58) US writer.
Discussing the difference in attitudes towards men and women in a tuberculosis hospital. *The Plague and I* [1948]

24 The War between Men and Women.
James Thurber (1894–1961) US humorist.
Title of a series of cartoons [1950s]

25 When a woman behaves like a man, why doesn't she behave like a nice man?
Edith Evans (1888–1976) British actress.
Observer, 'Sayings of the Week', 30 Sept 1956

26 Women want mediocre men, and men are working to be as mediocre as possible.
Margaret Mead (1901–78) US anthropologist.
Quote Magazine, 15 May 1958

27 Women have moved and shaken me, but I have been nourished by men.
May Sarton (1912–) Belgian-born US writer.
Mrs Stevens Hears the Mermaids Singing [1965]

28 I wonder if what makes men walk lordlike and speak so masterfully is having the love of women.
Alma Routsong (1924–) US writer and feminist.
A Place for Us [1969]

29 Women fail to understand how much men hate them.
Germaine Greer (1939–) Australian-born British writer and feminist.
The Female Eunuch [1970]

30 If men put from them in fear all that is 'womanish' in them, then long, of course, for that missing part in their natures, so seek to possess it by possessing us; because they have feared it in their own souls seek, too, to domi-

nate it in us – seek even to slay it – well, we're where we are now, aren't we?
Barbara Deming (1917–) US pacifist, feminist, and writer.
'Two Perspectives on Women's Struggles', *We Cannot Live Without Our Lives* [1974]

31 Man/Woman automatically means great/small, superior/inferior…the whole conglomeration of symbolic systems – everything, that is, that's spoken, everything that's organized as discourse, art, religion, the family, language, everything that seizes us, everything that acts on us – it is all ordered around hierarchical oppositions that come back to the man/woman opposition.
Hélène Cixous
Le Sexe ou la tête [1976]

32 Fighting is essentially a masculine idea; a woman's weapon is her tongue.
Hermione Gingold (1897–1987) British actress.
Attrib. [1987]

33 I don't think men and women were meant to live together. They are totally different animals.
Diana Dors (1931–84) British actress.
Remark, May 1988

34 Women expect decisions to be discussed first and made by consensus. They appreciate the discussion itself as evidence of involvement and communication. But many men feel oppressed by lengthy discussions about what they see as minor decisions, and they feel hemmed in if they can't just act without talking first. When women try to initiate a freewheeling discussion by asking, 'What do you think?' men often think they are being asked to decide.
Deborah Tannen US writer and professor of linguistics.
You Just Don't Understand [1990]

MENOPAUSE

1 When menstruation is about to cease, the period is called critical, 'the change, or turn of life, the climacteric period;' and many important changes take place in the constitution at this epoch…The cheeks and neck wither, the eyes recede in their sockets, and the countenance often becomes yellow, leaden-coloured, or florid, and the women become corpulent, and lose the mild peculiarities of their sex.
Dr Michael Ryan
A Manual of Midwifery [1841]

2 The change of life does not give talents, but it imparts a firmness of purpose to bring out effectively those that are possessed, whether it be to govern a household, to preside in a draw-

ing-room, or to thread and unravel political entanglements.
John Edward Tilt (1815–93) British doctor and president of the Obstetrical Society.
The Change of Life in Health and Disease [1857]

3 What happens during the climacteric is that the people she has served all her life stop making demands on her. She becomes a moon without an earth. What she wants is to be wanted and nobody wants her.
Germaine Greer (1939–) Australian-born British writer and feminist.
The Change [1991]

MENSTRUATION

1 And whosoever toucheth any thing that she sat upon shall wash his clothes, and bathe himself in water, and be unclean until the even. And if it be on her bed, or on any thing whereon she sitteth, when he toucheth it, he shall be unclean until the even. And if any man lie with her at all, and her flowers be upon him, he shall be unclean seven days; and all the bed whereon he lieth shall be unclean.
Bible: Leviticus
15:22–24

2 Because a man has more solid flesh than a woman, he is never so totally overfilled with blood that pain results if some of his blood does not exit each month.
Hippocrates (c. 460–c. 377 BC) Greek physician.
Diseases of Women, I [4th century BC]

3 In the case of very clean mirrors, if a woman who is menstruating looks into the mirror, the mirror's surface becomes bloody-dark, like a cloud…Eyes are affected like any other part of the body when the monthly period occurs, since by nature they happen to be full of blood vessels.
Aristotle (384–322 BC) Greek philosopher.
On Dreams [4th century BC]

4 But nothing could easily be found that is more remarkable than the monthly flux of women. Contact with it turns new wine sour, crops touched by it become barren, grafts die, seeds in gardens are dried up, the fruit of trees falls off, the bright surface of mirrors in which it is merely reflected is dimmed, the edge of steel and the gleam of ivory are dulled, hives of bees die, even bronze and iron are at once seized by rust, and a horrible smell fills the air; to taste it drives dogs mad and infects their bites with an incurable poison.
Pliny the Elder (Gaius Plinius Secundus; 23–79 AD) Roman scholar.
Natural History [1st century AD]

5 In women who have already menstruated often, each must be allowed to do according to her own custom. For some habitually take a rest, while others go on with moderate activities. But it is safer to rest and not to bathe especially on the first day.
Soranus of Ephesus (fl. 2nd century AD) Greek physician.
On Midwifery and the Diseases of Women [2nd century AD]

6 Whosoever shall lie in sexual intercourse with a woman who has an issue of blood; either out of the ordinary course or at the usual period, does no better deed than if he should burn the corpse of his own son, born of his own body, and killed by a spear, and drop its fat into the fire.
Fargard (Zoroastrian text) [c. 10th century]

7 Menstruating women carry with them a poison that could kill an infant in its cradle.
St Albert the Great (c. 1206–80) German Dominican bishop and philosopher, known as 'Doctor Universalis'.
On the Inner Secrets of Women [13th century]

8 Women are also monthly filled full of superfluous humours, and with them the melancholic blood boils; where of spring vapours, and are carried up, and conveyed through the nostrils and mouth, etc., to the bewitching of whatsoever it meet.
Reginald Scot (c. 1538–99) English writer.
The Discoverie of Witchcraft [1584]

9 The hygienic precautions relating to menstruation are scarcely ever duly attended to in this country. The young female, at the age of puberty, is not informed as to the change which is to occur to her; she is left ignorant on the subject; she is much astonished at the first eruption of the uterine secretion…She is not cautioned to avoid, during each periodical evacuation, exposure to cold, humidity, all strong emotions, violent exertions, walking, riding, dancing, etc., exciting aliments and drinks, etc., unless by the Hebrew persuasion.
Dr Michael Ryan
A Manual of Midwifery [1841]

10 She suffers from 'the custom of women', or she does not. In either case she is normally or abnormally ill. Thus every woman is, according to temperament and other circumstances, always more or less an invalid.
J. M. Allan
Journal of the Anthropological Society of London, 'On the Differences in the Minds of Men and Women' [1869]

11 Menstruation is not a disease, nor should it reduce to a state of even slight temporary invalidism.
Mrs E. B. Duffey
What Women Should Know [1873]

12 It is an undoubted fact that meat spoils when touched by menstruating women.
British Medical Journal, 1878

13 Dr Galabin showed the new ladies' sanitary towels manufactured by Messrs. Southall, Barclay, & Co., of Birmingham. They were extremely light and soft, and contained a pad of absorbent cotton wool...They were intended to supersede the ordinary diapers for use during the catamenia and after confinement. Dr Galabin thought that, whether or not they should come into ordinary use at catamenial periods, there could be no doubt that they would be very convenient for travelling.
Transactions of the Obstetrical Society of London, Vol. 22 [1880]

14 As a rule, in healthy girls under favourable circumstances neither the pain nor the discharge itself is sufficent to justify withdrawal from the usual duties and pleasures of life. The wise mother should know how to shield her child from undue exertion without making a monthly illness out of a natural function.
Mary Scharlieb (1845–1930) British gynaecological surgeon.
The Seven Ages of Woman [1915]

15 Reading and carrying the Koran and touching any part of the body to the edges or the spaces between the writings of the Koran as well as tinging with henna and the like are acts which are an abomination for a menstruating woman.
Ayatollah Ruholla Khomeini (1900–89) Iranian Shiite Muslim leader.
A Clarification of Questions [1980]

MISOGYNY

See also ATTITUDES; CONTEMPT

1 A man of straw is worth a woman of gold.
Proverb

2 But the leader of all wickedness is woman; 'tis she, cunning mistress of crime, besets our minds; 'tis by her foul adulteries so many cities smoke, so many nations war, so many peoples lie crushed beneath the ruins of their kingdoms, utterly o'erthrown. Let others be unnamed; Aegeus' wife alone, Medea, will prove that woman are an accursed race.
Seneca (c. 4 BC–65 AD) Roman author.
Hippolytus [1st century AD]

3 And remember, there's nothing these women won't do to satisfy
Their ever-moist groins: they've just one obsession – sex.
Juvenal (Decimus Junius Juvenalis; 60–130 AD) Roman satirist.
Satires, X [1st century AD]

4 The First Blast of the Trumpet Against the Monstrous Regiment of Women.
John Knox (c. 1513–72) Scottish religious reformer.
Title of pamphlet [1558]

5 Nature placed the female testicles internally...Woman is a most arrogant and extremely intractable animal; and she would be worse if she came to realize that she is no less perfect and no less fit to wear breeches than man...I believe that is why nature, while endowing her with what is necessary for our procreation, did so in such a way as to keep her from perceiving and ascertaining her sufficient perfection.
P. Borgarucci Italian anatomist.
Della contemplatione anatomica sopra tutte le parti del corpo umano [1564]

6 Brigands demand your money or your life; women require both.
Samuel Butler (1612–80) English satirist.
Attrib. [1680]

7 Of all the plagues with which the world is curst,
Of every ill, a woman is the worst.
George Granville (1667–1735) British poet and dramatist.
The British Enchanters

8 God created woman. And boredom did indeed cease from that moment – but many other things ceased as well! Woman was God's *second* mistake.
Friedrich Wilhelm Nietzsche (1844–1900) German philosopher.
The Antichrist [1895]

9 You will find that the woman who is really kind to dogs is always one who has failed to inspire sympathy in men.
Max Beerbohm (1872–1956) British writer.
Zuleika Dobson, Ch. 6 [1911]

10 A woman will always sacrifice herself if you give her the opportunity. It is her favourite form of self-indulgence.
W. Somerset Maugham (1874–1965) British novelist.
The Circle, III [1921]

11 I'd be equally as willing
For a dentist to be drilling

Than to ever let a woman in my life.
Alan Jay Lerner (1918–86) US songwriter.
My Fair Lady, I:2 [1956]

12 I enjoy fucking my wife. She lets me do it any way I want. No Women's Liberation for her. Lots of male chauvinist pig.
Joseph Heller (1923–   ) US novelist.
Something Happened [1974]

MITCHELL, Maria (1818–89)

US astronomer. A self-taught astronomer, she read mathematics and science while a librarian at the Nantucket Atheneum. In 1847 she discovered a comet, for which she received worldwide attention. In 1848 she became the first woman elected to the American Academy of Arts and Sciences. From 1865 she gained distinction as a professor of astronomy at Vassar College. In 1873, prompted by her concern for the professional status of women, she cofounded the Association for the Advancement of Women.

1 Why can not a man act himself, be himself, and think for himself? It seems to me that naturalness alone is power; that a borrowed word is weaker than our own weakness however small we may be.
Diary, 1867

2 For women there are, undoubtedly, great difficulties in the path, but so much the more to overcome. First, no woman should say, 'I am but a woman!' But a woman! what more can you ask to be?
Address to students, 1874

3 I do think, as a general rule, that teachers talk too much! A book is a very good institution! To read a book, to think it over, and to write out notes is a useful exercise; a book which will not repay some hard thought is not worth publishing.
Address to students, July 1887

MITFORD, Nancy (1904–73)

British writer. One of the talented Mitford sisters, she is noted for her witty depictions of the lives and idiosyncracies of the English aristocracy. Her most celebrated novel is *Love in a Cold Climate* (1949). One of her most widely read books was *Noblesse Oblige* (1956) in which she called attention to the distinction between U (upper class) and non-U (not upper class) modes of speech and behaviour. Other writings include *Pursuit of Love* (1945), which introduced the character of Lord Alconleigh (Uncle Matthew), based on her eccentric father Baron Redesdale (1878–1958) and *Don't Tell Alfred* (1960).

Quotation about Mitford

1 Nancy Mitford has lived for twenty years in Paris, yet when anyone bumps into her in the street they always look at her and say Sorry, in English.
The Sunday Times, Atticus, 28 Aug 1966

2 Nice cheap girl to take out for the evening. Costs you only eighteen and six for an orangeade in a night club.
Evelyn Waugh (1903–66) British novelist. *Memories* (Maurice Bowra)

Quotations by Mitford

3 An aristocracy in a republic is like a chicken whose head has been cut off: it may run about in a lively way, but in fact it is dead.
Noblesse Oblige

4 Some reviewers do get a bit sarky. One once said that I was like an ormolu clock, chiming away on the mantelpiece. He was probably being awfully rude, but I rather liked it. If you're an honest little clock, and tell the time properly, isn't that rather nice?
The Sunday Times, 28 Aug 1966

5 English women are elegant until they are ten years old, and perfect on grand occasions.
The Wit of Women (L. and M. Cowan)

MODESTY

1 Put off your shame with your clothes when you go in to your husband, and put it on again when you come out.
Theano (fl. c. 420s BC) Greek priestess.
Lives, Teachings, and Sayings of Famous Philosophers; Pythagoras, Bk VIII (Diogenes Laertius) [c. 420 BC]

2 Since, however, the law permits women to practise medicine and because it is better, out of consideration for morals and decency, for women rather than men to attend female patients, we grant her the licence to heal and to practise.
Charles, Duke of Calabria
Licence granted to Francesca of Salerno, 10 Sept 1321

3 The daughter-in-law of Pythagoras said that a woman who goes to bed with a man ought to lay aside her modesty with her skirt, and put it on again with her petticoat.
Michel de Montaigne (1533–92) French essayist.
Essais, I [1580–88]

4 Age will bring all things, and everyone knows, Madame, that twenty is no age to be a prude.
Molière (Jean Baptiste Poquelin; 1622–73) French dramatist.
Le Misanthrope, III:4 [1666]

5 The perfect hostess will see to it that the works of male and female authors be properly separated on her bookshelves. Their proximity, unless they happen to be married, should not be tolerated.
Lady Gough
Etiquette [1836]

6 She just wore
Enough for modesty – no more.
Robert Williams Buchanan (1841–1901) British poet and writer.
White Rose and Red, I [1871]

7 In some remote regions of Islam it is said, a woman caught unveiled by a stranger will raise her skirt to cover her face.
Raymond Mortimer (1895–1980) British literary critic and writer.
Colette

MONROE, Marilyn (Norma Jean Baker; 1926–62)

US actress and sex symbol. She made her debut in *Scudda-Hoo! Scudda-Hay!* but her first starring role came in *Don't Bother to Knock* (1952). A disclosure, in 1952, that she had posed as a nude model for a calendar photograph was used by the Hollywood publicity agents to turn her into a world-class sex symbol. In 1953 she made three successful films, *Niagara, Gentlemen Prefer Blondes*, and *How to Marry a Millionaire*. Despite her steadily deteriorating personal life she continued to appear in a series of highly acclaimed films, such as *The Seven Year Itch* (1955), *The Prince and the Showgirl* (1957), and *Some Like It Hot* (1959). In 1962 she died from an overdose of sleeping pills having been destroyed by the pressures of Hollywood. Although she is acclaimed as a fine comic actress, it is her image as a sex symbol and the various scandals associated with her widely publicized personal life which make her legend live on.

Quotations about Monroe

1 There's been an awful lot of crap written about Marilyn Monroe, and there may be an exact psychiatric term for what was wrong with her. I don't know – but truth to tell, I think she was quite mad.
George Cukor (1899–1983) US film director. *On Cukor* (Gavin Lambert)

2 The times being what they were, if she hadn't existed we would have had to invent her, and we did, in a way. She was the fifties' fiction, the lie that a woman has no sexual needs, that she is there to cater to, or enhance, a man's needs.
Molly Haskell *From Reverence to Rape*

3 Anyone can remember lines, but it takes an artist to come on the set and not know her lines and give the performance she did.
Billy Wilder (Samuel Wilder; 1906–) Austrian-born US film director.

Quotations by Monroe

4 I have too many fantasies to be a housewife...I guess I *am* a fantasy.
The First Ms Reader (ed. Francine Klagsbrun), 'Marilyn: The Woman Who Died Too Soon' (Gloria Steinem)

5 I've been on a calendar, but never on time.
Look, 16 Jan 1962

6 A sex symbol becomes a thing. I hate being a thing.
A Pictorial History of Sex in the Movies (Jeremy Pascall and Clive Jeavons)

MONTESSORI, Maria (1870–1952)

Italian doctor and educationalist. Born in Ancona, she studied medicine at the University of Rome and, in 1896, became the first woman in Italy to receive a medical degree. In 1907 she opened her first school in which she developed the system of child education that became known as the Montessori method. In 1909 she produced a book *Il metodo della pedagogia scientifica* (*The Montessori Method*; 1912) in which she set out her educational system. Her approach concentrated on development of the senses and stressed the importance of a child being allowed to progress at its own pace. She believed that voluntary learning, through a child's natural creative potential, rather than through compulsion, would increase a child's self-confidence and self-discipline. Many of her ideas are used in nursery- and infant-school education today, and there are also many Montessori kindergartens.

Quotations about Montessori

1 Like all great educators, she extended our sense of educability.
Brian Jackson (1933–83) British writer. *1000 Makers of the 20th Century*

2 Her almost unnoticed bequest was to change the toy culture of Western Europe so as to make it relevant not only to children's fantasy needs but to their manipulative and perceptual growth as well.
Brian Jackson (1933–83) British writer. *1000 Makers of the 20th Century*

Quotations by Montessori

3 We teachers can only help the work going on, as servants wait upon a master.
The Absorbent Mind

4 And if education is always to be conceived along the same antiquated lines of a mere transmission of knowledge, there is little to be hoped

from it in the bettering of man's future. For what is the use of transmitting knowledge if the individual's total development lags behind?
The Absorbent Mind

5 If help and salvation are to come, they can only come from the children, for the children are the makers of men.
The Absorbent Mind

6 And so we discovered that education is not something which the teacher does, but that it is a natural process which develops spontaneously in the human being.
The Absorbent Mind

MONTGOMERY, Lucy Maud (1874–1942)

Canadian writer, journalist, and teacher. Born in Clifton, Prince Edward Island, her mother died when she was a baby and she was brought up by her grandparents. In 1911 she married Reverend Ewan Macdonald and moved to Toronto. She is best known for her 'Anne' books, including *Anne of Green Gables* (1908), *Anne of Avonlea* (1909), *Anne of the Island* (1915), *Anne's House of Dreams* (1917), and *Anne of Windy Poplars* (1936), which take Anne from childhood to motherhood.

1 One spring I was looking over my notebook of plots…I found a faded entry written many years before: 'Elderly couple apply to orphan asylum for a boy. By mistake a girl is sent them.' I thought this would do. The result was *Anne of Green Gables*.
Contemporary Authors

2 Isn't it splendid to think of all the things there are to find out about? It just makes me feel glad to be alive – it's such an interesting world. It wouldn't be half so interesting if we knew all about everything, would it? There'd be no scope for imagination then, would there?
Anne of Green Gables, Ch. 2

3 There's such a lot of different Annes in me. I sometimes think that is why I'm such a troublesome person. If I was just one Anne it would be ever so much more comfortable, but then it wouldn't be half so interesting.
Anne of Green Gables, Ch. 20

4 When a man is alone he's mighty apt to be with the devil – if he ain't with God. He has to choose which company he'll keep, I reckon.
Anne's House of Dreams, Ch. 15

5 The point of good writing is knowing when to stop.
Anne's House of Dreams, Ch. 24

MORALITY

1 There is nothing in the whole world so unbecoming to a woman as a Nonconformist conscience.
Oscar Wilde (1854–1900) Irish-born British dramatist.
Lady Windermere's Fan, III [1891]

2 Nothing could be more grotesquely unjust than a code of morals, reinforced by laws, which relieves men from responsibility for irregular sexual acts, and for the same acts drives women to abortion, infanticide, prostitution and self-destruction.
Suzanne Lafollette (1893–) US politician, feminist, writer, and editor.
Concerning Women, 'Women and Marriage' [1926]

3 Nearly everybody sprouted a Canadian uncle, and there was inevitably a rise in the population. The resentment was always against the woman, however, and not the Canadian. 'No better than she should be, husband off at the war, and she'd done this' was the attitude.
Mary-Rose Murphy British teacher.
Don't You Know There's a War On? (Jonathan Croall) [c. 1944]

4 From the point of view of sexual morality the aeroplane is valuable in war in that it destroys men and women in equal numbers.
Ernest William Barnes (1874–1953) British clergyman and mathematician.
Rise of Christianity [1947]

5 A lady, that is an enlightened, cultivated, liberal lady – the only kind to be in a time of increasing classlessness – could espouse any cause: wayward girls, social diseases, unmarried mothers, andor birth control with impunity. But never by so much as the shadow of a look should she acknowledge her own experience with the Facts of Life.
Virgilia Peterson (1904–66) US writer and television personality.
A Matter of Life and Death [1961]

6 These were clever and beautiful women, often of good background, who through some breach of the moral code or the scandal of divorce had been socially ostracized but had managed to turn the ostracism into profitable account. Cultivated, endowed with civilized graces, they were frankly – kept women, but kept by one man only, or, at any rate, by one man at a time.
Cornelia Otis Skinner (1901–79) US writer, actress, and entertainer.
Elegant Wits and Grand Horizontals, Ch. 8 [1962]

7 Being a mother is a noble status, right? Right. So why does it change when you put 'unwed' or 'welfare' in front of it?

Florynce R. Kennedy (1916–) US lawyer, civil rights activist, and feminist.

Ms, 'The Verbal Karate of Florynce R. Kennedy, Esq.', Gloria Steinem, Mar 1973

8 Morality, like language, is an invented structure for conserving and communicating order. And morality is learned, like language, by mimicking and remembering.

Jane Rule (1931–) US-born Canadian writer.

Lesbian Images, 'Myth and Morality, Sources of Law and Prejudice' [1975]

MORE, Hannah (1745–1833)

British reformer. A writer and member of the Blue-stocking Circle she was befriended by Edmund Burke, Dr Johnson, and particularly David Garrick, who produced her plays *The Inflexible Captive* (1775) and *Percy* (1777). After the death of Garrick in 1779 she became steadily more pious and, through her friendship with the abolitionist William Wilberforce, was drawn to the Evangelicals. Deeply involved in trying to reform the conditions of the poor, she produced a series of treatises including *Thoughts on the Importance of the Manners of the Great to General Society* (1778) and *Cheap Repository Tracts* (1795–98), which sold over 2 million copies.

Quotations about More

1 She was born with a birch-broom in her hand, and worst of all was a shameless flatterer and insatiable of flattery. Her acceptance of a pension in compensation for a husband is a vile blot, never to be expunged from her character.

Caroline Bowles (1786–1854) British poet. Letter to Robert Southey, 21 Dec 1834

2 Much as I love your writings, I respect yet more your heart and your goodness. You are so good, that I believe you would go to heaven, even though there were no Sunday, and only six *working* days in the week.

Horace Walpole (1717–97) British writer. Letter to Mrs H. More, 1788

Quotations by More

3 Books, the Mind's food, not exercise!

The Bas Bleu

4 The roses of pleasure seldom last long enough to adorn the brow of him who plucks them; for they are the only roses which do not retain their sweetness after they have lost their beauty.

Essays on Various Subjects, 'On Dissipation'

5 If effect be the best proof of eloquence, then mine was a good speech.

Lives of Celebrated Women (Samuel Griswold Goodrich)

MOTHERHOOD

See also CHILDBIRTH; CHILDREN

1 MARIA. Maternal softness weakens my resolve,
And wakes new fears – thou dearest, best of men,
Torn from my side, I'm levell'd with my sex.
The wife – the mother – make me less than woman.

Mercy Otis Warren (1728–1814) US poet, historian, and playwright.

The Ladies of Castile, IV:5 [c. 1770]

2 Women, who are, beyond all doubt, the mothers of all mischief, also nurse that babe to sleep when he is too noisy.

R. D. Blackmore (1825–1900) British writer.

Lorna Doone [1869]

3 An author who speaks about his own books is almost as bad as a mother who talks about her own children.

Benjamin Disraeli (1804–81) British statesman.

Speech in Glasgow, 19 Nov 1873

4 Womanliness means only motherhood;
All love begins and ends there.

Robert Browning (1812–89) British poet.

The Inn Album [1875]

5 In my judgment it is a misfortune to all concerned when a woman…is either driven by poverty or lured by any generous ambition, to add to that great 'Profession of a Matron', any other systematic work; either as breadwinner to the family, or as a philanthropist or politician.

Frances Power Cobbe

The Duties of Women. A Course of Lectures [1881]

6 Though motherhood is the most important of all the professions – requiring more knowledge than any other department in human affairs – there was no attention given to preparation for this office.

Elizabeth Cady Stanton (1815–1902) US suffragette and abolitionist.

Eighty Years and More [1902]

7 Maternity is on the face of it an unsocial experience. The selfishness that a woman has learned to stifle or to dissemble where she alone is concerned, blooms freely and unashamed on behalf of her offspring.

Emily James Putnam (1865–1944) US educator, writer, and college administrator. First dean of Barnard College, New York.

The Lady, Introduction [1910]

8 Who has not watched a mother stroke her child's cheek or kiss her child *in a certain way* and felt a nervous shudder at the possessive outrage done to a free solitary human soul?
John Cowper Powys (1872–1963) British writer.
The Meaning of Culture [1930]

9 A mother! What are we worth really? They all grow up whether you look after them or not.
Christina Stead (c. 1900–) Australian writer.
The Man Who Loved Children, Ch. 10 [1940]

10 Sometimes we blame Mom too much for all that is wrong with her sons and daughters. After all, we might well ask, who started the grim mess? Who long ago made Mom and her sex 'inferior' and stripped her of her economic and political and sexual rights?
Lillian Smith (1897–1966) US writer and social critic.
Killers of the Dream, Pt II, Ch. 4 [1961]

11 If the expectant mother has come to terms with being a woman, which includes some lingering regrets at not having been born a man, she feels that her pregnancy is fulfilling her fate, completing her life as a woman and she knows a creativity that compensates for past restrictions and limitations.
T. Lidz
The Person: His Development Throughout the Life Cycle [1968]

12 Mother is the dead heart of the family, spending father's earnings on consumer goods to enhance the environment in which he eats, sleeps and watches the television.
Germaine Greer (1939–) Australian-born British writer and feminist.
The Female Eunuch [1970]

13 Now, as always, the most automated appliance in a household is the mother.
Beverly Jones (1927–) US writer and feminist.
The Florida Paper on Women's Liberation [1970]

14 No matter how old a mother is she watches her middle-aged children for signs of improvement.
Florida Scott-Maxwell (b. 1883) US-born British writer, psychologist, playwright, suffragette, and actress.
The Measure of My Days [1972]

15 It is misleading and unfair to imply that an intelligent woman must 'rise above' her maternal instincts and return to work when many intelligent, sensitive women have found that the reverse is better for them.
Sally E. Shaywitz (1942–) US paediatrician and writer.
The New York Times Magazine, 4 Mar 1973

16 The best thing that could happen to motherhood already has. Fewer women are going into it.
Victoria Billings (1945–) US journalist and writer.
Womansbook, 'Meeting Your Personal Needs' [1974]

17 Probably there is nothing in human nature more resonant with charges than the flow of energy between two biologically alike bodies, one of which has lain in amniotic bliss inside the other, one of which has laboured to give birth to the other. The materials are here for the deepest mutuality and the most painful estrangement.
Adrienne Rich (1929–) US poet and educator.
Of Woman Born [1976]

18 It is Nature itself that drives us to reproduce the species…Many would confirm that they could debate the matter disinterestedly, until they found themselves 'mated' and with some emotional security…then almost in spite of oneself comes the nest building and broody feeling.
Letter to the editor, *Observer*, Dec 1978

19 What is a mother? What elements of woman-ness does it hide and oppress? Either totally or at any rate enough so that an economic, political and symbolic system can feed off the mother to keep itself going, with the bosses exploiting the workers, the man-father exploiting the woman-mother, the name exploiting the body?
Psych et Po [1979]

20 When a child enters the world through you, it alters everything on a psychic, psychological and purely practical level. You're just not free anymore to do what you want to do. And it's not the same again. Ever.
Jane Fonda (1937–) US actress and political activist.
Los Angeles Weekly, 28 Nov–4 Dec 1980

21 The mother-child relationship is paradoxical and, in a sense, tragic. It requires the most intense love on the mother's side, yet this very love must help the child grow away from the mother and to become fully independent.
Erich Fromm (1900–80) US psychologist and philosopher.

22 Claudia…remembered that when she'd had her first baby she had realised with astonishment that the perfect couple consisted of a mother and child and not, as she had always supposed, a man and woman.
Alice Thomas Ellis (1932–) British writer.
The Other Side of the Fire [1983]

MURDOCH, Dame Iris (1919–)

British writer. Born in Dublin of Anglo-Irish parentage she studied classics at Somerville College, Oxford (1938). Despite their underlying philosophical themes, she has achieved wide readership of her novels, which include *The Sandcastle* (1957), *The Bell* (1958), *A Severed Head* (1961) which was made into a successful stage play, *The Sea, The Sea* (1978), which won the Booker prize, *The Good Apprentice* (1985), and *The Message to the Planet* (1989). She has also published a number of philosophical writings, including *Sartre, Romantic Rationalist* (1953) and a study of Plato, *The Fire and the Sun* (1977). She was made a DBE in 1987.

Quotations about Murdoch

1 A tousled heel-less, ladder-stockinged little lady – crackling with intelligence, but nothing at all of a prig.
George Lyttleton (1883–1962) British educationalist. *The Lyttleton Hart-Davis Letters*

2 She is like a character out of Hieronymus Bosch – the very nicest character.
The Times, 'Profile ', 25 Apr 1983

Quotations by Murdoch

3 Writing is like getting married. One should never commit oneself until one is amazed at one's luck.
The Black Prince, 'Bradley Pearson's Foreword'

4 'What are you famous *for*?'
'For nothing. I am just famous.'
The Flight from the Enchanter

5 He led a double life. Did that make him a liar? He did not feel a liar. He was a man of two truths.
The Sacred and Profane Love Machine

6 Only lies and evil come from letting people off.
A Severed Head

MUSICIANS

1 Listen: there was once a king sitting on his throne. Around him stood great and wonderfully beautiful columns ornamented with ivory, bearing the banners of the king with great honour. Then it pleased the king to raise a small feather from the ground and he commanded it to fly. The feather flew, not because of anything in itself but because the air bore it along. Thus am I.
Hildegard of Bingen (1098–1179) German composer, abbess, and mystic.
A feather on the breath of God... [12th century]

2 What you wrote to me about your musical occupations with reference to and in comparison with Felix was both rightly thought and expressed. Music will perhaps become his profession, whilst for *you* it can and must only be an ornament, never the root of your being and doing...it does you credit that you have always shown yourself good and sensible in these matters; and your very joy at the praise he earns proves that you might, in his place, have merited equal approval. Remain true to these sentiments and to this line of conduct; they are feminine, and only what is truly feminine is an ornament to your sex.
Abraham Mendelssohn
Letter to his daughter, Fanny, 16 July 1820

3 Clara has written a number of smaller pieces, which show a musicianship and tenderness of invention such as she has never before attained. But children, and a husband who is always living in the realms of imagination, do not go well with composition. She cannot work at it regularly, and I am often disturbed to think how many tender ideas are lost because she cannot work them out.
Robert Schumann (1810–56) German composer.
Referring to his wife Clara. Diary entry, Feb 1843

4 Singers in the church have a real liturgical office, and, therefore, women, as being incapable of exercising such office, cannot be admitted to form part of the choir or of the musical chapel.
Pius X (1835–1914) Italian pope (1903–14)
Attrib. [1914]

5 This temptation to pretend that women are non-existent musically, to ignore or damp down our poor little triumphs...is a microbe that will flourish comfortably, though perhaps surreptitiously, in the male organism, till there are enough women composers for it to die a natural death. Whereupon men will forget it ever existed. Have they not already forgotten their frenzied opposition to 'Votes for Women'?
Ethel Smyth (1858–1944) British composer.
A Final Burning of Boats [1928]

6 Probably the hardest of all the worlds that women have yet to conquer is that of The Arts, because there are no rules in that game, only chances to be given or withheld.
Ethel Smyth (1858–1944) British composer.
A Final Burning of Boats [1928]

7 Nature never intended the fair sex to become cornetists, trombonists, and players of wind instruments...Women cannot possibly play brass instruments and look pretty, and why should they spoil their good looks?
Gustave Kerker Musical director at the Casino Theatre, New York.
Remark, 1930

8 Women ruin music. If the ladies are ill-favoured the men do not want to play next to them, and if they are well-favoured they can't.
Sir Thomas Beecham (1879–1961) British conductor.
Attrib. [1961]

9 There are no women composers, never have been, and possibly never will be.
Thomas Beecham (1879–1961) British conductor.
Attrib. [1961]

10 Composing a piece of music is very feminine. It is sensitive, emotional, contemplative. By comparison, doing housework is positively masculine.
Barbara Kolb (1939–) US composer.
Time, 10 Nov 1975

NIGHTINGALE, Florence (1820–1910)

British nurse. Born in Florence, the daughter of wealthy parents, she received a broad classical education from her father. On 7 Feb 1837 she believed she heard the voice of God informing her that she had a mission, but it was not until some years later that she realized what that mission was. In 1850, after considerable family opposition, she entered the Institution of Protestant Deaconesses at Kaiserwerth, Germany to train as a nurse. In 1853 she was appointed superintendent of the Institution for the Care of Sick Gentlewomen in London. She became famous as the 'Lady of the Lamp' for her work during the Crimean War (1854–56), after which she brought about radical reforms in the army hospitals. In 1860 she set up the Nightingale School for Nurses at St Thomas's Hospital from funds raised by the public to commemorate her Crimean work. In 1907 she was awarded the Order of Merit – the first woman to receive this honour.

Quotations about Nightingale

1 Miss Nightingale did inspire awe, not because one felt afraid of her *per se*, but because the very essence of *Truth* seemed to emanate from her, and because of her perfect fearlessness in telling it.
William Richmond *The Richmond Papers*

2 What a comfort it was to see her pass. She would speak to one, and nod and smile to as many more; but she could not do it to all you know. We lay there by the hundreds; but we could kiss her shadow as it fell and lay our heads on the pillow again content.
A patient in the Crimean War. *Florence Nightingale* (Cecil Woodham-Smith)

Quotations by Nightingale

3 It may seem a strange principle to enunciate as the very first requirement in a Hospital that it should do the sick no harm.
Notes on Hospitals, Preface

4 No *man*, not even a doctor, ever gives any other definition of what a nurse should be than this – 'devoted and obedient.' This definition would do just as well for a porter. It might even do for a horse. It would not do for a policeman.
Notes on Nursing

5 The first possibility of rural cleanliness lies in *water supply*.
Letter to Medical Officer of Health, Nov 1891

OAKLEY, Annie (1860–1926)

US markswoman and entertainer. The inspiration for the musical *Annie Get Your Gun*, she was in real life an entertainer with 'Buffalo Bill's Wild West' show, in which she and her husband Frank Butler enthralled audiences with their sharp-shooting. Often called 'Little Sure Shot' she proved immensely popular and was given top billing in the Wild West show as 'Miss Annie Oakley, the Peerless Lady Wing-Shot'.

Quotation about Oakley

1 Little Sure-Shot.
Sitting Bull (c. 1834–90) US Sioux Indian chief. His nickname for Annie Oakley

Quotations by Oakley

2 I can shoot as well as you. I think I should be able to go on and trade shot for shot with you. You take one shot while I hold the object for you, and then I take the next one, you acting as holder for me.
Addressing her husband. *Annie Oakley: Woman at Arms* (Courtney Ryley Cooper), Ch. 4

O'BRIEN, Edna (1932–)

Irish writer. Born in the west of Ireland she is noted for her portrayal of young women attempting to escape from the confines of their upbringing, their sensual experiences, and also the pleasures, real or imagined, of the countryside. Her first novel *The Country Girls* (1960), which is largely autobiographical, was followed by *The Lonely Girl* (1962; screened as *The Girl with Green Eyes*, 1965). Later novels include *A Pagan Place* (1970), *Night* (1972), and *Johnny I Hardly Knew You* (1977; US title *I Hardly Knew You*, 1978), in which she expresses her despair over the enslavement of women. She received the Kingsley Amis First Novel Award (1962) and the Yorkshire Post Novel Award (1971).

1 I did not sleep. I never do when I am over-happy, over-unhappy, or in bed with a strange man.
The Love Object

2 Do you know what I hate about myself, I have never done a brave thing, I have never risked death.
A Scandalous Woman, 'Over'

3 To Crystal, hair was the most important thing on earth. She would never get married because you couldn't wear curlers in bed.
Winter's Tales, 8, 'Come into the Drawing Room, Doris'

4 The vote, I thought, means nothing to women. We should be armed.
Quoted as epigraph to *Fear of Flying* (Erica Jong), Ch. 16

OCCUPATIONS

See also WORK

1 We call a person the best midwife if she is trained in all branches of therapy (for some cases must be treated by diet, others by surgery, while still others must be cured by drugs); if she is moreover able to prescribe hygienic regulations for her patients, to observe the general and the individual features of the case, and from this to find out what is expedient.
Soranus of Ephesus (fl. 2nd century AD) Greek physician.
Gynaecology, I [2nd century AD]

2 Francesca, the wife of Matteo de Romana of Salerno, has explained to the Royal Court that she is reputed to be proficient in the art of surgery.
Charles, Duke of Calabria
Licence granted, 10 Sept 1321

3 There is another way in which the general opinion, that women are inferior to men, is manifested…I allude to the disproportionate value set on the time and the labor of men and women.
Sarah Moore Grimké (1792–1873) US abolitionist and women's rights pioneer.
Letter from Brookline, 1837

4 She knew that it is only in the eyes of the vulgar-minded and the foolish, that a woman is degraded by exerting her ingenuity or her talents as a means of support.
Eliza Leslie (1787–1858) US writer, editor, humorist, and cookery expert.
Pencil Sketches; or, Outlines of Character and Manners, 'Constance Allerton; or the Mourning Suits' [1837]

5 Every young woman in our land should be qualified by some accomplishment which she may teach, or some art or profession she can follow, to support her creditably, should the necessity occur.
Sarah Josepha Hale (1788–1879) US editor, writer, and poet.
Editorial, *Godey's Lady's Book*, Mar 1854

6 A devoted nurse, well taught in hygiene, and knowing practically the nature and accidents of various kinds of sickness, deserves, as Miss Nightingale has shown, a place next to the doctor, indeed medical treatment can only be effectively carried out through the agency of good nurses.
W. Farr
Census of England and Wales, 1861, 'Proposed Inquiry into the Occupations of the People: Medical Profession. Draft report'

7 They resumed the conversation started at dinner – the emancipation and occupations of women. Levin agreed with Dolly that a girl who did not marry could always find some feminine occupation in the family. He supported this view by saying that no family can get along without women to help them, that every family, poor or rich, had to have nurses, either paid or belonging to the family.
Leo Tolstoy (1828–1910) Russian writer.
Anna Karenina [1877]

8 The nurse and physician have different professions. The doctor is not a nurse, and only now and then is one found who fairly comprehends the actual matter-of-fact realities of the training school. On this fundamental difference rests the claim of the school to be ruled, as an educative and disciplinary body, by those of its origin.
Lavinia Dock US nurse.
Arguing, at the Chicago World's Fair in 1893, that nurses were more suitable than doctors to govern the nurses' school

9 We have no desire to say anything that might tend to encourage women to embark on accountancy, for although women might make excellent book-keepers there is much in accountancy proper that is, we think, unsuitable for them.
Accountant, English Institute of Chartered Accountants, 1912

10 The trained nurse has become one of the great blessings of humanity, taking a place beside the physician and the priest, and not inferior to either in her mission.
Sir William Osler (1849–1919) Canadian physician.
Aequanimitas, with Other Addresses, 'Nurse and Patient' [c. 1919]

11 For example, the women patients had to have their hair done in a certain way – it was parted in the centre in two plaits, one on each side, and that was the junior's job. If their hair wasn't tidy – the sister would just look down the row and if she saw a patient's head untidy, she made the nurse do it properly.

Report from an Australian nurse at Perth Public Hospital. *Nothing to Spare* (Jan Carter) [c. 1919]

12 But oh, what a woman I should be if an able young man would consecrate his life to me as secretaries and technicians do to their men employers.

Mabel Ulrich (b. 1882) US physician.

Scribner's Magazine, 'A Doctor's Diary, 1904–1932', June 1933

13 When the war came our daughter had just left school, and we said, 'Now you'll have to do some war work, what do you want to do? And to our astonishment she said, 'I'd like to learn nursing.' Her father was delighted, and so was I really. In fact she ought to have trained as a doctor, but it never entered our heads then that she might do that. It was only after the war, when she had done so well as a nurse, that we thought that. There were *some* women doctors, but they were rather rare.

Joyce Dennys British writer.

Don't You Know There's a War On? (Jonathan Croall) [c. 1939]

14 I don't pretend to be an ordinary housewife.

Elizabeth Taylor (1932–) British-born US actress.

Interview [c. 1980s]

15 Men, having kept work as their exclusive preserve for so long, *are* defensive with the women who try to enter it, and show a strong tendency to shunt us into the more traditional female roles – not managing director, but his PA; not headmaster, but deputy; not sales, but personnel, and so on.

Cathy Douglas

The Superwoman Trap

OLD AGE

1 After I am waxed old shall I have pleasure, my lord being old also?

Bible: Genesis

18:12

2 Gentle ladies, you will remember till old age what we did together in our brilliant youth!

Sappho (fl. c. 610–635 BC) Greek poet.

Distinguished Women Writers (Virginia Moore) [7th century BC]

3 When the first few wrinkles appear, When her skin goes dry and slack, when her teeth begin
To blacken, when her eyes turn lustreless, then: 'Pack

Your bags!' his steward will tell her. 'Be off with you!'

Juvenal (Decimus Junius Juveanlis; 60–130 AD) Roman satirist.

Satires, VI [1st century AD]

4 Alas! the colours of the flowers
Have faded in the long continued rain;
My beauty aging, too, as in this world
I gazed, engrossed, on things that were but vain.

Ono no Komachi (834–880) Japanese poet.

'The Colours of Flowers' [9th century]

5 Old age is woman's hell.

Ninon de Lenclos (1620–1705) French courtesan.

Attrib. [1705]

6 A woman would rather visit her own grave than the place where she had been young and beautiful after she is aged and ugly.

Corra May Harris (1869–1935) US writer.

Eve's Second Husband, Ch. 14 [1910]

7 That although artificial teeth are a great blessing, and although a suitable wig may be a charitable covering for a bald head, yet she is committing a sin against her personal appearance as well as against her self-respect if she dyes her hair.

Mary Scharlieb (1845–1930) British gynaecological surgeon.

The Seven Ages of Woman [1915]

8 Let's go out and buy playing-cards, good wine, bridge-scorers, knitting needles – all the paraphernalia to fill a gaping void, all that's required to disguise that monster, an old woman.

Colette (1873–1954) French writer.

Cheri [1920]

9 It is a terrible thing for an old woman to outlive her dogs.

Tennessee Williams (1911–83) US dramatist.

Camino Real [1953]

10 A diplomat is a man who always remembers a woman's birthday but never remembers her age.

Robert Frost (1875–1963) US poet.

Attrib. [1963]

11 Take a close-up of a woman past sixty! You might as well use a picture of a relief map of Ireland!

Nancy Astor (1879–1964) US-born British politician.

When asked for a close-up photograph. Attrib. [1964]

12 Being seventy is not a sin.

Golda Meir (1898–1978) Russian-born Israeli stateswoman.

Reader's Digest, July 1971, 'The Indestructible Golda Meir'

OPPRESSION

See also DOMINATION

1 Oppressed, degraded, enslaved, – must our unfortunate sex for ever submit to sacrifice their right, their pleasures, their *will*, at the altar of public opinion.
Maria Edgeworth (1767–1849) Irish novelist and essayist.
Angelina, Ch. 1 [c. 1799]

2 O! men with sisters dear,
O! men with mothers and wives!
It is not linen you're wearing out,
But human creatures' lives!
Thomas Hood (1799–1845) British poet.
The Song of the Shirt [1843]

3 Because the revolutionary tempest, in overturning at the same time the throne and the scaffold, in breaking the chain of the black slave, forgot to break the chain of the most oppressed of all – of Woman, the pariah of humanity.
Jeanne-Françoise Deroin (1805–94) French feminist.
Letter from Prison of St Lazare, Paris, 15 June 1851

4 With many women I doubt whether there be any more effectual way of touching their hearts than ill-using them and then confessing it. If you wish to get the sweetest fragrance from the herb at your feet, tread on it and bruise it.
Anthony Trollope (1815–82) British novelist.
Miss Mackenzie, Ch. 10 [1865]

5 In the early days, women were generally barmaids if they had nothing else they could do and if they were attractive…You see, it was really a form of prostitution, the women were supposed to oblige the men…Women held their jobs better if they were obliging. It's the same now in certain walks of life. Sometimes the barmaids were sacked if they weren't obliging, not if they weren't efficient.
Describing a woman's life in the Australian goldfields.
Nothing to Spare (Jan Carter) [c. 1906]

6 How men hate waiting while their wives shop for clothes and trinkets; how women hate waiting, often for much of their lives, while their husbands shop for fame and glory.
Thomas Szasz (1920–   ) US psychiatrist.
The Second Sin [1973]

7 Women in Africa work like beasts of burden, fetching firewood, carrying water, looking after the children and growing food. They are Africa's main food producers but have little time to devote to the task. Often they are not legally regarded as adults; they frequently have no land rights; and a husband can keep his wife's earnings.
New Internationalist, June 1990

8 In buses all over Kenya you will see women sitting together. They do this to try and avoid being molested by male passengers. Even educated middle-class women obediently stay at home at night while their husbands go out and spend money on their girlfriends. Occasionally they will write to newspaper agony columns; they are told to close their eyes and think of Kenya. They cannot be advised to leave their husbands, because under African customary law, which operates in most parts of the country, women are not allowed to own property and will get nothing from a divorce.
Peter Hillmore British journalist.
Observer Magazine, 24 Nov 1991

PANKHURST, Dame Christabel (1880–1958)

British suffragette. Daughter of Emmeline Pankhurst, she was in favour of using militant tactics to win the vote for women in Britain. In 1903 she cofounded (with her mother) the Women's Social and Political Union. Her militant campaign began in 1905 when, with Annie Kenney, she disrupted a Liberal Party meeting in Liverpool by unfurling a banner which read 'Votes for Women'. She was sent to jail for a technical assault on the police, thus drawing worldwide attention to the campaign. She continued with her campaign, organizing hungerstrikes, open-air rallies, and direct physical action, until the outbreak of World War I. The suffragette movement then decided to call a truce and Christabel Pankhurst became a leader of the women's war effort in Britain. She was made a DBE in 1936.

Quotations about Christabel Pankhurst

1 She knows everything and can see through everything.
Mrs Flora Drummond (1869–1949) British suffragette.
Suffragette, 12 Dec 1913

2 I heard Christabel Pankhurst the other day. She was very able, very clever, and very unpleasant. Her idea of progress is that females should meet together in masses and orate. But I agreed with most of her remarks, and her tone did not unconvert me.
E. M. Forster (1879–1970) British novelist. *Letters*, Vol. I

Quotations by Christabel Pankhurst

3 We are not ashamed of what we have done, because, when you have a great cause to fight for, the moment of greatest humiliation is the moment when the spirit is proudest.
Speech, Albert Hall, London, 19 Mar 1908

4 We are here to claim our rights as women, not only to be free, but to fight for freedom. It is

our privilege, as well as our pride and our joy, to take some part in this militant movement, which, as we believe, means the regeneration of all humanity.
Speech, 23 Mar 1911

5 What we suffragettes aspire to be when we are enfranchised is ambassadors of freedom to women in other parts of the world, who are not so free as we are.
Speech, Carnegie Hall, New York, 25 Oct 1915

PANKHURST, Emmeline (1858–1928)

British suffragette. After being educated in Manchester and Paris, in 1874 she married Richard Pankhurst, a barrister, who drafted the first British women's suffrage bill in the late 1860s, and the Married Women's Property Acts of 1870 and 1882. In 1889 she and her husband founded the Women's Franchise League which, in 1894, achieved the right for married women to vote in local elections.

Following her husband's death in 1898, Emmeline Pankhurst became registrar of births and deaths in a district of Manchester. In 1903 she cofounded (with her daughter, Christabel) the Women's Social and Political Union (WSPU) whose aim was to keep alive the cause of women's suffrage. From 1906 she directed WSPU activities from London, encouraging militant action, and campaigning and rallying people to the cause. She was jailed three times in 1908–09 and, in 1913, was arrested for inciting violence after the bombing of Lloyd George's home, and reimprisoned thirteen times under the 'Cat and Mouse Act' – the Prisoners (Temporary Discharge for Ill-Health) Act, 1913. With the outbreak of World War I, she and Christabel called off militant action, the government released all suffragette prisoners, and she directed her energies to recruiting women for the war effort.

After the war she lived for a time in America, returning to England in 1926, when she was chosen as Conservative candidate for Whitechapel. Her health failed before she could be elected. She died a few weeks after the passing of the Representation of the People Act (1928).

Quotations about Emmeline Pankhurst

1 What an extraordinary mixture of idealism and lunacy. Hasn't she the sense to see that the very worst method of campaigning for the franchise is to try and intimidate or blackmail a man into giving her what he would gladly give her otherwise.
David Lloyd George (1863–1945) British Liberal statesman. *Lloyd George* (Richard Lloyd George)

2 She was as she instinctively knew, cast for a great role. She had a temperament akin to genius. She could have been a queen on the Stage or in the Salon.
Emmeline Pethwick-Lawrence (1867–1954) British suffragette. *My Part in a Changing World*

Quotations by Emmeline Pankhurst

3 If civilisation is to advance at all in the future, it must be through the help of women, women freed of their political shackles, women with full power to work their will in society. It was rapidly becoming clear to my mind that men regarded women as a servant class in the community, and that women were going to remain in the servant class until they lifted themselves out of it.
My Own Story

4 Women had always fought for men, and for their children. Now they were ready to fight for their own human rights. Our militant movement was established.
My Own Story

5 I have no sense of guilt. I look upon myself as a prisoner of war. I am under no moral obligation to conform to, or in any way accept, the sentence imposed upon me.
Speech in court, Apr 1913. *The Fighting Pankhursts* (David Mitchell)

6 We have taken this action, because as women…we realize that the condition of our sex is so deplorable that it is our duty even to break the law in order to call attention to the reasons why we do so.
Speech in court, 21 Oct 1908. *Shoulder to Shoulder* (ed. Midge Mackenzie)

PANKHURST, Sylvia (1882–1960)

British suffragette. The daughter of Emmeline and Richard Pankhurst she was associated with her mother's movement although she, along with Keir Hardie, went further and espoused the socialist cause. Based in London, initially supporting herself as a freelance artist, she worked for the Women's Social and Political Union as an organizer and speaker, and visited the USA in 1911. She also designed the cover of *Votes for Women*, and wrote *The Suffragette* (1910). In 1912 she built up a democratic mass movement in London's East End, which from 1914 on was known as the East London Federation of the Suffragettes. During World War I the Federation organized maternity welfare clinics, a day nursery, a toy and clothing factory for unemployed women, and the League of Rights for Soldiers' and Sailors' Wives and Relatives. In the later part of her life she was occupied with fighting against fascism and for Ethiopian independence. She helped to set up the

Abyssinian Association and published *Ethiopia, A Cultural History* in 1955. The following year she moved to Addis Ababa where she remained until her death. She wrote the book *Suffragette Movement: An Intimate Account of Persons and Ideals* (1931), which is the source for much of the information we have on the movement's origins and history.

Quotation about Sylvia Pankhurst

1   She endured ten successive hunger and thirst strikes between June 1913 and June 1914. Such activity in and out of prison left her almost completely exhausted and with no time for painting.
Richard Pankhurst *Sylvia Pankhurst – Artist and Crusader*

Quotations by Sylvia Pankhurst

2   I could not give my name to aid the slaughter in this war, fought on both sides for grossly material ends, which did not justify the sacrifice of a single mother's son. Clearly I must continue to oppose it, and expose it, to all whom I could reach with voice or pen.
The Home Front, Ch. 25

3   My belief in the growth and permanence of democracy is undimmed. I know that the people will cast off the new dictatorships as they did the old. I believe as firmly as in my youth that humanity will surmount the era of poverty and war. Life will be happier and more beautiful for all. I believe in the GOLDEN AGE.
Myself When Young (ed. Margot Asquith)

4   We do not make beams from the hollow, decaying trunk of the fallen oak. We use the upsoaring tree in the full vigour of its sap.
Evening Standard, 5 Mar 1930

5   I have gone to war too…I am going to fight capitalism even if it kills me. It is wrong that people like you should be comfortable and well fed while all around you people are starving.
The Fighting Pankhursts (David Mitchell)

PARKER, Dorothy Rothschild (1893–1967)

US writer, humorist, and critic. A member of the Algonquin Round Table group, she is noted for her witty one-liners. She grew up in New York and, in 1916, started work as a theatre reviewer for *Vanity Fair*. She was sacked in 1920 for the acerbity of her reviews, and became a freelance writer. In 1926 her first volume of verse, *Enough Rope*, was published and proved to be a bestseller. Two later volumes of verse, *Sunset Gun* (1928) and *Death and Taxes* (1931), were collected with *Enough Rope* in *Collected Poems: Not So Deep as a Well* (1936). Her collections of short stories *Laments for the Living*

(1930) and *After Such Pleasures* (1933) were combined in *Here Lies* (1939). In 1933 she married her second husband, Alan Campbell and together they collaborated on film scripts, receiving credits for over 15 films, including *A Star Is Born*. In the 1950s she was named before the House Committee on Un-American Activities for having left-wing political affiliations, which she found affected her employment in the Hollywood studios. She also wrote two plays, *The Coast of Illyria* (1949) and *The Ladies of the Corridor* (1953).

Quotations about Parker

1   She has put into what she has written a voice, a state of mind, an era, a few moments of human experience that nobody else has conveyed.
Edmund Wilson (1895–1972) US critic and writer. Attrib.

2   She is a combination of Little Nell and Lady Macbeth.
Alexander Woollcott (1887–1943) US journalist. *While Rome Burns*

Quotations by Parker

3   Razors pain you
Rivers are damp;
Acids stain you;
And drugs cause cramp.
Guns aren't lawful;
Nooses give;
Gas smells awful;
You might as well live.
Enough Rope, 'Resumé'

4   All I say is, nobody has any business to go around looking like a horse and behaving as if it were all right. You don't catch horses going around looking like people, do you?
Horsie

5   Why is it no one ever sent me yet
One perfect limousine, do you suppose?
Ah no, it's always just my luck to get
One perfect rose.
One Perfect Rose

6   By the time you swear you're his,
Shivering and sighing,
And he vows his passion is
Infinite, undying –
Lady, make a note of this:
One of you is lying.
Unfortunate Coincidence

7   That should assure us of at least forty-five minutes of undisturbed privacy.
Pressing a button marked NURSE during a stay in hospital. *The Algonquin Wits* (R. Drennan)

8 If all the young ladies who attended the Yale promenade dance were laid end to end, no one would be the least surprised.
While Rome Burns (Alexander Woollcott)

9 Brevity is the soul of lingerie.
While Rome Burns (Alexander Woollcott)

10 It serves me right for putting all my eggs in one bastard.
Said on going into hospital to have an abortion. *You Might as Well Live* (J. Keats), Pt II, Ch. 3

11 How could they tell?
Reaction to news of the death of Calvin Coolidge, US President 1923–29; also attributed to H. L. Mencken. *You Might As Well Live* (J. Keats)

12 Check enclosed.
Giving her version of the two most beautiful words in the English language. Attrib.

PARTNERSHIP

1 Woman does not forget she needs the fecundator, she does not forget that everything that is born of her is planted in her.
Anaïs Nin (1903–77) French-born US writer.
The Diary of Anaïs Nin, Vol. II [Aug 1937]

2 I think it is a grave mistake for young girls to think that it has to be a career versus marriage, equality versus love. Partnership, not dependence, is the real romance in marriage.
Muriel Fox (1928–) US business executive and feminist.
New Woman, Oct 1971

3 Industrial relations are like sexual relations. It's better between two consenting parties.
Vic Feather (1908–76) British trade-union leader.
Guardian Weekly, 8 Aug 1976

4 Partners concerns and interests diverge over time more often than they converge, and the second half of life…can plunge people into a sense of isolation and despairing futility at once inescapable and totally unexpected.
David Smail British psychologist.
Taking Care [1986]

PARTURIER, Françoise (1919–)

French journalist. Born in Paris, she studied at Paris University and in 1947 married Jean Gatichon. She became a regular contributor to *Figaro* from 1956; using the pseudonym 'Nicole', she collaborated on three books with Josette Raoul-Duval. The first book written under her own name, *L'amant de cinq jours*, was published in 1959. Other works include *Lettre ouverte aux hommes* (1968), *L'amour? Le Plaisir?* (1968), and *Les Hauts de Ramatuelle* (1983).

1 To tell a woman using her mind that she is thinking with a man's brain means telling her that she can't think with her own brain; it demonstrates your ineradicable belief in her intellectual inadequacy.
Open Letter to Men

2 You men can't stand the truth, sir, as soon as it embarrasses your interests or your pleasure.
Open Letter to Men

3 We've never been in a democracy we've always been in a phallocracy!
Open Letter to Men

4 You say being a housewife is the noblest calling in the world…You remind me of those company executives who…praise the 'little guys' of their organization in their speeches.
Open Letter to Men

PAVLOVA, Anna (1881–1931)

Russian ballerina. Born in St Petersburg, she passed the entrance examination to the Ballet School (now the Kirov Theatre) in 1891, and was prima ballerina for the Russian Imperial Ballet by 1906. She left the Imperial Ballet in 1913 and the following year began touring the world with her own company. Her roles were largely classical and she is most famous for her performance in *Giselle* and in *Le Cygne* (*The Dying Swan*), which was choreographed especially for her by Michel Fokine. In 1912 she moved to London and established a dance school in Hampstead. In 1920 she founded a home for Russian refugee orphans in Paris.

Quotations about Pavlova

1 People waiting for her to leave the theatre never dreamed of daring to ask for her autograph, any more than they would ask royalty.
Sir Frederick Ashton (1904–88) British ballet dancer and choreographer. *Pavlova Impressions* (Margot Fonteyn)

2 The woman and artist I hold above all others in the history of the ballet.
Margot Fonteyn (1919–91) British ballet dancer. *Pavlova Impressions*

Quotations by Pavlova

3 Although one may fail to find happiness in theatrical life, one never wishes to give it up after having once tasted its fruits. To enter the School of the Imperial Ballet is to enter a convent whence frivolity is banned, and where merciless discipline reigns.
Pavlova: A Biography (ed. A. H. Franks), 'Pages of My Life'

4 As is the case in all branches of art, success depends in a very large measure upon individ-

ual initiative and exertion, and cannot be achieved except by dint of hard work.
Pavlova: A Biography (ed. A. H. Franks), 'Pages of My Life'

5 When a small child...I thought that success spelled happiness. I was wrong. Happiness is like a butterfly which appears and delights us for one brief moment, but soon flits away.
Pavlova: A Biography (ed. A. H. Franks), 'Pages of My Life'

PEACE

See also WAR

1 Woman, however, as the bearer and guardian of the new lives, has everywhere greater respect for life than man, who for centuries, as hunter and warrior, learned that the taking of lives may be not only allowed, but honourable.
Ellen Key (1849–1926) Swedish writer and feminist.
The Renaissance of Motherhood, Ch. 2 [1914]

2 The extent of their success (the Greenham women) in using woman power on behalf of a key woman's objective – peace – is to be found in the anger they arouse in the macho male.
Barbara Castle (1910–) British politician.
Guardian, 2 Oct 1984

PERÓN, Eva (1919–52)

Argentine politician. A beautiful and popular actress (known as Evita) whose charisma and charitable works did much for the cause of her husband, the president Juan Domingo Perón. Born in Los Toldos, she was educated in Junin and, in the 1930s and 1940s worked as a radio and film actress in Buenos Aires. In 1945 she married Juan Perón and took part in his presidential campaign of 1945–46. After his election she devoted much of her time and energy to alleviating poverty and improving social welfare. She was largely responsible for securing the vote for women, and formed the Peronista Feminist Party in 1949. She was nominated for the vice-presidency in 1951, but the Army forced her to withdraw her candidacy. She died the following year from cancer.

Quotations about Peron
1 A Court hairdresser who travels with her keeps her hair long and blonde and changes her hair style almost every day, swinging between a peak of high curls and a bun on the neck.
Robert Clyde *Daily Mail*, 4 July 1947

2 Wrapped in furs and sparkling with diamonds, she still addresses the workers of Buenos Aires as one of them: 'Nosotros los descamisados' – We the Shirtless. And in Argentina, if not in Europe, she gets away with it. To her own people, those from whom she sprang, she is a dream come true. Cinderella become Queen.
Observer, 'Profile', 13 July 1947

Quotations by Peron
3 I was very sad for many days when I discovered that in the world there were poor people and rich people; and the strange thing is that the existence of the poor did not cause me as much pain as the knowledge that at the same time there were people who were rich.
My Life's Cause

4 Our president has declared that the only privileged persons in our country are the children.
Speech, American Congress of Industrial Medicine, 5 Dec 1949

5 Almsgiving tends to perpetuate poverty; and does away with it once and for all. Almsgiving leaves a man just where he was before. Aid restores him to society as an individual worthy of all respect and not as a man with a grievance. Almsgiving is the generosity of the rich; social aid levels up social inequalities. Charity separates the rich from the poor; and raises the needy and sets him on the same level with the rich.
Speech, American Congress of Industrial Medicine, 5 Dec 1949

PIAF, Edith (Edith Giovanna Gassion; 1915–63)

French singer, cabaret artist, and songwriter. Born in Paris, her mother, a café singer, abandoned her at birth, and she was brought up by her grandmother. She became blind at the age of three, due to a complication of meningitis, but recovered her sight four years later. Piaf, Parisian slang for 'sparrow', was the name suggested to her by a cabaret owner who gave her her first nightclub job in 1935. She made her radio debut in 1936, and during World War II entertained French prisoners of war. In 1947 she toured America for the first time. She wrote about thirty songs herself, of which the best-known is 'La vie en rose'. She died at the age of forty-eight, her early death brought on by alcohol- and drug-abuse. An intensely popular cabaret and music-hall singer she sang with the same intensity and emotion as she lived her life. The song for which she is best remembered, 'Non, je ne regrette rien', was written by Charles Dumont, one of her many lovers.

Quotations about Piaf
1 Piaf, Dietrich and the tragically similar Garland were perhaps the only women entertainers

in mid-century able to unhinge an audience with emotion.
Derek Jewell (1927–85) British writer. *1000 Makers of the 20th Century*

2 One of her songs was *Je ne regrette rien* and that was how she was.
Derek Jewell (1927–85) British writer. *1000 Makers of the 20th Century*

Quotations by Piaf

3 You'll never make me believe that those big bouquets are bought with love; they're bought with money. You must have faith to buy a little bunch of violets, to dip your hand in your pocket and give them without feeling ridiculous. That's a real act of love.
Piaf (Simone Berteaut)

4 Any woman who lets a man walk over her is a dumb idiot and deserves no better.
Piaf (Simone Berteaut)

PLATH, Sylvia (1932–63)

US poet and novelist. Born in Boston, Massachusetts, she published her first poem at the age of eight. From 1955 to 1957 she attended Cambridge University on a Fulbright grant, where she met and married the British poet Ted Hughes. In 1959 she and Hughes settled permanently in Britain, and in 1960 she published her first book of poems, *The Colossus*. She had two children by Hughes, but in 1962 he left her to live with another woman. The remaining months of her life were ones of intense creativity, during which she published a novel, *The Bell Jar* (1963), under the pseudonym Victoria Lucas. However, they were also months of declining mental stability, and a month after its publication she committed suicide by gassing herself. Posthumous publications include *Ariel* (1965), *Crossing the War* (1971), and *Winter Trees* (1971). Her *Collected Poems* (1981) won a Pulitzer prize.

1 They all wanted to adopt me in some way and, for the price of their care and influence, have me resemble them.
The Bell Jar

2 Dying
is an art, like everything else.
I do it exceptionally well.
Lady Lazarus

3 The surgeon is quiet, he does not speak.
He has seen too much death, his hands are full of it.
Winter Trees, 'The Courage of Shutting-Up'

4 I am no shadow
Though there is a shadow starting from my feet.
I am a wife.

The city waits and aches. The little grasses
Crack through stone, and they are green with life.
Winter Trees, 'The Three Women'

POLITICS

1 Women in state affairs are like monkeys in glass-shops.
Proverb

2 The empress proceeded to use her authority in all matters of government, quite openly. Without the slightest embarrassment she assumed the duties of a man and she abandoned all pretence of acting through her ministers.
Michael Psellus (1018–96) Byzantine philospher and historian.
Referring to the reign of Theodora (1055–56). *Fourteen Byzantine Rulers (The Chronographia of Michael Psellus)* [11th century]

3 If things were even worse than they are after all this war they might have laid the blame upon the rule of a woman; but if such persons are honest they should blame only the rule of men who desire to play the part of kings. In future, if I am not any more hampered, I hope to show that women have a more sincere determination to preserve the country than those who have plunged it into the miserable condition to which it has been brought.
Catherine de Medici (1519–89) Italian queen.
Letter to the ambassador of Spain, 1570

4 I still love you, but in politics there is no heart, only head.
Napoleon I (Napoleon Bonaparte; 1769–1821) French emperor.
Referring to his divorce, for reasons of state, from the Empress Josephine [1809]. *Bonaparte* (C. Barnett)

5 I consider every attempt to induce women to think they have a just right to participate in the public duties of government as injurious to their best interests and derogatory to their character.
Sarah Josepha Hale (1788–1879) US editor, writer, and poet.
Editorial, *The Ladies' Magazine and Literary Gazette*, Feb 1832

6 If American politics are too dirty for women to take part in, there's something wrong with American politics.
Edna Ferber (1887–1968) US writer.
Cimarron, Ch. 23 [1929]

7 I cannot and will not cut my conscience to fit this year's fashions, even though I long ago came to the conclusion that I was not a political

person and could have no comfortable place in any political group.
Lillian Hellman (1906–) US playwright and writer.
Letter to the House Committee on Un-American Activities. *The Nation*, 31 May 1952

8 Women's function of homemaker, we once dreamed, would extend into politics and economics our highest creative and conserving instincts. Let us go back to the task of building that safe, decent and wholesome home for the entire human family to which we once pledged ourselves.
Rosika Schwimmer (1877–1948) Hungarian-born US pacifist and suffragette.
Speech, Centennial Celebration of Seneca Falls Convention of Women's Rights, July 1948

9 Too often the great decisions are originated and given form in bodies made up wholly of men, or so completely dominated by them that whatever of special value women have to offer is shunted aside without expression.
Eleanor Roosevelt (1884–1962) US First Lady, government official, writer, humanitarian, and lecturer.
Speech, United Nations, Dec 1952

10 And you're not going to have a society that understands its humanity if you don't have more women in government.
Bella Abzug (1920–) US lawyer and congresswoman.
Red Book, 'Impeachment?', Apr 1974

11 In politics women…type the letters, lick the stamps, distribute the pamphlets and get out the vote. Men get elected.
Clare Boothe Luce (1903–) US politician and writer.
Saturday ReviewWorld, 15 Sept 1974

12 I don't consider the Equal Rights Amendment a political issue. It is a moral issue as far as I am concerned. Where are women mentioned in the Constitution except in the Nineteenth Amendment, giving us the right to vote? When they said all *men* were created equal, they really meant it – otherwise, why did we have to fight for the Nineteenth Amendment?
Carol Burnett (c. 1936–) US comedienne and actress.
San Francisco Chronicle, 29 Apr 1979

13 Any woman who understands the problems of running a home will be nearer to understanding the problems of running a country.
Margaret Thatcher (1925–) British politician and prime minister (1979–90).
Observer, 8 May 1979

14 In politics, if you want anything said, ask a man; if you want anything done, ask a woman.
Margaret Thatcher (1925–) British politician and prime minister (1979–90).
The Changing Anatomy of Britain (Anthony Sampson) [1982]

PORNOGRAPHY

1 The fact remains that, no matter how disturbing violent fantasies are, as long as they stay within the world of pornography they are still only fantasies. The man masturbating in a theater showing a snuff film is still only watching a movie, not actually raping and murdering.
Deirdre English (1948–) US writer and editor.
Mother Jones, Apr 1980

2 She is the pinup, the centerfold, the poster, the postcard, the dirty picture, naked, half-dressed, laid out, legs spread, breast or ass protruding. She is the thing she is supposed to be: the thing that makes him erect.
Andrea Dworkin (1946–) US writer and journalist.
Pornography: Men Possessing Women [1981]

3 Women, for centuries not having access to pornography and unable to bear looking…are astonished. Women do not believe that men believe what pornography says about women. But they do. From the worst to the best of them, they do.
Andrea Dworkin (1946–) US writer and journalist.
Pornography: Men Possessing Women [1981]

PORTER, Katherine Anne (1890–1980)

US writer. Educated in a convent and at private schools, she worked as a newspaper woman in Chicago and Denver before settling in Mexico in 1920. Her only novel is *Ship of Fools* (1962), but she is known for her short stories which have been collected in *Flowering Judas* (1930), *Pale Horse, Pale Rider* (1939), and *The Leaning Tower* (1944). In 1965 she won the Pulitzer prize and National Book Award for her *Collected Short Stories*.

1 Nothing is mine, I have only nothing but it is enough, it is beautiful and it is all mine. Do I even walk about in my own skin or is it something I have borrowed to spare my modesty.
Pale Horse, Pale Rider

2 Miracles are instantaneous, they cannot be summoned, but come of themselves, usually at unlikely moments and to those who least expect them.
Ship of Fools, Pt III

3 The real sin against life is to abuse and destroy beauty, even one's own – even more, one's own, for that had been put in our care and we are responsible for its well-being.
Ship of Fools, Pt III

4 Such ignorance. All the boys were in military schools and all the girls were in the convent, and that's all you need to say about it.
Los Angeles Times, 'Lioness of Literature Looks Back' (Henry Allen), 7 July 1974

POWER

1 But nature be thanked, she has been so bountiful to us as we oftener enslave men than men enslave us. They seem to govern the world, but we really govern the world in that we govern men. For what man is he that is not governed by a woman, more or less?
Margaret Cavendish (c. 1623–c. 1673) English poet, playwright, and writer.
Sociable Letters [1664]

2 Women feel more; sensibility is the power of woman. They often rule more effectually, more sov'reignly, than man. They rule with tender looks, tears and sighs; but not with passion and threats; for if, or when, they so rule, they are no longer women, but abortions.
Johann Kaspar Lavater (1741–1801) Swiss writer and Protestant.
Essays on Physionomy [1775–78]

3 Obtain power, then, by all means; power is the law of man; make it yours.
Maria Edgeworth (1767–1849) Irish novelist and essayist.
An Essay on the Noble Science of Self-Justification [1787]

4 I do not wish them to have power over men; but over themselves.
Mary Wollstonecraft (1759–97) British writer.
Referring to women. *A Vindication of the Rights of Woman*, Ch. 4 [1792]

5 I know you do not make the laws but I also know that you are the wives and mothers, the sisters and daughters of those who do.
Angelina Grimké (1805–79) US writer and reformer.
The Anti-Slavery Examiner, 'Appeal to the Christian Women of the South', Sept 1836

6 The hand that rocks the cradle
Is the hand that rules the world.
William Ross Wallace (1819–81) US poet and songwriter.
John o'London's Treasure Trove [c. 1880]

7 A woman in authority is often unpopular, only because she is efficient.
Elaine Frances Burton (1904–) British politician and writer.
What of the Women? [1941]

8 It has profited civilization to develop and insist upon the myth of the dominance of biology rather than of ego in woman, thereby making of woman a distinctly separate and secondary citizen.
Vivian Gornick
SCUM Manifesto, Introduction (Valerie Solanas) [1970]

9 But powerlessness is still each woman's most critical problem, whether or not she is a social activist. It is at the root of most of her psychological disorders.
Toni Carabillo (1926–) US writer, editor, graphic designer, and feminist.
Address, 'Power Is the Name of the Game', California NOW State Conference, San Diego, 28 Oct 1973

10 Women rule the world…no man has ever done anything that a woman either hasn't allowed him to do or encouraged him to do.
Bob Dylan (Robert Allen Zimmerman; 1941–) US popular singer.
Rolling Stone, 21 June 1984

11 It seems that having information, expertise, or skill at manipulating objects is not the primary measure of power for most women. Rather, they feel their power enhanced if they can be of help.
Deborah Tannen US writer and professor of linguistics.
You Just Don't Understand [1990]

PRACTICALITY

1 I…chose my wife, as she did her wedding gown, not for a fine glossy surface, but such qualities as would wear well.
Oliver Goldsmith (1728–74) Irish-born British writer.
The Vicar of Wakefield, Preface [1761–62]

2 Any girl who was a lady would not even think of having such a good time that she did not remember to hang on to her jewelry.
Anita Loos (1891–1981) US novelist.
Gentlemen Prefer Blondes, Ch. 4 [1928]

3 We women ought to put first things first. Why should we mind if men have their faces on the money, as long as we get our hands on it?
Ivy Baker Priest (1905–53) US government official and writer.
Green Grows Ivy, Ch. 1 [1958]

4 Buy old masters. They fetch a better price than old mistresses.
Lord Beaverbrook (1879–1964) British newspaper owner and politician.
Attrib. [1964]

5 LASSI. Women! There isn't anything so bad that they don't soon start to enjoy it. Even if they lived in a barrel of shit they'd start making a home out of it, with everything nice and cozy.
Eeva-Liisa Manner (1921–) Finnish poet, writer, and playwright.
Snow in May, III:1 [1966]

PREGNANCY

1 If the child is a male, the mother has a better colour and an easier delivery; there is movement in the womb on the fortieth day. In a case of the other sex all the symptoms are the opposite: the burden is hard to carry, there is a slight swelling of the legs and groin, but the first movement is on the ninetieth day
Pliny the Elder (Gaius Plinius Secundus; 23–79 AD) Roman scholar.
Natural History, VII [1st century AD]

2 Thy ruddy face shall turn lean, and grow green as grass. Thine eyes shall be dusky, and underneath grow pale; and by the giddiness of thy brain, thy head shall ache sorely. Within thy belly, the uterus shall swell and strut out like a water bag; thy bowels shall have pains and there shall be stitches in thy flank, and pain rife in thy loins, heaviness in every limb. The burden of thy breast on thy two paps, and the streams of milk which trickle out of thee.
Hali Meidenhad [c. 1250]

3 It seems an insult to nature and to the Creator to imagine that pregnancy was ever intended to be a sickness…False states of society, false modes of dress, false habits of life, etc., all contribute to bring suffering at this time.
Mrs E. B. Duffey
What Women Should Know [1873]

4 Pregnancy is not a disease, and the pregnant woman should not consider herself a patient, but she should be more careful than ever to lead a really physiological life.
Mary Scharlieb (1845–1930) British gynaecological surgeon.
A Woman's Words to Women on the Care of their Health in England and in India [1895]

5 Dear Mary, We all knew you had it in you.
Dorothy Parker (1893–1967) US writer.
Telegram sent to a friend on the successful outcome of her much-publicized pregnancy [1915]

6 In men nine out of ten abdominal tumours are malignant; in women nine out of ten abdominal swellings are the pregnant uterus.
Rutherford Morison (1853–1939) British doctor.
The Practitioner, Oct 1965

7 It is the woman who is ultimately held responsible for pregnancy. While not being allowed to have control over her body, she is nevertheless held responsible for its products.
Carol Glassman (c. 1942–) US civil rights activist.
Sisterhood Is Powerful (ed. Robin Morgan) [1970]

PREJUDICE

See also DISCRIMINATION

1 No *man*, not even a doctor, ever gives any other definition of what a nurse should be than this – "devoted and obedient." This definition would do just as well for a porter. It might even do for a horse. It would not do for a policeman.
Florence Nightingale (1820–1910) British nurse.
Notes on Nursing [1860]

2 The woman who is really kind to dogs is always one who has failed to inspire sympathy in men.
Max Beerbohm (1872–1956) British writer.
Zuleika Dobson [1911]

3 He is pretty certain to come back into favour. One of the surest signs of his genius is that women dislike his books.
George Orwell (Eric Blair; 1903–50) British novelist.
Referring to Conrad. *New English Weekly*, 23 July 1936

4 There is perhaps one human being in a thousand who is passionately interested in his job for the job's sake. The difference is that if that one person in a thousand is a man, we say, simply, that he is passionately keen on his job; if she is a woman, we say she is a freak.
Dorothy L. Sayers (1893–1957) British writer.
Gaudy Night [1936]

5 Every form of bigotry can be found in ample supply in the legal system of our country. It would seem that Justice (usually depicted as a woman) is indeed blind to racism, sexism, war and poverty.
Florynce R. Kennedy (1916–) US lawyer, civil rights activist, and feminist.
'Instituionalized Oppression vs the Female', *Sisterhood Is Powerful* (ed. Robin Morgan) [1970]

6 She belongs to a Temperance Society and wears one of those badges in the shape of a bow of ribbon to show that she would never take a drink, not even brandy if she were dying. Of

course by temperance they all mean the opposite – total abstinence.
Elizabeth Taylor (1912–75) British writer.
Angel [1973]

PRIDE

1 If women be proud (or addicted to pride) it is ten to one to be laid, that it is the men that make them so; for like inchaunters, they do never leave or cease to bewitch & charme poore women with their flatteries.
Mary Tattlewell (fl. 1640) English writer.
'Epistle to the Reader: Long Megge of Westminster, hearing the abuse, offeres to women to riseth out of her grave and thus speaketh' [1640]

2 TREVES. In my experience, pride is a word often on women's lips – but they display little sign of it where love affairs are concerned.
Agatha Christie (1891–1975) British writer.
Toward's Zero, I [1957]

PROCREATION

1 I do not know how you appeared in my womb; it was not I who endowed you with breath and life, I had not the shaping of your every part.
It is the creator of the world, ordaining the process of man's birth and presiding over the origin of all things.
Bible: Maccabees
7:22–23

2 Only one woman in thousands has been endowed with the God-given aptitude to live in chastity and virginity…God fashioned her body so that she should be with a man, to have and to rear children. No woman should be ashamed of that for which God made and intended her.
Martin Luther (1483–1546) German Protestant.
Kritische Gesamtausgabe [1524]

3 Nature placed the female testicles internally…Woman is a most arrogant and extremely intractable animal; and she would be worse if she came to realize that she is no less perfect and no less fit to wear breeches than man…I believe that is why nature, while endowing her with what is necessary for our procreation, did so in such a way as to keep her from perceiving and ascertaining her sufficient perfection.
P. Borgarucci Italian anatomist.
Della contemplatione anatomica sopra tutte le parti del corpo umano [1564]

4 Scarce, sir. Mighty scarce.
Mark Twain (Samuel Langhorne Clemens; 1835–1910) US writer.
Responding to the question 'In a world without women what would men become?' Attrib. [1910]

5 The world cannot do without women, which is why there's resentment from men. They realise the future lies with us.
Joan Collins (1933–   ) British actress.
Claiming that men are no longer necessary because women can be impregnated by sperm stored in a bank.
Independent, 13 April 1991

PROGRESS

1 Modern inventions have banished the spinning-wheel, and the same law of progress makes the woman to-day a different woman from her grandmother.
Elizabeth Cady Stanton (1815–1902) US suffragette and abolitionist.
History of Woman Suffrage, Vol. I (with Susan B. Anthony and Mathilda Gage) [1881]

2 But this one thought stands, never goes – if I might but be one of those born in the future; then, perhaps, to be born a woman will not be to be branded.
Olive Schreiner (1855–1920) South African writer, feminist, and social critic.
The Story of an African Farm, 'Lyndall' [1883]

3 The original necessity for the ceaseless presence of the woman to maintain that altar fire – and it was an altar fire in very truth at one period – has passed with the means of prompt ignition; the matchbox has freed the housewife from that incessant service, but the *feeling* that women should stay at home is with us yet.
Charlotte Perkins Gilman (1860–1935) US writer and lecturer.
The Home, 'Two Callings', Pt II, Ch. 3 [1910]

4 It was very, very hard in those years, at the end of the war. It was all axe-work in those days, no bulldozers. I used to work with the axe until I couldn't do it any longer. I'd go out every day, even when I was pregnant. Women worked very hard, of course, then. When I look around now and see women who've got every convenience of every kind and think of the way women used to work hard on the farm, I often think what they owe to those women.
Description from an Australian farmer's wife. *Nothing to Spare* (Jan Carter) [1917]

5 It was difficult to decide whether the system that produced the kettle was a miracle of human ingenuity and co-operation or a colossal waste of resources, human and natural. Would we all be better off boiling our water in a pot hung over an open fire? Or was it the facility to do things at the touch of a button that freed men, and more particularly women, from servile labour and

made it possible for them to become literary critics?
David Lodge (1935–) British author.
Nice Work, V [1988]

PROMISCUITY

1 Lady Capricorn, he understood, was still keeping open bed.
Aldous Huxley (1894–1964) British novelist.
Antic Hay, Ch. 21 [1923]

2 I see – she's the original good time that was had by all.
Bette Davis (Ruth Elizabeth D.; 1908–89) US film star.
Referring to a starlet of the time [c. 1940]. *The Filmgoer's Book of Quotes* (Leslie Halliwell)

3 You know, she speaks eighteen languages. And she can't say 'No' in any of them.
Dorothy Parker (1893–1967) US writer.
Speaking of an acquaintance. Attrib. [1967]

4 My message to the businessmen of this country when they go abroad on business is that there is one thing above all they can take with them to stop them catching AIDS, and that is the wife.
Edwina Currie (1946–) British politician.
Observer, 15 Feb 1987

5 Every time you sleep with a boy you sleep with all his old girlfriends.
Government-sponsored AIDS advertisement, 1987

6 The strongest possible piece of advice I would give to any young woman is: Don't screw around, and don't smoke.
Edwina Currie (1946–) British politician.
Observer, 'Sayings of the Week', 3 Apr 1988

PROSTITUTION

1 Necessity never makes prostitution the business of men's lives; though numberless are the women who are thus rendered systematically vicious. This, however, arises, in a great degree from the state of idleness in which women are educated, who are always taught to look up to man for a maintenance, and to consider their persons as the proper return for his exertions to support them.
Mary Wollstonecraft (1759–97) British writer.
A Vindication of the Rights of Woman, Ch. 3 [1792]

2 We must go walk the streets, my sisters, love is our shameful trade,
Never complain though the hours be long and our work so poorly paid,
Fate has decreed that we serve men's need and forfeit our worthless life,

All to defend the family home and protect the virtuous wife.
Auguste Barbier (1805–82) French poet and dramatist.
Lazare [1837]

3 Prostitution is a blight on the human race…for if you men did not impose chastity on women as a necessary virtue while refusing to practise it yourselves, they would not be rejected by society for yielding to the sentiments of their hearts, nor would seduced, deceived and abandoned girls be forced into prostitution.
Flora Tristan (1803–44) French writer, feminist, and revolutionary socialist.
The London Journal of Flora Tristan [1842]

4 They are forbidden to practise their profession by day…They must be simple and decently dressed…They may not go about bare-headed. They are expressly forbidden to address men who are in the company of women or children. They must never, at any hour, show themselves at their windows but must keep these shut and curtained at all times.
A. J. B. Parent-Duchâtelet French historian.
Compulsory registration of prostitutes was established in France in 1816. Registered prostitutes were obliged to carry a card and to comply with the above conditions. *De la Prostitution dans la Ville de Paris* [1857]

5 Whether our reformers admit it or not, the economic and social inferiority of women is responsible for prostitution.
Emma Goldman (1869–1940) Russian-born US anarchist, political agitator and organizer, lecturer, and editor.
Anarchism and Other Essays, 'The Tragedy of Women's Emancipation', [1911]

6 This is virgin territory for whorehouses.
Al Capone (1899–1947) Italian-born US gangster.
Talking about suburban Chicago [c. 1925]. *The Bootleggers* (Kenneth Allsop), Ch. 16

7 What the proprietorship of these papers is aiming at is power, and power without responsibility – the prerogative of the harlot through the ages.
Stanley Baldwin (1867–1947) British statesman.
Attacking the press barons Lords Rothermere and Beaverbrook. It was first used by Kipling. Speech, election rally, 18 Mar 1931

8 Prostitution gives her an opportunity to meet people. It provides fresh air and wholesome exercise, and it keeps her out of trouble.
Joseph Heller (1923–) US novelist.
Catch-22, Ch. 33 [1961]

9 Romance without finance is a nuisance. Few men value free merchandise. Let the chippies fall where they may.
Sally Stanford (1904–82) US madam and writer.
The Lady of the House, Ch. 13 [1966]

10 There is something utterly nauseating about a system of society which pays a harlot 25 times as much as it pays its Prime Minister, 250 times as much as it pays its Members of Parliament, and 500 times as much as it pays some of its ministers of religion.
Harold Wilson (1916–) British politician and prime minister.
Referring to the case of Christine Keeler. Speech, House of Commons, June 1963

11 I have often noticed that a bribe…has that effect – it changes a relation. The man who offers a bribe gives away a little of his own importance; the bribe once accepted, he becomes the inferior, like a man who has paid for a woman.
Graham Greene (1904–91) British novelist.
The Comedians, Pt I, Ch. 4 [1966]

12 It is a silly question to ask a prostitute why she does it…These are the highest-paid 'professional' women in America.
Gail Sheehy (1937–) US writer and social critic.
Hustling, Ch. 4 [1971]

13 Punishing the prostitute promotes the rape of all women. When prostitution is a crime, the message conveyed is that women who are sexual are 'bad' and therefore legitimate victims of sexual assault. Sex becomes a weapon to be used by men.
Margo St James (1937–) US activist and prostitute.
San Francisco Examiner, 29 Apr 1979

14 They're whores, and that's not a term of abuse. It's a good honest biblical word for an honourable profession of ancient lineage. They make love with men for a living and don't you ever think badly of them for that. Any woman worthy of the name would do the same if her children were hungry. Remember, never judge someone until you've walked a mile in their moccasins.
Allegra Taylor
Prostitution: What's love got to do with it? [1991]

PUBERTY

1 All healthy persons, at the time of puberty, must certainly feel the passion of physical love. It is a part of their health, and as natural a consequence as hunger or thirst. It is the most delightful of all the passions, and makes the greater part of human happiness.
Dr Michael Ryan
A Manual of Midwifery [1831]

2 The commencement of menstruation is the borderline between childhood and womanhood, and this period of puberty is a most trying time. both as regards mental and bodily health.
Lionel A. Weatherly
The Young Wife's Own Book [1882]

3 Many a young life is battered and forever crippled in the breakers of puberty; if it cross these unharmed and is not dashed to pieces on the rock of childbirth, it may still ground on the ever-recurring shallows of menstruation, and lastly, upon the final bar of the menopause e'er protection is found in the unruffled waters of the harbor beyond reach of sexual storms.
George J. Engelmann (1809–84) US physician and botanist.
President's Address, American Gynecology Society, 1900

4 In the spring…your lovely Chloë lightly turns to one mass of spots.
Ronald Searle (1920–) British cartoonist.
The Terror of St Trinian's, Ch. 7 [1952]

RAMBERT, Dame Marie (Cyvia Rambam; 1888–1982)
Polish-born British ballet producer, director, and teacher. She studied eurhythmic dance with Emile Jacques-Dalcroze and, in 1913, was invited to join Diaghilev's Ballets Russes as a teacher of rhythmic technique. She became an assistant to Vaslav Nijinsky and influenced his controversial choreography of *L'Après-midi d'un faune* and *Le Sacre du printemps*. She continued her ballet training in London, staging her first ballet in 1917; in 1918, following her marriage to the playwright Ashley Dukes, she became a British citizen. In 1920 she opened a ballet school in London, producing her pupil Frederick Ashton's first ballet in 1926. Four years later she formed the Ballet Club, which, in 1935, became the Ballet Rambert, and helped to found the influential Camargo Society with Ninette de Valois. Over the next fifty years she relied mostly on British dancers, choreographers, and designers in her many productions, thus revitalizing national ballet. She was made a DBE in 1962.

Quotation about Rambert
1 Rambert's teaching has always combined technical excellence with the importance of the

individual dancer and his understanding of his role.

Richard Buckle (1916–) British writer and critic.
1000 Makers of the 20th Century

Quotations by Rambert

2 We want to create an atmosphere in which creation is possible.

Dancemagazine, 'Ballet Rambert: The Company That Changed Its Mind' (John Percival), Feb 1973

3 I don't do cartwheels any more, but I still do a *barre* to keep supple.

Dancemagazine, 'Old School Tights' (Beryl Hilary Ostlere), Feb 1973

RANKIN, Jeannette (1880–1973)

US suffragette and first woman member of Congress (1917–19, 1941–43). In 1909 she became a social worker in Seattle and for the next five years campaigned on behalf of women's suffrage in Washington, California, and Montana. In 1916 she was elected to the US House of Representatives, where she introduced the first bill that would have allowed women citizenship independent of their husbands. She lost popularity because of her stand against declaring war on Germany in 1917, which cost her the Republican Senate nomination in 1918. In 1940 she was again elected to the House, only to lose her seat by voting against the declaration of war on Japan, following the Pearl Harbour raid in 1941. She continued to be active in the peace movement after the war, urging women to demand a halt to US intervention in Vietnam.

1 We did not labor in suffrage just to bring the vote to women but to allow women to express their opinions and become effective in government.

American Political Women (Esther Stineman)

2 Men and women are like right and left hands: it doesn't make sense not to use both.

American Political Women (Esther Stineman)

3 As a woman I can't go to war, and I refuse to send anyone else.

Jeannette Rankin: First Lady in Congress (Hannah Josephson), Prologue

4 You can no more win a war than you can win an earthquake.

Jeannette Rankin: First Lady in Congress (Hannah Josephson), Ch. 8

RAPE

See also VIOLENCE

1 What they love to yield
They would often rather have stolen. Rough seduction

Delights them, the boldness of near rape
Is a compliment.

Ovid (Publius Ovidius Naso; 43 BC–17 AD) Roman poet.
The Art of Love [c. 16 BC]

2 It is little wonder that rape is one of the least-reported crimes. Perhaps it is the only crime in which the victim becomes the accused and, in reality, it is she who must prove her good reputation, her mental soundness, and her impeccable propriety.

Freda Adler (1934–) US educator.
Sisters in Crime, Ch. 9 [1975]

3 Rape is a form of mass terrorism…The fear of rape keeps women off the streets at night. Keeps women at home. Keeps women passive and modest for fear that they be thought provocative.

Susan Griffin (1943–) US poet, writer, and educator.
Women: a Feminist Perspective (ed. Jo Freeman) [1975]

4 However rape is a perfectly natural function. It means that a man so desires a woman that he takes her by force. Since a man is much stronger than a woman it does not necessarily involve much violence, and in many cases the woman duly submits.

Professor J. M. V. Browner
Vive la Différence [1981]

5 Women who say no do not always mean no. It is not just a question of saying no, it is a question of how she says it, how she shows and makes it clear. If she doesn't want it she only has to keep her legs shut and she would not get it without force and there would be marks of force being used.

David Wild (1927–) British judge.
Cambridge, 1982

6 Words such as 'beast', 'brute', 'monster' and 'sex fiend' are commonly used to describe the rapist. Yet we rarely see the simple word 'man', which the rapist invariably is.

Cambridge Rape Crisis Centre
Out of Focus [1987]

7 Women are entitled to dress attractively, even provocatively if you like, be friendly with casual acquaintances and still say no at the end of the evening without being brutally assaulted…This sort of brutal violence, particularly to women, has got to be dealt with severely. You broke her jaw just because she wasn't prepared to go to bed with you.

Richard Rougier (1932–) British judge.
Sentencing an attacker at the Old Bailey. *Daily Telegraph*, 4 Mar 1988

RELIGION

1 I am not giving permission for a woman to teach or tell a man what to do. A woman ought not to speak, because Adam was formed first and Eve afterwards, and it was not Adam who was led astray but the woman who was led astray and fell into sin. Nevertheless, she will be saved by childbearing.
Bible : I Timothy
2:12–15

2 And do you know that you are an Eve? God's sentence hangs over all your sex and His punishment weighs down upon you. You are the devil's gateway; it was you who first violated the forbidden tree and broke God's law. You coaxed your way around man whom the devil had not the force to attack. With what ease you shattered that image of God: man! Because of the death you deserved, the Son of God had to die. And yet you think of nothing but covering your gowns with jewellery? You should always go in mourning and rags.
Tertullian (Quintus Septimus Florens Tertullianus; c. 160–225 AD) Roman theologian.
De cultu feminarum (On Female Dress) [3rd century AD]

3 Go home and govern our children. I will not return to you, for the married will not see the kingdom of heaven.
Bertegund (fl. 530s) Merovingian nun.
She was talking to her husband. *Histoire Française*, Ch. 6 (Gregory of Tours) [c. 538]

4 Woman does not have a soul of a different sex from that which animates man. Both received a soul which is absolutely the same and of an equal condition. Women and men were equally endowed with the gifts of spirit, reason, and the use of words; they were created for the same end, and the sexual difference between them will not confer a different destiny.
Cornelius Heinrich Agrippa (c. 1486–1535) German physician and philosopher.
On the Nobility and Excellence of Women [1529]

5 A disturber of the peace am I? Yes indeed, of my own peace. Do you call this disturbing the peace that instead of spending my time in frivolous amusements I have visited the plague infested and carried out the dead?...I have never mounted the pulpit, but I have done more than any minister in visiting those in misery. Is this disturbing the peace of the church?
Katherine Zell (c. 1497–1562) German church worker and hymnist.
A Letter to the Citizency of the City of Strassburg, 1557

6 It is a mockery to allow women to baptise. Even the Virgin Mary was not allowed this.
John Calvin (1509–64) French Protestant reformer.
Institution de la religion Chrestienne [1560]

7 Complaint was forthwith made to William Pickering, then Mayor, that two women were preaching...He asked...their husbands' names. They told him: they had no husband but Jesus Christ and he sent them. Upon this the Mayor grew angry, called them whores and issued his warrant to the constable to whip them at the Market-Cross till the blood ran down their bodies.
Joseph Besse
A Collection of the Sufferings of the People called Quakers [1653]

8 A woman's preaching is like a dog's walking on his hinder legs. It is not done well; but you are surprised to find it done at all.
Samuel Johnson (1709–84) British lexicographer.
Life of Johnson, Vol. I (J. Boswell) [1763]

9 I am inclined to think, when we are admitted to the honor of studying Greek and Hebrew, we shall produce some various readings of the Bible a little different from those we now have.
Sarah Moore Grimké (1792–1873) US abolitionist and women's rights pioneer.
Letter from Haverhill, 17 July 1837

10 Woman owes her present elevation of character and condition to Christianity; in all countries where its benign holy influences is unfelt, she is still an unintellectual, a degraded being.
Louisa Caroline Tuthill (c. 1798–1879) US poet, writer, and playwright.
'Christianity' [c. 1850]

11 It is not Christianity, but priestcraft that has subjected woman as we find her. The Church and State have been united, and it is well for us to see it so.
Lucretia Mott (1793–1880) US abolitionist, Quaker, and suffragist.
Speech, Woman's Rights Convention, Philadelphia, 1854

12 Any Protestant woman in her senses would object to marrying a Roman Catholic...They prohibit the use of proper hygienic Birth Control methods preferring that a woman's health should be entirely ruined and that she should bring forth feeble, dying or imbecile infants rather than that proper hygienic methods should be used.
Marie Stopes (1880–1958) British birth-control campaigner.
Letter to an Irish Catholic, 18 Oct 1920

13 What is a woman? St Jerome replies that she is the door of the devil, the way of iniquity,

the sting of the scorpion...St Maximus calls the woman the shipwreck of man, the captivity of life, the lioness that embraces, the malicious animal.
From a handbook for priests. *Person and God in a Spanish Valley* (William A. Christian) [1924]

14 There is no objection to women members of pious associations and Catholic Action taking part with lighted candles in Catholic liturgical processions, provided they march after the celebrant and the proper order be observed so that the more worthy associations march nearer to the celebrant.
'Sacred Processions: Participation by Women', Canon Law, 1933

15 The earth as Mother, the womb from which all living things are born and to which all return at death, was perhaps the earliest representation of the divine in protohistoric religions.
Dena Justin (1912–   ) US writer and educator.
Natural History, 'From Mother Goddess to Dishwasher', Feb 1973

16 In our patriarchal world, we are all taught – whether we like to think we are or not – that God, being male, values maleness much more than he values femaleness...that in order to propitiate God, women must propitiate men.
Sonia Johnson (c. 1936–   ) US feminist and writer.
From Housewife to Heretic [1981]

17 When you go to a church where two men stand behind the Communion table, and ten men serve Communion, and another man stands at the lectern and reads the scripture, and another man stands up and preaches, and three more men stand in the aisles handing out bulletins, you hear a fairly loud statement about the nature of the Church.
Harold Dowler British churchman.
Ms, Mar 1982

18 Wedding day, well, is compulsory. Political women are tortured and raped before execution. Especially young women. They rape nine-year-old women in the prison because it is against God if they execute a virgin woman. Women are attacked in various horrific ways, such as acid being thrown in their faces, their hair being burnt if it is not covered. It means that just to be a woman in Iran is a political crime.
Selma James (1930–   ) US-born British feminist.
Strangers and Sisters: Women, Race and Immigration [1985]

19 The question of the rights of women to hold secular office is a quite separate matter and should not in any way be connected to or paralleled with the question of women's ordination.
Cardinal Willebrands (1909–   ) Dutch ecclesiastic.
Remark, June 1986

20 If women in the priesthood has come as a result of women's liberation, then I think it is satanic.
William Pwaisiho Malaitan churchman.
The Daily Telegraph, Aug 1988

21 More trouble in the Church of England over women priests is certain after the election tonight of the first woman bishop in the US Anglican Church.
The Daily Telegraph, 24 Sept 1988

22 The idea that only a male can represent Christ at the altar is a most serious heresy.
Dr George Carey (1935–   ) British churchman and Archbishop of Canterbury (1991–   ).
Reader's Digest, Apr 1991

23 As with Muslim child brides, it has been illegal for the past few years for girls to become temple prostitutes, to dedicate girls to goddesses. But tradition and old superstitions hold firm. The Bombay-based Indian Health Organisation estimates that 2,000 girls underwent *devadasi* initiation last year alone.
Peter Hillmore British journalist.
A *devadasi* is a Hindu temple prostitute. *Observer magazine*, 26 Jan 1992

RODDICK, Anita (1943–   )
British entrepreneur and founder of the Body Shop. Her concern for the environment led her to set up a nationwide chain of shops selling cosmetics and beauty products, using natural biodegradable ingredients and simple refillable packaging.

Quotation about Roddick
1 She is the phenomenon that will not go away.
Sunday Express, 9 June 1991

Quotations by Roddick
2 Most managers never get out from behind their desks to see how things are done. If that means I'm thought of as something of a hippie, I don't care.
Sunday Express, 9 June 1991

3 I loathe the cosmetics industry. It baffles me.
Sunday Express, 9 June 1991

4 We give customers a sense of theatre, a sense of the bizarre and we educate them.
Sunday Express, 9 June 1991

5 I hope to leave my children a sense of empathy and pity and a will to right social wrongs.
Sunday Express, 9 June 1991

ROOSEVELT, Eleanor (1884–1962)

United Nations diplomat and wife of President D. Roosevelt (1933–45). She was the niece of Theodore Roosevelt (president 1901–09), who married her distant cousin in 1905. In the early years of her marriage she was occupied with learning to be a political hostess and with raising her family of five children. From 1921 she provided help and inspiration for her husband, who was struggling against the crippling effects of poliomyelitis. At the same time she expanded her own role in public affairs, joining the Women's Trade Union League and serving as financial chairman (1924–28) of the women's division of the state Democratic Party. Throughout her political life she was a significant supporter of minority and educational causes. After her husband's death she was appointed chairman of the UN Commission on Human Rights (1946–51), playing a major role in the drafting of the Universal Declaration of Human Rights (1948).

Quotation about Roosevelt

1   Falsity withered in her presence. Hypocrisy left the room.
Adlai Stevenson (1900–65) US statesman. Address at the Democratic National Convention, 1962

Quotations by Roosevelt

2   No one can make you feel inferior without your consent.
This is My Story

3   I used to tell my husband that, if he could make *me* understand something, it would be clear to all the other people in the country.
Newspaper column, 'My Day', 12 Feb 1947

4   I have spent many years of my life in opposition and I rather like the role.
Letter to Bernard Baruch, 18 Nov 1952

RUBINSTEIN, Helena (1870–1965)

Polish-born US cosmetics manufacturer, business executive, and philanthropist. One of eight daughters of a Jewish family in Poland, she left in 1902 to visit relations in Australia. While there she opened a beauty salon in Melbourne, which proved an instant success. She took her business to Europe, where she studied under leading dermatologists, before opening the Maison de Beauté in London in 1908; another salon in Paris followed in 1912. During World War I she emigrated to America where she opened salons in New York and other cities. Her business was immensely successful, enabling her to establish the Helena Rubinstein Foundation, in 1953, which coordinated her gifts to such concerns as museums, colleges, and charities.

Quotation about Rubinstein

1   A great innovator, indefatigable worker, self-confessed matriarch and very much the *Grande Dame*.
Joan Price (1931–) US writer. *1000 Makers of the 20th Century*

Quotations by Rubinstein

2   I have always felt that a woman has the right to treat the subject of her age with ambiguity until, perhaps, she passes into the realm of over ninety. Then it is better she be candid with herself and with the world.
My Life for Beauty, Pt I, Ch. 1

3   There are no ugly women, only lazy ones.
My Life for Beauty, Pt II, Ch. 1

4   But what parent can tell when some such fragmentary gift of knowledge or wisdom will enrich her children's lives? Or how a small seed of information passed from one generation to another may generate a new science, a new industry – a seed which neither the giver nor the receiver can truly evaluate at the time.
My Life for Beauty, Pt I, Ch. 10

RUTHLESSNESS

1   …hung up naked the noblest and most distinguished of the women and then cut off their breats and sewed them to their mouths to make the victims appear to be eating them; afterwards they impaled the women on sharp skewers run lengthwise through the entire body.
Dio Cassius (c. 150–235) Roman historian.
Boadicea's alleged treatment of Roman women after attacking London. *Roman History* [60 AD]

2   When the Himalayan peasant meets the he-bear in his pride,
He shouts to scare the monster, who will often turn aside.
But the she-bear thus accosted rends the peasant tooth and nail
For the female of the species is more deadly than the male.
Rudyard Kipling (1865–1936) Indian-born British writer.
The Female of the Species

3   We are programmed (by biology or conditioning – who cares which?) to respond to social signals and pressures, and so find it almost impossible to be as single-mindedly ruthless as men.
Janet Daley British journalist.
The Times, 26 Nov 1991

SAGAN, Françoise (1935–)

French writer. She was born in Cahors, Lot, and educated in Paris. Her bestselling novel, *Bonjour Tristesse* (1954), was written when she was only 18 and immediately caused a furore with its precocious view of love. She has written many other novels since then, which examine the transitory nature of love; they include *Aimez-vous Brahms?* (1959), *Le Chien couchant* (1980), *The Still Storm* (1984), and *Un Sang d'aquarelle* (1987).

1 Every little girl knows about love. It is only her capacity to suffer because of it that increases.
Daily Express

2 It is healthier to see the good points of others than to analyze our own bad ones.
A Certain Smile, Pt I, Ch. 5

3 We had the same gait, the same habits and lived in the same rhythm; our bodies suited each other, and all was well. I had no right to regret his failure to make the tremendous effort required of love, and effort to know and shatter the solitude of another.
A Certain Smile, Pt II, Ch. 2

4 'Look here, why don't you love me? I should feel so much more peaceful. Why not put up that pane of glass called passion between us? It may distort things at times, but it's wonderfully convenient.' But no, we were two of a kind, allies and accomplices. In terms of grammar, I could not become the object, or he the subject. He had neither the capacity nor the desire to define our roles in any such way.
A Certain Smile, Pt II, Ch. 2

SAND, George (Aurore Dupin, Baronne Dudevant; 1804–76)

French writer. In 1822, after a convent upbringing, she married Casimir Dudevant. Although relations were happy to begin with, she soon tired of the marriage and began a passionate affair with a neighbour. In 1831 she moved to Paris and in 1832 published her first novel, *Indiana*, under the pseudonym, George Sand. In this novel, and in *Valentine* (1832) and *Lelia* (1833), she protested against the social conventions that tie a wife to her husband against her will. Popular during her lifetime, she is chiefly remembered for her cigar-smoking, loose-living image, and for her friendships and love affairs with some of the great artistic figures of her time, notably Chopin, Flaubert, and de Musset. Other works include *Le Mare au diable* (1846), *La Petite Fadette* (1849), *Histoire de ma vie* (1854–55), and *Contes d'une grand'mère* (1873).

Quotations about Sand

1 George Sand is as famous for her love affairs with such prominent artistic figures as Alfred de Musset and Frederic Chopin as she is for her writings.
William Rose Benét (1886–1950) US author. *The Reader's Encyclopedia*

2 How the devil did George Sand manage? That sturdy woman of letters found it possible to finish one novel and start another in the same hour. And she did not thereby lose either a lover or a puff of the narghile, not to mention a *Story of My Life* in 20 volumes, and I am overcome by astonishment.
Colette (1873–1954) French novelist. Remark, 1946

3 A great cow full of ink.
Gustav Flaubert (1821–80) French novelist. Attrib.

Quotations by Sand

4 One is happy as a result of one's own efforts, once one knows the necessary ingredients of happiness – simple tastes, a certain degree of courage, self denial to a point, love of work, and, above all, a clear conscience. Happiness is no vague dream, of that I now feel certain.
Correspondence, Vol. V

5 Liszt said to me today that God alone deserves to be loved. It may be true, but when one has loved a man it is very different to love God.
Intimate Journal

SAYINGS AND PROVERBS

1 As the goodman says, so say we; but as the good wife says, so must it be.

2 The bachelor is a peacock, the engaged man a lion and the married man a jackass.
German proverb

3 Behold, every one that useth proverbs shall use this proverb against thee, saying, As is the mother, so is her daughter.
Bible: Ezekiel
16:44–45

4 Better be an old man's darling than a young man's slave.

5 A clever man will build a city, a clever woman will lay it low.
Chinese proverb

6 Choose neither women nor linen by candle-light.

7 Every man can rule a shrew save he that has her.

8 A fair wife and a frontier castle breeds quarrels.

9 A fair woman without virtue is like palled wine.

10 The first wife is matrimony, the second company, the third heresy.

11 Forbid a thing, and that women will do.

12 The gist of a lady's letter is in the postscript.
The implication is that a woman's written communications are as rambling as her speech.

13 A good wife and health is a man's best wealth.

14 The gossip of two women will destroy two houses.
Arabic proverb

15 The hand that rocks the cradle rules the world.

16 He that has no wife, beats her oft.

17 He that will thrive must ask leave of his wife.
A wife is considered responsible for the household finances.

18 A horse, a wife, and a sword may be shewed, but not lent.

19 A maid oft seen, and a gown oft worn, are disesteemed and held in scorn.

20 Maidens should be seen, and not heard.

21 A man of straw is worth a woman of gold.

22 Man, woman, and devil, are the three degrees of comparison.

23 Marriages are made in heaven.

24 A married woman has nothing of her own but her wedding-ring and her hair-lace.

25 Marry in haste, and repent at leisure.

26 Men make houses, women make homes.

27 The more women look in their glass, the less they look to their house.

28 Never trust a woman, even if she has borne you seven children.
Japanese proverb

29 No mischief but a woman or a priest is at the bottom of it.

30 No war without a woman.

31 A poor beauty finds more lovers than husbands.

32 A sieve will hold water better than a woman's mouth a secret.

33 Swine, women, and bees cannot be turned.

34 Two daughters and a back door are three arrant thieves.
A reference to the expense of bringing up daughters.

35 When an ass climbs a ladder, we may find wisdom in women.

36 Who has a fair wife needs more than two eyes.

37 A wicked woman and an evil is three half-pence worse than the devil.

38 Wife and children are bills of charges.

39 A wife is sought for her virtue, a concubine for her beauty.
Chinese proverb

40 Woeful is the household that wants a woman.

41 A woman, a dog, and a walnut-tree, the more you beat them the better they be.

42 A woman cuts her wisdom teeth when she is dead.
Proverb

43 A woman has the form of an angel, the heart of a serpent, and the mind of an ass.
German proverb

44 A woman's mind and winter wind change oft.

45 A woman's place is in the home.

46 A woman's thoughts are afterthoughts.
Indian proverb

47 A woman's work is never done.

48 Women and sparrows twitter in company.
Japanese proverb

49 Women are like wasps in their anger.

50 Women are necessary evils.

51 Women are the devil's nets.

52 Women are the snares of Satan.

53 Women have long hair and short brains.
Proverb

54 Women in state affairs are like monkeys in glass-shops.

55 Women, priests, and poultry, have never enough.

56 Women will have the last word.

57 Women's counsel is cold.

58 You may ding the devil into a wife, but you'll never ding him out of her.
'Ding' means beat.

SCHUMANN, Clara (1819–96)

German pianist, teacher, and composer. Wife of Robert Schumann and daughter of Frederick Wieck she became one of the leading concert pianists of the 19th century, giving her first public recitals at the age of nine. She fell in love with Robert Schumann and, in the face of parental opposition, finally married him in 1840. Between 1841 and 1854 she bore him eight children. After the death of her husband in 1856, she edited the collected edition of his works (published 1881–93). She and her husband were largely responsible for the recognition of the genius of Brahms.

1 I too, have thought most seriously about the future. One thing I must say to you; I cannot be yours until circumstances have entirely altered. I do not want horses or diamonds, I am happy in possessing you, but I wish to lead a life free from care, and I see that I shall be unhappy if I cannot always work at my art, and that I cannot do if we have to worry over our daily bread.
Letter to Robert Schumann, 24 Nov 1837

2 I once thought that I possessed creative talent, but I have given up this idea; a woman must not desire to compose — not one has been able to do it, and why should I expect to? It would be arrogance, though indeed, my father led me into it in earlier days.
Diary entry, Nov 1839

3 There is nothing greater than the joy of composing something oneself, and then listening to it. There are some pretty passages in the trio, and I think it is fairly successful as far as form goes...Of course, it is only a woman's work, which is always lacking in force, and here and there in invention.
Diary entry, 2 Oct 1846

4 I always wish that the last movement of the Regenheder sonata might accompany me in my journey from here to the next world.
Said to Brahms. Attrib.

SEDUCTION

1 When she raises her eyelids it's as if she were taking off all her clothes.
Colette (1873–1954) French novelist.
Claudine and Annie [1903]

2 A lady is one who never shows her underwear unintentionally.
Lillian Day (b. 1893) US writer.
Kiss and Tell [1931]

3 Reality shows us that the real seducers are the daughters of Eve who sashay their way through God's world with their mini-skirts, low-cut and see-through blouses and tight-tight pants, for the sole purpose of exhibiting their curvaceous bodies to attract the attention and eyes of men.
Emerson Pereia Brazilian judge.
Brazil, 1975

SELF-CONFIDENCE

1 Why not be oneself? That is the whole secret of a successful appearance. If one is a greyhound why try to look like a Pekinese?
Edith Sitwell (1887–1964) British poet and writer.
Why I Look As I Do [c. 1915]

2 Speak up for yourself, or you'll end up a rug.
Mae West (1892–1980) US actress.
Attrib. [1980]

SELF-INDULGENCE

1 Sara could commit adultery at one end and weep for her sins at the other, and enjoy both operations at once.
Joyce Cary (1888–1957) British novelist.
The Horse's Mouth, Ch. 8 [1944]

2 I have looked on a lot of women with lust. I've committed adultery in my heart many times. God recognises I will do this and forgives me.
Jimmy Carter (1924–   ) US statesman and president.
Remark [1976]

SEX

1 In the case of women, it is my contention that when during intercourse the vagina is rubbed and the womb is disturbed, an irritation is set up in the womb which produces pleasure and heat in the rest of the body...Once intercourse has begun, she experiences pleasure throughout the whole time, until the man ejaculates. If her desire for intercourse is excited, she emits before the man, and for the remainder of the time she does not feel pleasure to the same extent; but if she is not in a state of excitement, then her pleasure terminates along with that of the man.
Hippocrates (c. 460–c. 377 BC) Greek physician.
On the Generating Seed and the Nature of the Child, IV [4th century BC]

2 Females are naturally libidinous, incite the males to copulation, and cry out during the act of coition.
Aristotle (384–22 BC) Greek philosopher.
Historia animalium [347–335 BC]

3 Lascivious movements are of no use whatever to wives. For a woman forbids herself to conceive and fights against it, if in her delight she aids the man's action with her buttocks, making undulating movements with all her breast limp; for she turns the share clean away from the furrow and makes the seed fail of its place. Whores indulge in such motions for their own purposes, that they may not often conceive and lie pregnant, and at the same time that their

intercourse may be more pleasing to men; which our wives evidently have no need for.
Lucretius (Titus Lucretius Carus; c. 99–c. 55 BC) Roman philosopher.
On the Nature of Things [1st century BC]

4 What they love to yield
They would often rather have stolen. Rough seduction
Delights them, the boldness of near rape
Is a compliment.
Ovid (Publius Ovidius Naso; 43 BC–17 AD) Roman poet.
The Art of Love [c. 16 BC]

5 For a priest to turn a man when he lies a-dying, is just like one that has a long time solicited a woman, and cannot obtain his end; at length makes her drunk, and so lies with her.
John Selden (1584–1654) English historian.
Table Talk [1689]

6 Have you not as yet observed that pleasure, which is undeniably the sole motive force behind the union of the sexes, is nevertheless not enough to form a bond between them? And that, if it is preceded by desire which impels, it is succeeded by disgust which repels? That is a law of nature which love alone can alter.
Pierre Choderlos de Laclos (1741–1803) French novelist.
Les Liaisons dangereuses, Letter 131 [1782]

7 In an uncorrupted woman the sexual impulse does not manifest itself at all, but only love; and this love is the natural impulse of a woman to satisfy a man.
Johann Fichte (1762–1814) German philosopher.
The Science of Rights [1796]

8 Ignorance of the necessity for sexual intercourse to the health and virtue of both man and woman, is the most fundamental error in medical and moral philosophy.
George Drysdale
The Elements of Social Science [1854]

9 Kissing don't last: cookery do!
George Meredith (1828–1909) British novelist.
The Ordeal of Richard Feverel, Ch. 28 [1859]

10 There are many females who never feel any sexual excitement whatever. The best mothers, wives, and managers of households, know little or nothing of sexual indulgences. Love of home, children, and domestic duties are the only passions they feel.
W. Acton
The Functions and Disorders of the Reproductive Organs [1865]

11 She burns and as it were, dries up the semen received by her from the male, and if by chance a child *is* conceived it is ill-formed and

does not remain nine months in the mother's womb.
John Davenport
Describing the result of orgasm in women. *Curiositates Eroticae Physiologiae* [1875]

12 The sole criterion of frigidity is the absence of the vaginal orgasm.
Sigmund Freud (1856–1939) Austrian psychoanalyst.
Three Essays on the Theory of Sexuality [1905]

13 When erotogenic susceptibility to stimulation has been successfully transferred by a woman from the clitoris to the vaginal orifice, it implies that she has adopted a new leading zone for the purpose of her later sexual activity.
Sigmund Freud (1856–1939) Austrian psychoanalyst.
Three Essays on the Theory of Sexuality [1905]

14 I discovered how girls were sent ignorant through life into marriage, and pleaded that they, like men, had a right to know themselves and what was the nature of the contract to which they were giving themselves for life – then I remember I was told by one, who herself had the care of daughters, that that ignorance formed too valuable an addition to the virginal charm of womanhood in the marriage market.
Laurence Housman (1865–1959) British artist and author.
The Immoral Effects of Ignorance in Sex Relations [1911]

15 I am happy now that Charles calls on my bedchamber less frequently than of old. As it is, I now endure but two calls a week and when I hear his steps outside my door I lie down on my bed, close my eyes, open my legs and think of England.
Lady Alice Hillingdon (1857–1940) Wife of 2nd Baron Hillingdon.
Often mistakenly attributed to Queen Victoria. *Journal* [1912]

16 Girls are taught from childhood that any exhibition of sexual feeling is unwomanly and intolerable; they also learn from an early age that if a woman makes a mistake it is upon her and upon her alone that social punishment will descend.
Mary Scharlieb (1845–1930) British gynaecological surgeon.
The Seven Ages of Woman [1915]

17 I do not believe that the normal man's sex needs are stronger than the normal woman's. The *average* man's undoubtedly are, owing to the utterly false repression of the woman's and

the utterly unnatural stimulation of the man's which have been current for so long.
Marie Stopes (1880–1958) British birth-control campaigner.
Letter, 17 Dec 1918

18 So many Englishwomen look upon sexual intercourse as abhorrent and not as a natural fulfilment of true love. My wife considered all bodily desire to be nothing less than animal passion, and that true love between husband and wife should be purely mental and not physical…Like so many Englishwomen she considered that any show of affection was not in keeping with her dignity as a woman and that all lovemaking and caresses should come entirely from the man and that the woman should be the passive receiver of affection.
Anonymous
Letter to Marie Stopes, 4 Apr 1921

19 When Eve ate this particular apple, she became aware of her own womanhood, mentally. And mentally she began to experiment with it. She has been experimenting ever since. So has man. To the rage and horror of both of them.
D. H. Lawrence (1885–1930) British novelist.
Fantasia of the Unconscious, Ch. 7 [1922]

20 It's all this cold-hearted fucking that is death and idiocy.
D. H. Lawrence (1885–1930) British novelist and poet.
Lady Chatterley's Lover, Ch. 14 [1928]

21 Sex is the tabasco sauce which an adolescent national palate sprinkles on every course in the menu.
Mary Day Winn (1888–1965) US writer.
Adam's Rib [1931]

22 A well-bred woman does not seek carnal gratification, and she is usually apathetic to sexual pleasures. Her love is physical or spiritual, rather than carnal, and her passiveness in regard to coition often amounts to disgust for it; lust is seldom an element in a woman's character, and she is the preserver of chastity and morality.
Dr O. A. Wall
Sex and Sex Worship [1932]

23 If all the young ladies who attended the Yale promenade dance were laid end to end, no one would be the least surprised.
Dorothy Parker (1893–1967) US writer.
While Rome Burns (Alexander Woollcott) [1934]

24 You know women as well as I do. They are only unwilling when you compel them, but after that they're as enthusiastic as you are.
Jean Giraudoux (1882–1944) French dramatist.
Tiger at the Gates [1935]

25 The residue of virility in the woman's organism is utilized by nature in order to eroticize her: otherwise the functioning of the maternal apparatus would wholly submerge her in the painful tasks of reproduction and motherhood.
Marie Bonaparte (1882–1962) French psychoanalyst, sexologist, educator, and writer.
International Journal of Psycho-Analysis, Vol. 16, 'Passivity, Masochism, and Femininity' [1935]

26 People will insist…on treating the *mons Veneris* as though it were Mount Everest.
Aldous Huxley (1894–1964) British novelist.
Eyeless in Gaza, Ch. 30 [1936]

27 But did thee feel the earth move?
Ernest Hemingway (1899–1961) US novelist.
For Whom the Bell Tolls, Ch. 13 [1940]

28 The Professor of Gynaecology began his course of lectures as follows: Gentlemen, woman is an animal that micturates once a day, defecates once a week, menstruates once a month, parturates once a year and copulates whenever she has the opportunity.
W. Somerset Maugham (1874–1965) British novelist.
A Writer's Notebook [1949]

29 The vagina walls are quite insensitive in the great majority of females…There is no evidence that the vagina is ever the sole source of arousal, or even the primary source of erotic arousal in any female.
Alfred Charles Kinsey (1894–1956) US zoologist and director of the Institute for Sex Research.
Sexual Behaviour in the Human Female [1953]

30 No sex without responsibility.
Lord Longford (1905–   ) British politician and social reformer.
Observer, 'Sayings of the Week', 3 May 1954

31 When I was young, I kissed my first woman, and smoked my first cigarette on the same day. Believe me, never since have I wasted any more time on tobacco.
Arturo Toscanini (1867–1957) Italian conductor.
Attrib. [1957]

32 Older women are best because they always think they may be doing it for the last time.
Ian Fleming (1908–64) British journalist and author.
Life of Ian Fleming (John Pearson) [1964]

33 So female orgasm is simply a nervous climax to sex relations…It may be thought of as a

sort of pleasure-prize like a prize that comes with a box of cereal. It is all to the good if the prize is there, but the cereal is valuable and nourishing if it is not.
Madeline Gray (1902–   ) US writer.
The Normal Woman [1967]

34   When women go wrong, men go right after them.
Mae West (1892–1980) US actress.
The Wit and Wisdom of Mae West (ed. J. Weintraub) [1967]

35   In the third stage they get their pleasure chiefly from the little penis that they have on the outside of their bodies, called the clitoris, and are mostly interested in having that organ stimulated. In the adult stage they get their greatest pleasure from the vagina, which can be used much more effectively to give pleasure to a male partner.
Eric Berne British doctor.
A Layman's Guide to Psychiatry and Psychoanalysis [1969]

36   If sex is such a natural phenomenon, how come there are so many books on how to?
Bette Midler (1944–   ) US actress and comedienne.
Attrib. [1970s]

37   Is sex dirty? Only if it's done right.
Woody Allen (Allen Stewart Konigsberg; 1935–   ) US film actor.
All You've Ever Wanted to Know About Sex [1972]

38   Because emotions rule all sexual responses (including orgasm) a woman needs to review carefully her own personal attitudes about sex, her feelings about her husband and their relationship together. In some cases, the inability of having an orgasm is simply the unconscious refusal to have one, in order to get revenge on the husband.
Dr David Reuben
Any Woman Can [1973]

39   'Sex,' she says, 'is a subject like any other subject. Every bit as interesting as agriculture.'
Muriel Spark (1918–   ) British writer and poet.
The Hothouse by the East River, Ch. 4 [1973]

40   Traditionally, sex has been a very private, secretive activity. Herein perhaps lies its powerful force for uniting people in a strong bond. As we make sex less secretive, we may rob it of its power to hold men and women together.
Thomas Szasz (1920–   ) US psychiatrist.
The Second Sin [1974]

41   ...the development of a female orgasm, which makes it easier for a female to be satisfied by one male, and which also operates psycho-

logically to produce a stronger emotional bond in the female.
George Pugh
Biological Origin of Human Values [1977]

42   SIECUS was founded in 1964, when one in two marriages was warped by sexual problems. Sex had to be brought out of the Victorian closet – freed from the guilt and fear, bigotry and misconceptions which shrouded it, if America was to recover from its deep-rooted sexual trouble.
Mary Calderone (1904–   ) US physician and sex educator.
SIECUS is an acronym for Sex Information and Education Council of the United States. SIECUS Fund-raising Letter, 1979

43   The orgasm has replaced the Cross as the focus of longing and the image of fulfilment.
Malcolm Muggeridge (1903–90) British writer.
The Most of Malcolm Muggeridge, 'Down with Sex'

44   It's not the men in my life that count; it's the life in my men.
Mae West (1892–1980) US actress.
Attrib. [1980]

45   What women want is not to be treated with respect and care. They want to be treated like shit. They seem to like it.
John Steed British rapist and murderer.
Referring to the rape and murder he comitted on the M4, 1986

46   Personally I know nothing about sex because I've always been married.
Zsa Zsa Gabor (1919–   ) Hungarian-born US film star.
Observer, 'Sayings of the Week', 16 Aug 1987

47   I know it does make people happy but to me it is just like having a cup of tea.
Cynthia Payne (1934–   ) London housewife
After her acquittal on a charge of controlling prostitutes in a famous 'sex-for-luncheon-vouchers' case, 8 Nov 1987

48   There was sex of course, but although both of them were extremely interested in sex, and enjoyed nothing better than discussing it, neither of them, if the truth be told, was quite so interested in actually having it, or at any rate in having it very frequently.
David Lodge (1935–   ) British author.
Nice Work, I [1988]

49   You think intercourse is a private act; it's not, it's a social act. Men are sexually predatory in life; and women are sexually manipulative. When two individuals come together and leave their gender outside the bedroom door, then they make love. If they take it inside with them,

they do something else, because society is in the room with them.
Andrea Dworkin US feminist.
Intercourse

50 As women have known since the dawn of our time, the primary site for stimulation to orgasm centers upon the clitoris. The revolution unleashed by the Kinsey report of 1953 has, by now, made this information available to men who, for whatever reason, had not figured it out for themselves by the more obvious routes of experience and sensitivity.
Stephen Jay Gould (1941–) US geologist and writer.
Bully for Brontosaurus [1991]

51 Dear Emmeline,
Don't laugh, OK? So I'm having a repetitive dream which I can't interpret. There are all these angry women who are booing and whistling me off the platform and shouting: 'Dora! Dora! Dora!'. What can it mean?
Yours anxiously,
Sigmund F,
Vienna
Emmeline replies: Surely you remember Dora? Your classic case study of hysteria? That 15 year-old girl whose strange aversion to sexual advances from her father's best friend was caused by her own secret sexual longing for her father and her jealousy over his liaison with another woman. Fitted in neatly with the Oedipus stuff didn't it? So neatly that you glossed over details indicating that she had for many years been sexually abused by her venereal diseased father, who was now eagerly passing on his beloved daughter to his best friend. Need I say more?
New Internationalist, Jan 1992

SEXISM
See ATTITUDES; DISCRIMINATION; MISOGYNY

SHELLEY, Mary Wollstonecraft (1797–1851)
British author. Daughter of William Godwin and Mary Wollstonecraft, she was the second wife of Percy Bysshe Shelley whom she married in 1816. Her most lasting monument is her novel *Frankenstein (or, the Modern Prometheus)* (1818), written as a result of an evening telling horror stories with her husband, Byron, and other friends in Switzerland. After her husband's death in 1822 she published his *Posthumous Poems* (1824) and edited his *Poetical Works* (1839). Her own works include *The Last Man* (1826), *The Fortunes of Perkin Warbeck* (1830), and *Rambles in Germany and Italy in 1840, 1842, and 1843* (1844).

Quotations about Shelley
1 Mrs. Shelley is very clever, indeed it would be difficult for her not to be so; the daughter of Mary Wollstonecraft and Godwin, and the wife of Shelley, could be no common person.
Lord Byron (1788–1824) British poet. *Conversations with Lord Byron* (Lady Blessington)

2 I am anxious that she should be brought up like a philosopher, even like a cynic. It will add greatly to the strength and worth of her character. I wish too that she should be *excited* to industry. She has occasionally great perseverance, but occasionally, too, she shows great need to be roused.
William Godwin was Mary Shelley's father. William Godwin (1756–1836) British novelist. Letter to William Baxter, June 1812

Quotations by Shelley
3 My dreams were all my own; I accounted for them to nobody; they were my refuge when annoyed – my dearest pleasure when free.
Frankenstein (or, the Modern Prometheus), Preface

4 Invention, it must be humbly admitted, does not consist in creating out of voice, but out of chaos.
Frankenstein (or, the Modern Prometheus)

SIDDONS, Sarah (née Kemble; 1755–1831)
British actress. Born into an acting family, the eldest of 12 children, she began making stage appearances as a child. While in her teens she fell in love with an actor, William Siddons, of whom her parents disapproved. She was sent to Bath to be a lady's maid, where she entertained in the servant's hall by giving recitals of Shakespeare and Milton. She also developed a talent for sculpture, which she developed in later life. Consent was finally given for her marriage to Siddons, which took place in Coventry in 1773. In 1775 David Garrick offered her a part in *The Merchant of Venice* at Drury Lane, London. However, she was a failure, and returned to touring the country as a tragic actress. In 1782 she again appeared at Drury Lane, at the request of Richard Brinsley Sheridan, and this time she had enormous success. In 1783 she was appointed elocution teacher to the royal children. She continued at Drury Lane until 1803, when she and her brother John Philip Kemble took over Covent Garden. Her notable performances include Katharine in *Henry VIII*, Constance in *King John*, Zara in *The Mourning Bride*, and Volumnia in *Coriolanus*. Her farewell performance in 1812 was in her most famous role as Lady Macbeth.

Quotations about Siddons

1 She was the stateliest ornament of the public mind.
William Hazlitt (1778–1830) British essayist. *Examiner*, 'Mrs. Siddons', 16 June 1816

2 Madam, you who so often occasion a want of seats to other people, will the more easily excuse the want of one yourself.
Speaking to Mrs. Siddons when she found there was no chair for her to sit down. Samuel Johnson (1709–84) British lexicographer. *Life of Johnson* (James Boswell)

Quotations by Siddons

3 Sorry am I to say I have often observed, that I have performed worst when I most ardently wished to do better than ever.
Letter to Rev. Whalley, 16 July 1781

4 I am, as you may observe, acting again…Our theatre is going on, to the astonishment of everybody. Very few of the actors are paid, and all are vowing to withdraw themselves: yet still we go on. Sheridan is certainly omnipotent.
Letter, 9 Nov 1796

SILLS, Beverley (Belle Silverman; 1929–)

US operatic soprano. She made her debut when only 19 with the Philadelphia Civic Opera. In 1955 she became a member of the New York City Opera Company, creating the role of Baby Doe in Douglas Moore's *The Ballad of Baby Doe* in 1956. She married Peter Bulkeley Greenough in this year, but was forced to leave the stage in 1961 after the births of their two children, one of whom was born deaf and the other mentally retarded. She returned in 1963 and has made several appearances in the major European opera houses. She was director of the New York City Opera from 1979 to 1989.

1 In a way, retarded children are satisfying. Everything is a triumph. Even getting Bucky to manage to get a spoon to his mouth was a triumph. God compensates.
Divas: Impressions of Six Opera Superstars (Winthrop Sargeant), 'Beverley Sills'

2 I would willingly give up my whole career if I could have just one normal child.
Divas: Impressions of Six Opera Superstars (Winthrop Sargeant), 'Beverley Sills'

3 A happy woman is one who has no cares at all; a cheerful woman is one who has cares but doesn't let them get her down.
Interview, *60 Minutes*, CBS-TV

4 My singing is very therapeutic. For three hours I have no troubles – I know how it's all going to come out.
Interview, *60 Minutes*, CBS-TV

SIN

1 I delight in sinning and hate to compose a mask
for gossip.
Sulpicia (fl. 63 BC–AD 14) Roman poet.
A Book of Women Poets (ed. Aliki and Willis Barnstone) [1st century AD]

2 Fashions in sin change.
Lillian Hellman (1906–) US playwright and writer.
Watch on the Rhine [1941]

3 Sin…has been made not only ugly but passé. People are no longer sinful, they are only immature or under privileged or frightened or, more particularly, sick.
Phyllis McGinley (1905–78) US poet and humorist.
The Province of the Heart, 'In Defense of Sin' [1959]

SINGLE WOMEN

1 Many times married women desire children, as maids do husbands, more for honour than for comfort or happiness, thinking it a disgrace to live old maids, and so likewise to be barren.
Margaret Cavendish (c. 1623–c. 1673) English poet, playwright, and writer.
Sociable Letters [1664]

2 Quite terrified with the dreadful name of old maid…she flies to some dishonourable match as her last, tho' much mistaken Refuge, to the disgrace of her Family, and her own irreparable Ruin.
Mary Astell (c. 1666–1731) English pamphleteer.
A Serious Proposal to the Ladies for the Advancement of their True and Greatest Interest [1694]

3 A single woman with a narrow income, must be a ridiculous, disagreeable old maid, the proper sport of boys and girls, but a single woman of fortune is always respectable, and may be as sensible and pleasant as anybody else.
Jane Austen (1775–1817) British novelist.
Emma [1816]

4 Of course the fate of the married woman is very much sadder than that of the spinster; at least the unmarried woman enjoys a certain freedom, she can enter society and travel with her family or with friends, whereas once a woman is married, she cannot stir from the house *without the permission of her husband*.
Flora Tristan (1803–44) French writer, feminist, and revolutionary socialist.
The London Journal of Flora Tristan [1842]

5 Molly remained a merry spinster all her days, one of the independent, brave and busy creatures of whom there is such need in the world to help take care of other people's wives

and children, and to do the many useful jobs that married folk have no time for.
Louisa May Alcott (1832–88) US writer and editor.
Jack and Jill [1880]

6 *Miss*, *n*. A title with which we brand unmarried women to indicate that they are in the market. Miss, Missis (Mrs) and Mister (Mr) are the three most distinctly disagreeable words in the language, in sound and sense. Two are corruptions of Mistress, the other of Master…If we must have them, let us be consistent and give one to the unmarried man. I venture to suggest Mush, abbreviated to Mh.
Ambrose Bierce (1842–?1914) US writer and journalist.
The Devil's Dictionary [1906]

7 The contempt with which the single woman has been regarded is different from that bestowed on her fallen sister, but it is no less real.
R. J. Campbell British churchman.
Christianity and the Social Order [1907]

8 It was so cold I almost got married.
Shelley Winters (1922–) US actress.
The New York Times, 29 Apr 1956

9 It is not to be supposed that Miss Brodie was unique…There were legions of her kind during the nineteen-thirties, women from the age of thirty and upward who crowded their war-bereaved spinsterhood with voyages of discovery into new ideas and energetic practices in art of social welfare, education or religion.
Muriel Spark (1918–) British writer and poet.
The Prime of Miss Jean Brodie, Ch. 3 [1961]

10 Being an old maid is like death by drowning, a really delightful sensation after you cease to struggle.
Edna Ferber (1887–1968) US writer.
Wit's End (R. E. Drennan), 'Completing the Circle' [1968]

11 Solitary women exhibit pseudo-masculine efficiency, a determined practical competence which they might expect or demand from a husband if only they had one.
Anthony Storr (1920–) British psychiatrist.
Human Aggression [1968]

12 Don't we realize we're a business, we single girls are? There are magazines for us, special departments in stores for us. Every building that goes up in Manhattan has more than fifty percent efficiency apartments…for the one million girls who have very little use for them.
Gail Parent (c. 1941–) US scenarist and writer.
Sheila Levine Is Dead and Living in New York, 'On Jobs and Apartments' [1972]

13 As she ages, the unmarried woman… appears to bring stronger psychological reserves to bear on the challenges of her position than those demonstrated by bachelor men.
Gail Sheehy (1937–) US writer and social critic.
Passages, Pt 5, Ch. 16 [1976]

SITWELL, Dame Edith (1887–1964)

British poet and critic, whose colourful poetry was matched by her exotic clothes and jewellery. A member of the celebrated Sitwell family, her childhood was unhappy as she did not fit into the conventional mould favoured by her parents. However, she was encouraged by her governess, Helen Rootham, to develop her talents. She and Miss Rootham took a flat together in 1914, and the following year her first volume of poetry, *The Mother*, was published. In 1916 she collaborated with her brothers Sir Osbert and Sacheverell on an annual anthology, *Wheels*, which attacked the prevailing poetry of the Georgians. The first performance of *Façade*, in which her poems were set to music by William Walton, was given in 1923. In the 1930s she lived for a while in Paris with Helen Rootham until the latter's death in 1938. Her writings include *Gold Coast Customs* (1929), *The English Eccentrics* (1933), *Street Songs* (1942), *Green Song* (1944), and *Song of the Cold* (1964). She was created a DBE in 1954.

Quotations about Sitwell

1 Then Edith Sitwell appeared, her nose longer than an ant-eater's, and read some of her absurd stuff.
Lytton Strachey (1880–1932) British writer. Letter to Dora Carrington, 28 June 1921

2 So you've been reviewing Edith Sitwell's latest piece of virgin dung, have you? Isn't she a poisonous thing of a woman, lying, concealing, flipping, plagiarising, misquoting, and being as clever a crooked literary publicist as ever.
Dylan Thomas (1914–53) Welsh poet. Letter to Glyn Jones, 1934

Quotations by Sitwell

3 My poems are hymns of praise to the glory of life.
Collected Poems, 'Some Notes on My Poetry'

4 A lady asked me why, on most occasions, I wore black. 'Are you in mourning?'
'Yes.'
'For whom are you in mourning?'
'For the world.'
Taken Care Of, Ch. 1

5 A pompous woman of his acquaintance, complaining that the head-waiter of a restaurant had not shown her and her husband

immediately to a table, said, 'We had to tell him who we were.' Gerald, interested, enquired, 'And who were you?'
Taken Care Of, Ch. 15

SMITH, Margaret Chase (1897–)

US politician. Educated at Skowhegan High School she began her career as a teacher, moving to journalism in 1919, to work on the *Independent Reporter*. In 1940 she was elected to the House of Representatives and from 1948 to 1972 was the Senator for Maine.

1 In these perilous hours, I fear that the American people are ahead of their leaders in realism and courage – but behind them in knowledge of the facts because the facts have not been given to them.
Address, US Senate, 21 Sept 1961

2 Before you can become a statesman you first have to get elected, and to get elected you have to be a politician pledging support for what the voters want.
Declaration of Conscience, 'Nuclear Test Ban Treaty', 1972

3 We are rapidly approaching a day when the United States will be subject to all sorts of diplomatic blackmail and a strategy of terror waged by the Soviet Union.
Reader's Digest, 'It's Time to Speak Up for National Defense', Mar 1972

4 The key to security is public information.
Reader's Digest, 'It's Time to Speak Up for National Defense', Mar 1972

SOCIETY

1 There is little point in girls of common extraction learning to read as well as young ladies or being taught as fine a pronunciation or knowing what a period is, etc. It is the same with writing. All they need is enough to keep their accounts and memoranda; you don't need to teach them fine hand-writing or talk to them of style: a little spelling will do. Arithmetic is different. They need it.
Mme de Maintenon (Françoise d'Aubigné, Marquise de M.; c. 1635–1719) Second wife of Louis XIV of France.
Lettres sur l'éducation des filles [1713]

2 Then let the society man has made be blamed for this aberration of nature, and let woman be exonerated. As long as she remains the slave of man and the victim of prejudice, as long as she is refused training in a profession, as

long as she is deprived of her civil rights, there can be no moral law for her.
Flora Tristan (1903–44) French writer, feminist, and revolutionary socialist.
The London Journal of Flora Tristan [1842]

3 Women are the real architects of society.
Harriet Beecher Stowe (1811–96) US writer and social critic.
Atlantic Monthly, 'Dress, or Who Makes the Fashions' [1864]

4 Old-fashioned ways which no longer apply to changed conditions are a snare in which the feet of women have always become readily entangled.
Jane Addams (1860–1935) US social worker.
Newer Ideals of Peace, 'Utilization of Women in City Government' [1892]

5 The world in the past has been ruled by force, and man has dominated over woman by reason of his more forceful and aggressive qualities both of body and mind. But the balance is already shifting; force is losing its dominance, and mental alertness, intuition, and the spiritual qualities of love and service, which in women is strong, are gaining ascendancy.
'Abdu'l-Bahá (1844–1921) Persian leader of the Baha'i faith.
Bahá'u'lláh and the New Era (J. E. Esslemont) [c. 1921]

6 For the first time, she realised that conversation might have been entirely satisfactory if women had been allowed to admit they understood the limited number of subjects men were interested in, and she was so excited by her idea that she almost committed the social crime of allowing a conversation to pause.
Frances Newman (c. 1883–1928) US writer and librarian.
The Hard-Boiled Virgin [1926]

7 In society it is etiquette for ladies to have the best chairs and get handed things. In the home the reverse is the case. That is why ladies are more sociable than gentlemen.
Virginia Graham (1912–) US writer and broadcaster.
Say Please, Ch. 1 [1949]

8 Clearly, society has a tremendous stake in insisting on a woman's natural fitness for the career of mother: the alternatives are all too expensive.
Ann Oakley (1944–) British sociologist and writer.
Woman's Work: The Housewife, Past and Present, Ch. 8 [1974]

9 Women serve as guardians of culture, upholders of society.
Patricia Meyer Spacks (1929–) US literary critic, educator, and editor.
The Female Imagination, Ch. 7 [1975]

SOMERVILLE, Mary (1780–1872)

British astronomer and physical geographer. The daughter of a naval officer, she received one year of formal education before her marriage to a cousin in 1804. After his death in 1807 she married W. Somerville, another cousin, in 1812. Her second husband encouraged her interest in science, which enabled her to become a respected figure in the scientific circles of London. In 1831 she published her translation of Pierre Simon de Laplace's *Mécanique Céleste* (*The Mechanism of the Heavens*). In 1834 she published her own work *On the Connexion of the Physical Sciences*, which proved popular, and led to her being granted a government pension of £300 a year. In 1840 she moved to Europe, where she produced her final two works *Physical Geography* (1848), which was widely used as a university text book until the end of the century, and *On Molecular and Microscopic Science* (1869). Somerville College, Oxford, opened in 1879 for the education of women, was named after her.

1 One of the greatest improvements in education is that teachers are now fitted for their duties by being taught the art of teaching.
Physical Geography, 'Benevolence'

2 And who shall declare the time allotted to the human race, when the generation of the most insignificant insect existed for unnumbered ages? Yet man is also to vanish in the ever-changing course of events. The earth is to be burnt up, and the elements to melt with fervent heat – to be again reduced to chaos – possibly to be renovated and adorned for other races of beings. These stupendous changes may be but cycles in those great laws of the universe, where all is variable but the laws themselves and He who ordained them.
Physical Geography, 'God and His Works'

3 The moral disposition of the age appears in the refinement of conversation.
Physical Geography, 'Influence of Christianity'

4 No circumstance in the natural world is more inexplicable than the diversity of form and colour in the human race.
Physical Geography, 'Varieties of the Human Race'

SONTAG, Susan (1933–)

US writer and critic. She graduated from the University of Chicago in 1951, where she went on to study English literature before moving to Harvard to study philosophy. She subsequently taught philosophy at several colleges and universities until the publication of her first novel, *The Benefactor* (1963). Her best-known work is *Illness as a Metaphor* (1979). Other publications include *Death Kit* (1967), *On Photography* (1977), *Under the Sign of Saturn* (1980), and *AIDS and Its Metaphors* (1988).

1 It is only the fear of malpractice that keeps doctors candid in this country.
The Dick Cavett Show, PBS-TV, 14 June 1978

2 Fatal illness has always been viewed as a test of moral character, but in the nineteenth century there is a great reluctance to let anybody flunk the test.
Illness as Metaphor, Ch. 5

3 Illness is the night-side of life, a more onerous citizenship. Everyone who is born holds dual citizenship, in the kingdom of the well and in the kingdom of the sick. Although we all prefer to use only the good passport, sooner or later each of us is obliged, at least for a spell, to identify ourselves as citizens of that other place.
Illness as Metaphor

4 A photograph is not only an image (as a painting is an image), an interpretation of the real; it is also a trace, something directly stencilled off the real, like a footprint or a death mask.
On Photography

SORROW

1 My eye cried and woke me.
The night was pain.
Al-Khansa (575–646) Arabic poet.
'The Night' [7th century]

2 Have you any idea
How long a night can last, spent
Lying alone and sobbing?!
Mother of Michitsuna (fl. 954–974) Japanese diarist.
One Hundred Poems from the Japanese [c. 974]

3 A woman's heart always has a burned mark.
Louise Labé (c. 1524–66) French poet, linguist, feminist, and soldier.
Oeuvres, Sonnet II [1555]

4 Does anybody wonder so many women die. Grief and constant anxiety kill nearly as many women as men die on the battlefield.
Mary Chesnut (1823–86) US diarist.
Diary from Dixie, 9 June 1862

5 It is only the women whose eyes have been washed clear with tears who get the broad vision that makes them little sisters to all the world.

Dorothy Dix (Elizabeth Meriwether Gilmer; 1861–1951) US journalist and writer.
Dorothy Dix, Her Book, Introduction [1926]

6 If I am ever unhappy, my remedy is to retire to my bathroom, soak in a scented bath, light a candle, and maybe cry.

Natalia Makarova (1940–   ) Russian ballerina.
Independent, 'Quote Unquote', 30 Nov 1991

SPARK, Muriel (1918–   )

British writer. Born in Edinburgh and educated at James Gillespie's School and the Heriot Watt College, she spent some years in Africa until her marriage to S. O. Spark in 1938. During World War II she worked in the political intelligence department of the Foreign Office (1944–45) and later edited *Poetry Review* (1947–49). Her fiction-writing career began in 1951 when she won the *Observer* short-story competition. Her conversion to Catholicism in 1954 influenced much of her subsequent work, particularly *The Mandelbaum Gate* (1965), which won the James Tait Black Prize. Her most celebrated novel is *The Prime of Miss Jean Brodie* (1961), which also enjoyed success as a play (1966) and a film (1969). Other works include *The Girls of Slender Means* (1963), *The Only Problem* (1984), and *Symposium* (1990).

Quotation about Spark

1 Her prose is like a bird darting from place to place, palpitating with nervous energy; but a bird with a bright beady eye and a sharp beak as well.
Francis Hope *Observer*, 28 Apr 1963

Quotations by Spark

2 Parents learn a lot from their children about coping with life.
The Comforters, Ch. 6

3 Being over seventy is like being engaged in a war. All our friends are going or gone and we survive amongst the dead and the dying as on a battlefield.
Memento Mori, Ch. 4

4 Give me a girl at an impressionable age, and she is mine for life.
The Prime of Miss Jean Brodie, Ch. 1

5 One's prime is elusive. You little girls, when you grow up, must be on the alert to recognize your prime at whatever time of your life it may occur. You must then live it to the full.
The Prime of Miss Jean Brodie, Ch. 1

6 Do you think it pleases a man when he looks into a woman's eyes and sees a reflection of the British Museum Reading Room?
The Wit of Women (L. and M. Cowan)

STANHOPE, Lady Hester (1776–1839)

British traveller. Despite her early success as a political hostess and housekeeper to her uncle, William Pitt the Younger, she left Britain in 1810 and settled in Djoun in what is now the Lebanon. Here she led an extremely exotic existence, building herself an oriental palace, taking a Syrian lover, and dressing in Turkish male attire. She developed an interest in astrology which led some people to credit her with prophetic powers. She was also influential in the politics of the area, later giving sanctuary to Europeans after the battles of Navarino (1827) and Acre (1832). Her final years were spent as a recluse, marked by increasing debts, until she died in poverty.

Quotations about Stanhope

1 Her habits grew more and more eccentric. She lay in bed all day and sat up all night, talking unceasingly for hour upon hour to Dr Meryon, who alone of her English attendants remained with her.
Lytton Strachey (1880–1932) British writer. *Books and Characters* 'Lady Hester Stanhope'

2 She had a remarkable talent for divining characters by the conformation of men. It was founded both on the features of the face and on the shape of the head, body and limbs. Some indications she went by were taken from a resemblance to animals; and wherever such indications existed, she inferred that the dispositions peculiar to these animals were to be found in the person.
John Tomb (1882–1950) British civil servant. *English Eccentrics*

Quotations by Stanhope

3 At twenty my complexion was like alabaster, and at five paces distant the sharpest eyes could not discover my pearl necklace from my skin.
Little Memoirs of the Nineteenth Century (George Paston), Pt I

4 If you were to take every feature in my face, and lay them one by one on the table, there is not one single one that would bear examination. The only thing is that, put together and lighted up, they look well enough. It is homogeneous ugliness, and nothing more.
Little Memoirs of the Nineteenth Century (George Paston), Pt I

5 I am reckoned here the first politician in the world, and by some a sort of prophet.
Referring to her position in Syria. Letter to Dr Meryon, 1836

STANTON, Elizabeth Cady (1815–1902)

US reformer and leader of the woman suffrage movement. In 1840 she married Henry Brewster Stanton, a journalist and abolitionist, and attended the international slavery convention in London. The exclusion of women from the floor of this convention was an important factor in rousing Elizabeth Stanton to organize women to win greater equality. In 1848 she and Mrs Lucretia Mott organized the first women's rights convention, which was held at Seneca Falls, New York. In the same year she circulated petitions to secure the passage of a law giving married women property rights. From 1850 Elizabeth Stanton and Susan B. Anthony cooperated in compiling *The Revolution*, a women's rights newspaper, the *Women's Bible*, and, with Mathilda Gage, the first three volumes of *The History of Woman Suffrage*. She was president of the National American Woman Suffrage Association from 1865–90.

Quotations about Stanton

1 Heigh! ho! the carrion crow
Mrs Stanton's all the go:
Twenty tailors take the stitches,
Mrs Stanton wears the breeches.
Anonymous

2 If Mrs Stanton would attend a little more to her domestic duties and a little less to those of the great public, perhaps she would exalt her sex quite as much as she does by quixotically fighting windmills in their gratuitous behalf, and might possibly set a notable example of domestic felicity. No married woman can convert herself into a feminine Knight of the Rueful Visage and ride about the country attempting to redress imaginary wrongs without leaving her own household in a neglected condition that must be an eloquent witness against her.
Anonymous *New York Sunday Times*, Jan 1868

3 As usual when she had fired her gun she went home and left me to finish the battle.
Susan B. Anthony (1820–1905) US editor. Remark after Mrs Stanton had addressed a convention on the subject of divorce, June 1860

4 Mrs Stanton is my sentence maker, my pen artist.
Susan B. Anthony *Life and Work of Susan B. Anthony* (Ida Hasted Harper)

5 That such mental powers must be hampered with such a *clumsy body* – oh – if we could only give her elasticity of limbs – and locomotive powers.
Susan B. Anthony (1820–1906) US editor. Letter to Elizabeth Smith Miller, 15 Feb 1892

Quotations by Stanton

6 I have been into many of the ancient cathedrals – grand, wonderful, mysterious. But I always leave them with a feeling of indignation because of the generations of human beings who have struggled in poverty to build these altars to the unknown god.
Diary

7 Man in his lust has regulated his whole question of sexual intercourse. Long enough! Let the mother of mankind, whose prerogative it is to set bounds to his indulgence, rouse up and give this matter a thorough fearless examination.
The Emancipation of American Women (A. Sinclair)

8 We still wonder at the stolid incapacity of all men to understand that woman feels the invidious distinctions of sex exactly as the black man does those of color, or the white man the more transient distinctions of wealth, family, position, place, and power; that she feels as keenly as man the injustice of disfranchisement.
History of Woman Suffrage (with Susan B. Anthony and Mathilda Gage), Vol. I

9 It is impossible for one class to appreciate the wrongs of another.
History of Woman Suffrage (with Susan B. Anthony and Mathilda Gage), Vol. I

10 *Declaration of Sentiments:*…We hold these truths to be self-evident: that all men and women are created equal…
History of Woman Suffrage (with Susan B. Anthony and Mathilda Gage), Vol. I

11 The prolonged slavery of women is the darkest page in human history.
History of Woman Suffrage (with Susan B. Anthony and Mathilda Gage), Vol. I

12 Womanhood is the great fact in her life; wifehood and motherhood are but incidental relations.
History of Woman Suffrage (with Susan B. Anthony and Mathilda Gage), Vol. I.

STARK, Freya Madeline (1893–)

British traveller and writer. Born in Paris, she spent her childhood between Devonshire (with her father) and Italy (with her mother). During World War I she joined the Red Cross and nursed in Italy. In the 1920s, in an attempt to escape from her demanding mother, she decided to travel to the East. In 1927, having learnt Arabic, she set off for Beirut. She spent most of World War II in the Middle East, working for the ministry of information. Her best-known works include *The Valley of the Assassins* (1934), *The Southern Gates of Arabia* (1936), which describe her travels in the Middle East, *A Winter in Arabia* (1940), *The Coast of*

Incense (1953), and *Rome on the Euphrates* (1966). A volume of selected letters, *Over the Rim of the World*, was published in 1988.

1 I am not so much of a pacifist that I would not fight for Peace!
The Coast of Incense

2 I have come to the conclusion that it is more flattering to be a 'man's woman' than a 'woman's woman': a man's woman has to be unselfish and agreeable at any rate in conversation – with a mind broader than her shop, as men have the supreme merit of not always wanting to talk shop.
The Coast of Incense

3 The great and almost only comfort about being a woman is that one can always pretend to be more stupid than one is, and no one is surprised.
The Valley of the Assassins

4 The true wanderer, whose travels are happiness…goes out not to shun, but to seek.
Lives of Modern Women (Caroline Moorehead)

STEAD, Christina (1902–83)
Australian writer. Born in Australia and educated at New South Wales Teachers College, she spent most of her life abroad, living in the United States, Paris, and London. In 1952 she married the writer William Blake, with whom she settled in London. However, in 1974 she returned to Australia. Her best-known book is *The Man Who Loved Children* (1940), which depicts marriage as a state of continuous warfare, and which reveals the author's concern with the human need for the apparently irreconcilable qualities of personal freedom and love. Her other works include *House of All Nations* (1938), *The People with the Dogs* (1952), *The Little Hotel* (1973), and *Miss Herbert* (1976).

Quotation about Stead
1 She'd first known she was a 'word-stringer' when she produced an essay at the age of ten, on the life-cycle of the frog.
Lorna Sage (1943–) British journalist. *The Salzburg Tales*, Introduction

Quotations by Stead
2 A self-made man is one who believes in luck and sends his son to Oxford.
House of All Nations, 'Credo'

3 'Pity them, the English are so poor now, the most unfortunate people on earth,' my papa says, 'and yet they cannot lose their pride, their tradition, their history.'
The Little Hotel

4 It is a grimmer version of human affairs than that of real tragedy where at least there is some resolution, some feeling of significance.
A Little Tea, a Little Chat

5 I know your breed; all your fine officials debauch the young girls who are afraid to lose their jobs: that's as old as Washington.
The Man Who Loved Children, Ch. 4

STEIN, Gertrude (1874–1946)
US writer. She graduated from Radcliffe College in 1897, where she studied psychology under the psychologist and philosopher William James. She followed this with several years spent studying the anatomy of the brain, but eventually grew tired of her studies and decided to follow her brother, Leo, to Europe. There, they began buying the paintings of Matisse, Braque, and Picasso before they were well known, enabling her, so she thought, to take credit for the later growth of Cubism. In Paris, where she lived from 1903 with her life-long companion Alice B. Toklas, she presided over a salon, which included such writers as Sherwood Anderson and Ernest Hemingway, as well as many of the experimental painters. She is best remembered for the influence she had on the writers around her rather than her own work. Her writings include *Three Lives* (1909), *Tender Buttons* (1914), and the libretto for an opera by Virgil Thomson, *Four Saints in Three Acts* (1934).

Quotations about Stein
1 Reading Gertrude Stein at length is not unlike making one's way through an interminable and badly printed game book.
Richard Bridgeman *Gertrude Stein in Pieces*

2 Miss Stein was a past master in making nothing happen very slowly.
Clifton Fadiman (1904–) US writer and broadcaster. *The Selected Writings of Clifton Fadiman*, 'Puzzlements'

Quotations by Stein
3 Besides Shakespeare and me, who do you think there is?
Speaking to a friend she considered knew little about literature. *Charmed Circle* (J. Mellow)

4 The Jews have produced only three originative geniuses: Christ, Spinoza, and myself.
Charmed Circle (J. Mellow)

5 That's what you are. That's what you all are. All of you young people who served in the war. You are a lost generation.
A Moveable Feast (E. Hemingway)

STEINEM, Gloria (1934–)

US writer, journalist, and feminist. She graduated from Smith College in 1956 and began publishing freelance articles while studying in India. In 1960 she moved to New York, where she worked as a writer and journalist, and where she became involved in the women's liberation movement. In 1971 she helped found the National Women's Political caucus (which encouraged women to run for political office) and in 1972 founded *Ms*, the magazine that treated contemporary issues from a feminist viewpoint. Her writings include *The Thousand Indias* (1957) and *Marilyn* (1986).

1 The first problem for all of us, men and women, is not to learn, but to unlearn.
The New York Times, 'A New Egalitarian Life Style', 26 Aug 1971

2 The definition of woman's work is shitwork.
Writer's Digest, 'Freelancer with No Time to Write' (John Brady), Feb 1974

3 If the men in the room would only think how they would feel graduating with a 'spinster of arts' they would see how important this is.
Referring to language reform. Speech Yale University, Sept 1981

STOPES, Marie (1880–1958)

British botanist and social worker. Born in Edinburgh, she gained a degree in botany and geology from University College, London in 1902, and in 1904 her PhD from Munich University. In the same year she was appointed assistant lecturer in botany at Manchester University and, after receiving her DSc in 1905, was appointed lecturer in palaeobotany. After her marriage she moved to London in 1911, and was appointed to a similar position at University College, London (1913–20). Her first marriage was annulled in 1916, after she claimed she was still a virgin, a condition that is said to have led her to write her book *Married Love* (1918), which deals with the problems of sexuality within marriage. In 1918 she married H. V. Roe, an aircraft manufacturer, with whose encouragement she set up the Mothers' Clinic for Birth Control in Holloway, London, in 1921. *Contraception: Its Theory, History and Practice*, published in 1923, was the first comprehensive work on the subject. Although her work evoked violent opposition, particularly from Roman Catholics, she had a great influence on the gradual relaxation of the Church of England's stand against birth control and the acceptance of family planning as a vital concept throughout the world.

Quotations about Stopes

1 A fascinating combination of scientist and would-be poet, of mystic and crank, of propagandist and neurotic, Marie Stopes splendidly embraced the challenge of society and set up her first birth-control clinic in London in 1921, but she completely failed to write a poem of any consequence.
Keith Briant *Marie Stopes*

2 Her frontal attacks on old taboos, her quasi-prophetic tone, her flowery fervour, aroused strong opposition from those who disagreed with her for religious reasons or felt that she had overstepped the bounds of good taste.
Daily Telegraph, Obituary, 3 Oct 1958

3 Dr Marie Stopes made contraceptive devices respectable in a somewhat gushing book, *Married Love*. For this she deserves to be remembered among the great benefactors of the age.
A. J. P. Taylor (1906–90) British historian. *English History 1914–45*

Quotations by Stopes

4 An impersonal and scientific knowledge of the structure of our bodies is the surest safeguard against prurient curiosity and lascivious gloating.
Married Love, Ch. 5

5 Each coming together of man and wife, even if they have been mated for many years, should be a fresh adventure; each winning should necessitate a fresh wooing.
Married Love, Ch. 10

6 We are not much in sympathy with the typical hustling American business man, but we have often felt compunction for him, seeing him nervous and harassed, sleeplessly, anxiously hunting dollars and all but overshadowed by his overdressed, extravagant and idle wife, who sometimes insists that her spiritual development necessitates that she shall have no children...Yet such wives imagine that they are upholding women's emancipation.
The Fighting Pankhursts (David Mitchell)

STOWE, Harriet Beecher (1811–96)

US writer and philanthropist. The daughter of Congregationalist minister, Lyman Beecher, she married a clergyman, Calvin Ellis Stowe, in 1836. In 1843 she published *The Mayflower; or, Sketches of Scenes and Characters Among the Descendants of the Pilgrims*. She lived for 18 years in Cincinnati, close to a slave-holding community, where she came into contact with fugitive slaves. In 1850 she and her husband moved to Maine, where she wrote the book for which she is now remembered *Uncle Tom's Cabin; or Life Among the Lowly* (1852). The book proved immensely popular and has been translated into at least 23 languages.

Quotations about Stowe

1 Harriet Beecher Stowe, whose *Uncle Tom's Cabin* was the first evidence to America that no hurricane can be so disastrous to a country as a ruthlessly humanitarian woman.
Sinclair Lewis (1885–1951) US novelist. *Henry Ward Beecher: An American Portrait* (Paxton Hibben), Introduction

2 To her who in our evil time
Dragged into light the nation's crime
With strength beyond the strength of men
And, mightier than their sword, her pen.
John Greenleaf Whittier (1807–92) US poet. *Runaway to Heaven, the Story of Harriet Beecher Stowe* (Johanna Johnston)

Quotations by Stowe

3 The bitterest tears shed over graves are for words left unsaid and deeds left undone.
Little Foxes, Ch. 3

4 'Do you know who made you?' 'Nobody, as I knows on,' said the child, with a short laugh…'I 'spect I grow'd.'
Uncle Tom's Cabin, Ch. 20

5 I did not write it. God wrote it. I merely did his dictation.
Referring to *Uncle Tom's Cabin*. Attrib.

STRENGTH

1 CANDIDA. Ask James's mother and his three sisters what it cost to save James the trouble of doing anything but be strong and clever and happy. Ask me what it costs to be James's mother and three sisters and wife and mother of his children all in one.
George Bernard Shaw (1836–1950) Irish dramatist and critic.
Candida [1898]

2 Wonderful women! Have you ever thought how much we all, and women especially, owe to Shakespeare for his vindication of women in these fearless, high-spirited, resolute and intelligent heroines?
Ellen Terry (1847–1928) British actress.
Four Lectures on Shakespeare, 'The Triumphant Women' [1911]

3 The world in the past has been ruled by force, and man has dominated over woman by reason of his more forceful and aggressive qualities both of body and mind. But the balance is already shifting; force is losing its dominance, and mental alertness, intuition, and the spiri-

tual qualities of love and service, in which women is strong, are gaining ascendancy.
'Abdu'l-Bahá (1844–1921) Persian leader of the Baha'i faith.
Bahá'u'lláh and the New Era (J. E. Esslemont) [c. 1921]

4 I'm the foe of moderation, the champion of excess. If I may lift a line from a die-hard whose identity is lost in the shuffle, 'I'd rather be strongly wrong than weakly right.'
Tallulah Bankhead (1903–68) US actress.
Tallulah, Ch. 1 [1952]

5 Within the context of most human societies to date, women of strength and achievement are exceptions to the rule. This is reflected in novels about the past or present. Science fiction and fantasy, on the other hand, allow one to imagine and write about worlds where strong independent women *are* the rule, or to construct a society whose features can illuminate the workings of our own.
Pamela Sargent
Frontiers [1977]

STYLE

1 Glamour is what makes a man ask for your telephone number. But it also is what makes a woman ask for the name of your dressmaker.
Lilly Daché (1904–   ) French-born US fashion designer and writer.
Woman's Home Companion, July 1955

2 There goes a woman who knows all the things that can be taught and none of the things that cannot be taught.
Coco Chanel (1883–1971) French dress designer.
Coco Chanel, Her Life, Her Secrets (Marcel Haedrich) [1965]

3 English women are elegant until they are ten years old, and perfect on grand occasions.
Nancy Mitford (1904–73) British writer.
The Wit of Women (L. and M. Cowan) [1973]

SUBJECTION
See also DOMINATION; OPPRESSION

1 By bringing them into crowded places, by permitting them to take part in men's affairs, one destroys that submissiveness and modesty which is natural to them and ends up by encouraging brazenness. Moreover, to do this is also, in a certain sense, to wrong men; for what else is it but a wrong, a grievous wrong, to cause the female sex to meddle in matters which pertain uniquely to men?
Leo the Wise (886–912) Byzantine emperor.
The Novels of Leo (P. Noailles and A. Dain) [10th century]

2 Adam and Lilith never found peace together; for when he wished to lie with her, she took offence at the recumbent posture he demanded. 'Why must I lie beneath you?' she asked. 'I also was made from dust, and am therefore your equal.' But Adam tried to make her obedient to him by force. And Lilith, in a rage, uttered the magic name of God, rose into the air and left him.

Numera Rabba
Medieval midrash on Adam's first wife, Lilith – Eve was his third. [c. 1200]

3 Whoever rightly considers the order of things may plainly see the whole race of woman-kind is by nature, custom, and the laws, made subject to man, to be governed according to his discretion: therefore it is the duty of every one of us that desires to have ease, comfort, and repose, with those men to whom we belong, to be humble, patient, and obedient, as well as chaste.

Giovanni Boccaccio (1313–75) Italian writer and poet.
Decameron, 'The Ninth Day' [1349–51]

4 Item: Man does not exist for the sake of woman, but woman exists for the sake of man and hence there shall be this difference that a man shall love his wife, but never be subject to her, but the wife shall honour and fear the husband.

Martin Luther (1483–1546) German Protestant.
Vindication of Married Life [16th century]

5 Woman's authority is nil; let her in all things be subject to the rule of man...Adam was beguiled by Eve, not she by him. It is right that he whom woman led into wrongdoing should have her under his direction, so that he may not fail a second time through female levity.

Corpus Juris Canonici [*The Body of Canon Law*; 16th century]

6 Woman is under man's dominion and has no authority, nor can she teach, give evidence, make a contract nor be a judge.

Baltasar Gracian (1601–58) Spanish Jesuit.
[1658]

7 Wife and servant are the same
But only differ in the name,
For when that fatal knot is tied,
Which nothing, nothing can divide,
When she the word *obey* has said,
And man by law supreme has made,
Then all that's kind is laid aside,
And nothing left but state and pride.

Mary Lee (1656–1710) English poet and writer.
The Ladies Defence, 'To the Ladies' [1701]

8 Our servile Tongues are taught to cry for Pardon
Ere the weak Senses know the Use of Words:
Our little Souls are tortur'd by Advice;
And moral Lectures stun our Infant Years:
Thro' check'd Desires, Threatnings, and Restraint
The Virgin runs; but ne'er outgrows her Shackles
They still will fit her, even to hoary Age.

Mary Leapor (1722–46) British playwright, poet, and servant.
Poems Upon Several Occasions, Vol. II [c. 1746]

9 A man must know how to defy opinion; a woman how to submit to it.

Germaine de Staël (1766–1817) French novelist, literary critic, and feminist.
Delphine [1802]

10 What a misfortune it is to be born a woman!...Why seek for knowledge, which can prove only that our wretchedness is irremediable? If a ray of light break in upon us, it is but to make darkness more visible; to show us the now limits, the Gothic structure, the impenetrable barriers of our prison.

Maria Edgeworth (1767–1849) Irish novelist and essayist.
Leonora, Letter I [1805]

11 Man was created independent because destined to govern the family, society, and nature; while woman was made dependent, tied to hearth and home by a long chain of never-ending infirmities.

John Edward Tilt (1815–93) British doctor and president of the Obstetrical Society.
On the Preservation of the Health of Women [1851]

12 The wife who submits to sexual intercourse against her wishes or desires, virtually commits suicide; while the husband who compels it, commits murder.

Victoria Claflin Woodhull (1838–1927) US feminist, political activist, writer, and editor.
Speech, 'The Elixir of Life', American Association of Spiritualists, 1873

13 They resumed the conversation started at dinner – the emancipation and occupations of women. Levin agreed with Dolly that a girl who did not marry could always find some feminine occupation in the family. He supported this view by saying that no family can get along without women to help them, that every family, poor or rich, had to have nurses, either paid or belonging to the family.

Leo Tolstoy (1828–1910) Russian writer.
Anna Karenina [1877]

14 It takes a brave man to face a brave woman, and man's fear of women's creative energy has

never found expression more clear than in the old German clamor, renewed by the Nazis, of 'Kinder, Kuchen und Kirche' for women.
Pearl Buck (1892–1973) US novelist.
To My Daughters with Love [1967]

15   The fact is that men need women more than women need men; and so, aware of this fact, man has sought to keep woman dependent upon him economically as the only method open to him of making himself necessary to her.
Elizabeth Gould Davis ((1925–74) US librarian and writer.
The First Sex, Pt IV, Ch. 22 [1971]

16   Therefore, women should not be pushed forward or allowed to have prominence in those spheres where Allah has assigned them an inferior position. This is vital for decency and for maintaining equilibrium in the Society; otherwise there will be moral chaos, social imbalance and corruption as is being witnessed today because of the prominence of women in economic, political and social pursuits.
Muhammad Imran
Ideal Women in Islam [1979]

SUCCESS

1   A woman who is loved always has success.
Vicki Baum (1888–1960) Austrian-born US writer, playwright, and scenarist.
Grand Hotel [1931]

2   Nothing fails like success; nothing is so defeated as yesterday's triumphant Cause.
Phyllis McGinley (1905–78) US poet and humorist.
The Province of the Heart, 'How to Get Along with Men' [1959]

3   The secret of my success is that no woman has ever been jealous of me.
Elsa Maxwell (1883–1963) US songwriter, broadcaster, and actress.
The Natives were Friendly (Noël Barber) [1963]

4   I don't think success is harmful, as so many people say. Rather, I believe it indispensable to talent, if for nothing else than to increase the talent.
Jeanne Moreau (1929–   ) French actress.
The Egotists (Oriana Fallaci) [1963]

5   Unusual excellence in women was clearly associated for them with the loss of femininity, social rejection, personal or societal destruction or some combination of the above.
Matina Horner (c. 1929–   ) US psychiatrist, educator, college administrator, and writer.
Women and Success: the Anatomy of Achievement [1964]

6   The real demon is success – the anxieties engendered by this quest are relentless, degrading, corroding. What is worse, there is no end to this escalation of desire.
Marya Mannes (1904–   ) US writer.
Journal of Neuropsychiatry, 'The Roots of Anxiety in Modern Women', May 1964

7   But my biggest problem all my life was men. I never met one yet who could compete with the image the public made out of Bette Davis.
Bette Davis (Ruth Elizabeth D.; 1908–89) US actress.
Conversations in the Raw, 'Bette Davis' (Rex Reed) [1969]

8   The idea has gained currency that women have often been handicapped not only by a fear of failure – not unknown to men either – but by a fear of success as well.
Sonya Rudikoff US writer.
Commentary, 'Women and Success', Oct 1974

9   Powerful men often succeed through the help of their wives. Powerful women only succeed in spite of their husbands.
Linda Lee-Potter British journalist.
Daily Mail, 16 May 1984

10   She knows there's no success like failure
And that failure's no success at all.
Bob Dylan (Robert Allen Zimmerman; 1941–   ) US popular singer.
Love Minus Zero No Limit

SUFFRAGETTES

1   No vote can be given by lunatics, idiots, minors, aliens, females, persons convicted of perjury, subornation of perjury, bribery treating or undue influence, or by those tainted of felony or outlawed in a criminal suit.
Sir William Blackstone (1723–80) British jurist.
Commentaries on the Laws of England [1780]

2   'I wish I had a vote', said Dame Harrald. 'The women have no votes', said Mrs Collins mournfully.
'The more's the shame', said gossip Faddle.
'In this world the men have it all their own way', remarked Dame Harrald pensively.
Benjamin Disraeli (1804–81) British statesman.
A Year at Hartlebury [1834]

3   The right to vote will yet be swallowed up in the real question, viz: has woman a right to herself? It is very little to me to have the right to vote, to own property, etc., if I may not keep my body, and its uses, in my absolute right.
Lucy Stone (1818–93) US suffragette, abolitionist, editor, and lecturer.
Letter to Antoinette Brown, 1855

4   If the disenfranchised woman should still be compelled to remain the servile, docile, meekly-acquiescent, self-immolated and self-

abnegative wife, there would be no difficulty about the voting.
Tennessee Claflin (1845–1923) US feminist, writer, and editor.
'Constitutional Equality, a Right of Women' [1871]

5 As when the slaves who got their freedom had to take it over or under or through the unjust forms of the law, precisely so now must women take it to get their right to a voice in this government.
Susan B. Anthony (1820–1906) US suffragette and editor. Founder of Woman's State Temperance Society of New York.
Courtroom Speech, 18 June 1873

6 One would wish for every girl who is growing up to womanhood that it might be brought home to her by some refined and ethically-minded member of her own sex how insufferable a person woman becomes when, like a spoilt child, she exploits the indulgence of man; when she proclaims that it is his duty to serve her and to share with her his power and possessions; when she makes an outcry when he refuses to part with what is his own; and when she insists upon thrusting her society upon men everywhere.
Almroth Edward Wright (1861–1947) British bacteriologist.
The Unexpurgated Case Against Woman Suffrage [c. 1900]

7 If civilisation is to advance at all in the future, it must be through the help of women, women freed of their political shackles, women with full power to work their will in society. It was rapidly becoming clear to my mind that men regarded women as a servant class in the community, and that women were going to remain in the servant class until they lifted themselves out of it.
Emmeline Pankhurst (1858–1928) British suffragette.
My Own Story [c. 1903]

8 Women had always fought for men, and for their children. Now they were ready to fight for their own human rights. Our militant movement was established.
Emmeline Pankhurst (1858–1928) British suffragette.
My Own Story [c. 1903]

9 Give women the vote, and in five years there will be a crushing tax on bachelors.
George Bernard Shaw (1856–1950) Irish dramatist and critic.
Man and Superman, Preface [1903]

10 If all women were enfranchised they would at once swamp the votes of men.
Samuel Evans MP for Glamorgan, Wales.
House of Commons, 1906

11 If you mean that noisiness and hysteria are proofs of unfitness for public life then every Parliament in the world should close, every election meeting be prohibited, every sex be disfranchised. Did Englishmen ever get their voting right save by noisiness and hysteria?
Israel Zangwill (1864–1926) Jewish author and philanthropist.
Letter to the editor, *The Times*, 29 Oct 1906

12 We have taken this action, because as women…we realize that the condition of our sex is so deplorable that it is our duty even to break the law in order to call attention to the reasons why we do so.
Emmeline Pankhurst (1858–1928) British suffragette.
Speech in court, 21 Oct 1908 *Shoulder to Shoulder* (ed. Midge Mackenzie)

13 The man's world must become a man's and a woman's world. Why are we afraid? It is the next step forward on the path to the sunrise, and the sun is rising over a new heaven and a new earth.
Martha Thomas (1857–1935) US educator, suffragette, writer, and college administrator.
Address, North American Woman Suffrage Association, Buffalo, New York, Oct 1908

14 Nothing would induce me to vote for giving women the franchise. I am not going to be henpecked into a question of such importance.
Winston Churchill (1874–1965) British statesman.
The Amazing Mr Churchill (Robert Lewis Taylor) [c. 1910]

15 The food, so delicious, so tempting, is offered by man to the woman, representative of her sex, and for the sake of her sex, she must refuse even to taste it. So the woman triumphs over the man. The offering is the lesser sin, but the acceptance is the greater, in this revolution of womanhood each woman strives to remove the old stigma of the story of Adam and Eve. She refuses to accept the position of subjection so disastrous to the race, both morally and physically, so great a barrier to progress and evolution.
Helen Gordon Liddle
The Prison: A Sketch (An Experience of Forcible Feeding) [1911]

16 We are here to claim our rights as women, not only to be free, but to fight for freedom… Nothing but contempt is due to those people who ask us to submit to unmerited oppression. We shall not do it.

Christabel Pankhurst (1880–1958) British suffragette, evangelist, and writer.

Speech, 23 Mar 1911

17 I blushed with shame that the cup of tea should have such power over me. Would one little sip matter. Quite possibly no one was hunger striking. I stretched my tongue and curling it let it touch the level of the tea, in some sort as a cat lappeth, and drew it in…About ten minutes later the door swung open. My head was still buried in my hands in abject shame. A wardress tore off the coverings and handed the untasted (?) refreshment to a wardress outside. 'That's the seventeenth that hasn't touched anything,' I heard her say in gruesome tones to the other.

S. I. Stevenson

No Other Way [c. 1911]

18 Are you who are in authority at the Home Office unaware that the modern woman writes as well as sews? Perhaps you may be anxious to press upon us some permanent prejudice of your own in the form of the needle rather than the pen as a suitable implement for women. If this be so may I beg you to choose some other time and place for exalting the needle at the expense of the pen?

Marion Wallace-Dunlop

Written during her imprisonment for suffragist activities. Letter to the home secretary, 5 Dec 1911

19 It always seems to me when the anti-suffrage members of the Government criticize militancy in women that it is very like beasts of prey reproaching the gentler animals who turn in desperate resistance when at the point of death.

Emmeline Pankhurst (1858–1928) British suffragette, founder of Women's Social and Political Union (1905).

Speech, 'I Incite This Meeting to Rebellion', 17 Oct 1912

20 Over one thousand women have gone to prison in the course of this agitation, have suffered their imprisonment, have come out of prison injured in health, weakened in body, but not in spirit.

Emmeline Pankhurst (1858–1928) British suffragette, founder of Women's Social and Political Union (1905).

Speech to the Court, 2 Apr 1913

21 It is better, as far as getting the vote is concerned I believe, to have a small, united group than an immense debating society.

Alice Paul (1885–1977) US suffragette.

Letter to Eunice R. Oberly, 6 Mar 1914

22 What we suffragettes aspire to be when we are enfranchised is ambassadors of freedom to women in other parts of the world, who are not so free as we are.

Christabel Pankhurst (1880–1958) British suffragette, evangelist, and writer.

Speech, 'America and the War', Carnegie Hall, New York, 25 Oct 1915

23 We want the vote so that we may serve our country better. We want the vote so that we shall be more faithful and more true to our allies. We want the vote so that we may help to maintain the cause of Christian civilisation for which we entered this war. We want the vote so that in future such wars if possible may be averted.

Emmeline Pankhurst (1858–1928) British suffragette, founder of Women's Social and Political Union (1905).

Speech, Queen's Hall, 23 Apr 1917

24 Prison. It was not prison for me. Hunger-strikes. They had no fears for me. Cat and Mouse Act. I could have laughed. A prison cell was quiet – no telephone, no paper, no speeches, no sea sickness, no sleepless nights. I could lie on my plank bed all day and all night and return once more to my day dreams.

Annie Kenney (fl. 1910s) English suffragist.

Memoirs of a Militant [1924]

25 The vote, I thought, means nothing to women. We should be armed.

Edna O'Brien (1936–) Irish novelist.

Quoted as epigraph to *Fear of Flying* (Erica Jong), Ch. 16 [1973]

SULLIVAN, Annie (1866–1936)

US teacher. Partially-sighted, she graduated from the Perkins Institution for the Blind in Boston in 1886. The following year she was engaged as a governess to Helen Keller, who had been made blind and deaf by a childhood illness. She succeeded in teaching Helen Keller to communicate and, in the following years, gained an international reputation as Keller displayed a gifted intelligence graduating, with Annie Sullivan's help, from Radcliffe College, in 1904. After an unsuccessful marriage, Annie Sullivan and her pupil embarked on a number of worldwide lecture trips, increasing public awareness of the problems of the blind.

1 I am beginning to suspect all elaborate and special systems of education. They seem to me to be built upon the supposition that every child is a kind of idiot who must be taught to think.

Letter, 8 May 1887

2 It is a rare privilege to watch the birth, growth, and first feeble struggles of a living mind.

Letter, 22 May 1887

3 It's queer how ready people always are with advice in any real or imaginary emergency, and no matter how many times experience has shown them to be wrong, they continue to set forth their opinions, as if they had received them from the Almighty!
Letter, 12 June 1887

4 Language grows out of life, out of its needs and experiences...*Language* and *knowledge* are indissolubly connected; they are interdependent. Good work in language presupposes and depends on a real knowledge of things.
Speech, American Association to Promote the Teaching of Speech to the Deaf, July 1894

SUPERIORITY

1 Spare your ships, and do not risk a battle; for these people are as much superior to your people in seamanship, as men to women.
Artemisia (fl. 480 BC) Carian queen of Halicarnassus and military leader.
The people she was referring to were the Greeks. *The Persian Wars*, Bk VIII (Herodotus) [c. 480 BC]

2 You are quite right in maintaining the general inferiority of the female sex; at the same time many women are in many things superior to many men, though speaking generally what you say is true.
Plato (427–347 BC) Greek philosopher.
Republic [4th century BC]

3 I am surprised, my only love, that contrary to custom in letter-writing and, indeed, to the natural order, you have thought fit to put my name before yours in the greeting which heads your letter, so that we have woman before man.
Heloise (c.1100–c. 1163) French abbess.
The Letters of Abelard and Heloise [12th century]

4 It is an amazing thing to see in our city the wife of a shoemaker, or a butcher, or a porter dressed in silk with chains of gold at the throat, with pearls and a ring of good value...and then in contrast to see her husband cutting the meat, all smeared with cow's blood, poorly dressed... but whoever considers this carefully will find it reasonable, because it is necesary that the lady, even if low-born and humble, be draped with such clothes for her natural excellence and dignity, and that the man less adorned as if a slave, or a little ass, born to her service.
Lucrezia Marinella (fl. 1600) Italian writer.
The Nobility and Excellence of Women together with the Defects and Deficiencies of Men [1600]

5 For to make woman our superior in all the qualities proper to her sex, and to make her our equal in all the rest, what is this but to transfer to the woman the superiority which nature has given to her husband?
Jean-Jacques Rousseau (1712–78) French philosopher.
Émile [1762]

6 It is apparent that we cannot speak of inferiority and superiority, but only of specific differences in aptitudes and personality between the sexes. These differences are largely the result of cultural and other experiential factors.
Anne Anastasi (1908–) US educator.
Differential Psychology [1937]

7 There was, I think, never any reason to believe in any innate superiority of the male, except his superior muscle.
Bertrand Russell (1872–1970) British philosopher.
Unpopular Essays [1950]

8 Society, being codified by man, decrees that woman is inferior: she can do away with this inferiority only by destroying the male's superiority.
Simone de Beauvoir (1908–86) French writer and feminist.
Le Deuxième Sexe (*The Second Sex*) [1949]

9 When you are born and they tell you 'what a pity that you are so clever, so intelligent, so beautiful but you are not a man', you are ashamed of your conditon as a woman. I wanted to act like a man because the man was the master.
Melina Mercouri (c. 1925–) Greek actress and political activist.
Ms, Oct 1973

10 With the old rules for masculine superiority fading in the public sphere, how can men face the feminine superiority they have posited in the private world?
Elizabeth Janeway (1913–) US writer.
Between Myth and Morning [1974]

11 Freud, living at a time when women were proving their heads were no different from men's, substituted the penis for the head as the organ of male superiority, an organ women could never prove they had.
Una Stannard (1927–) US educator and writer.
Mrs Man [1977]

12 It might be marvellous to be a man – then I could stop worrying about what's fair to women and just cheerfully assume I was superior, and that they had all been born to iron my shirts. Better still, I could be an Irish man – then I would have all the privileges of being male without giving up the right to be wayward, temperamental and an appealing minority.
Katharine Whitehorn (1926–) British journalist.
Observer, 29 June 1980

TALENT AND GENIUS
See also INTELLECT; INTELLECTUALS; INTELLIGENCE

1 Taste is the feminine of genius.
Edward Fitzgerald (1809–83) British poet.
Letter to J. R. Lowell, Oct 1877

2 A career is born in public – talent in privacy.
Marilyn Monroe (Norma Jean Baker; 1926–62) US actress.
The First Ms Reader (ed. Francine Klagsbrun) [1972]

TAXATION
1 I am humbly following in your footsteps and having a row with the Government over the iniquity of the Marriage Tax in the form of super-tax…our incomes being added together we are liable for supertax which we are refusing to pay on the grounds of morality as I consider in a Christian country it is an immoral and outrageous act to tax me because I am living in Holy matrimony instead of as my husband's mistress.
Marie Stopes (1880–1958) British birth-control campaigner.
Letter to George Bernard Shaw, 29 June 1925

2 A woman's income chargeable to tax shall…for any year during which she is a married woman living with her husband be deemed for income tax purposes to be his income and not to be her income.
Income and Corporation Taxes Act, 1970

3 I earn and pay my own way as a great many women do today. Why should unmarried women be discriminated against – unmarried men are not.
Dinah Shore (1920–) US singer and actress.
Los Angeles Times, 16 Apr 1974

4 The IRS has stolen from me over the past 20 years because I am single. It is unconstitutional to impose a penalty tax of 40 percent on me because I have no husband.
Vivien Kellems (1896–1975) US industrialist, feminist, and lecturer.
Reader's Digest, Oct 1975

5 It is ironic that the wife who made Britain great again, and who is the leader of the Western World, has to get her husband to sign her tax form.
Jacqui Lait
Referring to Margaret Thatcher. Speech, Oct 1987

6 Ever since I was first married it had struck me as ridiculous that my husband should be legally responsible for dealing with the Inland Revenue on my behalf.
Lee Crooke British housewife.
Referring to the new taxation law in Britain, effective from Apr 1990, that married women should be taxed separately from their husbands. *Money Factor*, Aug 1990

TERESA, Mother (Agnes Gonxha Bajahiu; 1910–)
Albanian-born Roman Catholic nun and missionary, now an Indian citizen. After deciding to be a missionary at the age of 12, she joined the Sisters of Loretto in Ireland in 1928, shortly afterwards sailing for India as a teacher. After nursing training, she founded her Order of Missionaries of Charity (1948) in a pilgrim hostel given to her by the municipal authorities of Calcutta. Her order received official recognition from the Catholic Church in 1950. The order opened many centres to serve the blind, aged, crippled, and dying; the leper colony of Shanti Nagar (Town of Peace) was built near Asanol, partly funded by the proceeds from Pope Paul VI's car, which he donated to Mother Teresa on a visit to India in 1964 and which she immediately raffled. In 1968 she was summoned to Rome, where she founded a home staffed primarily by Indian nuns. The Missionaries of Charity now operate around 60 centres in Calcutta, and more than 200 centres worldwide. For her work she received the Nobel Peace prize (1979), the Bharat Ratna (Star of India; 1980), and an honorary OM (1983).

Quotations about Mother Teresa
1 She is among the last of the great missionary superstars.
Arun Chacko *The Times*, 14 Aug 1983

2 Without her faith Mother Teresa would be remarkable only for her ordinariness, and she rejoices in this fact for it is evidence of the power for which she and many others with her are but channels.
Kathryn Spink *For the Brotherhood of Man Under the Fatherhood of God*, 1981

Quotations by Mother Teresa
3 The poor are our brothers and sisters…people in the world who need love, who need care, who have to be wanted.
Time, 'Saints Among Us', 29 Dec 1975

4 Loneliness and the feeling of being unwanted is the most terrible poverty.
Time, 'Saints Among Us', 29 Dec 1975

5 To keep a lamp burning we have to keep putting oil in it.
Time, 'Saints Among Us', 29 Dec 1975

6 I would not give a baby from one of my homes for adoption to a couple who use contraception. People who use contraceptives do not understand love.

Radio broadcast, while on a visit to London.

7 This is not for me. The honour is for the poor.

Said on receiving the Order of Merit, 24 Nov 1983. *The Sunday Times*, 3 Dec 1989

TERESA OF AVILA, St (1515–82)

Spanish Carmelite nun; feast day October 15. In 1529 her mother died and, despite her father's opposition, she entered the Carmelite Convent of the Incarnation at Ávila in around 1535. She remained in the convent until 1555, when she underwent a religious awakening. This led to her concentrating on reforming the Carmelite order, restoring its life to the original observance of austerity. In 1562 she opened St Joseph's, the first convent of the Carmelite Reform, where she insisted on poverty and complete withdrawal from life. In 1567 she met St John of the Cross (a poet and mystic) whom she encouraged to initiate Carmelite Reform for men. She spent the rest of her life in establishing 16 more convents throughout Spain. Her writings include *Book of the Foundations* (1610), which describes the establishment of her convents, *The Way of Perfection* (1583), and *The Interior Castle* (1588). She was canonized in 1622, and in 1970 Pope Paul VI elevated her to doctor of the church, the first women to be honoured in this way.

1 Be gentle to all and stern with yourself.

Selected Writings of St Teresa of Avila (ed. William J. Doheny), 'The Book of Foundations'

2 Humility must always be doing its work like a bee making its honey in the hive: without humility all will be lost.

Selected Writings of St Teresa of Avila (ed. William J. Doheny), 'Interior Castle'

3 There seem to me a great many blessings which come from true poverty and I should be sorry to be deprived of them.

Selected Writings of St Teresa of Avila (ed. William J. Doheny), 'Spiritual Relations'

4 The hour I have long wished for is now come.

Last words. *Distinguished Women Writers* (Virginia Moore)

TERRY, Dame Ellen (1847–1928)

British actress. Born in Coventry, she was the second surviving daughter of a theatrical family. She made her debut at the age of nine as Mamillius in *The Winter's Tale*. The play was produced by Charles Kean, with whose company she remained until 1859, when she joined the repertory company playing at the Theatre Royal, Bristol. In 1864 she left the stage to marry the artist G. F. Watts, but within a year the marriage failed and she returned to the stage, appearing opposite Henry Irving in *The Taming of the Shrew* in 1867. Her comeback was not successful, and in 1868 she again gave up the theatre, this time to live with the architect and theatrical designer Edward Godwin, by whom she had two children. In 1875 they parted and she returned to the stage to support her children. In 1878 she began her long distinguished association with Henry Irving, playing opposite him in all the major Shakespearean and other classical roles. In the 1890s she began her renowned correspondence with Bernard Shaw and, after parting from Irving in 1902, appeared in several of Shaw's plays, notably in the role of Lady Cecily Wayneflete in *Captain Brassbound's Conversion* (1905), which he wrote with her in mind. In 1907 she married the US actor James Carew, with whom she remained until 1910. In her later years she acted less and turned to lecturing on Shakespeare, touring America and Australia in 1910 and 1911, respectively. Her final performance was in *Crossings* in 1925, at the Lyric, Hammersmith. She was made a DBE in the same year.

Quotations about Terry

1 She was an extremely beautiful girl and as innocent as a rose. When Watts kissed her, she took for granted she was going to have a baby.

George Bernard Shaw (1856–1950) Irish dramatist and critic. *Days with Bernard Shaw* (Stephen Winston)

2 One may say that her marriages were adventures and her friendships enduring.

George Bernard Shaw (1856–1950) Irish dramatist and critic. *Ellen Terry and Bernard Shaw, A Correspondence* (ed. C. St J. Constable)

Quotations by Terry

3 Wonderful women! Have you ever thought how much we all, and women especially, owe to Shakespeare for his vindication of women in these fearless, high-spirited, resolute and intelligent heroines?

Four Lectures on Shakespeare, 'The Triumphant Women'

4 Imagination! imagination! I put it first years ago, when I was asked what qualities I thought necessary for success upon the stage.

The Story of My Life, Ch. 2

5 What is a diary as a rule? A document useful to the person who keeps it, dull to the contemporary who reads it, invaluable to the student, centuries afterwards, who treasures it!

The Story of My Life, Ch. 14

THATCHER, Margaret Hilda (1925–)

British Conservative politician. Born in Grantham, the daughter of a grocer, she was educated locally and then studied chemistry followed by law at Somerville College, Oxford. She became a member of parliament in 1959, being appointed minister of pensions and national insurance in 1961. From 1970 to 1974 she was secretary of state for education. In 1975, while in opposition, she successfully challenged Edward Heath for the Conservative Party leadership. In 1979 she became the first woman prime minister of the United Kingdom, a post she held until her resignation in 1990.

She is chiefly remembered for her strong personality and her right-wing policies. At home she favoured an economic policy of monetarism, low government spending, and privatization. Abroad she had a reputation as a strong leader, mainly based on her stand during the Falklands War (1982). Her attitudes earned her a number of nicknames including the (originally Russian) epithet 'the Iron Lady'.

Quotations about Thatcher

1 Mrs Thatcher is a woman of common views but uncommon abilities.

Julian Critchley (1930–) British Conservative politician. *The Times*, 'Profile'

2 Attila the Hen.

Clement Freud (1924–) British Liberal politician and broadcaster. BBC Radio programme, *The News Quiz*

3 She approaches the problems of our country with all the one-dimensional subtlety of a comic-strip.

Denis Healey (1917–) British Labour politician. Speech, House of Commons, 22 May 1979

4 Margaret Thatcher's great strength seems to be the better people know her, the better they like her. But, of course, she has one great disadvantage – she is a daughter of the people and looks trim, as the daughters of the people desire to be. Shirley Williams has such an advantage over her because she's a member of the upper-middle class and can achieve that kitchen-sink-revolutionary look that one cannot get unless one has been to a really good school.

Rebecca West (Cicely Isabel Fairfield; 1892–1983) British novelist and journalist. Said in an interview with Jilly Cooper. *The Sunday Times*, 25 July 1976

Quotations by Thatcher

5 If a woman like Eva Peron with no ideals can get that far, think how far I can go with all the ideals that I have.

The Sunday Times, 1980

6 U-turn if you want to. The lady's not for turning.

Speech, Conservative Conference, 1980

7 No one would have remembered the Good Samaritan if he'd only had good intentions. He had money as well.

Television interview, 1980

8 Pennies do not come from heaven. They have to be earned here on earth.

Sunday Telegraph, 1982

9 I don't mind how much my ministers talk – as long as they do what I say.

The Times, 1987

10 I fight on, I fight to win.

Statement, 21 Nov 1990

11 Having consulted widely among colleagues, I have concluded that the unity of the Party and the prospects of victory in a General Election would be better served if I stood down to enable Cabinet colleagues to enter the ballot for the leadership.

Statement, 22 Nov 1990

TOLERANCE

1 Do you know why God withheld the sense of humour from women?
That we may love you instead of laughing at you.

Mrs Patrick Campbell (1865–1940) British actress. To a man [1940]. *The Life of Mrs Pat* (M. Peters)

2 Women receive
the insults of men
with tolerance
having been bitten
in the nipple
by their toothless gums.

Dilys Laing (1906–60) Canadian poet. *Collected Poems*, 'Veterans' [1967]

TRUTH

1 There was altogether too much candour in married life; it was an indelicate modern idea, and frequently led to upsets in a household, if not divorce.

Muriel Spark (1918–) British writer and poet. *Memento Mori*, Ch. 12 [1959]

2 I tore myself away from the safe comfort of certainities through my love for truth; and truth rewarded me.

Simone de Beauvoir (1908–86) French writer and feminist. *All Said and Done* [1974]

UNFAITHFULNESS

See also ADULTERY

1 Why should marriage bring only tears?
All I wanted was a man
With a single heart,

And we would stay together
As our hair turned white,
Not somebody always after wriggling fish
With his big bamboo rod.
Chuo Wên-chūn (?179–117 BC) Chinese poet.
Orchid Boat, Women Poets of China (Kenneth Rexroth and Ling Chung) [2nd century BC]

2 No man worth having is true to his wife, or can be true to his wife, or ever was, or ever will be so.
John Vanbrugh (1664–1726) English architect and dramatist.
The Relapse, III:2 [1696]

3 Translations (like wives) are seldom faithful if they are in the least attractive.
Roy Campbell (1901–57) South African poet.
Poetry Review [1949]

4 To the man-in-the-street, who, I'm sorry to say
Is a keen observer of life,
The word Intellectual suggests straight away
A man who's untrue to his wife.
W. H. Auden (1907–73) British poet.
Note on Intellectuals

5 Reading someone else's newspaper is like sleeping with someone else's wife. Nothing seems to be precisely in the right place, and when you find what you are looking for, it is not clear then how to respond to it.
Malcolm Bradbury (1932–) British academic and novelist.
Stepping Westward, Bk I, Ch. 1 [1975]

VICTORIA (1819–1901)

Queen of Great Britain (1837–1901) and Empress of India (1876–1901). Daughter of Edward, Duke of Kent, she succeeded her uncle William IV. On 10 October 1839 she met her cousin, Prince Albert, for the first time. She proposed to him five days later and they were married on 10 February 1840. She was devoted to her husband, by whom she had nine children although she hated both childbirth and motherhood. After Albert's death in 1861 she retired into seclusion, from which she did not emerge until her Golden Jubilee in 1887. In the early years of her reign she was greatly influenced by the Whig prime minister Lord Melbourne but after her marriage, Albert became the greatest influence on her political views. Her reign saw the transition of Britain to a mass democracy and a decline in royal power. Although she was unpopular for parts of her reign, especially during her years of seclusion, in her last years she was seen as the symbol of imperial unity, which enabled her to restore dignity and popularity to the monarchy.

Quotations about Victoria

1 Queen Victoria in her eighties was more known, more revered, and a more important part of the life of the country than she had ever been. Retirement, for a monarch, is not a good idea.
Charles, Prince of Wales (1948–) Eldest son of Elizabeth II

2 Nothing could be more amiable and agreeable than she was. Can you wish for a better account of a little tit of 18 made all at once into a Queen?
Thomas Creevey (1768–1838) British politician and diarist. Letter to Elizabeth Ord, 5 Aug 1837

3 She's more of a man than I expected.
Henry James (1843–1916) US novelist. *Diary* (E. M. Forster)

4 Nowadays a parlourmaid as ignorant as Queen Victoria was when she came to the throne would be classed as mentally defective.
George Bernard Shaw (1856–1950) Irish dramatist and critic.

Quotations by Victoria

5 I will be good.
On learning that she would succeed to the throne. Remark to her governess, Louise (afterwards Baroness) Lehzen, 11 Mar 1830

6 He speaks to Me as If I was a public meeting.
Referring to Gladstone. *Collections and Recollections* (G. W. E. Russell), Ch. 14

7 A strange, horrible business, but I suppose good enough for Shakespeare's day.
Giving her opinion of *King Lear*. *Living Biographies of Famous Rulers* (H. Thomas)

8 Move Queen Anne? Most certainly not! Why it might some day be suggested that *my* statue should be moved, which I should much dislike.
Said at the time of her Diamond Jubilee (1897), when it was suggested that the statue of Queen Anne should be moved from outside St. Paul's. *Men, Women and Things* (Duke of Portland), Ch. 5

9 We are not amused!
Attrib.

VIOLENCE

See also RAPE

1 In a number of cases men may be excused for the injuries they inflict on their wives, nor should the law intervene. Provided he neither kills nor maims her, it is legal for a man to beat his wife when she wrongs him – for instance, when she is about to surrender her body to another man, when she contradicts or abuses him, or when she refuses, like a decent woman, to obey his reasonable commands.
Philippe de Beaumanoir (1246–96) French jurist.
Customs of the People of Beauvais [13th century]

2 Blows are fitter for beasts than for rational creatures.
Hannah Wooley (1623–c. 1675) English pioneer educator and governess.
The Gentlewoman's Companion [1675]

3 Brute force, the law of violence, rules to a great extent in the poor man's domicile; and woman is little more than his drudge.
Sarah Moore Grimké (1792–1873) US abolitionist and women's rights pioneer.
Letter from Brookline, Sept 1837

4 'Can I have a black eye, too, Ma?' asks the little girl. 'Wait till you're old enough to get married, pet,' says her mother.
Cartoon caption [1896]

5 CELINE. Don't you read the paper? Don't you know that men don't hit their wives any more?
Christiane Rochefort (1917–   ) French scenarist, filmmaker, and writer.
Les Stances à Sophie [1970]

6 The man has both the right and duty to chastise his girlfriend or wife in certain circumstances. Indeed, it is perfectly natural.
Professor J. M. V. Browner
Vive la Différence [1981]

7 'I never talked to anyone about it because I didn't think they'd believe me. When everyone says how nice your husband is, you begin to think that it's you that must be in the wrong. I was embarrassed and ashamed when it all came out but at the same time I was relieved because it showed I wasn't crackers.
Report of the battered wife who suffered for eight years before she threatened her husband with divorce. *Independent on Sunday*, 24 Nov 1991

8 The Canadians have declared that domestic violence is not a feminist issue but a matter of human rights.
Caroline Moorehead British journalist.
Independent Magazine, 7 Dec 1991

VIRGINITY

1 As a result of visions, many people choke to death, more women than men, for the nature of women is less courageous and is weaker. And virgins who do not take a husband at the appropriate time for marriage experience these visions more frequently, especially at the time of their first monthly period.
Hippocrates (c. 460–c. 377 BC) Greek physician.
On Virgins [4th century BC]

2 The error of Jovian consisted in holding virginity not to be preferable to marriage. This error is refuted above all by the example of Christ Who both chose a virgin for His mother and remained Himself a virgin.
St Thomas Aquinas (1225–74) Italian theologian.
Summa Theologica [13th century]

3 It is one of the superstitions of the human mind to have imagined that virginity could be a virtue.
Voltaire (François-Marie Arouet; 1694–1778) French writer.
Notebooks [1778]

4 With regard to sexual relations, we should note that in giving herself to intercourse, the girl renounces her honour. This is not, however, the case with men, for they have yet another sphere for their ethical activity beyond that of the family.
Hegel (1770–1831) German philospher.
Referring to unmarried girls. *The Philosophy of Right* [1821]

5 Although it is true that the hymen is often relaxed in virgins, or broken and diminished by accidents independent of all coition, such accidents are very rare, and the absence of the hymen is assuredly a good ground of strong suspicion.
T. Bell British doctor.
Kalogynomia [1821]

6 A simple maiden in her flower
Is worth a hundred coats-of-arms.
Alfred, Lord Tennyson (1809–92) British poet.
Lady Clara Vere de Vere, II [1833]

7 Nothing is more horrible than the terror, the sufferings, and the revulsion of a poor girl, ignorant of the facts of life, who finds herself raped by a brute. As far as possible we bring them up as saints, and then we hand them over as if they were fillies.
George Sand (Aurore Dupin, Baronne Dudevant; 1804–76) French novelist.
Letter to Hippolyte Chatiron, 1843

8 After the operator has cut out the clitoris and the lips of the labia…she then sews up the parts with a pack needle and a thread of sheepskin, while a tin tube is inserted for the passage of urine. Before marriage the bridegroom trains himself for a month on beef, honey, and milk; for if he can open the bride with his natural weapon he is a mighty sworder. If he fails, he tries penetration with his fingers, and by way of last resort, whips out his knife and cuts the parts open. The sufferings of the bride must be severe.
Richard Burton (1821–90) British explorer and scholar.
Referring to the circumcision of Arab women. *Love, War, and Fancy; Notes to the Arabian Nights* [c. 1888]

9 Are there still virgins? One is tempted to answer no. There are only girls who have not yet crossed the line, because they want to preserve their market value…Call them virgins if you wish, these travelers in transit.
Françoise Giroud (1916–) Swiss-born French politician, journalist, editor, and French Minister of Women.
Coronet, Nov 1960

10 I used to be Snow White…but I drifted.
Mae West (1892–1980) US actress.
The Wit and Wisdom of Mae West (ed. J. Weintraub) [1967]

11 I'll wager you that in 10 years it will be fashionable again to be a virgin.
Barbara Cartland (1902–) British romantic novelist.
Observer, 'Sayings of the Week', 20 June 1976

12 I said 10 years ago that in 10 years time it would be smart to be a virgin. Now everyone is back to virgins again.
Barbara Cartland (1902–) British romantic novelist.
Observer, 'Sayings of the Week', 12 July 1987

13 The men you meet aren't naive enough to expect virgins but they certainly don't want to hear about the 'ghosts' of your past life. Yet I can't imagine a man sticking around much after two or three months if you hadn't slept together.
Sacha Cowlam (1963–)
Out of the Doll's House (Angela Holdsworth) [1988]

VIRTUE

1 A fair woman without virtue is like palled wine.
Proverb

2 Who can find a virtuous woman? for her price is far above rubies
The heart of her husband doth safely trust in her, so that he shall have no need of spoil.
She will do him good and not evil all the days of her life.
Bible: Proverbs
31:10–12

3 You see, leaving women to do what they like is not just to lose *half* the battle (as it may seem): a woman's natural potential for virtue is inferior to a man's, so she's proportionately a greater danger, perhaps even twice as great.
Plato (429–347 BC) Greek philosopher.
Laws, VI [4th century BC]

4 MRS. PLOTWELL. Virtue, thou shining Jewel of my Sex – Thou precious Thing, that none knows how to value as they ought, while they enjoy it, but like spendthrift Heirs, when they have wasted all their Store, wou'd give the World they cou'd retrieve their lost Estate.
Susannah Centlivre (c. 1667–1723) English poet, playwright, and actress.
The Beau's Duel, V:1 [1700]

5 Unhappy as the event must be for Lydia, we may draw from it this useful lesson: that loss of virtue in a female is irretrievable; that one false step involves her in endless ruin; that her reputation is no less brittle than it is beautiful; and that she cannot be too much guarded in her behavior towards the undeserving of the other sex.
Jane Austen (1775–1817) British novelist.
Pride and Prejudice, Ch. 47 [1813]

6 Prostitution is a blight on the human race…for if you men did not impose chastity on women as a necessary virtue while refusing to practise it yourselves, they would not be rejected by society for yielding to the sentiments of their hearts, nor would seduced, deceived and abandoned girls be forced into prostitution.
Flora Tristan (1803–44) French writer, feminist, and revolutionary socialist.
The London Journal of Flora Tristan [1842]

7 Be good, sweet maid, and let who can be clever;
Do lovely things, not dream them, all day long;
And so make Life, and Death, and that For Ever,
One grand sweet song.
Charles Kingsley (1819–75) British writer.
A Farewell. To C. E. G.

8 Most good women are hidden treasures who are only safe because nobody looks for them.
Dorothy Parker (1893–1967) US writer.
The New York Times, Obituary, 8 June 1967

9 Woman's virtue is man's greatest invention.
Cornelia Otis Skinner (1901–79) US stage actress.
Attrib. [1979]

VOTE

See EMANCIPATION; SUFFRAGETTES

WAR

1 He is wanted and must go. You and I, Kate, have also service to do. Food must be prepared for the hungry; for before to-morrow night, hundreds, I hope thousands, will be on their way to join the continental forces.
Mary Draper (c. 1718–1810) US patriot.
She was referring to her son; Kate was her daughter. Response to a call to arms [1776]

2 There is no force in the plea, that 'if women vote they must fight.' Moreover, war is not the normal state of the human family in its higher

development, but merely a feature of barbarism lasting on through the transition of the race, from the savage to the scholar.
Elizabeth Cady Stanton (1815–1902) US suffragette and abolitionist.
History of Woman Suffrage, Vol. I (with Susan B. Anthony and Mathilda Gage) [1881]

3 We have always borne part of the weight of war, and the major part…Men have made boomerangs, bows, swords, or guns with which to destroy one another; we have made the men who destroyed and were destroyed!…*We pay the first cost on all human life.*
Olive Schreiner (1855–1920) South African writer, feminist, and social critic.
Woman and Labor, Ch. 4 [1911]

4 Where do all the women who have watched so carefully over the lives of their beloved ones get the heroism to send them to face the canon?
Käthe Kollwitz (1867–1945) German painter, sculptor, and graphic artist.
Diary entry, 27 Aug 1914

5 Suddenly, without any warning a German plane flew in low over the house and released a bomb. I shouted to the photographer who was under the black velvet cloth trying to take the photo, 'Look out, he's dropping bombs.' The man just shouted back from the cloth, 'Never mind about the bomb – just SMILE.' One of the bombs fell quite near, hitting a Church a little way up the road. My veil was torn when I tried to get to shelter in our Church. As we walked down the nave to the drone of planes and the noise of gunfire overhead, I heard Christopher's Mother trying to whistle the wedding march for us. Even she realised how we longed for all the trimmings.
Joan Veazey (1914–) British calligraphist.
Describing her war-time wedding. *People at War* (ed. Michael Moynihan) [1940]

6 As a woman I can't go to war, and I refuse to send anyone else.
Jeannette Rankin (1880–1973) US suffragette, pacifist, and politician.
Jeannette Rankin: First Lady in Congress, Prologue [c. 1941]

7 Don't worry because you can't give the children the foods you used to give them, foods such as fruit and meat. A meal of bread, margarine, cheese, milk, and a salad of raw, shredded vegetables is grand for children. This is, in fact, the Health Meal…which greatly improved the health of the Norwegian school-children before the war. The Health Meal is ship-saving, fuel-saving, and easy to prepare.
Pamphlet from the Ministry of Food. *Food Facts*, 109 [c. 1942]

8 I am not elevating women to sainthood, nor am I suggesting that all women share the same views, or that all women are good and all men bad. Women have screamed for war. Women, like men, have stoned black children going to integrated schools. Women have been and are prejudiced, narrowminded, reactionary, even violent. *Some* women. They, of course, have a right to vote and a right to run for office. I will defend that right, but I will not support them or vote for them.
Bella Abzug (1920–) US lawyer and congresswoman.
Speech, National Women's Political Caucus, Washington, DC, 10 July 1971

9 Everyone is always talking about our defense effort in terms of defending women and children, but no one ever asks the women and children what they think.
Patricia Schroeder (1940–) US politician, lawyer, and educator.
American Political Women [1980]

WEALTH

1 A poor beauty finds more lovers than husbands.
Proverb

2 Wealth covers sin – the poor
Are naked as a pin.
Kassia (fl. c. 840) Byzantine poet.
Women Poets of the World (eds Joanna Bankier and Deirdre Lashgari) [c. 840]

3 Nothing melts a Woman's Heart like gold.
Susannah Centlivre (c. 1667–1723) English poet, playwright, and actress.
The Basset-Table, IV [1705]

4 Maidens, like moths, are ever caught by glare,
And Mammon wins his way where Seraphs might despair.
Lord Byron (1788–1824) British poet.
Childe Harold's Pilgrimage, I [1812]

5 I think people still want to marry rich. Girls especially…It's simple. Don't date poor boys. Go where the rich are…You don't have to be rich to go where they go.
Sheilah Graham (c. 1908–) British-born US writer.
Los Angeles Times, 13 Oct 1974

6 If one is rich and one's a woman, one can be quite misunderstood.
Katharine Graham (1917–) US newspaper publisher and editor.
Ms, 'The Power That Didn't Corrupt', Oct 1974

7 If women didn't exist, all the money in the world would have no meaning.
Aristotle Onassis (1906–75) Greek businessman. Attrib. [1975]

WEBB, Beatrice (1858–1943)

British economist and socialist. The eighth daughter of a wealthy and influential family, she questioned, at an early age, the conventions of her father's business world. This suspicion of privilege led her into social work in London, where she soon learned of the realities of lower-class life; this experience enabled her to assist her cousin, Charles Booth, to research his study *The Life and Labour of the People of London*. In 1891 she published *The Cooperative Movement* in Britain. In 1892 she married the socialist Sidney Webb, with whom she produced *The History of Trade Unionism* (1894) and its sequel *Industrial Democracy* (1897). They established the London School of Economics in 1895 and the *New Statesman* in 1913. In 1914 she and her husband became members of the Labour Party; Beatrice also held a number of responsible positions, including membership of the War Cabinet Committee on Women in Industry (1918–19), being a JP in London (1919–27), and serving on the Lord Chancellor's Advisory Committee for Women Justices (1919–20). Her *Constitution for the Socialist Commonwealth of Great Britain* was published in 1920. In 1932 she and her husband visited Russia, where they were so impressed by the workings of a socialist state that they spent the next three years writing *Soviet Communism: A New Civilisation* (1935). In 1928 they retired to their Hampshire home, where Beatrice died.

Quotations about Webb

1 When a man said to Beatrice Webb, 'Much of this talk about feminism is nonsense; any woman would rather be beautiful than clever,' she replied, 'Quite true. But that is because so many men are stupid and so few are blind'.
Daily Express, 14 Oct 1947

2 Cold, commanding, too often right to be pleasant.
Hesketh Pearson (1887–1964) British biographer. *Bernard Shaw*

3 There's no more mysticism in Beatrice than in a steam engine.
H. G. Wells (1866–1946) British writer. 'The Webbs as I Saw Them' (Desmond MacCarthy)

Quotations by Webb

4 Religion is love; in no case is it logic.
My Apprenticeship, Ch. 2

5 If I ever felt inclined to be timid as I was going into a room full of people, I would say to myself, 'You're the cleverest member of one of the cleverest families in the cleverest class of the cleverest nation in the world, why should you be frightened?'
Portraits from Memory (Bertrand Russell), 'Sidney and Beatrice Webb'

WEIL, Simone (1909–43)

French revolutionary, writer, and philosopher. Born in Paris, she showed a social awareness at a very young age. During World War I, when offered sugar, she refused because the French soldiers at the Front had none. This identification with the poor and deprived was a recurrent theme throughout her life. She worked for a year on the shopfloor in a Renault factory (1934–35), then for the International Brigade in Spain (1936). Here, her pacifist principles would not allow her to fight although she did become the camp cook. During World War II she worked with the resistance movement in England. She died from tuberculosis as a result of her resolution to restrict herself to the same diet as the inmates of the Nazi labour camps. Her works, most of which were published posthumously, include *La Pesanteur et la grâce* (1949; *Gravity and Grace*, 1952) and *Cahiers* (1952–55; *Notebooks*, 1956).

1 Culture is an instrument wielded by professors to manufacture professors, who when their turn comes will manufacture professors.
The Need for Roots

2 The word 'revolution' is a word for which you kill, for which you die, for which you send the labouring masses to their death, but which does not possess any content.
Oppression and Liberty, 'Reflections Concerning the Causes of Liberty and Social Oppression'

3 But not even Marx is more precious to us than the truth.
Oppression and Liberty, 'Revolution Proletarienne'

4 The future is made of the same stuff as the present.
On Science, Necessity, and the Love of God (ed. Richard Rees), 'Some Thoughts on the Love of God'

WELDON, Fay (1931–)

British novelist, dramatist, and screenwriter. Born in Worcester and educated at St Andrews University, she worked in advertising before becoming a full-time writer. She is best known for her novels, including *The Fat Woman's Joke* (1967), *Praxis* (1978), *The Life and Loves of a She-Devil* (1983), *Leader of the Band* (1988), and *Darcy's Utopia* (1990). Her novels reflect the rising feminist consciousness of the 1970s, and deal with women's feelings and relationships.

1 We shelter children for a time; we live side by side with men; and that is all. We owe them nothing, and are owed nothing. I think we owe our friends more, especially our female friends.
Praxis

2 'Perhaps,' thought Praxis, 'that was the whole trouble. I was too nearly Willie's equal. He did his best: stopping my education, forbidding me to earn, reducing me to whoredom: yes, he certainly did his best. Except, alas, that to blame Willie for these things is ridiculous. He didn't do them. He pointed a finger, and I ran, willingly, in the direction he pointed.'
Praxis

WEST, Mae (1892–1980)

US actress. Born in Brooklyn, New York, she began in show business as a child. Early stage successes included *À la Broadway* (1941) and *Sometime* (1913). In 1926 she appeared in the first play that she had written, *Sex* – it was considered so shocking that it was closed down and she was imprisoned for ten days for obscenity. However, her public appeal grew and she delighted her fans with both her comic talent and her unashamedly sensual and vulgar performances. She wrote and acted in several other plays, including *Diamond Lil* (1928) and *The Constant Sinner* (1931), making a particular impact when appearing with W. C. Fields in *My Little Chickadee* (1940). Other films include *Night After Night* (1932), *She Done Him Wrong* (1933), *Myra Breckinridge* (1970), and *Sextette* (1977). During World War II soldiers named their inflatable life jackets 'Mae Wests' as a tribute to her figure.

Quotations about West

1 In a non-permissive age, she made remarkable inroads against the taboos of her day, and did so without even lowering her neckline.
Leslie Halliwell (1929–) British journalist and author. *The Filmgoer's Book of Quotes*

2 She stole everything but the cameras.
George Raft (1895–1980) US actor. Attrib.

Quotations by West

3 A gold rush is what happens when a line of chorus girls spot a man with a bank roll.
Klondike Annie, film 1936

4 I always did like a man in uniform. And that one fits you grand. Why don't you come up sometime and see me?
Often misquoted as 'Come up and see me some time'.
She Done Him Wrong, film 1933

5 I used to be Snow White...but I drifted.
The Wit and Wisdom of Mae West (ed. J. Weintraub)

6 When women go wrong, men go right after them.
The Wit and Wisdom of Mae West (ed. J. Weintraub)

7 I'm glad you like my Catherine. I like her too. She ruled thirty million people and had three thousand lovers. I do the best I can in two hours.
After her performance in *Catherine the Great*. Speech from the stage

WEST, Dame Rebecca (Cicily Isabel Fairchild; 1892–1983)

British writer. Of Anglo-Irish descent, Rebecca West was educated at Watson's Ladies College in Edinburgh. She trained as an actress in London, but from 1911 became involved in women's suffrage and journalism. In 1913 she began a ten-year affair with H. G. Wells, which led to the birth of her son Anthony West. Her first significant work, a critical biography of Henry James, was published in 1916. After breaking with Wells in 1923 she went to the USA, where her journalistic talent was soon recognized. She also began writing novels, including *The Judge* (1922) and *Harriet Hume* (1929). Travelling with her husband, Henry Maxwell Adams, who she married in 1930, she wrote a book about Yugoslavia, *Black Lamb and Grey Falcon* (1941). After World War II she reported on the trial of 'Lord Haw-Haw' (William Joyce) for the *New Yorker*, which led to *The Meaning of Treason* (1949), a study of the psychology of traitors. Her reports of the Nuremberg trials of German war criminals were collected in *A Train of Powder* (1955). She was made a DBE in 1959.

Quotations about West

1 Miss West sent H. G. Wells an ultimatum. He must choose. Either he could leave Jane and marry her, go on living with her, with a guarantee of £3000 a year; or say goodbye. She knew that the last was the only possible choice.
Norman and Jeanne Mackenzie *The Time Traveller: The Life of H. G. Wells*

2 She regarded me as a piece of fiction – like one of her novels – that she could edit and improve.
Anthony West is her son. Anthony West (1914–) British author. *Heritage*

Quotations by West

3 The point is that nobody likes having salt rubbed into their wounds, even if it is the salt of the earth.
The Salt of the Earth, Ch. 2

4 God forbid that any book should be banned. The practice is as indefensible as infanticide.
The Strange Necessity, 'The Tosh Horse'

5 There is no such thing as conversation. It is an illusion. There are intersecting monologues, that is all.
There Is No Conversation, Ch. 1

WIDOWHOOD

1 Well, a widow, I see, is a kind of sinecure.
William Wycherley (1640–1716) English dramatist.
The Plain Dealer, V:3 [1676]

2 Widows are accountable to none for their Actions.
Susannah Centlivre (c. 1667–1723) English poet, playwright, and actress.
The Basset-Table, I [1705]

3 Hail! thou state of widowhood,
State of those that mourn to God;
Who from earthly comforts torn,
Only live to pray and mourn.
Isabella Graham (1742–1814) US poet, letter writer, educator, and philanthropist.
'Widowhood' [1774]

4 Widow. The word consumes itself.
Sylvia Plath (1932–63) US poet and writer.
Crossing the Water, 'Widow' [1963]

5 She *was* a widow, that strange feminine entity who had once been endowed with a dual personality and was now only half of what she had been.
Agnes Sligh Turnbull (1888–) US writer.
The Flowering, Ch. 1 [1972]

6 'Widow' is a harsh and hurtful word. It comes from the Sanskrit and it means 'empty'. I have been empty too long.
Lynn Caine (c. 1927–) US writer and publicist.
Widow [1974]

WILLARD, Emma (1787–1870)

US teacher and poet. In 1808 she became principal of a girls' academy in Vermont and in 1814 opened her own boarding school. In 1819 she appealed to the New York state legislature, in an address 'Plan for Improving Female Education', for state aid in founding schools for girls and for educational equality for women. Although the plan was rejected, Governor De Witt Clinton was impressed and invited her to move her school to Waterford. In 1821 the school was moved to Troy and named the Troy Female Seminary (now the Emma Willard School). In 1854, together with Henry Barnard, she represented the United States at the World's Educational Convention in London.

1 Rocked in the cradle of the deep
I lay me down in peace to sleep;
Secure I rest upon the wave,
For Thou, O Lord! hast power to save.
Written at sea. 'The Ocean Hymn', 14 July 1831

2 Take care of health. Would you enjoy life? Take care of health; for without it, existence is, for every purpose of enjoyment, worse than a blank.
A Treatise for the Motive Powers which Produce the Circulation of the Blood, 'Care of Health. – To Young Ladies'

3 The human mind will wander to future times.
Address on behalf of the Greek Normal School

4 He is not necessarily the best teacher who performs the most labour; makes his pupils work the hardest, and bustles the most. A hundred cents of copper, though they make more clatter and fill more space, have only a tenth of the value of one eagle of gold.
Address to the Columbian Association, 'How to Teach'

WISDOM

1 She must be enduringly, incorruptibly good; instinctively, infallibly wise – wise not for self-development, but for self-renunciation: wise, not that she may set herself above her husband, but that she may never fail from his side: wise, not with the narrowness of insolent and love-less pride, but with the passionate gentleness of an infinitely variable, because infinitely applicable, modesty of service – the true changefulness of woman.
John Ruskin (1819–1900) British art critic and writer.
Sesame and Lilies [1865]

2 Women never have young minds. They are born three thousand years old.
Shelagh Delaney (1939–) British dramatist.
A Taste of Honey, I:1 [1958]

WITCHES

1 Thou shalt not suffer a witch to live.
Bible: Exodus
22:18

2 They have slippery tongues, and are unable to conceal from their fellow-women those things which by evil arts they know; and, since they are weak, they find an easy and secret manner of vindicating themselves by witchcraft.
Heinrich Kramer and James Sprenger German Dominican monks.
Explaining why there are more female than male witches. *Malleus Maleficarum* [1486]

3 For my part, I have ever believed, and do now know, that there are witches.
Thomas Browne (1605–82) English physician and writer.
Religio Medici, Pt I [1642]

4 A witch is a rebel in physics, and a rebel is a witch in politics. The one acts against nature, the other against order, the rule of it. For both are in league with the devil.
Thomas Vaughan (1622–66) British chemist and mystic.
[c. 1650]

5 When the sergeants had brought the said witch-finder on horseback to town...Thirty women were brought into the townhall and stript, and then openly had pins thrust into their bodies, and most of them was found guilty, near twenty-seven of them, by him and set aside.
Ralph Gardiner
England's Grievance Discovered [1655]

6 Although the witch, incarnate or in surrogate mother disguise, remains a universal bogey, pejorative aspects of the wizard, her masculine counterpart, have vanished over the patriarchal centuries. The term *wizard* has acquired reverential status – wizard of finance, wizard of diplomacy, wizard of science.
Dena Justin (1912–) US writer and educator.
Natural History, 'From Mother Goddess to Dishwasher', Feb 1973

7 The girl is lost; she is burnt flesh.
Umberto Eco (1932–) Italian semiologist and writer.
Referring to a suspected witch. *The Name of the Rose* [1981]

WOLFF, Charlotte (1904–86)

Born in Germany, she studied at the universities of Freiburg and Munich, receiving her MD from Berlin University in 1928. After escaping from Nazi persecution she became a psychiatrist in private practice in England from 1951. Her writings include *The Human Hand* (1942), *A Psychology of Gesture* (1942), *On the Way to Myself* (1969), and *Love Beween Women* (1971).

1 Women have always been the guardians of wisdom and humanity which makes them natural, but usually secret, rulers. The time has come for them to rule openly, but together with and not against men.
Bisexuality: A Study, Ch. 2

2 I have no doubt that lesbianism makes a woman virile and open to *any* sexual stimulation, and that she is more often than not a more adequate and lively partner in bed than a 'normal' woman.
Love Between Women

3 A niggling feeling of discomfort and unease follows masturbation, even in those who do not feel guilty about it.
Love Between Women

WOLLSTONECRAFT, Mary (1759–97)

British writer. A passionate advocate of social and educational equality for women her first work was *Thoughts on the Education of Daughters* (1787). In 1792 her most celebrated pamphlet, *A Vindication of the Rights of Woman*, was published. In the same year she went to Paris to observe the French Revolution, travelling as the wife of her lover, Gilbert Imlay. In the spring of 1794 she gave birth to a daughter, Fanny. The following year her relationship with Imlay ended and she returned to London, where she became one of an influential radical group that included William Godwin, Thomas Paine, William Blake, and William Wordsworth. In 1796 she began an affair with Godwin and the following year, realizing that she was pregnant, they were married. She died 11 days after the birth of her second daughter, Mary. *See* MARY SHELLEY.

Quotations about Wollstonecraft

1 In all probability had she been married well in early life, she had then been a happy woman and universally respected.
Monthly Visitor, Feb 1798

2 Among the writers whose extravagant doctrines have not only been published in this country, but circulated with uncommon avidity, loaded with extravagant praise and insinuated into every recess, the name of Mary Wollstonecraft has obtained a lamentable distinction.
Jane West *Letters to a Young Man*

Quotations by Wollstonecraft

3 The *divine right* of husbands, like the divine right of kings, may, it is hoped, in this enlightened age, be contested without danger.
A Vindication of the Rights of Woman, Ch. 3

4 I do not wish them to have power over men; but over themselves.
Referring to women. *A Vindication of the Rights of Woman*, Ch. 4

5 I know what you are thinking of, but I have nothing to communicate on the subject of religion.
Last words, spoken to her husband.

WOMANHOOD

1 Those two conflicting qualities, those warring contradictions, womanhood and anger, which accord so ill together, fought a hard battle in her breast. When anger in Isolde's breast was about to slay her enemy, sweet womanhood intervened. 'No, don't!' it softly whispered.
Gottfried von Strassburg (fl. 1210) German poet.
Tristan [c. 1210]

2 Our trouble is not our womanhood, but the artificial trammels of custom under false conditions.
Elizabeth Cady Stanton (1815–1902) US suffragette and abolitionist.
Diary entry, 1890

3 We have in us the blood of a womanhood that was never bought and never sold; that wore no veil and had no foot bound; whose realized ideal of marriage was sexual companionship and an equality in duty and labor.
Olive Schreiner (1855–1920) South African writer, feminist, and social critic.
Woman and Labor [1911]

4 Wonderful women! Have you ever thought how much we all, and women especially, owe to Shakespeare for his vindication of women in these fearless, high-spirited, resolute and intelligent heroines?
Ellen Terry (1847–1928) British actress.
Four Lectures on Shakespeare, 'The Triumphant Women' [1911]

5 It will be found that there are womanly concerns, of profound importance to a girl and therefore to an empire, which demand no less of the highest mental and moral qualities than any of the subjects in a man's curriculum, and the pursuit of which in reason does not compromise womanhood, but only ratifies and empowers it.
C. W. Saleeby
Woman and Womanhood [1912]

6 When Eve ate this particular apple, she became aware of her own womanhood, mentally. And mentally she began to experiment with it. She has been experimenting ever since. So has man. To the rage and horror of both of them.
D. H. Lawrence (1885–1930) British novelist.
Fantasia of the Unconscious, Ch. 7 [1922]

7 It seems to me impossible to judge to how great a degree the unconscious motives for the flight from womanhood are reinforced by the actual social subordination of women.
Karen Horney (1885–1952) German-born US psychiatirst, writer, and educator.
'The Flight from Womanhood', *Feminine Psychology* [1926]

8 The art of being a woman can never consist of being a bad imitation of a man.
Olga Knopf (b. 1888) Austrian-born US psychiatrist and writer.
The Art of Being A Woman [1932]

9 One is not born a woman, one becomes one.
Simone de Beauvoir (1908–86) French writer.
Le Deuxième Sexe (*The Second Sex*) [1949]

WOMAN'S NATURE
See also ATTITUDES; FEMININITY

1 A fickle thing and changeful is woman always.
Virgil (Publius Vergilius Maro; 70–19 BC) Roman poet.
Aeneid [29–19 BC]

2 The Blessed One said, 'Amrapali, the mind of a woman is easily disturbed and misled. She yields to her desires and surrenders to jealousy more easily than a man. Therefore it is more difficult for a woman to follow the Noble Path.'
The Teachings of Buddha [5th century BC]

3 Since revenge is ever the pleasure of a paltry spirit, a weak and abject mind! Draw this conclusion at once from the fact that no one delights in revenge more than a woman.
Juvenal (Decimus Junius Juvenalis; 60–130 AD) Roman satirist.
Satires [2nd century AD]

4 In her particular nature, woman is defective and misbegotten...the production of woman is due to a weakness in the generative force or imperfection in the pre-existing matter or even from some external influences, for example the humid winds from the south.
St Thomas Aquinas (1225–74) Italian theologian.
Summa theologica [1266–73]

5 Woman is a wheedling and secret enemy. And that she is more perilous than a snare does not speak of the snares of hunters, but of devils.
Jacob Sprenger and Hendrich Kramer
The indispensable handbook for the Inquisition. *Malleus Maleficarum* [1489]

6 But if, Amazon-like, you attack your gallants,
And put us in fear of our lives,
You may do very well for sisters and aunts,
But, believe me, you'll never be wives.
William Whitehead (1715–85) British writer.
'Song for Ranelagh' [1774]

7 Any great and unusual exhibition of bravery by a woman, or violent excitement, especially the loud intemperate language of quarrel, with vehement gestures, or manual conflict, almost always causes hysterical reaction, most injurious to health, dangerous, and sometimes fatal: conclusive testimony that woman was never intended to rival man, either in politics or war.
James McGrigor Allan
Woman Suffrage Wrong [1890]

8 The meaning of woman is to be meaningless. She represents negation, the opposite pole from the Godhead, the other possibility of humanity.
Otto Weininger (1880–1903) Philosopher who influenced the Nazi movement.
Sex and Character [1903]

9 To the woman falls the larger share of the work of adjustment: she leaves the initiative to the man and out of her own need renounces originality.
Helene Deutsch (1884–1982) US psychiatrist.
Psychology of Women, I [1946]

10 The incentive for girls to equip themselves for marriage and home-making is genetic.
Kathleen Ollerenshaw (1912–) British educational theorist.
Education for Girls [1961]

WOMAN'S ROLE

See also DUTY; MARTYRDOM

1 A woman's place is in the home.
Proverb

2 A woman's virtue may be easily described: her virtue is to order her house, and keep what is indoors, and obey her husband.
Plato (429–347 BC) Greek philospher.
Meno [4th century BC]

3 Caesar's wife must be above suspicion.
Julius Caesar (100–44 BC) Roman general and statesman.
Said in justification of his divorce from Pompeia, after she was unwittingly involved in a scandal. *Lives*, 'Julius Caesar' (Plutarch) [c. 62 BC]

4 For is there anything better than a wife who is chaste, domestic, a good housekeeper, a rearer of children; one to gladden you in health, to tend you in sickness; to be your partner in good fortune, to console you in misfortune; to restrain the mad passion of youth, and to temper the unseasonable harshness of old age?
Dio Cassius (c. 150–235 AD) Roman historian.
Dio's Roman History (E. Cary) [3rd century AD]

5 Whoever rightly considers the order of things may plainly see the whole race of woman-kind is by nature, custom, and the laws, made subject to man, to be governed according to his discretion: therefore it is the duty of every one of us that desires to have ease, comfort, and repose, with those men to whom we belong, to be humble, patient, and obedient, as well as chaste.
Giovanni Boccaccio (1313–75) Italian writer and poet.
Decameron, 'Ninth Day' [c. 1353]

6 Cherish your husband's person and make sure you keep him in clean linen, this being your office. For men have to look after things outside the house and husbands have to go abroad in all sorts of weather, at times getting soaked in rain, at times dry, and sometimes bathed in sweat.
Anonymous
Le Ménagier de Paris [1393]

7 Men have broad and large chests, and small narrow hips, and more understanding than women, who have but small and narrow breasts, and broad hips, to the end they should remain at home, sit still, keep house, and bear and bring up children.
Martin Luther (1483–1546) German Protestant reformer.
Table Talk, 'Of Marriage and Celibacy' [16th century]

8 Many a man has been a wonder to the world, whose wife and valet have seen nothing in him that was even remarkable. Few men have been admired by their servants.
Michel de Montaigne (1533–92) French essayist.
Essais, III [1580–88]

9 Get thee to a nunnery: why wouldst thou be a breeder of sinners?
William Shakespeare (1564–1616) English dramatist.
Hamlet, III:1 [1599]

10 A man is in general better pleased when he has a good dinner upon his table, than when his wife talks Greek.
Samuel Johnson (1709–84) British lexicographer.
Johnsonian Miscellanies, Vol. II (ed. G. B. Hill) [1784]

11 To man belong professions, dignities, authorities, and pleasures; for woman, there remain only duties, domestic virtue, and perhaps as the result of these, the happiness of tranquil submission.
Sarah Wentworth Morton (1759–1846) US poet.
My Mind and Its Thoughts, 'The Sexes' [1823]

12 Maids must be wives and mothers, to fulfill
The entire and holiest end of woman's being.
Fanny Kemble (1809–93) British actress, writer, and poet.
'Woman's Heart' [1839]

13 God made the woman for the man,
And for the good and increase of the world.
Alfred, Lord Tennyson (1809–92) British poet.
'Edwin Morris' [1842]

14 Women exist in the main solely for the propagation of the species.
Arthur Schopenhauer (1788–1860) German philosopher.
Attrib. [1860]

15 I should like to know what is the proper function of women, if it is not to make reasons for husbands to stay at home, and still stronger reasons for bachelors to go out.
George Eliot (Mary Ann Evans; 1819–80) British novelist.
The Mill on the Floss, Ch. 6 [1860]

16 As a general rule, a modest woman seldom desires any sexual gratification for herself. She submits to her husband, but only to please him; and, but for the desire of maternity, would far rather be relieved from his attentions.
W. Acton
The Functions and Disorders of the Reproductive Organs [1865]

17 It is a man's place to rule, and a woman's to yield. He must be held up as the head of the house, and it is her duty to bend so unmurmuringly to his wishes, that the rest of the household will follow her example, and treat him with the due respect his sex demands.
Sarah Ann Sewell (fl. 1870s) British writer and social critic.
Woman and the Times We Live In [1869]

18 For men must work, and women must weep,
And there's little to earn, and many to keep,
Though the harbour bar be moaning.
Charles Kingsley (1819–75) British writer.
The Three Fishers

19 Womanhood is the great fact in her life; wifehood and motherhood are but incidental relations.
Elizabeth Stanton (1815–1902) US suffragette.
History of Woman Suffrage, Vol. I (with Susan B. Anthony and Mathilda Gage) [1880]

20 The silliest woman can manage a clever man; but it needs a very clever woman to manage a fool.
Rudyard Kipling (1865–1936) Indian-born British writer.
Plain Tales from the Hills, 'Three and – an Extra' [1888]

21 In all languages the words, Wife, Mother, are spoken with reverence, and associated with the highest, holiest functions of woman's

earthly life. To man belongs the kingdom of the head: to woman the empire of the heart!
James McGrigor Allan
Woman Suffrage Wrong [1890]

22 Man should be trained for war and woman for the recreation of the warrior; all else is folly.
F. W. Nietzsche (1844–1900) German philosopher.
Thus Spake Zarathustra [1883–92]

23 If we can alleviate sufferings and at the same time comfort the many aching and anxious hearts at home, shall we not be fulfilling our greatest mission in life? These are 'Women's Rights' in the best sense of the word. We need no others.
Jennie Jerome Churchill (1854–1921) British hostess, editor, and playwright.
Speech, First Meeting of General Committee for Hospital Ship, 18 Nov 1899

24 Woman is unrivaled as a wet nurse.
Mark Twain (Samuel Langhorne Clemens; 1835–1910) US writer.
Attrib. [1910]

25 Are you who are in authority at the Home Office unaware that the modern woman writes as well as sews? Perhaps you may be anxious to press upon us some permanent prejudice of your own in the form of the needle rather than the pen as a suitable implement for women. If this be so may I beg you to choose some other time and place for exalting the needle at the expense of the pen?
Marion Wallace-Dunlop
Written during her imprisonment for suffragist activities. Letter to the home secretary, 5 Dec 1911

26 To the old saying that man built the house but woman made of it a 'home' might be added the modern supplement that woman accepted cooking as a chore but man has made of it a recreation.
Emily Post (1873–1960) US writer.
Etiquette, Ch. 34 [1922]

27 Women have served all these centuries as looking-glasses possessing the magic and delicious power of reflecting the figure of man at twice its natural size.
Virginia Woolf (1882–1941) British novelist.
A Room of One's Own [1929]

28 'Did little girls have to be as good as that?' Laura asked, and Ma said: 'It was harder for little girls. Because they had to behave like little ladies all the time, not only on Sundays. Little girls could never slide downhill, like boys. Little girls had to sit in the house and stitch on samplers.'
Laura Ingalls Wilder (1867–1957) US writer.
Little House in the Big Woods, Ch. 5 [1932]

29 A woman must learn to obey. We must not ask why. We cannot help our birth. We must accept it and do the duty that is ours in this lifetime.
Pearl S. Buck (1892–1973) US writer.
'The First Wife', *First Wife and Other Stories* [1933]

30 It is possible, of course, that the only effect of...sheltering is to create in women a generalized dependency which will then be transferred to the husband and which will enable her all the more readily to accept the role of wife in a family which still has many patriarchal features.
Mirra Komarovsky (1906–) Russian-born US educator and writer.
American Sociological Review, 'Functional Analysis of Sex Roles', Aug 1950

31 There was such a thing as women's work and it consisted chiefly, Hilary sometimes thought, in being able to stand constant interruption and keep your temper.
May Sarton (1912–) Belgian-born US writer.
Mrs Stevens Hears the Mermaids Singing [1965]

32 AGNES. There are many things a woman does: she bears the children – if there *is* that blessing. Blessing? Yes, I suppose, even with the sadness. She runs the house, for what that's worth: makes sure there's food, and not just anything, and decent linen; looks well; assumes whatever duties are demanded – if she is in love, or loves; and plans.
Edward Albee (1928–) US dramatist.
A Delicate Balance [1966]

33 The overemphasis on protecting girls from strain or injury and underemphasis on developing skills and experiencing teamwork fits neatly into the pattern of the second sex...Girls are the spectators and the cheerleaders...Perfect preparation for the adult role of woman – to stand decoratively on the sidelines of history and cheer on the men who make the decisions.
Kathryn Clarenbach (c. 1925–) US educator and feminist.
Sex Role Stereotyping in the Schools [1973]

34 Women are emotional and an emotional approach is the best approach...Reiterate that the prime function in life is to reproduce; that is what God placed her on earth for.
Training booklet used by the Royal Canadian Mounted Police (The Mounties), 1975

35 A woman's place is in the home looking after the family, not out working.
John Paul II (Karol Wojtyla; 1920–) Pope (1978–).
Speech, 1981

36 My mother said it was simple to keep a man, you must be a maid in the living room, a cook in the kitchen and a whore in the bedroom.

I said I'd hire the other two and take care of the bedroom bit.
Jerry Hall US model and actress.
Remark, Oct 1985

WOMEN'S LIBERATION MOVEMENT
See also FEMINISM

1 The so-called women's question is a whole people question...Our uprising is the most terrible to the conservative, precisely because it is so important for the revolution. The opposition to the women is always more intense than that towards any other group, and it is always expressed in the most hysterical terms.
Sheila Rowbotham
Once a Feminist (Michelene Wandor) [1969]

2 A woman needs a man like a fish needs a bicycle.
Graffiti; often attributed to Gloria Steinem [1970s]

3 WOMEN'S RIGHTS NOW!!
Followed by 'Yes Dear'.
Exchange of graffiti [1970s]

4 Because woman's work is never done and is underpaid or unpaid or boring or repetitious and we're the first to get the sack and what we look like is more important than what we do and if we get raped it's our fault and if we get bashed we must have provoked it and if we raise our voices we're nagging bitches and if we enjoy sex we're nymphos and if we don't we're frigid and if we love women it's because we can't get a 'real' man and if we ask our doctor too many questions we're neurotic and/or pushy and if we expect community care for children we're selfish and if we stand up for our rights we're aggressive and 'unfeminine' and if we don't we're typical weak females and if we want to get married we're out to trap a man and if we don't we're unnatural and because we still can't get an adequate safe contraceptive but men can walk on the moon and if we can't cope or don't want a pregnancy we're made to feel guilty about abortion and...for lots and lots of other reasons we are part of the women's liberation movement.
Taken from a leaflet/poster produced by the NUS Women's Campaign

5 The point of Women's Liberation is not to stand at the door of the male world, beating our fists, and crying: 'Let me in, damn you, let me in!' The point is to walk away from that world and concentrate on creating a new woman.
Vivian Gornick
SCUM Manifesto, Introduction (Valerie Solanas) [1970]

6 We whose hands have rocked the cradle, are now using our heads to rock the boat.
Wilma Scott Heide (1926–) US nurse and feminist.
NOW Official Biography [1971]

7 This movement…is the last stage of the drive for equality for women. We are determined that our daughters and granddaughters will live as free human beings, secure in their personhood, and dedicated to making this nation and the world a humane place in which to live.
Aileen Clarke Hernandez (1926–) US business executive, public affairs counsellor, and feminist. President of NOW (1970–71).
Address, National Conference of NOW, Los Angeles, 3–6 Sept 1971

8 The rumblings of women's liberation are only one pointer to the fact that you already have a discontented work force. And if conditions continue to lag so far behind the industrial norm and the discomfort increases, you will find…that you will end up with an inferior product.
Elaine Morgan (1920–) British writer.
The Descent of Woman, Ch. 11 [1972]

9 I'm furious about the Women's Liberationists. They keep getting up on soapboxes and proclaiming that women are brighter than men. That's true, but it should be kept very quiet or it ruins the whole racket.
Anita Loos (1891–1981) US novelist.
Observer, 'Sayings of the Year', 30 Dec 1973

10 Emancipation means equal status for different roles…Liberation… is a demand for the abolition of wife and mother, the dissolution of the family.
Arianna Stassinopoulos (1950–) Greek writer.
The Female Woman, 'The Family Woman' [1973]

11 The uniqueness of today's Women's Liberation Movement is that it dares to challenge what is, including the male chauvinism not only under capitalism but within the revolutionary movement itself.
Raya Dunayevskaya (c. 1911–) US author and philosopher.
Philosophy and Revolution, Ch. 9 [1973]

12 We're seeing women organize together… with the realization that collective or organized action is much more important than individual change.
Patricia Carbine (1931–) US editor.
AFTRA Magazine, Summer 1974

13 Women's liberation is the liberation of the feminine in the man and the masculine in the woman.
Corita Kent (1918–) US graphic artist and ex-nun.
Los Angeles Times, 'A Time of Transition for Corita Kent', 11 July 1974

14 The modern woman is the curse of the universe. A disaster, that's what. She thinks that before her arrival on the scene no woman ever did anything worthwhile before, no woman was ever liberated until her time, no woman really ever amounted to anything.
Adela Rogers St Johns (1894–) US writer and journalist.
Los Angeles Herald-Examiner, 'Some Are Born Great', 13 Oct 1974

15 I know a twenty-eight-year-old woman, a recent graduate of Harvard Business School. She asked me the other day if I wasn't afraid of what people will say if I associate with the women's movement. What she doesn't understand is that it's because of the movement and people like me that it's now not as difficult for her to make it.
Muriel Siebert (c. 1928–) US securities analyst.
Women at Work (Betty Medsger) [1975]

16 Women's Liberation is just a lot of foolishness. It's the men who are discriminated against. They can't bear children. And no one's likely to do anything about that.
Golda Meir (1898–1978) Russian-born Israeli stateswoman.
Attrib. [1978]

17 The only good thing about Hammerfall, women's lib was dead milliseconds after Hammerstrike.
Larry Niven (1938–) US science-fiction writer.
'Hammerfall' was a fictional collision in the late 1970s between the Earth and a large comet that destroyed civilization. *Lucifer's Hammer*, Pt III (with Jerry Pournelle) [1978]

18 In redefining femininity women were recovering their own strength and power, but they were also rediscovering the meaningfulness of life in the notions of sisterhood.
Victor Seidler British writer and sociologist.
Achilles Heel, June 1979

19 I think a lot of the women's lib movement came from the war. The women who were growing up then are the mothers of today, and I'm sure they've been affected by the fact that their mothers worked then. For my age group you felt very inhibited about wanting to work. Before the war, if you heard people talking about education, it was always, 'Oh, of course, the boy must go,' and 'The girl, well, she's only going to be a housewife anyway, so she's no time for that.'

Mary Wolfard British radio journalist.

Don't You Know There's a War On? (Jonathan Croall) [1988]

WOOLF, Virginia (*born* Stephen; 1882–1941)

British novelist. She was a central figure of the Bloomsbury group (a group of writers and artists active in the 1910s and 1920s), which included the writer Leonard Woolf, who she married in 1912. Her novel *Jacob's Room* (1922) established her reputation as an innovative novelist – a reputation which was secured by her major novels, *Mrs Dalloway* (1925), *To the Lighthouse* (1927), and *The Waves* (1931). She was also a literary critic and journalist; her interest in feminism is acknowledged in *A Room of One's Own* (1929) and its sequel, *Three Guineas* (1938). Virginia Woolf suffered bouts of acute depression from the time of her mother's death in 1895. These became increasingly incapacitating and, in the spring of 1941, she drowned herself.

Quotations about Woolf

1 Virginia Woolf is dead, a grey, highly-strung woman of dignity and charm, but she was unstable and often had periods of madness. She led the Bloomsbury movement, did much to make England so Left – yet she always remained a lady, and was never violent. She could not stand human contacts, and people fatigued her.

Sir Henry Channon (1897–1958) British politician and writer. Diary, 5 Apr 1941

2 I do not believe that she wrote one word of fiction which does not put out boundaries a little way; one book which does not break new ground and form part of the total experiment.

Susan Hill (1942–) British novelist and playwright. *Daily Telegraph* 5 May 1974

3 I enjoyed talking to her, but thought *nothing* of her writing. I considered her 'a beautiful little knitter'.

Edith Sitwell (1887–1964) British poet and writer. Letter to G. Singleton

Quotations by Woolf

4 Those comfortably padded lunatic asylums which are known, euphemistically, as the stately homes of England.

The Common Reader, 'Lady Dorothy Nevill'

5 Few people can be so tortured by writing as I am. Only Flaubert, I think.

Diary, Vol. 5, 1936–41

6 If you do not tell the truth about yourself you cannot tell it about other people.

The Moment and Other Essays

7 The older one grows the more one likes indecency.

Monday or Tuesday

8 When one reads of a witch being ducked, of a woman possessed by devils, of a wise woman selling herbs, or even of a very remarkable man who had a mother, then I think we are on the track of a lost novelist, a suppressed poet, of some mute and inglorious Jane Austen, some Emilty Brontë who dashed her brains out on the moor or mopped and mowed about the highways crazed with the torture her gift had put her to. Indeed I would venture that Anon, who wrote so many poems without signing them, was a woman.

A Room of One's Own

9 If we didn't live venturously, plucking the wild goat by the beard, and trembling over precipices, we should never be depressed, I've no doubt; but already should be faded, fatalistic and aged.

A Writer's Diary, 26 May 1924

10 Dearest, I feel certain that I am going mad again: I feel we cant go through another of those terrible times. And I shant recover this time. I begin to hear voices, and cant concentrate. So I am doing what seems the best thing to do…If anybody could have saved me it would have been you. Everything has gone from me but the certainty of your goodness. I cant go on spoiling your life any longer.

I dont think two people could have been happier than we have been.

Suicide note to her husband, ?18 Mar 1941

WORK

1 O! men with sisters dear,
O! men with mothers and wives!
It is not linen you're wearing out,
But human creatures' lives!

Thomas Hood (1799–1845) British poet.
The Song of the Shirt [1843]

2 Women must remain in industry despite all narrow-minded caterwauling; in fact the circle of their industrial activity must become broader and more secure daily.

Clara Zetkin (1857–1933) German political activist.
The Question of Women Workers and Women at the Present Time [1889]

3 The history of women's work in this country shows that legislation has been the only force

which has improved the working conditions of any large number of women wage-earners.
Helen L. Sumner (1876–1933) US government official and children's rights activist.
Senate Report, *History of Women in Industry in the United States*, Vol. IX [1911]

4 One event I covered for the BBC was a big meeting at the Albert Hall of women workers from all over the country…I think every minister in the government attended, to speak to the women about the war effort, and to pat them on the back and say, 'Thank you, duckies, we shan't need you later, but at the moment we do, so come in and get on with it.' They depended on women to get production up.
Mary Wolfard British radio journalist.
Don't You Know There's a War On? (Jonathan Croall) [c. 1943]

5 So after the war going away to work became acceptable, instead of being a confession that you were unable to find a job near home…Of course at the end of the war the attitude to women working changed again – witness the way day nurseries were shut down. But I think people soon realized that many women didn't want to scuttle back to the kitchen and the social round.
Joan Collins British teacher and social worker.
Don't You Know There's a War On? (Jonathan Croall) [c. 1945]

6 I blame the women: they stay home all day, they set the tone. Many look back with regret to the days when they worked in an office. Their work kept them alert. Home and childminding can have a blunting effect on a woman's mind. But only she can sharpen it.
Betty Jerman British journalist.
The article that inspired Maureen Nicol to form the National Housewives' Register. *Guardian*, 1960

7 No man can call himself liberal, or radical, or even a conservative advocate of fair play, if his work depends in any way on the unpaid or underpaid labor of women at home, or in the office.
Gloria Steinem (1934–) US writer, feminist, and editor.
The New York Times, 26 Aug 1971

8 To love what you do and feel that it matters – how could anything be more fun?
Katharine Graham (1917–) US newspaper publisher and editor.
Ms, 'The Power That Didn't Corrupt', Oct 1974

WRITERS

1 I am obnoxious to each carping tongue
Who says my hand a needle better fits,
A Poet's pen all scorn I should thus wrong,
For such despite they cast on Female wits:
If what I do prove well, it won't advance,
They'll say it's stolen, or else it was by chance.
Anne Bradstreet (c. 1612–72) English-born US poet and essayist.
Several Poems Compiled with Great Variety of Wit and Learning, Prologue [1678]

2 All I ask, is the privilege for my masculine part, the poet in me…if I must not, because of my sex, have this freedom, I lay down my quill and you shall hear no more of me.
Aphra Behn (1640–89) English novelist, dramatist, poet, translator, and spy.
The Lucky Chance, Preface [1686]

3 Alas! a woman that attempts the pen,
Such an intruder on the rights of men,
Such a presumptuous creature, is esteemed,
The fault can by no virtue be redeemed.
Anne Finch (1661–c. 1722) English poet.
Miscellany Poems, Written by a Lady [1713]

4 When Women write, the Criticks, now-a-days,
Are ready, e'er they see, to damn their Plays,
Wit, as the Men's Prerogative, they claim,
And with one Voice, the bold Invader blame.
Mary Davys (1674–1732) English playwright and novelist.
The Self-Rival; A Comedy, Prologue [1725]

5 Regularity and Decorum. 'Tis what we Women-Authors, in particular, have been thought greatly deficient in; and I shou'd be concern'd to find it an Objection not to be remov'd.
Elizabeth Cooper (fl. 1730s) British playwright and anthologist.
The Rival Widows; or, Fair Libertine, Preface [1735]

6 Dear reader, here is something for you to read. To be sure, it is not written by a great, scholarly man. Oh, no! It is by a mere woman whose name you scarcely know and for whose station in life you have to look among the most humble of people, for she is nothing but a comedian…If any one asks you who helped her, you had better answer, 'I don't know' – for it may very well be that she did it all herself.
Friederika Karoline Neuber (1697–1760) German actress, theatre manager, and playwright.
Vorspiel [c. 1750]

7 A female poet, a female author of any kind, ranks below an actress, I think.
Charles Lamb (1775–1834) British essayist.

8 Literature cannot be the business of a woman's life, and it ought not to be. The more she is engaged in her proper duties, the less lei-

sure will she have for it, even as an accomplishment and a recreation.
Robert Southey (1774–1843) British poet.
Letter [c. 1843]

9 If we search the polemic writings of the most militant feminists, we can nowhere find expressions which compare in venom and ruthlessness with the woman-eating sentiments of certain medieval 'saints' and modern 'philosophers'.
Katharine Anthony (1877–1965) US writer and educator.
Feminism in Germany and Scandinavia, Ch. 9 [1915]

10 Just as it is still in her close personal relationships that woman most naturally uses her human genius and her artistry in life, so it is still in the portrayal of those relationships that she perfects her most characteristic genius in writing.
Elizabeth Drew (1887–1965) British-born US writer and literary critic.
'Is There a "Feminine" Fiction?', *The Modern Novel* [1926]

11 I would venture to guess that Anon, who wrote so many poems without signing them, was often a woman.
Virginia Woolf (1882–1941) British novelist.
A Room of One's Own [1929]

12 To be a woman and a writer
is double mischief, for

the world will slight her
who slights 'the servile house,' and who would rather
make odes than beds.
Dilys Laing (1906–60) Canadian poet.
Collected Poems, 'Sonnet to a Sister in Error' [1967]

13 Be born anywhere, little embryo novelist, but do not be born under the shadow of a great creed, not under the burden of original sin, not under the doom of salvation.
Pearl S. Buck (1892–1973) US writer.
'Advice to Unborn Novelists' [1972]

14 These…women…wrote in a world which was controlled by men, a world in which women's revelations, if they were anything but conventional, might not be welcomed, might not be recognized, and they wrote nevertheless.
Joan Goulianos (1939–) US writer, educator and literary critic.
By a Woman Writt, Introduction [1973]

15 On the whole the Female Wits wrote big, fat fabulous plays with breadth and depth of the kind you don't see today. Their themes were universal: love, greed, jealousy, human follies and foibles, the only things that are the slightest bit interesting in life.
Fidelis Morgan
Referring to female Restoration writers. *Independent*, 19 Nov 1991

KEYWORD INDEX

References are to themes or to
people in the Thematic Section or
to quotations in the Chronology
(marked CHRON). The references
are to quotation numbers, not page
numbers.

A

abandonment Voluntary death would be an a. of our present post BLAVATSKY, E, 2

abhorrent Englishwomen look upon sexual intercourse as a. SEX, 18

abilities a. of women are far inferior CHRON, 225
the sheer power of her interpretative a. CALLAS, M, 1

able She was very a., very clever, and very unpleasant PANKHURST, C, 2

abolished veil has been a. CHRON, 684

abolition Liberation...a. of wife
WOMEN'S LIBERATION MOVEMENT, 10

abominable neither unnatural, nor a., nor mad LESBIANISM, 2

abomination a. for a menstruating woman MENSTRUATION, 15

abortion A. leads to...trivialization of the act of procreation ABORTION, 8
a. the human rights of the mother ABORTION, 6
a. would be a sacrament ABORTION, 10
first a. that woman begins to 'know' ABORTION, 5
folklore of a. ABORTION, 11
greatest destroyer of peace is a. ABORTION, 13
No woman has an a. for *fun* ABORTION, 15
practice of a. is as old as pregnancy CHRON, 610
revise the a. laws...modern conditions and ideas CHRON, 538
right to a. and improved contraception transformed many women's lives CHRON, 718
we demand freedom of a. CHRON, 632; ABORTION, 7
without risking death in an illegal a. FEMINISM, 20

abortions A. will not let you forget ABORTION, 4
right to determine which American women can have a. ABORTION, 14

absence total a. of humour COLETTE, 3

absolute he is the A. – she is the Other CHRON, 577
insist upon retaining an a. power over Wives CHRON, 195

absurd a. talk about a woman's sphere CHRON, 335
Edith Sitwell...read some of her a. stuff SITWELL, E, 1

abundant a. shower of curates BRONTË, C, 8

abuse stand the chance of violent sexual a. LAW, 17
whores, and that's not a term of a. PROSTITUTION, 14

accomplices two of a kind, allies and a. CHRON, 588
two of a kind, allies and a. SAGAN, F, 4

accomplished A. girls...were made into governesses CHRON, 235

accomplishment Every young woman...should be qualified by some a. OCCUPATIONS, 5
qualified by some a. which she may teach CHRON, 286

accouchement husband being present at the a. of his wife CHILDBIRTH, 7

accountable Widows are a. to none WIDOWHOOD, 2

accountancy much in a. proper that is...unsuitable for them OCCUPATIONS, 9

accounts enough to keep their a. and memoranda SOCIETY, 1

accuracy neither the a. nor the attention for success in the exact sciences CHRON, 188

accurate No woman should ever be quite a. about her age AGE, 7

accursed woman are an a. race MISOGYNY, 2

accustomed trot merrily off in his old a. gait CHRON, 479

achieve girls plan for whom they will a. and attain MEN AND WOMEN, 11

achieved women have not a. as much as men ACHIEVEMENT, 4

achievement first-rate a. is no longer inhibited CHRON, 602

acquiesce half the human race does a. CHRON, 253

acquiescence Adam's ready a. with his wife's proposal GRIMKÉ, S, 2

act A. by yourself FONDA, J, 3
expect us to a. like a lady FLYNN, E, 2

acting A. is role-playing ACTING, 2
I am...a. again SIDDONS, S, 4

action girls cannot be beaten in a. CHRON, 547
most men...interested in a. DISAPPOINTMENT, 3
time is right for a. CHRON, 747

active Man is a. CHRON, 20

activity hindering healthful and varied a. HEALTH AND HEALTHY LIVING, 4

actor a. is something less than a man ACTING, 3

actress An a.'s life is so transitory HAYES, H, 4
I am not a versatile a. GARBO, G, 6
no other a....could escape unfavourable comparison EVANS, E, 1
she was the greatest a. in the world BERNHARDT, S, 1

Adam A.'s ready acquiescence with his wife's proposal GRIMKÉ, S, 2
not A. who was led astray but the woman CHILDBIRTH, 3; RELIGION, 1

Addams Jane A. is...sacrificing all for the masses ADDAMS, J, 3

adieu bid a. to the muses CHRON, 183

administer as married women, control and a. their own property CHRON, 370

administrator I am an agitator, not an a. ASTOR, N, 4

admired Few men have been a. by their servants WOMAN'S ROLE, 8

admit refuse to a. that I am more than fifty-two AGE, 9

adopt They all wanted to a. me PLATH, S, 1

adult What is an a. BEAUVOIR, S, 3

adulterated an a. Christianity BROWN, O, 3

adultery commit a. at one end SELF-INDULGENCE, 1
guilty of incestuous a....or of rape DIVORCE, 6
have no rights to bring criminal accusations for a. ADULTERY, 3
I've committed a. in my heart SELF-INDULGENCE, 2
petition for a husband's a. DIVORCE, 7
take your wife in a....put her to death ADULTERY, 2
Wives have no right to bring criminal accusations for a. CHRON, 56

advance If civilisation is to a....it must be through...women PANKHURST, E, 3
women must a. and fulfill their mission EQUALITY, 14

advanced tame an a. young woman EMANCIPATION, 9

advantage women still have an a. simply because they *are* women CHRON, 620

advantages granting to females the a. of a systematic and thorough education CHRON, 234
very Infancy debarr'd those a. CHRON, 171

adventure coming together of man and wife...should be a fresh a. STOPES, M, 5

adventures her marriages were a. and her friendships enduring TERRY, E, 2

adverse there are always compensations for every a. experience BROWN, O, 1

advice how ready people always are with a. SULLIVAN, A, 3

Our little Souls are tortur'd by A.   SUBJECTION, 8

woman seldom asks a.   ATTITUDES, 9

aerodromes She hung around a.   JOHNSON, A, 1

aeroplane a. is valuable...destroys men and women
   MORALITY, 4

Wonderful Amy the A. Girl   JOHNSON, A, 2

affair The a. between Margot Asquith and Margot
Asquith   ASQUITH, M, 2

affairs conduct a....in accordance with random opinions   CHRON, 223

tide in the a. of women   ATTITUDES, 16

Women in state a. are like monkeys in glass-shops
   POLITICS, 1; SAYINGS AND PROVERBS, 54

affections A different taste in jokes is a...strain on the
a.   ELIOT, G, 5

desert the a. of an innocent female   BETRAYAL, 2

afraid a. of what people will say
   WOMEN'S LIBERATION MOVEMENT, 15

a. of women knowing as much as themselves
   CHRON, 198

Africa Women in A. work like beasts of burden
   OPPRESSION, 7

age A child blown up by a.   BEAUVOIR, S, 1

A. changes our relationship with time   CHRON, 635

A. will bring all things   MODESTY, 4

a woman has the right to treat...her a. with ambiguity   RUBINSTEIN, H, 2

lady of a certain a.   AGE, 3

No woman should ever be quite accurate about her
a.   AGE, 7

The moral disposition of the a.   SOMERVILLE, M, 3

treat...her a. with ambiguity   AGE, 10

who tells one her real a.   AGE, 6

aged after she is a. and ugly   OLD AGE, 6

but already should be faded, fatalistic and a.
   WOOLF, V, 9

aggressions violent a. of bodily torment towards the
unhappy wife   CHRON, 320

agitation women have gone to prison in the course of
this a.   SUFFRAGETTES, 20

agitator I am an a., not an administrator   ASTOR, N, 4

agreeable I do not want people to be very a.   AUSTEN, J, 13

man says what he knows, a woman what is a.
   CHRON, 196

agriculture Sex...interesting as a.   SEX, 39

Aids A. pandemic is a classic own-goal   AIDS, 3

stop them catching A....the wife   PROMISCUITY, 4

to stop them catching A.   AIDS, 1

Aikin immunities which Miss A. may rightfully plead
   AIKIN, L, 1

Miss Lucy A....pert as a pear-monger   AIKIN, L, 2

aim Marriage is the a. and end of all sensible girls
   CHRON, 438

what is the a. in the training of girls   EDUCATION, 23

air my spirit found outlet in the a.   JOHNSON, A, 3

aisle A.. Altar. Hymn   MARRIAGE, 67

alabaster my complexion was like a.   STANHOPE, H, 3

alcohol a. is a weakening and deadening force
   DRINKING, 6

A. was a threat to women   DRINKING, 9

alimony Judges...in the matter of arranging a.   DIVORCE, 11

A. is one way of compensating women for those
financial disabilities   CHRON, 646

alive ascertain...possible to keep me a. in prison
   CHRON, 450

We intend to remain a.   MEIR, G, 5

all 'Is this a.?'   CHRON, 597

allies two of a kind, a. and accomplices
   CHRON, 588; SAGAN, F, 4

women...natural a. of the present era   CHRON, 455

all-thing a. that is good and comfortable
   JULIAN OF NORWICH, 1

almonds Don't eat too many a.   COLETTE, 7

almsgiving A. tends to perpetuate poverty   PERÓN, E, 5

alone I want to be a.   GARBO, G, 4; 5

Lying a. and sobbing?!   SORROW, 2

Oh, to be a.   CHRON, 397

She sleeps a. at last   EPITAPHS, 4

altar Aisle. A.. Hymn   MARRIAGE, 67

Amazon A.-like, you attack your gallants
   WOMAN'S NATURE, 6

ambassadors we suffragettes aspire to be when we are
enfranchised is a.   SUFFRAGETTES, 22

ambiguity a woman has the right to treat...her age with
a.   AGE, 10; RUBINSTEIN, H, 2

ambition all things unseemly, which they call a.
   CHRON, 375

fruitful mother of children was the happiest a.
   CHRON, 325

I confess my a. is restless   AMBITION, 2

amendment This a....would be like a beacon   CHRON, 689

America Growing up female in A.   JONG, E, 3

woman governs A.   FEMINISM, 9

American serenely throned as queen among her A. sisters   HOWE, J, 1

American Negro adult A. female emerges a formidable
character   CHRON, 616

ample a comely, a. woman with no outward traces of
brilliance   CHRISTIE, A, 2

amused how to be a. rather than shocked   BUCK, P, 5

one has to be very old before one learns how to be a.
   BUCK, P, 5

We are not a.   VICTORIA, 9

anaesthesia proof of the usefulness of a.   CHILDBIRTH, 10

anatomy he has studied a. and dissected at least one
woman   MARRIAGE, 29

anesthetized so a. by your own pain   JOHNSON, L, 3

angel woman yet think him an a.   LOVE, 40

Known as the 'A. of the prison'   FRY, E, 1

anger A. repressed can poison a relationship   ANGER, 6

warring contradictions, womanhood and a.
   ANGER, 2; WOMANHOOD, 1

wasps in their a.   ANGER, 1; SAYINGS AND PROVERBS, 49

anguish drinking deep of that divinest a.   BRONTË, E, 7

animal less strongly developed a. passions of girls
   EDUCATION, 23

poor nature becomes so very a.   CHILDBIRTH, 13

animals give my wisdom and experience to a.
   MATURITY, 4

ankles art of lifting her /skirt over her a.   CHRON, 14

Anne a lot of different A.s in me   MONTGOMERY, L, 3

cold calculation than of passion in A.'s attitude
   BOLEYN, A, 2

annulled as slave...had to be a. as woman   CHRON, 629

annuls her her marriage utterly a.   CHRON, 208

Anon I would...guess that A....was often a woman
   WOOLF, V, 8; WRITERS, 11

antifeminists A....want women to specialise in virtue
   CHRON, 435

anxiety Grief and constant a. kill nearly as many
women   SORROW, 4

apart she shall be put a. seven days   CHRON, 6

appearance bore a man's spirit under the a. of a
woman ACHIEVEMENT, 2
secret of a successful a. SELF-CONFIDENCE, 1
trivial concerns – to do with physical a. APPEARANCE, 19
appeared how you a. in my womb PROCREATION, 1
appetite not created merely to gratify the a. of man
EDUCATION, 16
Women are there to feed an a. APPEARANCE, 16
applause Glorious bouquets and storms of a.
MARKOVA, A, 1
apple When Eve ate this particular a.
SEX, 19; WOMANHOOD, 6
apprehension a. the steady rise in the number of female
factory employees CHRON, 399
approved A Work generally a....and made most profitable and necessary for all men CHRON, 165
archaeologist An a. is the best husband CHRISTIE, A, 7
arch-enemy love...has one a. – and that is life LOVE, 58
architects real a. of society SOCIETY, 3
architecture Fashion is a. CHANEL, C, 6
arguments a. in opposition to the Equal Rights Amendment CHRON, 682
aristocracy An a. in a republic is like a chicken whose
head has been cut off MITFORD, N, 3
arithmetic A. is different SOCIETY, 1
armed We should be a. SUFFRAGETTES, 25
arms For the theatre one needs long a. BERNHARDT, S, 2
arrogant most a. and extremely intractable animal
MISOGYNY, 5; PROCREATION, 3
art a. of being a woman WOMANHOOD, 8
a. of lifting her /skirt over her ankles CHRON, 14
a. of woman must be born CHRON, 540
cannot always work at my a. SCHUMANN, C, 1
Dying /is an a. PLATH, S, 2
I have discovered the a....lost for two thousand years
DUNCAN, I, 3
process of home-making...an a. and a profession
CHRON, 297
artificial a. trammels of custom WOMANHOOD, 2
artist A woman a. must be...capable of making the primary sacrifices CASSATT, M, 1
Remember I'm an a. ARTISTS, 3
The...a. I hold above all others in...the ballet
PAVLOVA, A, 2
The a....is...somewhat apart HINKLE, B, 2
artists she comes at a time...when a. are working in a
vacuum HEPWORTH, B, 2
arts worlds that women have yet to conquer is that of
The A. MUSICIANS, 6
ashamed embarrassed and a. VIOLENCE, 7
not a. of having been in love LOVE, 22
We are not a. of what we have done
CHRON, 409; PANKHURST, C, 3
aspect her a. was terrifying BOADICEA, 1
Meet in her a. BEAUTY, 9
aspire those who a. to higher things AMBITION, 4
ass a. climbs a ladder, we may find wisdom
SAYINGS AND PROVERBS, 35
mind of an a. INTELLIGENCE, 2; SAYINGS AND PROVERBS, 43
assert women should a. their rights as human beings
CHRON, 367
astray not Adam who was led a. but the woman
CHILDBIRTH, 3; RELIGION, 1
asunder let not man put a. MARRIAGE, 7
asylums Those comfortably padded lunatic a....the
stately homes WOOLF, V, 4

Athens A. holds sway over all Greece DOMINATION, 1
athletes Women can be great a. EQUAL OPPORTUNITIES, 4
atmosphere The conductor and director must create
the a. CALDWELL, S, 2
attacks Her frontal a. on old taboos STOPES, M, 2
attain man attaining to a higher eminence...than
woman can a. INTELLECT, 7
attainments rare a....but...can she spin
CHRON, 132; FEMININITY, 4
Attila A. the Hen THATCHER, M, 2
attitude end of the war the a. to women working
changed WORK, 5
scope for change...women's a. to themselves
FEMINISM, 8
the largest scope for change still lies in men's a. to
women BRITTAIN, V, 2
attractive if they are in the least a. UNFAITHFULNESS, 3
want in life but to be as a. as possible to men
APPEARANCE, 3
attractively Women are entitled to dress a. RAPE, 7
aura woman has the same a. of isolation CHILDBIRTH, 19
Austen More can be learnt from Miss A. AUSTEN, J, 1
Australia So you're going to A. MELBA, N, 3
author An a. who speaks about his own books
MOTHERHOOD, 3
female a....ranks below an actress WRITERS, 7
Mrs Behn was the first woman...to earn her living as
an a. BEHN, A, 3
the a. of my pain CHILDBIRTH, 18
authoress the a....whose books have set all London...speculating BRONTË, C, 2
authority however great the a. of the husband CHRON, 129
right and a. of the husband CHRON, 31
The defiance of established a. ARENDT, H, 3
woman in a. is often unpopular POWER, 7
Woman's a. is nil SUBJECTION, 5
authors more daring than most male a. JONG, E, 1
autocrat be an a.: that's my trade CATHERINE THE GREAT, 6
the portrayal of her as a ruthless natural a. GANDHI, I, 2
autograph asked me for my a. BLACK, S, 2
to ask for her a., any more than they would ask royalty PAVLOVA, A, 1
automated a. appliance...is the mother MOTHERHOOD, 13
avenues New a. for higher culture...are opening before
them CHRON, 339
average a. man in the long run, the mental superior of
the a. woman INTELLIGENCE, 9
rare, man who is as steadily intelligent,...as the a.
woman INTELLIGENCE, 13
aversion Her friendships were flames of extravagant
passion ending in a. ANNE, 2
awake The lilies and roses were all a. COMPLIMENTS, 4

B

babies have their b. with gravity CHILDBIRTH, 23
making b. I think is a huge penitence CHRON, 81
she is thoroughly feminine...made for nothing but to
mother b. ELIOT, G, 2
women who are past the menopause to have b.
CHRON, 744
baby next thing, a b. was there CHRON, 463
Rock-a-bye, b., for father is near CHRON, 372
bachelors reasons for b. to go out
CHRON, 302; ELIOT, G, 6; WOMAN'S ROLE, 15
back The b. is fitted to the burden COURAGE, 3

background woman is always in the b.
MEN AND WOMEN, 16

backlash force of the b. CHRON, 747
violent b. against feminism FEMINISM, 23

bad b. woman...bit of goodness GOOD AND EVIL, 2
no worse evil than a b. woman ATTITUDES, 3
Wit in women is apt to have b. consequences
HUMOUR, 1

Balaklava days at B. have been so busy CHRON, 288

ballet The...artist I hold above all others in...the b.
PAVLOVA, A, 2

To enter the...B. is to enter a convent PAVLOVA, A, 3

bamboo after wriggling fish /With his big b. rod
ADULTERY, 1

banned any book should be b. WEST, R, 4

baptise mockery to allow women to b. RELIGION, 6

barbarity the...b. of war...forces men...to commit acts
KEY, E, 4

barbarous b. custom of wresting from women whatever she possesses CHRON, 250
b. custom that forbids the maid to make advances in
love CHRON, 230

Bardot The myth of B. is finished BARDOT, B, 5

barge b. with gilded stern CLEOPATRA VII, 3

barrage chemical b. has been hurled against the fabric
of life CARSON, R, 3

barrenness quarrels which vivify its b. GREER, G, 4

barriers sex b....those that exist in their own minds
CHRON, 669

barring guardian angel b. the way CHRON, 526

barrister b. had objected because 11 members of the
jury were women LAW, 16

bastard all my eggs in one b. ABORTION, 3
eggs in one b. PARKER, D, 10

bath sit in a b. of a decoction of linseed ABORTION, 1

bathe safer to rest and not to b. MENSTRUATION, 5

battle b. for women's rights EQUALITY, 21
march into b. together with the men COURAGE, 5
she went home and left me to finish the b.
STANTON, E, 3

battle-axe all in white...a little b. in her hand
JOAN OF ARC, 2

battlefield we survive amongst the dead and the dying
as on a b. SPARK, M, 3

beacon This amendment...would be like a b. CHRON, 689

bear b. and rear the majestic race MARTYRDOM, 2
Grant I may not b. a child CHRON, 495
women...should remain at home...and b. and bring
up children WOMAN'S ROLE, 7

beard b. I would have been the King DISCRIMINATION, 2

bearing hard travail in child b. CHILDBIRTH, 1

beasts Men are b. BARDOT, B, 6
men use us but a degree above b. CHRON, 160
Women in Africa work like b. of burden OPPRESSION, 7

beat more you b. them the better they be
SAYINGS AND PROVERBS, 41
neither kills nor maims her, it is legal for a man to b.
his wife VIOLENCE, 1
not for *every* cause is it right to b. her CHRON, 102

beaten girls cannot be b. in action CHRON, 547

beatings b. of the lonely heart LONELINESS, 3

beats has no wife, b. her oft SAYINGS AND PROVERBS, 16

beauties reality contains unparalleled b. ABBOTT, B, 3

beautiful a name as b. as the *Equal Rights* Amendment
CHRON, 691

an extremely b. girl and as innocent as a rose
TERRY, E, 1
b. woman in the act of cooking dinner for someone
she loves ATTITUDES, 23
Life will be happier and more b. PANKHURST, S, 3
lovely as to be b. BEAUTY, 6
not be half so b. if she was as great at mathematics
INTELLIGENCE, 4
Rich men's houses are seldom b. ASQUITH, M, 6
She is neither young nor b. GASKELL, E, 2
she would have given all her genius and all her fame
to be b. BRONTË, C, 3
the most b. woman I've ever seen BEAUTY, 13
What is b. is good GOOD AND EVIL, 1
when a woman isn't b. BEAUTY, 11

beauty B. and brains just can't be entertained BEAUTY, 15
B. in distress BEAUTY, 7
B. in London is so cheap BEAUTY, 8
b. is only skin deep BEAUTY, 12
b. of a woman is only skin-deep CHRON, 74
B. with all the Helps of Art, /is of no long Date
COSMETICS, 2
better to be first with an ugly woman than the hundredth with a b. LOVE, 57
But b.'s self she is, /When all her robes are gone
BEAUTY, 3
Character contributes to b. CHARACTER, 5
concubine for her b. BEAUTY, 1; SAYINGS AND PROVERBS, 39
dressed in womanly b. BEAUTY, 2
her b. made /The bright world dim BEAUTY, 10
images of female b. have come to weigh upon us
CHRON, 745
Love built on b. LOVE, 12
My b. aging, too OLD AGE, 4
She walks in b. BEAUTY, 9
sin against life is to...destroy b. PORTER, K, 3
the overwhelming b. of endurance COURAGE, 6
to inquire, /Would cloud our b. CHRON, 173
Who is't that to women's b. would submit BEHN, A, 5

bed distinguish her Husbands B. from anothers
CHRON, 163
in b. with a strange man O'BRIEN, E, 1
Lady Capricorn,...was...keeping open b.
PROMISCUITY, 1
on my b. I can still do something DIX, D, 5
woman who goes to b. with a man MODESTY, 3

beds rather make odes than b. WRITERS, 12

bees Swine, women, and b. SAYINGS AND PROVERBS, 33

befallen shadow of justice in the fate that has b.
women CHRON, 217

behaviour highest standards of b. without any law
CHRON, 30

behind In the dusk, with a light b. her AGE, 4

beneath Let the matron...stay b. the husband EQUALITY, 2
Why must I lie b. you SUBJECTION, 2

benefit mutual and satisfied sexual act is of great b. to
the average woman CHRON, 473

benefits ERA means that women who serve will get
equal b. CHRON, 679

benevolence husband render unto the wife due b.
MARRIAGE, 4

best all that's b. of dark and bright BEAUTY, 9
b. thing that could happen to motherhood
MOTHERHOOD, 16
she did her b. EPITAPHS, 3

best-trained care of children...better left to the b. practitioners CHRON, 619

betrothed a bride's attitude towards her b. MARRIAGE, 67

better b. to have loved and lost LOVE, 39
b. to marry than to burn MARRIAGE, 5
for b. for worse MARRIAGE, 15
more you beat them the b. they be SAYINGS AND PROVERBS, 41
No b. than she should be MORALITY, 3

Bible B. and Church have been the greatest stumbling block EMANCIPATION, 5
Outsold only by the B. and Shakespeare CHRISTIE, A, 1
various readings of the B. RELIGION, 9

bicycle fish needs a b. WOMEN'S LIBERATION MOVEMENT, 1

big unrepentant creature, b. with child is not such an outrageous sight CHRON, 490

bills She Paid the B. EPITAPHS, 5

biological male is a b. accident CHRON, 609

biology the dominance of b. POWER, 8

bird Her prose is like a b. SPARK, M, 1

birds spring now comes unheralded by the return of the b. CARSON, R, 4
worn b. in their hats for years CONSERVATION, 1

birth B. may be a matter of a moment CHILDBIRTH, 22
From b. to age eighteen, a girl needs good parents MATURITY, 2
married Four years...given b. for the Fifth time CHRON, 501
profound experience of the b. of the child CHILDBIRTH, 20

birth control instead of b. every one would preach drink control BIRTH CONTROL, 8; DRINKING, 7
No law in England can make B. BIRTH CONTROL, 7
prohibit the use of proper hygienic B. methods BIRTH CONTROL, 5; RELIGION, 12
scandalous to call Dr Marie Stopes B. method an experiment CHRON, 493

birthday A diplomat...always remembers a woman's b. OLD AGE, 10

birthright There is no b. in the white skin BESANT, A, 2

bishop blonde to make a b. kick a hole APPEARANCE, 9

bitch gives her opinion she's a b. DISCRIMINATION, 8
say 'spic' and 'b.' with impunity CHRON, 742
word b. can be frequently employed LANGUAGE, 5

bizarre her source material...sometimes refreshing, sometimes b. CHRISTINE DE PISAN, 2

black A lady asked me why...I wore b. SITWELL, E, 4

black eye b., too, Ma VIOLENCE, 4

blackmail United States...subject to all sorts of diplomatic b. SMITH, M, 3

blame b. Mom too much MOTHERHOOD, 10
b. only the rule of men POLITICS, 3
who can b. my woe DEATH, 1

blaming no use b. the men – we made them what they are CHRON, 494

blank Pain – has an Element of B. DICKINSON, E, 5

blast The First B. of the Trumpet CHRON, 116

blessings a world of b. by good Queen Elizabeth CHRON, 115
b. which come from true poverty TERESA OF AVILA, 3

blight Prostitution is a b. on the human race PROSTITUTION, 3; VIRTUE, 6

blind love is b. LOVE, 16
so many men are stupid and so few are b. WEBB, B, 1
union of a deaf man to a b. woman MARRIAGE, 24

blindness the...world was stumbling...in social b. KELLER, H, 4

blockade Women under b.,...survive...more successfully than men EMOTION, 2

blocking by b. the careers of so many other singers MELBA, N, 1

blonde A b. to make a bishop kick a hole APPEARANCE, 9

blondes Gentlemen always seem to remember b. LOOS, A, 1

blood b. of a womanhood that was never bought WOMANHOOD, 3
lie in sexual intercourse with a woman who has an issue of b. MENSTRUATION, 6
Shamed, dishonored, wading in b. CHRON, 478
so much Christian b.,...as under the said Queen Mary CHRON, 114
'Twas red with the b. of freemen HOWE, J, 5

bloodiness The sink is the great symbol of the b. of family life FAMILY, 10

bloom It's a sort of b. on a woman CHARM, 3

Bloomsbury She led the B. movement WOOLF, V, 1

blows B. are fitter for beasts than for rational creatures. VIOLENCE, 2

blue-stocking English b. adolescents CHRON, 615

blunting childminding can have a b. effect WORK, 6

blurred commenced drinking alone...b. sharp things DRINKING, 8

Boadicea B. put an end to her life by poison BOADICEA, 1

boat in the same b....not a chance of recording the vote CHRON, 406

bodies had pins thrust into their b. WITCHES, 5
scientific knowledge of the structure of our b. STOPES, M, 4
take for our b. /A master EXPLOITATION, 1
women gazed out of the slumped and sagging b. APPEARANCE, 14
women's b. are softer than men's, so their understanding is sharper CHRISTINE DE PISAN, 4

body b. of a weak and feeble woman CHRON, 125; ELIZABETH I, 11
I draw what I feel in my b. HEPWORTH, B, 4
woman keeps her b. intact CHASTITY, 2

bogey witch...remains a universal b. LANGUAGE, 6; WITCHES, 6

bomb Never mind about the b. – just smile WAR, 5

bonny good heart will help...a b. face BRONTË, E, 8

boobs the female...is all b. and buttocks GREER, G, 5

book an interminable and badly printed game b. STEIN, G, 1
any b. should be banned WEST, R, 4
I do not believe that she wrote...one b. which does not break new ground WOOLF, V, 2
library that hadn't a b. AUSTEN, J, 3
this b. is in future to be regarded as an indecent document CHRON, 496

books An author who speaks about his own b. MOTHERHOOD, 3
B., the Mind's food MORE, H, 3
permitted no b. but such as tend to the...effeminating of the mind CHRON, 177
the authoress...whose b. have set all London...speculating BRONTË, C, 2
women dislike his b. PREJUDICE, 3

bored When you're b. with yourself MARRIAGE, 61

bores I have the sort of face that b. me ASQUITH, M, 4

boring b. to be too much in the sun DU PRÉ, J, 4

born art of woman must be b.   CHRON, 540
Be b. anywhere, little embryo novelist   WRITERS, 13
joy that a man is b. into the world
    CHRON, 58; CHILDBIRTH, 2
misfortune it is to be b. a woman   SUBJECTION, 10
One is not b. a woman
    CHRON, 576; BEAUVOIR, S, 3; WOMANHOOD, 9
borrowed I have b. to spare my modesty   PORTER, K, 1
bough Loaf of Bread beneath the B.   LOVE, 41
bought blood of a womanhood that was never b.
    WOMANHOOD, 3
b. things because she wanted 'em   EDUCATION, 12
bound b. hand and foot by love and motherhood
    CHRON, 655
bouquets Glorious b. and storms of applause
    MARKOVA, A, 1
bow I b. before your rights as wife   CHRON, 11
boy b. commands the better price   CHRON, 523
rarely...one can see in a little b. the promise of a
man   MEN AND WOMEN, 14
boys B. will be b.   MEN AND WOMEN, 13
teach them the same subjects as are taught to b.
    CHRON, 97
Where...b. plan for what...young girls plan for
whom   GILMAN, C, 3
bracelet diamond and safire b. lasts forever   LOOS, A, 3
braces I had b. on my teeth and got high marks
    APPEARANCE, 11
brain if woman possessed a b. equal to man's
    INTELLIGENCE, 9
masculine disillusionment...woman has a b.
    INTELLECT, 10
parts of the b....less well developed in women
    CHRON, 400; INTELLIGENCE, 11
the skilled hands and cultural b. of women   GAGE, M, 2
To overload a woman's b.   CHRON, 349
brains a girl with b. ought to do something else
    INTELLIGENCE, 14; LOOS, A, 2
Beauty and b. just can't be entertained   BEAUTY, 15
b. as fruitful as our bodies   CHRON, 162
bred in schools to mature our b.   INTELLECT, 2
elephants' b. were even larger than men's   CHRON, 741
half the b. in the country...are not being used
    CHRON, 680
witches are usually old women of...small b.   CHRON, 120
Women have long hair and short b.
    INTELLIGENCE, 3; SAYINGS AND PROVERBS, 53
brand Miss, n. A title with which we b. unmarried
women   LANGUAGE, 2; SINGLE WOMEN, 6
branded woman...born b.   PROGRESS, 2
brandy must have b. on her apple dumplings   DRINKING, 3
brass Women cannot possibly play b. instruments and
look pretty   MUSICIANS, 7
brave nothing b. women cannot do if they are only
given the chance   CHRON, 405
We could never learn to be b....if there were only joy
    KELLER, H, 3
breach b. of promise   BETRAYAL, 3
bread Loaf of B. beneath the Bough   LOVE, 41
millions of women who earn their b. by the sweat of
their brows   CHRON, 335
breadwinner b. to the family   MOTHERHOOD, 5
break duty even to b. the law   CHRON, 410
breakfast she must not reheat his sins for b.
    FORGIVENESS, 3
breasts they add weight to the b.   COLETTE, 7

breats cut off their b. and sewed them to their mouths
    RUTHLESSNESS, 1
breeches Mrs Stanton wears the b.   STANTON, E, 1
Plenty of women to wear the b.   BLOOMER, A, 2
breeder b. of sinners   WOMAN'S ROLE, 9
brevity B. is the soul of lingerie   CLOTHES, 9; PARKER, D, 9
bribe The man who offers a b.   PROSTITUTION, 11
bricklayers B. kick their wives to death   MARRIAGE, 42
bride a b.'s attitude towards her betrothed   MARRIAGE, 67
It helps...to remind your b. that you gave up a
throne for her   MARRIAGE, 66
open the b. with his natural weapon he is a mighty
sworder   VIRGINITY, 8
bridled once a woman was b. it was out of the question for her to indulge   CHASTITY, 4
brigands B. demand your money   MISOGYNY, 6
bright her beauty made /The b. world dim   BEAUTY, 10
brighter proclaiming that women are b. than men
    LOOS, A, 5
brilliance a comely, ample woman with no outward
traces of b.   CHRISTIE, A, 2
brilliant remember till old age...our b. youth   OLD AGE, 2
bringeth when she b. forth a little girl   CHRON, 102
British Museum a reflection of the B. Reading Room
    INTELLIGENCE, 17; SPARK, M, 6
broken Esteem of men as of a b. reed   MEN, 1
Our spinning wheels are all b.   CHRON, 424
women had not b. the law of the Koran   CHRON, 720
Brontës Literary criticism of the B.   THE BRONTËS, 1
the B., as women and as writers   BRONTË, A, 3
broody in spite of oneself comes the nest building and
b. feeling   MOTHERHOOD, 18
brothers eagerness to learn with your b.   EDUCATION, 5
Sisters should be always willing to attend their b.
    DUTY, 2; FAMILY, 3
The poor are our b. and sisters   TERESA, MOTHER, 3
bruise sweetest fragrance from the herb...tread on it
and b. it   OPPRESSION, 4
brute Because man is a b., woman has to be locked up
    CHRON, 382
women in prison refuse to let b. force rule the world
    CHRON, 449
buds the darling b. of May   BEAUTY, 5
build clever man will b. a city   SAYINGS AND PROVERBS, 5
building human organism needs...good b. material
    HEALTH AND HEALTHY LIVING, 7
twenty years of marriage make her...like a public b.
    MARRIAGE, 37
bulrushes England may as well dam...the Nile with b.
    CHILD, L, 3
burden The back is fitted to the b.   COURAGE, 3
Women...shouldered the double b. unquestioningly
    CHRON, 709
burdens both sexes would continue to share the b. of
house-keeping   CHRON, 536
bureaucracy without freedom of the press,...b. rises
    CHRON, 480
burn better to marry than to b.   MARRIAGE, 5
She is very unpopular with the clergy...we long to b.
her alive   FRY, E, 2
burned woman's heart...b.   SORROW, 3
burning To keep a lamp b.   TERESA, MOTHER, 5
burns She b. and...dries up the semen   SEX, 11
burnt she is b. flesh   WITCHES, 7
Troy to be b. in flames   CHRON, 42
business a b., we single girls   SINGLE WOMEN, 12

ancestors did not want women to conduct any...b.
without a guardian CHRON, 32
a woman's b. to get married MARRIAGE, 41
B....may bring money AUSTEN, J, 5
Literature cannot be the b. of a woman's life WRITERS, 8
businessmen My message to the b. of this country AIDS, 1
busybody presumptuous /Flat-chested b..../Gate-crash-
ing all-male meetings CHRON, 49
but I am b. a woman CHRON, 330
butter-flies unfashionable employment of pursuing B.
CHRON, 170
butterfly Happiness is like a b. PAVLOVA, A, 5
buttock B. fetishism is comparatively rare GREER, G, 6
buttocks the female...is all boobs and b. GREER, G, 5
buying Marrying a man is like b. MARRIAGE, 60

C

cabinet woman Prime Minister...the best man in the c.
CHRON, 730
Caesar C.'s wife must be above suspicion
CHRON, 40; DIVORCE, 1; WOMAN'S ROLE, 3
cake Let them eat c. MARIE ANTOINETTE, 5
want your c. while you eat it too BIRTH CONTROL, 11
calamities learned woman is the greatest of all c.
INTELLECTUALS, 2
calculation cold c. than of passion in Anne's attitude
BOLEYN, A, 2
calendar on a c., but never on time MONROE, M, 5
cameras She stole everything but the c. WEST, M, 2
campaign it may tire out the workers and destroy...the
c. CATT, C, 3
candour too much c. in married life TRUTH, 1
canon heroism to send them to face the c. WAR, 4
canopy c. of cloth of gold, dressed as Venus
CLEOPATRA VII, 3
cant love – all the wretched c. of it GREER, G, 4
capitalism I am going to fight c. CHRON, 489; PANKHURST, S, 5
Militarism...is one of the chief bulwarks of c.
KELLER, H, 2
Capitol I shall administer justice on the C.
CLEOPATRA VII, 5
Capricorn Lady C...was...keeping open bed
PROMISCUITY, 1
captive have reserved Cleopatra as a c. to adorn his
Triumph CLEOPATRA VII, 4
care abandon the c. of their offspring CHRON, 244
yet she hathe but c. and woo CHRON, 106
career c. is born in public TALENT AND GENIUS, 1
c. woman...encounters a new obstacle: the hostility
of men CHRON, 612
caress is better than a c. CHRON, 535
her life and c. still seem to have been dreamed up by
one of her script-writers BOW, C, 2
how to combine marriage and a c. CHRON, 706
no other c. possible...is a flagrant social injustice
CHRON, 283
careerists despicable and self-seeking c. IBARRURI, D, 1
careers by blocking the c. of so many other singers
MELBA, N, 1
To get to the top...put their c. and companies first
CHRON, 704
cares a cheerful woman is one who has c. SILLS, B, 3
caress c. is better than a career CHRON, 535
careth he that is married c....how he may please his
wife MARRIAGE, 6

carnal c. lust which in women is insatiable LUST, 1
well-bred woman does not seek c. gratification SEX, 22
cars 50 Saudi women drove a convoy of c. CHRON, 720
cartwheels I don't do c. any more RAMBERT, M, 3
caste measure the social c. of a person MARRIAGE, 54
castle fair wife...frontier c. SAYINGS AND PROVERBS, 8
castrate Charlotte might 'c.' them or Emily 'unman'
them with her passion THE BRONTËS, 1
cat What c.'s averse to fish ATTITUDES, 12
catastrophe When a man confronts c....a woman looks
in her mirror MEN AND WOMEN, 18
catchwords Man is a creature who lives...by c.
DISCRIMINATION, 5
caterwauling remain in industry despite all narrow-
minded c. CHRON, 357
Cather Miss C....the new frontier she found it in the
mind CATHER, W, 2
the whole range of C.'s values, standards, tastes, and
prejudices CATHER, W, 1
Catherine I'm glad you like my C.
CATHERINE THE GREAT, 2; WEST, M, 7
cattle God intended women only as a finer sort of c.
CHRON, 159
cause women have been the c. of many troubles
CHRON, 107
cavaliers a nation of men of honour and of c.
MARIE ANTOINETTE, 2
celibacy no intermediary situation between marriage
and c. CHRON, 73
cello born to play the c. DU PRÉ, J, 1
cells These little grey c. CHRISTIE, A, 5
censurid shall be c. by my owne *Sex* CHRON, 147
chain the flesh to feel the c. BRONTË, E, 6
chair feminism has almost been equated with a tiresome insistence on 'c.' LANGUAGE, 10
challenge Women's Liberation Movement...dares to c.
what is CHRON, 642
chambermaid a man would be as happy in the arms of
a c. ATTITUDES, 14
chamois springing from blonde to blonde like the c. of
the Alps MARRIAGE, 70
chance nothing brave women cannot do if they are
only given the c. CHRON, 405
no women have had a fair c. CHRON, 271
Chanel C. epitomised the New Woman CHANEL, C, 2
change Most women set out to try to c. a man MEN, 5
My love...will c. LOVE, 36
scope for c....women's attitude to themselves
FEMINISM, 8
the largest scope for c. still lies in men's attitude to
women BRITTAIN, V, 2
changeful c. is woman always WOMAN'S NATURE, 1
change of life c. does not give talents MENOPAUSE, 2
changing Woman is always fickle and c.
CHRON, 43; CONTRARINESS, 2
chaos Invention,...out of c. SHELLEY, M, 4
character a person's c. lies in their own hands
FRANK, A, 7
C. contributes to beauty CHARACTER, 5
I had become a woman of...c. MATURITY, 1
no differences save by merit of c. BESANT, A, 4
the very nicest c. MURDOCH, I, 2
woman, whose c. has been the subject of so much
controversy BORGIA, L, 2
characters for divining c. by the conformation of men
STANHOPE, H, 2

Most women have no c.   CHARACTER, 2
charge Men are in c. of women   CHRON, 67
charity C. separates the rich from the poor   PERÓN, E, 5
charm C. is a delusion   CHARM, 1
charms C. by accepting, by submitting sways
      DOMINATION, 4
Whose c. all other maids surpass   CHARM, 2
chaste anything better than a wife who is c.
      WOMAN'S ROLE, 4
insist that a young girl should be pure, c. and innocent   HYPOCRISY, 2
modest and c. woman   CHRON, 229
poverty /Kept Latin women c.   CHASTITY, 1
to be c. a woman must not be clever
      CHRON, 128; JARS, M, 3
Women that are c.   CONTRARINESS, 3
chastise man has both the right and duty to c. his
girlfriend or wife   VIOLENCE, 6
chastity aptitude to live in c. and virginity
      CHASTITY, 3; PROCREATION, 2
impose c. on women as a necessary virtue
      PROSTITUTION, 3; VIRTUE, 6
virtues of women are reserve, quiet, c., orderliness
      FEMININITY, 1
women more esteemed by the opposite sex than c.
      CHASTITY, 5
chastity belt Female circumcision is a physiological c.
      CHASTITY, 7
cheap Beauty in London is so c.   BEAUTY, 8
Nice c. girl to take out for the evening   MITFORD, N, 2
underpaying women and using them as a reserve c.
labor supply   CHRON, 654
check C. enclosed   PARKER, D, 12
dreadful is the c.   BRONTË, E, 6
cheerful a c. woman is one who has cares   SILLS, B, 3
chemical c. barrage has been hurled against the fabric
of life   CARSON, R, 3
cheque to sign a little c.   MELBA, N, 2
cherish to love and to c.   MARRIAGE, 15
C. your husband's person...this being your office
      WOMAN'S ROLE, 6
cherry Till 'C. ripe' themselves do cry   APPEARANCE, 4
chieftain I am a c. of war   CHRON, 103
child c. enters the world through you   MOTHERHOOD, 20
Grant I may not bear a c.   CHRON, 495
man can say that the c. belongs to him by law
      CHRON, 510
perfect couple consisted of a mother and c.
      MOTHERHOOD, 22
stronger than a man simpler than a c.   BRONTË, E, 1
The mother-c. relationship is paradoxical
      MOTHERHOOD, 21
There are only two things a c. will share willingly
      CHILDREN, 8
childbearing gracious to her in her c..   CHRON, 70
no small consolation, that of c.   CHRON, 64
she will be saved by c.   CHILDBIRTH, 3; RELIGION, 1
Women have c. equipment   BIRTH CONTROL, 16
childbirth a matter of High Tech versus natural c.
      CHILDBIRTH, 24
c. is a heavy strain on the physique of any woman
      CHRON, 531
C. is that natural process   CHILDBIRTH, 11
painless c. does not exist as a matter of course.
      CHILDBIRTH, 17
the male equivalent of c.   CHILDBIRTH, 21

childcare France...c. is subsidised by the government
      CHILDREN, 11
procreation and c. are considered as one and the
same thing   CHRON, 626
childminding c. can have a blunting effect   WORK, 6
children achieve victory and return to our c.
      IBARRURI, D, 6
all c. would be conceived by artificial insemination
      CHRON, 710
all right until you start having c.   CHRON, 709
better reasons for having c. than not knowing how to
prevent them   BIRTH CONTROL, 9
care of c....better left to the best-trained practitioners
      CHRON, 619
c., and a husband...do not go well with composition
      MUSICIANS, 3
c. cease to be altogether desirable   CHRON, 515
Do you hear the c. weeping   BROWNING, E, 5
forming of the minds of c.   CHRON, 245
He that loves not his wife and c.   FAMILY, 2
'I have four nice c., and hope to have eight.'
      AMBITION, 3
in sorrow thou shalt bring forth c.   CHRON, 4
not much about having c.   CHILDREN, 9
one interest in common...c.   CHILDREN, 5
only privileged persons in our country are the c.
      PERÓN, E, 4
Parents learn a lot from their c.   SPARK, M, 2
patriarchal society...make c. of women   CHRON, 623
She...had better mind the kitchen and the c.
      BROWNING, E, 1
she watches her middle-aged c.   MOTHERHOOD, 14
stop believing and making their c. believe...that rain
is sent to us by Jesus   CHRON, 334
the c. are the makers of men   MONTESSORI, M, 5
The early marriages of silly c.   MARRIAGE, 25
We are transfused into our c.   CHILDREN, 4
We shelter c. for a time   WELDON, F, 1
Wife and c.   SAYINGS AND PROVERBS, 38
wives for the production of full-blooded c.   CHRON, 29
Women of the working class...should not have more
than two c.   CHRON, 472
women...should remain at home..., and bear and
bring up c.   WOMAN'S ROLE, 7
Chinese How did C. women,...discover they could run
      FRIEDAN, B, 5
chivalry another side to c.   CHIVALRY, 5
the age of c. is gone   MARIE ANTOINETTE, 2
True c. respects all womanhood   CHIVALRY, 1
Chloë In the spring...your lovely C.   PUBERTY, 4
chloroform that blessed C....delightful beyond measure
      CHILDBIRTH, 12
choir women...cannot be admitted to form part of the
c.   MUSICIANS, 4
choke result of visions, many people c. to death, more
women than men   VIRGINITY, 1
choose allowed women...to c. their own future
      CHRON, 717
the sound of men demanding their right to c.
      CHRON, 710
chore one more c. had to be done   CATHER, W, 5
chores multiple monotonous c. that are her daily lot
      CHRON, 580
chorus a dozen are only a c.   APPEARANCE, 10
Christ only a male can represent C....serious heresy
      CHRON, 729; RELIGION, 22

The Jews have produced...C., Spinoza, and myself
STEIN, G, 4

Christian good a C. as Mahomet ELIZABETH I, 3
several young women...would render the C. life
intensely difficult MARRIAGE, 55

Christianity Woman owes her present elevation...to C.
RELIGION, 10

Christian Science C. explains all cause and effect as
mental EDDY, M, 3

chronicler c. of contemporary Britain DRABBLE, M, 1
c. of her times BRITTAIN, V, 1

Church Bible and C. have been the greatest stumbling
block EMANCIPATION, 5
fairly loud statement about the nature of the C.
RELIGION, 17

Church of England trouble in the C. over women priests
RELIGION, 21

cigar a good c. is a smoke CONTEMPT, 2

cigarette I kissed my first woman, and smoked my
first c. SEX, 31

cigarettes emancipation of today displays itself mainly
in c. and shorts CHRON, 517

Cinderella A sort of literary C. BRONTË, A, 1

circulation Nancy, had a wider c. than both papers
ASTOR, N, 2

circumcision Female c., a traditional practice CHASTITY, 8
Female c. is a physiological chastity belt CHASTITY, 7

citizen status of a full and equal person and c.
CHRON, 605
woman a...secondary c. POWER, 8

citizens individual well-being is for private c. JARS, M, 2

city clever man will build a c. SAYINGS AND PROVERBS, 5

civilisation If c. is to advance...it must be
through...women PANKHURST, E, 3

civilization C. is a method of living ADDAMS, J, 6

civilized Woman will be the last thing c. by Man
CONTEMPT, 3
C. woman...paying too high a price DRABBLE, M, 4

Clara Bow C....was totally representative of...the flapper BOW, C, 3

clashes the c. and jars which we feel most keenly
ADDAMS, J, 4

class for one c. to appreciate the wrongs of another
STANTON, E, 9
promiscuous assemblage of the sexes in the same c.
is a dangerous innovation CHRON, 304

cleanliness The first possibility of rural c. lies in *water
supply.* NIGHTINGALE, F, 5

clear if he could make *me* understand...it would be c.
to all ROOSEVELT, E, 3

clenched You cannot shake hands with a c. fist
GANDHI, I, 5

Cleopatra Had C.'s nose been shorter
APPEARANCE, 5; CLEOPATRA VII, 2

clergy She is very unpopular with the c....we long to
burn her alive FRY, E, 2

clergyman a good deal of the c.'s wife about her
GASKELL, E, 2

clerks poor male c. whose living they are doing their
utmost to take CHRON, 428

clever as c. a crooked literary publicist as ever
SITWELL, E, 2
Be good, sweet maid, and let who can be c.
HAPPINESS, 2; VIRTUE, 7
c. man will build a city SAYINGS AND PROVERBS, 5
Mrs. Shelley is very c. SHELLEY, M, 1

She was very able, very c., and very unpleasant
PANKHURST, C, 2

strong and c. and happy STRENGTH, 1
to be chaste a woman must not be c.
CHRON, 128; JARS, M, 3

cleverest You're the c. member of...the c. nation in the
world WEBB, B, 5

cling nature of a woman...to c. to the man CHRON, 231
tendency to c. to their own sex HOMOSEXUALITY, 2

clitoris stimulation to orgasm centers upon the c. SEX, 50
successfully transferred...from the c. to the vaginal
orifice SEX, 13

clock One once said that I was like an ormolu c.
MITFORD, N, 4

close c. their eyes and think of Kenya OPPRESSION, 8

clothes as if she were taking off all her c.
COLETTE, 4; SEDUCTION, 1
bought her wedding c. ATTITUDES, 9
c. possess an influence more powerful CLOTHES, 4
draped with such c. for her natural excellence
CLOTHES, 2; SUPERIORITY, 4
Put off your shame with your c. MODESTY, 1

cloud fiend hid in a c. CHILDBIRTH, 5

club cruel a weapon as the cave man's c.
CONSERVATION, 4

clumsy That such mental powers must be hampered
with such a c. *body* STANTON, E, 5

cock He was like a c. ELIOT, G, 4

cold C., commanding, too often right WEBB, B, 2
counsel is c. SAYINGS AND PROVERBS, 57
husband be or become of so c. a nature DIVORCE, 3
so c. I almost got married SINGLE WOMEN, 8
The Irish,...are needed in this c. age CHILD, L, 2

collapse glom on to men so that they can c. with relief
CHRON, 596

college c....a substitute for...marriage EDUCATION, 28

colour the c. bar and all it implies are largely due to
thoughtlessness BESANT, A, 3
the diversity of...c. in the human race SOMERVILLE, M, 4

come Why don't you c. up sometime and see me
WEST, M, 4

comet learned woman is thought to be a c. CHRON, 157

comfort c. about being a woman...always pretend to
be more stupid STARK, F, 3
What a c. it was to see her pass NIGHTINGALE, F, 2

comforts War C. meeting was a solemn affair CHRON, 552

comic-strip one-dimensional subtlety of a c.
THATCHER, M, 3

command male is naturally more fitted to c. CHRON, 24

commanding Cold, c., too often right WEBB, B, 2
Men's courage is shown in c. CHRON, 23

commerce Friendship is a disinterested c. between
equals LOVE AND FRIENDSHIP, 4

commit woman alone, can...c. them ATTITUDES, 18

commitment Her total c.,..., spontaneity and fearlessness CASTLE, B, 2
Total c. to family COMMITMENT, 4

common recognise that there is a woman's c. ground
CHRON, 733
woman of c. views but uncommon abilities
THATCHER, M, 1

commonwealth insane persons, confined within this c.
DIX, D, 2

communicate I have nothing to c. on the subject of religion WOLLSTONECRAFT, M, 5

communicated knowledge...should be c. to women no less than men CHRON, 336

Communist need of being a member of the C. Party JUSTICE, 2

community Marriage...a c....making in all two MARRIAGE, 43

true c. consists of individuals CHRON, 608

companies To get to the top...put their careers and c. first CHRON, 704

companion your queen and c., far beyond my desert or desire BOLEYN, A, 3

companions c. for middle age MARRIAGE, 11

compare c. thee to a summer's day BEAUTY, 5

comparison Man, woman, and devil, are the three degrees of c. SAYINGS AND PROVERBS, 22

no other actress...could escape unfavourable c. EVANS, E, 1

comparisons c. are odious COMPLIMENTS, 1

compass my heart shall be /The faithful c. CONSTANCY, 2

compassion c. without condescension ADDAMS, J, 2

compel Liberation would c. women into male roles CHRON, 653

only unwilling when you c. them SEX, 24

compels law c. her to bear everything from him CHRON, 320

compensation c. will only be four-fifths of ours CHRON, 564

compensations housekeeping cares bring...endearing c. HOUSEKEEPING, 1

there are always c. for every adverse experience BROWN, O, 1

compleat inward and outward Vertues...in a C. Woman CHRON, 165

complexion my c. was like alabaster STANHOPE, H, 3

compliments She could exchange c. or insults...with dukes or dockers ASTOR, N, 1

compose woman must not desire to c. SCHUMANN, C, 2

composers enough women c. for it to die a natural death MUSICIANS, 5

There are no women c. MUSICIANS, 9

composing C....is very feminine MUSICIANS, 10

nothing greater than the joy of c. SCHUMANN, C, 3

woman's c. is like a dog's walking on his hind legs CHRON, 516

composition children, and a husband...do not go well with c. MUSICIANS, 3

compromise not a question that leaves much room for c. MEIR, G, 5

compulsion seized by the stern hand of C. CONTRARINESS, 8

computer masculine preserve, as in c. science CHRON, 716

conceal C. whatever learning she attains CHRON, 186

concealed highest injustice our knowledge must rest c. CHRON, 185

conceive every woman who was married would automatically want to c. CHRON, 574

conception aids in preventing c. BIRTH CONTROL, 2

demands to know how to prevent c. CHRON, 462

if the parts be smooth c. is prevented BIRTH CONTROL, 1

preventing c. shocks the mind of a woman BIRTH CONTROL, 3

concern Such matters are men's c. CHRON, 47

concerns trivial c. – to do with physical appearance APPEARANCE, 19

concubine c. for her beauty BEAUTY, 1; SAYINGS AND PROVERBS, 39

concubines selling of young girls as c. CHRON, 543

condescension compassion without c. ADDAMS, J, 2

condition c. of our sex is so deplorable CHRON, 410; PANKHURST, E, 6

conditioning totality of their c. DISCRIMINATION, 6

condolence a prolific writer of notes of c. DICKINSON, E, 2

conductor The c. and director must create the atmosphere CALDWELL, S, 2

confess obliged to c. the supremacy of the other sex CHRON, 251

confessing women...ill-using them and then c. it OPPRESSION, 4

confine c. themselves to making puddings and knitting stockings CHRON, 272

confirmed marriages shall be c. by a nuptial blessing CHRON, 73

conform c. to the classic and traditional images CHRON, 603

conformation for divining characters by the c. of men STANHOPE, H, 2

confusion Nurses all in c. CHRON, 288

conquer worlds that women have yet to c. is that of The Arts MUSICIANS, 6

conquered c. by female fury CHRON, 31

conquers He who angers you, c. you KENNY, E, 4

conscience a Nonconformist c. MORALITY, 1

not cut my c. to fit this year's fashions DETERMINATION, 1; POLITICS, 7

conscientious objectors there were women c....during the war CHRON, 560

consciously I have never c. exploited the fact that I am a woman CASTLE, B, 5

consensus expect decisions to be...made by c. MEN AND WOMEN, 34

consent No one can make you feel inferior without your c. ROOSEVELT, E, 2

consequences men never violate the laws of God without suffering the c. CHILD, L, 1

consider C. your sex and spare me CHRON, 86

consolation no small c., that of childbearing CHRON, 64

Consort resolution, to please her C....and the Nation CATHERINE THE GREAT, 1

conspicuous be most c. when she is with her husband CHRON, 52

consumes Widow. The word c. itself WIDOWHOOD, 4

contemplative Between women love is c. CHRON, 578

contempt c. with which the single woman has been regarded SINGLE WOMEN, 7

sexual shyness...arouses the c. of decent ones CHRON, 562

continuance housewives as mothers...ensuring the adequate c. of the British race CHRON, 555

contraception a terrific story about oral c. BIRTH CONTROL, 19

right to abortion and improved c. transformed many women's lives CHRON, 718

contraceptive c. pill may reduce the importance of sex CHRON, 611

Dr Marie Stopes made c. devices respectable STOPES, M, 3

contraceptives use c. do not understand love TERESA, MOTHER, 6

C. should be used BIRTH CONTROL, 13

contract law expressly forbids...women from being able to make a c. CHRON, 25

contradiction Woman's at best a c. CONTRARINESS, 4

contradictions warring c., womanhood and anger
ANGER, 2; WOMANHOOD, 1
contributory she was guilty of a great deal of c. negligence LAW, 18
control a woman must first c. herself ANTRIM, M, 4
controversy woman, whose character has been the subject of so much c. BORGIA, L, 2
convenience women who've got every c. of every kind PROGRESS, 4
convent Such ignorance. All the boys were in military schools and all the girls were in the c. PORTER, K, 4
To enter the…Ballet is to enter a c. PAVLOVA, A, 3
conversation c. is primarily a language of rapport LANGUAGE, 9
female c. to the last new publication CHRON, 224
There is no such thing as c. WEST, R, 5
cookery c. do SEX, 9
cooking beautiful woman in the act of c. dinner for someone she loves ATTITUDES, 23
woman accepted c.…but man…made of it a recreation CHRON, 492; WOMAN'S ROLE, 26
C., baking and washing…duties…have to undertake herself CHRON, 368
corrupt rotten and c. to the marrow MANN, E, 2
corrupted one whom fame has not c. CURIE, M, 2
corruption social imbalance and c.…because of the prominence of women SUBJECTION, 16
corset c. must be looked upon as distinctly prejudicial to health CLOTHES, 7; HEALTH AND HEALTHY LIVING, 5
cosmetic sunlight as a kind of c. effulgence COSMETICS, 7
cosmetics c. names seemed obscenely obvious COSMETICS, 11
I loathe the c. industry RODDICK, A, 3
In the factory we make c. COSMETICS, 10
cost pay the first c. on all human life WAR, 3
costs a woman to cling to her standards at all c. CAVELL, E, 1
costume c. of women should be suited to her wants and necessities BLOOMER, A, 5
counsel c. is cold SAYINGS AND PROVERBS, 57
counteroffensive today's power structure…to mount a c. against women CHRON, 746
country c. a man's c. CHRON, 413
it's not so much a c. as an experience JHABVALA, R, 3
law of this c. has made you my master CHRON, 238
understanding the problems of running a c. HOUSEKEEPING, 10; POLITICS, 13
couple perfect c. consisted of a mother and child MOTHERHOOD, 22
courage ahead of their leaders in realism and c. SMITH, M, 1
C.! I have shown it for years MARIE ANTOINETTE, 4
C. is the price…for granting peace EARHART, A, 1
In c. and honor ANTHONY, S, 2
Men's c. is shown in commanding CHRON, 23
course c. of true love never did run smooth LOVE, 15
married for a c. or two at mealtimes ADULTERY, 10
court A C. hairdresser who travels with her PERÓN, E, 1
courtship C. is to marriage MARRIAGE, 17
cow A great c. full of ink SAND, G, 3
coward better to be the widow of a hero than the wife of a c. IBARRURI, D, 5
No c. soul is mine BRONTË, E, 4
cowards make c. of men as the liquor power DRINKING, 4
the future…makes c. of us DIX, D, 2

cows daring…to explain…that c. can be eaten GANDHI, I, 4
cradle hands have rocked the c. WOMEN'S LIBERATION MOVEMENT, 6
The hand that rocks the c. POWER, 6
crazy He never regarded himself as c. JONG, E, 2
They think I am a c. woman and never molest me CALAMITY JANE, 1
create c. in women a generalized dependency WOMAN'S ROLE, 30
created c. /Forgiveness but to speak FORGIVENESS, 1
gods c. woman for the indoors functions CHRON, 27
creation an atmosphere in which c. is possible RAMBERT, M, 2
an ugly *woman* is a blot on the fair face of c. BRONTË, C, 5
her intellect is not for invention or c. CHRON, 308
men from their first c. usurped a supremacy CHRON, 160
creative man's fear of women's c. energy FEAR, 1; SUBJECTION, 14
Woman is a being dominated by the c. urge HINKLE, B, 1
creator c. would purposely make half the whole race imperfect MEN AND WOMEN, 2
The c.…desires to subdue other minds HINKLE, B, 4
creeds Vain are the thousand c. BRONTË, E, 5
cricket I do love c. – it's so very English BERNHARDT, S, 3
crimes No punishment…prevent the commission of c. ARENDT, H, 4
rape is one of the least-reported c. RAPE, 2
criminal neither am I as a militant Suffragist a c. CHRON, 429
Wives have no right to bring c. accusations for adultery CHRON, 56
criminals regarding them as c. and lunatics CHRON, 430
criticism Literary c. of the Brontës THE BRONTËS, 1
criticks Women write, the C.…damn their Plays WRITERS, 4
crooked as clever a c. literary publicist as ever SITWELL, E, 2
crop watering the last year's c. ELIOT, G, 3
Cross 'Lead him to the C..' JOAN OF ARC, 2
The orgasm has replaced the C. SEX, 43
crossed a girl likes to be c. in love a little now and then LOVE, 30
crosses series of c. for us mothers CHRON, 484
crow sun had risen to hear him c. ELIOT, G, 4
crown he who placed the c. of Egypt upon my head. CHRON, 35
cruel c. a weapon as the cave man's club CONSERVATION, 4
c. to bother people who want to be left in peace GARBO, G, 3
She is irresponsible and immoral, but not deliberately c. BARDOT, B, 2
crushing c. and numbing force of the bare struggle for life CHRON, 387
cry bring them softness, teach them how to c. BAEZ, J, 3
I often want to c. MEN AND WOMEN, 20
She likes stories that make her c. KELLER, H, 1
the only advantage women have over men…they can c. MEN AND WOMEN, 20
cultivation prevent the c. of the female understanding CHRON, 203
proper c. of all her powers FEMINISM, 2

cultural Our c. world is the product of male consciousness   CHRON, 665
the skilled hands and c. brain of women   GAGE, M, 2
culture C. is an instrument wielded by professors
    WEIL, S, 1
guardians of c.   SOCIETY, 9
New avenues for higher c....are opening before them
    CHRON, 339
to change the toy c.   MONTESSORI, M, 2
curates abundant shower of c.   BRONTË, C, 8
cures Smiths, Weavers, and Women, boldly and
accustomably took upon them great C.   CHRON, 131
curfew c., let the men stay home   CHRON, 663
curriculum highest mental and moral qualities...in a
man's c.   EDUCATION, 25; WOMANHOOD, 5
curse modern woman is the c. of the universe
    WOMEN'S LIBERATION MOVEMENT, 14
curvaceousness c....incompatible with the life of the
mind   INTELLIGENCE, 18
custom artificial trammels of c.   WOMANHOOD, 2
barbarous c. of wresting from women whatever she
possesses   LAW, 9
c. has plac'd us in   CHRON, 170
c. has pronounced necessary for their sex   CHRON, 272
c. in letter-writing   SUPERIORITY, 3
c. of women   MENSTRUATION, 10
the restraint of law and that of c.   CATT, C, 2
customers We give c. a sense of theatre   RODDICK, A, 4
cuts c. her wisdom teeth when she is dead
    INTELLIGENCE, 1; SAYINGS AND PROVERBS, 42
cynic she should be brought up like a philosopher,
even like a c.   SHELLEY, M, 2

D

dad They fuck you up, your mum and d.   FAMILY, 12
daily multiple monotonous chores that are her d. lot
    CHRON, 580
dainty D. skirts and delicate blouses   CHRON, 460
damn Women write, the Criticks...d. their Plays
    WRITERS, 4
damnation there would be no d.   ATTITUDES, 7
damned d. if you do   BREASTFEEDING, 6
dance I have discovered the d.   DUNCAN, I, 3
dancer the importance of the individual d.   RAMBERT, M, 1
danger Euthanasia is a long, smooth-sounding word,
and...conceals its d.   BUCK, P, 4
I realized there was a measure of d.   EARHART, A, 4
she is her husband's partner in d.   CHRON, 53
dangerous d. for women to use such things against
their husbands   EDUCATION, 5
man is a d. creature   ADAMS, A, 3
dangers without the wickedness of women...world
would remain proof against innumerable d.
    CHRON, 105
daring more d. than most male authors   JONG, E, 1
darkness the d. inside houses   DELANEY, S, 1
daughter As is the mother, so is her d.
    SAYINGS AND PROVERBS, 3
inheritance goes to the son, not the d.   CHRON, 66
my d. all her life   CHILDREN, 6
the earth is free for every son and d. of mankind
    CHRON, 142
daughters d. are but branches which by marriage are
broken off from the root   CHRON, 151

Education of their Children as well D. as Sons
    CHRON, 169
important...preparing the d. of the land to be good
mothers   CHRON, 240
Two d....are...arrant thieves   SAYINGS AND PROVERBS, 34
Words are men's d.   CHRON, 182; ATTITUDES, 11
dawn They sighed for the d. and thee   COMPLIMENTS, 4
day compare thee to a summer's d.   BEAUTY, 5
from this d. forward   MARRIAGE, 15
dead cuts her wisdom teeth when she is d.
    INTELLIGENCE, 1; SAYINGS AND PROVERBS, 42
Mother is the d. heart of the family
    CHRON, 624; GREER, G, 3
we survive amongst the d. and the dying as on a battlefield   SPARK, M, 3
women's lib was d. milliseconds after Hammerstrike
    WOMEN'S LIBERATION MOVEMENT, 17
Dead Political equality is D. Sea fruit   CHRON, 530
deadly the female of the species is more d. than the
male   ATTITUDES, 19; RUTHLESSNESS, 2
deaf union of a d. man to a blind woman   MARRIAGE, 24
death Because I could not stop for D.   DICKINSON, E, 3
d. you merited, the Son of God had to die
    APPEARANCE, 2
enough women composers for it to die a natural d.
    MUSICIANS, 5
He has seen too much d.   PLATH, S, 3
I have never risked d.   O'BRIEN, E, 2
I shall but love thee better after d.
    BROWNING, E, 7; LOVE, 38
keep d. in my line of sight   DEATH, 3
many herbs against the early d. of woman   CHRON, 385
men of her town shall stone her to d.   CHRON, 8
Mrs Browning's d. is rather a relief to me
    BROWNING, E, 1
Sickness, sin and d....do not originate in God
    EDDY, M, 5
Sin brought d.   EDDY, M, 4
take your wife in adultery,...put her to d.   ADULTERY, 2
the d. of the American family   BOMBECK, E, 4
The thought of d. came   DEATH, 2
till d. us do part   MARRIAGE, 15
Voluntary d. would be an abandonment of our present post   BLAVATSKY, E, 2
without risking d. in an illegal abortion   FEMINISM, 20
debauch your fine officials d. the young girls   STEAD, C, 5
debauchery theft to foist heirs born of d. on an entire
family   CHRON, 154
debt Posterity has paid its d. to her   BRONTË, E, 2
run into d. with Nature   CHRON, 316
deceit useth much more machination and d. than a
man   CHRON, 95
deceive Women...weeping,...meanes...to d.   DECEPTION, 1
decent earn a d. living at other occupations   CHRON, 451
ejected from all d. society   BEHN, A, 1
I do not think it is delicate or d.   CHILDBIRTH, 9
decide d. how you're going to live   LIFE, 3
I leave before being left. I d.   BARDOT, B, 4
Women d. the larger questions of life   INTELLIGENCE, 13
decisions expect d. to be...made by consensus
    MEN AND WOMEN, 34
Declaration principles of the D. of Independence
    EQUALITY, 7
decline d. from the standard of morals   CAULKINS, F, 2
decorum Regularity and D.....Women-
Authors...greatly deficient in   WRITERS, 5

deep beauty is only sin d. BEAUTY, 12
deer Shall the dog lie where the d. once couched GWYNN, N, 5
deface liberal education of women is to d. the image of God CHRON, 158
defeat every victory turns into a d. BEAUVOIR, S, 4
defect this fair d. /Of nature CHRON, 153
defective woman is d. and misbegotten WOMAN'S NATURE, 4
defense d. effort in terms of defending women WAR, 9
deferred long d. and often wished for BRONTE, C, 4
defiance The d. of established authority ARENDT, H, 3
deficient Regularity and Decorum....Women-Authors...greatly d. in WRITERS, 5
definition This d....would not do for a policeman CHRON, 300; NIGHTINGALE, F, 4
degraded d. class of labor in the market CHRON, 392
woman is d. by exerting her ingenuity CHRON, 252
degrading middle-class hold housewifely work as d. CHRON, 348
degree men use us but a d. above beasts CHRON, 160
delicacy d. of the national manners in point of this kind CHRON, 266
old-fashioned notions of d. or propriety CHILDBIRTH, 6
delicate Dainty skirts and d. blouses CHRON, 460
I do not think it is d. or decent CHILDBIRTH, 9
Young ladies are d. plants HEALTH AND HEALTHY LIVING, 1
delight I d. in sinning SIN, 1
delivery child is a male, the mother has a better colour and an easier d. PREGNANCY, 1
demand d. what we want for women CHRON, 498
we d. freedom of abortion CHRON, 632; ABORTION, 7
demanded assumes whatever duties are d. WOMAN'S ROLE, 32
demanding stopped d. so much respeckt for ourselves HUMILITY, 7
democracy never...a d....a phallocracy PARTURIER, F, 3
demon real d. is success SUCCESS, 6
denied heroic actions, public employments,...d. our sex CHRON, 148
depend d. on men to sort out financial things INDEPENDENCE, 3
make it...unnecessary that women should d. on men CHRON, 283
depended d. on women to get production up WORK, 4
dependence show their consciousness of d. CHRON, 248
dependency create in women a generalized d. WOMAN'S ROLE, 30
dependent man...keep woman d. upon his economically SUBJECTION, 15
now d. on the man's labour CHRON, 242
she is financially less d. on a job CHRON, 712
she must not be d. on her husband's bounty INDEPENDENCE, 2; LAW, 8
woman was made d. CHRON, 281; SUBJECTION, 11
deplorable condition of our sex is so d. CHRON, 410; SUFFRAGETTES, 12
depressed If we didn't live venturously,...we should never be d. WOOLF, V, 9
what partiality!...one exalted and the other d. EDUCATION, 15
deserters every year there are new d. CASSATT, M, 3
deserves dumb idiot and d. no better PIAF, E, 4
desideratum great d. the mother's milk CHRON, 322
designed industry has not d. itself...to help women CHRON, 721

man is d. to walk three miles EQUALITY, 23
use of her that nature d. for her LUST, 2
desirability unsatisfied mother who unduly stressed the d. of professional careers CHRON, 615
desirable children cease to be altogether d. CHRON, 515
desire Those who restrain D. LUST, 4
woman must not d. to compose SCHUMANN, C, 2
your queen and companion, far beyond my desert or d. BOLEYN, A, 3
desolate d. and sick of an old passion LOVE, 48
despicable d. and self-seeking careerists IBARRURI, D, 1
despises A woman d. a man for loving her LOVE, 46
destiny 'anatomy is d.' CHRON, 618
destroyer greatest d. of peace is abortion ABORTION, 13
desultory intellectually more d. and volatile than men INTELLECT, 5
detested d. women's gossip GOSSIP, 2
developed parts of the brain...less well d. in women CHRON, 400; INTELLIGENCE, 11
development higher mental d. of woman INTELLECTUALS, 3
school education ignores,...healthy d. BLACKWELL, E, 2
devil ding the d. SAYINGS AND PROVERBS, 58
it's just to kill the d. BLACKWELL, E, 4
Man, woman, and d., are the three degrees of comparison SAYINGS AND PROVERBS, 22
The D.'s in her tongue BEHN, A, 8
the door of the d. RELIGION, 13
three halfpence worse than the d. SAYINGS AND PROVERBS, 37
Women are the d.'s nets SAYINGS AND PROVERBS, 51
You are the d.'s gateway CHRON, 62
devoted definition of...a nurse...'d. and obedient' CHRON, 300; NIGHTINGALE, F, 4
nurse should be...d. and obedient PREJUDICE, 1
diamonds Wrapped in furs and sparkling with d. PERON, E, 2
diary Her d. endures FRANK, A, 1
What is a d. as a rule TERRY, E, 5
dictation I did not write it. God wrote it. I merely did his d. STOWE, H, 5
Dido D. and the Trojan chief CHRON, 44
die better to d. on your feet than to live on your knees IBARRURI, D, 4
dies marries or d....kindly spoken of AUSTEN, J, 4
dieting Unnecessary d. BEAUTY, 14; HEALTH AND HEALTHY LIVING, 6
difference schoolroom...d. of sex...need to be forgotten CHRON, 391
the d. of sex, if there is any ANTHONY, S, 4
value lies in their d. CHRON, 722
differences education to bring out and fortify the d. CHRON, 525
different Arithmetic is d. SOCIETY, 1
d., not because he is illegitimate ILLEGITIMACY, 2
Women are equal because...not d. CHRON, 586
difficulties there are,..., great d. in the path MITCHELL, M, 2
diffident I am naturally timid and d. DIX, D, 3
dignity aware of liberty and d. and true reason MANN, E, 3
ding d. the devil SAYINGS AND PROVERBS, 58
dinner A man is...better pleased when he has a good d. upon his table CHRON, 197; INTELLIGENCE, 6; WOMAN'S ROLE, 10
wife may not be present at d. CHRON, 37
diplomat A d....always remembers a woman's birthday OLD AGE, 10

diplomatic United States...subject to all sorts of d. blackmail SMITH, M, 3

direction d. belongs to the man CHRON, 72

director The conductor and d. must create the atmosphere CALDWELL, S, 2

dirty American politics are too d. for women POLITICS, 6
Is sex d. SEX, 37
politics are too d. for women CHRON, 520

disappointment one hope – that I will not be a d. CALLAS, M, 3

disciple a d....of the fiend, called the Pucelle JOAN OF ARC, 1

discontents the family...source of all our d. FAMILY, 11

discriminated Why should unmarried women be d. against CHRON, 666
Why should unmarried women be d. against TAXATION, 3

discrimination Legislation is not going to change d. CHRON, 686

disdain d. /Our being your equals CHRON, 133

disease Pregnancy is not a d. PREGNANCY, 4

diseases These d....they're purely psychic JHABVALA, R, 1

disfranchisement injustice of d. CHRON, 346
woman...feels as keenly as man the injustice of d. STANTON, E, 8

disgrace d. for women to be sexually responsible CHRON, 676
d. to live old maids SINGLE WOMEN, 1
no d. in the dust CHRON, 348

disgraceful d. but common to see women...unable to pronounce what they read EDUCATION, 10

disgust passionate woman, with d. MEN AND WOMEN, 7

disgusting d. as a woman who acts the freethinker INTELLIGENCE, 5

disillusionment masculine d....woman has a brain INTELLECT, 10

dislike that *my* statue should be moved, which I should much d. VICTORIA, 8

disparagement need not call for the help of a Man-Midwife, which is a d. CHRON, 146

disposition the d. for...a wife CHARACTER, 3

disproportionate d. value set on the time and labor of men and women CHRON, 260

dissatisfied the strange, d. voice stirring within her FRIEDAN, B, 3

distinction chief d. in the intellectual powers of the two sexes CHRON, 326
not believe in sex d. in literature, law, politics, or trade CHRON, 466

distinctions invidious d. of sex CHRON, 346
woman feels the invidious d. of sex STANTON, E, 8

distrust stay together, but we d. one another MARRIAGE, 69

diverge Partners concerns and interests d. over time PARTNERSHIP, 4

divided person who d. society into two parts HYPATIA, 2

divine The d. *right* of husbands CHRON, 202; MARRIAGE, 20; WOLLSTONECRAFT, M, 3

divorce d....Blame our obsolete sex roles CHRON, 657
d. has increased one thousand percent DIVORCE, 12
d. is obtainable only by the very rich DIVORCE, 4
notice of d. to her husband on trumped-up grounds CHRON, 63
only good thing about d. DIVORCE, 10
scandal of d. had been socially ostracized MORALITY, 6

do wanted women to d....certain things such as join up EXPLOITATION, 2

docile remain the servile, d.,...self-abnegative wife SUFFRAGETTES, 4

dockers She could exchange compliments or insults...with dukes or d. ASTOR, N, 1

doctor A devoted nurse,..., deserves,..., a place next to the d. OCCUPATIONS, 6
ought to have trained as a d. OCCUPATIONS, 13
The d. is not a nurse OCCUPATIONS, 8
woman is incompetent to be a lawyer, minister or d. CHRON, 343

doctors few D., either male or female, as possible CHRON, 303
women D. can get practice CHRON, 338

doctrines writers whose extravagant d. have...been published WOLLSTONECRAFT, M, 2

does many things a woman d. WOMAN'S ROLE, 32

dog A woman's preaching is like a d.'s walking on his hinder legs CHRON, 189; CONTEMPT, 1; RELIGION, 8
d., and a walnut-tree SAYINGS AND PROVERBS, 41
Shall the d. lie where the deer once couched GWYNN, N, 5
woman's composing is like a d.'s walking on his hind legs CHRON, 516

dogma the existence of Satan a d. of the church BLAVATSKY, E, 4

dogs The woman who is really kind to d. PREJUDICE, 2
woman who is...kind to d. MISOGYNY, 9

dollar Nothing that costs only a d. is worth having ARDEN, E, 3

domestic could not make my dream of d. contentment come true CHRON, 693
d. tabby-cat-woman CHRON, 447
in d. service CHRON, 456
there remain only duties, d. virtue CHRON, 226
zeal in the holy cause of humanity...infringe on those d. duties CHRON, 222

dominance man's economic d. over women CHRON, 470

dominated man has d. over woman SOCIETY, 5; STRENGTH, 3

domination d. of women...most fundamental of links DOMINATION, 7
wrong in the world to male d. CHRON, 521

domineer nor must woman d. over man CHRON, 60

dominion lust of d. DOMINATION, 5
Woman is under man's d. SUBJECTION, 6

done One never notices what has been d. CURIE, M, 7
speak of what I have d. ACHIEVEMENT, 1

door no d. to slam BEAUTY, 16

doormat feminist whenever I express sentiments that differentiate me from a d. or a prostitute CHRON, 592

doubtful name of a woman makes one d. ARTISTS, 1

downfall women...brought on their own d. DOMINATION, 8

downtrodden most d. and sweated workers CHRON, 381

dozen a d. are only a chorus APPEARANCE, 10

draw I d. what I feel in my body HEPWORTH, B, 4

drawbacks One of the d. of Fame MELBA, N, 5

dreadful d. is the check BRONTË, E, 6
d. name of old maid SINGLE WOMEN, 2

dream could not make my d. of domestic contentment come true CHRON, 693
Happiness is no vague d. SAND, G, 4

dreams My d. were all my own SHELLEY, M, 3

dress Elegance...not...a new d. CLOTHES, 13
I have no d. except the one I wear CURIE, M, 6

no such thing as a moral d.   CLOTHES, 8
dressed d. in womanly beauty   BEAUTY, 2
Today I d. to meet my father's eyes   CLOTHES, 1
drink instead of birth control every one would preach
    d. control   BIRTH CONTROL, 8; DRINKING, 7
she would never take a d.   PREJUDICE, 6
drinking commenced d. alone...blurred sharp things
    DRINKING, 8
    d. deep of that divinest anguish   BRONTË, E, 7
drowning Being an old maid is like death by d.
    SINGLE WOMEN, 10
drudgery Women in d. knew   MARTYRDOM, 3
drunk What, when d. one sees in other women, one
sees in Garbo sober   GARBO, G, 2
dukes She could exchange compliments or
    insults...with d. or dockers   ASTOR, N, 1
dull a very d. Play   MARRIAGE, 17
dumb d. blonde because of the way I look
    APPEARANCE, 17
    d. idiot and deserves no better   PIAF, E, 4
duress women dwell...on the d.   CHRON, 692
dusk In the d., with a light behind her   AGE, 4
dust Excuse my d.   EPITAPHS, 6
no disgrace in the d.   CHRON, 348
dusting fill in their space time washing out the offices
and d. same   CHRON, 428
duties assumed the d. of a man   POLITICS, 2
assumes whatever d. are demanded   WOMAN'S ROLE, 32
justify withdrawal from the usual d. and pleasures
of life   MENSTRUATION, 14
Mrs Stanton would attend...to her domestic d.
    STANTON, E, 2
there remain only d.   CHRON, 226; WOMAN'S ROLE, 11
duty absolute d.,...., to suckle her infant   BREASTFEEDING, 4
done my d. to my Country having had 13 children
    BIRTH CONTROL, 6
d. and privilege to fill in the scale of society
    CHRON, 232
d. even to break the law   CHRON, 410
D. is ours and events are God's   GRIMKÉ, A, 3
highest and eternal d. of women   DUTY, 1
man has both the right and d. to chastise his
girlfriend or wife   VIOLENCE, 6
most sacred d. which devolves upon the sex
    CHRON, 245
the condition of our sex is so deplorable that it is our
d....to break the law   PANKHURST, E, 6
dwell d. at home without their husbands   CHRON, 100
women d....on the duress   CHRON, 692
dyes committing a sin...against her self-respect if she
d. her hair   APPEARANCE, 8; OLD AGE, 7
dying D. /is an art   PLATH, S, 2
For a priest to turn a man when he lies a-d.
    DECEPTION, 2; SEX, 5
we survive amongst the dead and the d. as on a battlefield   SPARK, M, 3
dyke never said I was a d.   LESBIANISM, 7
dynamic class people as static and d.
    CHRON, 519; MEN AND WOMEN, 19

E

ear the e. begins to hear   BRONTË, E, 6
earn mothers who must e....no leisure time problem
    CHRON, 446
ears guard over your eyes and e.   BRONTË, A, 7

earth becomes a moon without an e.   MENOPAUSE, 3
But did thee feel the e. move   SEX, 27
draining the e. of its /priceless and irreplaceable
resources   CONSERVATION, 5
e. as Mother   RELIGION, 15
the e. is free for every son and daughter of mankind
    CHRON, 142
eat average woman may not e. at the same table with
the husband   CHRON, 502
Don't e. too many almonds   COLETTE, 7
want your cake while you e. it too   BIRTH CONTROL, 11
eaten daring...to explain...that cows can be e.
    GANDHI, I, 4
eats e., sleeps and watches the television
    CHRON, 624; GREER, G, 3
eccentric Her habits grew more and more e.
    STANHOPE, H, 1
economic an e., political and symbolic system can feed
off the mother   MOTHERHOOD, 19
Black women need e. equality   FEMINISM, 12
leads to e. equality   CHRON, 530
man's e. dominance over women   CHRON, 470
threatening to fragile American manhood...feminist
drive for e. equality   FEMINISM, 21
women are e. factors in society   CHRON, 373
economically assumption that a woman is e. helpless
    CHRON, 508
man...keep woman dependent upon him e.
    SUBJECTION, 15
economy cannot have the same e. of space as if there
are men only   CHRON, 553
running the home,...helping to run the e., too
    CHRON, 726
edit She regarded me as a piece of fiction...that she
could e. and improve   WEST, R, 2
educability she extended our sense of e.   MONTESSORI, M, 1
educate e. a woman you e. a family   EDUCATION, 27
educated being e. she will be evilly spoken of   JARS, M, 4
e. in terms of their own social function   CHRON, 601
few people really wish women to be e.   CHRON, 313
educating What are we e. women for   CHRON, 583
education e. for women has progressed   CHRON, 370
e. is a leading out of what is...in the pupil's soul
    EDUCATION, 29
e. is...a natural process   MONTESSORI, M, 6
E. of their Children as well Daughters as Sons
    CHRON, 169
e. to bring out and fortify the differences   CHRON, 525
Elementary e. for girls must therefore be obligatory
    EDUCATION, 21
granting to females the advantages of a systematic
and thorough e.   CHRON, 234
if e. is...a mere transmission of knowledge
    MONTESSORI, M, 4
liberal e. of women is to deface the image of God
    CHRON, 158
more expensive e.   CHRON, 168
right E. of the Female Sex   CHRON, 163
school e. ignores,...healthy development
    BLACKWELL, E, 2
suspect all...special systems of e.   SULLIVAN, A, 1
woman of e.   EDUCATION, 12
women having equal e. with men   CHRON, 156
educational e. objectives...geared exclusively to the
vocational patterns of men   CHRON, 599

effeminate e. man...who dislikes woman and fears her
emancipation EMANCIPATION, 8
effeminating permitted no books but such as tend to
the...e. of the mind CHRON, 177
efficient be e. if you're going to be lazy HOUSEKEEPING, 8
efforts One is happy as a result of one's own e.
SAND, G, 4
eggs all my e. in one bastard ABORTION, 3
e. in one bastard PARKER, D, 10
ego male e....is elephantine MEN, 6
egoistic The emancipation of women is...the greatest
e. movement KEY, E, 1
Egypt he who placed the crown of E. upon my head.
CHRON, 35
Egyptian I, an E., am to seek that favour CHRON, 36
eight 'I have four nice children, and hope to have e.'
AMBITION, 3
eighteen From birth to age e., a girl needs good parents
MATURITY, 2
she speaks e. languages. And she can't say 'No' in
any of them PROMISCUITY, 3
ejected e. from all *decent* society BEHN, A, 1
elected Men get e. POLITICS, 11
electoral want the e. franchise CHRON, 376
electorate reject from the e. public-spirited workers...is a folly CHRON, 371
elegance E....not...a new dress CLOTHES, 13
elegant English women are e. MITFORD, N, 5; STYLE, 3
elephantine male ego...is e. MEN, 6
elephants e.' brains were even larger than men's
CHRON, 741
elevation removal of all the hindrances to her e.
CHRON, 277
eloquence effect be the best proof of e. MORE, H, 5
elusive One's prime is e. SPARK, M, 5
emancipated e. on condition that they don't upset men
CHRON, 697
emancipating necessity of e. herself from emancipation
CHRON, 419
woman is...e. herself from emancipation
EMANCIPATION, 7
emancipation Conditional e. CHRON, 694
effeminate man...who dislikes woman and fears her
e. EMANCIPATION, 8
e. and occupations of women
OCCUPATIONS, 7; SUBJECTION, 13
e. of today displays itself mainly in cigarettes and
shorts CHRON, 517
e. of woman can be brought about only by paid work
CHRON, 533
e. of woman...was stale stuff EMANCIPATION, 10
e. of women EMANCIPATION, 6
imagine that they are upholding women's e.
STOPES, M, 6
most effective is unconditional e. CHRON, 385
The e. of women is...the greatest egoistic movement
KEY, E, 1
Western light...harbinger of e. CHRON, 341
embarrassed e. and ashamed VIOLENCE, 7
embattled e. gates to equal rights CHRON, 641
emergence e. of woman as a political force CHRON, 649
Emily Brontë E. remains the sphinx of literature
BRONTË, E, 3
eminence man attaining to a higher e.,...than woman
can attain INTELLECT, 7

emotion Isadora Duncan...the...development of e. at
the expense of intellect DUNCAN, I, 2
unhinge an audience with e. PIAF, E, 1
emotional The physiological differences...create
intense e. problems FLYNN, E, 1
Women are e. EMOTION, 4; WOMAN'S ROLE, 34
empathy a sense of e. and pity RODDICK, A, 5
empire to woman the e. of the heart WOMAN'S ROLE, 21
employ State must continue to e. them CHRON, 474
employed e. females exclusively at his power-looms
CHRON, 270
employees depressed wages because women are the
chief e. EQUAL OPPORTUNITIES, 3
some occupations have depressed wages because
women are the chief e. CHRON, 647
employment nearly every remunerative e. is engrossed
by men only CHRON, 295
unfashionable e. of pursuing Butter-flies CHRON, 170
young females should possess some e. CHRON, 310
employments heroic actions, public e.,...denied our
sex CHRON, 148
story of women's work in gainful e. CHRON, 425
enclosed Check e. PARKER, D, 12
endangered feminist because I feel e. FEMINISM, 14
endurance the overwhelming beauty of e. COURAGE, 6
endures Her diary e. FRANK, A, 1
enduring her marriages were adventures and her
friendships e. TERRY, E, 2
enemy left me as an e. ANGER, 3
Woman is a wheedling and secret e. WOMAN'S NATURE, 5
energy exhausted my e. in tirades INJUSTICE, 5
enfranchised If all women were e.
CHRON, 395; SUFFRAGETTES, 10
want to see the women of this country e. CHRON, 442
engine no more mysticism in Beatrice than in a steam
e. WEBB, B, 3
engineering girls...could undertake e. jobs CHRON, 558
engineers *Toilets* was always the reason women
couldn't become e. CHRON, 701
England E. is the paradise of women CHRON, 127
Every woman in E. is longing for her political freedom CHRON, 394
ready to do for the happiness or prosperity of E.
ANNE, 4
English E. women are elegant MITFORD, N, 5; STYLE, 3
I do love cricket – it's so very E. BERNHARDT, S, 3
If the E. language had been properly organized
LANGUAGE, 3
they always look at her and say Sorry, in E.
MITFORD, N, 1
engross I must have something to e. my thoughts
BLACKWELL, E, 2
enjoyment husband...obstacle to the e. of many things.
DOMINATION, 1
enlightened in this e. age WOLLSTONECRAFT, M, 3
enlightenment organization and e. of working women
CHRON, 358
enmity clamour for political rights...sexual e. CHRON, 360
enough patriotism is not e. CAVELL, E, 4
Women, priests, and poultry, have never e.
SAYINGS AND PROVERBS, 55
enslave e. someone – you *are* enslaved CHRON, 664
enslaved Oppressed, degraded, e. OPPRESSION, 1
entangled a snare in which the feet of
women...become...e. ADDAMS, J, 5

entertainer the most popular e. the world has ever
known CHRISTIE, A, 1
entitled Women are e. to dress attractively EQUALITY, 11; STANTON, E, 10
envy real genuine, hard-working e. JEALOUSY, 3
equal all men and women are created e.
EQUALITY, 11; STANTON, E, 10
an attitude of e. respect for all men ADDAMS, J, 6
don't believe in e. opportunity
CHRON, 715; EQUAL OPPORTUNITIES, 5
embattled gates to e. rights CHRON, 641
e. interest with the men of this Nation CHRON, 143
E. pay for e. work CHRON, 647
e. right with himself CHRON, 364
female mind with e. powers and faculties EQUALITY, 6
feminist goals will not have been realised until all
human beings are e. CHRON, 702
fool who didn't agree with e. rights and pay
FEMINISM, 19
in the womb are we all e. EQUALITY, 19
I was too nearly Willie's e. WELDON, F, 2
principle of women working with e. status CHRON, 514
status of a full and e. person and citizen CHRON, 605
woman is the e. of man CHRON, 318
Woman must be regarded as e. to man CHRON, 595
Women are e. because...not different CHRON, 586
women having e. education with men CHRON, 156
equality absolute e. is impossible CHRON, 620
achieved e., they will be your masters CHRON, 33
Assume an e., plead your passion CHRON, 230
Created in perfect e. CHRON, 259
E. may perhaps be a right, but no...fact CHRON, 239
E. of rights under the law shall not be abridged...on
account of sex CHRON, 662
e. of shared necessity CHRON, 622
juridical e. between men and women CHRON, 269
last stage of the drive for e.
WOMEN'S LIBERATION MOVEMENT, 7
married state there should be the strictest e. CHRON, 274
Political e. is Dead Sea fruit CHRON, 530
promoting e. of opportunity between men and
women CHRON, 681
really great in favor of e. CHRON, 518
strongest arguments against the alleged e. of the
sexes EQUALITY, 10
theoretical acceptance of e. has always remained
CHRON, 594
There never will be...e. until women...make laws
ANTHONY, S, 3
true e. of the sexes CHRON, 491
vote is the symbol of freedom and e. CHRON, 440
woman's asking for e. in the church CHRON, 613
work to see that e. exists CHRON, 571
years of working towards e. between men and
women CHRON, 724
equall neare his heart, to be his e. CHRON, 135
equal pay idea of e. now has majority support CHRON, 711
principle of e. for equal work CHRON, 511
Equal Rights Amendment a name as beautiful as the *E.*
CHRON, 691
arguments in opposition to the E. CHRON, 682
E....a moral issue POLITICS, 12
equals disdain /Our being your e. CHRON, 133
Our being your e. EQUALITY, 4
treat women as subjects instead of e. CHRON, 470
equipped Mothers who can share their children's interests...far better e. CHRON, 537

equitably all family duties must be shared e. CHRON, 333
equivalents always true e. CHRON, 332
era forming a new e. in female history CHRON, 210
ERA Anybody against...the E. CHRON, 687
E. means that women who serve will get equal benefits CHRON, 679
erotic primary source of e. arousal SEX, 29
erudition dazzling appearance, e. and fondness for
sharp repartee GREER, G, 1
essence the very e. of *Truth* seemed to emanate from
her NIGHTINGALE, F, 1
establishment marrying merely to get an e. MARRIAGE, 23
estate low e. of his handmaiden CHRON, 57
personal e. of the wife...be vested in the wife
CHRON, 344
esteem E. of men as of a broken reed MEN, 1
esteemed women more e. by the opposite sex than
chastity CHASTITY, 5
estrangement deepest mutuality and the most painful
e. MOTHERHOOD, 17
eternal My love...resembles the e. rocks LOVE, 36
eternity He has made his impress on e. HYPATIA, 5
etiquette e. for ladies to have the best chairs SOCIETY, 7
euthanasia E. is a long, smooth-sounding word,
and...conceals its danger BUCK, P, 4
Eva Peron If a woman like E. with no ideals
THATCHER, M, 5
Eve E....the mother of all living CHRON, 5
mother E., who flouted the first prohibition FREEDOM, 1
real seducers are the daughters of E. SEDUCTION, 3
remove the old stigma of the story of Adam and E.
SUFFRAGETTES, 15
When E. ate this particular apple SEX, 19; WOMANHOOD, 6
you are an E. CHRON, 62
Everest treating the *mons Veneris* as...Mount E. SEX, 26
everything She knows e. PANKHURST, C, 1
evidence forbid women's e. LAW, 4
evil no worse e. than a bad woman ATTITUDES, 3
Only lies and e. come from letting people off
MURDOCH, I, 6
Romans endured much e. through Cleopatra
CLEOPATRA VII, 1
those things which by e. arts they know WITCHES, 2
evilly being educated she will be e. spoken of JARS, M, 4
evils many e. associated with the nefarious traffic
CHRON, 523
woman's hands raised the lid...scattered the e.
CHRON, 12
Women are necessary e. SAYINGS AND PROVERBS, 50
exalted what partiality!...one e. and the other
depressed EDUCATION, 15
excellence draped with such clothes for her natural e.
CLOTHES, 2; SUPERIORITY, 4
e. in women...loss of femininity SUCCESS, 5
exciting look both moral and e. APPEARANCE, 12
exclusively employed females e. at his power-looms
CHRON, 270
excuse E. my dust EPITAPHS, 6
execute against God if they e. a virgin woman
CHRON, 707; RELIGION, 18
executioner the e. is very good and I have a little neck
BOLEYN, A, 5
executive the e. expression of human immaturity
BRITTAIN, V, 5
exercise Prostitution...provides fresh air and wholesome e. PROSTITUTION, 8

exertion success depends...upon individual initiative and e.   PAVLOVA, A, 4

exhibited I *will not* be e. in his Triumph CLEOPATRA VII, 7

exile New York...where every one is an e.   GILMAN, C, 2

exist painless childbirth does not e. as a matter of course.   CHILDBIRTH, 17

existed if she hadn't e. we would have had to invent her   MONROE, M, 2

existence A married woman in English law has no legal e.   LAW, 10

blame for the e. of humanity on women   INJUSTICE, 6

exists woman e. for the sake of man   SUBJECTION, 4

expect people e. me to neigh, grind my teeth   ANNE, PRINCESS, 3

expected what more could be e. of any woman   CHRON, 340

expensive more e. education   CHRON, 168

experience E. is a good teacher   ANTRIM, M, 2

it's not so much a country as an e.   JHABVALA, R, 3

love like other arts requires e.   LOVE, 32

she has written...a few moments of human e.   PARKER, D, 1

there are always compensations for every adverse e.   BROWN, O, 1

The triumph of hope over e.   MARRIAGE, 18

experiences the child should be allowed to meet the real e. of life   KEY, E, 2

experiment scandalous to call Dr Marie Stopes Birth Control method an e.   CHRON, 493

exploited I have never consciously e. the fact that I am a woman   CASTLE, B, 5

exploits e. the indulgence of man   CHRON, 445

insufferable a person woman becomes when...she e. the indulgence of man   SUFFRAGETTES, 6

expression the executive e. of human immaturity   BRITTAIN, V, 5

extension e. of women's rights CHRON, 218; FEMINISM, 1

extol E. her for the fruit of her toil   CHARM, 1

extraordinary e. women...*male* spirits, confined by mistake in female frames   ACHIEVEMENT, 3

extravagant a wild, impetuous and e. creature   DUNCAN, I, 1

writers whose e. doctrines have...been published   WOLLSTONECRAFT, M, 2

ex-wife no fury like an e. searching for a new lover   ANGER, 4

eyelids When she raises her e. COLETTE, 4; SEDUCTION, 1

eyes glances sidelong at him, thus showing her e.   CHRON, 542

guard over your e. and ears   BRONTË, A, 7

Look not in my e., for fear /They mirror true the sight I see   LOVE, 49

Mine e. have seen the glory of the coming of the Lord   HOWE, J, 3

the king's great appetite, and her e., which are black and beautiful and take great effect.   BOLEYN, A, 1

Eyre I wish you had not sent me Jane E.   EDUCATION, 19

F

fabric chemical barrage has been hurled against the f. of life   CARSON, R, 3

fabrics right and wrong in f.   ASHLEY, L, 1

face a garden in her f.   APPEARANCE, 4

I have the sort of f. that bores me   ASQUITH, M, 4

My f. is my fortune, sir, she said   MARRIAGE, 19

faces men have their f. on the money   PRACTICALITY, 3

faction Mrs President...of a f.   ADAMS, A, 2

factory In the f. we make cosmetics   COSMETICS, 10

narrowness and lack of freedom of the f.   CHRON, 420

F. females have in general much lower wages than males   CHRON, 244

facts poor girl, ignorant of the f. of life   VIRGINITY, 7

Facts of Life acknowledge her own experience with the F.   MORALITY, 5

faded but already should be f., fatalistic and aged   WOOLF, V, 9

fails Nothing f. like success   SUCCESS, 2

failure no success like f.   SUCCESS, 10

F. meant poverty   DU MAURIER, D, 2

fair All is f.   LOVE, 1

demand f. and honest reporting for all women   CHRON, 703

f. wife...frontier castle   SAYINGS AND PROVERBS, 8

f. wife needs more than two eyes   SAYINGS AND PROVERBS, 36

f. woman is a paradise to the eye   BEAUTY, 4

f. woman without virtue   SAYINGS AND PROVERBS, 9; VIRTUE, 1

no women have had a f. chance EQUAL OPPORTUNITIES, 1

stop worrying about what's f. to women SUPERIORITY, 12

Fair Sex F. may be encourag'd to attempt Mathematics   CHRON, 180

faith And f. shines equal   BRONTË, E, 4

f. to buy a little bunch of violets   PIAF, E, 3

no need for any other f. than...faith in human beings   BUCK, P, 7

faithful my heart shall be /The f. compass CONSTANCY, 2

Translations (like wives) are seldom f.   UNFAITHFULNESS, 3

faithlessness f. of his wife   ADULTERY, 5

fallen Humility becomes our f. nature   HUMILITY, 6

false She wore f. hair and that red   ELIZABETH I, 2

falsity F. withered in her presence   ROOSEVELT, E, 1

fame One of the drawbacks of F.   MELBA, N, 5

one whom f. has not corrupted   CURIE, M, 2

she would have given all her genius and all her f. to be beautiful   BRONTË, C, 3

familiarity F. between men and women is apt to turn to virtue's disadvantage   FRIENDSHIP, 1

families All happy f. resemble one another FAMILY, 5

Keep them at home to look after their f.   CHRON, 257

family all f. duties must be shared equitably CHRON, 333

educate a woman you educate a f.   EDUCATION, 27

Mother is the dead heart of the f.   CHRON, 624; GREER, G, 3; MOTHERHOOD, 12

no f. can get along without women to help   OCCUPATIONS, 7; SUBJECTION, 13

real sin when a young married woman refuses to bear a f.   BIRTH CONTROL, 4

run the house, bring up a f. and...work   HEALTH AND HEALTHY LIVING, 9

taught anything at all but the management of a f.   EDUCATION, 30

the death of the American f.   BOMBECK, E, 4

the f....source of all our discontents   FAMILY, 11

theft to foist heirs born of debauchery on an entire f.   CHRON, 154

The sink is the great symbol of the bloodiness of f. life   FAMILY, 10

Total commitment to f.   COMMITMENT, 4

Women choose for the f.   FAMILY, 14

famous as f. for her love affairs   SAND, G, 1
What are you f. *for*   MURDOCH, I, 4
fanaticism f. built up unnecessary hostility   BESANT, A, 1
fantasies stay within the world of pornography…only
   f.   PORNOGRAPHY, 1
too many f. to be a housewife   MONROE, M, 4
fantastic woman's complete historical subjection…most f. myths   CHRON, 569
fantasy Her rampant sexuality made her a f. figure for
   men   BARDOT, B, 3
Science fiction and f.,…, allow one to imagine…strong independent women   STRENGTH, 5
She is every man's f. mistress   GARBO, G, 1
farewell bid f. to sin and sorrow   AGE, 2
Fascism F. recognizes women as a part of the life force
   CHRON, 541
fashion f. is born by small facts   CLOTHES, 10
her approach to everything concerning f.   CHANEL, C, 1
true to you, darlin', in my f.   CONSTANCY, 3
F. is architecture   CHANEL, C, 6
fashions not cut my conscience to fit this year's f.
   DETERMINATION, 1; POLITICS, 7
F. in sin change   SIN, 2
fat Female Wits wrote big, f. fabulous plays   WRITERS, 15
fatal F. illness has…been viewed as a test   SONTAG, S, 2
fatalistic but already should be faded, f. and aged
   WOOLF, V, 9
fate f. of the married woman
   MARRIAGE, 26; SINGLE WOMEN, 4
hostages given to f.   FAMILY, 1
F. has not been kind to Mrs Browning   BROWNING, E, 3
father No man is responsible for his f.   FAMILY, 7
Today I dressed to meet my f.'s eyes   CLOTHES, 1
fathers interest…involved either in that of their f. or in
   that of their husbands   CHRON, 227
interests of our f., husbands, and brothers, ought to
   be ours   CHRON, 263
fattening lettuce has been f. all along   BOMBECK, E, 1
fault The fundamental f. of the female character
   CHRON, 278; CHARACTER, 4
favours Whether a pretty woman grants or withholds
   her f.   CHRON, 45
fawning men who can be gratified by the f. fondness of
   spaniel-like affection   INDEPENDENCE, 1
fear f. of success as well.   SUCCESS, 8
f. of women   CHRON, 604
male reviewers who f. female sexuality   FEAR, 2
man's f. of women's creative energy
   FEAR, 1; SUBJECTION, 14
feared force of a woman…is less f. by men   CHRON, 69
fearlessness Her total commitment…spontaneity and f.
   CASTLE, B, 2
fears have a woman's f.   COURAGE, 2
fecundator she needs the f.   PARTNERSHIP, 1
fed f. on feeding   BREASTFEEDING, 5
feeble-minded woman…so vicious, or so f., that she cannot withstand temptation   BRONTË, A, 5
feed an economic, political and symbolic system can
   f. off the mother   MOTHERHOOD, 19
better to f. the child with maternal milk
   BREASTFEEDING, 1
Women are there to f. an appetite   APPEARANCE, 16
feeding fed on f.   BREASTFEEDING, 5
feel women f. just as men f.   CHRON, 272
feeling A man is as old as he's f.   AGE, 5

feet better to die on your f. than to live on your knees
   IBARRURI, D, 4
housewife on her f. from dawn till dark
   HOUSEKEEPING, 4
felicity likely to mar the general f.   MARRIAGE, 44
fellowship such a f. of good knights shall never be
   together   FRIENDSHIP, 2
female f. inmates of our prisons   CHRON, 233
f. is an empty thing and easily swayed   CHARACTER, 1
f. is less perfect than the male   CHRON, 55
f. sex to meddle in matters which pertain uniquely
   to men   SUBJECTION, 1
few Doctors, either male or f., as possible   CHRON, 303
forming a new era in f. history   CHRON, 210
Growing up f. in America   JONG, E, 3
in Christ Jesus there is neither male nor f.   GRIMKÉ, A, 4
Midwives to the perpetual honour of the f. Sex
   CHRON, 155
right Education of the F. Sex   CHRON, 163
stigmatize the f. mind   INJUSTICE, 3
the f. character…has no sense of justice   CHARACTER, 4
the f. of the species is more deadly than the male
   ATTITUDES, 19; RUTHLESSNESS, 2
The fundamental fault of the f. character
   CHRON, 278; CHARACTER, 4
there needs must be a f.   CHRON, 54
What f. heart can gold despise   ATTITUDES, 12
works of male and f. authors be properly separated
   MODESTY, 5
females human f. become sterile in the forties
   FERTILITY, 1
No vote can be given by lunatics…f.
   LAW, 7; SUFFRAGETTES, 1
Feme Every F. Covert is a sort of infant   LAW, 5
feminine Composing…is very f.   MUSICIANS, 10
Gordian knot of a seemingly insoluble f. dilemma
   CHRON, 587
intellectuality…paid for by the loss of valuable f.
   qualities   CHRON, 570
men face the f. superiority   SUPERIORITY, 10
only what is truly f. is an ornament to your sex
   MUSICIANS, 2
purely f. affairs…women may testify   LAW, 4
she is thoroughly f.…made for nothing but to mother
   babies   ELIOT, G, 2
strange f. entity…half of what she had been
   WIDOWHOOD, 5
Taste is the f. of genius   TALENT AND GENIUS, 1
Women's liberation is the liberation of the f. in the
   man   WOMEN'S LIBERATION MOVEMENT, 13
femininity excellence in women…loss of f.   SUCCESS, 5
most lesbians…seek to cultivate…their f.   LESBIANISM, 3
where in the world did I put my f.   FEMININITY, 11
feminism f. has almost been equated with a tiresome
   insistence on 'chair'   LANGUAGE, 10
F.…not just a laundry list   FEMINISM, 16
important task of modern f. is to accept and proclaim sex   CHRON, 500
menace just as threatening…as Hitlerism – F.
   CHRON, 556
Modern young women…show a strong hostility to
   the word 'f.   CHRON, 539
rid England of all traces of f.   FEMINISM, 5
violent backlash against f.   FEMINISM, 23
what…f. has achieved for women   FRIEDAN, B, 1

feminist best home for a f. was in another person's lab
FEMINISM, 10
f. because I feel endangered FEMINISM, 14
f. goals will not have been realised until all human
beings are equal CHRON, 702
f. rhetoric, rigidified in reaction FEMINISM, 15
f. struggle being a peripheral kind of thing FEMINISM, 13
f. whenever I express sentiments that differentiate
me from a doormat or a prostitute CHRON, 592
f. whenever I express sentiments that differentiate
me FEMINISM, 17
I'm proud to be a f. CHRON, 698
The most influencial f. FRIEDAN, B, 2
feminists stridency of the f. CHRON, 740
F. think only in terms of social power FEMINISM, 22
fertility The management of f. FERTILITY, 2
fetishism Buttock f. is comparatively rare GREER, G, 6
fetters movement for women's rights has broken many
old f. CHRON, 418
fickle Woman is always f. and changing
CHRON, 43; CONTRARINESS, 2
fiction She regarded me as a piece of f....that she
could edit and improve WEST, R, 2
She was the fifties' f. MONROE, M, 2
field Man for the f. and woman for the hearth
MEN AND WOMEN, 9
vaster f. for their imaginations to rove EDUCATION, 11
Your wives are your f. DOMINATION, 2
fiend a f. hid in a cloud CHILDBIRTH, 5
fifty-two refuse to admit that I am more than f. AGE, 9
fight a great cause to f. for CHRON, 409; PANKHURST, C, 3
born women and as such do not f. with men CHRON, 15
I f. to win THATCHER, M, 10
if women vote they must f..' WAR, 2
not so much of a pacifist that I would not f. for Peace
STARK, F, 1
fighting no end to f. till the Vote is won CHRON, 436
fig leaves they sewed f. together CHRON, 2
figures shows you that f. can lie APPEARANCE, 7
filthy woman with cut hair is a f. spectacle
APPEARANCE, 6
finance Romance without f. is a nuisance PROSTITUTION, 9
financial Alimony is one way of compensating women
for those f. disabilities CHRON, 646
depend on men to sort out f. things INDEPENDENCE, 3
Women's battle for f. equality has barely been joined
CHRON, 678
financially she is f. less dependent on a job CHRON, 712
finer God intended women only as a f. sort of cattle
CHRON, 159
fire you may sit by my f. and read GILMAN, C, 4
first f. woman...strong enough to turn the world
upside down CHRON, 282
f. woman to do anything ACHIEVEMENT, 5
The F. Blast of the Trumpet CHRON, 116
fiscal a keen sense of her own f. value MELBA, N, 2
fish f. needs a bicycle WOMEN'S LIBERATION MOVEMENT, 2
queen did f. for men's souls ELIZABETH I, 1
What cat's averse to f. ATTITUDES, 12
fist You cannot shake hands with a clenched f.
GANDHI, I, 5
fitted male is naturally more f. to command CHRON, 24
flapper Clara Bow...was totally representative of...the
f. BOW, C, 3
Miss Bow, the emergent f. BOW, C, 1

flatterer a shameless f. and insatiable of flattery
MORE, H, 1
flattering more f. to be a 'man's woman' STARK, F, 2
flattery a shameless flatterer and insatiable of f.
MORE, H, 1
frailty of our sex to be fond of f. FAILINGS, 1
woman is infallibly to be gained by...f. ATTITUDES, 13
fleas the f. in my bed were as good COMPLIMENTS, 2
flesh f. to feel the chain BRONTË, E, 6
she is burnt f. WITCHES, 7
they raze the skin and rend the f. of her body
HYPATIA, 3
flight f. from womanhood WOMANHOOD, 2
flirt f. with their own husbands LOVE AND MARRIAGE, 5
flood-tide a just cause reaches its f. CATT, C, 4
flouted mother Eve, who f. the first prohibition
FREEDOM, 1
flowers any man lie with her at all, and her f. be upon
him, he shall be unclean MENSTRUATION, 1
flux monthly f. of women. Contact with it turns new
wine sour MENSTRUATION, 4
fly learned to f. JOHNSON, A, 1
folklore f. of abortion ABORTION, 11
follies lovers cannot see the pretty f. LOVE, 16
folly checking this mad, wicked f. of 'Woman's Rights'
EMANCIPATION, 3
reject from the electorate public-spirited workers...is
a f. CHRON, 371
source of female f. and vice CHRON, 203
the slightest f. /That ever love did make thee run
into LOVE, 17
When lovely woman stoops to f. BETRAYAL, 1
food Books, the Mind's f. MORE, H, 3
fool A f. bolts pleasure, then complains of...indiges-
tion ANTRIM, M, 1
clever woman to manage a f. WOMAN'S ROLE, 20
Love is the wisdom of the f. LOVE, 28
foolhardy vows most women are made to take are very
f. CHRON, 206
foolishness Women's Liberation is just a lot of f.
WOMEN'S LIBERATION MOVEMENT, 16
fools I am two f. LOVE, 20
forbid f. women's evidence LAW, 4
My sex is usually f. studies of this nature CHRON, 177
F. a thing, and that women will do
CONTRARINESS, 1; SAYINGS AND PROVERBS, 11
forbidden expressly f. to address men who are in the
company of women or children PROSTITUTION, 4
forbids law expressly f....women from being able to
make a contract CHRON, 25
force as base as to use f. HYPATIA, 6
f. of a woman...is less feared by men CHRON, 69
strong as the f. of love CHILDREN, 3
foreign to be a woman F. Minister MEIR, G, 1
forfeit we serve men's need and f. our worthless life
CHRON, 249; PROSTITUTION, 2
forget Abortions will not let you f. ABORTION, 4
forgive She intended to f. FORGIVENESS, 2
forgiven Once a woman has f. her man FORGIVENESS, 3
forgiveness created /F. but to speak FORGIVENESS, 1
forgives Man f. woman anything save the wit to outwit
him ANTRIM, M, 3
forgotten schoolroom...difference of sex...need to be f.
CHRON, 391
formidable adult American Negro female emerges a f.
character CHRON, 616

G

generations g. of human beings who have struggled in poverty STANTON, E, 6

genetic home-making is g. WOMAN'S NATURE, 10

genitals he *will* remove your g. CHRON, 668

genius most characteristic g. in writing WRITERS, 10
She had a temperament akin to g. PANKHURST, E, 2
she would have given all her g. and all her fame to be beautiful BRONTË, C, 3
Since when was g....respectable BROWNING, E, 4
Taste is the feminine of g. TALENT AND GENIUS, 1
women approach g. they also approach masculinity INTELLIGENCE, 15
works of g. are beyond her reach CHRON, 188

gentility woman's road to g....doing nothing at all CHRON, 416

gentle a g., quiet, rather subdued person BRONTË, A, 2
find that all the g. sex this process is unsexing CHRON, 349
g. to all and stern with yourself TERESA OF AVILA, 1

gentleman A g....wouldn't hit a woman with his hat on CHIVALRY, 4
God is a g. FEMININITY, 10

gentlemen extremely difficult to behave like g. ATTITUDES, 24
Good-morning, g. both ELIZABETH I, 6
G....remember blondes LOOS, A, 1

gifts doubtful value to enlist the g. of women CHRON, 575
God's g. put man's best g. BROWNING, E, 6

gin No man is genuinely happy, married, who has to drink worse g. MARRIAGE, 46
G. was mother's milk DRINKING, 5

girl Every little g. knows about love LOVE, 61; SAGAN, F, 1
From birth to age eighteen, a g. needs good parents MATURITY, 2
g. with brains INTELLIGENCE, 14; LOOS, A, 2
Give me a g. at an impressionable age SPARK, M, 4
insist that a young g. should be pure, chaste and innocent HYPOCRISY, 2
one can...see in a little g. the threat of a woman MEN AND WOMEN, 14
One g. can be pretty APPEARANCE, 10
to call a g. off from making a pie GRIMKÉ, S, 3
when she bringeth forth a little g. CHRON, 102

girls Elementary education for g. must therefore be obligatory EDUCATION, 21
G. are so much prettier ARTISTS, 5
G. are so queer CONTRARINESS, 5
g. from being g. MEN AND WOMEN, 13
g....say No when they mean Yes CONTRARINESS, 5
g. who wear glasses APPEARANCE, 15
It was harder for little g. WOMAN'S ROLE, 28
the...rift between the sexes is...widened by...teaching...to the g. DISCRIMINATION, 5
When you see what some g. marry MARRIAGE, 40
Where...boys plan for what...young g. plan for whom GILMAN, C, 3

gist The g. of a lady's letter is in the postscript SAYINGS AND PROVERBS, 12

give like the grave, cries 'G.,' ADAMS, A, 3

glamour G....man ask for your telephone number STYLE, 1

glass look in their g., the less they look to their house SAYINGS AND PROVERBS, 27
pane of g. called passion between us CHRON, 588

glasses girls who wear g. APPEARANCE, 15

glass-shops Women in state affairs are like monkeys in g. POLITICS, 1; SAYINGS AND PROVERBS, 54

glom g. on to men so that they can collapse with relief CHRON, 596

glorification g. of the 'woman's role' CHRON, 598

glorious no g. renown in a woman's punishment CHRON, 42

glory greatest g. of a woman is to be least talked about by men CHRON, 19
It is a great g. in a woman ATTITUDES, 1
long hair, it is a g. to her APPEARANCE, 1
Mine eyes have seen the g. of the coming of the Lord HOWE, J, 3

God Duty is ours and events are G.'s GRIMKÉ, A, 3
G. alone deserves to be loved SAND, G, 5
G., being male, values maleness RELIGION, 16
G. did send me JOAN OF ARC, 6
G., in whom I do not believe BEAUVOIR, S, 6
G. is a gentleman FEMININITY, 10
G.'s gifts put man's best gifts BROWNING, E, 6
I did not write it. G. wrote it. I merely did his dictation STOWE, H, 5
I try to do G.'s will...he visits me with misfortune BORGIA, L, 5
'Resistance to tyranny is obedience to G..' ANTHONY, S, 6
Sickness, sin and death...do not originate in G. EDDY, M, 5
Those who marry G....can become domesticated too MARRIAGE, 62
when one has loved a man it is very different to love G. SAND, G, 5
woman is not made in G.'s image CHRON, 83
your voice speaking an assured word for G. and Immortality EDDY, M, 1

gods a place where g. strode the earth CALDWELL, S, 3

gold Were't not for g. and women ATTITUDES, 7
What female heart can g. despise ATTITUDES, 12
Woman's Heart like g. WEALTH, 3

golden perhaps, the g. rule MARRIAGE, 34

gold rush A g. is what happens when WEST, M, 3

good all-thing that is g. and comfortable JULIAN OF NORWICH, 1
Be g., sweet maid, and let who can be clever HAPPINESS, 2; VIRTUE, 7
g. women are the obedient CHRON, 67
g. writing is knowing when to stop MONTGOMERY, L, 5
healthier to see the g. points SAGAN, F, 3
I will be g. VICTORIA, 5
only g. thing about divorce DIVORCE, 10
The king has been very g. to me BOLEYN, A, 4
What is beautiful is g. GOOD AND EVIL, 1

goodness bad woman...bit of g. GOOD AND EVIL, 2
I respect yet more your heart and your g. MORE, H, 2
strong feeling of g. about Jackie DU PRÉ, J, 2
the certainty of your g. WOOLF, V, 10

goods isn't a bad bit of g., the Queen COMPLIMENTS, 2

Gordian G. knot of a seemingly insoluble feminine dilemma CHRON, 587

gossip detested women's g. GOSSIP, 2
g. of two women GOSSIP, 1; SAYINGS AND PROVERBS, 14
G. is the opiate of the oppressed JONG, E, 4

govern Man was created independent because destined to g. SUBJECTION, 11
still for moderation and will g. by it ANNE, 5
to yield, is the only way to g. GRIMKÉ, S, 4

we really g. the world　　　　　　　POWER, 1
governance beseemeth wives to be wise and of great g.
　　　　　　　　　　　　　　　CHRON, 100
governed g. by a woman, instead of a man, was
　improper　　　　　　　　　　CHRON, 77
　way in which women are g. in this Republic
　　　　　　　　　　　　　　　CHRON, 246
governesses Accomplished girls...were made into g.
　　　　　　　　　　　　　　　CHRON, 235
government do not think women are safe guides in g.
　　　　　　　　　　　　　　　CHRON, 398
　duties of g....injurious to their best interests CHRON, 236
　g. by men only is not an appeal to reason　CHRON, 458
　more women in g.　　　　　　　POLITICS, 10
　right to a voice in this g.　　　SUFFRAGETTES, 5
　When women stand at the head of g.　CHRON, 223
gracious g. to her in her child-bearing.　CHRON, 70
graduating g. with a 'spinster of arts' degree　CHRON, 695
grand that g. word 'woman'　　　LANGUAGE, 1
Grande Dame very much the G.　RUBINSTEIN, H, 1
grapes He is trampling out the vintage where the g. of
　wrath　　　　　　　　　　　HOWE, J, 3
grasp exceed the g. of my woman's mind　CHRON, 75
grasper I never was any greedy, scraping g.
　　　　　　　　　　　　　　ELIZABETH I, 12
grasping that power..., is ever g.　ADAMS, A, 3
gratified men who can be g. by the fawning fondness
　of spaniel-like affection　　　INDEPENDENCE, 1
gratify not created merely to g. the appetite of man
　　　　　　　　　　　　　　EDUCATION, 16
gratitude fill her soul with g. to God and to the Man
　　　　　　　　　　　　LOVE AND MARRIAGE, 4
grave like the g., cries 'Give, give.'　ADAMS, A, 3
graves The bitterest tears shed over g.　STOWE, H, 3
gravity have their babies *with* g.　CHILDBIRTH, 23
great really g. in favor of equality　CHRON, 518
greater nothing g. than the joy of composing
　　　　　　　　　　　　　SCHUMANN, C, 3
Greece Athens holds sway over all G.　DOMINATION, 1
green 'G.-Eyed Monster' causes much woe　JEALOUSY, 4
grey These little g. cells　　　CHRISTIE, A, 5
grief G. and constant anxiety kill nearly as many
　women　　　　　　　　　　SORROW, 4
　g. of mothers who are denied the privilege of nurs-
　ing their infants　　　　　　CHRON, 322
　Hope of the world in g. and wrong　HOWE, J, 4
　we take all the g. from man　MEN AND WOMEN, 3
grimmer a g. version of human affairs　STEAD, C, 4
grounds notice of divorce to her husband on trumped-
　up g.　　　　　　　　　　CHRON, 63
grow'd 'I 'spect I g..'　　　　STOWE, H, 4
guardian ancestors did not want women to conduct
　any...business without a g.　　CHRON, 32
guardians g. of culture　　　SOCIETY, 9
　Women...the g. of wisdom　　EQUALITY, 16
guide God sent a voice to g. me　JOAN OF ARC, 5
guides do not think women are safe g. in government
　　　　　　　　　　　　　　CHRON, 398
guilt depressing to admit g. and to repent　GUILT, 3
　dwell on g. and misery　　　AUSTEN, J, 6
　g. of having a nice body　　DRABBLE, M, 6
　I have no sense of g.　　　PANKHURST, E, 5
　Tears would be an admission of g.　DU MAURIER, D, 3
guilty g. skunk she made me feel　GUILT, 2
　how steadily do they who are g. shrink from reproof
　　　　　　　　　　　　　BLOOMER, A, 4

she was g. of a great deal of contributory negligence
　　　　　　　　　　　　　　LAW, 18
gynaeceum remote part of the house called 'the g.'
　　　　　　　　　　　　　　CHRON, 37

H

habit A h. the pleasure of which increases with practise　　　　　　　　　　　ADAMS, A, 5
habits Curious things, h.　　CHRISTIE, A, 6
　errors in the h. of mothers　　CHRON, 293
　Her h. grew more and more eccentric　STANHOPE, H, 1
had you h. it in you　　　　PREGNANCY, 5
hair if a woman have long h.　APPEARANCE, 1
　long h., it is a glory to her　APPEARANCE, 1
　To Crystal, h. was the most important
　　　　　　　　　　MARRIAGE, 63; O'BRIEN, E, 3
　woman with cut h. is a filthy spectacle　APPEARANCE, 6
　Women have long h. and short brains
　　　　　　INTELLIGENCE, 3; SAYINGS AND PROVERBS, 53
　women patients had to have their h. done in a cer-
　tain way　　　　　　　OCCUPATIONS, 11
　you have lovely h.　　　　BEAUTY, 11
hairdresser A Court h. who travels with her　PERÓN, E, 1
half leaves out h. the human race it cannot be as main
　　　　　　　　　　EQUAL OPPORTUNITIES, 6
　strange feminine entity...h. of what she had been
　　　　　　　　　　　　WIDOWHOOD, 5
Hallelujah Here lies my wife,.../H.　EPITAPHS, 2
Hammerstrike women's lib was dead milliseconds after
　H.　　　　　WOMEN'S LIBERATION MOVEMENT, 17
hand The h. that rocks the cradle
　　　　　　　　SAYINGS AND PROVERBS, 15
handbag she disliked the imitations of her trumpet
　tone in the famous line 'A h.'　EVANS, E, 2
handicap completely triumphed over the h. of her sex
　　　　　　　　　　　　　　CHRON, 82
handmaiden low estate of his h.　CHRON, 57
hands a person's character lies in their own h.
　　　　　　　　　　　　　FRANK, A, 7
　Men and women are like right and left h.　RANKIN, J, 2
　You cannot shake h. with a clenched fist　GANDHI, I, 5
happiness a man is always seeking for h.
　　　　　　　　　　DIX, D, 3; MARRIAGE, 48
　can speak of h.　　　　　BROWN, O, 4
　h. /comes to a person, not a gender　HAPPINESS, 1
　H. in marriage　　　　　AUSTEN, J, 9
　H. is like a butterfly　　PAVLOVA, A, 5
　H. is no vague dream　　SAND, G, 4
　I thought that success spelled h.　PAVLOVA, A, 5
　one h....to love and be loved.　HAPPINESS, 3
　one may fail to find h. in theatrical life　PAVLOVA, A, 3
　success spelled h.　　　HAPPINESS, 4
happy a h. woman and universally respected
　　　　　　　　　WOLLSTONECRAFT, M, 1
　be h. later on, but it's much harder　BEAUVOIR, S, 5
　h. families resemble each other　FAMILY, 5
　One is h. as a result of one's own efforts　SAND, G, 4
　We all live with the objective of being h.　FRANK, A, 5
harbinger Love's a h. of pain　LOVE, 55
　Western light...h. of emancipation　CHRON, 341
hard it is better for h. words to be on paper　FRANK, A, 3
　it is h. work, not a woman's work　CHRON, 728
harder It was h. for little girls　WOMAN'S ROLE, 28
harem subservient womanhood is the nearest...to the
　spiritual delights of the h.　CHRON, 434

harlot society…pays a h. 25 times as much as it pays its Prime Minister PROSTITUTION, 10
the prerogative of the h. through the ages PROSTITUTION, 7
harm the very first requirement in a Hospital that it should do the sick no h. NIGHTINGALE, F, 3
harsh 'Widow' is a h. and hurtful word WIDOWHOOD, 6
hat A gentleman…wouldn't hit a woman with his h. on CHIVALRY, 4
hate how much men h. them MEN AND WOMEN, 29
I h. a learned woman EDUCATION, 1
hating patriotism which consists in h. all other nations GASKELL, E, 5
hats worn birds in their h. for years CONSERVATION, 1
have To h. and to hold MARRIAGE, 15
hazard an occupational h. of being a wife ANNE, PRINCESS, 4
head in politics there is no heart, only h. POLITICS, 4
shorter by a h. ELIZABETH I, 7
When women stand at the h. of government CHRON, 223
heads Freud…substituted the penis for the h. SUPERIORITY, 11
head-waiter A pompous woman…complaining that the h. SITWELL, E, 5
health corset must be looked upon as distinctly prejudicial to h. CLOTHES, 7; HEALTH AND HEALTHY LIVING, 5
good wife and h. is a man's best wealth SAYINGS AND PROVERBS, 13
in sickness and in h. MARRIAGE, 15
Take care of h. WILLARD, E, 2
The H. Meal is ship-saving WAR, 7
Women want work both for the h. of their minds CHRON, 294
You can no more separate Mrs. Eddy from Science and H. EDDY, M, 2
healthful hindering h. and varied activity HEALTH AND HEALTHY LIVING, 4
healthier h. to see the good points SAGAN, F, 2
hear ear begins to h. BRONTË, E, 6
heard Maidens should be seen, and not h. SAYINGS AND PROVERBS, 20
heart beatings of the lonely h. LONELINESS, 3
dead h. of the family FAMILY, 13
good h. will help…a bonny face BRONTË, E, 8
h. and stomach of a King CHRON, 125; ELIZABETH I, 11
in politics there is no h., only head POLITICS, 4
I respect yet more your h. and your goodness MORE, H, 2
Mother is the dead h. of the family CHRON, 624; GREER, G, 3
my h. shall be /The faithful compass CONSTANCY, 2
my soul in the midst of my h. JULIAN OF NORWICH, 4
neare his h., to be his equall CHRON, 135
Once a woman has given you her h. LOVE, 24
The history of every country begins in the h. CATHER, W, 4
to woman the empire of the h. WOMAN'S ROLE, 21
woman's h.…burned SORROW, 3
Woman's H. like gold WEALTH, 3
hearth Man for the field and woman for the h. MEN AND WOMEN, 9
heaven Marriage is…excluded from h. MARRIAGE, 44
married will not see the kingdom of h. RELIGION, 3
Parting is all we know of h. DICKINSON, E, 4
Pennies do not come from h. THATCHER, M, 8

heesh If John or Mary comes h. will want to play LANGUAGE, 3
hell all we need of h. DICKINSON, E, 4
h. a fury like a woman scorned HATE, 2
Old age is woman's h. OLD AGE, 5
the h. of horses CHRON, 127
help power enhanced if they can be of h. POWER, 11
helped who h. her WRITERS, 6
herb sweetest fragrance from the h.…tread on it and bruise it OPPRESSION, 4
herbs induce h. or other means to cause miscarriage ABORTION, 2
many h. against the early death of woman CHRON, 385
here h. today and gone tomorrow BEHN, A, 7
heresy only a male can represent Christ…serious h. CHRON, 729; RELIGION, 22
hermit I, who so love a h. life BLACKWELL, E, 3
hero better to be the widow of a h. than the wife of a coward IBARRURI, D, 5
heroic h. actions, public employments,…denied our sex CHRON, 148
heroine the magnanimous pity of a h. JOAN OF ARC, 3
heroines H. are, then, heroic COURAGE, 6
heroism h. to send them to face the canon WAR, 4
herself has woman a right to h. CHRON, 289
hesitant h. about encouraging a woman as a protégé CHRON, 712
hesitate A leader who doesn't h.…is not fit to be a leader MEIR, G, 2
hide stay at home and h. herself CHRON, 52
highbrow What is a h. INTELLECTUALS, 4
higher not made for the h. forms of science INTELLIGENCE, 8
those who aspire to h. things AMBITION, 4
High Tech a matter of H. versus natural childbirth CHILDBIRTH, 24
hindrances legal and material h. BEAUTY, 17
removal of all the h. to her elevation CHRON, 277
hippie I'm thought of as something of a h. RODDICK, A, 2
history The h. of every country begins in the heart CATHER, W, 4
their pride, their tradition, their h. STEAD, C, 3
women's h. is fragmented, interrupted DUTY, 5
hit men don't h. their wives any more VIOLENCE, 5
Hitler the H. Youth organization MANN, E, 4
hold To have and to h. MARRIAGE, 15
home efficient care and management of the h. CHRON, 503
H. is the girl's prison FAMILY, 6
Keep them at h. to look after their families CHRON, 257
lived in a barrel of shit they'd start making a h. PRACTICALITY, 5
prefer to have women in the h. and not as airline pilots CHRON, 631
running the h.,…helping to run the economy, too CHRON, 726
stay at h. and hide herself CHRON, 52
woman's place is in the h. WOMAN'S ROLE, 35
woman's role in the h. new status CHRON, 650
woman was made dependent, tied to hearth and h. SUBJECTION, 11
women…should remain at h.…, and bear and bring up children WOMAN'S ROLE, 7
homemaker function of h.,…extend into politics POLITICS, 8
home-making h. is genetic WOMAN'S NATURE, 10

marriage and h. is genetic CHRON, 593
process of h....an art and a profession CHRON, 297
The whole process of h., housekeeping and cooking
HOUSEKEEPING, 2
homes Men make houses, women make h.
SAYINGS AND PROVERBS, 26
homicide prove that her husband is a h. CHRON, 63
homo The 'h.' is the legitimate child CHRON, 487
honest demand fair and h. reporting for all women
CHRON, 703
honor In courage and h. ANTHONY, S, 2
honour a nation of men of h. and of cavaliers
MARIE ANTOINETTE, 2
giving herself to intercourse, the girl renounces her
h. VIRGINITY, 4
h. is for the poor TERESA, MOTHER, 7
H. to Womankind CHRISTINE DE PISAN, 5
Midwives to the perpetual h. of the female Sex
CHRON, 155
treated unjustly, her desire for h. JUSTICE, 1
we're fighting for this woman's h. CHIVALRY, 2
wife shall h. and fear the husband SUBJECTION, 4
hope H. of the world in grief and wrong HOWE, J, 4
one h. – that I will not be a disappointment
CALLAS, M, 3
Only h. stayed where it was CHRON, 12
The triumph of h. over experience MARRIAGE, 18
horrible A strange, h. business,...good enough for
Shakespeare's day VICTORIA, 7
horror The nightmare dreamer is delivered up to the
h. MANN, E, 1
horse h., a wife, and a sword SAYINGS AND PROVERBS, 18
nobody has any business to go around looking like a
h. PARKER, D, 4
horses England...hell of h. CHRON, 127
hospital the very first requirement in a H. that it
should do the sick no harm NIGHTINGALE, F, 3
hostages h. given to fate FAMILY, 1
h. to fortune MARRIAGE, 10
hostility career woman...encounters a new obstacle:
the h. of men CHRON, 612
fanaticism built up unnecessary h. BESANT, A, 1
Modern young women...show a strong h. to the
word 'feminism' CHRON, 539
hour The h. I have long wished for TERESA OF AVILA, 1
hours What are her *h. of labour* CHRON, 363
house Cleaning your h. while your kids are still growing HOUSEKEEPING, 6
look in their glass, the less they look to their h.
SAYINGS AND PROVERBS, 27
run the h., bring up a family and...work
HEALTH AND HEALTHY LIVING, 9
housecraft h. has not been generally regarded as a
skilled occupation CHRON, 503
household h. labor...not usually considered as 'real
work' CHRON, 617
Woeful is the h. SAYINGS AND PROVERBS, 40
housekeep To h., one had to plan ahead HOUSEKEEPING, 5
housekeeping both sexes would continue to share the
burdens of h. CHRON, 536
H. ain't no joke CHRON, 317; HOUSEKEEPING, 3
h. cares bring...endearing compensations
HOUSEKEEPING, 1
The whole process of home-making, h. and cooking
HOUSEKEEPING, 2

houses Men make h., women make homes
SAYINGS AND PROVERBS, 26
Rich men's h. are seldom beautiful ASQUITH, M, 6
the darkness inside h. DELANEY, S, 1
housewife being a h. is the noblest calling in the world
PARTURIER, F, 4
being a h. is the noblest call in the world CHRON, 614
demise of the h. is entirely to be welcomed CHRON, 738
don't pretend to be an ordinary h. OCCUPATIONS, 14
h. on her feet from dawn till dark HOUSEKEEPING, 4
matchbox has freed the h. PROGRESS, 3
picture of a woman, a h. CHRON, 683
too many fantasies to be a h. MONROE, M, 4
housewifely middle-class hold h. work as degrading
CHRON, 348
housewives h. as mothers...ensuring the adequate continuance of the British race CHRON, 555
H. and mothers seldom find it practicable to come
out on strike CHRON, 638
human abortion the h. rights of the mother ABORTION, 6
a grimmer version of h. affairs STEAD, C, 4
domestic violence...a matter of h. rights VIOLENCE, 8
Friendship is far more h. FRIENDSHIP, 3
half the h. race does acquiesce CHRON, 253
no need for any other faith than...faith in h. beings
BUCK, P, 7
not linen you're wearing out, /But h. creatures' lives
CHRON, 268; OPPRESSION, 2; WORK, 1
pay the first cost on all h. life WAR, 3
sculptures nearly always suggest a h. presence
HEPWORTH, B, 1
humanely warriors...are treated h. CHRON, 10
humanitarian as a ruthlessly h. woman STOWE, H, 1
humanity blame for the existence of h. on women
INJUSTICE, 6
Women have always been the guardians of wisdom
and h. WOLFF, C, 1
zeal in the holy cause of h....infringe on those
domestic duties CHRON, 222
human race the diversity of...colour in the h.
SOMERVILLE, M, 4
the time allotted to the h. SOMERVILLE, M, 2
humble He'll h. her MARRIAGE, 64
h. in character and submissive HUMILITY, 3
h. work of an obscure woman CHRON, 75; HUMILITY, 1
humiliation the moment of greatest h. is...when the
spirit is proudest CHRON, 409; PANKHURST, C, 3
humility born to base h. HUMILITY, 5
without h. all will be lost TERESA OF AVILA, 2
H. becomes our fallen nature HUMILITY, 6
humor we have no sense of h. HUMOUR, 2
humour God withheld the sense of h. from women
TOLERANCE, 1
Total absence of h. COLETTE, 3
hump A woman...without a positive h., may marry
whom she likes MARRIAGE, 27
hunger striking no one was h. CHRON, 444
possibly no one was h. SUFFRAGETTES, 17
hunt motto be:– H. BRONTË, C, 5
hunted tell the others by their h. expression DUTY, 3
hurt Those have most power to h. us that we love
LOVE, 21
husband acts through the medium of her h. CHRON, 261
adorn the h.'s reign CHRON, 176
a h. whom I could have loved CATHERINE THE GREAT, 3
An archaeologist is the best h. CHRISTIE, A, 7

appreciation of the h....falling in love with the wife
LA FAYETTE, M, 2
Being a h. is a whole-time job MARRIAGE, 45
be most conspicuous when she is with her h.
CHRON, 52
children, and a h....do not go well with composition
MUSICIANS, 3
distrust herself and to obey her h. CHRON, 179
happened unawares to look at her h. AUSTEN, J, 12
h. and wife are one person in law CHRON, 191
h. being present at the accouchement of his wife
CHILDBIRTH, 7
h. be or become of so cold a nature DIVORCE, 3
h. *be present during the labour* CHILDBIRTH, 14
h. must be constantly worshipped as a god MARRIAGE, 2
h....obstacle to the enjoyment of many things.
DOMINATION, 3
h. render unto the wife due benevolence MARRIAGE, 4
I do not want to involve my h. in my actions
CHRON, 276
I was your h. LA FAYETTE, M, 4
Let the matron...stay beneath the h. EQUALITY, 2
light wife doth make a heavy h. MARRIAGE, 13
necessary for the wife to *ask* her h. for money
CHRON, 329
not getting a h.,...may find...without resources
CHRON, 301
'passion shooting' by h. of a wife LAW, 15
penalty tax of 40 percent on me because I have no h.
CHRON, 677; TAXATION, 4
permitting the 'passion shooting' by a h. of a wife
CHRON, 627
prove that her h. is a homicide CHRON, 63
she must not be dependent on her h.'s bounty
INDEPENDENCE, 2; LAW, 8
submits to her h., but only to please him
CHRON, 305; WOMAN'S ROLE, 16
superiority which nature has given to her h.
SUPERIORITY, 5
virgins who do not take a h. at the appropriate time
VIRGINITY, 1
wife is entirely under the power...of her h. CHRON, 110
wife shall honour and fear the h. SUBJECTION, 4
husbands dangerous for women to use such things
against their h. EDUCATION, 5
distinguish her H. Bed from anothers CHRON, 163
divine right of h. CHRON, 202
dwell at home without their h. CHRON, 100
flirt with their own h. LOVE AND MARRIAGE, 5
h. and wives...belong to different sexes
DIX, D, 4; MEN AND WOMEN, 21
h. and wives make shipwreck of their lives
DIX, D, 3; MARRIAGE, 48
h., love your wives MARRIAGE, 3
h. to stay at home CHRON, 302; ELIOT, G, 6; WOMAN'S ROLE, 15
interest...involved either in that of their fathers or in
that of their h. CHRON, 227
My h. have been very unlucky BORGIA, L, 4
poor beauty finds more lovers than h.
SAYINGS AND PROVERBS, 31; WEALTH, 1
Powerful women only succeed in spite of their h.
SUCCESS, 9
some are just h. killing their wives LAW, 14
Teaching poor h. the way they should go CHRON, 372
The *divine right* of h. MARRIAGE, 20; WOLLSTONECRAFT, M, 3
willing to let their h. vote for them CHRON, 356

huswifery good h.,...other learning a woman needs not
CHRON, 138
hut Love in a h. LOVE, 34
hygienic h. precautions relating to menstruation are
scarcely ever duly attended to MENSTRUATION, 9
hymen h. is often relaxed in virgins VIRGINITY, 5
Torch of H. serves but to light the Pyre LAW, 12
Love and H. would seldom meet CHRON, 199
hymn Aisle. Altar. H. MARRIAGE, 67
hymns My poems are h. of praise SITWELL, E, 3
hypocrisy saved from the necessity of h. HYPOCRISY, 1
H. left the room ROOSEVELT, E, 1
hysteria noisiness and h. are proofs of unfitness for
public life SUFFRAGETTES, 11
H. is a natural phenomenon EMOTION, 3
hysterical they are too h. CHRON, 398

I

idea One clear i. is too precious a treasure to lose
GILMAN, C, 1
ideal at fourteen every boy should be in love with
some i. woman...on a pedestal LOVE, 65
i. exposes marriages to new strains CHRON, 585
i. woman changes...to suit the taste of man
FEMININITY, 8
patriarchal system is the i. for which he longs
CHRON, 434
idealism an extraordinary mixture of i. and lunacy
PANKHURST, E, 1
passionate i. and daring imagination CHRON, 430
ideals think how far I can go with all the i. that I have
THATCHER, M, 5
ideological Wars and revolutions...have outlived all
their i. justifications ARENDT, H, 5
idiocy denounce the i. of religious scriptures
LESBIANISM, 6
idiots Society is a cage of i. JARS, M, 1
idle i. woman is a badge of superior social status
CHRON, 590
idleness passing one's whole life in moral i.
BLAVATSKY, E, 1
ignorance keeping women in a state of i.
CHRON, 213; EDUCATION, 14
Such i.. All the boys were in military schools and all
the girls were in the convent PORTER, K, 4
weakness of their sex as well as their i. of business
matters LAW, 1
wife in i....that she has become the victim of venereal disease CHRON, 415
women were kept in Turkish i. CHRON, 207
ignorant a parlourmaid as i. as Queen Victoria
VICTORIA, 4
poor girl, i. of the facts of life VIRGINITY, 7
illegitimate different, not because he is i. ILLEGITIMACY, 2
There are no i. children ILLEGITIMACY, 1
illness I. is the night-side of life SONTAG, S, 3
image A photograph is not only an i. SONTAG, S, 4
i. *they* supply...the Rock And Roll Slut APPEARANCE, 18
woman is not made in God's i. CHRON, 83
imagination I.!...I put it first years ago TERRY, E, 4
inflamed the i. even of women and peasants
CHRON, 292
I. was trusted more than judgment CAULKINS, F, 3
passionate idealism and daring i. CHRON, 430
There'd be no scope for i. then MONTGOMERY, L, 2

imaginations vaster field for their i. to rove EDUCATION, 11
imagining How reconcile this world...with...my i.
KELLER, H, 4
imbalance social i. and corruption...because of the prominence of women SUBJECTION, 16
imitates Photography can never grow up if it i.
ABBOTT, B, 1
imitation either a token woman or an i. man CHRON, 730
imitations she disliked the i. of her trumpet tone in the famous line 'A handbag' EVANS, E, 2
immaturity the executive expression of human i.
BRITTAIN, V, 5
immoral She is irresponsible and i., but not deliberately cruel BARDOT, B, 2
immortal giving life to an i. soul CHILDBIRTH, 13
Immortality just ourselves /And I. DICKINSON, E, 3
your voice speaking an assured word for God and I.
EDDY, M, 1
imperfect creator would purposely make half the whole race i. MEN AND WOMEN, 2
imperiously masculine society i. breeds in woman its own corrective CHRON, 566
impetuous a wild, i. and extravagant creature
DUNCAN, I, 1
impolite we thought it was i. to let the man pour the tea CHRON, 727
important It makes them feel i. to think they are in love CATHER, W, 3
most i. thing women have to do EMANCIPATION, 2
One doesn't recognize...the really i. moments...until it's too late CHRISTIE, A, 3
imposed serious mental strain is now being i. upon girls CHRON, 431
impossible i. to be as single-mindedly ruthless as men
RUTHLESSNESS, 3
impressionable Give me a girl at an i. age SPARK, M, 4
impressions subduing all her i. as a woman ARTISTS, 2
improper governed by a woman, instead of a man, was i. CHRON, 77
I only hope it is not i. GASKELL, E, 4
improve She regarded me as a piece of fiction...that she could edit and i. WEST, R, 2
improvements Debarred from all i. of the mind
CHRON, 174
in you had it i. you PREGNANCY, 5
inadequacy belief in her intellectual i. PARTURIER, F, 1
incapable woman is i. of receiving a training similar to that of man CHRON, 318
incapacity her i. to make honorable provision for herself ADULTERY, 7
inch against odds, the women i. forward FEMINISM, 6
incidental she is the i. CHRON, 577
inclinations conduct affairs...in accordance with random opinions and i. INTELLECT, 3
income deemed for i. tax purposes to be his i.
TAXATION, 2
single woman with a narrow i. SINGLE WOMEN, 3
incompetent woman is i. to be a lawyer, minister or doctor CHRON, 343
inconstancy Man with that i. was born BEHN, A, 4
incroach Women i. too much upon their Prerogatives
CHRON, 147
incubator passive i. of his seed CHRON, 20
incubators jobs for which no man is qualified are human i. EQUAL OPPORTUNITIES, 2

indecency The older one grows the more one likes i.
WOOLF, V, 7
indecent this book is in future to be regarded as an i. document CHRON, 496
independence i. of one-half the nation CHRON, 347
principles of the Declaration of I. CHRON, 256; EQUALITY, 7
talk...means to preserve i. LANGUAGE, 9
independent I am i. CASSATT, M, 2
i., brave and busy creatures SINGLE WOMEN, 5
Man was created i. because destined to govern
SUBJECTION, 11
one must do some work seriously and must be i.
CURIE, M, 3
Science fiction and fantasy,..., allow one to imagine...strong i. women STRENGTH, 5
to become fully i. MOTHERHOOD, 21
indignation a feeling of i. STANTON, E, 6
indiscriminately practising i. between the sexes
CHRON, 314
indissoluble union is i. CHRON, 265
individual i. well-being is for private citizens JARS, M, 2
the importance of the i. dancer RAMBERT, M, 1
individuals true community consists of i. CHRON, 608
indoors gods created woman for the i. functions
CHRON, 27
indulge once a woman was bridled it was out of the question for her to i. CHASTITY, 4
indulgence exploits the i. of man CHRON, 445
irregular i. of a natural impulse CHRON, 323
indulgences best mothers, wives,..., know little or nothing of sexual i. SEX, 10
industrial I. relations are like sexual relations
PARTNERSHIP, 3
industry don't think a woman's place is in i. CHRON, 534
drive women out of i. altogether CHRON, 511
i. has not designed itself...to help women CHRON, 721
remain in i. despite all narrow-minded caterwauling
CHRON, 357
Women must remain in i. WORK, 2
inelegance continual state of i. AUSTEN, J, 11
inequality laws and prejudices submit women to the most revolting i. CHRON, 267
Infancy very I. debarr'd those advantages CHRON, 171
infant Every Feme Covert is a sort of i. LAW, 5
infanticide as indefensible as i. WEST, R, 4
inferior abilities of women are far i. CHRON, 225
female in point of strength is, in general, i. to the male CHRON, 201
i. to men as regards justice INTELLECT, 4
No one can make you feel i. without your consent
ROOSEVELT, E, 2
Society...decrees that woman is i. SUPERIORITY, 8
woman's natural potential for virtue is i. to a man's
VIRTUE, 3
inferiority cannot speak of i. and superiority
SUPERIORITY, 6
claiming of superiority and imputing of i. CHRON, 524
general i. of the female sex SUPERIORITY, 2
i. of women...enforced by law CHRON, 440
sense of i. is one of the prime requisites for...subjection CHRON, 475
social i....responsible for prostitution PROSTITUTION, 5
infidelity woman's i. has graver results CHRON, 154
influence clothes possess an i. more powerful CLOTHES, 4
influential The most i. feminist FRIEDAN, B, 2
information solid i. is unbecoming her sex CHRON, 225

The key to security is public i.   SMITH, M, 4
ingenuity a woman is degraded by exerting her i.
   OCCUPATIONS, 4
woman is degraded by exerting her i.   CHRON, 252
inheritance a widow shall have her marriage portion
and her i.   CHRON, 87
i. goes to the son, not the daughter   CHRON, 66
inhibited first-rate achievement is no longer i.   CHRON, 602
initiative she leaves the i. to the man   WOMAN'S NATURE, 9
success depends…upon individual i. and exertion
   PAVLOVA, A, 4
injured i. Woman! rise   CHRON, 228
injustice highest i. our knowledge must rest concealed
   CHRON, 185
i. of disfranchisement   CHRON, 346
no other career possible…is a flagrant social i.
   CHRON, 283
ink A great cow full of i.   SAND, G, 3
Inland Revenue husband should be legally responsible
for dealing with the I.   TAXATION, 6
innate never any reason to believe in any i. superiority
of the male   SUPERIORITY, 7
innocent an extremely beautiful girl and as i. as a rose
   TERRY, E, 1
desert the affections of an i. female   BETRAYAL, 2
innovation promiscuous assemblage of the sexes in the
same class is a dangerous i.   CHRON, 304
inquire to i., /Would cloud our beauty   CHRON, 173
insane i. persons, confined within this commonwealth
   DIX, D, 2
liable to be regarded as i.   CHRON, 422
she may be regarded as 'logically i.'   INTELLECT, 8
insanity the twentieth century men had reached a
peak of i.   BAEZ, J, 2
insatiable carnal lust which in women is i.   LUST, 1
insemination all children would be conceived by artificial i.   CHRON, 710
insensitive vagina walls are quite i.   SEX, 29
instantaneous Miracles are i.   PORTER, K, 2
instinct soul of a sex is emerging from the dim chamber of i.   FEMINISM, 4
woman's i. than a man's reason   CHRON, 512
institution An i. or reform movement that is not selfish
   BARTON, C, 2
institutions women, being the victims of all social i.
   EMOTION, 1
insufferable i. a person woman becomes when…she
exploits the indulgence of man   SUFFRAGETTES, 6
insult A man should not i. his wife publicly
   MARRIAGE, 58
insults i. of men…having been bitten…by their toothless gums.   TOLERANCE, 2
She could exchange compliments or i.…with dukes
or dockers   ASTOR, N, 1
insurrection She was involved in an i. of slaves   BEHN, A, 2
intact woman keeps her body i.   CHASTITY, 2
intellect her i. is not for invention or creation   CHRON, 308
i. never was given to be…buried in the earth
   GRIMKÉ, A, 2
Isadora Duncan…the…development of emotion at
the expense of i.   DUNCAN, I, 2
woman have her i. in vain   INTELLECT, 1
Women's i., who wants it   CHRON, 694
intellectual belief in her i. inadequacy   PARTURIER, F, 1
chief distinction in the i. powers of the two sexes
   CHRON, 326

i. woman is masculinized   CHRON, 570
I. women are the most modest inquirers after truth
   GILMAN, C, 2
never an i.   INTELLECTUALS, 5
The word I. suggests   UNFAITHFULNESS, 4
intelligence crackling with i., but nothing at all of a
prig   MURDOCH, I, 1
You ask whether woman possesses any natural i.
   CHRISTINE DE PISAN, 3
intelligent i. woman…reads the marriage contract
   DUNCAN, I, 5
unfair to imply that an i. woman must 'rise above'
her maternal instincts   CHRON, 651
intense opposition to the women is always more i.
   WOMEN'S LIBERATION MOVEMENT, 1
intercourse giving herself to i., the girl renounces her
honour   VIRGINITY, 4
have i. with her during her period of menstruation
   CHRON, 7
i. is a private act   SEX, 49
Once i. has begun, she experiences pleasure throughout   SEX, 1
Social i.   BLACKWELL, E, 1
interest one i. in common…children   CHILDREN, 5
women take so little i. in…the world   CHRON, 393
interested limited number of subjects men were i. in
   SOCIETY, 6
The average man is…i. in a woman who is i. in him
   MEN, 4
interests duties of government…injurious to their best
i.   CHRON, 236
i. of our fathers, husbands, and brothers, ought to be
ours   CHRON, 263
i. of women will be represented as well   CHRON, 337
intermarriage By i. and by every means in his power
   CHRON, 84
interminable an i. and badly printed game book
   STEIN, G, 1
international science is essentially i.   CURIE, M, 4
interpreter The soul fortunately, has an i.   BRONTË, C, 6
intractable most arrogant and extremely i. animal
   MISOGYNY, 5; PROCREATION, 3
intuition with woman the powers of i.…more strongly
marked   INTELLECT, 6
invalid every woman is…, always more or less an i.
   MENSTRUATION, 10
invent if she hadn't existed we would have had to i.
her   MONROE, M, 2
invention her intellect is not for i. or creation   CHRON, 308
I.,…out of chaos   SHELLEY, M, 1
last-minute i. of The Pill   BIRTH CONTROL, 18; CHRON, 671
Woman's virtue is man's greatest i.   VIRTUE, 9
inventions Modern i. have banished the spinning-
wheel   PROGRESS, 1
involve I do not want to i. my husband in my actions
   CHRON, 276
Iran woman in I. is a political crime
   CHRON, 707; RELIGION, 18
Ireland a picture of a relief map of I.
   ASTOR, N, 5; OLD AGE, 11
Irish The I.…are needed in this cold age   CHILD, L, 2
iron also wash and i. them   EQUALITY, 20
irresponsible She is i. and immoral, but not deliberately cruel   BARDOT, B, 2
irretrievable loss of virtue in a female is i.   VIRTUE, 5
Islam In some remote regions of I.   MODESTY, 7

isolation woman has the same aura of i. CHILDBIRTH, 19
issues no such things as women's i. CHRON, 630
ivory little bit...of i. AUSTEN, J, 14

J

jackass married man a j. SAYINGS AND PROVERBS, 2
Jane Eyre J. strikes us as a personage...from the head of a man BRONTË, C, 1
jars the clashes and j. which we feel most keenly ADDAMS, J, 4
jealous j. and malignant eye on a woman of great parts CHRON, 192
jealousy j. be produced by love JEALOUSY, 2
surrenders to j. more easily than a man WOMAN'S NATURE, 2
Jew Pessimism is a luxury that a J. never can allow himself MEIR, G, 7
jewellery Don't ever wear artistic j. COLETTE, 6
j....wrecks a woman's reputation COLETTE, 6
jewelry she did not remember...her j. LOOS, A, 4; PRACTICALITY, 2
Jewish poignant symbol of J. suffering FRANK, A, 2
Jews not enough prisons...in Palestine to hold all the J. MEIR, G, 8
The J. have produced...Christ, Spinoza, and myself STEIN, G, 4
job Being a husband is a whole-time j. MARRIAGE, 45
j. becomes a woman's j. CHRON, 716
woman's ability to stick to a j. DETERMINATION, 4
jobs j. for which no man is qualified are human incubators EQUAL OPPORTUNITIES, 2
many women are doing two j. in society CHRON, 726
very few j....require a penis or vagina CHRON, 661
women end up doing two j. CHRON, 673
joined what...God hath j. together MARRIAGE, 7
join up wanted women to do...certain things such as j. EXPLOITATION, 2
joke Housekeeping ain't no j. CHRON, 317; HOUSEKEEPING, 3
jokes A different taste in j. is a...strain on the affections ELIOT, G, 5
journalist A capable, bustling novelist of the j. school BUCK, P, 1
journey my j. from here to the next world SCHUMANN, C, 4
joy glittering like the morning star full of life and splendour and j. MARIE ANTOINETTE, 1
I have j. in my submission JHABVALA, R, 2
We could never learn to be brave...if there were only j. KELLER, H, 3
joys j. of parents are secret CHILDREN, 2
judgment Imagination was trusted more than j. CAULKINS, F, 3
jury barrister had objected because 11 members of the j. were women LAW, 16
just a j. cause reaches its flood-tide CATT, C, 4
is it not j. that this sex should partake of the sufferings CHRON, 187
j. and merciful as Nero ELIZABETH I, 3
justice inferior to men as regards j. INTELLECT, 4
I seek j.,...now while I live CHRON, 689
I shall administer j. on the Capitol CLEOPATRA VII, 5
J....blind to racism, sexism, war and poverty PREJUDICE, 5
j. is the sword I carry JUSTICE, 3
shadow of j. in the fate that has befallen women CHRON, 217

the female character...has no sense of j. CHARACTER, 4
justifications Wars and revolutions...have outlived all their ideological j. ARENDT, H, 5

K

kept Married women are k. women CHRON, 532; MARRIAGE, 50
not a stigma for the woman to be k. by a man CHRON, 715
kettle system that produced the k. PROGRESS, 5
keys all the k. should hang from the belt of one woman CHRON, 94
kids Cleaning your house while your k. are still growing HOUSEKEEPING, 6
kill a man can't step up and k. a woman CHIVALRY, 3
If it's natural to k. BAEZ, J, 1
it's just to k. the devil BLACKWELL, E, 4
The word 'revolution' is a word for which you k. WEIL, S, 2
killing no difference between...k. and making decisions that...kill MEIR, G, 4
some are just husbands k. their wives LAW, 14
kills neither k. nor maims her, it is legal for a man to beat his wife VIOLENCE, 1
kindly marries or dies...k. spoken of AUSTEN, J, 4
kindness Their k. cheer'd his drooping soul AIKIN, L, 3
king The k. has been very good to me BOLEYN, A, 4
the k.'s great appetite, and her eyes, which are black and beautiful and take great effect. BOLEYN, A, 1
heart and stomach of a K. CHRON, 125; ELIZABETH I, 11
kings queens...compare favorably with the k. GAGE, M, 3
kiss we could k. her shadow as it fell NIGHTINGALE, F, 2
kissed Wherever one wants to be k. CHANEL, C, 5
kissing K. don't last SEX, 9
kitchen She...had better mind the k. and the children BROWNING, E, 1
Kitchener If K. was not a great man, he was...a great poster ASQUITH, M, 3
knew I k. what I wanted DETERMINATION, 3
knights' sorrier for my good k. loss than for...my fair queen FRIENDSHIP, 2
knitter a beautiful little k. WOOLF, V, 3
knitting confine themselves to making puddings and k. stockings CHRON, 272
didn't get it for k. more socks CHRON, 557
women takes to welding as readily as she takes to k. CHRON, 554
know first abortion that woman begins to 'k.' ABORTION, 5
knowing afraid of women k. as much as themselves CHRON, 198
A woman, especially if she have the misfortune of k. anything INTELLIGENCE, 7
knowledge fragmentary gift of k. or wisdom RUBINSTEIN, H, 4
highest injustice our k. must rest concealed CHRON, 185
if education is...a mere transmission of k. MONTESSORI, M, 4
k....should be communicated to women no less than men CHRON, 336
knows a woman who k. all...that can be taught CHANEL, C, 3; STYLE, 2
man says what he k., a woman what is agreeable CHRON, 196
She k. everything PANKHURST, C, 1

Koran women had not broken the law of the K.
CHRON, 720

L

lab best home for a feminist was in another person's l.
FEMINISM, 10

label Lesbian is a l. invented by the man   LESBIANISM, 4

labor degraded class of l. in the market   CHRON, 392

disproportionate value set on the time and l. of men and women   CHRON, 260

disproportionate value set on the time and the l. of men and women.   OCCUPATIONS, 3

underpaid l. of women   WORK, 7

labour husband be present during the l.   CHILDBIRTH, 14

more skilled l. which women can supply   CHRON, 299

now dependent on the man's l.   CHRON, 242

society wants from women is not l.   CHRON, 296

What are her *hours of l.*   CHRON, 363

ladder ass climbs a l., we may find wisdom
SAYINGS AND PROVERBS, 35

ladies etiquette for l. to have the best chairs   SOCIETY, 7

l. are only admitted to the library if accompanied by a Fellow   CHRON, 526

Young l. are delicate plants
HEALTH AND HEALTHY LIVING, 1

lady a l. and yet be thoroughly political   CHRON, 582

expect us to act like a l.   FLYNN, E, 2

l., better run   ADULTERY, 9

l. of a certain age   AGE, 3

The l.'s not for turning   THATCHER, M, 6

ladylike did not consider it l. for women to drink pints
DRINKING, 10

Lady Macbeth combination of Little Nell and L.
PARKER, D, 2

laid all the young ladies who attended the Yale promenade dance were l. end to end   PARKER, D, 8; SEX, 23

lamp To keep a l. burning   TERESA, MOTHER, 5

land l., like women, was meant to be possessed
CHRON, 658

landscape thinking of large works in a l.   HEPWORTH, B, 3

language conversation is primarily a l. of rapport
LANGUAGE, 9

L. grows out of life   SULLIVAN, A, 4

liberation of l.   LANGUAGE, 8

she knows her l. better than most ladies do
EDUCATION, 19

She studied l. as the soldier guards his sword   DIX, D, 1

writer who combines scientific ability...with a command of the English l.   CARSON, R, 1

languages she speaks eighteen l.. And she can't say 'No' in any of them   PROMISCUITY, 3

large thinking of l. works in a landscape   HEPWORTH, B, 3

lascivious L. movements are of no use whatever to wives   SEX, 3

lass On Richmond Hill there lives a l.   CHARM, 2

late One doesn't recognize...the really important moments...until it's too l.   CHRISTIE, A, 3

laughed Few women care to be l. at   HUMOUR, 3

laughing cannot be always l. at a man   AUSTEN, J, 10

laughter you can draw l. from an audience   MARRIAGE, 56

laundry Feminism...not just a l. list   FEMINISM, 16

law A married woman in English l. has no legal existence   LAW, 10

duty even to break the l.   CHRON, 410

Equality of rights under the l. shall not be abridged...on account of sex   CHRON, 662

eyes of the l. her personal liberty and her status are *nil*   CHRON, 351

husband and wife are one person in l.   CHRON, 191

inferiority of women...enforced by l.   CHRON, 440

iniquitous l....over the person and property of another   CHRON, 237

keep their place as l. directs   CHRON, 59

l. holds...property is of greater value than life   FRY, E, 3

l. where it concerns women, is a slavish one.   LAW, 12

No l. in England can make Birth Control
BIRTH CONTROL, 7

not believe in sex distinction in literature, l., politics, or trade   CHRON, 466

the condition of our sex is so deplorable that it is our duty...to break the l.   PANKHURST, E, 6

the l. is a ass   CHRON, 258

the restraint of l. and that of custom   CATT, C, 2

two people marry...in the eyes of the l. one person
CHRON, 670

lawful lower their gaze before the men at whom it is not l. for them to look   HUMILITY, 2

not be l....to bring home another wife   CHRON, 34

laws know you do not make the l.   CHRON, 247

l. were man's l.   CHRON, 413

Love is above the l.   LOVE, 31

severe l. of men no longer prevent women from...the sciences   CHRON, 112

she cannot submit to l. made without women's participation   CHRON, 275

There never will be...equality until women...make l.
ANTHONY, S, 3

unquestioning obedience to l. she had no share in making   CHRON, 364

voice in making the l.   CHRON, 337

women themselves help to make l.   EQUALITY, 13

you do not make the l.   GRIMKÉ, A, 1; POWER, 5

lawyer woman is incompetent to be a l., minister or doctor   CHRON, 343

lazy be efficient if you're going to be l.   HOUSEKEEPING, 8

There are no ugly women, only l. ones
COSMETICS, 9; RUBINSTEIN, H, 3

leader A l. who doesn't hesitate...is not fit to be a l.
MEIR, G, 2

leapt Into the dangerous world I l.   CHILDBIRTH, 5

learn eagerness to l. with your brothers   EDUCATION, 5

not to l., but to unlearn   STEINEM, G, 1

We could never l. to be brave...if there were only joy
KELLER, H, 3

woman must l. to obey   WOMAN'S ROLE, 29

learned I hate a l. woman   EDUCATION, 1

L. ladies are not to my taste   EDUCATION, 6

l. woman is the greatest of all calamities
INTELLECTUALS, 2

l. woman is thought to be a comet
CHRON, 157; INTELLECTUALS, 1

maiden...have come forth...in this radiance of l.
HUMILITY, 4

men   morality is l.   MORALITY, 8

Vehement exclamation against L. Women   CHRON, 184

learner Woman must be a l.   CHRON, 60

learning Conceal whatever l. she attains   CHRON, 186

free to set son or daughter to take l.   CHRON, 99

Girls study for prizes and not for l.   CHRON, 331

good huswifery,...other l. a woman needs not
CHRON, 138

woman should acquire l. CHRON, 96

learnt More can be l. from Miss Austen AUSTEN, J, 1

leave I l. before being left. I decide BARDOT, B, 4

thrive must ask l. of his wife SAYINGS AND PROVERBS, 17

lectures went to men's l., unless the professor objected
CHRON, 402

left better to be l. than never to have been loved
LOVE, 25

I leave before being l.. I decide BARDOT, B, 4

l. me as an enemy ANGER, 3

legal abandons all claims to consider woman as a l.
person CHRON, 208

l. and material hindrances BEAUTY, 17

l. status of the Mohammedan woman CHRON, 359

marriage the very being or l. existence of woman is
suspended LAW, 6

neither kills nor maims her, it is l. for a man to beat
his wife VIOLENCE, 1

no l. slaves – except for the woman in every man's
home LAW, 11

legally husband should be l. responsible for dealing
with the Inland Revenue TAXATION, 6

marriage...made l. cannot be unmade CHRON, 71

legislation l. has been the only force which has
improved the working conditions WORK, 3

l....improved the working conditions CHRON, 426

L. is not going to change discrimination CHRON, 686

legs If she doesn't want it she only has to keep her l.
shut RAPE, 5

woman's composing is like a dog's walking on his
hind l. CHRON, 516

leisure mothers who must earn...no l. time problem
CHRON, 446

peace and l. of the days in *purdah* CHRON, 600

women form the l. class CHRON, 506

lesbian L. is a label invented by the man LESBIANISM, 4

lesbianism l. makes a woman virile
LESBIANISM, 5; WOLFF, C, 2

L....a political stance CHRON, 634

L. is not a matter of sexual preference LESBIANISM, 8

lesbians most l....seek to cultivate...their femininity
LESBIANISM, 3

less equal rights, nothing more but nothing l.
EQUALITY, 18

lesson A l. for the wyfe CHRON, 108

letter The gist of a lady's l. is in the postscript
SAYINGS AND PROVERBS, 12

letters His sayings are generally like women's l.
ATTITUDES, 17

man who teaches women l. feeds more poison
EDUCATION, 3

That sturdy woman of l. SAND, G, 2

lettuce l. has been fattening all along BOMBECK, E, 1

levity l. of mind CHRON, 17

liar He did not feel a l. MURDOCH, I, 5

liars let us be revenged by proving them to be l.
CATHERINE THE GREAT, 5

liberated l. woman...renounce the desire of being a sex
object FEMINISM, 11

liberation l. of language LANGUAGE, 8

L....abolition of wife WOMEN'S LIBERATION MOVEMENT, 10

L. would compel women into male roles CHRON, 653

regard the Women's L. movement as a serious threat
CHRON, 652

Women's L. is just a lot of foolishness CHRON, 685

Women's L. Movement...dares to challenge what is
CHRON, 642

Liberationists I'm furious about the Women's L.
CHRON, 645; LOOS, A, 5

liberty aware of l. and dignity and true reason MANN, E, 3

eyes of the law her personal l. and her status are *nil*
CHRON, 351

Poor, – yet blest with l. AIKIN, L, 4

selling the l. of other women CHRON, 408

liberty-loving right of private contract...dear to a l. people CHRON, 354

libidinous Females are naturally l. SEX, 2

library ladies are only admitted to the l. if accompanied by a Fellow CHRON, 526

l. that hadn't a book AUSTEN, J, 3

lid woman's hands raised the l....scattered the evils
CHRON, 12

lie shows you that figures can l. APPEARANCE, 7

Why must I l. beneath you SUBJECTION, 2

lies Only l. and evil come from letting people off
MURDOCH, I, 6

life a keen observer of l. UNFAITHFULNESS, 4

chemical barrage has been hurled against the fabric
of l. CARSON, R, 3

Fascism recognizes women as a part of the l. force
CHRON, 541

giving l. to an immortal soul CHILDBIRTH, 13

her l. and career still seem to have been dreamed up
by one of her script-writers BOW, C, 2

hymns of praise to the glory of l. SITWELL, E, 3

I approach the end of my l. with pleasure BORGIA, L, 3

Illness is the night-side of l. SONTAG, S, 3

law holds...property is of greater value than l. FRY, E, 3

l. deserves the protection of society ABORTION, 12

l. may not be prolonged beyond the power of usefulness AIKIN, L, 5

l. today is dedicated to the *removal of risk* BLACK, S, 3

L. will be happier and more beautiful PANKHURST, S, 3

love...has one arch-enemy – and that is l. LOVE, 58

meaningfulness of l. in the notions of sisterhood
WOMEN'S LIBERATION MOVEMENT, 18

Mrs John Smith, her l. is one long slavery CHRON, 363

really don't know l. at all LIFE, 4

she is mine for l. SPARK, M, 4

sickness need not be a part of l.
HEALTH AND HEALTHY LIVING, 8

Than to ever let a woman in my l. MISOGYNY, 11

The Book of L. begins LIFE, 1

the child should be allowed to meet the real experiences of l. KEY, E, 2

The first rule in opera is the first rule in l. MELBA, N, 6

they get about ten percent out of l. DUNCAN, I, 7

Woman...has everywhere greater respect for l. than
man PEACE, 1

worked all the time for her whole l. ASHLEY, L, 2

your wife! /And I have no other l. CHRON, 397

light content with l. and easily broken ties ELIOT, G, 7

lightened brooding tragedy and its dark shadows can
be l. GANDHI, I, 6

liking it saves me the trouble of l. them AUSTEN, J, 13

lilies The l. and roses were all awake COMPLIMENTS, 4

limb perils...of wind and l. CONSTANCY, 1

limited l. number of subjects men were interested in
SOCIETY, 6

linen It is not l. you're wearing out OPPRESSION, 2; WORK, 1

washing one's clean l. in public   LOVE AND MARRIAGE, 5
women nor l.   SAYINGS AND PROVERBS, 6
lines not know her l. and give the performance she
did   MONROE, M, 3
lingerie Brevity is the soul of l.   CLOTHES, 9; PARKER, D, 9
linguistic l. sexism is intact   LANGUAGE, 7
linseed sit in a bath of a decoction of l.   ABORTION, 1
lioness A natural unassuming woman whom
they...spoil by making a l. of her   GASKELL, E, 1
feeds a l. at home   FAMILY, 2
lips her l. narrow and her teeth black   ELIZABETH I, 2
pride is a word often on women's l. – but they display little sign of it where love affairs are concerned.   PRIDE, 2
liquor make cowards of men as the l. power   DRINKING, 4
literary A sort of l. Cinderella   BRONTË, A, 1
It's l. suicide   BOMBECK, E, 3
L. criticism of the Brontës   THE BRONTËS, 1
unreasonable prejudice...against a l. and scientific
education for women   CHRON, 328
literature Emily Brontë remains the sphinx of l.   BRONTË, E, 3
L. cannot be the business of a woman's life   WRITERS, 8
L. is mostly about having sex   CHILDREN, 9
not believe in sex distinction in l., law, politics, or
trade   CHRON, 466
little These l. grey cells   CHRISTIE, A, 5
The woman's mind is l.   MEN AND WOMEN, 23
Little Nell combination of L. and Lady Macbeth   PARKER, D, 2
live better to die on your feet than to l. on your knees   IBARRURI, D, 4
Come l. with me   LOVE, 13; 19
decide how you're going to l.   LIFE, 3
easier to l. through someone else   FRIEDAN, B, 6
I have learned to l. each day as it comes   DIX, D, 2
I seek justice,...now while I l.   CHRON, 689
People do not l. nowadays   DUNCAN, I, 7
To l. with thee, and be thy love   LOVE, 14
We all l. with the objective of being happy   FRANK, A, 5
You might as well l.   PARKER, D, 3
lived She...has never l.   LOVE, 26
living God of practical American life: Can the man
make a l.   CHRON, 421
make love with men for a l.   PROSTITUTION, 14
poor male clerks whose l. they are doing their
utmost to take   CHRON, 428
loaves l. are set down by our very door   CHRON, 424
locked Because man is a brute, woman has to be l. up   CHRON, 382
logically she may be regarded as 'l. insane'   INTELLECT, 8
loneliness L....is the most terrible poverty   TERESA, MOTHER, 4
lonely Housework...inhumanely l.   HOUSEKEEPING, 7
look dumb blonde because of the way I l.   APPEARANCE, 17
looking-glasses Women have served...as l.   WOMAN'S ROLE, 27
looks A woman as old as she l.   AGE, 5
Lord L.! hast power to save   WILLARD, E, 1
Mine eyes have seen the glory of the coming of the
L.   HOWE, J, 3
placed over her as master, L. and tyrant   CHRON, 401
lordlike what makes men walk l.   MEN AND WOMEN, 28
lords None ought to be l. or landlords over another   CHRON, 142

loss intellectuality...paid for by the l. of valuable feminine qualities   CHRON, 570
lost better to have loved and l.   LOVE, 39
I have discovered the art...l. for two thousand years   DUNCAN, I, 3
never to have l. at all   LOVE, 50
You are a l. generation   STEIN, G, 5
lot disappointment is the l. of women   DISAPPOINTMENT, 1
love a girl likes to be crossed in l. a little now and
then   LOVE, 30
All mankind l. a lover   LOVE, 35
all the world and l. were young   LOVE, 14
ashamed of having been in l.   LOVE, 22
barbarous custom that forbids the maid to make
advances in l.   CHRON, 230
Because women can do nothing except l.   ATTITUDES, 21; LOVE, 53
Between women l. is contemplative   CHRON, 578
bound hand and foot by l. and motherhood   CHRON, 655
Come live with me, and be my l.   LOVE, 13
Every little girl knows about l.   LOVE, 61; SAGAN, F, 1
folly...l. did make thee run into   LOVE, 17
How do I l. thee   LOVE, 37
husbands, l. your wives   MARRIAGE, 3
if men and women marry those whom they do not l.   LOVE AND MARRIAGE, 3
I shall but l. thee better after death   BROWNING, E, 7; LOVE, 38
It makes them feel important to think they are in l.   CATHER, W, 3
jealousy be produced by l.   JEALOUSY, 2
law of nature which l. alone can alter   LUST, 3; SEX, 6
live with me, and be my l.   LOVE, 19
l. – all the wretched cant of it   GREER, G, 4
L. and Hymen would seldom meet   CHRON, 199
l., an...intercourse between tyrants and slaves   LOVE AND FRIENDSHIP, 2
L. built on beauty   LOVE, 12
L. ceases to be a pleasure   BEHN, A, 6; LOVE, 23
l. children always suffer   CHRON, 490
l. dwells in gorgeous palaces   LOVE, 11
l....has one arch-enemy – and that is life   LOVE, 58
L. in a hut   LOVE, 34
L. is above the laws   LOVE, 31
L. is based on a view of women   ATTITUDES, 25
l. is blind   LOVE, 16
L. is like the measles   LOVE, 47
L. is moral even without...marriage   KEY, E, 3
L. is not love /Which alters   LOVE, 18
L. is the wisdom of the fool   LOVE, 28
L. laughs at locksmiths   LOVE, 3
l., like a running brook, is disregarded   LOVE, 56
l. like other arts requires experience   LOVE, 32
L. makes the world   LOVE, 4
L. means never having to say   LOVE, 63
L. means the pre-cognitive flow   LOVE AND FRIENDSHIP, 5
L.'s like the measles   LOVE, 42
L.'s pleasure lasts but a moment   LOVE, 29
L....the gift of oneself   LOVE, 59
L. will find a way   LOVE, 5
l. what you do   WORK, 8
make l. with men for a living   PROSTITUTION, 14
Many a man has fallen in l. with a girl   LOVE, 60
My L. in her attire doth show her wit   BEAUTY, 3
My l....resembles the eternal rocks   LOVE, 36
My l....will change   LOVE, 36

No l. like the first l. LOVE, 7
Nuptial l. maketh mankind LOVE AND MARRIAGE, 2
of vegetables as if they were l. objects COLETTE, 1
one happiness...to l. and be loved. HAPPINESS, 3
qualities of l. and service, in which women is strong
STRENGTH, 3
qualities of l. and service, which in women is strong
SOCIETY, 5
rather they make l. CHRON, 607
Religion is l. WEBB, B, 4
She makes l. just like a woman MATURITY, 3
strong as the force of l. CHILDREN, 3
Such ever was l.'s way LOVE, 43
the most intense l. on the mother's side
MOTHERHOOD, 21
Those have most power to hurt us that we l.
LOVE, 21; LOVE, 21
To live with thee, and be thy l. LOVE, 14
to l. and to cherish MARRIAGE, 15
use contraceptives do not understand l.
TERESA, MOTHER, 6
vanity and l....universal characteristics
MEN AND WOMEN, 5
what a mischievous devil L. is LOVE, 52
when one has loved a man it is very different to l.
God SAND, G, 5
love-affair evils of an illicit l. ADULTERY, 6
love affairs as famous for her l. SAND, G, 1
loved a husband whom I could have l.
CATHERINE THE GREAT, 3
better to be left than never to have been l. LOVE, 25
better to have l. and lost LOVE, 39; 50
God alone deserves to be l. SAND, G, 5
never to have l. at all LOVE, 39
She who has never l. has never lived LOVE, 26
lovely l. as to be beautiful BEAUTY, 6
lovemaking keep young people away from l.
LA FAYETTE, M, 1
l. and caresses should come entirely from the man
SEX, 18
rosy l. and marrying LOVE AND MARRIAGE, 6
lover All mankind love a l. LOVE, 35
an ex-wife searching for a new l. ANGER, 4
no true l., no true friend LOVE AND FRIENDSHIP, 3
satisfied with her l.'s mind LOVE, 44
lovers l. cannot see /The pretty follies LOVE, 16
poor beauty finds more l. than husbands
SAYINGS AND PROVERBS, 31; WEALTH, 1
those of us meant to be l. LOVE, 64
loves He that l. not his wife and children FAMILY, 2
I have reigned with your l. CHRON, 130; ELIZABETH I, 4
loving A woman despises a man for l. her LOVE, 46
most l. mere folly LOVE AND FRIENDSHIP, 1
luck A self-made man...believes in l. STEAD, C, 2
just my l. to get /One perfect rose PARKER, D, 5
lucky L. at cards LOVE, 6
lunacy an extraordinary mixture of idealism and l.
PANKHURST, E, 1
lunatic Those comfortably padded l. asylums...the
stately homes WOOLF, V, 4
lunatics No vote can be given by l.
CHRON, 190; LAW, 7; SUFFRAGETTES, 1
regarding them as criminals and l. CHRON, 430
lust Man in his l. STANTON, E, 7
lying One of you is l. PARKER, D, 6

M

Macbeth refused the part of Lady M. EVANS, E, 3
machination useth much more m. and deceit than a
man CHRON, 95
machine new social relationships of the men and
women around the m. CHRON, 628
mad I am going m. again WOOLF, V, 10
I think she was quite m. MONROE, M, 1
neither unnatural, nor abominable, nor m.
LESBIANISM, 2
madame Call me m. LANGUAGE, 4
Madame Bovary All I could think of...was: M.
ADULTERY, 8
made 'Do you know who m. you?' STOWE, H, 4
m. myself up morally COSMETICS, 4
tape, ribbon,...heretofore was m. by poore aged woemen CHRON, 137
magazines ministers realized that women's m. had an
influence CHRON, 549
magnanimous the m. pity of a heroine JOAN OF ARC, 3
magnetic Her m. stage personality CALLAS, M, 2
Mahomet good a Christian as M. ELIZABETH I, 3
maid await news of the M. JOAN OF ARC, 4
Being an old m. is like death by drowning
SINGLE WOMEN, 10
m. oft seen...disesteemed SAYINGS AND PROVERBS, 19
Surrender to the M. CHRON, 103
maiden A simple m. in her flower VIRGINITY, 6
m....have come forth...in this radiance of learned
men HUMILITY, 4
maids M. must be wives WOMAN'S ROLE, 12
main leaves out half the human race it cannot be as
m. EQUAL OPPORTUNITIES, 6
maintenance always taught to look up to man for a m.
EDUCATION, 17; PROSTITUTION, 1
majestic bear and rear the m. race MARTYRDOM, 2
majority idea of equal pay now has m. support
CHRON, 711
make and mend moral little booklet 'M.' CHRON, 559
makers the children are the m. of men MONTESSORI, M, 5
maladies five worst m. that afflict the female mind
CHRON, 179
male all the privileges of being m. SUPERIORITY, 12
child is a m., the mother has a better colour and an
easier delivery PREGNANCY, 1
dare not reveal the difficulties of their sicknesses to
a m. doctor CHRON, 78
female is less perfect than the m. CHRON, 55
few Doctors, either m. or female, as possible
CHRON, 303
God, being m., values maleness RELIGION, 16
in Christ Jesus there is neither m. nor female
GRIMKÉ, A, 4
In the sex-war thoughtlessness is the weapon of the
m. MEN AND WOMEN, 22
Liberation would compel women into m. roles
CHRON, 653
m. is a biological accident CHRON, 609
m. is by nature superior CHRON, 22
more deadly than the m. ATTITUDES, 19; RUTHLESSNESS, 2
only a m. can represent Christ...serious heresy
CHRON, 729; RELIGION, 22
Our cultural world is the product of m. conscious-
ness CHRON, 665

solid united front of m. clubbability · CHRON, 723
State which regards the purposes of life solely from the m. standpoint · CHRON, 476
the peculiar situation of the human m. · BEAUVOIR, S, 2
venereal pleasure is almost entirely on the side of the m. · CHRON, 306
works of m. and female authors be properly separated · MODESTY, 5
males m. in the paternal line shall succeed · LAW, 2
m. should deposit their sperm in a sperm bank · CHRON, 710

malignant jealous and m. eye on a woman of great parts · CHRON, 192
malpractice the fear of m. · SONTAG, S, 1
Mammon M. wins his way where Seraphs might despair · WEALTH, 4
man a m. is always seeking for happiness · DIX, D, 3; MARRIAGE, 48
A m. is only as old as the woman · AGE, 8
A m....is *so* in the way · GASKELL, E, 3
A m. of straw · MISOGYNY, 1; SAYINGS AND PROVERBS, 21
assumed the duties of a m. · POLITICS, 2
called Woman, because she was taken out of M. · CHRON, 1
cannot be always laughing at a m. · AUSTEN, J, 10
coming together of m. and wife...should be a fresh adventure · STOPES, M, 5
direction belongs to the m. · CHRON, 72
Every m. can rule a shrew · SAYINGS AND PROVERBS, 7
fill her soul with gratitude to God and to the M. · LOVE AND MARRIAGE, 4
God made the woman for the m. · WOMAN'S ROLE, 13
If a m. stays away from his wife · MARRIAGE, 35
It takes...twenty years to make a m. · MEN AND WOMEN, 17
Jane Eyre strikes us as a personage...from the head of a m. · BRONTË, C, 1
M. for the field and woman for the hearth · MEN AND WOMEN, 9
M. has his will · MEN AND WOMEN, 10
M. in his lust · STANTON, E, 7
m. is a dangerous creature · ADAMS, A, 3
m. is as old as he's feeling · AGE, 5
m. is designed to walk three miles · EQUALITY, 23
M.'s love is of man's life a thing apart · LOVE, 33; MEN AND WOMEN, 6
M. to command and woman to obey · MEN AND WOMEN, 9
m. who's untrue to his wife · UNFAITHFULNESS, 4
M. with that inconstancy was born · BEHN, A, 4
M. with the head and woman with the heart · MEN AND WOMEN, 9
M., woman, and devil, are the three degrees of comparison · SAYINGS AND PROVERBS, 22
more flattering to be a 'm.'s woman' · STARK, F, 2
My mother said it was simple to keep a m. · WOMAN'S ROLE, 36
not created merely to gratify the appetite of m. · EDUCATION, 16
only place where a m. can feel...secure · GREER, G, 2
rarely...one can see in a little boy the promise of a m. · MEN AND WOMEN, 14
She's more of a m. than I expected · VICTORIA, 3
simple word 'm.', which the rapist invariably is · CHRON, 714; RAPE, 6
some meannesses...too mean even for m. · ATTITUDES, 18
stronger than a m. simpler than a child · BRONTË, E, 1

Susan Anthony...has striven long and earnestly to become a m. · ANTHONY, S, 1
Think me all m. · EQUALITY, 5
'Tis strange what a m. may do · LOVE, 40
To the m.-in-the-street, who · UNFAITHFULNESS, 4
we have woman before m. · SUPERIORITY, 3
we take all the grief from m. · MEN AND WOMEN, 3
When a woman behaves like a m. · MEN AND WOMEN, 25
Why can't a woman be more like a m. · ATTITUDES, 26
why doesn't she behave like a nice m. · EVANS, E, 5
woman exists for the sake of m. · SUBJECTION, 4
woman in name, but in spirit she is a m. · CHRON, 85
woman stands on an even platform with m. · GAGE, M, 1
woman the shipwreck of m. · RELIGION, 13
Women who love the same m. · LOVE, 51
young m. not yet · MARRIAGE, 12
manage clever woman to m. a fool · WOMAN'S ROLE, 20
management efficient care and m. of the home · CHRON, 503
manager Men marry...to get a m. for the house · CHRON, 28; MARRIAGE, 1
Manderley Last night I went to M. · DU MAURIER, D, 4
manhood clothes...reconstructing their diminished m. · CLOTHES, 11
threatening to fragile American m....feminist drive for economic equality · FEMINISM, 21
manipulative women are sexually m. · SEX, 49
mankind the earth is free for every son and daughter of m. · CHRON, 142
the mother of m. · STANTON, E, 7
Man-Midwife need not call for the help of a M., which is a disparagement · CHRON, 146
manners delicacy of the national m. in point of this kind · CHRON, 266
M. are...the need of the plain · APPEARANCE, 13
man-rule m.,...has implied to woman · CHRON, 401
map a picture of a relief m. of Ireland · ASTOR, N, 5; OLD AGE, 11
mar likely to m. the general felicity · MARRIAGE, 44
march m. into battle together with the men · COURAGE, 5
mare farmer's m. has a foal she is turned out to rear it in idleness · CHILDBIRTH, 15
Margot Asquith The affair between M. and M. · ASQUITH, M, 2
Marilyn Monroe There's been an awful lot of crap written about M. · MONROE, M, 1
mark an ever-fixed m. · LOVE, 18
market man enjoys the right to lead his wife to m. with a rope about her neck · CHRON, 219
markets join the noisy throng in the busy m. of the world · CHRON, 296
marriage a widow shall have her m. portion and her inheritance · CHRON, 87
daughters are but branches which by m. are broken off from the root · CHRON, 151
expect of m. that it shall be an equal partnership · CHRON, 585
Happiness in m. · AUSTEN, J, 9
her m. utterly annuls her · CHRON, 208
how to combine m. and a career · CHRON, 706
In no country...are the m. laws so iniquitous as in England · CHRON, 255
intelligent woman...reads the m. contract · DUNCAN, I, 5
Love is moral even without...m. · KEY, E, 3
man avoids /M. and all the troubles women bring · MARRIAGE, 9

M....a community...making in all two MARRIAGE, 43
m....a condition of slavery for women CHRON, 276
m. and home-making is genetic CHRON, 593
M. and motherhood should not be for sale CHRON, 447
M....a woman's best investment MARRIAGE, 65
m. bring only tears ADULTERY, 1
m. had always been her object MARRIAGE, 22
M. in modern times is regarded as a partnership CHRON, 735
M. is a wonderful invention MARRIAGE, 75
M. is...excluded from heaven MARRIAGE, 44
M. is for women the commonest mode of livelihood CHRON, 522
M. is the aim and end of all sensible girls CHRON, 438
m....made legally cannot be unmade CHRON, 71
m. may be a failure spiritually DIVORCE, 9
m. of true minds LOVE, 18
m....the arrangements of property CHRON, 254
M....the best of opiates MARRIAGE, 51
m. the very being or legal existence of woman is suspended LAW, 6
no intermediary situation between m. and celibacy CHRON, 73
office...his by m., like the rest of his wife's property CHRON, 209
property earned during m. belongs wholly to the husband CHRON, 369
Sexual intercourse in m. CHRON, 306
She'll wear the pants in that m. ANNE, PRINCESS, 2
she needs m. and he does not MARRIAGE, 52
state of m. CHRON, 287
training women to consider m. as the sole object EDUCATION, 18
twenty years of m. make her...like a public building MARRIAGE, 37
undesired sex...greater in m. than in prostitution CHRON, 522
virginal charm of womanhood in the m. market SEX, 14
virgin who is not pledged in m. CHRON, 9
wasn't told anythink about m. CHRON, 463
what does man gain by m. MARRIAGE, 30
Why should m. bring only tears UNFAITHFULNESS, 1
Women...care fifty times more for a m. than a ministry CHRON, 312; MARRIAGE, 32
marriages her m. were adventures and her friendships enduring TERRY, E, 2
M. are made in heaven SAYINGS AND PROVERBS, 23
The early m. of silly children MARRIAGE, 25
Marriage Tax iniquity of the M. in the form of supertax TAXATION, 1
married A m. woman in English law has no legal existence LAW, 10
as m. women, control and administer their own property CHRON, 370
a woman's business to get m. MARRIAGE, 41
don't sleep with m. men ADULTERY, 11
every woman who was m. would automatically want to conceive CHRON, 574
greater amount of happiness...in the m. state CHRON, 265
he that is m. careth...how he may please his wife MARRIAGE, 6
I m. beneath me ASTOR, N, 3; MARRIAGE, 38
I would have m. for money LONGWORTH, A, 3
m. for a course or two at mealtimes ADULTERY, 10
M. life is a woman's profession CHRON, 301

m....like jumping into a hole in the ice MARRIAGE, 39
m. past redemption MARRIAGE, 16
m. people should have the same kind of partnership in property CHRON, 50
m. state there should be the strictest equality CHRON, 274
m. will not see the kingdom of heaven RELIGION, 3
m. woman has nothing of her own but her wedding-ring SAYINGS AND PROVERBS, 24
M. women are kept women CHRON, 532; MARRIAGE, 50
never contemplated...right of voting...for m. women CHRON, 264
No man is genuinely happy, m., who has to drink worse gin MARRIAGE, 46
not made m. woman subservient to have her be polluted CHRON, 111
principle of m. women so working CHRON, 514
Reader, I m. him BRONTË, C, 7
so cold I almost got m. SINGLE WOMEN, 8
woman can get m. or not as she likes CHRON, 717
Writing is like getting m. MARRIAGE, 68
marries m. or dies...kindly spoken of AUSTEN, J, 4
marry as easy to m. a rich woman as a poor woman MARRIAGE, 28
A woman...may m. whom she likes MARRIAGE, 27
best thing a woman can do is to m. CHRON, 690
better to m. than to burn MARRIAGE, 5
Every woman should m. MARRIAGE, 33
if men and women m. those whom they do not love LOVE AND MARRIAGE, 3
if only you could persuade him to m. MARRIAGE, 55
may m. or you may not CHRON, 596
Men m.,...to get a manager for the house CHRON, 28
Men m....to get a manager for the house MARRIAGE, 1
M. in haste SAYINGS AND PROVERBS, 25
No man should m. MARRIAGE, 29
No widow shall be compelled to m. CHRON, 88
no woman should m. a teetotaller MARRIAGE, 34
Then I can't m. you, my pretty maid MARRIAGE, 19
Those who m. God...can become domesticated too MARRIAGE, 62
To m. a man out of pity is folly ASQUITH, M, 5
two people m....in the eyes of the law one person CHRON, 670
when a man should m. MARRIAGE, 12
When you see what some girls m. MARRIAGE, 40
woman holding public office were to m. CHRON, 209
marrying first her name is lost as to her particular in m. CHRON, 150
M. a man is like buying MARRIAGE, 60
m. merely to get an establishment MARRIAGE, 23
rosy love-making and m. LOVE AND MARRIAGE, 6
martyr Now he will raise me to be a m. BOLEYN, A, 4
martyrdom retold history as a story of their long M. CHRON, 529
Marx not even M. is more precious...than the truth WEIL, S, 3
Mary so much Christian blood,...as under the said Queen M. CHRON, 114
masculine Fighting is essentially a m. idea MEN AND WOMEN, 32
m. mythology suppressing...facts of women's sexual CHRON, 464
m. part, the poet in me CHRON, 166
m. preserve, as in computer science CHRON, 716

m. society imperiously breeds in woman its own corrective   CHRON, 566
partly from m. clannishness   MEN, 2
Solitary women exhibit pseudo-m. efficiency
      SINGLE WOMEN, 11
masculinity women approach genius they also
approach m.   INTELLIGENCE, 15
masculinized intellectual woman is m.   CHRON, 570
master a past m. in making nothing happen very
slowly   STEIN, G, 2
law of this country has made you my m.   CHRON, 238
lie down mistress, and get up m.
      DOMINATION, 6; FREEDOM, 2
man was the m.   SUPERIORITY, 9
placed over her as m., Lord and tyrant   CHRON, 401
take for our bodies /A m.   EXPLOITATION, 1
wife ought to suffer, and let the husband…be m.
      CHRON, 93
masters achieved equality, they will be your m.
      CHRON, 33
Buy old m.   PRACTICALITY, 4
masturbation feeling of…unease follows m.   WOLFF, C, 3
matchbox m. has freed the housewife   PROGRESS, 3
maternal better to feed the child with m. milk
      BREASTFEEDING, 1
M. softness weakens my resolve   MOTHERHOOD, 1
Physiology has specified the nature of the m. role
      CHRON, 705
To shingle was to cut loose from the m. pattern
      CHRON, 488
unfair to imply that an intelligent woman must 'rise
above' her m. instincts   CHRON, 651; MOTHERHOOD, 15
maternity M. is…an unsocial experience   MOTHERHOOD, 7
mathematics avoid pregnancy by…m.   BIRTH CONTROL, 12
Fair Sex may be encourag'd to attempt M.   CHRON, 180
female professor of m. is…a monstrosity   CHRON, 350
not be half so beautiful if she was as great at m.
      INTELLIGENCE, 4
matrimony m., which I always thought a highly overrated performance   DUNCAN, I, 6
my first experience with m.   MARRIAGE, 47
matron Let the m….stay beneath the husband
      EQUALITY, 2
matter Women represent…m. over mind
      MEN AND WOMEN, 12
matters Such m. are men's concern   CHRON, 47
mature bred in schools to m. our brains   INTELLECT, 2
m. woman in the media   AGE, 11
May darling buds of M.   BEAUTY, 5
me Besides Shakespeare and m., who do you think
there is   STEIN, G, 3
meals three m. a day   CHRON, 694
meannesses some m….too mean even for man
      ATTITUDES, 18
measles Love is like the m.   LOVE, 47
Love's like the m.   LOVE, 42
meddle female sex to m. in matters which pertain
uniquely to men   SUBJECTION, 1
Women…m. with Politicks   CHRON, 152
media mature woman in the m.   AGE, 11
mediocre Women want m. men   MEN AND WOMEN, 26
medium acts through the m. of her husband   CHRON, 261
a m. is represented by nature   ABBOTT, B, 2
meet We only part to m. again   CONSTANCY, 2
meeting as If I was a public m.   VICTORIA, 6

memoranda enough to keep their accounts and m.
      SOCIETY, 1
memories limits his vision to his m. of yesterday
      LANGTRY, L, 1
men been nourished by m.   MEN AND WOMEN, 27
biggest problem all my life was m.   SUCCESS, 7
don't sleep with married m.   ADULTERY, 11
England…purgatory of m.   CHRON, 127
equal interest with the m. of this Nation   CHRON, 143
expressly forbidden to address m. who are in the
company of women or children   PROSTITUTION, 4
I don't think m. and women were meant to live
together   MEN AND WOMEN, 33
If women be proud…m. that make them so   PRIDE, 1
It's not the m. in my life that count   SEX, 44
M. and women are like right and left hands   RANKIN, J, 2
m. and women are wretched   EQUALITY, 17
M. are beasts   BARDOT, B, 6
M. are not often unreasonable   GILMAN, C, 3
M. know that women are an overmatch for them
      CHRON, 198
m. ought to be doing the work instead of the women
      CHRON, 534
m. represent…mind over morals   MEN AND WOMEN, 12
m. who…thank God He did not make them women
      CHRON, 639
O! m. with sisters dear   CHRON, 268; OPPRESSION, 2; WORK, 1
power over m.   CHRON, 204; WOLLSTONECRAFT, M, 4
proclaiming that women are brighter than m.
      LOOS, A, 5
so many m. are stupid and so few are blind   WEBB, B, 1
superior…as m. to women   SUPERIORITY, 1
the largest scope for change still lies in m.'s attitude
to women   BRITTAIN, V, 2
the only advantage women have over m. they can
cry   MEN AND WOMEN, 20
the sound of m. demanding their right to choose
      CHRON, 710
The War between M. and Women   MEN AND WOMEN, 24
Why are women…so much more interesting to m.
      MEN, 3
With strength beyond the strength of m.   STOWE, H, 2
Women…are either better or worse than m.
      MEN AND WOMEN, 4
Women had always fought for m.   PANKHURST, E, 4
Women have smaller brains than m.   INTELLIGENCE, 20
world the m. have it all their own way   SUFFRAGETTES, 2
menace m. just as threatening…as Hitlerism – Feminism   CHRON, 556
menopause women who are past the m. to have babies
      CHRON, 744
menstruating woman who is m. looks into the mirror
      MENSTRUATION, 3
menstruation commencement of m. is the borderline
      PUBERTY, 2
ever-recurring shallows of m.   CHRON, 377; PUBERTY, 3
have intercourse with her during her period of m.
      CHRON, 7
hygienic precautions relating to m. are scarcely ever
duly attended to   MENSTRUATION, 9
M. is not a disease   MENSTRUATION, 11
mental Christian Science explains all cause and effect
as m.   EDDY, M, 3
higher m. development of woman   INTELLECTUALS, 3
highest m. and moral qualities…in a man's curriculum   EDUCATION, 25; WOMANHOOD, 5

average man in the long run, the m. superior of the
average woman INTELLIGENCE, 9
m. and moral condition of prostitutes CHRON, 284
serious m. strain is now being imposed upon girls
CHRON, 431
That such m. powers must be hampered with such a
clumsy body STANTON, E, 5
mentality feminine m. manifests...primitive character
INTELLECT, 9
merciful just and m. as Nero ELIZABETH I, 3
mercy to know our self, and ask m. JULIAN OF NORWICH, 3
mere m. woman whose name you scarcely know
WRITERS, 6
merit no differences save by m. of character BESANT, A, 4
merited death you m., the Son of God had to die
APPEARANCE, 2
midwife best m. if she is trained in all branches of therapy OCCUPATIONS, 1
midwifery force women to take up *M.* CHRON, 338
midwives few sensible m. are to be found CHILDBIRTH, 4
M. to the perpetual honour of the female Sex
CHRON, 155
militancy Government criticize m. in women
SUFFRAGETTES, 19
militant neither am I as a m. Suffragist a criminal
CHRON, 429
militarism M....is one of the chief bulwarks of capitalism KELLER, H, 2
milk Gin was mother's m. DRINKING, 5
great desideratum the mother's m. CHRON, 322
mind A short neck denotes a good m. INTELLIGENCE, 16
A woman's m. and winter wind change oft
SAYINGS AND PROVERBS, 44
curvaceousness...incompatible with the life of the
m. INTELLIGENCE, 18
Debarred from all improvements of the m. CHRON, 174
exceed the grasp of my woman's m. CHRON, 75
female m. with equal powers and faculties EQUALITY, 6
first feeble struggles of a living m. SULLIVAN, A, 2
five worst maladies that afflict the female m.
CHRON, 179
human m. will wander to future times WILLARD, E, 3
levity of m. CHRON, 17
men represent...m. over morals MEN AND WOMEN, 12
m. is not sex-typed INTELLECT, 11
m. of an ass INTELLIGENCE, 2; SAYINGS AND PROVERBS, 43
Miss Cather...the new frontier she found it in the m.
CATHER, W, 2
The woman's m. is little MEN AND WOMEN, 23
To know the *m.* of a woman LOVE AND FRIENDSHIP, 5
Women represent...matter over m. MEN AND WOMEN, 12
minds forming of the m. of children CHRON, 245
marriage of true m. LOVE, 18
m. have no sex CHRON, 164
sex barriers...those that exist in their own m.
CHRON, 669
Some m. remain open KENNY, E, 3
Women want work both for the health of their m.
CHRON, 294
minister I have done more than any m. RELIGION, 5
to be a woman Foreign M. MEIR, G, 1
woman is incompetent to be a lawyer, m. or doctor
CHRON, 343
ministers I don't mind how much my m. talk
THATCHER, M, 9

ministry Women...care fifty times more for a marriage
than a m. CHRON, 312; MARRIAGE, 32
she left the M. for Overseas Development CASTLE, B, 1
Miracles M. are instantaneous PORTER, K, 2
mirror Look not in my eyes, for fear /They m. true the
sight I see LOVE, 49
When a man confronts catastrophe...a woman looks
in her m. MEN AND WOMEN, 18
woman who is menstruating looks into the m.
MENSTRUATION, 3
misbegotten woman is defective and m.
WOMAN'S NATURE, 4
miscarriage induce herbs or other means to cause m.
ABORTION, 2
mischief m. but a woman or a priest
SAYINGS AND PROVERBS, 29
Women...the mothers of all m. MOTHERHOOD, 2
mischievous what a m. devil Love is LOVE, 52
misery dwell on guilt and m. AUSTEN, J, 6
misfortune I try to do God's will...he visits me with m.
BORGIA, L, 5
m. it is to be born a woman CHRON, 216; SUBJECTION, 10
misrepresentation gross m. of the women's peace camp
CHRON, 703
Miss *M., n.* A title with which we brand unmarried
women LANGUAGE, 2; SINGLE WOMEN, 6
missionary the last of the great m. superstars
TERESA, MOTHER, 1
mistake extraordinary women...*male* spirits, confined
by m. in female frames ACHIEVEMENT, 3
franchise to women in this country would be a political m. CHRON, 461
Woman was God's *second* m. MISOGYNY, 8
mistakes Why don't you learn from my m. DELANEY, S, 4
mistress a m., and only then a friend
LOVE AND FRIENDSHIP, 4
lie down m., and get up master
DOMINATION, 6; FREEDOM, 2
She is every man's fantasy m. GARBO, G, 1
mistresses a better price than old m. PRACTICALITY, 4
Wives are young men's m. MARRIAGE, 11
mixture an extraordinary m. of idealism and lunacy
PANKHURST, E, 1
mockery m. to allow women to baptise RELIGION, 6
moderation foe of m. STRENGTH, 4
still for m. and will govern by it ANNE, 5
modern m. woman is the curse of the universe
WOMEN'S LIBERATION MOVEMENT, 14
You're a m. woman CHRON, 505
modest m. and chaste woman CHRON, 229
modesty a woman...ought to lay aside...m. with her
skirt MODESTY, 3
destroys that submissiveness and m. which is natural SUBJECTION, 1
endeavoured to keep all M., and a due Reverence to
Nature CHRON, 172
Enough for m. MODESTY, 6
I have borrowed to spare my m. PORTER, K, 1
lay aside...m....and put it on again with her petticoat MODESTY, 3
sexual systems of plants can accord with female m.
CHRON, 211
Mohammedan legal status of the M. woman CHRON, 359
molest They think I am a crazy woman and never m.
me CALAMITY JANE, 1
Mom blame M. too much MOTHERHOOD, 10

monarch Retirement, for a m., is not a good idea
VICTORIA, 1

monarchy *Helm* of this Imperial M. CHRON, 119

money Brigands demand your m. or your life
MISOGYNY, 6

Business...may bring m. AUSTEN, J, 5

except for large sums of m. HUMOUR, 3

Good Samaritan...had m. as well THATCHER, M, 7

If women didn't exist,...m....no meaning WEALTH, 7

I would have married for m. LONGWORTH, A, 3

men have their faces on the m. PRACTICALITY, 3

necessary for the wife to *ask* her husband for m.
CHRON, 329

Where large sums of m. are concerned...trust
nobody CHRISTIE, A, 4

monkeys Women in state affairs are like m. in glass-
shops POLITICS, 1; SAYINGS AND PROVERBS, 54

mons treating the *m. Veneris* as...Mount Everest SEX, 26

monster that m., an old woman OLD AGE, 8

monstrosity female professor of mathematics is...a m.
CHRON, 350

monstrous First Blast of the Trumpet...M. Regiment of
Women CHRON, 116; MISOGYNY, 4

monthly without making a m. illness out of a natural
function MENSTRUATION, 14

Women are also m. filled full of superfluous
humours MENSTRUATION, 8

moon becomes a m. without an earth MENOPAUSE, 3

moral Equal Rights Amendment...a m. issue POLITICS, 12

highest mental and m. qualities...in a man's curriculum EDUCATION, 25; WOMANHOOD, 5

look both m. and exciting APPEARANCE, 12

Love is m. even without...marriage KEY, E, 3

Men make the m. code CHRON, 453

mental and m. condition of prostitutes CHRON, 284

m. little booklet 'Make and Mend' CHRON, 559

no such thing as a m. dress CLOTHES, 8

passing one's whole life in m. idleness BLAVATSKY, E, 1

The m. disposition of the age SOMERVILLE, M, 3

morality m. is learned MORALITY, 8

morally made myself up m. COSMETICS, 4

morals code of m....which relieves men from responsibility for irregular sexual acts CHRON, 507

decline from the standard of m. CAULKINS, F, 2

men represent...mind over m. MEN AND WOMEN, 12

mother abortion the human rights of the m. ABORTION, 6

a friend can't take a m.'s place FRANK, A, 4

A m....ought to supply nature's food BREASTFEEDING, 3

And Her M. Came Too FAMILY, 9

an economic, political and symbolic system can feed
off the m. MOTHERHOOD, 19

As is the m., so is her daughter SAYINGS AND PROVERBS, 3

automated appliance...is the m. MOTHERHOOD, 13

Being a m. is a noble status MORALITY, 7

chose a virgin for His m. VIRGINITY, 2

earth as M. RELIGION, 15

Eve...the m. of all living CHRON, 5

fundamental human right of the m. to bear life
gladly or not at all CHRON, 465

gives his own name and that of his m. CHRON, 18

I was born...at an extremely tender age because my
m. needed a fourth at meals CHILDBIRTH, 16

m. as a social servant CHRON, 374

M. is far too clever to understand
DECEPTION, 3; INTELLIGENCE, 12

M. is the dead heart of the family
CHRON, 624; GREER, G, 3; MOTHERHOOD, 12

m. – make me less than woman MOTHERHOOD, 1

m.! What are we worth really? They all grow up
whether you look after them or not. MOTHERHOOD, 9

My m. said it was simple to keep a man
WOMAN'S ROLE, 36

natural vocation for every woman is that of wife and
m. EDUCATION, 26

perfect couple consisted of a m. and child
MOTHERHOOD, 22

she is thoroughly feminine...made for nothing but to
m. babies ELIOT, G, 2

the most intense love on the m.'s side MOTHERHOOD, 21

The m.-child relationship is paradoxical
MOTHERHOOD, 21

the m. of mankind STANTON, E, 7

The woman is uniformly sacrificed to the wife and
m. GAGE, M, 4

this war,...which did not justify the sacrifice of a single m.'s son PANKHURST, S, 2

unsatisfied m. who unduly stressed the desirability
of professional careers CHRON, 615

motherhood best thing that could happen to m.
MOTHERHOOD, 16

bound hand and foot by love and m. CHRON, 655

highest obligation to the State, viz., M. CHRON, 399

Marriage and m. should not be for sale CHRON, 447

m. is the most important of all the professions
MOTHERHOOD, 6

painful tasks of reproduction and m. SEX, 25

sacred responsibilities of m. INJUSTICE, 6

wifehood and m. STANTON, E, 12

Womanliness means only m. MOTHERHOOD, 4

mother-in-law What a marvellous place to drop one's
m. FAMILY, 8

mothers best m., wives...know little or nothing of sexual indulgences SEX, 10

errors in the habits of m. CHRON, 293

Housewives and m. seldom find it practicable to
come out on strike CHRON, 638

housewives as m....ensuring the adequate continuance of the British race CHRON, 555

important...preparing the daughters of the land to be
good m. CHRON, 240

make better wives and m. and citizens CHRON, 565

m. become producers FERTILITY, 4

m. should nurse their own children BREASTFEEDING, 2

M. who can share their children's interests...far better equipped CHRON, 537

O! men with m. and wives
CHRON, 268; OPPRESSION, 2; WORK, 1

series of crosses for us m. CHRON, 484

socially pernicious...consequences of the working of
m. CHRON, 448

sons were taken from their m. CHRON, 604

women become like their m. MEN AND WOMEN, 15

Women...the m. of all mischief MOTHERHOOD, 2

mothers-in-law Two m. FAMILY, 1

motto m. be:– Hunt BRONTË, C, 5

mounts The parent is he who m. CHRON, 16

mourning always go in m. and rags RELIGION, 2

in m....for the world SITWELL, E, 4

move But did thee feel the earth m. SEX, 27

movement the pioneers in the woman m. CATT, C, 1

nicest the very n. character   MURDOCH, I, 2
night Last n. I went to Manderley   DU MAURIER, D, 4
nightmare The n. dreamer is delivered up to the horror
    MANN, E, 1
nil eyes of the law her personal liberty and her status
are *n.*   CHRON, 351
Nile England may as well dam...the N. with bulrushes
    CHILD, L, 3
Nineteenth Amendment fight for the N.   POLITICS, 12
no Spell n. for me   CONTRARINESS, 6
girls...say N. when they mean Yes   CONTRARINESS, 5
she speaks eighteen languages. And she can't say
'N.' in any of them   PROMISCUITY, 3
Nobel wins the N. prize   INTELLECTUALS, 6
noblest being a housewife is the n. calling in the
world   PARTURIER, F, 4
being a housewife is the n. call in the world   CHRON, 614
nobody N. asked you, sir, she said   MARRIAGE, 19
non-achievers describe the women they treat as 'n.'
    FERTILITY, 3
Nonconformist a N. conscience   MORALITY, 1
Norma Jean Goodbye N.   EPITAPHS, 7
nose Cleopatra's n. been shorter
    APPEARANCE, 5; CLEOPATRA VII, 2
nothing married woman has n. of her own but her
wedding-ring   SAYINGS AND PROVERBS, 24
N. that costs only a dollar is worth having   ARDEN, E, 3
woman's road to gentility...doing n. at all   CHRON, 416
notices One never n. what has been done   CURIE, M, 7
nourished been n. by men   MEN AND WOMEN, 27
novelist A capable, bustling n. of the journalist school
    BUCK, P, 1
Be born anywhere, little embryo n.   WRITERS, 13
nunnery Get thee to a n.   WOMAN'S ROLE, 9
nuptial marriages shall be confirmed by a n. blessing
    CHRON, 73
nurse A devoted n....deserves...a place next to the
doctor   OCCUPATIONS, 6
definition of...a n....'devoted and obedient'   CHRON, 300
mothers should n. their own children   BREASTFEEDING, 2
Nature's gentle n.   KENNY, E, 2
No *man*...gives any other definition of...a
n....than...'devoted and obedient'
    NIGHTINGALE, F, 4; PREJUDICE, 1
Panic plays no part in the training of a n.   KENNY, E, 1
The doctor is not a n.   OCCUPATIONS, 8
The trained n....one of the great blessings of humanity   OCCUPATIONS, 10
nurses old men's n.   MARRIAGE, 11
N. all in confusion   CHRON, 288
nursing grief of mothers who are denied the privilege
of n. their infants   CHRON, 322
nurture true vocation, the n. of the coming race
    EDUCATION, 22

O

obedience 'Resistance to tyranny is o. to God.'
    ANTHONY, S, 6
unquestioning o. to laws she had no share in making
    CHRON, 364
obedient definition of...a nurse...'devoted and o.'
    CHRON, 300; NIGHTINGALE, F, 4
good women are the o.   CHRON, 67
obey distrust herself and to o. her husband   CHRON, 179
obeying him as a wife should o.   CHRON, 34

she the word o. has said   SUBJECTION, 7
woman must learn to o.   WOMAN'S ROLE, 29
Woman...was made to serve and o. man   CHRON, 118
obeying virtuous wife rules her husband by o. him
    CHRON, 41
object A necessary o., woman   CHRON, 90
liberated woman...renounce the desire of being a sex
o.   FEMINISM, 11
marriage had always been her o.   MARRIAGE, 22
training women to consider marriage as the sole o.
    EDUCATION, 18
obligation highest o. to the State, viz., Motherhood
    CHRON, 399
oblige women were supposed to o. the men
    OPPRESSION, 5
obscenely cosmetics names seemed o. obvious
    COSMETICS, 11
obscure humble work of an o. woman   CHRON, 75
humble work of an o. woman   HUMILITY, 1
obsession just one o. – sex   MISOGYNY, 3
obsolete divorce...Blame our o. sex roles   CHRON, 657
obstacle career woman...encounters a new o.: the hostility of men   CHRON, 612
husband...o. to the enjoyment of many things.
    DOMINATION, 3
sex of the former should no longer be an o.   CHRON, 243
occasion Mrs Gandhi never gives a performance less
than the o. demands   GANDHI, I, 3
you who so often o. a want of seats to other people
    SIDDONS, S, 2
occupation housecraft has not been generally regarded
as a skilled o.   CHRON, 503
occupations earn a decent living at other o.   CHRON, 451
emancipation and o. of women
    OCCUPATIONS, 7; SUBJECTION, 13
some o. have depressed wages because women are
the chief employees   CHRON, 647
ocean The o. is a place of paradoxes   CARSON, R, 5
odds against o., the women inch forward   FEMINISM, 6
odes rather /make o. than beds   WRITERS, 12
odious comparisons are o.   COMPLIMENTS, 1
Oedipus Fitted in neatly with the O. stuff   SEX, 51
office Cherish your husband's person...this being your
o.   WOMAN'S ROLE, 6
woman holding public o. were to marry   CHRON, 209
official goods & evils of the position of a woman...in o.
life   CHRON, 291
offspring abandon the care of their o.   CHRON, 244
old After I am waxed o.   OLD AGE, 1
Better be an o. man's darling   SAYINGS AND PROVERBS, 4
In days of o....The women ruled the men   CHRON, 497
man...as o. as the woman he feels   AGE, 8
one has to be very o. before one learns how to be
amused   BUCK, P, 5
such a paradise for o. women   AGE, 1
terrible thing for an o. woman to outlive her dogs
    OLD AGE, 9
that monster, an o. woman   OLD AGE, 8
witches are usually o. women of...small brains
    CHRON, 120
You're as o. as you feel   ARDEN, E, 4
older The o. one grows the more one likes indecency
    WOOLF, V, 7
old-fashioned O. ways...a snare in which the feet of
women   SOCIETY, 4
old maid dreadful name of o.   SINGLE WOMEN, 2

old maids disgrace to live o. SINGLE WOMEN, 1
one-half independence of o. the nation CHRON, 347
opening New avenues for higher culture…are o. before them CHRON, 339
opera I approach an o. as though I didn't know it CALDWELL, S, 1
The first rule in o. is the first rule in life MELBA, N, 6
opiate Gossip is the o. of the oppressed JONG, E, 4
opiates Marriage…the best of o. MARRIAGE, 51
opinion give him my o. MARRIAGE, 31
gives her o. she's a bitch DISCRIMINATION, 8
opportunity promoting equality of o. between men and women CHRON, 681
the full o. for women to become free FLYNN, E, 4
opposed o. to the use of women in uniform CHRON, 567
opposition I have spent many years…in o. ROOSEVELT, E, 4
o. to the women is always more intense WOMEN'S LIBERATION MOVEMENT, 1
o. to women pilots to start with CHRON, 563
oppressed Gossip is the opiate of the o. JONG, E, 4
O., degraded, enslaved OPPRESSION, 1
oppression intruding vandals bent only on the o. of womankind CHRON, 644
the o. they represented FLYNN, E, 3
oral a terrific story about o. contraception BIRTH CONTROL, 19
orator her gifts as a popular o. IBARRURI, D, 2
orderliness virtues of women are reserve, quiet, chastity, o. FEMININITY, 1
ordinariness Without her faith Mother Teresa would be remarkable only for her o. TERESA, MOTHER, 2
ordinary talent for describing the…characters of o. life AUSTEN, J, 2
organism human o. needs…good building material HEALTH AND HEALTHY LIVING, 7
organization o. and enlightenment of working women CHRON, 358
organize We're seeing women o. together WOMEN'S LIBERATION MOVEMENT, 12
orgasm development of a female o. SEX, 41
female o….a sort of pleasure-prize SEX, 33
inability of having an o. is simply the unconscious refusal to have one SEX, 38
modern woman discovered the o. CHRON, 636
stimulation to. centers upon the clitoris SEX, 50
The o. has replaced the Cross SEX, 43
ormolu One once said that I was like an o. clock MITFORD, N, 4
ornament only what is truly feminine is an o. to your sex MUSICIANS, 2
the stateliest o. of the public mind SIDDONS, S, 1
ostracized scandal of divorce had been socially o. MORALITY, 6
other he is the Absolute – she is the O. CHRON, 577
others tell the o. by their hunted expression DUTY, 3
ourselves be o. and free CHRON, 696
outrageous unrepentant creature, big with child is not such an o. sight CHRON, 490
out-ranks title human being…precedes and o. every other EQUALITY, 12
outwit Man forgives woman anything save the wit to o. him ANTRIM, M, 3
overcome 'Thou shalt not be o..' JULIAN OF NORWICH, 5
overdressed overshadowed by his o., extravagant and idle wife STOPES, M, 6
overload To o. a woman's brain CHRON, 349

overmatch Men know that women are an o. for them CHRON, 198
overrated matrimony, which I always thought a highly o. performance DUNCAN, I, 6
owned not o. our freedom long enough FREEDOM, 4
own-goal Aids pandemic is a classic o. AIDS, 3; ANNE, PRINCESS, 6

P

pa 'tis p. sings to you CHRON, 372
pacifist not so much of a p. that I would not fight for Peace STARK, F, 1
paid emancipation of woman can be brought about only by p. work CHRON, 533
men were p. more than the women CHRON, 568
She P. the Bills EPITAPHS, 5
pain came not in the world without our p. EQUALITY, 4
Love's a harbinger of p. LOVE, 55
P. – has an Element of Blank DICKINSON, E, 5
so anesthetized by your own p. JOHNSON, L, 3
the author of my p. CHILDBIRTH, 18
paint Spring hills p. themselves COSMETICS, 1
painted not as young as they're p. COSMETICS, 3
palace Love in a p. LOVE, 34
Palestine not enough prisons…in P. to hold all the Jews MEIR, G, 8
panic P. plays no part in the training of a nurse KENNY, E, 1
paper it is better for hard words to be on p. FRANK, A, 3
paradise England is the p. of women CHRON, 127
fair woman is a p. to the eye BEAUTY, 4
such a p. for old women AGE, 1
Wilderness is P. enow LOVE, 41
paradoxes The ocean is a place of p. CARSON, R, 5
paragraph she hardly knew how to write a full p. ADAMS, A, 1
parasites groan because we are p. CHRON, 573
p. – we women – because we produce nothing FEMINISM, 7
pardon God may p. you, but I never can ELIZABETH I, 5
Our servile Tongues are taught to cry for P. SUBJECTION, 8
parent The p. is he who mounts CHRON, 16
parents From birth to age eighteen, a girl needs good p. MATURITY, 2
joys of p. are secret CHILDREN, 2
P….bones on which children sharpen their teeth CHILDREN, 10
P. learn a lot from their children SPARK, M, 2
pariah Woman, the p. of humanity CHRON, 280; OPPRESSION, 3
parking lot Sunnybrook Farm is now a p. BLACK, S, 1
parlourmaid a p. as ignorant as Queen Victoria VICTORIA, 4
part till death us do p. MARRIAGE, 15
We only p. to meet again CONSTANCY, 2
partiality what p.!…one exalted and the other depressed EDUCATION, 15
participate p. in the public duties of government POLITICS, 5
parting P. is all we know of heaven DICKINSON, E, 4
partner Most woman…do not…support a married p. CHRON, 572
she is her husband's p. in danger CHRON, 53
partners p. in business and in thoughts EQUALITY, 8

P. concerns and interests diverge over time
PARTNERSHIP, 4
partnership expect of marriage that it shall be an equal
p. CHRON, 585
Marriage in modern times is regarded as a p.
CHRON, 735
married people should have the same kind of p. in
property CHRON, 50
P....real romance in marriage PARTNERSHIP, 2
party In our p., being a woman is no problem CHRON, 674
pass p. for forty-three AGE, 4
They shall not p. IBARRURI, D, 3
passé Sin...not only ugly but p. SIN, 3
passes Men seldom make p. APPEARANCE, 15
passion Assume an equality, plead your p. CHRON, 230
cold calculation than of p. in Anne's attitude
BOLEYN, A, 2
desolate and sick of an old p. LOVE, 48
Her friendships were flames of extravagant p. ending
in aversion ANNE, 2
pane of glass called p. between us CHRON, 588
'p. shooting' by husband of a wife LAW, 15
permitting the 'p. shooting' by a husband of a wife
CHRON, 627
time of puberty, must certainly feel the p. of physical love PUBERTY, 1
You complete each other, p. and romance aside
FONDA, J, 4
passionate p. woman, with disgust MEN AND WOMEN, 7
passive Woman... is p. CHRON, 20
past mentioning some woman whom he knew in the
p. JEALOUSY, 1
thanksgiving for the p....warnings for the future
CAULKINS, F, 1
The p. is still too close to us DU MAURIER, D, 5
woman can shed her p. CHRON, 390
paternal males in the p. line shall succeed LAW, 2
patient your intention is not to help me as a p.
CHRON, 450
patients women p. had to have their hair done in a certain way OCCUPATIONS, 11
patriarchal p. society...make children of women
CHRON, 623
p. system is the ideal for which he longs CHRON, 434
patriotism p. is not enough CAVELL, E, 4
p. of woman; not to thunder in senates CHRON, 309
p. which consists in hating all other nations
GASKELL, E, 5
p. which has nerved women to endure torture in
prison CHRON, 454
Pavlova P. contemplates her swans COMMITMENT, 2
pay Equal p. for equal work CHRON, 647
What does he think they p. me for EVANS, E, 4
peace Courage is the price...for granting p. EARHART, A, 1
cruel to bother people who want to be left in p.
GARBO, G, 3
greatest destroyer of p. is abortion ABORTION, 13
gross misrepresentation of the women's p. camp
CHRON, 703
in time of p. we must prepare for war BARTON, C, 1
not so much of a pacifist that I would not fight for P.
STARK, F, 1
p. and leisure of the days in *purdah* CHRON, 600
using woman power on behalf of a key woman's
objective – p. PEACE, 2

peasants inflamed the imagination even of women
and p. CHRON, 292
peculiar the p. situation of the human male BEAUVOIR, S, 2
peculiarities the mild p. of their sex MENOPAUSE, 1
pedestal at fourteen every boy should be in love with
some ideal woman...on a p. LOVE, 65
pen woman that attempts the p. WRITERS, 3
penis Freud...substituted the p. for the head
SUPERIORITY, 11
very few jobs...require a p. or vagina CHRON, 661
penitence making babies I think is a huge p. CHRON, 81
pennies P. do not come from heaven THATCHER, M, 8
people stopped short of treating women as p. CHRON, 589
two p. with one pulse LOVE, 62
women are p., too CHRON, 737
perfect female is less p. than the male CHRON, 55
performance Mrs Gandhi never gives a p. less than the
occasion demands GANDHI, I, 3
not know her lines and give the p. she did
MONROE, M, 3
performed p. worst when I...wished to do better
SIDDONS, S, 3
perfume sad woman who buys her own p. COSMETICS, 8
peripheral feminist struggle being a p. kind of thing
FEMINISM, 13
permanence do nothing that has p. FAILINGS, 1
pernicious socially p....consequences of the working of
mothers CHRON, 448
persecution P. for opinion DISCRIMINATION, 4
personality Her magnetic stage p. CALLAS, M, 2
pert Miss Lucy Aikin...p. as a pear-monger AIKIN, L, 2
pessimism P. is a luxury that a Jew never can allow
himself MEIR, G, 7
petition p. for a husband's adultery DIVORCE, 7
petticoat lay aside...modesty...and put it on again
with her p. MODESTY, 3
phallocracy never...a democracy...a p. PARTURIER, F, 3
phenomenon Hysteria is a natural p. EMOTION, 5
the p. that will not go away RODDICK, A, 1
philosopher she should be brought up like a p., even
like a cynic SHELLEY, M, 2
philosophy I have a simple p. LONGWORTH, A, 1
photograph A p. is not only an image SONTAG, S, 4
photography P. can never grow up if it imitates
ABBOTT, B, 1
physical women possess but one class of p. organs
HEALTH AND HEALTHY LIVING, 3
physically Girls are p. and mentally more precocious
EQUALITY, 10
physicians As teachers...the first work for women p.
BLACKWELL, E, 3
physiological The p. differences...create intense emotional problems FLYNN, E, 1
physiology P. has specified the nature of the maternal
role CHRON, 705
Picardy Roses are flowering in P. COMPLIMENTS, 5
pickle as if he had been weaned on a p. LONGWORTH, A, 2
pie to call a girl off from making a p. GRIMKÉ, S, 3
pill contraceptive p. may reduce the importance of
sex BIRTH CONTROL, 14
of course the p. CHRON, 618
last-minute invention of The P.
CHRON, 671; BIRTH CONTROL, 18
Protestant women may take the P. BIRTH CONTROL, 15
pilots opposition to women p. to start with CHRON, 563

prefer to have women in the home and not as airline
p.   CHRON, 631
pins find out witches by pricking them with p.
     CHRON, 145
  had p. thrust into their bodies   WITCHES, 5
pint one cannot put a quart in a p. cup   GILMAN, C, 1
pints did not consider it ladylike for women to drink
p.   DRINKING, 10
pinup p., the centerfold, the poster   PORNOGRAPHY, 2
pioneer a p. in an industry   ARDEN, E, 1
pioneers the p. in the woman movement   CATT, C, 1
piping Helpless, naked, p. loud   CHILDBIRTH, 5
pith all the p. is in the postscript   ATTITUDES, 17
pity a sense of empathy and p.   RODDICK, A, 5
  the magnanimous p. of a heroine   JOAN OF ARC, 3
  To marry a man out of p. is folly   ASQUITH, M, 5
place all right in our p.   AMBITION, 4
  don't think a woman's p. is in industry   CHRON, 534
  keep their p. as law directs   CHRON, 59
  love a p. the less for having suffered in it   AUSTEN, J, 7
  time that the women took their p. in Imperial politics   CHRON, 423
  woman's p. is in the home   WOMAN'S ROLE, 35
plain Manners are...the need of the p.   APPEARANCE, 13
plaisir *P. d'amour*   LOVE, 29
plan If women cannot p. their pregnancies, they can
p. little else   CHRON, 648
  To housekeep, one had to p. ahead   HOUSEKEEPING, 5
plants sexual systems of p. can accord with female
modesty   CHRON, 211
platform woman stands on an even p. with man
     GAGE, M, 1
Plato explained publicly the writings of P.   HYPATIA, 1
play woman can't p. as a man plays   DU PRÉ, J, 3
please he that is married careth...how he may p. his
wife   MARRIAGE, 6
  submits to her husband, but only to p. him   CHRON, 305
pleasure A fool bolts p., then complains of...indiges-
tion   ANTRIM, M, 1
  greatest p. from the vagina...used much more effectively to give p. to a male   SEX, 35
  I approach the end of my life with p.   BORGIA, L, 3
  Love ceases to be a p.   BEHN, A, 6; LOVE, 23
  Once intercourse has begun, she experiences p.
throughout   SEX, 1
  that p., which is undeniably the sole motive force
behind the union of the sexes   LUST, 3
  that p., which is undeniably the sole motive force
behind the union of the sexes   SEX, 6
  The roses of p. seldom last long   MORE, H, 4
  venereal p. is almost entirely on the side of the male
     CHRON, 306
pleasure-loving p. girl...the centre of the Vatican circle
     BORGIA, L, 1
pleasure-prize female orgasm...a sort of p.   SEX, 33
pleasures justify withdrawal from the usual duties and
p. of life   MENSTRUATION, 14
pluck weak women, without p. and grit   CHRON, 366
plumes no p. waved upon their heads   CONSERVATION, 3
plundering persist in your wicked resolution of p.
  those women of their lives and fortunes   CHRON, 39
pocket smile I could feel in my hip p.   LUST, 7
poems My p. are hymns of praise   SITWELL, E, 3
  that Anon, who wrote so many p.
     WOOLF, V, 8; WRITERS, 11

poet A fascinating combination of scientist and
would-be p.   STOPES, M, 1
  masculine part, the p. in me   CHRON, 166
  privilege for...the p. in me   WRITERS, 2
poetry debar'd from sense, and sacred p.   INJUSTICE, 2
poison Anger repressed can p. a relationship   ANGER, 6
  Boadicea put an end to her life by p.   BOADICEA, 1
  Menstruating women carry with them a p.
     MENSTRUATION, 7
  remorse is the p. of life   GUILT, 1
poisoned I could have p. you   CLEOPATRA VII, 6
poisonous Isn't she a p. thing of a woman   SITWELL, E, 2
  the addition of p. substances   DRINKING, 3
policeman This definition...would not do for a p.
     CHRON, 300
  This definition...would not do for a p.   NIGHTINGALE, F, 4
political a lady and yet be thoroughly p.   CHRON, 582
  clamour for p. rights...sexual enmity   CHRON, 360
  emergence of woman as a p. force   CHRON, 649
  Every woman in England is longing for her p. freedom   CHRON, 394
  founded a Women's Social and P. Union   CHRON, 396
  franchise to women in this country would be a p.
mistake   CHRON, 461
  Lesbianism...a p. stance   CHRON, 634
  P. equality is Dead Sea fruit   CHRON, 530
  woman in Iran is a p. crime   CHRON, 707; RELIGION, 18
  women freed of their p. shackles
     CHRON, 411; SUFFRAGETTES, 7
  women...p. slaves   CHRON, 347
politician She was the ablest Labour p. of her generation   CASTLE, B, 3
  the first p....a sort of prophet   STANHOPE, H, 5
politicks Women...meddle with P.   CHRON, 152
politics American p. are too dirty for women   POLITICS, 6
  field of p. should be left to men   CHRON, 263
  function of homemaker,...extend into p.   POLITICS, 8
  In p....ask a woman   CHRON, 699; POLITICS, 14
  in p. there is no heart, only head   POLITICS, 4
  not believe in sex distinction in literature, law, p., or
trade   CHRON, 466
  p. are too dirty for women   CHRON, 520
  time that the women took their place in Imperial p.
     CHRON, 423
  women get too tired and dull to bother with p.
     CHRON, 509
pompous A p. woman...complaining that the head-
waiter   SITWELL, E, 5
poor Charity separates the rich from the p.   PERÓN, E, 5
  in the world there were p. people and rich people
     PERÓN, E, 3
  p. beauty finds more lovers than husbands
     SAYINGS AND PROVERBS, 31; WEALTH, 1
  P., – yet blest with liberty   AIKIN, L, 4
  The p. are our brothers and sisters   TERESA, MOTHER, 3
poorer for richer for p.   MARRIAGE, 15
popped all of a sudden out p. a baby   CHRON, 544
pornography stay within the world of p....only fantasies   PORNOGRAPHY, 1
  what p. says about women   PORNOGRAPHY, 3
portrayal the p. of her as a ruthless natural autocrat
     GANDHI, I, 2
position goods & evils of the p. of a woman...in official
life   CHRON, 291
possessed land, like women, was meant to be p.
     CHRON, 658

prevent better reasons for having children than not knowing how to p. them BIRTH CONTROL, 9
p. the cultivation of the female understanding CHRON, 203
severe laws of men no longer p. women from...the sciences CHRON, 112
price a better p. than old mistresses PRACTICALITY, 4
boy commands the better p. CHRON, 523
Civilized woman...paying too high a p. DRABBLE, M, 4
Courage is the p....for granting peace EARHART, A, 1
her p. is far above rubies VIRTUE, 2
pricking find out witches by p. them with pins CHRON, 145
pride More p., you women CHRON, 383
p. is a word often on women's lips – but they display little sign of it where love affairs are concerned. PRIDE, 2
their p., their tradition, their history STEAD, C, 3
the p. of race BESANT, A, 3
priest For a p. to turn a man when he lies a-dying DECEPTION, 2; SEX, 5
mischief but a woman or a p. SAYINGS AND PROVERBS, 29
priestcraft p. that has subjected woman RELIGION, 11
priests trouble in the Church of England over women p. RELIGION, 21
prig crackling with intelligence, but nothing at all of a p. MURDOCH, I, 1
prime One's p. is elusive SPARK, M, 5
Prime Minister It will be years...before a woman will...become P. CHRON, 667
society...pays a harlot 25 times as much as it pays its P. PROSTITUTION, 10
woman P....the best man in the cabinet CHRON, 730
primitive feminine mentality manifests...p. character INTELLECT, 9
Princess Anne P....receptive to chat about tanks ANNE, PRINCESS, 1
principle p. of women working with equal status CHRON, 514
prison ascertain...possible to keep me alive in p. CHRON, 450
enduring a long period of privation and solitary confinement in p. CHRON, 437
Home is the girl's p. FAMILY, 6
Known as the 'Angel of the p.' FRY, E, 1
Over one thousand women have gone to p. CHRON, 443
patriotism which has nerved women to endure torture in p. CHRON, 454
p. cell was quiet SUFFRAGETTES, 24
women have gone to p. in the course of this agitation SUFFRAGETTES, 20
women in p. refuse to let brute force rule the world CHRON, 449
prison-cell women's symbolic militancy punished with a p. CHRON, 453
prisoner given her a p.'s proficiency in handling these virtues CHRON, 485
prisoners school in Newgate for the children of the poor p. CHRON, 220
prisons not enough p....in Palestine to hold all the Jews MEIR, G, 8
privacy right to p. and reproductive control CHRON, 659
That should assure us of...forty-five minutes of undisturbed p. PARKER, D, 7
private right of p. contract...dear to a liberty-loving people CHRON, 354

sex has been a very p., secretive activity SEX, 40
privilege duty and p. to fill in the scale of society CHRON, 232
grief of mothers who are denied the p. of nursing their infants CHRON, 322
p. for...the poet in me WRITERS, 2
privileged only p. persons in our country are the children PERÓN, E, 4
Sundays being p. from the needle CHRON, 181
privileges all the p. of being male SUPERIORITY, 12
prizes Girls study for p. and not for learning CHRON, 331
problem biggest p. all my life was men SUCCESS, 7
In our party, being a woman is no p. CHRON, 674
powerlessness is still each woman's most critical p. POWER, 9
whole p. of women's role in society CHRON, 583
problems sincere attempts to help a woman solve her p. MEN, 9
procreation Abortion leads to...trivialization of the act of p. ABORTION, 8
p. and childcare are considered as one and the same thing CHRON, 626
produce parasites – we women – because we p. nothing FEMINISM, 7
producers mothers become p. FERTILITY, 4
production depended on women to get p. up WORK, 4
profession forbidden to practise their p. by day PROSTITUTION, 4
Married life is a woman's p. CHRON, 301
not proper for women to be of this p. CHRON, 155
process of home-making...an art and a p. CHRON, 297
professional unsatisfied mother who unduly stressed the desirability of p. careers CHRON, 615
professions motherhood is the most important of all the p. MOTHERHOOD, 6
professor went to men's lectures, unless the p. objected CHRON, 402
professors Culture is an instrument wielded by p. WEIL, S, 1
profitable A Work generally approved...and made most p. and necessary for all men CHRON, 165
profound p. experience of the birth of the child CHILDBIRTH, 20
progressed education for women has p. CHRON, 370
prohibit p. the use of proper hygienic Birth Control methods BIRTH CONTROL, 5; RELIGION, 12
prohibition mother Eve, who flouted the first p. FREEDOM, 1
prolonged life may not be p. beyond the power of usefulness AIKIN, L, 5
prominence social imbalance and corruption...because of the p. of women SUBJECTION, 16
promiscuous p. assemblage of the sexes in the same class is a dangerous innovation CHRON, 304
promise rarely...one can see in a little boy the p. of a man MEN AND WOMEN, 14
pronounce disgraceful but common to see women...unable to p. what they read EDUCATION, 10
proof p. of virginity in her CHRON, 8
without the wickedness of women...world would remain p. against innumerable dangers CHRON, 105
propagation Women exist...solely for the p. of the species WOMAN'S ROLE, 14
proper not p. for women to be of this profession CHRON, 155
properties ten p. of a woman FEMININITY, 2

property as married women, control and administer their own p. CHRON, 370

iniquitous law...over the person and p. of another CHRON, 237

law holds...p. is of greater value than life FRY, E, 3

marriage...the arrangements of p. CHRON, 254

married people should have the same kind of partnership in p. CHRON, 50

office...his by marriage, like the rest of his wife's p. CHRON, 209

p. earned during marriage belongs wholly to the husband CHRON, 369

women are not allowed to own p. OPPRESSION, 8

prophet the first politician...a sort of p. STANHOPE, H, 5

propogation meerly intended for the Worlds p. CHRON, 162

proportion larger p. of women remain unmarried CHRON, 299

propriety old-fashioned notions of delicacy or p. CHILDBIRTH, 6

prose Her p. is like a bird SPARK, M, 1

prosperity ready to do for the happiness or p. of England ANNE, 4

received true p. from the golden Muses CHRON, 13

prostitute ask a p. why does it PROSTITUTION, 12

feminist whenever I express sentiments that differentiate me from a doormat or a p. CHRON, 592

I don't think a p. is more moral MARRIAGE, 74

prostitutes comparison to be made between p. and the men CHRON, 323

girls to become temple p. RELIGION, 23

mental and moral condition of p. CHRON, 284

prostitution Necessity never makes p. the business of men's lives EDUCATION, 17; PROSTITUTION, 1

P. is a blight on the human race PROSTITUTION, 3; VIRTUE, 6

P....keeps her out of trouble PROSTITUTION, 8

P....provides fresh air and wholesome exercise PROSTITUTION, 8

social inferiority...responsible for p. PROSTITUTION, 5

undesired sex...greater in marriage than in p. CHRON, 522

protect Every man I meet wants to p. me CHIVALRY, 6

protected our sex is p. by greater sobriety DRINKING, 2

protection life deserves the p. of society ABORTION, 12

protégé hesitant about encouraging a woman as a p. CHRON, 712

Protestant I am the P. whore GWYNN, N, 3

P. women may take the Pill BIRTH CONTROL, 15

proud If women be p....men that make them so PRIDE, 1

proudest the moment of greatest humiliation is...when the spirit is p. CHRON, 409; PANKHURST, C, 3

proved British women have p. themselves in this war CHRON, 557

provision her incapacity to make honorable p. for herself ADULTERY, 7

prude twenty is no age to be a p. MODESTY, 4

prudery He will not call it purity, he will call it p. CHRON, 528

psychic These diseases...they're purely p. JHABVALA, R, 1

psychological unmarried woman...stronger p. reserves SINGLE WOMEN, 13

puberty period of p. is a most trying time PUBERTY, 2

time of p., must certainly feel the passion of physical love PUBERTY, 1

public career is born in p. TALENT AND GENIUS, 2

participate in the p. duties of government POLITICS, 5

the stateliest ornament of the p. mind SIDDONS, S, 1

twenty years of marriage make her...like a p. building MARRIAGE, 37

publication female conversation to the last new p. CHRON, 224

publicist as clever a crooked literary p. as ever SITWELL, E, 2

publicly explained p. the writings of Plato HYPATIA, 1

published writers whose extravagant doctrines have...been p. WOLLSTONECRAFT, M, 2

Pucelle a disciple...of the fiend, called the P. JOAN OF ARC, 1

pulse two people with one p. LOVE, 62

punishment capital p. tend to the security of the people FRY, E, 3

no glorious renown in a woman's p. CHRON, 42

No p....prevent the commission of crimes ARENDT, H, 4

P. is not for revenge FRY, E, 4

puppy Frogs and snails /And p.-dogs' tails MEN AND WOMEN, 8

purdah peace and leisure of the days in *p.* CHRON, 600

pure insist that a young girl should be p., chaste and innocent HYPOCRISY, 2

purgatory the p. of men CHRON, 127

purify dearest task it is to soften, to bless, and to p. our imperfect nature CHRON, 262

purity He will not call it p., he will call it prudery CHRON, 528

p. of the virgin be maintained CHASTITY, 6

purposes State which regards the p. of life solely from the male standpoint CHRON, 476

Q

qualified Every young woman...should be q. by some accomplishment OCCUPATIONS, 5

qualities q....necessary for success upon the stage TERRY, E, 4

Q. in which women predominate CHRON, 550

quarrel utter unpredictability of a q. ANGER, 5

quarrels q. which vivify its barrenness GREER, G, 4

quart one cannot put a q. in a pint cup GILMAN, C, 1

queen I am your anointed Q. CHRON, 124; ELIZABETH I, 8

isn't a bad bit of goods, the Q. COMPLIMENTS, 2

made all at once into a Q. VICTORIA, 2

q. did fish for men's souls ELIZABETH I, 1

serenely throned as q. among her American sisters HOWE, J, 1

sorrier for my good knights' loss than for...my fair q. FRIENDSHIP, 2

your q. and companion, far beyond my desert or desire BOLEYN, A, 3

Queen Anne Move Q.? Most certainly not VICTORIA, 8

queens for q. I might have enough FRIENDSHIP, 2

q....compare favorably with the kings GAGE, M, 3

queer Girls are so q. CONTRARINESS, 5

question this whole q. of sexual intercourse LUST, 5

questions Women decide the larger q. of life INTELLIGENCE, 13

quiescent woman may determine not to remain q. CHRON, 361

quiet cannot expect the Suffragettes to give you a q. life CHRON, 436

R

race the pride of r.   BESANT, A, 3

racism Justice...blind to r., sexism, war and poverty
           PREJUDICE, 5

racist expressing in sexist terms...in r. terms...would
deny   CHRON, 660

radiance maiden...have come forth...in this r. of
learned men   HUMILITY, 4

rags always go in mourning and r.   RELIGION, 2

raise Now he will r. me to be a martyr   BOLEYN, A, 4

rake every woman is at heart a r.   ATTITUDES, 10

random conduct affairs...in accordance with r. opinions   CHRON, 223; INTELLECT, 3

rape guilty of incestuous adultery,...or of r.   DIVORCE, 6
R. is a form of mass terrorism   RAPE, 3
r. is a perfectly natural function   RAPE, 4
r. is one of the least-reported crimes   RAPE, 2
regale her mind with scenes of r., orgy, adultery and
prostitution   HYPOCRISY, 2

rapist r. remains a r....irrespective of his relationship
with his victim   CHRON, 734
simple word 'man', which the r. invariably is
         CHRON, 714; RAPE, 6

rapists All men are r.   MEN, 8

rapport conversation is primarily a language of r.
         LANGUAGE, 9

rare r., man who is as steadily intelligent,...as the
average woman   INTELLIGENCE, 13

rats I see some r. have got in   CHRON, 407

raze they r. the skin and rend the flesh of her body
         HYPATIA, 3

razors R. pain you   PARKER, D, 3

read not suitable for a female to know how to r.
         EDUCATION, 4
you may sit by my fire and r.   GILMAN, C, 4

reader R., I married him   BRONTË, C, 7

reading two full years r. at the said public school
         CHRON, 167

readings various r. of the Bible   RELIGION, 9

real household labor...not usually considered as 'r.
work'   CHRON, 617

realism ahead of their leaders in r. and courage
         SMITH, M, 1

reality r. contains unparalleled beauties   ABBOTT, B, 3
She simply inhabits r.   ADDAMS, J, 1

rear farmer's mare has a foal she is turned out to r. it
in idleness   CHILDBIRTH, 15

rearing most successful mode of r. girls   CHRON, 355

reason government by men only is not an appeal to r.
         CHRON, 458
such as say our Sex is void of R.   CHRON, 144
things by r. of my sexe, I may not doe   CHRON, 126
woman's instinct than a man's r.   CHRON, 512
woman's r.   ATTITUDES, 4

rebel witch is a r. in physics   WITCHES, 4

rebellious gave the vote to the older women who were
deemed less r.   CHRON, 499

reconcile How r. this world...with...my imagining
         KELLER, H, 4

recreation woman accepted cooking...but man...made
of it a r.   CHRON, 492; WOMAN'S ROLE, 26
woman for the r. of the warrior   WOMAN'S ROLE, 22

red She wore false hair and that r.   ELIZABETH I, 2

redemption married past r.   MARRIAGE, 16

reflection a r. of the British Museum Reading Room
         INTELLIGENCE, 17; SPARK, M, 6

reform An institution or r. movement that is not selfish   BARTON, C, 2

refreshing her source material...sometimes r., sometimes bizarre   CHRISTINE DE PISAN, 2

refusal inability of having an orgasm is simply the
unconscious r. to have one   SEX, 38

regiment the Monstrous R. of Women   CHRON, 116

regratery trade of r. belongeth by right the rather to
women   CHRON, 95

regret with them I can r. nothing   MARIE ANTOINETTE, 3

regularity R. and Decorum....Women-Authors...greatly
deficient in   WRITERS, 5

reign adorn the husband's r.   CHRON, 176

reigned I have r. with your loves   CHRON, 130; ELIZABETH I, 4
r. a virgin and died a virgin   ELIZABETH I, 9

reject Learn to r. friendship   FRIENDSHIP, 4

rejoice new sights of Nature made me r.   CURIE, M, 5

relations a certain stupidity in her personal r.   ANNE, 3

relationship Age changes our r. with time   CHRON, 635
rapist remains a rapist...irrespective of his r. with
his victim   CHRON, 734

relationships new social r. of the men and women
around the machine   CHRON, 628

relative education of women should be r. to man
         EDUCATION, 13

relief Mrs Browning's death is rather a r. to me
         BROWNING, E, 1

religion I have nothing to communicate on the subject
of r.   WOLLSTONECRAFT, M, 5
preparing herself not for r. but for fornication
         CHRON, 79
R. is love   WEBB, B, 4
women to have been the founders of r.   CHRON, 46

religious denounce the idiocy of r. scriptures
         LESBIANISM, 6

remarkable Without her faith Mother Teresa would be
r. only for her ordinariness   TERESA, MOTHER, 2

remember she did not r....her jewelry
     LOOS, A, 4; PRACTICALITY, 2

remorse r. for what you have thought about your wife
         MARRIAGE, 49
r. is the poison of life   GUILT, 1

remote the impression of something as unique and r.
as Undine   DICKINSON, E, 1

removal life today is dedicated to the r. of risk
         BLACK, S, 3

remove he *will* r. your genitals   CHRON, 668

remunerative nearly every r. employment is engrossed
by men only   CHRON, 295

rend they raze the skin and r. the flesh of her body
         HYPATIA, 3

render husband r. unto the wife due benevolence
         MARRIAGE, 4

repartee dazzling appearance, erudition and fondness
for sharp r.   GREER, G, 1

repel not right to r. minds which are virtuous and
brave   CHRON, 122

repent depressing to admit guilt and to r.   GUILT, 3

representation Laws in which we have no voice, or R.
         CHRON, 193

representatives women ought to have r.   CHRON, 205

represented interests of women will be r. as well
         CHRON, 337

repression utterly false r. of the woman's   SEX, 17

reproaching men refrain from r. women   CHRON, 98
reproduce Nature itself that drives us to r. the species
                                         MOTHERHOOD, 18
prime function in life is to r.
                          EMOTION, 4; WOMAN'S ROLE, 34
reproduction painful tasks of r. and motherhood   SEX, 25
reproductive r. capacity is diminished in various
degrees   EDUCATION, 24
right to privacy and r. control   CHRON, 659
reproof how steadily do they who are guilty shrink
from r.   BLOOMER, A, 4
republic An aristocracy in a r. is like a chicken whose
head has been cut off   MITFORD, N, 3
way in which women are governed in this R.
                                             CHRON, 246
repugnant Woman to bear rule...is r. to Nature
                                             CHRON, 117
reputation against a woman who wants to rise to a
man's r.   CHRON, 214
it wrecks a woman's r.   COLETTE, 6
my r. as a rider and quick shot was well known
                                        CALAMITY JANE, 2
reserve virtues of women are r., quiet, chastity, orderliness   FEMININITY, 1
resistance 'R. to tyranny is obedience to God.'
                                           ANTHONY, S, 6
resolve This is a woman's r.   BOADICEA, 3
resources draining the earth of its priceless and
irreplaceable r.   CONSERVATION, 5
not getting a husband,...may find...without r.
                                             CHRON, 301
respeckt stopped demanding so much r. for ourselves
                                             HUMILITY, 7
respect an attitude of equal r. for all men   ADDAMS, J, 6
Woman...has everywhere greater r. for life than man
                                              PEACE, 1
respectable Dr Marie Stopes made contraceptive
devices r.   STOPES, M, 3
single woman of fortune is always r.   SINGLE WOMEN, 3
respected a happy woman and universally r.
                                       WOLLSTONECRAFT, M, 1
responsibility code of morals...which relieves men
from r. for irregular sexual acts   CHRON, 507
ennobling influence of national r.   CHRON, 376
love r. and I don't mind unpopularity   CASTLE, B, 6
No sex without r.   SEX, 30
power without r.   PROSTITUTION, 7
prime r. of a woman   DUTY, 4
responsible No man is r. for his father   FAMILY, 7
woman...held r. for pregnancy   PREGNANCY, 7
rest get rid of the r. of her   LOVE, 24
safer to r. and not to bathe   MENSTRUATION, 5
restless I confess my ambition is r.   AMBITION, 2
restraint Thro' check'd Desires, Threatnings, and R.
                                           SUBJECTION, 8
restructure R. your life   FONDA, J, 3
retarded r. children are satisfying   SILLS, B, 1
retirement R., for a monarch, is not a good idea
                                            VICTORIA, 1
Revelations It ends with R.   LIFE, 1
revenge no one delights in r. more than a woman
                                        WOMAN'S NATURE, 3
Punishment is not for r.   FRY, E, 4
revenged let us be r. by proving them to be liars
                                      CATHERINE THE GREAT, 5

reverence endeavoured to keep all Modesty, and a due
R. to Nature   CHRON, 172
revolution r. of womanhood...remove the old stigma of
the story of Adam and Eve   SUFFRAGETTES, 15
The word 'r.' is a word for which you kill   WEIL, S, 2
revolutionary I am a r.   FONDA, J, 5
revolutions Wars and r....have outlived all their ideological justifications   ARENDT, H, 5
rewarded truth r. me   TRUTH, 2
rib the r....made he a woman   CHRON, 1
ribbon tape, r.,...heretofore was made by poore aged
woemen   CHRON, 137
rich as easy to marry a r. woman as a poor woman
                                           MARRIAGE, 28
Charity separates the r. from the poor   PERÓN, E, 5
divorce is obtainable only by the very r.   DIVORCE, 4
Go where the r. are   WEALTH, 5
in the world there were poor people and r. people
                                            PERÓN, E, 3
r. and one's a woman   WEALTH, 6
R. men's houses are seldom beautiful   ASQUITH, M, 6
richer for r. for poorer   MARRIAGE, 15
Richmond On R. Hill there lives a lass   CHARM, 2
rien Je ne regrette r.   PIAF, E, 2
rifled this r. and bleeding womb   ABORTION, 5
rift the...r. between the sexes is...widened by...teach-
ing...to the girls   DISCRIMINATION, 5
right all r. in our place   AMBITION, 4
fundamental human r. of the mother to bear life
gladly or not at all   CHRON, 465
has woman a r. to herself   CHRON, 289
learned how to ask for their support in the r. way
                                            FEMINISM, 18
man has both the r. and duty to chastise his
girlfriend or wife   VIOLENCE, 6
never contemplated...r. of voting...for married
women   CHRON, 264
r. and authority of the husband   CHRON, 31
r. to determine which American women can have
abortions   ABORTION, 14
The *divine* r. of husbands   WOLLSTONECRAFT, M, 3
time is r. for action   CHRON, 747
Women would rather be r. than reasonable
                                         CONTRARINESS, 7
rights battle for women's r.   EQUALITY, 21
claim our r. as women   SUFFRAGETTES, 16
equal r., nothing more but nothing less   EQUALITY, 18
extension of women's r.   CHRON, 218
have no r. to bring criminal accusations for adultery
                                            ADULTERY, 3
I do not ask for my r.   CHRON, 285
movement for women's r. has broken many old fetters   CHRON, 418
Poor woman has her r. as well as you   CHRON, 215
These are 'Women's R.'   WOMAN'S ROLE, 23
We are here to claim our r. as women   PANKHURST, C, 4
We want r.   CHRON, 290
women should assert their r. as human beings
                                            CHRON, 367
WOMEN'S R. NOW   WOMEN'S LIBERATION MOVEMENT, 3
women their r. and nothing less
                             ANTHONY, S, 5; EQUALITY, 9
Women...were ready to fight for their own human r.
                                            CHRON, 412
women who want women's r.   FEMINISM, 3
Women will have...the fullest r.   CHRON, 513

rigidified feminist rhetoric, r. in reaction   FEMINISM, 15
rise against a woman who wants to r.
    CHRON, 214; DISCRIMINATION, 3
apprehension the steady r. in the number of female
  factory employees   CHRON, 399
injured Woman! r.   CHRON, 228
risk life today is dedicated to the *removal of r.*
    BLACK, S, 3
rival conclusive testimony that woman was never
  intended to r. man   WOMAN'S NATURE, 7
robbery stupendous system of organized r.   CHRON, 365
rock-a-bye R., baby, for father is near   CHRON, 372
rocked hands have r. the cradle
    WOMEN'S LIBERATION MOVEMENT, 6
rocks The hand that r. the cradle   POWER, 6
rod after wriggling fish /With his big bamboo r.
    ADULTERY, 1
role adult r. of woman   WOMAN'S ROLE, 33
glorification of the 'woman's r.'   CHRON, 598
whole problem of women's r. in society   CHRON, 583
woman's r. in the home new status   CHRON, 650
role-playing Acting is r.   ACTING, 2
roles strong tendency to shunt us into the more traditional female r.   OCCUPATIONS, 15
romance Partnership...real r. in marriage   PARTNERSHIP, 2
R. without finance is a nuisance   PROSTITUTION, 9
Twenty years of r. make a woman look like a ruin
    MARRIAGE, 37
You complete each other, passion and r. aside
    FONDA, J, 4
root daughters are but branches which by marriage
  are broken off from the r.   CHRON, 151
Music...never the r. of your being   MUSICIANS, 2
rose an extremely beautiful girl and as innocent as a r.
    TERRY, E, 1
A r. without a thorn   CHARM, 2
just my luck to get /One perfect r.   PARKER, D, 5
never crave the r.   BRONTË, A, 4
roses I would like my r. to see you   COMPLIMENTS, 3
R. are flowering in Picardy   COMPLIMENTS, 5
The lilies and r. were all awake   COMPLIMENTS, 4
The r. of pleasure seldom last long   MORE, H, 4
rotten r. and corrupt to the marrow   MANN, E, 2
rouge intoxication of r.   COSMETICS, 5
royalty to ask for her autograph, any more than they
  would ask r.   PAVLOVA, A, 1
rubies her price is far above r.   VIRTUE, 2
rug you'll end up a r.   SELF-CONFIDENCE, 2
ruin Twenty years of romance make a woman look
  like a r.   MARRIAGE, 37
rule blame only the r. of men   POLITICS, 3
Every man can r. a shrew   SAYINGS AND PROVERBS, 7
he shall r. over thee   CHRON, 4
man's place to r.   CHRON, 321; WOMAN'S ROLE, 17
The first r. in opera is the first r. in life   MELBA, N, 6
woman's power is not for r.   CHRON, 308
Women r. the world   POWER, 10
ruled In days of old,.../The women r. the men
    CHRON, 497
school to be r.   OCCUPATIONS, 8
rulers Women...natural, but usually secret, r.   CHRON, 581
rules law of violence, r....in the poor man's domicile
    VIOLENCE, 3
no make-a da r.   BIRTH CONTROL, 17
the hand that r. the world   POWER, 6
virtuous wife r. her husband by obeying him   CHRON, 41

run How did Chinese women,...discover they could r.
    FRIEDAN, B, 5
lady, better r.   ADULTERY, 9
Russia R. still writhed and stumbled   CHRON, 469
ruthless impossible to be as single-mindedly r. as men
    RUTHLESSNESS, 3
the portrayal of her as a r. natural autocrat   GANDHI, I, 2
ruthlessly as a r. humanitarian woman   STOWE, H, 1

S

sacrament abortion would be a s.   ABORTION, 10
sacred most s. duty which devolves upon the sex
    CHRON, 245
s. responsibilities of motherhood   INJUSTICE, 6
sacrifice A woman will always s. herself   MISOGYNY, 10
submit to s. their right   CHRON, 212
this war,...which did not justify the s. of a single
  mother's son   PANKHURST, S, 2
upheld by s.   MARTYRDOM, 1
sacrificed The woman is uniformly s. to the wife and
  mother   GAGE, M, 4
sacrifices A woman artist must be...capable of making
  the primary s.   CASSATT, M, 1
sacrificing Jane Addams is...s. all for the masses
    ADDAMS, J, 3
sainthood not elevating women to s.   WAR, 8
saints woman-eating sentiments of certain medieval
  's.'   WRITERS, 9
sale offering herself for s. •   LOVE AND MARRIAGE, 1
salt nobody likes having s. rubbed into their wounds
    WEST, R, 3
S. water and absence   LOVE, 8
Samaritan No one would have remembered the Good
  S.   THATCHER, M, 7
sanctity prose lifts sensuousness to the pitch of s.
    COLETTE, 2
sanguine should not be s. when...one in four women
    CHRON, 739
sanitary towels new ladies' s.   MENSTRUATION, 13
Santa Claus stopped believing in S.   BLACK, S, 2
Satan S. first addressed himself to woman   CHRON, 123
the existence of S. a dogma of the church
    BLAVATSKY, E, 4
Women are the snares of S.   SAYINGS AND PROVERBS, 52
satisfaction but work *gives* s.   FRANK, A, 6
satisfying retarded children are s.   SILLS, B, 1
Saudi 50 S. women drove a convoy of cars   CHRON, 720
say afraid of what people will s.
    WOMEN'S LIBERATION MOVEMENT, 15
sayings His s. are generally like women's letters
    ATTITUDES, 17
says man s. what he knows, a woman what is agreeable   CHRON, 196
scandalous s. to call Dr Marie Stopes Birth Control
  method an experiment   CHRON, 493
scarce S., sir. Mighty s.   PROCREATION, 4
school two full years reading at the said public s.
    CHRON, 167
schoolroom in the s....does the difference of sex...need
  to be forgotten   ANTHONY, S, 4
s....difference of sex...need to be forgotten   CHRON, 391
science not made for the higher forms of s.
    INTELLIGENCE, 8
s. is essentially international   CURIE, M, 4

You can no more separate Mrs. Eddy from S. and
Health   EDDY, M, 2
science fiction S. and fantasy,..., allow one to imagine...strong independent women   STRENGTH, 5
sciences neither the accuracy nor the attention for success in the exact s.   CHRON, 188
severe laws of men no longer prevent women
from...the s.   CHRON, 112
scientific s. knowledge of the structure of our bodies
                                                      STOPES, M, 4
unreasonable prejudice...against a literary and s.
education for women   CHRON, 328
writer who combines s. ability...with a command of
the English language   CARSON, R, 1
scientist A fascinating combination of s. and would-be
poet   STOPES, M, 1
scorned fury like a woman s.   HATE, 2
screw Don't s. around, and don't smoke   PROMISCUITY, 6
script-writers her life and career still seem to have been
dreamed up by one of her s.   BOW, C, 2
sculptures s. nearly always suggest a human presence
                                                    HEPWORTH, B, 1
sea For all at last return to the s.   CARSON, R, 2
seasons two s. winter and winter   DELANEY, S, 3
seats you who so often occasion a want of s. to other
people   SIDDONS, S, 2
secret joys of parents are s.   CHILDREN, 2
when it ceases to be a s.   BEHN, A, 6; LOVE, 23
secretaries s. and technicians do to their men
                                                   OCCUPATIONS, 12
secretive As we make sex less s., we may rob it of its
power   SEX, 40
secure only place where a man can feel...s.   GREER, G, 2
security The key to s. is public information   SMITH, M, 4
seducers real s. are the daughters of Eve   SEDUCTION, 3
seduction Rough s. /Delights them   RAPE, 1; SEX, 4
see new way to s.   BEAUTY, 16
Why don't you come up sometime and s. me
                                                       WEST, M, 4
seed passive incubator of his s.   CHRON, 20
seen Maidens should be s., and not heard
                                          SAYINGS AND PROVERBS, 20
self to know our s., and ask mercy   JULIAN OF NORWICH, 3
self-consciousness completely devoid of s.   HAYES, H, 2
self-indulgence her favourite form of s.   MISOGYNY, 10
selfish An institution or reform movement that is not
s.   BARTON, C, 2
self-made A s. man...believes in luck   STEAD, C, 2
self-renunciation wise not for self-development, but for
s.   FEMININITY, 7; WISDOM, 1
self-respect committing a sin...against her s. if she dyes
her hair   APPEARANCE, 8; OLD AGE, 7
selling s. of young girls as concubines   CHRON, 543
semen She burns and...dries up the s.   SEX, 11
senates patriotism of woman; not to thunder in s.
                                                     CHRON, 309
sense debar'd from s., and sacred poetry   INJUSTICE, 2
sensibility s. is the power of woman   POWER, 2
sensible Marriage is the aim and end of all s. girls
                                                     CHRON, 438
sensuousness prose lifts s. to the pitch of sanctity
                                                     COLETTE, 2
sentence God's s. hangs over all your sex   RELIGION, 2
sentimentalist The s. ages   LANGTRY, L, 2
sentiments *Declaration of S.*   STANTON, E, 10

Seraphs Mammon wins his way where S. might
despair   WEALTH, 4
seriously one must do some work s. and must be independent   CURIE, M, 3
servant mother is still the unchartered s. of the future
                                                     CHRON, 483
Wife and s. are the same   CHRON, 178; SUBJECTION, 7
servants book you would even wish your wife or your
s. to read   CHRON, 591
Few men have been admired by their s.
                                               WOMAN'S ROLE, 8
We teachers can only help...as s.   MONTESSORI, M, 3
serve ERA means that women who s. will get equal
benefits   CHRON, 679
want the vote so that we may s. our country better
                                                     CHRON, 471
we s. men's need and forfeit our worthless life
                                       CHRON, 249; PROSTITUTION, 2
Woman...was made to s. and obey man   CHRON, 118
served better s. if I stood down   THATCHER, M, 11
service have also s. to do   WAR, 1
life goes in the s. of the nation   GANDHI, I, 7
qualities of love and s., which in women is strong
                                    SOCIETY, 5; STRENGTH, 3
servile remain the s., docile,...self-abnegative wife
                                                  SUFFRAGETTES, 4
seventy Being over s. is like being engaged in a war
                                                     SPARK, M, 3
Being s. is not a sin   MEIR, G, 6; OLD AGE, 12
sewed cut off their breats and s. them to their mouths
                                                  RUTHLESSNESS, 1
sews modern woman writes as well as s.
                   CHRON, 427; SUFFRAGETTES, 18; WOMAN'S ROLE, 25
sex As we make s. less secretive, we may rob it of its
power   SEX, 40
both of them were extremely interested in s.   SEX, 48
condition of our s. is so deplorable   CHRON, 410
Consider your s. and spare me   CHRON, 86
contraceptive pill may reduce the importance of s.
                                       CHRON, 611; BIRTH CONTROL, 14
if s. isn't the most important, what is   DRABBLE, M, 2
If s. is such a natural phenomenon   SEX, 36
important task of modern feminism is to accept and
proclaim s.   CHRON, 500
in the schoolroom...does the difference of s....need
to be forgotten   ANTHONY, S, 4
In the s.-war thoughtlessness is the weapon of the
male   MEN AND WOMEN, 22
invidious distinctions of s.   CHRON, 346
Is s. dirty   SEX, 37
Literature is mostly about having s.   CHILDREN, 9
minds have no s.   CHRON, 164
nicest women in our 'society' are raving s. maniacs
                                                     CHRON, 607
no more weakness than is natural to her s.   ATTITUDES, 1
normal man's s. needs are stronger   SEX, 17
No s. without responsibility   SEX, 30
not have a soul of a different s.   EQUALITY, 3; RELIGION, 4
only as the vassals of your S.   ADAMS, A, 4
Personally I know nothing about s.   MARRIAGE, 72; SEX, 46
pitting of s. against s.   CHRON, 524
right...to vote shall not be denied...on account of s.
                                                     CHRON, 482
S. becomes a weapon   PROSTITUTION, 13
S. had to be brought out of the Victorian closet   SEX, 42
s. has been a very private, secretive activity   SEX, 40

S....interesting as agriculture — SEX, 39
S. is the tabasco sauce — SEX, 21
s. of the former should no longer be an obstacle — CHRON, 243
such as say our S. is void of Reason — CHRON, 144
the condition of our s. is so deplorable that it is our duty...to break the law — PANKHURST, E, 6
the difference of s., if there is any — ANTHONY, S, 4
the mild peculiarities of their s. — MENOPAUSE, 1
The total deprivation of s. — BLACKWELL, E, 1
tortuous road that led to the s. war — CHRON, 637
treat us only as the vassals of your S. — CHRON, 194
undesired s....greater in marriage than in prostitution — CHRON, 522
wife is one who has made a permanent s. bargain — CHRON, 441
woman feels the invidious distinctions of s. — STANTON, E, 8
sex discrimination unlawful certain kinds of s. — CHRON, 681
sexe things by reason of my s., I may not doe — CHRON, 126
sexes husbands and wives...belong to different s. — DIX, D, 4; MEN AND WOMEN, 21
practising indiscriminately between the s. — CHRON, 314
that pleasure, which is undeniably the sole motive force behind the union of the s. — LUST, 3
that pleasure, which is undeniably the sole motive force behind the union of the s. — SEX, 6
the...rift between the s. is...widened — DISCRIMINATION, 5
sexism Justice...blind to racism, s., war and poverty — PREJUDICE, 5
linguistic s. is intact — LANGUAGE, 7
sexist expressing in s. terms...in racist terms...would deny — CHRON, 660
sex symbol A s. becomes a thing — MONROE, M, 6
Being a s. is a heavy load to carry — BOW, C, 4
sex-typed mind is not s. — INTELLECT, 11
sexual beyond reach of s. storms — CHRON, 377
beyond reach of s. storms — PUBERTY, 3
code of morals...which relieves men from responsibility for irregular s. acts — CHRON, 507
Industrial relations are like s. relations — PARTNERSHIP, 3
Lesbianism is not a matter of s. preference — LESBIANISM, 8
lie in s. intercourse with a woman who has an issue of blood — MENSTRUATION, 6
majority of women...are not very much troubled with s. feelings — CHRON, 305
many females who never feel any s. excitement — SEX, 10
masculine mythology suppressing...facts of women's s. — CHRON, 464
mutual and satisfied s. act — CHRON, 473; LUST, 6
s. shyness...arouses the contempt of decent ones — CHRON, 562
s. systems of plants can accord with female modesty — CHRON, 211
uncorrupted woman the s. impulse does not manifest itself — SEX, 7
sexual intercourse Englishwomen look upon s. as abhorrent — SEX, 18
S. in marriage — CHRON, 306
submits to s. against her wishes — SUBJECTION, 12
this whole question of s. — LUST, 5
sexuality Her rampant s. made her a fantasy figure for men — BARDOT, B, 3
male reviewers who fear female s. — FEAR, 2

sexually disgrace for women to be s. responsible — CHRON, 676
women are s. manipulative — SEX, 49
shackles women freed of their political s. — SUFFRAGETTES, 7
shadow I am no s....I am a wife — PLATH, S, 4
we could kiss her s. as it fell — NIGHTINGALE, F, 2
shadows brooding tragedy and its dark s. can be lightened — GANDHI, I, 6
She could aways discover sunlight behind the s. — HOWE, J, 2
Shakespeare A strange, horrible business,...good enough for S.'s day — VICTORIA, 7
Besides S. and me, who do you think there is — STEIN, G, 3
Outsold only by the Bible and S. — CHRISTIE, A, 1
Wonderful women!...how much we...owe to S. — STRENGTH, 2; TERRY, E, 3; WOMANHOOD, 4
shame blushed with s. that the cup of tea should have such power — SUFFRAGETTES, 17
Put off your s. with your clothes — MODESTY, 1
shamed S., dishonored, wading in blood — CHRON, 478
shameful fuddled woman is a s. sight — DRINKING, 1
shameless a s. flatterer and insatiable of flattery — MORE, H, 1
share Mothers who can s. their children's interests...far better equipped — CHRON, 537
s. in all his possession — EQUALITY, 1
sharper women's bodies are softer than men's, so their understanding is s. — CHRISTINE DE PISAN, 4
shed woman can s. her past — CHRON, 390
Shelley Mrs. S. is very clever — SHELLEY, M, 1
S.'s nature is utterly womanish — FEMININITY, 9
shelter We s. children for a time — WELDON, F, 1
shingle To s. was to cut loose from the maternal pattern — CHRON, 488
ship-saving The Health Meal is s. — WAR, 7
shipwreck husbands and wives make s. of their lives — DIX, D, 3; MARRIAGE, 48
shit lived in a barrel of s. they'd start making a home — PRACTICALITY, 5
want to be treated like s. — SEX, 45
shocked how to be amused rather than s. — BUCK, P, 5
shocks preventing conception s. the mind of a woman — BIRTH CONTROL, 3
shoot I can s. as well as you — OAKLEY, A, 2
shorter s. by a head — ELIZABETH I, 7
shoulder women stand s. to s. with the men to win the common victory — CHRON, 457
shouldered Women...s. the double burden unquestioningly — CHRON, 709
shrew Every man can rule a s. — SAYINGS AND PROVERBS, 7
shun true wanderer,......goes out not to s. — STARK, F, 4
shunted value women have to offer is s. aside — POLITICS, 9
shut If she doesn't want it she only has to keep her legs s. — RAPE, 5
sick the very first requirement in a Hospital that it should do the s. no harm — NIGHTINGALE, F, 3
sickness in s. and in health — MARRIAGE, 15
s. need not be a part of life — HEALTH AND HEALTHY LIVING, 8
S., sin and death...do not originate in God — EDDY, M, 5
sicknesses dare not reveal the difficulties of their s. to a male doctor — CHRON, 78
sidelong glances s. at him, thus showing her eyes — CHRON, 542
sieve s. will hold water — SAYINGS AND PROVERBS, 32

sighed They s. for the dawn and thee COMPLIMENTS, 4
sight keep death in my line of s. DEATH, 3
Silvia Who is S.? What is she FEMININITY, 3
simpler stronger than a man s. than a child BRONTË, E, 1
sin beauty is only s. deep BEAUTY, 12
Being seventy is not a s. MEIR, G, 6; OLD AGE, 12
committing a s....against her self-respect if she dyes her hair APPEARANCE, 8; OLD AGE, 7
Fashions in s. change SIN, 2
real s. when a young married woman refuses to bear a family BIRTH CONTROL, 4
Sickness, s. and death...do not originate in God EDDY, M, 5
s. against life is to...destroy beauty PORTER, K, 3
S. brought death EDDY, M, 4
Wealth covers s. WEALTH, 2
sincere women have a more s. determination to preserve the country CHRON, 121
sinecure a widow...is a kind of s. WIDOWHOOD, 1
singers by blocking the careers of so many other s. MELBA, N, 1
single a business, we s. girls SINGLE WOMEN, 12
contempt with which the s. woman has been regarded SINGLE WOMEN, 7
s. man in possession of a good fortune AUSTEN, J, 8; MARRIAGE, 21
s. woman with a narrow income SINGLE WOMEN, 3
sings 'tis pa s. to you CHRON, 372
sink The s. is the great symbol of the bloodiness of family life FAMILY, 10
sinners breeder of s. WOMAN'S ROLE, 9
sinning I delight in s. SIN, 1
sins marriage and with that name veils her s. CHRON, 44
she must not reheat his s. for breakfast FORGIVENESS, 3
sisterhood meaningfulness of life in the notions of s. WOMEN'S LIBERATION MOVEMENT, 18
sisters all the lovely s. CHRON, 633
little s. to all the world DIX, D, 1; SORROW, 5
O! men with s. dear CHRON, 268; OPPRESSION, 2; WORK, 1
S. should be always willing to attend their brothers DUTY, 2; FAMILY, 3
sixty close-up of a woman past s. ASTOR, N, 5; OLD AGE, 11
skilled more s. labour which women can supply CHRON, 299
skirt art of lifting her /s. over her ankles CHRON, 14
a woman...ought to lay aside...modesty with her s. MODESTY, 3
skunk guilty s. she made me feel GUILT, 2
slam no door to s. BEAUTY, 16
slave as s....had to be annulled as woman CHRON, 629
condition of a s. CHRON, 287
s. of man and the victim of prejudice SOCIETY, 2
supplication of the freed s. CHRON, 253
slavery marriage...a condition of s. for women CHRON, 276
Mrs John Smith, her life is one long s. CHRON, 363
prolonged s. of women CHRON, 345; EMANCIPATION, 4; STANTON, E, 11
wretchedness and s. of women CHRON, 295
slaves love, an...intercourse between tyrants and s. LOVE AND FRIENDSHIP, 2
no legal s. – except for the woman in every man's home LAW, 11
She was involved in an insurrection of s. BEHN, A, 2
slavish law where it concerns women, is a s. one. LAW, 12

sleep better to s. with a pretty boy HOMOSEXUALITY, 1
Every time you s. with a boy AIDS, 2; PROMISCUITY, 5
I believe s. was never more welcome ANNE, 1
I did not s. O'BRIEN, E, 1
sleeps eats, s. and watches the television CHRON, 624; GREER, G, 3
She s. alone at last EPITAPHS, 4
slumped women gazed out of the s. and sagging bodies APPEARANCE, 14
slut image *they* supply...the Rock And Roll S. APPEARANCE, 18
small Man...s. MEN AND WOMEN, 31
virtue's still far too s. COLETTE, 5
smile a s. I could feel in my hip pocket LUST, 7
Never mind about the bomb – just s. WAR, 5
smiles She is Venus when she s. FEMININITY, 5
smoke Don't screw around, and don't s. PROMISCUITY, 6
no woman should marry...a man who does not s. MARRIAGE, 34
smooth course of true love never did run s. LOVE, 15
if the parts be s. conception is prevented BIRTH CONTROL, 1
smothered let her be s. in mire DIVORCE, 2
snails Frogs and s. /And puppy-dogs' tails MEN AND WOMEN, 8
snakes The women are all s. CALAMITY JANE, 3
snare a s. in which the feet of women...become...entangled ADDAMS, J, 5
Old-fashioned ways...a s. in which the feet of women SOCIETY, 4
snares Women are the s. of Satan SAYINGS AND PROVERBS, 52
Snow I used to be S. White VIRGINITY, 10; WEST, M, 5
snub Her weapon is the s. GANDHI, I, 1
sobbing Lying alone and s.?! SORROW, 2
sober What, when drunk one sees in other women, one sees in Garbo s. GARBO, G, 2
sobriety our sex is protected by greater s. DRINKING, 2
social educated in terms of their own s. function CHRON, 601
existing s. arrangements which structure inequality CHRON, 702
Feminists think only in terms of s. power FEMINISM, 22
mother as a s. servant CHRON, 374
S. intercourse BLACKWELL, E, 1
the...world was stumbling...in s. blindness KELLER, H, 4
Working women want...to improve the s. laws CHRON, 371
Socialist Said the S. to the Suffragist CHRON, 417
Social Security plan for S. puts a premium on marriage CHRON, 555
society duty and privilege to fill in the scale of s. CHRON, 232
many women are doing two jobs in s. CHRON, 726
person who divided s. into two parts HYPATIA, 2
real architects of s. SOCIETY, 3
she insists upon thrusting her s. upon men everywhere CHRON, 445
S....decrees that woman is inferior SUPERIORITY, 8
s....insisting on a woman's natural fitness SOCIETY, 8
S. is a cage of idiots JARS, M, 1
s....pays a harlot 25 times as much as it pays its Prime Minister PROSTITUTION, 10
s. wants from women is not labour CHRON, 296
women are economic factors in s. CHRON, 373
socks didn't get it for knitting more s. CHRON, 557

sofa rather lie on a s. than sweep beneath it
HOUSEKEEPING, 8
soften dearest task it is to s., to bless, and to purify our imperfect nature CHRON, 262
softer women's bodies are s. than men's, so their understanding is sharper CHRISTINE DE PISAN, 4
softness bring them s., teach them how to cry BAEZ, J, 3
soldier She studied language as the s. guards his sword DIX, D, 1
soldiers militant Suffragettes stand in an analogous position to s. CHRON, 429
solid man has more s. flesh than a woman
MENSTRUATION, 2
solitary S. women exhibit pseudo-masculine efficiency SINGLE WOMEN, 11
solitude to know and shatter the s. of another SAGAN, F, 3
solve sincere attempts to help a woman s. her problems MEN, 9
sombrero sunbonnet as well as the s. COURAGE, 4
someone like sleeping with s. else's wife
UNFAITHFULNESS, 5
sometime Why don't you come up s. and see me
WEST, M, 4
son inheritance goes to the s., not the daughter
CHRON, 66
the earth is free for every s. and daughter of mankind CHRON, 142
sons I have a wife, I have s. FAMILY, 1
s. were taken from their mothers CHRON, 604
sorcery false enchantments and s. JOAN OF ARC, 1
sorrow bid farewell to sin and s. AGE, 2
in s. thou shalt bring forth children CHRON, 4
when she is in travail hath s. CHRON, 58
sorry they always look at her and say S., in English
MITFORD, N, 1
soul education is a leading out of what is…in the pupil's s. EDUCATION, 29
fill her s. with gratitude to God and to the Man
LOVE AND MARRIAGE, 4
my s. in the midst of my heart JULIAN OF NORWICH, 4
No coward s. is mine BRONTË, E, 4
not have a s. of a different sex EQUALITY, 3; RELIGION, 4
possessive outrage done to a free solitary human s.
MOTHERHOOD, 8
s. of a sex is emerging from the dim chamber of instinct FEMINISM, 4
Their kindness cheer'd his drooping s. AIKIN, L, 3
The s. fortunately, has an interpreter BRONTË, C, 6
souls queen did fish for men's s. ELIZABETH I, 1
The s. of women are so small ATTITUDES, 8
sour monthly flux/ of women. Contact with it turns new wine s. MENSTRUATION, 4
space cannot have the same economy of s. as if there are men only CHRON, 553
spaniel curls like…ears of a water s. BROWNING, E, 2
sparrows Women and s. twitter in company
SAYINGS AND PROVERBS, 48
speak s. of what I have done ACHIEVEMENT, 1
When I think, I must s. ATTITUDES, 5
spear pass from the s. to the spindle LAW, 2
special Women are not a s. interest group CHRON, 656
species Women exist…solely for the propagation of the s. WOMAN'S ROLE, 14
speculating the authoress…whose books have set all London…s. BRONTË, C, 2
speculum constant use of the s. CHRON, 284

speech An after-dinner s. should be like a lady's dress
CLOTHES, 12
sperm males should deposit their s. in a s. bank
CHRON, 710
sphere absurd talk about a woman's s. CHRON, 335
sphinx Emily Brontë remains the s. of literature
BRONTË, E, 3
spic say 's.' and 'bitch' with impunity CHRON, 742
spice Sugar and s. /And all that's nice MEN AND WOMEN, 8
spin rare attainments…but…can she s.
CHRON, 132; FEMININITY, 4
spindle pass from the spear to the s. LAW, 2
spinning Our s. wheels are all broken CHRON, 424
spinning-wheel Modern inventions have banished the s. PROGRESS, 1
Spinoza The Jews have produced…Christ, S., and myself STEIN, G, 4
spinster graduating with a 's. of arts' degree CHRON, 695
s. of arts STEINEM, G, 3
spinsterhood war-bereaved s. with voyages of discovery SINGLE WOMEN, 9
spirit bore a man's s. under the appearance of a woman ACHIEVEMENT, 2
my s. found outlet in the air JOHNSON, A, 3
woman in name, but in s. she is a man CHRON, 85
spiritually marriage may be a failure s. DIVORCE, 9
spite Powerful women only succeed in s. of their husbands SUCCESS, 9
splendour glittering like the morning star full of life and s. and joy MARIE ANTOINETTE, 1
spoils meat s. when touched by menstruating women
MENSTRUATION, 12
spontaneity Her total commitment,…, . and fearlessness CASTLE, B, 2
spring In the s.…your lovely Chloë PUBERTY, 4
s. now comes unheralded by the return of the birds
CARSON, R, 4
staff a high-handed attitude with her s. ARDEN, E, 2
stage last s. of the drive for equality
WOMEN'S LIBERATION MOVEMENT, 7
qualities…necessary for success upon the s. TERRY, E, 4
stale emancipation of woman…was s. stuff
EMANCIPATION, 10
standards a woman to cling to her s. at all costs
CAVELL, E, 1
highest s. of behaviour without any law CHRON, 30
Stanton Mrs S. would attend…to her domestic duties
STANTON, E, 2
star glittering like the morning s. full of life and splendour and joy MARIE ANTOINETTE, 1
start it is far easier to s. something EARHART, A, 3
starve Let not poor Nelly s. GWYNN, N, 1
starving all around you people are s.
CHRON, 489; PANKHURST, S, 5
state Women in s. affairs are like monkeys in glassshops POLITICS, 1; SAYINGS AND PROVERBS, 54
stateliest the s. ornament of the public mind
SIDDONS, S, 1
stately homes Those comfortably padded lunatic asylums…the s. WOOLF, V, 4
static class people as s. and dynamic
CHRON, 519; MEN AND WOMEN, 19
statue that *my* s. should be moved, which I should much dislike VICTORIA, 8
status eyes of the law her personal liberty and her s. are *nil* CHRON, 351

s. of woman CHRON, 605
term *wizard* has acquired reverential s.
LANGUAGE, 6; WITCHES, 6
sterile human females become s. in the forties
FERTILITY, 1
stern gentle to all and s. with yourself TERESA OF AVILA, 1
stigma not a s. for the woman to be kept by a man
CHRON, 715
revolution of womanhood each woman strives to
remove the old s. of the story of Adam and Eve
SUFFRAGETTES, 15
s. for a man to be unemployed EQUAL OPPORTUNITIES, 5
stigmatize s. the female mind INJUSTICE, 3
stir s. up the zeal of women themselves CHRON, 319
stirring the strange, dissatisfied voice s. within her
FRIEDAN, B, 3
stockings a whole garment and an unladdered pair of
s. to wear CASTLE, B, 4
stole She s. everything but the cameras WEST, M, 2
stone men of her town shall s. her to death CHRON, 8
stones There are two kinds of s. EARHART, A, 2
stood better served if I s. down THATCHER, M, 11
stoops When lovely woman s. to folly BETRAYAL, 1
stories She likes s. that make her cry KELLER, H, 1
storms beyond reach of sexual s. CHRON, 377
beyond reach of sexual s. PUBERTY, 3
strain childbirth is a heavy s. on the physique of any
woman CHRON, 531
strains ideal exposes marriages to new s. CHRON, 585
strange A s., horrible business,...good enough for
Shakespeare's day VICTORIA, 7
streets We must go walk the s. CHRON, 249
strength difference in s. between men and women
EQUALITY, 15
female in point of s. is, in general, inferior to the
male CHRON, 201
With s. beyond the s. of men STOWE, H, 2
stridency s. of the feminists CHRON, 740
strike Housewives and mothers seldom find it practicable to come out on s. CHRON, 638
strong s. and clever and happy STRENGTH, 1
stronger normal man's sex needs are s. SEX, 17
s. than a man simpler than a child BRONTË, E, 1
structure existing social arrangements which s.
inequality CHRON, 702
struggle crushing and numbing force of the bare s. for
life CHRON, 387
struggled suburban wife s. with it alone CHRON, 597
struggles first feeble s. of a living mind SULLIVAN, A, 2
strut uterus shall swell and s. out like a water bag
PREGNANCY, 2
studies My sex is usually forbid s. of this nature
CHRON, 177
study Girls s. for prizes and not for learning CHRON, 331
We must prepare and s. truth BLAVATSKY, E, 3
stuff Edith Sitwell...read some of her absurd s.
SITWELL, E, 1
The future is made of the same s. WEIL, S, 4
to s. a mushroom CHRON, 675
stumbling the...world was s....in social blindness
KELLER, H, 4
stumbling block Bible and Church have been the greatest s. EMANCIPATION, 5
stupid comfort about being a woman...always pretend
to be more s. STARK, F, 3
She has been called s. ANNE, 3

so many men are s. and so few are blind WEBB, B, 1
sturdy That s. woman of letters SAND, G, 2
styles change their s. and talk like men CHRON, 725
subconscious American women know far more about
the s. CHRON, 481
subdue The creator...desires to s. other minds
HINKLE, B, 4
subdued a gentle, quiet, rather s. person BRONTË, A, 2
subduing s. all her impressions as a woman ARTISTS, 2
subjected priestcraft that has s. woman RELIGION, 11
subjection *God* has determined s. to be women's lot
CHRON, 161
sense of inferiority is one of the prime requisites
for...s. CHRON, 475
token of s. CHRON, 139
woman's complete historical s....most fantastic
myths CHRON, 569
subjects teach them the same s. as are taught to boys
CHRON, 97
treat women as s. instead of equals CHRON, 470
submission I have joy in my s. JHABVALA, R, 2
s. to the woman CHRON, 72
submissive humble in character and s. HUMILITY, 3
submissiveness destroys that s. and modesty which is
natural SUBJECTION, 1
submit she cannot s. to laws made without women's
participation CHRON, 275
Who is't that to women's beauty would s. BEHN, A, 5
woman how to s. to it SUBJECTION, 9
submits s. to her husband, but only to please him
CHRON, 305; WOMAN'S ROLE, 16
s. to sexual intercourse against her wishes
SUBJECTION, 12
submitting Charms by accepting, by s. sways
DOMINATION, 4
subordinate women are made s. by traditions CHRON, 743
subservient not made married woman s. to have her be
polluted CHRON, 111
refuses to be s. CHRON, 433
s. womanhood is the nearest...to the spiritual
delights of the harem CHRON, 434
subsidised France...childcare is s. by the government
CHILDREN, 11
subsistence adult Englishwomen work for s. CHRON, 298
substitute college...a s. for...marriage EDUCATION, 28
subtlety one-dimensional s. of a comic-strip
THATCHER, M, 3
suburban s. wife struggled with it alone CHRON, 597
suburbs The selling of the s. BOMBECK, E, 2
succeed those who ne'er s. DICKINSON, E, 6
success fear of s. as well. SUCCESS, 8
I don't think s. is harmful SUCCESS, 4
I thought that s. spelled happiness PAVLOVA, A, 5
I was never affected by the question of the s. MEIR, G, 3
neither the accuracy nor the attention for s. in the
exact sciences CHRON, 188
no s. like failure SUCCESS, 10
Nothing fails like s. SUCCESS, 2
real demon is s. SUCCESS, 6
secret of my s. SUCCESS, 3
s....by dint of hard work PAVLOVA, A, 4
s. depends...upon individual initiative and exertion
PAVLOVA, A, 4

S. is counted sweetest DICKINSON, E, 6
s. spelled happiness HAPPINESS, 4
woman who is loved...has s. SUCCESS, 1

successful most s. mode of rearing girls   CHRON, 355
suckle absolute duty,..., to s. her infant   BREASTFEEDING, 4
suffer love children always s.   CHRON, 490
 wife ought to s., and let the husband...be master
   CHRON, 93
suffered love a place the less for having s. in it
   AUSTEN, J, 7
suffering foundation of bitter s.
   CLOTHES, 3; HEALTH AND HEALTHY LIVING, 2
 poignant symbol of Jewish s.   FRANK, A, 2
 some degree of s. is connected with child-birth
   CHILDBIRTH, 11
sufferings If we can alleviate s.   WOMAN'S ROLE, 23
 is it not just that this sex should partake of the s.
   CHRON, 187
suffragette riot-ridden s. movements in the Western
 countries   CHRON, 672
suffragettes cannot expect the S. to give you a quiet
 life   CHRON, 436
 militant S. stand in an analogous position to soldiers
   CHRON, 429
 we s. aspire to be...ambassadors of freedom to
 women   PANKHURST, C, 5
 we s. aspire to be/ when we are enfranchised is
 ambassadors   SUFFRAGETTES, 22
Suffragist Said the Socialist to the S.   CHRON, 417
suffragists s. did influence voters   CHRON, 404
sugar S. and spice /And all that's nice   MEN AND WOMEN, 8
suicide It's literary s.   BOMBECK, E, 3
suit in a light so dim he would not have chosen a s.
 by it   LOVE, 60
suitable not s. for a female to know how to read
   EDUCATION, 4
sun boring to be too much in the s.   DU PRÉ, J, 4
 s. had risen to hear him crow   ELIOT, G, 4
sunbonnet s. as well as the sombrero   COURAGE, 4
sunlight She could aways discover s. behind the shadows   HOWE, J, 2
 s. as a kind of cosmetic effulgence   COSMETICS, 7
Sunnybrook Farm S. is now a parking lot   BLACK, S, 1
superfluous Women are also monthly filled full of s.
 humours   MENSTRUATION, 8
superior idle woman is a badge of s. social status
   CHRON, 590
 male is by nature s.   CHRON, 22
 must she account him her s.   MARRIAGE, 14
 s....as men to women   SUPERIORITY, 1
superiority cannot speak of inferiority and s., but only
 of specific differences   SUPERIORITY, 6
 claiming of s. and imputing of inferiority   CHRON, 524
 futile argument as to the relative s. of men and
 women   EMANCIPATION, 8
 men face the feminine s.   SUPERIORITY, 10
 never any reason to believe in any innate s. of the
 male   SUPERIORITY, 7
superstars the last of the great missionary s.
   TERESA, MOTHER, 1
superstition Men will fight for a s....as for a living truth
   HYPATIA, 4
superstitions s. of the human mind   VIRGINITY, 3
supertax iniquity of the Marriage Tax in the form of s.
   TAXATION, 1
supplication s. of the freed slave   CHRON, 253
support learned how to ask for their s. in the right way
   FEMINISM, 18
 Most woman...do not...s. a married partner   CHRON, 572

supported look forward to being themselves s.
   CHRON, 572
supremacy men from their first creation usurped a s.
   CHRON, 160
 obliged to confess the s. of the other sex   CHRON, 251
Sure-Shot Little S.   OAKLEY, A, 1
survive Women under blockade,...s....more successfully than men   EMOTION, 2
Susan Anthony S....has striven long and earnestly to
 become a man   ANTHONY, S, 1
suspect s. all...special systems of education
   SULLIVAN, A, 1
suspended marriage the very being or legal existence
 of woman is s.   LAW, 6
suspicion Caesar's wife must be above s.
   CHRON, 40; DIVORCE, 1; WOMAN'S ROLE, 3
swains all our s. commend her   FEMININITY, 3
swans Pavlova contemplates her s.   COMMITMENT, 2
swayed female is an empty thing and easily s.
   CHARACTER, 1
sweat millions of women who earn their bread by the
 s. of their brows   CHRON, 335
sweated most downtrodden and s. workers   CHRON, 381
sweet woman is a tender and s. person   CHRON, 640
sweetest Success is counted s.   DICKINSON, E, 6
swell uterus shall s. and strut out like a water bag
   PREGNANCY, 2
swellings nine out of ten abdominal s. are the pregnant
 uterus   PREGNANCY, 6
swine S., women, and bees   SAYINGS AND PROVERBS, 33
sword horse, a wife, and a s.   SAYINGS AND PROVERBS, 18
 justice is the s. I carry   JUSTICE, 3
 She studied language as the soldier guards his s.
   DIX, D, 1
symbol poignant s. of Jewish suffering   FRANK, A, 2
 veil is seen as the s. of independence from the Western values   CHRON, 713
 vote is the s. of freedom and equality   CHRON, 440
symbolic women's s. militancy punished with a prison-
 cell   CHRON, 453
sympathy enlist the s. of women...against the wanton
 slaughter of birds   CONSERVATION, 2
 failed to inspire s. in men   MISOGYNY, 9
 she wants s.   DISAPPOINTMENT, 3
system stupendous s. of organized robbery   CHRON, 365
 s. that produced the kettle   PROGRESS, 5
systematic granting to females the advantages of a s.
 and thorough education   CHRON, 234

T

tabasco Sex is the t. sauce   SEX, 21
table A man is...better pleased when he has a good
 dinner upon his t.
   CHRON, 197; INTELLIGENCE, 6; WOMAN'S ROLE, 10
taboos Her frontal attacks on old t.   STOPES, M, 2
take just t. 'em, and not be talkin' about it   CHRON, 307
taken called Woman, because she was t. out of Man
   CHRON, 1
talent Everyone has t.   JONG, E, 5
 t. for describing the...characters of ordinary life
   AUSTEN, J, 2
talents change of life does not give t.   MENOPAUSE, 2
talk change their styles and t. like men   CHRON, 725
 my ministers t. – as long as they do what I say
   THATCHER, M, 9

One has to grow up with good t.   HAYES, H, 1
t....means to preserve independence   LANGUAGE, 9
teachers t. too much   MITCHELL, M, 3
talked greatest glory of a woman is to be least t. about
by men   CHRON, 19
talkin just *take 'em,* and not be t.' about it   CHRON, 307
tame t. an advanced young woman   EMANCIPATION, 9
tanks Princess Anne...receptive to chat about t.
    ANNE, PRINCESS, 1
task dearest t. it is to soften, to bless, and to purify
our imperfect nature   CHRON, 262
hard t. it is   CHILDBIRTH, 8
taste A different t. in jokes is a...strain on the affections   ELIOT, G, 5
ideal woman changes...to suit the t. of man
    FEMININITY, 8
T. is the feminine of genius   TALENT AND GENIUS, 1
tastes the whole range of Cather's values, standards,
t., and prejudices   CATHER, W, 1
taught a woman who knows all...that can be t.
    CHANEL, C, 3; STYLE, 2
t. anything at all but the management of a family
    EDUCATION, 30
woman t. once, and ruined all   CHRON, 64
tax penalty t. of 40 percent on me because I have no
husband   CHRON, 677; TAXATION, 4
taxes Why should we pay t.   CHRON, 38
tea it is just like having a cup of t.   SEX, 47
Mum,...I want my t.   CHRON, 504
teach qualified by some accomplishment which she
may t.   CHRON, 286
t. them the same subjects as are taught to boys
    CHRON, 97
teacher Experience is a good t.   ANTRIM, M, 2
not necessarily the best t.   WILLARD, E, 4
teachers As t.,...the first work for women physicians
    BLACKWELL, E, 3
t. talk too much   MITCHELL, M, 3
We t. can only help...as servants   MONTESSORI, M, 3
teaches man who t. women letters feeds more poison
    EDUCATION, 3
teaching being taught the art of t.   SOMERVILLE, M, 1
tears marriage bring only t.   ADULTERY, 1
T. would be an admission of guilt   DU MAURIER, D, 3
The bitterest t....are for words...unsaid   STOWE, H, 1
the women whose eyes have been washed...with t.
    DIX, D, 1; SORROW, 5
technicians secretaries and t. do to their men
    OCCUPATIONS, 12
teeth artificial t. are a great blessing
    APPEARANCE, 8; OLD AGE, 7
cuts her wisdom t. when she is dead
    INTELLIGENCE, 1; SAYINGS AND PROVERBS, 42
her lips narrow and her t. black   ELIZABETH I, 2
I had braces on my t. and got high marks
    APPEARANCE, 11
taking out his false t. and hurling them at his wife
    MARRIAGE, 36
teetotaller no woman should marry a t.   MARRIAGE, 34
television eats, sleeps and watches the t.
    CHRON, 624; GREER, G, 3
tell How could they t.   PARKER, D, 11
temperament She had a t. akin to genius   PANKHURST, E, 2
temperance by t. they all mean the opposite   PREJUDICE, 6
She belongs to a T. Society   PREJUDICE, 6
tempests That looks on t.   LOVE, 18

temptation virtue is only elicited by t.   BRONTÉ, A, 5
tendency invariable t. to shut women out   CHRON, 432
strong t. to shunt us into the more traditional female
roles   OCCUPATIONS, 15
tender woman is a t. and sweet person   CHRON, 640
terrifying her aspect was t.   BOADICEA, 2
terrorism Rape is a form of mass t.   RAPE, 3
test Fatal illness has...been viewed as a t.   SONTAG, S, 2
testicles Nature placed the female t. internally
    MISOGYNY, 5; PROCREATION, 3
women...have t.   CHRON, 113
testify purely feminine affairs...women may t.   LAW, 4
testimony conclusive t. that woman was never
intended to rival man   WOMAN'S NATURE, 7
thanksgiving t. for the past...warnings for the future
    CAULKINS, F, 1
Thatcher Margaret T.'s great strength   THATCHER, M, 4
theatre For the t. one needs long arms   BERNHARDT, S, 2
We give customers a sense of t.   RODDICK, A, 4
theatrical one may fail to find happiness in t. life
    PAVLOVA, A, 3
theft t. to foist heirs born of debauchery on an entire
family   CHRON, 154
themselves power...over t.   WOLLSTONECRAFT, M, 4
therapeutic My singing is very t.   SILLS, B, 4
thick Through t. and thin   CONSTANCY, 1
thieves Two daughters...are...arrant t.
    SAYINGS AND PROVERBS, 34
thin Through thick and t.   CONSTANCY, 1
thing A sex symbol becomes a t.   MONROE, M, 6
think close their eyes and t. of Kenya   OPPRESSION, 8
I t. him so, because I t. him so   ATTITUDES, 4
T. me all man   EQUALITY, 5
t. with our wombs   INTELLIGENCE, 19
Third World one in six training places goes to T.
women   DISCRIMINATION, 9
thirst earned his t. and the right to quench it
    MARRIAGE, 64
thorn A rose without a t.   CHARM, 2
Thou Book of Verse – and T.   LOVE, 41
thoughtlessness In the sex-war t. is the weapon of the
male   MEN AND WOMEN, 22
the colour bar and all it implies are largely due to t.
    BESANT, A, 3
thoughts I must have something to engross my t.
    BLACKWELL, E, 2
partners in business and in t.   EQUALITY, 8
woman's t. are afterthoughts   SAYINGS AND PROVERBS, 46
threat Alcohol was a t. to women   DRINKING, 9
one can...see in a little girl the t. of a woman
    MEN AND WOMEN, 14
regard the Women's Liberation movement as a serious t.   CHRON, 652
three halfpence t. worse than the devil
    SAYINGS AND PROVERBS, 37
thrive t. must ask leave of his wife
    SAYINGS AND PROVERBS, 17
throne It helps...to remind your bride that you gave
up a t. for her   MARRIAGE, 66
throned serenely t. as queen among her American sisters   HOWE, J, 1
throng join the noisy t. in the busy markets of the
world   CHRON, 296
thrusting she insists upon t. her society upon men
everywhere   CHRON, 445
tide t. in the affairs of women   ATTITUDES, 16

ties content with light and easily broken t.　ELIOT, G, 7

time disproportionate value set on the t. and labor of
men and women　CHRON, 260; OCCUPATIONS, 3
the original good t. that was had by all　PROMISCUITY, 2
T. was away and somewhere else　LOVE, 62

timid I am naturally t. and diffident　DIX, D, 3

tirades exhausted my energy in t.　INJUSTICE, 5

tired women get too t. and dull to bother with politics
CHRON, 509

title t. human being…precedes and out-ranks every
other　EQUALITY, 12

tobacco never since have I wasted any more time on t.
SEX, 31

to-day here t., and gone tomorrow　BEHN, A, 7

toil Extol her for the fruit of her t.　CHARM, 1

toilets T. was always the reason women couldn't
become engineers　CHRON, 701

token either a t. woman or an imitation man　CHRON, 730

told wasn't t. anythink about marriage　CHRON, 463

tolerance insults of men with t. having been bitten in
the nipple by their toothless gums.　TOLERANCE, 2

tomboy you had to…be a t. or whatever　FONDA, J, 2

tomorrow here today and gone t.　BEHN, A, 7
there was never going to be a t.　JOHNSON, L, 2

tongue One t. is sufficient for a woman
CHRON, 149; EDUCATION, 9
The Devil's in her t.　BEHN, A, 8

top To get to the t.…put their careers and companies
first　CHRON, 704

torch T. of Hymen serves but to light the Pyre　LAW, 12

tortuous t. road that led to the sex war　CHRON, 637

torture patriotism which has nerved women to endure
t. in prison　CHRON, 454

totality t. of their conditioning　DISCRIMINATION, 6

toucheth whosoever t. her shall be unclean　CHRON, 6

toy to change the t. culture　MONTESSORI, M, 2

trade not believe in sex distinction in literature, law,
politics, or t.　CHRON, 466

tradition their pride, their t., their history　STEAD, C, 3
women's movement…changed t.　CHRON, 688

traditional Female circumcision, a t. practice　CHASTITY, 8
strong tendency to shunt us into the more t. female
roles　OCCUPATIONS, 15

traditions women are made subordinate by t.　CHRON, 743

tragedy brooding t. and its dark shadows can be lightened　GANDHI, I, 6
That is their t.　MEN AND WOMEN, 15

trained best midwife if she is t. in all branches of therapy　OCCUPATIONS, 1
girls must be t. in precisely the same way　EDUCATION, 2
ought to have t. as a doctor　OCCUPATIONS, 13

training one in six t. places goes to Third World
women　DISCRIMINATION, 9
t. women to consider marriage as the sole object
EDUCATION, 18
what is the aim in the t. of girls　EDUCATION, 23
woman is incapable of receiving a t. similar to that
of man　CHRON, 318

trampling He is t. out the vintage where the grapes of
wrath　HOWE, J, 3

transitory An actress's life is so t.　HAYES, H, 4

translations T. (like wives) are seldom faithful
UNFAITHFULNESS, 3

travail when she is in t. hath sorrow　CHRON, 58

travelling very convenient for t.　MENSTRUATION, 13

treason in trust I have found t.　ELIZABETH I, 10

treasure One clear idea is too precious a t. to lose
GILMAN, C, 1

treated want to be t. like shit　SEX, 45

tree The woman…gave me of the t.　CHRON, 3

trimmings longed for all the t.　WAR, 5

triumph have reserved Cleopatra as a captive to adorn
his T.　CLEOPATRA VII, 4
I *will not* be exhibited in his T.　CLEOPATRA VII, 7

triumphed completely t. over the handicap of her sex
CHRON, 82

Trojan Dido and the T. chief　CHRON, 44

trot I don't t. it out and about　COLETTE, 5
t. merrily off in his old accustomed gait　CHRON, 479

trouble a woman is on a…hunt for t.
DIX, D, 3; MARRIAGE, 48
it saves me the t. of liking them　AUSTEN, J, 13
Prostitution…keeps her out of t.　PROSTITUTION, 8

troubled majority of women…are not very much t.
with sexual feelings　CHRON, 305

troubles man avoids /Marriage and all the t. women
bring　MARRIAGE, 9
women have been the cause of many t.　CHRON, 107

Troy T. to be burnt in flames　CHRON, 42

true No man worth having is t. to his wife
UNFAITHFULNESS, 2
therefore they must be t. ether to other　CHRON, 109
t. to you, darlin', in my fashion　CONSTANCY, 3
T. love never grows old　LOVE, 9

trumpet she disliked the imitations of her t. tone in
the famous line 'A handbag'　EVANS, E, 2
The First Blast of the T.　CHRON, 116; MISOGYNY, 4

trust in t. I have found treason　ELIZABETH I, 10
never t. a woman　AGE, 6; SAYINGS AND PROVERBS, 28
Where large sums of money are concerned,…t.
nobody　CHRISTIE, A, 4

truth a t. universally acknowledged　MARRIAGE, 21
If you do not tell the t. about yourself　WOOLF, V, 6
Intellectual women are the most modest inquirers
after t.　GILMAN, C, 2
Men will fight for a superstition…as for a living t.
HYPATIA, 4
not even Marx is more precious…than the t.　WEIL, S, 3
She can't help writing t.　ADDAMS, J, 1
the very essence of T. seemed to emanate from her
NIGHTINGALE, F, 1
to follow t. wherever it might lead　BROWN, O, 2
t. rewarded me　TRUTH, 2
t. universally acknowledged　AUSTEN, J, 8
We must prepare and study t.　BLAVATSKY, E, 3
You men can't stand the t.　PARTURIER, F, 2

truths He was a man of two t.　MURDOCH, I, 5

Turkish women were kept in T. ignorance　CHRON, 207

turning The lady's not for t.　THATCHER, M, 6

twentieth the t. century men had reached a peak of
insanity　BAEZ, J, 2
Victorian versus t. values　BUCK, P, 2

tyranny 'Resistance to t. is obedience to God.'
ANTHONY, S, 6
Under conditions of t.　ARENDT, H, 2
Women are the creatures of an organised t. of men
CHRON, 353

tyrant placed over her as master, Lord and t.　CHRON, 401

tyrants love, an…intercourse between t. and slaves
LOVE AND FRIENDSHIP, 2

U

ugliness It is homogeneous u.   STANHOPE, H, 4
ugly after she is aged and u.   OLD AGE, 6
an u. *woman* is a blot on the fair face of creation
    BRONTË, C, 5
better to be first with an u. woman   BUCK, P, 6; LOVE, 57
Sin...not only u. but passé   SIN, 3
There are no u. women, only lazy ones
    COSMETICS, 9; RUBINSTEIN, H, 3
ultimatum Miss West sent H. G. Wells an u.   WEST, R, 1
unassuming A natural u. woman whom they...spoil by
making a lioness of her   GASKELL, E, 1
unawares happened u. to look at her husband
    AUSTEN, J, 12
unbecoming nothing...so u. to a woman   MORALITY, 1
solid information is u. her sex   CHRON, 225
unchivalrous just a bit u.   CHIVALRY, 3
unclean any man lie with her at all, and her flowers be
upon him, he shall be u.   MENSTRUATION, 1
whosoever toucheth her shall be u.   CHRON, 6
uncommon woman of common views but u. abilities
    THATCHER, M, 1
unconditional most effective is u. emancipation
    CHRON, 385
uncorrupted u. woman the sexual impulse does not
manifest itself   SEX, 7
underdeveloped If Canada is u.   BARDOT, B, 1
underpaid u. labor of women   WORK, 7
underpaying u. women and using them as a reserve
cheap labor supply   CHRON, 654
understand if he could make *me* u....it would be clear
to all   ROOSEVELT, E, 3
understanding prevent the cultivation of the female u.
    CHRON, 203
women's bodies are softer than men's, so their u. is
sharper   CHRISTINE DE PISAN, 4
undertake Cooking, baking and washing...duties...have to u. herself   CHRON, 368
underwear never shows her u. unintentionally
    SEDUCTION, 2
Undine the impression of something as unique and
remote as U.   DICKINSON, E, 1
unemployed stigma for a man to be u.
    EQUAL OPPORTUNITIES, 5
talk about u. women   CHRON, 352
unfair u. to imply that an intelligent woman must 'rise
above' her maternal instincts
    CHRON, 651; MOTHERHOOD, 15
unfavourable no other actress...could escape u. comparison   EVANS, E, 1
unfeminine to pity the neurotic, u., unhappy women
    FRIEDAN, B, 4
unfitness noisiness and hysteria are proofs of u. for
public life   SUFFRAGETTES, 11
unfortunate most u. creatures   EXPLOITATION, 1
women show more sympathy for the u. than men
    CHRON, 221
unhappy each u. family is u. in its own way   FAMILY, 5
unheralded spring now comes u. by the return of the
birds   CARSON, R, 4
unhinge u. an audience with emotion   PIAF, E, 1
uniform opposed to the use of women in u.   CHRON, 567
unintentionally never shows her underwear u.
    SEDUCTION, 2

union that pleasure, which is undeniably the sole
motive force behind the u. of the sexes   LUST, 3; SEX, 6
u. is indissoluble   CHRON, 265
unions women to join various u.   CHRON, 504
unique the impression of something as u. and remote
as Undine   DICKINSON, E, 1
united solid u. front of male clubbability   CHRON, 723
universally a happy woman and u. respected
    WOLLSTONECRAFT, M, 1
truth u. acknowledged   AUSTEN, J, 8
universe In this unbelievable u....no absolutes BUCK, P, 3
university it is necessary to go to a u....to become a successful writer   BRITTAIN, V, 3
To women the enjoyment of U. life   CHRON, 386
unjust denial of the franchise to women is u.   CHRON, 379
unjustly treated u., her desire for honour   JUSTICE, 1
unlawful u. certain kinds of sex discrimination
    CHRON, 681
unlearn not to learn, but to u.   STEINEM, G, 1
unlucky My husbands have been very u.   BORGIA, L, 4
unman Charlotte might 'castrate' them or Emily 'u.'
them with her passion   THE BRONTËS, 1
unmarried an u. mother   ILLEGITIMACY, 3
larger proportion of women remain u.   CHRON, 299
to keep u.   MARRIAGE, 41
u. woman...stronger psychological reserves
    SINGLE WOMEN, 13
Why should u. women be discriminated against
    CHRON, 666; TAXATION, 3
unnatural neither u., nor abominable, nor mad
    LESBIANISM, 2
unpleasant She was very able, very clever, and very u.
    PANKHURST, C, 2
unpopular She is very u. with the clergy...we long to
burn her alive   FRY, E, 2
woman in authority is often u.   POWER, 7
unpopularity love responsibility and I don't mind u.
    CASTLE, B, 6
unpredictability utter u. of a quarrel   ANGER, 5
unreasonable Men are not often u.   GILMAN, C, 3
unrepentant u. creature, big with child is not such an
outrageous sight   CHRON, 490
unsaid The bitterest tears...are for words...u. STOWE, H, 3
unseemly all things u., which they call ambition
    CHRON, 375
unsexing find that all the gentle sex this process is u.
    CHRON, 349
unsocial Maternity is...an u. experience   MOTHERHOOD, 7
unsuitable much in accountancy proper that is...u. for
them   OCCUPATIONS, 9
unwomanly sexual feeling is u. and intolerable   SEX, 16
upper-middle Shirley Williams...a member of the u.
class   THATCHER, M, 4
use Lascivious movements are of no u. whatever to
wives   SEX, 3
u. of her that nature designed for her   LUST, 2
usefulness life may not be prolonged beyond the
power of u.   AIKIN, L, 5
uterus condition of her u.   DISCRIMINATION, 7
u. shall swell and strut out like a water bag
    PREGNANCY, 2
U-turn U. if you want to   THATCHER, M, 6

V

v. of women are reserve, quiet, chastity, orderliness
FEMININITY, 1
virtuous v. wife rules her husband by obeying him
CHRON, 41
who can find a v. woman VIRTUE, 2
vision limits his v. to his memories of yesterday
LANGTRY, L, 1
visions result of v., many people choke to death, more
women than men VIRGINITY, 1
vivify quarrels which v. its barrenness GREER, G, 4
vocation love...to women a v. LOVE, 27
natural v. for every woman is that of wife
CHRON, 459; EDUCATION, 26
true v., the nurture of the coming race EDUCATION, 22
vocational educational objectives...geared exclusively
to the v. patterns of men CHRON, 599
voice God sent a v. to guide me JOAN OF ARC, 5
Laws in which we have no v., or Representation
CHRON, 193
only v. in the affairs of the nation CHRON, 378
right to a v. in this government SUFFRAGETTES, 5
v. in making the laws CHRON, 337
void such as say our Sex is v. of Reason CHRON, 144
volatile intellectually more desultory and v. than men
INTELLECT, 5
voluntary v. removal of the veil by Egyptian women
CHRON, 584
V. death would be an abandonment of our present
post BLAVATSKY, E, 2
vote gave the v. to the older women who were
deemed less rebellious CHRON, 499
getting the v. is concerned SUFFRAGETTES, 21
Give women the v. SUFFRAGETTES, 9
if women v. they must fight.' WAR, 2
in the same boat...not a chance of recording the v.
CHRON, 406
No v. can be given by lunatics CHRON, 190
ought to have a v. for Westminster CHRON, 324
reasons for giving women the v. CHRON, 311
right...to v. shall not be denied...on account of sex
CHRON, 482
The v., I thought, means nothing to women
O'BRIEN, E, 4
to bring the v. to women RANKIN, J, 1
v. is the symbol of freedom and equality CHRON, 440
want the v. so that we may serve our country better
CHRON, 471
We want the v. SUFFRAGETTES, 23
willing to let their husbands v. for them CHRON, 356
no end to fighting till the V. is won CHRON, 436
voters suffragists did influence v. CHRON, 404
support for what the v. want SMITH, M, 2
votes V. for Women CHRON, 403; CHRON, 452
voting never contemplated...right of v....for married
women CHRON, 264
vows v. most women are made to take are very foolhardy CHRON, 206

W

wage-earning a w. woman DUNCAN, I, 4
wages depressed w. because women are the chief
employees EQUAL OPPORTUNITIES, 3
Factory females have in general much lower w. than
males CHRON, 244

some occupations have depressed w. because
women are the chief employees CHRON, 647
women are used to bring down w. CHRON, 384
waist encloses the w. of a girl in these cruel contrivances CLOTHES, 3; HEALTH AND HEALTHY LIVING, 2
walk We must go w. the streets CHRON, 249
We must go w. the streets PROSTITUTION, 2
walks She w. in beauty BEAUTY, 9
walnut-tree dog, and a w. SAYINGS AND PROVERBS, 41
wander Why do people so love to w. CASSATT, M, 4
wanderer true w....goes out not to shun STARK, F, 4
want demand what we w. for women CHRON, 498
What does a woman w. ATTITUDES, 22
wanted bought things because she w. 'em EDUCATION, 12
I knew what I w. DETERMINATION, 3
wanton enlist the sympathy of women...against the w.
slaughter of birds CONSERVATION, 2
wants costume of women should be suited to her w.
and necessities BLOOMER, A, 5
nobody w. her MENOPAUSE, 3
war a lot of the women's lib movement came from the
w. WOMEN'S LIBERATION MOVEMENT, 19
As a woman I can't go to w. RANKIN, J, 3; WAR, 6
Being over seventy is like being engaged in a w.
SPARK, M, 3
British women have proved themselves in this w.
CHRON, 557
I am a chieftain of w. CHRON, 103
in time of peace we must prepare for w. BARTON, C, 1
Justice...blind to racism, sexism, w. and poverty
PREJUDICE, 5
the...barbarity of w....forces men...to commit acts
KEY, E, 4
there were women conscientious objectors...during
the w. CHRON, 560
The W. between Men and Women MEN AND WOMEN, 24
this w.,....which did not justify the sacrifice of a single mother's son PANKHURST, S, 2
w. without a woman SAYINGS AND PROVERBS, 30
women were awfully keen to do w. work CHRON, 551
You can no more win a w. RANKIN, J, 4
warnings thanksgiving for the past...w. for the future
CAULKINS, F, 1
warrior woman for the recreation of the w.
WOMAN'S ROLE, 22
warriors w....are treated humanely CHRON, 10
wars W. and revolutions...have outlived all their ideological justifications ARENDT, H, 5
war workers need came for women 'w.' CHRON, 456
wash also w. and iron them EQUALITY, 20
washing fill in their space time w. out the offices and
dusting same CHRON, 428
wasps w. in their anger ANGER, 1; SAYINGS AND PROVERBS, 49
water sieve will hold w. SAYINGS AND PROVERBS, 32
The first possibility of rural cleanliness lies in w.
supply. NIGHTINGALE, F, 5
watering a-w. the last year's crop ELIOT, G, 3
waxed After I am w. old OLD AGE, 1
way A man...is *so* in the w. GASKELL, E, 3
woman has her w. MEN AND WOMEN, 10
world the men have it all their own w. SUFFRAGETTES, 2
weak w. women, without pluck and grit CHRON, 366
weakening alcohol is a w. and deadening force
DRINKING, 6
weakens Maternal softness w. my resolve MOTHERHOOD, 1
weaker the w. vessel CHRON, 61; MARRIAGE, 8

weakness a borrowed word is weaker than our own w.
MITCHELL, M, 1

no more w. than is natural to her sex ATTITUDES, 1

through my w. of body that I become pregnant
CHRON, 501

w. of their sex as well as their ignorance of business matters LAW, 1

wealth good wife and health is a man's best w.
SAYINGS AND PROVERBS, 13

W. covers sin WEALTH, 2

weaned as if he had been w. on a pickle LONGWORTH, A, 2

weapon Her w. is the snub GANDHI, I, 1

In the sex-war thoughtlessness is the w. of the male
MEN AND WOMEN, 22

open the bride with his natural w. he is a mighty sworder VIRGINITY, 8

Sex becomes a w. PROSTITUTION, 13

wear I...chose my wife...for...such qualities as would w. well PRACTICALITY, 1

wedding-ring married woman has nothing of her own but her w. SAYINGS AND PROVERBS, 24

weeds Worthless as wither'd w. BRONTË, E, 5

weep For men must work, and women must w.
WOMAN'S ROLE, 18

w. for her sins at the other SELF-INDULGENCE, 1

weeping Do you hear the children w. BROWNING, E, 5

weigh images of female beauty have come to w. upon us CHRON, 745

welding women takes to w. as readily as she takes to knitting CHRON, 554

well will to do w., which women may have
AMBITION, 1; CHRON, 141

well-bred w. woman does not seek carnal gratification
SEX, 22

well-dressed consciousness of being w. CLOTHES, 5

Wells Miss West sent H. G. W. an ultimatum WEST, R, 1

Westminster ought to have a vote for W. CHRON, 324

wheedling Woman is a w. and secret enemy
WOMAN'S NATURE, 5

when w. a man should marry MARRIAGE, 12

white all in w....a little battle-axe in her hand
JOAN OF ARC, 2

I used to be Snow W. VIRGINITY, 10

There is no birthright in the w. skin BESANT, A, 2

Who W. is Silvia FEMININITY, 3

whole if she knew the w. of it LOVE, 44

whore a w. in the kitchen and a cook in bed
MARRIAGE, 59

I am the Protestant w. GWYNN, N, 3

whoredom women be guilty of w. ADULTERY, 4

whorehouses virgin territory for w. PROSTITUTION, 6

whores w., and that's not a term of abuse
PROSTITUTION, 14

why ask a prostitute w. she does it PROSTITUTION, 12

wicked Of wommen.../Seyn they be w. CHRON, 101

persist in your w. resolution of plundering those women of their lives and fortunes CHRON, 39

wickedness leader of all w. is woman MISOGYNY, 2

without the w. of women...world would remain proof against/ innumerable dangers CHRON, 105

widow a w....is a kind of sinecure WIDOWHOOD, 1

better to be the w. of a hero than the wife of a coward IBARRURI, D, 5

No w. shall be compelled to marry CHRON, 88

Walk wide o' the W. at Windsor CHRON, 342

'W.' is a harsh and hurtful word WIDOWHOOD, 6

W.. The word consumes itself WIDOWHOOD, 4

you, my dear, will be my w. MARRIAGE, 57

widows W. are accountable to none WIDOWHOOD, 2

wife A loving w. will do anything MARRIAGE, 53

A man should not insult his w. publicly MARRIAGE, 58

A man who's untrue to his w. UNFAITHFULNESS, 4

an occupational hazard of being a w. ANNE, PRINCESS, 4

anything better than a w. who is chaste
WOMAN'S ROLE, 4

appreciation of the husband...falling in love with the w. LA FAYETTE, M, 2

better to be the widow of a hero than the w. of a coward IBARRURI, D, 5

book you would even wish your w. or your servants to read CHRON, 591

Caesar's w. must be above suspicion
CHRON, 40; DIVORCE, 1; WOMAN'S ROLE, 3

chose my w....for...qualities as would wear well
PRACTICALITY, 1

coming together of man and w....should be a fresh adventure STOPES, M, 5

faithlessness of his w. ADULTERY, 5

fit to be a man's w. CHRON, 134

good w. and health is a man's best wealth
SAYINGS AND PROVERBS, 13

good w. says, so must it be SAYINGS AND PROVERBS, 1

Here lies my w. EPITAPHS, 1; 2

he that is married careth...how he may please his w.
MARRIAGE, 6

He that loves not his w. and children FAMILY, 2

husband and w. are one person in law CHRON, 191

I am no shadow...I am a w. PLATH, S, 4

I bow before your rights as w. CHRON, 11

If a man stays away from his w. MARRIAGE, 35

I have a w., I have sons FAMILY, 1

light w. doth make a heavy husband MARRIAGE, 13

man enjoys the right to lead his w. to market with a rope about her neck CHRON, 219

Margot is a good w. MARRIAGE, 71

natural vocation for every woman is that of w.
CHRON, 459; EDUCATION, 26

necessary for the w. to *ask* her husband for money
CHRON, 329

No man worth having is true to his w.
UNFAITHFULNESS, 2

not be lawful...to bring home another w. CHRON, 34

obeying him as a w. should obey CHRON, 34

overshadowed by his overdressed, extravagant and idle w. STOPES, M, 6

permitting the 'passion shooting' by a husband of a w. CHRON, 627

personal estate of the w....be vested in the w.
CHRON, 344

remorse for what you have thought about your w.
MARRIAGE, 49

single man...must be in want of a w. MARRIAGE, 21

stop them catching AIDS...the w. PROMISCUITY, 4

taking out his false teeth and hurling them at his w.
MARRIAGE, 36

the disposition for...a w. CHARACTER, 3

The first w. is matrimony SAYINGS AND PROVERBS, 10

the w....the weaker vessel CHRON, 61; MARRIAGE, 8

the w. who made Britain great again,...has to get her husband to sign her tax form TAXATION, 5

The woman is uniformly sacrificed to the w. and mother GAGE, M, 4

thrive must ask leave of his w. SAYINGS AND PROVERBS, 17
violent aggressions of bodily torment towards the
unhappy w. CHRON, 320
When a man opens the car door for his w. MARRIAGE, 73
W. and children SAYINGS AND PROVERBS, 38
W. and servant are the same CHRON, 178; SUBJECTION, 7
w. is one who has made a permanent sex bargain
CHRON, 441
w. ought not to make friends of her own CHRON, 51
w. shall honour and fear the husband SUBJECTION, 4
with a w. to tell him what to do MEN, 7
your w.! /And I have no other life CHRON, 397
wifehood w. and motherhood STANTON, E, 12
wilderness W. is Paradise enow LOVE, 41
will Man has his w. MEN AND WOMEN, 10
w. to do well, which women may have
AMBITION, 1; CHRON, 141
Williams Shirley W....a member of the upper-middle
class THATCHER, M, 4
win I fight to w. THATCHER, M, 10
wind A woman's mind and winter w. change oft
SAYINGS AND PROVERBS, 44
of w. and limb CONSTANCY, 1
Windsor Here is a sad slaughter at W. GWYNN, N, 4
Walk wide o' the Widow at W. CHRON, 342
wine A Flask of W. LOVE, 41
wins he who goes ahead...w. CATHERINE THE GREAT, 4
winter two seasons w. and w. DELANEY, S, 3
wisdom ass climbs a ladder, we may find w.
SAYINGS AND PROVERBS, 35
cuts her w. teeth when she is dead
INTELLIGENCE, 1; SAYINGS AND PROVERBS, 42
fragmentary gift of knowledge or w. RUBINSTEIN, H, 4
Love is the w. of the fool LOVE, 28
w. never comes from women CHRON, 123
Women have always been the guardians of w. and
humanity WOLFF, C, 1
Women...the guardians of w. EQUALITY, 16
wise beseemeth wives to be w. and of great governance CHRON, 100
w. not for self-development, but for self-renunciation FEMININITY, 7; WISDOM, 1
wiser boys are naturally w. than you CHRON, 273
wished long deferred and often w. for BRONTË, C, 4
wit Man forgives woman anything save the w. to outwit him ANTRIM, M, 3
W. in women is apt to have bad consequences
HUMOUR, 1
witch thou shalt not suffer a w. to live WITCHES, 1
w. is a rebel in physics WITCHES, 4
w....remains a universal bogey LANGUAGE, 6; WITCHES, 6
witches find out w. by pricking them with pins
CHRON, 145
I have ever believed,...that there are w. WITCHES, 3
w. are usually old women of...small brains CHRON, 120
witchlike Beneath a bony, w. head ASQUITH, M, 1
withdrawal justify w. from the usual duties and
pleasures of life MENSTRUATION, 14
witness not to be accepted as a w.: a woman LAW, 3
wits Female W. wrote big, fat fabulous plays WRITERS, 15
witty a very w. prologue MARRIAGE, 17
Pretty, w. Nell GWYNN, N, 2
wives aim of English w. is MARRIAGE, 30
beseemeth w. to be wise and of great governance
CHRON, 100

best mothers, w.,..., know little or nothing of sexual
indulgences SEX, 10
Bricklayers kick their w. to death MARRIAGE, 42
husbands and w....belong to different sexes
DIX, D, 4; MEN AND WOMEN, 21
husbands and w. make shipwreck of their lives
DIX, D, 3; MARRIAGE, 48
husbands, love your w. MARRIAGE, 3
insist upon retaining an absolute power over W.
CHRON, 195
Maids must be w. WOMAN'S ROLE, 12
make better w. and mothers and citizens CHRON, 565
men don't hit their w. any more VIOLENCE, 5
no sort of work in the home strictly reserved for 'the
w.' HOUSEKEEPING, 9
not account their w. as their vassals CHRON, 136
O! men with mothers and w.
CHRON, 268; OPPRESSION, 2; WORK, 1
The others were only my w. MARRIAGE, 57
they don't make good w. COMMITMENT, 1
Translations (like w.) are seldom faithful
UNFAITHFULNESS, 3
W. are young men's mistresses MARRIAGE, 11
w. for the production of full-blooded children
CHRON, 29
W. have no right to bring criminal accusations for
adultery CHRON, 56
you do not make the laws but...are the w....of those
who do GRIMKÉ, A, 1
Your w. are your field DOMINATION, 2
wizard term *w.* has acquired reverential status
LANGUAGE, 6; WITCHES, 6
woe 'Green-Eyed Monster' causes much w. JEALOUSY, 4
who can blame my w. DEATH, 1
woeful W. is the household SAYINGS AND PROVERBS, 40
woman A diplomat...always remembers a w.'s birthday OLD AGE, 10
all the keys should hang from the belt of one w.
CHRON, 94
A man is only as old as the w. AGE, 8
And a w. is only a w. CONTEMPT, 2
an ugly *w.* is a blot on the fair face of creation
BRONTË, C, 5
Any w. who understands the problems of running a
home HOUSEKEEPING, 10; POLITICS, 13
a w. is on a...hunt for trouble DIX, D, 3; MARRIAGE, 48
a w....ought to lay aside...modesty with her skirt
MODESTY, 3
A w.'s place is in the home
SAYINGS AND PROVERBS, 45; WOMAN'S ROLE, 1
a w.'s reason ATTITUDES, 4
A w.'s work SAYINGS AND PROVERBS, 47
A w. will always sacrifice herself MISOGYNY, 10
a w. yet think him an angel LOVE, 40
body of a weak and feeble w. CHRON, 125; ELIZABETH I, 11
called W., because she was taken out of Man CHRON, 1
close-up of a w. past sixty ASTOR, N, 5; OLD AGE, 11
educate a w. you educate a family EDUCATION, 27
every w. is at heart a rake ATTITUDES, 10
Every w. should marry MARRIAGE, 33
Frailty, thy name is w. ATTITUDES, 6
God made the w. for the man
CHRON, 279; WOMAN'S ROLE, 13
goods & evils of the position of a w....in official life
CHRON, 291

he has studied anatomy and dissected at least one w.
MARRIAGE, 29

hell a fury like a w. scorned HATE, 2

I am a...w. – nothing more FEMININITY, 6

I am a w.? When I think, I must speak ATTITUDES, 5

if a w. have long hair APPEARANCE, 1

If a w. like Eva Peron with no ideals THATCHER, M, 5

I had become a w. of...character MATURITY, 1

It is a great glory in a w. ATTITUDES, 1

It's a sort of bloom on a w. CHARM, 3

I would...guess that Anon...was often a w. WRITERS, 11

I would venture that Anon, who wrote so many
poems without signing them, was a w. WOOLF, V, 8

Man for the field and w. for the hearth
MEN AND WOMEN, 9

mentioning some w. whom he knew in the past
JEALOUSY, 1

mother – make me less than w. MOTHERHOOD, 1

name of a w. makes one doubtful ARTISTS, 1

No one delights more in vengeance than a w.
CHRON, 48; ATTITUDES, 2; HATE, 1

No w. should ever be quite accurate about her age
AGE, 7

Old age is w.'s hell OLD AGE, 5

Once a w. has given you her heart LOVE, 24

one can...see in a little girl the threat of a w.
MEN AND WOMEN, 14

One is not born a w.
CHRON, 576; BEAUVOIR, S, 3; WOMANHOOD, 9

One tongue is sufficient for a w.
CHRON, 149; EDUCATION, 9

rich and one's a w. WEALTH, 6

She makes love just like a w. MATURITY, 3

Than to ever let a w. in my life MISOGYNY, 11

that grand word 'w.' LANGUAGE, 1

the most beautiful w. I've ever seen BEAUTY, 13

the rib...made he a w. CHRON, 1

the sort of w. who lives for others DUTY, 3

the w. who is really kind to dogs MISOGYNY, 9

The w. who outranks us all ANTHONY, S, 2

This is a w.'s resolve BOADICEA, 3

To know the *mind* of a w. LOVE AND FRIENDSHIP, 5

Twenty years of romance make a w. look like a ruin
MARRIAGE, 37

we have w. before man SUPERIORITY, 3

What does a w. want CHRON, 486

When a w. becomes a scholar INTELLIGENCE, 10

When a w. behaves like a man MEN AND WOMEN, 25

When lovely w. stoops to folly BETRAYAL, 1

who can find a virtuous w. VIRTUE, 2

Why can't a w. be more like a man ATTITUDES, 26

Why...was I born a w. DISCRIMINATION, 1

will not stand...being called a w. in my own house
CONTEMPT, 4

w. alone, can...commit them ATTITUDES, 18

w. a...secondary citizen POWER, 8

w. as old as she looks AGE, 5

w. governs America FEMINISM, 9

w. has her way MEN AND WOMEN, 10

w. in Iran is a political crime CHRON, 707; RELIGION, 18

W. is always fickle and changing
CHRON, 43; CONTRARINESS, 2

w. is an animal that CHRON, 579; SEX, 28

w. is a tender and sweet person CHRON, 640

W. is unrivaled as a wet nurse WOMAN'S ROLE, 24

w....knowing anything INTELLIGENCE, 7

w. of education EDUCATION, 12

w.'s composing is like a dog's walking on his hind
legs CHRON, 516

w. seldom asks advice ATTITUDES, 9

w....so vicious, or so feeble-minded, that she cannot
withstand temptation BRONTË, A, 5

W.'s at best a contradiction CONTRARINESS, 4

W.'s virtue is man's greatest invention VIRTUE, 9

w.'s weapon is her tongue MEN AND WOMEN, 32

w.'s whole existence LOVE, 33; MEN AND WOMEN, 6

w. taught once, and ruined all CHRON, 64

w. that attempts the pen WRITERS, 3

w. the shipwreck of man RELIGION, 13

wrecks a w.'s reputation COLETTE, 6

W. to bear rule...is repugnant to Nature CHRON, 117

W. was God's *second* mistake MISOGYNY, 8

W. will be the last thing civilized by Man CONTEMPT, 3

woman-eating w. sentiments of certain medieval
'saints' WRITERS, 9

womanhood blood of a w. that was never bought
WOMANHOOD, 3

by virtue of their common w. BLACKWELL, E, 4

flight from w. WOMANHOOD, 7

True chivalry respects all w. CHIVALRY, 1

warring contradictions, w. and anger
ANGER, 2; WOMANHOOD, 1

W. is the great fact in her life
STANTON, E, 12; WOMAN'S ROLE, 19

womanish men...fear all that is 'w.' MEN AND WOMEN, 30

womankind Honour to W. CHRISTINE DE PISAN, 5

whole race of w. is...made subject to man
SUBJECTION, 3; WOMAN'S ROLE, 5

womanliness W. means only motherhood MOTHERHOOD, 4

womanly cast aside all w. decency CHRON, 104

there are w. concerns EDUCATION, 25; WOMANHOOD, 5

woman's rights the short dress and w. were inseparably
connected BLOOMER, A, 3

womb how you appeared in my w. PROCREATION, 1

in the w. are we all equal EQUALITY, 19

this rifled and bleeding w. ABORTION, 5

wombs think with our w. INTELLIGENCE, 19

women all men and w. are created equal STANTON, E, 10

all w. do ASTOR, N, 3; MARRIAGE, 38

battle for w.'s rights CHRON, 700

Because w. can do nothing except love
ATTITUDES, 21; LOVE, 53

comely to w. to nourish their hair CHRON, 139

defense effort in terms of defending w. WAR, 9

fear of w. CHRON, 604

Few w. care to be laughed at HUMOUR, 3

Give w. the vote CHRON, 388

God withheld the sense of humour from w.
TOLERANCE, 1

I don't think men and w. were meant to live together
MEN AND WOMEN, 33

If civilisation is to advance...it must be through...w.
PANKHURST, E, 3

If men knew how w. pass their time ATTITUDES, 20

If w. didn't exist,...money...no meaning WEALTH, 7

imagine that they are upholding w.'s emancipation
STOPES, M, 6

In days of old,.../The w. ruled the men CHRON, 497

make it...unnecessary that w. should depend on
men CHRON, 283

men and w. are wretched EQUALITY, 17

Men know that w. are an overmatch for them
CHRON, 198
Most good w. are hidden treasures VIRTUE, 8
most important thing w. have to do CHRON, 319
Most w. have no characters CHARACTER, 2
Most w. set out to try to change a man MEN, 5
no family can get along without w. to help
OCCUPATIONS, 7; SUBJECTION, 13
Older w. are best SEX, 32
Plenty of w. to wear the breeches BLOOMER, A, 2
prefer to have w. in the home and not as airline
pilots CHRON, 631
proclaiming that w. are brighter than men LOOS, A, 5
prolonged slavery of w. STANTON, E, 11
proper function of w.
CHRON, 302; ELIOT, G, 6; WOMAN'S ROLE, 15
several young w....would render the Christian life
intensely difficult MARRIAGE, 55
souls of w. are so small ATTITUDES, 8
Suffer the w. whom ye divorce CHRON, 68
The emancipation of w. is...the greatest egoistic
movement KEY, E, 1
the largest scope for change still lies in men's
attitude to w. BRITTAIN, V, 2
the Monstrous Regiment of W. CHRON, 116
the only advantage w. have over men –...they can
cry MEN AND WOMEN, 20
The question of the rights of w. RELIGION, 19
There are two kinds of w. ATTITUDES, 27; EXPLOITATION, 3
There never will be...equality until w....make laws
ANTHONY, S, 3
The vote, I thought, means nothing to w. O'BRIEN, E, 4
The War between Men and W. MEN AND WOMEN, 24
the w. whose eyes have been washed...with tears
DIX, D, 1; SORROW, 5
The world cannot do without w. PROCREATION, 5
Votes for W. CHRON, 403
We are here to claim our rights as w. PANKHURST, C, 4
Were't not for gold and w. ATTITUDES, 7
we suffragettes aspire to be...ambassadors of free-
dom to w. PANKHURST, C, 5
When w. go wrong SEX, 34; WEST, M, 6
Why are w....so much more interesting to men MEN, 3
W....are either better or worse than men
MEN AND WOMEN, 4
W. are much more like each other MEN AND WOMEN, 5
w. are people, too CHRON, 737
W. become like their mothers MEN AND WOMEN, 15
W. cannot be part of the Institute of France CURIE, M, 1
W....care fifty times more for a marriage than a min-
istry CHRON, 312; MARRIAGE, 32
w. defend themselves so poorly ATTITUDES, 15
w. dislike his books PREJUDICE, 3
W. exist...solely for the propagation of the species
WOMAN'S ROLE, 14
w. feel just as men feel CHRON, 272
W. had always fought for men PANKHURST, E, 4
W. have always been the guardians of wisdom and
humanity WOLFF, C, 1
W. have served all these centuries CHRON, 527
W. have served...as looking-glasses WOMAN'S ROLE, 27
W. have smaller brains than men INTELLIGENCE, 20
w....ill-using them and then confessing it OPPRESSION, 4
W....men hate them CHRON, 625
W....natural, but usually secret, rulers CHRON, 581
W. never have young minds DELANEY, S, 2; WISDOM, 2

w. nor linen SAYINGS AND PROVERBS, 6
W., priests, and poultry, have never enough
SAYINGS AND PROVERBS, 55
W. represent...matter over mind MEN AND WOMEN, 12
w. require both MISOGYNY, 6
w. should assert their rights as human beings
CHRON, 367
w. show more sympathy for the unfortunate than
men CHRON, 221
w. still have an advantage simply because they are
women CHRON, 620
w. their rights and nothing less ANTHONY, S, 5
w. were going to remain in the servant class CHRON, 411
W....were ready to fight for their own human rights
CHRON, 412
w. who have done something with their lives
ACHIEVEMENT, 6
W. who love the same man LOVE, 51
w. who moan at the lack of opportunities CHRON, 719
W. would rather be right than reasonable
CONTRARINESS, 7
Wonderful w.!...how much we...owe to Shakespeare
STRENGTH, 2; TERRY, E, 3; WOMANHOOD, 4
women's lib a lot of the w. movement came from the
war WOMEN'S LIBERATION MOVEMENT, 19
women's liberation No W. for her MISOGYNY, 12
point of W. WOMEN'S LIBERATION MOVEMENT, 5
rumblings of w. WOMEN'S LIBERATION MOVEMENT, 8
The uniqueness of today's W. Movement
WOMEN'S LIBERATION MOVEMENT, 11
W. is the liberation of the feminine in the man
WOMEN'S LIBERATION MOVEMENT, 13
Women's Liberationists furious about the W.
WOMEN'S LIBERATION MOVEMENT, 9
wonder Many a man has been a w. to the world
WOMAN'S ROLE, 8
woo yet she hathe but care and w. CHRON, 106
Woolf Virginia W. is dead WOOLF, V, 1
word a borrowed w. is weaker than our own weak-
ness MITCHELL, M, 1
Women will have the last w. SAYINGS AND PROVERBS, 56
words The bitterest tears...are for w....unsaid
STOWE, H, 3
W. are men's daughters CHRON, 182; ATTITUDES, 11
w. left unsaid and deeds left undone STOWE, H, 3
word-stringer she was a 'w.' STEAD, C, 1
wore w. enough for modesty MODESTY, 6
work adult Englishwomen w. for subsistence CHRON, 298
but w. gives satisfaction FRANK, A, 6
cannot always w. at my art SCHUMANN, C, 1
For men must w., and women must weep
WOMAN'S ROLE, 18
it is hard w., not a woman's w. CHRON, 728
men ought to be doing the w. instead of the women
CHRON, 534
no sort of w. in the home strictly reserved for 'the
wives' HOUSEKEEPING, 9
principle of equal pay for equal w. CHRON, 511
regulation of their w. in the hands of men CHRON, 379
story of women's w. in gainful employments
CHRON, 425
success...by dint of hard w. PAVLOVA, A, 4
such a thing as women's w. WOMAN'S ROLE, 31
they must hate to w. for a living MARRIAGE, 40
woman's w. is shitwork STEINEM, G, 2
Women...may freely use and w. CHRON, 92

Women want w. both for the health of their minds
CHRON, 294
worked w. all the time for her whole life ASHLEY, L, 2
workers it may tire out the w. and destroy…the campaign
CATT, C, 3
reject from the electorate public-spirited w.…is a folly
CHRON, 371
working end of the war the attitude to women w. changed
WORK, 5
legislation…improved the w. conditions
CHRON, 426; WORK, 3
organization and enlightenment of w. women
CHRON, 358
socially pernicious…consequences of the w. of mothers
CHRON, 448
Women of the w. class…should not have more than two children
CHRON, 472
W. women want…to improve the social laws
CHRON, 371
works thinking of large w. in a landscape HEPWORTH, B, 3
world All the w. loves a lover LOVE, 2
a w. where there is so much to be done DIX, D, 4
came not in the w. without our pain EQUALITY, 4
child enters the w. through you MOTHERHOOD, 20
first woman…strong enough to turn the w. upside down
CHRON, 282
in mourning…for the w. SITWELL, E, 4
Into the dangerous w. I leapt CHILDBIRTH, 5
joy that a man is born into the w.
CHRON, 58; CHILDBIRTH, 2
little sisters to all the w. DIX, D, 1; SORROW, 5
Many a man has been a wonder to the w.
WOMAN'S ROLE, 8
the hand that rules the w. POWER, 6
The w. cannot do without women PROCREATION, 5
think about the nature of the w. ARENDT, H, 1
women take so little interest in…the w. CHRON, 393
w. must become a man's and a woman's
SUFFRAGETTES, 13
worrying stop w. about what's fair to women
SUPERIORITY, 12
worse for better for w. MARRIAGE, 15
worshipped husband must be constantly w. as a god
MARRIAGE, 2
worst a woman is the w. MISOGYNY, 7
worth mother! What are we w. really? They all grow up whether you look after them or not.
MOTHERHOOD, 9
worthy more w. associations march nearer to the celebrant
RELIGION, 14
womane is a w. wyght CHRON, 106
wrath He is trampling out the vintage where the grapes of w.
HOWE, J, 3
wresting barbarous custom of w. from women whatever she possesses
CHRON, 250
wretched love – all the w. cant of it GREER, G, 4
wretchedness w. and slavery of women CHRON, 295

wriggling after w. fish /With his big bamboo rod
ADULTERY, 1
wrinkles When the first few w. appear OLD AGE, 3
write she hardly knew how to w. a full paragraph
ADAMS, A, 1
Women w., the Criticks…damn their Plays WRITERS, 4
writer a prolific w. of notes of condolence DICKINSON, E, 2
it is necessary to go to a university…to become a successful w.
BRITTAIN, V, 3
writers privileges enjoyed by good w. AIKIN, L, 1
the Brontës, as women and as w. BRONTË, A, 3
writes modern woman w. as well as sews CHRON, 427
modern woman w. as well as sews
SUFFRAGETTES, 18; WOMAN'S ROLE, 25
writhed Russia still w. and stumbled CHRON, 469
writing Few people can be so tortured by w. WOOLF, V, 5
good w. is knowing when to stop MONTGOMERY, L, 5
I found out in the first two pages that it was a woman's w.
ELIOT, G, 1
most characteristic genius in w. WRITERS, 10
W. is like getting married MARRIAGE, 68; MURDOCH, I, 3
written she has w.…a few moments of human experience
PARKER, D, 1
wrong right and w. in fabrics ASHLEY, L, 1
When women go w. SEX, 34; WEST, M, 6
wrongs for one class to appreciate the w. of another
STANTON, E, 9
their 'w.' will be redressed CHRON, 327
undertake to discuss the w. of women CHRON, 241
wrote they w. nevertheless WRITERS, 14
wyfe A lesson for the w. CHRON, 108
wyght womane is a worthy w. CHRON, 106

Y

Yale all the young ladies who attended the Y. promenade dance were laid end to end PARKER, D, 8; SEX, 23
yes girls…say No when they mean Y. CONTRARINESS, 5
yet A young man not y. MARRIAGE, 12
yield man's place to rule…woman's to y.
WOMAN'S ROLE, 17
to y., is the only way to govern GRIMKÉ, S, 4
young not as y. as they're painted COSMETICS, 3
She is neither y. nor beautiful GASKELL, E, 2
yourself If you do not tell the truth about y. WOOLF, V, 6
youth remember till old age…our brilliant y. OLD AGE, 2
y. so glutted with freedom FREEDOM, 3
the Hitler Y. organization MANN, E, 4
Y. is something very new CHANEL, C, 4

Z

zeal stir up the z. of women themselves CHRON, 319
z. in the holy cause of humanity…infringe on those domestic duties
CHRON, 222

BIOGRAPHICAL INDEX

References are either to the thematic headings in the Thematic Section under which the author or speaker appears, or to a quotation in the Chronology. Entries set in bold indicate biographical entries in the Thematic Section. These are listed in their normal alphabetical position. The references are to quotation numbers, not page numbers.